Programming with Microsoft®

Visual Basic® 4.0

JOE McGREW
h (610-622-6483) -
w (302-886-3947)

for Windows™

Diane Zak

College of DuPage

A DIVISION OF COURSE TECHNOLOGY

ONE MAIN STREET, CAMBRIDGE, MA 02142

an International Thomson Publishing company I(T)P®

Cambridge • Albany • Bonn • Boston • Cincinnati • London • Madrid • Melbourne • Mexico City
New York • Paris • San Francisco • Singapore • Tokyo • Toronto • Washington

Programming with Microsoft® Visual Basic® 4.0 for Windows™ is published by CTI.

Managing Editor	Wendy Welch Gordon
Product Manager/Developmental Editor	Kim T. M. Crowley
Production Editor	Jean Bermingham
Text and Cover Designer	Kim Munsell
Cover Illustrator	Douglas Goodman

© 1997 CTI.
A Division of Course Technology— I(T)P®

For more information contact:

Course Technology, Inc.
One Main Street
Cambridge, MA 02142

International Thomson Editores
Campos Eliseos 385, Piso 7
Col. Polanco
11560 Mexico D.F. Mexico

International Thomson Publishing Europe
Berkshire House 168-173
High Holborn
London WCIV 7AA
England

International Thomson Publishing GmbH
Konigswinterer Strasse 418
53227 Bonn
Germany

Thomas Nelson Australia
102 Dodds Street
South Melbourne, 3205
Victoria, Australia

International Thomson Publishing Asia
211 Henderson Road
#05-10 Henderson Building
Singapore 0315

Nelson Canada
1120 Birchmount Road
Scarborough, Ontario
Canada M1K 5G4

International Thomson Publishing Japan
Hirakawacho Kyowa Building, 3F
2-2-1 Hirakawacho
Chiyoda-ku, Tokyo 102
Japan

Trademarks
Course Technology and the open book logo are registered trademarks and CourseKits is a trademark of Course Technology. Custom Editions is a registered trademark of International Thomson Publishing, Inc.

I(T)P® The ITP logo is a registered trademark of International Thomson Publishing.
Microsoft, Visual Basic, and Windows are registered trademarks, and are trademarks of Microsoft Corporation.

Some of the product names and company names used in this book have been used for identification purposes only, and may be trademarks or registered trademarks of their respective manufacturers and sellers.

Disclaimer
CTI reserves the right to revise this publication and make changes from time to time in its content without notice.

ISBN 0-7600-3530-X

Printed in the United States of America

10 9 8 7 6 5 4

Preface

Programming with Microsoft Visual Basic 4.0 for Windows is designed for a beginning programming course. This book uses Visual Basic (using Windows 95 or Windows 3.1), an object-oriented/event-driven language, to teach programming concepts. This book capitalizes on the energy and enthusiasm students naturally have for Windows-based applications and clearly teaches students how to take full advantage of Visual Basic's power. It assumes students have learned basic Windows skills and file management from Course Technology's *New Perspectives on Microsoft Windows 95-Brief*, *New Perspectives on Microsoft Windows 3.1-Brief* or from *an equivalent book*.

Organization and Coverage

Programming with Microsoft Visual Basic 4.0 for Windows contains an Overview and ten tutorials that present hands-on instruction. In these tutorials students with no previous programming experience learn how to plan and create their own interactive Windows applications. Using this book, students will be able to do more advanced tasks sooner than they would using other introductory texts; a perusal of the table of contents affirms this. By the end of the book, students will have learned how to write If...Then...Else, Select Case, Do...While, Do...Until, and For...Next statements, as well as how to create and manipulate sequential access files, random access files, and arrays. Students will also learn how to create executable files and how to include multiple forms in a project. GUI design skills are emphasized, and advanced skills such as accessing information in a database and using OLE are taught.

Approach

Programming with Microsoft Visual Basic 4.0 for Windows distinguishes itself from other Windows textbooks because of its unique two-pronged approach. First, it motivates students by demonstrating why they need to learn the concepts and skills. This book teaches programming concepts using a task-driven, rather than a command-driven, approach. By working through the tutorials—which are each motivated by a realistic case—students learn how to use programming applications they are likely to encounter in the workplace. This is much more effective than memorizing a list of commands out of context. Second, the content, organization, and pedagogy of this book exploit the Windows environment. The material presented in the tutorials capitalizes on Visual Basic's power to perform complex programming tasks earlier and more easily than was possible under DOS.

Features

Programming with Microsoft Visual Basic 4.0 for Windows is an exceptional textbook because it also includes the following features:

- **"Read This Before You Begin" Page** This page is consistent with Course Technology's unequaled commitment to helping instructors introduce technology into the classroom. Technical considerations and assumptions about hardware, software, and default settings are listed in one place to help instructors save time and eliminate unnecessary aggravation.

- **Tutorial Cases** Each tutorial begins with a programming-related problem that students could reasonably expect to encounter in business, followed by a demonstration of an application that could be used to solve the problem. Showing the students the completed application before they learn how to create it is motivational and instructionally sound. By allowing the students to see the type of application they will be able to create after completing the tutorial, the students will be more motivated to learn because they can see how the programming concepts that they are about to learn can be used and, therefore, why the concepts are important.
- **Lessons** Each tutorial is divided into three lessons—A, B, and C. Lesson A introduces the programming concepts that will be used in the completed application. In Lessons B and C, the student creates the application required to solve the problem specified in the Tutorial Case.
- **Step-by-Step Methodology** The unique Course Technology methodology keeps students on track. They click or press keys always within the context of solving the problem posed in the Tutorial Case. The text constantly guides students, letting them know where they are in the process of solving the problem. The numerous illustrations include labels that direct students' attention to what they should look at on the screen.
- **Help?** paragraphs anticipate the problems students are likely to encounter and help them resolve these problems on their own. This feature facilitates independent learning and frees the instructor to focus on substantive conceptual issues rather than on common procedural errors.
- **TIPS** provide additional information about a procedure—for example, an alternative method of performing the procedure.
- **GUI Design Tips** contain guidelines and recommendations for designing applications that follow Windows standards, as outlined in *The Windows® Interface Guidelines for Software Design*, published by Microsoft Press.
- **Windows 3.1 Notes** indicate when steps or screenshots differ if students are using Windows 3.1.
- **Summaries** Following each lesson is a Summary, which recaps the programming concepts, commands, and controls covered in the lesson.
- **Questions and Exercises** Each lesson concludes with meaningful, conceptual Questions that test students' understanding of what they learned in the lesson. The Questions are followed by Exercises, which provide students with additional practice of the skills and concepts they learned in the lesson.
- **Discovery Exercises** Unlike DOS, the Windows environment allows students to learn by exploring and discovering what they can do. The Discovery Exercises are designated by the word "Discovery" in the margin. They encourage students to challenge and independently develop their own programming skills while exploring the capabilities of Visual Basic.
- **Debugging Techniques and Exercises** One of the most important programming skills a student can learn is the ability to correct problems in an existing application. The Debugging Techniques and Exercises at the end of each tutorial introduce various bug-detecting techniques and then provide an opportunity for students to apply the techniques to detect and correct errors in an existing application.

Microsoft® Visual Basic® Programming System for Windows™

Microsoft® Visual Basic® Programming System for Windows™, known as the Visual Basic 4.0 Working Model, is a limited version of the software which is bundled free with each copy of this text. This programming system has all the functionality of the commercial version of Visual Basic excluding the MAKE.EXE capability (compiler), Crystal Reports Controls, SetUp Wizard, and the VB Icon Library. This version also has a two-form limit, and a limited number of controls. The inclusion of this Working Model allows students to take their learning home with them and further explore programming concepts and Visual Basic. Due to the limited functionality of the Working Model, students will need access to a computer with the full commercial version of Visual Basic 4.0 for Windows to complete some of the tutorials. This is indicated in affected tutorials.

The Supplements

- **Instructor's Manual** The Instructor's Manual has been written by the author and has been quality assurance tested. It is available in printed form and through the CTI Faculty Online Companion on the World Wide Web. (Call your customer service representative for the URL and your password.) The Instructor's Manual contains the following items:
  - Additional coverage of Visual Basic concepts such as Sorting and Binary Search.
  - Cases which can be assigned as semester projects.
  - Answers to all of the questions and solutions to all of the exercises. Suggested solutions are also included for Discovery Exercises.
  - Tutorial Notes, which contain background information from the author about the Tutorial Case and the instructional progression of the tutorial.
  - Technical Notes, which include troubleshooting tips as well as information on how to customize the students' screens to closely emulate the screen shots in the book.
- **Electronic Test Bank** The Electronic Test Bank allows instructors to create custom tests by editing individual test questions, selecting questions individually or at random, and printing out scrambled versions of the same test.
- **Solutions Files** Solutions Files contain every file students are asked to create or modify in the tutorials, Exercises, and Debugging Techniques and Exercises.
- **Student Files** Student Files, containing all of the data that students will use for the tutorials, Exercises, and Debugging Techniques and Exercises, are provided through CTI's Online Companion, as well as on disk. A Readme file includes technical tips for lab management. See the inside covers of this book and the "Read This Before You Begin" page before the Overview for more information on Student Files.

Acknowledgments

I would like to thank all of the people who helped to make this book a reality, especially Kim Crowley, my Development Editor and Product Manager. You have been so kind, patient, understanding, helpful, and fun. I know I could not have made it without you.

Thanks also to Wendy Gordon, Managing Editor; Jean Bermingham, Production Editor; and the Quality Assurance testers—Len Emma, Gina Griffiths, and Chris Lathrop—managed by Jim Valente and U Jin Wong. I am grateful to the many reviewers who provided invaluable comments on the first edition of this book, in particular: Jon E. Juarez, Dona Ana Branch Community College; Ronald Burgher, Metropolitan Community College; Mary Amundson-Miller, Greenville Technical College, and Dave Cooper of New River Community College.

Finally, I dedicate this book to my father, Henry.

Diane Zak

Contents

tutorial 3
USING VARIABLES AND CONSTANTS *VB 155*

t u t o r i a l 4

THE SELECTION STRUCTURE *VB 235*

t u t o r i a l   5
THE REPETITION STRUCTURE *VB 333*

t u t o r i a l   6

SEQUENTIAL ACCESS FILES AND MENUS *VB 423*

case ▶ The PAO Application

Read This Before You Begin

To the Student

Student Disks

To complete the tutorials, Exercises, and Debugging Techniques and Exercises in this book, you need Student Disks. Your instructor will either provide you with Student Disks or ask you to make your own.

If you are told to make your own Student Disks, you will need 3 blank, formatted high-density disks. You will need to copy a set of folders from a file server or standalone computer onto your disks. Your instructor will tell you which computer, drive letter, and folders contain the files you need. The following table shows you which folders go on each of your disks, so that you will have enough disk space to complete all the tutorials, Exercises, and Debugging Techniques and Exercises:

Student Disk	Write this on the disk label	Put these folders on the disk
1	Overview, Tutorials 1–2	*Overview* *Tut01* *Tut02*
2	Tutorials 3–6	*Tut03* *Tut04* *Tut05* *Tut06*
3	Tutorials 7–10 and Appendices A & B	*Tut07* *Tut08* *Tut09* *Tut10* *TutApA*

When you begin each tutorial, be sure you are using the correct Student Disk. See the inside front or inside back cover of this book for more information on Student Disk files, or ask your instructor or technical support person for assistance.

Using Your Own Computer

If you are going to work through this book using your own computer, you will need:
- **Computer System** Microsoft Visual Basic 4.0 Standard Edition or Professional Edition for Windows 3.1 or Windows 95 must be installed on your computer. This book assumes a complete installation of Microsoft Visual Basic 4.0.
- **Microsoft Visual Basic Programming System for Windows,** known as the Visual Basic 4.0 Working Model, is provided with each copy of this book. The following system requirements apply.

  - Personal computer with 386DX/25 or higher processor (486 or higher recommended)
  - Microsoft Windows 95 or Windows NT Workstation 3.51 or later operating system
  - 6 MB of memory (8 MB or more recommended) if using Windows 95; 16 MB if using Windows NT Workstation
  - Available hard-disk space; minimum installation 20 MB
  - A CD-ROM drive (the Visual Basic Working Model is only available on CD-ROM)
  - VGA or higher resolution monitor
  - Microsoft Mouse or compatible pointing device

This programming system has all the functionality of the commercial version of Visual Basic excluding the MAKE.EXE capability (compiler), Crystal Reports Controls, SetUp Wizard, and the VB Icon Library. This version also has a two-form limit, and a limited number of custom controls. Due to the limited functionality of the

Visual Basic Working Model, you will need access to a computer with the full commercial version of Visual Basic 4.0 for Windows to complete some of the tutorials in this book.
- **Student Disks** Ask your instructor or lab manager for details on how to get Student Disks. You will not be able to complete the tutorials or exercises in this book using your own computer until you have Student Disks. The student files may also be obtained electronically through the Internet. See the inside front or back cover of this book for more details.

Visit Our World Wide Web Site

Additional materials designed especially for you are available on the World Wide Web. Go to **http://coursetools.com.**

To the Instructor

To complete the tutorials in this book, your students must use a set of student files. These files are included in the Instructor's Resource Kit. They may also be obtained electronically through the Internet. See the inside front or back cover of this book for more details. Follow the instructions in the Readme file to copy the student files to your server or standalone computer. You can view the Readme file using a text editor such as WordPad or Notepad.

Once the files are copied, you can make Student Disks for the students yourself, or tell students where to find the files so they can make their own Student Disks. Make sure the files get copied correctly onto the Student Disks by following the instructions in the Student Disks section above, which will ensure that students have enough disk space to complete all the tutorials, Exercises, and Debugging Techniques and Exercises.

CTI Student Files

You are granted a license to copy the Student Files to any computer or computer network used by students who have purchased this book.

OVERVIEW

objectives

This overview contains basic definitions and background information, including:

- A brief description of Visual Basic
- A brief history of programming languages
- A Visual Basic demonstration
- Information on using the tutorials effectively

An Overview of Visual Basic:

A History and a Demonstration

A Brief Description of Visual Basic

Although computers appear to be amazingly intelligent machines, they cannot yet think on their own. Computers still rely on human beings to give them directions. These directions are called **programs,** and the people who write the programs are called **programmers.**

Just as human beings communicate with each other through the use of languages such as English, Spanish, Hindi, or Chinese, programmers use a variety of special languages, called **programming languages**, to communicate with the computer. Some popular programming languages are COBOL (Common Business Oriented Language), Pascal, C, BASIC (Beginner's All-Purpose Symbolic Instruction Code), and Visual Basic. As its name implies, Visual Basic is more visually oriented than most other programming languages. In fact, you might think of Visual Basic as a sort of sign language. Visual Basic represents a new way to write computer programs.

A Brief History of Programming Languages

It is difficult to appreciate the Visual Basic language, and to understand its impact on the future of programming, without looking back at the programming languages that preceded it. In the next sections, you will take a quick look at the forerunners to Visual Basic.

Machine Languages

Within a computer, all data is represented by microscopic electronic switches that can be either off or on. The off switch is designated by a 0, and the on switch is designated by a 1. Because computers can understand only these on and off switches, the first programmers had to write the program instructions using nothing but combinations of 0s and 1s. Instructions written in 0s and 1s are called **machine language** or **machine code**. The machine languages (each type of machine has its own language) represent the only way to communicate directly with the computer. Figure 1 shows a program written in a machine language.

```
0100
001101   100000   001101   110001
00101    10001    10000
01110
111001
111001   001   11000   001
11000
0011100
100010   00110
```

Figure 1: Machine language

As you can imagine, programming in machine language is very tedious and error-prone; it also requires highly trained programmers.

Assembly Languages

Slightly more advanced programming languages are called **assembly languages**. Figure 2 shows a program written in an assembly language.

```
main proc pay
    mov ax, dseg
    mov ax, 0b00h
    add ax, dx
    mov a1, b1
    mul b1, ax
    mov b1, 04h
```

Figure 2: Assembly language

The assembly languages simplify the programmer's job by allowing the programmer to use mnemonics in place of the 0s and 1s in the program. **Mnemonics** are memory aids—in this case, alphabetic abbreviations for instructions. For example, most assembly languages use the mnemonic ADD to represent an add operation and the mnemonic MUL to represent a multiply operation. Programs written in an assembly language require an **assembler**, which is also a program, to convert the assembly instructions into machine code—the 0s and 1s the computer can understand. Although it is much easier to write programs in assembly language than in machine language, programming in assembly language still is tedious and requires highly trained programmers.

High-Level Languages

High-level languages, which allow the programmer to use instructions that more closely resemble the English language, represent the next advance in programming languages. High-level languages require either an interpreter or a compiler to convert the English-like instructions into the 0s and 1s the computer can understand. Like assemblers, both interpreters and compilers are separate programs. An **interpreter** translates the high-level instructions into machine code, line by line, as the program is running; a **compiler** translates the entire program into machine code before running the program. Like their predecessors, most high-level languages are procedure oriented.

Procedure-Oriented High-Level Languages

In **procedure-oriented high-level languages**, the emphasis of a program is on *how* to accomplish a task. The programmer must instruct the computer every step of the way, from the start of the task to its completion. The programmer determines and controls the order in which the computer should process the instructions. COBOL, BASIC, Pascal, and C are popular procedure-oriented languages.

Figure 3 shows a program written in BASIC. Notice how closely the instructions resemble the English language. Even if you do not know the BASIC language, it is easy to see that the program shown in Figure 3 tells the computer, step by step, *how* to compute and print an employee's net pay.

```
input "Enter Name";names$
input "Enter Hours";hours
input "Enter Rate";rate
gross = hours * rate
fwt = .2 * gross
socsec = .07 * gross
state = .06 * gross
net = gross - fwt - socsec - state
print names$, net
end
```

Figure 3: BASIC—a procedure-oriented high-level language

In all procedure-oriented programs, the order of the instructions is extremely important. For example, in the program shown in Figure 3, you could not put the instruction to print the net pay before the instruction to calculate the net pay and expect the computer to print the correct results. When writing programs in a procedure-oriented language, the programmer must determine not only the proper instructions to give the computer, but the correct sequence of those instructions as well.

Procedure-oriented high-level languages are a vast improvement over machine languages and assembly languages. Many of the high-level languages do not require a great amount of technical expertise; you do not need to be a professional programmer to write a program using these languages.

The Introduction of Windows

As you know, Windows software provides an easy-to-use **graphical user interface**, referred to as a **GUI**, with which a user can interact. This GUI is common to all applications written for the Windows environment. It is this standard interface that makes Windows applications so popular: once you learn one Windows application, it is very easy to learn another.

Although the standard interface found in all Windows applications makes the user's life much easier, it complicates the programmer's life a great deal. In the beginning, writing programs for the Windows environment was extremely tedious. Programmers found themselves spending countless hours writing instructions to create the buttons, scroll bars, dialog boxes, and menus needed in all Windows applications. Because the programmer has no control over which button the user will click in a Windows application, or which scroll bar the user will employ, the first Windows programmers had to write instructions that could handle any combination of actions the user might take. Tasks that used to take a few lines of program code now needed pages. Because programming Windows applications required a great amount of expertise, it appeared that the beginning of the Windows environment meant the end of the do-it-yourself, nonprofessional programmer. But then a new category of high-level languages emerged—the object-oriented/event-driven programming languages.

Object-Oriented/Event-Driven High-Level Languages

The object-oriented/event-driven high-level languages simplified the task of programming applications for Windows. In **object-oriented/event-driven languages**, the emphasis of a program is on the *objects* included in the user interface (such as scroll bars and buttons) and the *events* (such as scrolling and clicking) that occur when those objects are used.

Visual Basic is an object-oriented/event-driven programming language that is easy enough for a nonprogrammer to use, yet sophisticated enough to be used by professional programmers. (C++ and Smalltalk are also object-oriented/event-driven programming languages.) With Visual Basic it takes just a few clicks of the mouse to include standard Windows objects such as buttons, list boxes, scroll bars, and icons in your Windows application. Once the objects are created, the programmer then concentrates on writing the specific instructions telling each object how to respond when clicked, double-clicked, scrolled, and so on. For example, Figure 4 shows the Visual Basic instructions that direct an object to end the application when the user clicks the object. (In this case the object is an Exit button.)

```
Private Sub cmdExit_Click ()
    End
End Sub
```

Figure 4: Visual Basic—an object-oriented/event-driven language

In the next section you will run a Visual Basic application that will give you a quick look at some of the objects you will learn how to create in the following tutorials.

A Visual Basic Demonstration

The Visual Basic application you are about to run will show you only some of the objects you will learn how to create in the tutorials. For now, it is not important for you to understand how these objects were created or why the objects perform the way they do. Those questions will be answered in the tutorials.

To run the Visual Basic application:

1 If necessary, start Windows, then place your Student Disk in the appropriate drive. Click the **Start** button on the taskbar, then click **Run** on the Start menu. The Run dialog box opens. Click the **Browse** button in the Run dialog box. The Browse dialog box opens. You want to run the Month95(month95.exe) file, which is located in the Overview folder on your Student Disk.

If necessary, start Windows, then place your Student Disk in the appropriate drive. Make sure the Program Manager window is open. Click File on the menu bar, then click Run in the File menu. The Run dialog box opens. Click the Browse button. The Browse dialog box opens. You want to run the Month31.exe file, which is located in the Overview folder on your Student Disk.

2 Click the **Look in** list arrow, then click the drive containing your Student Disk. Click the **Overview** folder, then click the **Open** button to open the Overview folder. Click **Month95**(month95.exe) in the list of file names, then click the **Open** button. The Browse dialog box closes and the Run dialog box appears again. The Run box should display either A:\OVERVIEW\MONTH95.EXE or B:\OVERVIEW\MONTH95.EXE. Click the **OK** button. After a few moments, Visual Basic displays the application shown in Figure 5.

WINDOWS 3.1

Click the Drives list arrow, then click the drive containing your Student Disk. Click the a:\ (or b:\) folder in the Directories box, then click the OK button to open the folder. You want to run the Month31.exe file, which is located in the Overview folder on your Student Disk. Click the Overview folder, then click the OK button to open the Overview folder. Click month31.exe in the list of file names, then click the OK button. The Browse dialog box closes and the Run dialog box appears again. The Command Line should display either A:\OVERVIEW\MONTH31.EXE or B:\OVERVIEW\MONTH31.EXE. Click the OK button. After a few moments, Visual Basic displays the application shown in Figure 5.

menu

text box

list box

option buttons

label control

command button

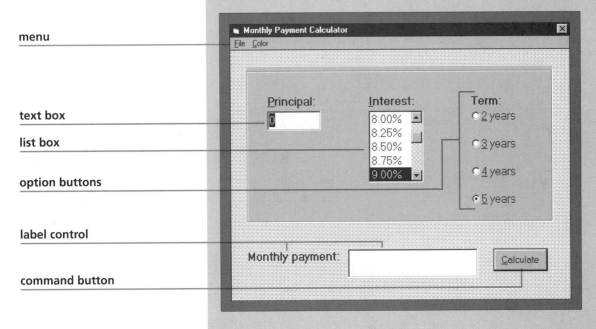

Figure 5: Monthly payment application

Figure 5 identifies some of the different objects appearing in the application's interface. Notice that the interface contains a text box, a list box, a command button, option buttons, label controls, and a menu. You can use this application to calculate the monthly payment for a car loan. For example, what would your monthly payment be if you wanted to borrow $30,000 at 8% interest for five years?

To compute the monthly car payment:

1   Type **30000** in the Principal text box, then click **8.00%** in the Interest list box. Notice that Visual Basic highlights the 8.00% entry in the list box.

2   The option button corresponding to the five-year term is already selected, so you just need to click the **Calculate** button to compute the monthly payment. Visual Basic computes and displays the monthly payment, as shown in Figure 6.

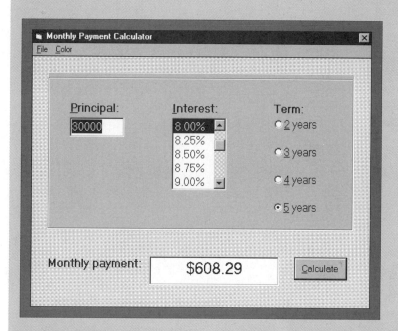

Figure 6: Computed monthly payment

Now determine what your monthly payment would be if you wanted to borrow $10,000 at 7.25% interest for four years.

3   Type **10000** in the Principal text box. Notice that the 10000 replaces the previously highlighted 30000.

4   Scroll the Interest list box until the 7.25% rate is visible, then click **7.25%**.

5   Click the **4 years** option button. Notice that Visual Basic deselects the five-year option button as it selects the four-year option button.

6   Click the **Calculate** button to compute the monthly payment. Visual Basic computes and displays the monthly payment of $240.62.

Notice that the application's menu bar has two menus: File and Color. See what options are on both menus.

To view the options on the Color and File menus:

1   Click **Color**. The Color menu opens and displays two options: Background and Information Box.

You use the Background option to change the background color of the screen.

2   Click **Background**. The Color dialog box opens. Click a color of your choice, then click the **OK** button. The application's background changes accordingly.

If you don't like the current color, you can use the Background option on the Color menu to select a different color. Now see what the Information Box option on the Color menu does.

3   Click **Color**, then click **Information Box**. The Color dialog box opens. Click a color of your choice, then click the **OK** button. The color of the information box changes accordingly. (The information box is the box in which you enter the principal, interest, and term information.)

If you don't like the current color, you can use the Information Box option on the Color menu to select a different color. Now view the options on the File menu.

4   Click **File**. The File menu opens and shows two options: Print and Exit.

You use the Print option to print the monthly payment screen. (If you chose a dark color for the background and/or the information box, you should change the dark color to a light color before printing; otherwise your printout may be unreadable.)

5   If your computer is connected to a printer, click **Print**. The monthly payment screen prints on the printer.

You use the Exit option on the File menu to end the demonstration application.

6   Click **File**, then click **Exit**. The demonstration is now finished.

In the tutorials you will learn how to create Visual Basic applications that you can run directly from Windows, just as you did in the demonstration.

As you can see, programming languages have come a long way since the first machine languages. This brief history and demonstration should give you a better appreciation for the Visual Basic programming language.

Using the Tutorials Effectively

The tutorials in this book will help you learn about Microsoft Visual Basic Version 4.0. They are designed to be used at your computer. Begin by reading the text that explains the concepts. Then when you come to the numbered steps, follow the steps on your computer. Read each step carefully and completely before you try it.

As you work, compare your screen with the figures to verify your results. Don't worry if your screen display differs slightly from the figures. The important parts of the screen display are labeled in each figure. Just be sure you have these parts on your screen. The figures in the book show how your screen will look if you are using Windows 95. If you are using Windows 3.1, however, you will notice that the differences between the figures and your screen are minor. For example, the Control menu box in Windows 3.1 has been replaced with a Close button in Windows 95, and the Minimize, Maximize, and Restore buttons have a different look in Windows 95. When the tutorials direct you to "Close the window," "Minimize the window," "Maximize the window," and "Restore the window," you simply need to use the method appropriate for your version of Windows.

Don't worry about making mistakes; that's part of the learning process. Help? notes identify common problems and explain how to get back on track. You should complete the steps in the Help? box only if you are having the problem described. Tip boxes provide additional information about a procedure—for example, an alternative method of performing the procedure.

Each tutorial is divided into three lessons. You might want to take a break between lessons. Following each lesson is a Summary section that lists the important elements of the lesson. After the Summary section are multiple-choice questions and exercises designed to review and reinforce that lesson's concepts. You should complete all of the end-of-lesson questions and exercises before going on to the next lesson. You can't learn Visual Basic without a lot of practice, and future tutorials assume that you have mastered the information found in the previous tutorials. Some of the end-of-lesson exercises are Discovery exercises, which allow you to both "discover" the solutions to problems on your own and experiment with material that is not covered in the tutorial.

At the end of each tutorial you will find a Debugging section. In programming, the term **debugging** refers to the process of finding and fixing the errors in a program. Each Debugging section includes debugging tips, as well as exercises designed to let you practice debugging applications.

Throughout the book you will find GUI (Graphical User Interface) boxes. These boxes contain guidelines and recommendations for designing applications. You should follow these guidelines and recommendations so that your applications follow the Windows standard.

Before you begin the tutorials, you should know how to use Microsoft Windows 95. This book assumes you have learned basic Windows-navigation and file-management skills from Course Technology's *New Perspectives on Microsoft Windows 95 Brief*, *New Perspectives on Microsoft Windows 3.1 Brief*, or an *equivalent* book.

QUESTIONS

1. The set of directions given to a computer is called _____ .
   a. computerese
   b. commands
   c. instructions
   d. a program
   e. rules

2. Instructions written in 0s and 1s are called _____ .
   a. assembly language
   b. booleans
   c. computerese
   d. machine code
   e. mnemonics

3. _____ languages allow the programmer to use mnemonics, which are alphabetic abbreviations for instructions.
   a. Assembly
   b. High-level
   c. Machine
   d. Object
   e. Procedure

4. _____ languages allow the programmer to use instructions that more closely resemble the English language.
   a. Asembly
   b. High-level
   c. Machine
   d. Object
   e. Procedure

5. A(n) _____ translates high-level instructions into machine code, line by line, as the program is running.
   a. assembler
   b. compiler
   c. interpreter
   d. program
   e. translator

6. A(n) _____ translates the entire high-level program into machine code before running the program.
   a. assembler
   b. compiler
   c. interpreter
   d. program
   e. translator

7. A(n) _____ converts assembly instructions into machine code.
   a. assembler
   b. compiler
   c. interpreter
   d. program
   e. translator

8. Visual Basic is a(n) _____ language.
   a. assembler
   b. mnemonic
   c. object-oriented/event-driven
   d. procedure-oriented

9. In procedure-oriented languages, the emphasis of a program is on how to accomplish a task.
   a. True
   b. False

10. In object-oriented languages, the emphasis of a program is on the objects included in the user interface and the events that occur on those objects.
    a. True
    b. False

TUTORIAL

1

An Introduction to Visual Basic

Creating a Copyright Screen

case▶ Interlocking Software Company, a small firm specializing in custom programs, hires you as a programmer trainee. In that capacity, you will learn to write Windows applications using the Visual Basic language, an object-oriented/event-driven programming language.

On your second day of work, Chris Statton, the senior programmer at Interlocking Software, assigns you your first task: create a copyright screen. Chris explains that every custom application created at Interlocking Software must display a copyright screen when the application is started. The copyright screen identifies the application's author and copyright year and includes the Interlocking Software Company logo. A sketch of the copyright screen is shown in Figure 1-1.

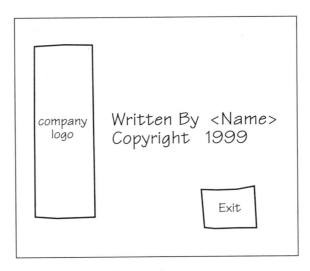

Figure 1-1: Sketch of the copyright screen

Although this first task is small, the copyright screen will give you an opportunity to learn the fundamentals of Visual Basic without having to worry about the design issues and programming concepts necessary for larger applications.

Previewing the Copyright Screen

Before starting the first lesson, you will preview a completed copyright screen that was created using Visual Basic. (If you are using the Professional Edition of Visual Basic, you will add sound to this copyright screen in Lesson C.)

To preview the completed copyright screen:

1   If necessary, start Windows, then place your Student Disk in the appropriate drive. Click the **Start** button on the taskbar. The Start menu opens. Click **Run** in the Start menu. The Run dialog box opens. Click the **Browse** button in the Run dialog box. The Browse dialog box opens. You want to run the Copy95(Copy95.exe) file, which is located in the Tut01 folder on your Student Disk.

If necessary, start Windows, then place your Student Disk in the appropriate drive. Make sure the Program Manager window is open. Click File on the menu bar. The File menu opens. Click Run in the File menu. The Run dialog box opens. Click the Browse button. The Browse dialog box opens. You want to run the Copy31(Copy31.exe) file, which is located in the Tut01 folder on your Student Disk.

2   If necessary, click the **Look in** list arrow, then click the drive containing your Student Disk. Click the **Tut01** folder, then click the **Open** button to open the Tut01 folder. Click **Copy95 (Copy95.exe)** in the list of filenames. (Depending on how Windows 95 is set up on your computer, you may see the .exe extension on the filename. If you do, click the Copy95.exe filename.) Click the **Open** button. The Browse dialog box closes and the Run dialog box appears again. The Run box should display either A:\TUT01\COPY95.EXE or B:\TUT01\COPY95.EXE. Click the **OK** button. After a short time, a copyright screen appears, as shown in Figure 1-2.

Click the Drives list arrow, then click the drive containing your Student Disk. Click the a:\ (or b:\) folder in the Directories list box, then click the OK button to open the folder. Click the Tut01 folder, then click the OK button to open the Tut01 folder. Click Copy31.exe in the list of filenames, then click the OK button. The Browse dialog box closes and the Run dialog box appears again. The command line should display either A:\TUT01\COPY31.EXE or B:\TUT01\COPY31.EXE. Click the OK button. After a short time, a copyright screen appears, as shown in Figure 1-2.

Figure 1-2: Copyright screen

3   Click the **Exit** button. The application ends.

Now you will create your own copyright screen.

Tutorial 1 is designed to get you comfortable with the Visual Basic environment. You will also learn about the Visual Basic language. Remember, each tutorial contains three lessons. You should complete a lesson in full and do the end-of-lesson questions and exercises before moving on to the next lesson.

In this lesson you will learn how to:

■ Start and exit Visual Basic

■ Identify the components of the Visual Basic display

■ Set the properties of an object

■ Create, save, run, and stop a Visual Basic application

■ Open both a new project and an existing project

Creating a New Project

Starting Visual Basic

Before you can begin creating your copyright screen, you must start Visual Basic.

To start Visual Basic:

1 If necessary, start Windows, then place your Student Disk in the appropriate disk drive. Click the **Start** button on the Windows 95 taskbar. The Start menu appears. Point to **Programs** in the Start menu. The Programs menu appears to the right of the Start menu. Point to **Visual Basic 4.0** in the Programs menu. The Visual Basic menu appears to the right of the Programs menu. Click **Visual Basic 4.0** (Visual Basic 4.0 Working Model) in the Visual Basic 4.0 menu. The Visual Basic copyright screen appears momentarily, and then the Visual Basic startup screen appears. Hide the taskbar. (If you don't know how to hide the Windows 95 taskbar, read the HELP? statement below.)

HELP? To hide the Windows 95 taskbar, click the Start button, point to Settings, then click taskbar to display the taskbar Properties window. On the taskbar Options tab, click the Auto hide check box. A check mark appears in the check box. Click the OK button to remove the taskbar Properties window. The taskbar is now hidden from view; only a thin line appears in its place at the bottom of the screen. (Depending on how you have Windows 95 set up, your taskbar could be at the top, right, left, or bottom edge of the screen. The thin line will appear in the location of the taskbar. This book assumes that the taskbar is located at the bottom of the screen.) To display the hidden taskbar temporarily, move the mouse pointer to a location below the thin line at the bottom of the screen. To hide the taskbar again, move the mouse pointer back to a location above the thin line at the bottom of the screen.

If necessary, start Windows, then place your Student Disk in the appropriate disk drive. The Program Manager window should be open. To reduce some of the screen clutter, you will first instruct Windows to minimize the Program Manager to an icon when you start Visual Basic. To do so, click Options. The Options menu opens. If the Minimize on Use option is not checked, then click Minimize on Use to check that option. If the Options menu is still open, click Options again to close it. Double-click the Visual Basic 4.0 (16-bit) group icon in the Program Manager window. The Visual Basic group window opens. Double-click the Visual Basic 4.0 (16-bit) icon in the Visual Basic group window.

Important Note: In the future, you will be instructed simply to "start Visual Basic."

The Visual Basic startup screen is shown in Figure 1-3. Your screen might not look identical to Figure 1-3, but it should have all the parts labeled in the figure.

Project window

main window

Toolbox window (your toolbox may include some additional tools)

Form window

Properties window

Figure 1-3: Visual Basic startup screen

HELP? Recall that the figures in these tutorials show Windows 95 screens. If you are using Windows 3.1, your screen will differ slightly from Figure 1-3. The title bar, for example, now has a Close button ☒ instead of a Control menu box ▭. The Minimize and Maximize buttons also have a different look in Windows 95.

The Visual Basic Startup Screen

As Figure 1-3 shows, the Visual Basic startup screen contains five separate windows: the Visual Basic main window, the Toolbox window, the Form window, the Properties window, and the Project window. You can't see all of the Properties window and the Project window right now because the Form window overlaps them. You will learn how to display those windows in a little while. For now, take a closer look at Visual Basic's main window, Form window, and Toolbox window.

HELP? If the Toolbox window is not displayed on the screen, click View on the menu bar, then click Toolbox. Your Toolbox window may include some additional tools. If the Properties window is not displayed on the screen, click View, then click Properties. If the Project window is not displayed, click View, then click Project.

The Main Window

The Visual Basic main window, at the top of the screen, contains the title bar, the menu bar, and the toolbar. Figure 1-4 shows these parts of the Visual Basic display.

title bar
menu bar
toolbar

Figure 1-4: Visual Basic main window

HELP? If the toolbar is not displayed on the screen, click View on the menu bar, then click Toolbar.

The title bar indicates that Microsoft Visual Basic is currently working in **design time,** which means it is waiting for you to design your application. The title bar also shows that the name of the current application is Project1. Below the Visual Basic title bar is the menu bar. The **menu bar** displays the commands you will use to build your application. Buttons on the **toolbar,** located below the menu bar, provide quick access to the most commonly used menu commands.

The Form Window

A Visual Basic Form window, one of many objects you can create in Visual Basic, appears in the center of the screen, as shown in Figure 1-5.

default caption

title bar
Minimize button
Maximize/Resize button
Close button

Figure 1-5: Visual Basic Form window

A Visual Basic **Form window** is a window in which you design the user interface for your application. As you might recall, a **user interface** is what you see and interact with when running a Windows application. Notice that the Form window (or form) already contains its own title bar, as well as Minimize ▼, Maximize ▲, and Close ☒ buttons.

The Form window in Windows 3.1 also contains Minimize ▼ and Maximize ▲ buttons, but has a Control menu box ▭ instead of a Close button.

Visual Basic assigns the default caption, Form1, to the first form. This caption appears in the form's title bar.

In these tutorials, you will learn how to customize a form by attaching other objects, such as buttons, boxes, and scroll bars, to the form. (Notice that a form is an object that can contain other objects.) During design time, Visual Basic displays dots in the form to assist you in aligning these objects. The dots are not visible when you run the application.

The Toolbox Window

On the left of the screen is the Toolbox window. The **toolbox** contains the set of tools you use when designing a Visual Basic application. These tools allow you to place objects (also called **controls**) such as buttons, boxes, and scroll bars on the form. Figure 1-6 describes the purpose of each of the basic tools. (Your toolbox may include some additional tools.)

Tool	Control	Purpose
	Check box	Displays a box that is either checked or unchecked
	Combo box	Combines and displays a text box with a list box
	Command button	Performs a command when clicked
	Data	Displays information from a database
	Directory list box	Displays a list of directories from which the user can select
	Drive list box	Displays a list of drives from which the user can select
	File list box	Displays a list of filenames from which the user can select
	Frame	Provides a visual and functional container for controls
	Horizontal scroll bar	Displays a horizontal scroll bar containing a range of values
	Image	Displays a picture; simpler version of the Picture box control
	Label	Displays text that the user cannot change
	Line	Draws lines on a form
	List box	Displays a list of choices from which a user can select
	OLE	Allows object linking and embedding
	Option button	Displays a button that can be either on or off
	Picture box	Displays a picture
	Pointer	Allows you to move and size forms and controls
	Shape	Draws a circle, ellipse, square, or rectangle on a form
	Text box	Accepts or displays text that the user can change
	Timer	Displays a clock that performs events at specified time intervals
	Vertical scroll bar	Displays a vertical scroll bar containing a range of values

tips

If you have trouble distinguishing the tools in the toolbox, you can display the tool's name by resting the mouse pointer on the tool.

Figure 1-6: List of tools in the toolbox

Take a look at the Project window next.

The Project Window

An application (project) can contain many files. The Project window lists the names of the files included in the application you are currently creating. Display the Project window to see the names of the files included in this application.

To display the Project window:

You can also display the Project window by using the Project command on the View menu.

1   Position the mouse pointer on the **Project** button ⊠ on the toolbar. After a few seconds a **tooltip**, which contains the button's name, appears; in this case, the tooltip says Project. If you have trouble distinguishing the icons in the toolbar buttons, you can always display a button's name by resting the mouse pointer on a button. Click the **Project** button ⊠ on the toolbar. The Project window displays with its title bar highlighted, indicating that it is the currently selected window.

2   If necessary, position the mouse pointer on the Project window's bottom border until it becomes a double arrow, then drag the bottom border up until it matches Figure 1-7. (Remember, dragging means holding the left mouse button down while you move the mouse.) Position the mouse pointer on the Project window's title bar and drag the Project window to the bottom of the screen, as shown in Figure 1-7.

HELP? When dragging a window, be sure to place the mouse pointer on the window's title bar.

displays the code for
the selected file

displays the form
associated with the
selected file

Project window

Figure 1-7: Location of the Project window

Whenever you run Visual Basic or whenever you create a new project, Visual Basic automatically creates a default project named Project1. The name appears in the title bar of the Project window. The default project contains the Form1 file, which is the default filename for the form appearing on the screen. If you don't change the name of the form when you save it, this is the name Visual Basic will use to save the form. (A Visual Basic project can contain many different files, as you will see in future tutorials.)

Notice that the Project window also contains two buttons labeled, respectively, View Form and View Code. The **View Form** button displays the form associated with the selected file. Use this button to view the various forms included in a project or to display a form you closed unintentionally. The **View Code** button displays the program instructions, called code, associated with the selected file.

So far you have learned about four of the five Visual Basic windows: the main window, the Form window, the Toolbox window, and the Project window. The Properties window is next.

The Properties Window

Each object in Visual Basic has a set of characteristics, called **properties**, associated with it. These properties, listed in the **Properties window**, control the object's appearance and behavior. Before you can display the Properties window, you must select an object. In this case, you will select the form, which is the only object in the current application.

tips

▶ You can also display the Properties window by pressing the F4 key or by using the Properties command in the View menu.

To display the Properties window:

1   Click the **form's title bar** to select the form. The form's title bar is now highlighted, which indicates that it is the selected object.

2   Click the **Properties** button 🗗 on the toolbar. The Properties window appears on the screen with its title bar highlighted, indicating that it is the currently selected window.

Now arrange the screen so the Properties window does not overlap the Form window.

3   If necessary, position the mouse pointer on the Properties window's title bar and drag the Properties window to match Figure 1-8. You may also need to drag the bottom border of the Properties window to match Figure 1-8.

4   Click the **form's title bar** to select the form. Position the mouse pointer on the right border of the form until the pointer turns into a double arrow, then drag the border to match Figure 1-8. Position the mouse pointer on the bottom border of the form until the pointer turns into a double arrow, then drag the border to match Figure 1-8. If necessary, position the mouse pointer on the left border of the form until the pointer turns into a double arrow, then drag the border to match Figure 1-8.

Properties window
title bar

Object box

Properties list

settings box

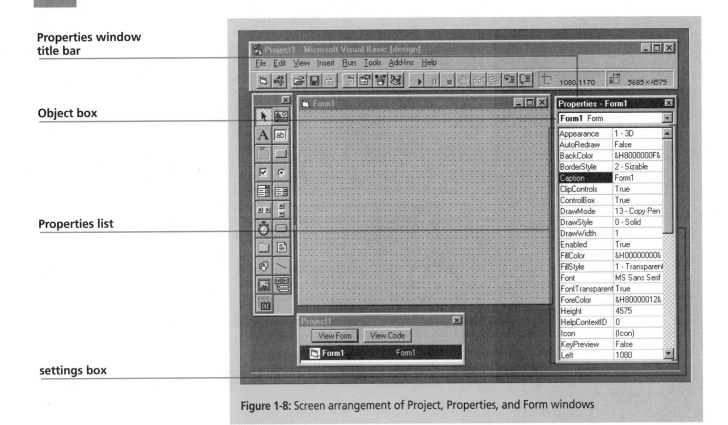

Figure 1-8: Screen arrangement of Project, Properties, and Form windows

As indicated in Figure 1-8, the Properties window includes an Object box and a Properties list. The **Object box**, located immediately below the Properties window's title bar, displays the name and type of the selected object—in this case, Form1 Form. You can use the Object box to select an object in the user interface. You must select an object before you can either display or change the value of its properties. (You'll learn more about the Object box in Lesson B.)

The **Properties list** in the Properties window has two columns. The left column displays all the properties associated with the selected object (in this case, the form). The right column, called the **Settings box**, displays the current value, or setting, of each of those properties. For example, the current value of the Caption property is Form1.

tips

••••••••••••••••••

▶ You can also use ↓ and ↑ on your keyboard, as well as the Home, End, Page Down, and Page Up keys to scroll the Properties window, but you must first make the Properties window the active window.

To view the properties in the Properties window:

1 Click the **down scroll arrow** in the Properties window's vertical scroll bar to scroll through the entire Properties list. As you scroll, notice the various properties associated with a form.

2 Drag the scroll box to the top of the vertical scroll bar to display the beginning of the Properties list once again.

Notice that the currently selected property in the Properties list is highlighted. In this case, the currently selected property is the Caption property; the value of the Caption property is Form1.

HELP? If the Caption property is not highlighted, click Caption in the Properties list.

You can change the setting for many of the listed properties by simply typing a new value in the property's Settings box. Some properties, however, have predefined settings. If a property has predefined settings, either a list arrow or an ellipsis (...) will appear in the Settings box when the property is selected. When you click the list arrow, either a list or a color palette appears containing the valid predefined settings for that property; you then select the setting you want from that list or color palette. Clicking the ellipsis in the Settings box displays a dialog box in which you select the settings for the property. You will get a chance to practice with both the list arrow and ellipsis as you change various properties throughout this lesson. You will begin by changing the Caption property, which is the currently selected property.

Setting the Caption Property

Programmers who create applications for the Windows environment need to be aware of the conventions used in Windows applications. One such convention is that the name of the application usually appears in the application window's title bar. Notice, for example, that "Project1 - Microsoft Visual Basic [design]" appears in the title bar of Visual Basic's window. Because the form on the screen will become your application's window when the application is run, its title bar should display an appropriate name.

In Visual Basic the **Caption property** controls the text displayed in the form's title bar. If you are using Windows 95, the Caption property is also displayed on the application's button on the taskbar when the application is running.

WINDOWS **3.1**

If you are using Windows 3.1, the Caption property is also displayed below the form's icon when the form is minimized.

As you've already seen, Visual Basic automatically assigns the default caption Form1 to the first form in a project. A better, more descriptive caption would be "Interlocking Software Company"—the name of the company responsible for the copyright screen application.

To set the Caption property for the selected form:

1   Verify that the Caption property is the currently selected property in the Properties window.

Notice that the Settings box does not contain either the list arrow or the ellipsis, which means this property does not have any predefined settings.

> **HELP?** If the Caption property is not highlighted, click Caption in the Properties list.

2   Type **Interlocking Software Company** and press the **Enter** key. The new caption appears in the Settings box to the right of the Caption property; it also appears in the form's title bar.

Notice that you do not have to erase the old caption before entering the new caption. You simply need to select the appropriate property and then type the new value; the new value replaces the old value for the selected property.

You will change the form's Name property next.

Setting the Name Property

Visual Basic automatically assigns a default name to every object it creates. For example, the default name for the first form in a project is Form1, the default name for the second form in a project is Form2, and so on. Because a project can contain many objects, it is a good practice to give each one a more meaningful name; this will help you keep track of the various objects in the application.

An object's name must begin with a letter and it must contain only letters, numbers, and the underscore character. You cannot use punctuation characters or spaces in an object's name, and the name cannot exceed 40 characters. One popular naming convention is to have the first three characters in the name represent the object's type (form, scroll bar, and so on), and the remainder of the name represent the object's purpose. For example, a more descriptive name for this form would be frmCopyright. The "frm" identifies the object as a form, and the "Copyright" reminds you of the form's purpose. Figure 1-9 contains a list of the three characters usually associated with the form and the basic tools (objects) in the toolbox. (The pointer is not really a control; it simply provides a way to move and resize forms and controls.)

Object	ID	Object	ID
Check Box	chk	Label	lbl
Combo Box	cbo	Line	lin
Command Button	cmd	List Box	lst
Data	dat	OLE	ole
Directory List Box	dir	Option Button	opt
Drive List Box	drv	Picture	pic
File List Box	fil	Shape	shp
Form	frm	Text Box	txt
Frame	fra	Timer	tmr
Horizontal Scroll Bar	hsb	Vertical Scroll Bar	vsb
Image	img		

Figure 1-9: Objects and their three-character IDs for the Name property

You assign a new name to an object by setting the object's **Name property**. Although you can type the entire name in uppercase letters, lowercase letters, or a combination of uppercase and lowercase letters, it is a common practice to type the three-character ID in lowercase and capitalize just the first letter in the part of the name that identifies the purpose. For example, you will capitalize only the "C" in "frmCopyright."

tips

• • • • • • • • • • • • • • • •

You can also press ↓ and ↑ on your keyboard, as well as the Home, End, Page Down, and Page Up keys to scroll the Properties window, but you must first make the Properties window the active window.

To set the Name property for the Form1 form, which is the currently selected object:

1 Scroll the Properties window until the Name property is visible, then click **Name** in the Properties list to select that property. The Name property is now highlighted.

Notice that the Name property does not have any predefined settings as its Settings box does not contain a list arrow or an ellipsis. That means that you can simply type the new name into the Settings box.

2 Type **frmCopyright** and press the **Enter** key. (Remember, you can't use spaces in the name.) The new name, frmCopyright, is displayed in both the Properties and Project windows, as shown in Figure 1-10.

form object name

default project name

filename for
form on disk

form name

Figure 1-10: Name changes in Project window and in Properties window

Notice that Visual Basic makes two changes in the Project window. It replaces the default filename Form1 with frmCopyright and the default form name Form1 with frmCopyright.

It can be very easy to confuse the Name property with the Caption property. Recall that the form's Caption property controls the text displayed in the form's title bar. It also controls the text displayed on the application's taskbar button when the application is running in Windows 95, or below the minimized icon in Windows 3.1. The Name property, however, assigns a name to an object. When writing Visual Basic instructions (called code), you use an object's name, not its caption, to refer to the object. In other words, the name is used by the programmer, whereas the caption is read by the user.

Programmers typically give names to the form and to any controls that will either be coded or referred to in code. Controls that are not coded and are not referred to in code are usually not given names. You will name all of the controls in this lesson for practice only.

Next you will make the copyright screen more interesting by adding some color to it.

Setting the BackColor Property

The **BackColor property** controls the background color of an object. Unlike the Caption and Name properties, the BackColor property has predefined settings.

To change the background color of an object:

1 As the Object box in the Properties window shows, the form is the currently selected object, so you just need to scroll the Properties window until the BackColor property is visible in the Properties list.

2 Click **BackColor** in the Properties list. Notice the list arrow in the Settings box.

3 Click the **Settings box** list arrow. A color palette displays.

4 If you have a color monitor, click a **light blue square**. The background color of the form changes to a light blue. If you do not have a color monitor, click the **Settings box** list arrow to close the color palette.

You will now learn how to save the work you have done so far.

tips

....

▶ You can also save a new project by using both the Save File As and the Save Project As commands from the File menu. You must, however, be sure to save the form before saving the project. In other words, you must use the Save File As command before the Save Project As command.

WINDOWS 3.1

Saving a Visual Basic Project

It is a good practice to save the current project every 10 or 15 minutes so you won't lose a lot of work if the computer loses power. When you save a project for the first time, Visual Basic asks you for a name for the form file and a name for the project file. The project file will contain the names of the files appearing in the Project window, along with their location on the disk. The project file also records information on how the windows are arranged and sized when you open the project.

The easiest way to save the form and the project is to click the Save Project button on the toolbar.

To save a Visual Basic project:

1 Click the **Save Project** button 🖫 on the toolbar. The Save File As dialog box opens.

The dialog box prompts you for the name of the form file first; you can tell that by looking in the Save as type text box.

In Windows 3.1, the name of the text box is Save File as Type.

Notice that the name appearing in the File name box is the name you assigned to the form with the Name property. You can keep the name that Visual Basic offers in the File name box or, if you prefer, you can change the name. In this case, to keep the files you create in these tutorials grouped together in a meaningful way, you will save this form file as laCopy. The "laCopy" indicates that the Copyright application was created or saved in Lesson A.

2 Type **laCopy** in the File name box. (Be sure to use the lowercase "l" and not the number one.) Visual Basic will automatically add a .frm extension when it saves this file. The ".frm" extension indicates that the file is a form.

You want to save the form file in the Tut01 folder on your Student Disk.

3 If necessary, click the **Save in** list arrow, then click **the drive containing your Student Disk**. Click the **Tut01** folder, then click the **Open** button to open the Tut01 folder. The Tut01 folder opens, as shown in Figure 1-11.

If necessary, click the Drives list arrow, then click the drive containing your Student Disk. Click the a:\ (or b:\) folder Directories box, then click the OK button. Click the Tut01 folder, then click the OK button to open the Tut01 folder. The Tut01 folder opens.

WINDOWS   3.1

current folder

Figure 1-11: Save File As dialog box

You can also double-click a folder to open it.

WINDOWS   3.1

4 Click the **Save** button to save the laCopy form file. Visual Basic saves the laCopy form file in the Tut01 folder on your Student Disk.

Click the OK button to save the laCopy form file. Visual Basic saves the laCopy form file in the Tut01 folder on your Student Disk.

HELP? If this is the second or subsequent time you are practicing this lesson, Visual Basic will display a dialog box that asks if you want to replace the existing file. Click the Yes button.

Now that the form is saved, Visual Basic displays the Save Project As dialog box, which prompts you for the project name. The File name text box shows that the default project is named Project1. You should change the default project name, Project1, to a more descriptive name. To keep the files grouped together in a meaningful way, you will name the project file laCopy also. Visual Basic automatically adds the .vbp extension when it saves a project file. The ".vbp" stands for "Visual Basic project." (It is not necessary for the project file to have the same name as the form file, as you will see in later tutorials.)

The information in the Save Project As dialog box is the same as for the form file, except for the filename.

5 Type **laCopy** in the File name box and click the **Save** button to save the project. Visual Basic saves the laCopy project file in the Tut01 folder on your Student Disk.

Type laCopy in the File name box and click the OK button to save the project. Visual Basic saves the laCopy project file in the Tut01 folder on your Student Disk.

HELP? If this is the second or subsequent time you are practicing this lesson, Visual Basic will display a dialog box that asks if you want to replace the existing file. Click the Yes button.

Notice the changes in the Project window displayed in Figure 1-12.

project name for the project on your Student Disk

name of the form file on your Student Disk

form object name

Figure 1-12: Project window

The Project window's title bar now indicates that the name of the project is laCopy. The laCopy project contains the names of all files included in the project—in this case, only the laCopy.frm file. The name of the form contained in the laCopy.frm file is frmCopyright. (laCopy.frm is the name of the form file on your Student disk; frmCopyright is the name of the form object itself.)

Now that the form and the project are saved, you can run the project to see what you have accomplished so far.

Starting and Ending a Visual Basic Project

The only way you can tell if your application works is by starting (running) it. When you run the application, Visual Basic displays the user interface you created.

tips

You can also start an application by pressing the F5 key or by using the Start command on the Run menu.

To start (run) the copyright screen application:

1 Click the **Start** button ▶ on the toolbar. Visual Basic enters run time, as shown in Visual Basic's title bar, and the user interface appears.

Notice that the user interface does not fill the entire screen, as you would like it to. You will need to stop the application and return to the design screen to fix this problem.

2 Click the **End** button ■ on the toolbar to end the application. Visual Basic leaves run time and returns to design time, as Visual Basic's title bar now indicates.

tips

You can also end an application by using the End command on the Run menu.

You can make a form fill the entire screen by setting the form's WindowState property.

Setting the WindowState Property

The **WindowState property** determines the visual state of a Form window during run time. The property has three valid settings: Normal, Minimized, and Maximized. The default setting is Normal. If you change the setting of this property to Minimized, Visual Basic will not display the form on the screen when the application is run; rather, the application will appear as a button on the Windows 95 taskbar.

The application will display as a Minimized icon when the application is run in Windows 3.1.

Setting the value of this property to Maximized enlarges the form to its maximum size when the application is run. Because you want the form to fill the entire screen, you will set the value of the WindowState property to Maximized.

WINDOWS 3.1

▶ It is a good practice to save the project before running it.

To set the value of the WindowState property, and then save and run the application:

1 Scroll the Properties window until the WindowState property is visible, then click **WindowState** in the Properties list. Notice the list arrow in the Settings box; the list arrow indicates that this property has predefined settings.

2 Click the **Settings box** list arrow to display the valid settings for this property, then click **2-Maximized**.

3 Click the **Save Project** button 🔲 on the toolbar. Visual Basic saves the form and the project using the names you specified earlier.

▶ You can also start an application by pressing F5 or by using the Start command on the Run menu.

4 Click the **Start** button ▶ on the toolbar. The form now fills the entire screen.

Notice that you can't see the End button ■ or the menu bar when the form is maximized. You can, however, use either the form's Close button or its Resize button to end the application; the buttons are located in the form's title bar.

WINDOWS 3.1

You can use either the form's Control menu box ▭ or its Restore button 🔲 to end the application; both buttons are located in the form's title bar.

The Close button ✕ (*Control menu box ▭ in Windows 3.1*) will end the application immediately. The Resize button 🔲 (*Restore button 🔲 in Windows 3.1*), on the other hand, will return the form to its standard size. You will then be able to see Visual Basic's main window, which includes the End button ■ and the menu bar. Although the ✕ button (▭ *in Windows 3.1*) is the easiest of the two methods because it ends the application immediately, it does have a limitation: you won't be able to use it to end an application that stops running because of an error. In those cases, you will need to use the 🔲 button instead. See how this button can be used to end an application.

▶ You can also stop an application by using the End command on the Run menu. Another way to display the main window is to press Alt.

5 Click the **Resize** button 🔲 to restore the form to its standard size, then click the **End** button ■.

Click the Restore button ⬍ to restore the form to its standard size, then click the End button ■.

WINDOWS 3.1

Before finishing Lesson A, you will learn how to begin a new project and how to open an existing project. Both of these skills will help you complete the end-of-lesson exercises.

Opening a New Project

When you are finished with one project and want to begin another project, you can simply click File, then click New Project. You can open a new project while a previous project is on the screen. When you open the new project, Visual Basic closes the previous project. Try opening a new project now.

To open a new project:

1   Click **File**, then click **New Project**. The laCopy project is closed and a new project opens.

Now you will open a project that was previously saved.

Opening an Existing Project

If you want to continue working on an existing project, you simply click the Open Project button on the toolbar and then tell Visual Basic which project you want to open. Open the existing laCopy project and change the form's BackColor property to a light gray.

To open an existing project:

1   Click the **Open Project** button ⊠ on the toolbar. The Open Project dialog box opens.

   HELP? If you were working on a project before choosing the Open Project option and you did not save that form and/or project, Visual Basic will display one or more dialog boxes asking if you want to save the current form and/or project before opening another project. In this case, you don't want to save the current form and project, so click the No button. After you click the No button, the Open Project dialog box will appear.

You want to open the laCopy project file, which is located in the Tut01 folder on your Student Disk.

2   The Tut01 folder on your Student Disk should be open, so simply click **laCopy** (laCopy.vbp) in the list of project filenames. The laCopy (laCopy.vbp) filename appears in the File name box. Click the **Open** button to open the laCopy project. The laCopy Project window opens.

   The Tut01 folder on your Student Disk should be open, so simply click lacopy.vbp in the list of project filenames. The lacopy.vbp filename appears in the File name text box. Click the OK button to open the lacopy.vbp project. The laCopy Project window opens.

WINDOWS 3.1

3   Click the **View Form** button in the Project window to display the frmCopyright form.

4   Set the form's BackColor property to a light gray.

5   Click the **Save Project** button 🖫 to save the application.

Although the application is not completed, it's time for a break. You will complete the copyright screen in the remaining two lessons.

Exiting Visual Basic

As in most Windows applications, you exit an application using either the Close button (*Control menu box in Windows 3.1*) or the Exit command on the File menu.

To exit Visual Basic:

1 Click the **Close** button ☒ on the Visual Basic title bar, then redisplay the Windows 95 taskbar.

Click the Control menu box ▬ on the Visual Basic title bar, then click Close. Restore the Program Manager window by double-clicking the Program Manager icon at the bottom of the screen.

HELP? To redisplay the Windows 95 taskbar, move the mouse pointer to the thin line at the bottom of the screen until the taskbar appears. Click the Start button, point to Settings, then click Taskbar. Click the Auto hide check box on the taskbar Options tab. No check mark should appear in the Auto hide check box. Click the OK button.

WINDOWS 3.1

You can also close Visual Basic by using the Exit command on the File menu. If you did not save the current form and/or project before exiting Visual Basic, Visual Basic will display one or more dialog boxes asking if you want to save the current form and/or project before exiting.

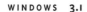

Now you can either take a break or complete the end-of-lesson questions and exercises.

S U M M A R Y

To start Visual Basic using Windows 95:

■ Start Windows 95 and place your Student Disk in the appropriate drive.

■ Click the Start button on the Windows 95 taskbar. The Start menu appears.

■ Point to Programs in the Start menu, then point to Visual Basic 4.0 in the Programs menu. The Visual Basic 4.0 menu appears.

■ Click Visual Basic 4.0 (Visual Basic 4.0 Working Model) in the Visual Basic 4.0 menu. The Visual Basic startup screen appears.

■ If you prefer, you can hide the Windows 95 taskbar to show more of the Visual Basic screen.

WINDOWS 3.1

To start Visual Basic using Windows 3.1:

■ *Start Windows 3.1 and place your Student Disk in the appropriate drive. The Program Manager window should be open.*

■ *Click Options to open the Options menu. If the Minimize on Use check box is not checked, then click Minimize on Use to check that option. If the Options menu is still open, click Options again to close it.*

■ *Double-click the Visual Basic 4.0 (16-bit) group icon in the Program Manager window to open the Visual Basic group window.*

■ *Double-click the Visual Basic 4.0 (16-bit) icon in the Visual Basic group window.The Visual Basic startup screen appears.*

To hide the Windows 95 taskbar permanently:

■ Click the Start button on the Windows 95 taskbar, point to Settings, then click Taskbar to display the taskbar Properties window.

■ Click the Auto hide check box in the taskbar Options tab. A check mark appears in the box next to the Auto hide option. Click the OK button to remove the taskbar Properties window. The Windows 95 taskbar is now hidden from view; only a thin line appears in its place at the bottom of the screen.

To display/rehide the Windows 95 taskbar temporarily:

■ To temporarily display the hidden taskbar, move the mouse pointer to a location below the thin line at the bottom of the screen until you see the taskbar.

■ To rehide the hidden taskbar, move the mouse pointer back to a location above the thin line at the bottom of the screen until the taskbar is hidden again.

To display the hidden Windows 95 taskbar permanently:

■ Move the mouse pointer to a location below the thin line at the bottom of the screen until the Windows 95 taskbar displays. Click the Start button on the Windows 95 taskbar. Point to Settings, then click Taskbar to display the taskbar Properties window.

■ Click the Auto hide check box on the taskbar Options tab. No check mark should appear in the Auto hide check box. Click the OK button to remove the taskbar Properties window. Windows 95 redisplays the taskbar.

To display the toolbar:

■ Click View, then click Toolbar.

To display the toolbox:

■ Click View, then click Toolbox.

To display the Project window:

■ Click the Project button 🖳 on the toolbar. You can also click View, then click Project.

To display the Properties window:

■ Click the Properties button 🗒 on the toolbar. You can also press the F4 key, or click View then click Properties.

To set the value of a property:

■ Select the object whose property you want to set.
■ Display the Properties window.
■ Select the property whose value you want to set.

If a list arrow appears in the Settings box:

■ Click the list arrow in the Settings box, then click the desired value in either the list or the palette.

If an ellipsis (...) appears in the Settings box:

■ Click the ellipsis, then enter the appropriate information in the dialog box.

If the Settings box does not display either a list arrow or an ellipsis:

■ Enter the new value into the Settings box.

To control the text appearing in the form's title bar, and on the application's button in the Windows 95 taskbar when the application is running, and below the form when the form is minimized in Windows 3.1 :

■ Set the form's Caption property.

To give a more meaningful name to an object:

■ Set the object's Name property.

To change the background color of an object:

■ Set the object's BackColor property.

To control the visual state of a form during run time:

■ Set the form's WindowState property.

To save a new Visual Basic project:

■ Click the Save Project button ▦ on the toolbar. Enter a filename for the form in the File name text box, then select the appropriate drive and folder, and then click the Save button to save the form file. Enter a filename for the project in the File name text box, then click the Save button to save the project file.
or

■ Click File, then click Save File As. Enter a filename for the form in the File name text box, then select the appropriate drive and folder, and then click the Save button to save the form file. Click File, then click Save Project As. Enter a filename for the project in the File name text box, then click the Save button to save the project file.

■ *Click the Save Project button ▦ on the toolbar. Enter a filename for the form in the File name text box, then select the appropriate drive and folder, and then click the OK button to save the form file. Enter a filename for the project in the File name text box, then click the OK button to save the project file.*
or

■ *Click File, then click Save File As. Enter a filename for the form in the File name text box, then select the appropriate drive and folder, and then click the OK button to save the form file. Click File, then click Save Project As. Enter a filename for the project in the File name text box, then click the OK button to save the project file.*

To run a Visual Basic application:

■ Click the Start button ▸ on the toolbar. You can also press the F5 key, or click Run then click Start.

To stop running a Visual Basic application:

■ If necessary, click the form's Resize button ▣ so that the Visual Basic menu bar and toolbar are visible. Click the End button ▪ on the toolbar. You can also click Run, then click End.

   or

■ Click the form's Close button ✕. You may not be able to use ✕ to end an application that stops because of an error. You will need to use the Resize button ▣ instead.

■ *If necessary, click the form's Restore button ▴ so that the Visual Basic menu bar and toolbar are visible. Click the End button ▪ on the toolbar. You can also click Run, then click End.*

   or

■ *Click the form's Control menu box ▬, then click Close. You may not be able to use ▬ to end an application that stops because of an error. You will need to use the Restore button ▴ instead.*

To open a new project:

■ Click File, then click New Project. (If you were working on a project before choosing the Open Project option and you did not save that form and/or project, Visual Basic will display one or more dialog boxes asking if you want to save the current form and/or project before opening another project.)

To open an existing project:

■ Click the Open Project button 🖻 on the toolbar. You can also click File, then click Open Project. Select the appropriate drive and folder. Click the project name in the list of files, then click the Open button (*OK button in Windows 3.1*) to open the project. (If you were working on a project before choosing the Open Project option and you did not save that form and/or project, Visual Basic will display one or more dialog boxes asking if you want to save the current form and/or project before opening another project.)

■ Click the View Form button in the Project window.

To exit Visual Basic:

■ Click the Close button ✕ on the Visual Basic title bar. You can also click File, then click Exit.

■ *Click the Control menu box ▬ on the Visual Basic title bar, then click Close. You can also double-click ▬, or click File then click Exit.*

QUESTIONS

1. You design your user interface in a _____ .
   a. design bar
   b. form
   c. menu bar
   d. Properties window
   e. toolbar

2. The tools you use when designing your application are found in the _____ .
   a. design bar
   b. toolbox
   c. toolbar
   d. user interface
   e. user screen

3. In which window do you set the characteristics that control an object's appearance and behavior?
   a. Main
   b. Form
   c. Project
   d. Properties
   e. Toolbox

4. When you save a form, which of the following extensions does Visual Basic add to the filename you enter?
   a. .ffr
   b. .ffl
   c. .for
   d. .form
   e. .frm

5. When you save a project, which of the following extensions does Visual Basic add to the filename you enter?
   a. .frm
   b. .prg
   c. .prj
   d. .pro
   e. .vbp

6. The _____ property controls the background color of an object.
   a. BackColor
   b. BackGround
   c. BelowColor
   d. Color
   e. FormColor

7. The _____ property controls the visual state of a form window when the application is run.
   a. FormState
   b. FormWindow
   c. StateForm
   d. StateWindow
   e. WindowState

8. The _____ property controls the text appearing in the form's title bar.
   a. Caption
   b. Name
   c. Text
   d. Title
   e. Window

9. The _____ property controls the text that appears on the application's button on the Windows 95 taskbar when the application is running, and below the icon when the form is minimized in Windows 3.1.
   a. Application
   b. Button
   c. Caption
   d. Name
   e. Text

10. You give an object a more meaningful name by setting the object's _____ property.
    a. Application
    b. Caption
    c. Form
    d. Name
    e. Text

11. When coding an application, you use the _____ property to refer to an object.
    a. Application
    b. Caption
    c. Form
    d. Name
    e. Text

12. Refer to Figure 1-13. Identify the location of the following Visual Basic components by writing the appropriate letter on the line to the left of the component.
    ___ Form window   ___ Properties list
    ___ Main window   ___ Properties window
    ___ Menu bar   ___ Settings box
    ___ Object box   ___ Toolbar
    ___ Project window   ___ Toolbox window

A
B
C
D
E

F

G
H
I
J

Figure 1-13: Visual Basic screen

13. Explain the difference between a form's Caption property and a form's Name property.

14. Explain how to open a new project.

15. Explain how to open an existing project.

16. Explain how to display the Project window and the Properties window.

E X E R C I S E S

1. In this exercise, you will change the properties of an existing form.
   a. If necessary, start Visual Basic. Your Student Disk should be in the appropriate drive.
   b. Open the la1 (Lesson A, Exercise 1) project, which is located in the Tut01 folder on your Student Disk. View the form. (Notice that the form contains some text. You will learn how to include text in a form in Lesson B.)
   c. Size and arrange the windows so they do not overlap each other.
   d. Set the following properties for the form:

Caption:	Charities Unlimited
BackColor:	Dark blue
Name:	frmCharity
WindowState:	2-Maximized
   e. Run the application. (You do not need to save the application.) Stop the application. If necessary, correct any errors and repeat this step again.

f. Click File, then click Print. When the Print dialog box opens, click the Form As Text check box, then click the OK button. The Form As Text option will print the properties of the form. You do not need to save this application.

2. In this exercise, you will change the properties of an existing form.
   a. If necessary, start Visual Basic. Your Student Disk should be in the appropriate drive.
   b. Open the la2 (Lesson A, Exercise 2) project, which is located in the Tut01 folder on your Student Disk. View the form. (Notice that the form contains a picture. You will learn how to include a picture in a form in Lesson C.)
   c. Size and arrange the windows so they do not overlap each other.
   d. The form's title bar should say Photos Inc. (be sure to type the period). Set the appropriate property.
   e. Give the form a more meaningful name. Call it frmPhotos.
   f. Change the form's background color to red.
   g. You want the form to fill the entire screen when the application is run. Set the appropriate property.
   h. Run the application. (You do not need to save the application.) Then stop the application. If necessary, correct any errors and repeat this step again.
   i. Click File, then click Print. When the Print dialog box opens, click the Form As Text check box, then click the OK button. The Form As Text option will print the properties of the form. You do not need to save this application.

3. As you learned in Lesson A, some properties have predefined settings and some do not. You can tell if a property has predefined settings by first selecting the property in the Properties list, and then looking in the Settings box next to the selected property. Use the following key to complete Exercise 3.

   A   This property has no predefined settings.

   B   This property has predefined settings. The list arrow in the Settings box will display either a list of the valid choices or a palette.

   C   This property has predefined settings. The ellipsis in the Settings box will display a dialog box.

Below are the names of 10 properties for a form. If necessary, start Visual Basic and open a new project. Select each of the 10 properties, one at a time, in the Properties list. On the line to the left of the property, write A, B, or C, according to the key mentioned above.

___ Caption   ___ ForeColor
___ Enabled   ___ Icon
___ FillColor   ___ Left
___ FillStyle   ___ Name
___ Font   ___ Picture

In this lesson you will learn how to:

- Access Visual Basic Help
- Add a label control to a form
- Move and size a control
- Delete a control from a form
- Select multiple controls
- Save files under a different name

Working with Controls

Getting Help in Visual Basic

You will begin this lesson by spending some time looking at Visual Basic's on-line Help system. If you encounter any problems during the tutorials or if you have any questions, you will then be able to get help on your own.

To start this lesson:

1 Start Visual Basic, if necessary, and make sure your Student Disk is in the appropriate drive.

2 Use the Open Project button 🖻 on the toolbar to open the laCopy project that you created in Lesson A. Recall that the file is in the Tut01 folder on your Student Disk.

3 Click the **View Form** button to view the frmCopyright form.

You can access Visual Basic Help by using either the F1 key or the Help menu. You can practice with both of these methods right now, beginning with the Help menu.

To access Help through the Help menu:

1 Click **Help**. The Help menu opens. Click **Search For Help On**. Visual Basic displays the Visual Basic Help dialog box, which contains three tabs labeled Contents, Index, and Find. The Index tab, which is the frontmost tab, allows you to search for information on specific topics. You will learn how to use the Index tab in this tutorial; you will get a chance to practice with the Contents and Find tabs in a Discovery exercise at the end of this lesson. The Index tab is shown in Figure 1-14.

Click Help. The Help menu opens. Click Search For Help On. Visual Basic displays the Search dialog box.

Figure 1-14: Index tab in Visual Basic Help dialog box

The Index tab in Windows 95 and the Search dialog box in Windows 3.1 are organized like the index in a book. Both contain an alphabetical list of keywords for topics, which allows you to search quickly for information. You will search for information on the Name property.

To access Help on a particular topic, you can either type a topic (or just the first few letters of the topic) in the box at the top of the window or select one of the topics from the list.

2 Type **name p** in the box at the top of the Index tab. The selection bar moves to the Name property topic. Click the **Display** button in the Visual Basic Help dialog box. The Topics Found dialog box opens and shows a list of Help windows for the Name property. The Name Property (Visual Basic Help) topic is already selected in the list, so you just need to click the **Display** button in the Topics Found dialog box to display the Help window for the Name property. (Be sure to click the Display button in the Topics Found dialog box.) The Help window for the Name property opens, as shown in Figure 1-15.

WINDOWS   3.1

Type n (the lowercase letter n) in the box at the top of the Search dialog box. The selection bar moves to the Name property topic. Click the Show Topics button in the Search dialog box. The Name property topic is highlighted in the box at the bottom of the Help screen. Click the Go To button. The Help window for the Name Property opens.

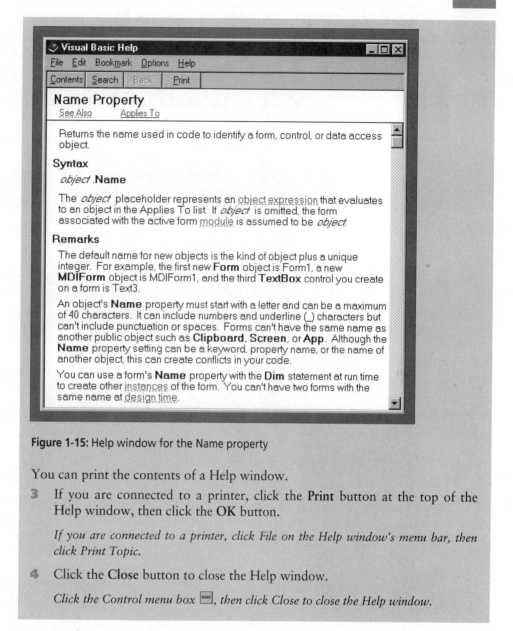

Figure 1-15: Help window for the Name property

You can print the contents of a Help window.

3 If you are connected to a printer, click the **Print** button at the top of the Help window, then click the **OK** button.

WINDOWS   3.1

If you are connected to a printer, click File on the Help window's menu bar, then click Print Topic.

4 Click the **Close** button to close the Help window.

WINDOWS   3.1

Click the Control menu box ⊟, then click Close to close the Help window.

In addition to using the Search For Help On command in the Help menu, you can also access Visual Basic Help by pressing F1.

Using F1

The F1 key provides you with context-sensitive help. That means Visual Basic displays a Help window for whatever is currently selected. In many instances, using the F1 key is a faster way of getting help. You can use the F1 key, for example, to display the Help window for the Name property, but you must first select that property in the Properties window.

> To use the F1 key to display the Help window for the Name property:
>
> **1**   If necessary, scroll the Properties window until the Name property is visible in the Properties list. Click **Name** in the Properties list, then press the **F1** key to display a Help window for the Name property. The same Help window shown earlier in Figure 1-15 appears on the screen.
>
> **Important Note: In future steps you will not be instructed, specifically, to scroll the Properties window to locate a property; instead, you will be told to simply click the property. If you do not see the property in the Properties list, you will need to scroll the Properties window until the property is visible.**
>
> **2**   Close the Help window.

In summary, you use the F1 key to obtain context-sensitive help. You can use the Help menu to obtain help on specific topics. Be sure to refer to Help if you have any questions or problems while you are working in Visual Basic.

Now you will add some objects to the current form.

Adding a Control to a Form

The tools in the toolbox allow you to add graphical objects, called **controls**, to a form. The terms "object" and "control" are often used interchangeably in Visual Basic. Technically, however, a control refers to an object placed on a form. Although the form itself is an object, it is not a control. (The tutorials in this book use "object" to refer both to a form and a control; "control" refers only to the objects placed on the form—not the form itself.)

The first tool you will use is the Label tool—the large letter A in the toolbox. The **Label tool** creates a label control (graphical object) that you can use to display text you don't want the user to modify. In other words, when your application is run, Visual Basic will not allow the user to make any changes to the contents of a label control. In this application, you do not want the user to modify the information on the copyright screen, so a label control is the correct control to use.

> To create a default-size label control in the center of the form:
>
> **1**   Double-click the **Label tool** Ⓐ in the toolbox. A default-size label control appears in the center of the form, with the default caption Label1. Click **Caption** in the Properties list. See Figure 1-16.

default caption

sizing handles

Figure 1-16: Default-size label control added to form

HELP? If a label control does not appear in the center of the form, double-click the Label tool again. If a different control appears, press the Delete key to remove the incorrect control, then repeat Step 1.

Notice that a label control's caption—in this case, Label1—appears inside the control. Visual Basic also assigns Label1 as the default setting of this control's Name property. You can verify that, if you want, by scrolling the Properties window until you see the Name property in the Properties list.

In order to use Visual Basic efficiently, you must know how to size, move, and delete the controls you've placed on the form. You will learn these three skills next.

Sizing, Moving, and Deleting a Control

You size, move, and delete a Visual Basic control in the same manner as you do in any Windows application. First, you must select the control that you want to size, move, or delete. You select a control by clicking it; when a control is selected, sizing handles appear around it. For example, notice the sizing handles around the Label1 control in Figure 1-16, indicating that the control is selected. Practice sizing, moving, and deleting the Label1 control.

To size, move, and then delete the Label1 control, which is currently selected:

1 Place the mouse pointer on the label control's lower-right sizing handle until the mouse pointer becomes a double arrow, then drag the sizing handle until the object is a little larger than the default size. (You don't need to worry about the exact size.) When the control is the desired size, release the mouse button.

Now move the Label1 control.

tips

· · · · · · · · · · · · · · ·

▶ In order to delete a control, the control must be selected in the form and the Form window must be the active window. In other words, you can't delete a control if either the main, Properties, Project, or toolbox title bar is highlighted. To avoid any problems with deleting controls, make it a practice to click the control in the form before you press the Delete key.

2   To move the Label1 control, position the mouse pointer anywhere on the Label1 control, except on a sizing handle. Drag the Label1 control to the upper-left corner of the screen, then release the mouse button. (Don't worry about the exact location.)

Next, delete the Label1 control.

3   The Label1 control should still be selected; press the **Delete** key to delete the control.

Now that you know how to add, size, move, and delete controls, you can continue building the copyright screen.

Adding Label Controls to the Copyright Screen

The copyright screen application requires two label controls: one for the name of the application's author and the other for the copyright year.

To add two label controls to the copyright screen:

1   Double-click the **Label** tool [A] in the toolbox. The Label1 control appears in the center of the form.

2   Drag the Label1 control to the upper-left corner of the screen. (Don't worry about the exact location.)

3   Double-click the **Label** tool [A] in the toolbox again. The Label2 control appears in the center of the form.

4   Drag the Label2 control to a location immediately below the Label1 control.

Now that the controls are on the form, the next step is setting their properties.

Setting the Properties of a Label Control

The first property you will set is the Name property. Recall that you use the Name property to assign meaningful names to objects. Following the naming convention discussed earlier, you will assign the name lblAuthor to the first label control and the name lblYear to the second label control. The "lbl" identifies the objects as label controls, and "Author" and "Year" indicate each control's purpose in the form.

Important Note: Programmers usually don't give names to controls that are not either being coded or referred to in code. You are naming these two label controls for practice only.

To set the Name property of the two label controls:

1   Click the **Label1** control in the form to select it. Sizing handles appear around the control. The Object box in the Properties window also shows that the Label1 control is the currently selected object. (Recall that the Object box is located below the Properties window's title bar.)

2 Click **Name** in the Properties list, then type **lblAuthor** and press the **Enter** key to enter a new name for this control. lblAuthor appears as the value of the Name property in the Properties list; it also appears in the Object box.

3 Select the Label2 control, then set its Name property to **lblYear**.

Like forms, label controls also have a Caption property, which controls the text that appears inside the label control. The lblAuthor control's caption is currently Label1; the lblYear control's caption is currently Label2. In this application you want the words "Written By" and your name to appear in the lblAuthor control, and the words "Copyright Year" and the year 1999 to appear in the lblYear control, so you will need to set both controls' Caption properties accordingly.

To set the Caption property for the two label controls:

1 The lblYear control is currently selected, so just click **Caption** in the Properties list, then type **Copyright Year 1999** and press the **Enter** key. The new caption appears in the lblYear control.

Because the caption is longer than the width of the control, some of the information wraps around to the next line. You can use the sizing handles to size the label control until the entire caption appears on one line, or you can change the label control's AutoSize property. The **AutoSize property** does just what its name implies: it automatically sizes the control to fit its current contents. You will set the AutoSize property.

2 Click **AutoSize** in the Properties list. A list arrow appears in the Settings box. Recall that the list arrow means this property has predefined settings.

3 Click the **Settings box** list arrow to see the valid settings for the AutoSize property. A list appears.

As the list indicates, Visual Basic allows you to set the AutoSize property to either True or False. Many of the other properties shown in the Properties list also have only these two settings. (These settings are called **Boolean** values, named after the English mathematician George Boole.) The True setting turns the property on; the False setting turns the property off. To tell Visual Basic to size the selected control automatically, you will set the control's AutoSize property to True.

4 Click **True** in the list. The lblYear control automatically stretches to fit the contents of the Caption property.

5 Select the lblAuthor label control and set its AutoSize property to **True**.

6 Click **Caption** in the Properties list to select the Caption property for the lblAuthor control.

7 Type **Written By** and press the **spacebar**, then type your name and press the **Enter** key.

Now specify the placement of these two label controls on the form.

Setting the Left and Top Properties

Recall that you can drag a control to any position on the form. So that your screen agrees with the figures in the book, however, you will sometimes be given the value of each control's **Left property** and **Top property**. These two properties control the position of the upper-left corner of the object. You will use the Left and Top properties to move the lblYear control to its proper position on the form. This time, instead of selecting the control by clicking it on the form, you will use the Object box to select the control.

To select a control using the Object box, and then set the control's Left property and its Top property:

1 Click the **Object box** list arrow, located immediately below the Properties window's title bar, to display its list. The list shows the name and type of the three objects included in the form.

2 Click **lblYear Label** in the list to select that label control. The lblYear control is now selected, as the sizing handles indicate.

3 Click **Left** in the Properties list to select that property.

The location of an object in a form is measured in twips from the edges of the form. A **twip** is 1/1440 of an inch. If you set the Left property to 1440, Visual Basic positions the control 1" from the left edge of the form. (Actual physical distances on the screen vary according to the size of the monitor.) Position the lblYear control 3.5" from the left edge of the form.

4 Type **5040** as the Left property and press the **Enter** key to position the selected control 3.5" from the left edge of the form. Visual Basic moves the lblYear control accordingly.

Now position the lblYear control 3" from the top of the form.

5 Click **Top** in the Properties list, type **4320** and press the **Enter** key to position the selected control 3" from the top of the form. Visual Basic positions the control lblYear control accordingly. (Don't worry if the control is not visible. You will see the control when you maximize the form in the next section.)

Next, you will position the lblAuthor control 2.5" from the top of the form and 3.5" from the left edge of the form.

6 Select the lblAuthor control, then set its Top property to **3600** and its Left property to **5040**.

The final modification you will make to these label controls is to set their Font property. As you will see in the next section, you can set the Font property for both controls at the same time.

Changing the Property for More Than One Control At a Time

You can change the appearance of many of the objects in your user interface by changing the object's Font property. The **Font property** allows you to change the type of font used to display the text in the object, as well as the style and size of the font. A **font** is the general shape of the characters in the text. Courier and MS Sans Serif are examples of font types; regular, bold, and italic are examples of font styles. The size of a font is measured in points, with one **point** equaling 1/72 of an inch; 8, 10, and 18 are examples of font sizes.

One reason for changing a font is to bring attention to a specific part of the screen. In the copyright application, for example, you can make the text in the two label controls more noticeable by increasing the size of the font Visual Basic uses. You can change the size for both controls at the same time by clicking one control and then pressing and holding down the Control key as you click the other control in the form. (You must hold down the Control key as you click the control in the form; you can't hold down the Control key and click the control's name in the Object box.) You can use the Control-click method to select as many controls as you want. You cancel the selection by clicking on the form or on any unselected control in the form.

To select both label controls, then set their Font property:

1   The lblAuthor control should still be selected. Verify that by looking in the Object box in the Properties window or by looking for sizing handles around the control in the form. (If the lblAuthor control is not selected, then use the Object box to select it now.)

2   Maximize the form so that you can see the lblYear control. The form fills the entire screen.

3   Press and hold down the **Ctrl** key as you click the **lblYear control**. Both label controls are now selected, as shown in Figure 1-17. Notice that the sizing handles appear in a lighter shade of gray.

both label controls are selected

Figure 1-17: Both label controls selected

4   Press the **F4** key to display the Properties window, then click **Font** in the Properties list. The ellipsis, which appears in the Settings box, indicates that this property has predefined settings. When you click the ellipsis, a dialog box will appear. You will need to enter the appropriate information in the dialog box.

5   Click the ... (ellipsis) in the Settings box to display the dialog box. The Font dialog box shown in Figure 1-18 opens.

Figure 1-18: Font dialog box

The default font is typically the regular style of the MS Sans Serif font. The default font size is 8 points, or 1/9 of an inch. (Recall that one point is 1/72 of an inch.) To make the text in the two label controls more noticeable, you will increase the font size to 12 points, or 1/6 of an inch. You will also select the bold style of the MS Sans Serif font.

6   Click **Bold** in the Font style list box to change the font style to Bold. Click **12** in the Size list box to increase the font size to 12 points. Click the **OK** button. The text in the two label controls displays in the new font style and size.

7   Click the **form** to cancel the selection of the label controls, then restore the form to its standard size.

Saving Files Under a Different Name

Before ending Lesson B, you will save what you have completed so far and then run the application to see how it looks. Usually you save the form and the project using its original name. In this case, however, you will give the form and the project a different name. By saving the form and the project under a different name, you can repeat this lesson as often as you want because the original files from Lesson A will still be on your Student Disk. One very important note: When saving forms and projects, you always save the form first, then save the project.

To save the form and the project under a different name:

1 Click **File**, then click **Save File As** to save the form under a new name. The Save File As dialog box opens with the current name of the form (either laCopy or laCopy.frm), offered in the File name box. The open folder is Tut01.

2 Change the filename to **lbCopy**, then click the **Save** button to save the form under the new name. A copy of the frmCopyright form is now saved as lbCopy.frm on your Student Disk.

Change the filename to lbcopy.frm, then click the OK button to save the form under the new name. A copy of the frmCopyright form is now saved as lbcopy.frm on your Student Disk.

HELP? If this is the second or subsequent time you are practicing this lesson, Visual Basic will display a dialog box that asks if you want to replace the existing file. Click the Yes button.

Notice that Visual Basic updates the Project window to reflect the new name of the form file, lbCopy.frm. That's why you must give the form a new name before giving the project a new name; when you save the project, Visual Basic saves the information that is currently listed in the Project window. (Notice that the name of the form object within the .frm file, however, is still frmCopyright.) You can now save the project under a new name.

3 Click **File**, then click **Save Project As** to save the project under a new name. The Save Project As dialog box appears with the current name of the project (either laCopy or laCopy.vbp) showing in the File name text box. The open folder is Tut01.

4 Change the filename to **lbCopy**, then click the **Save** button to save the project under the new name. A copy of the project is now saved as lbCopy.vbp on your Student Disk. Now that the files are saved, you can run the project.

Change the filename to lbcopy.vbp, then click the OK button to save the project under the new name. A copy of the project is now saved as lbcopy.vbp on your Student Disk. Now that the files are saved, you can run the project.

HELP? If this is the second or subsequent time you are practicing this lesson, Visual Basic will display a dialog box that asks if you want to replace the existing file. Click the Yes button.

5 Click the **Start** button on the toolbar. The copyright screen appears as shown in Figure 1-19. (Recall that the copyright screen will display your name instead of Diane Zak.)

tips

▶ **You can also use either the F5 key or the Start command on the Run menu to run an application.**

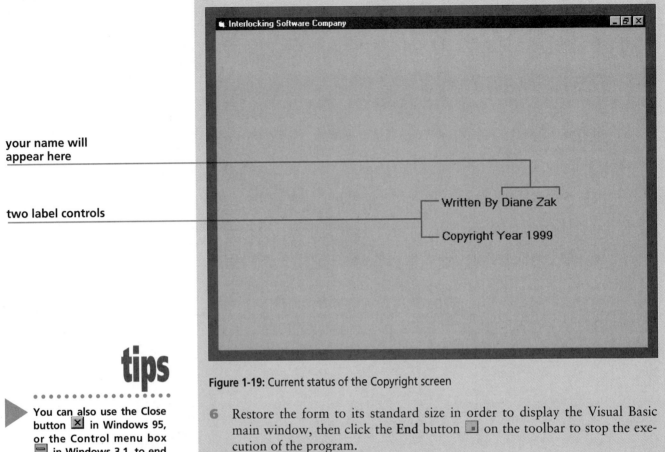

your name will
appear here

two label controls

Written By Diane Zak

Copyright Year 1999

Figure 1-19: Current status of the Copyright screen

6   Restore the form to its standard size in order to display the Visual Basic main window, then click the **End** button ▣ on the toolbar to stop the execution of the program.

Now you can either exit Visual Basic and take a break, or complete the end-of-lesson questions and exercises. (If necessary, remember to redisplay the Windows 95 taskbar or restore the Windows 3.1 Program Manager.) In Lesson C you will complete the copyright screen.

S U M M A R Y

To access the Visual Basic Help windows:

■   Click Help on the menu bar, then click either the Search for Help On or the Contents command. The Visual Basic Help dialog box appears. Use the Contents tab to search for information on general topics. Use the Index tab to search for information on specific topics. Use the Find tab to search for words or phrases that may be contained in the Help windows.

   or

■   Click the object, window, property, and so on for which you want to display a Help window, then press the F1 key. The F1 key provides you with context-sensitive help, which means Visual Basic displays a Help window for whatever is currently selected.

To add a control to a form:

- In the toolbox, double-click the tool representing the control you want to add to the form.
- Move the control and/or size the control as necessary.

To select an object:

- Click the object. Sizing handles will appear around the object.
  or
- Display the Properties window, click the Object box list arrow, then click the name of the object in the list. Sizing handles will appear around the object.

To size an object:

- Select the object you want to size. Then position the mouse pointer on one of the sizing handles and drag until the object is the desired size.

To move an object:

- Position the mouse pointer on the object you want to move, being careful not to position the pointer on any of the sizing handles. Then drag the object to its new location.

To delete a control:

- Select the control you want to delete, then press the Delete key. Be sure to select the proper control in the form. In order to delete a control, the Form window must be the active window.

To select multiple controls:

- Click the first control you want to select in the form.
- Press and hold down the Control (Ctrl) key as you click the other controls you want to select. You must select the controls directly on the form, not their names in the Object box.

To cancel the selection of one of the selected controls:

- Press and hold down the Ctrl key as you click the control.

To cancel the selection of all of the selected controls:

- Click on the form or on any unselected control in the form.

To control the position of an object's left edge:

- Set the object's Left property.

To control the position of an object's top edge:

- Set the object's Top property.

To automatically size a label control to fit its current contents:

- Set the label control's AutoSize property to True.

To control the type, style, and size of the font used to display text in an object:

■   Set the object's Font property.

To save the open form and project using a different name:

■   Click File, then click Save File As to save the form. Enter the new name for the form in the File name text box, select the appropriate drive and folder in the Save in list box, then click the Save button. If a file with that name already exists on the disk, Visual Basic will display a dialog box asking if you want to replace the existing file. If you want to replace the form file on the disk with the current form, click the Yes button; otherwise, click the No button.

■   Click File, then click Save Project As to save the project. Enter the new name for the project in the File name text box, select the appropriate drive and folder in the Save in list box, then click the Save button. If a file with that name already exists on the disk, Visual Basic will display a dialog box asking if you want to replace the existing file. If you want to replace the project file on the disk with the current project, click the Yes button; otherwise, click the No button.

WINDOWS   3.1

■   *Click File, then click Save File As to save the form. Enter the new name for the form in the File name text box, select the appropriate drive in the Drives list box and the appropriate folder in the Directories list box. Click the OK button. If a file with that name already exists on the disk, Visual Basic will display a dialog box asking if you want to replace the existing file. If you want to replace the form file on the disk with the current form, click the Yes button; otherwise, click the No button.*

■   *Click File, then click Save Project As to save the project. Enter the new name for the project in the File name text box, select the appropriate drive in the Drives list box and the appropriate folder in the Directories list box. Click the OK button. If a file with that name already exists on the disk, Visual Basic will display a dialog box asking if you want to replace the existing file. If you want to replace the project file on the disk with the current project, click the Yes button; otherwise, click the No button.*

To display the Visual Basic main menu when a maximized form is running:

■   Restore the form to its standard size, or press Alt.

Q U E S T I O N S

1.   You can open context-sensitive Help windows by selecting an object and pressing _____ .
     a.   F1
     b.   F2
     c.   F3
     d.   F4
     e.   F5

2.   The _____ tool creates a control in which you display text that you don't want the user to change.
     a.   Caption
     b.   Command
     c.   Control
     d.   Label
     e.   Text

3. The location of an object in a form is measured in _____ from the edges of the form.
   a. characters
   b. inches
   c. points
   d. twips
   e. twups

4. The size of a font is measured in _____ .
   a. characters
   b. inches
   c. points
   d. twips
   e. twups

5. Which of the following properties tells a label control to adjust automatically to the size of its caption?
   a. AutoAdjust
   b. AutoCaption
   c. AutoControl
   d. AutoLblSize
   e. AutoSize

6. In order to delete a control on a form, the _____ window must be the active window, which means that its title bar must be highlighted.
   a. Form
   b. main
   c. Project
   d. Properties
   e. Toolbox

7. Explain how to a) select more than one control at a time, b) deselect one of the selected controls, and c) deselect all of the selected controls.

8. Explain how to size, move, and delete a control on a form.

9. Explain how to save an existing form file and an existing project file under a different name.

10. Explain the difference between the Contents tab and the Index tab in the Visual Basic Help dialog box.

11. Explain how to use the F1 key to access Visual Basic Help.

E X E R C I S E S

1. In this exercise, you will add a label control to a form. You will also change the properties of the form and its objects.
   a. If necessary, start Visual Basic and open a new project. Your Student Disk should be in the appropriate drive. Size and arrange the windows so they do not overlap each other.
   b. Save the form and the project as lb1Done in the Tut01 folder on your Student Disk. Remember to save the form *before* saving the project.
   c. Set the following properties for the form:
      Caption: IMA
      BackColor: White
      Name: frmIMA
      WindowState: 2-Maximized

    d. Add a label control to the form. Set the following properties for the label control:

Caption:	International Mechanics Association
Name:	lblTitle
Left:	800 twips
Font:	12 points, bold
AutoSize:	True
Top:	1000 twips

    e. Save and run the application. Then stop the application. If necessary, correct any errors and repeat this step again.

    f. Click File, then click Print. When the Print dialog box opens, click the Form As Text check box, then click the OK button. The Form As Text option will print the properties of the form.

2. In this exercise, you will add label controls to a form. You will also change the properties of the form and its objects.

    a. If necessary, start Visual Basic and open a new project. Size and arrange the windows so they do not overlap each other. Your Student Disk should be in the appropriate drive.

    b. Save the form and the project as lb2Done in the Tut01 folder on your Student Disk. Remember to save the form *before* saving the project.

    c. The form's title bar should say Jefferson Cleaning Inc. (include the period). Set the appropriate property.

    d. Give the form a more meaningful name. Call it frmJefferson.

    e. Change the form's background color to a light blue.

    f. You want the form to fill the entire screen when the application is run. Set the appropriate property.

    g. Add two label controls to the form. The size of both label controls should adjust automatically to their contents, so you will need to set the appropriate property.

    h. Give the label controls more meaningful names. Call them lblLine1 and lblLine2.

    i. The lblLine1 control should say Welcome To. The lblLine2 control should say Jefferson Cleaning Inc. (with the period).

    j. Set the font size for both controls to 24 points.

    k. Maximize the form, then drag both label controls to the center of the screen, with the lblLine1 control first and lblLine2 control below it.

    l. Set the BackColor for both label controls to white. Set the ForeColor to red.

    m. Save and run the application. Then stop the application. If necessary, correct any errors and repeat this step again.

    n. Maximize the form, then press Ctrl + P. (Press and hold down the Ctrl key as you press the letter p.) When the Print dialog box appears, click both the Form Image and the Form As Text check boxes, then click the OK button. The Form Image option will print the maximized form and the Form As Text option will print the properties of the form.

3. In this exercise, you will create the user interface shown in Figure 1-20.

    a. If necessary, start Visual Basic and open a new project. Size and arrange the windows so they do not overlap each other. Your Student Disk should be in the appropriate drive.

    b. Save the form and the project as lb3Done in the Tut01 folder on your Student Disk. Remember to save the form *before* saving the project.

    c. Create the user interface shown in Figure 1-20. You can use any names for the objects, as long as they are meaningful and follow the naming convention you learned in this tutorial. You can also use any font type, style, and size. You can also choose any color for the form and the label controls in the form. Be sure that the form fills the entire screen when the application is run.

two label controls

Figure 1-20

d. Save and run the application. Then stop the application. If necessary, correct any errors and repeat this step again.

e. Maximize the form, then press Ctrl + P. (Hold down the Ctrl key as you press the letter p.) When the Print dialog box appears, click both the Form Image and the Form As Text check boxes, then click the OK button. The Form Image option will print the maximized form and the Form As Text option will print the properties of the form.

Exercise 4 is a Discovery Exercise, which allows you to both "discover" the solutions to problems on your own and to experiment with material that is not covered in the tutorial. *You can complete Exercise 4 only if you are using Windows 95.*

discovery ▶ 4. In this exercise, you will practice with both the Find and Contents tabs in the Visual Basic Help dialog box.

a. Use the Search For Help On option on the Visual Basic Help menu to view the Find tab in the Visual Basic Help dialog box. Experiment with the Find tab by using it to look up topics. Write a one-paragraph summary explaining a) the purpose of the Find tab and b) how to use the Find tab.

b. Now practice with the Contents tab. Click Help, then click Search For Help On, and then click the Contents tab.

The Contents tab displays a list of general topics for which Help is available. The tab contains three buttons: Display, Print, and Cancel. You use the Display button to display the selected Help window. You use the Print button to print the contents of the selected Help window. The Cancel button closes Visual Basic Help.

Notice the icons to the left of each topic. Three different icons can appear in the Contents tab: a Help icon (indicated by a question mark), a closed book icon, and an open book icon. If the Help icon appears next to a topic, it means that you can display that topic's Help window by simply selecting the topic, and then clicking

tips

You can also maximize a Help window to read more of its contents.

the Display button. See how that works by displaying the Help window for the Read Me topic.

c. The Read Me topic should be selected, so you just need to click the Display button. The Help window for the Read Me topic opens.

Remember that, in Windows you can view additional Help windows for an underlined word or phrase by simply clicking the word or phrase.

d. Position the mouse pointer on <u>Questions and Answers About Microsoft Visual Basic for Windows 4.0</u>. The mouse pointer turns into ⬚. Click <u>Questions and Answers About Microsoft Visual Basic for Windows 4.0</u>. The Help window opens.

e. Close the Help window.

f. Click Help, then click Search For Help On, and then click the Contents tab.

Notice that the closed book icon appears next to two of the topics. If the closed book icon appears next to a topic, it means that the topic contains subtopics. To display the list of subtopics, you need to open the closed book. In order to open the book for the Visual Basic Help topic, you need to select the Visual Basic Help topic.

g. Click Visual Basic Help. Notice that the Display button becomes an Open button when you select a topic that is associated with the closed book icon.

h. Click the Open button. The closed book icon changes to an open book icon, and Visual Basic displays the list of subtopics for the Visual Basic Help topic.

Notice that the closed book icon appears next to two of the subtopics in the list. The closed book icon tells you that these subtopics have their own list of topics. You can display the additional list by clicking the subtopic and then clicking the Open button. Most of the subtopics in the Help window, however, are represented by the Help icon. Recall that the Help icon means that the topic represents a Help window that can be displayed by simply selecting the topic and then clicking the Display button. Display the Help window for the Glossary topic; you can use the Glossary Help window to look up the definitions of words.

i. Click Glossary. The Open button changes to a Display button. Click the Display button. The Glossary Help window, which displays an alphabetical list of words, appears.

Now suppose that you want to look up the word "event." One way to do so would be to scroll the Help window until the words beginning with the letter "e" appear. An easier way, however, is to use the lettered buttons at the top of the Help window. To look up, quickly, the word "event," you simply need to click the E button.

j. Position the mouse pointer on the E button at the top of the Help window. The mouse pointer turns to ⬚.

k. Click the E button. The Help window now displays words that begin with the letter E.

l. Click <u>event</u> in the list. The definition of the term "event" appears.

m. Click anywhere in the Glossary Help window to remove the definition.

n. Close the Help window.

LESSON C
objectives

In this lesson you will learn how to:

■ Add an image control to the form

■ Add a Command button to the form

■ Enter code in a Code window

■ Use the Multimedia Control to add sound to an application

■ Print the form, the properties of the objects in the form, and the code

■ Make an executable file

Writing Code

Adding an Image Control to the Form

According to the sketch of the copyright screen (see Figure 1-1), you need to include the Interlocking Software Company logo in your application. You can use either the Image tool or the Picture box tool to add a picture (or icon) to a form. One advantage of the Image tool over the Picture box is that the Image tool requires less of the computer's memory. You will use the Image tool to create an image control for the copyright screen.

tips

▶ You can also use the Open Project command on the File menu to open an existing project.

To add an image control to the form:

1 Start Visual Basic, if necessary, and make sure your Student Disk is in the appropriate drive.

2 Use the Open Project button on the toolbar to open the lbCopy project that you created in Lesson B. Recall that the project file is in the Tut01 folder on your Student Disk.

You will now save the form and the project under a different name so that both the lbCopy form file and the lbCopy project file remain intact. This approach will allow you to practice Lesson C as often as you like.

3 Use both the Save File As and the Save Project As commands on the File menu to save the form and the project, respectively, as lcCopy. (Recall from Lesson B that you must save the form before you save the project.)

HELP? If this is the second or subsequent time you are practicing this lesson, Visual Basic will display a dialog box that asks if you want to replace the existing file. Click the Yes button.

4 Click the **View Form** button to view the frmCopyright form.

5 Position the mouse pointer on the **Image** tool 🖼 in the toolbox. After a few seconds a tooltip, which contains the tool's name, appears; in this case the tooltip says Image. If you have trouble distinguishing the tools in the toolbox, you can always display the tool's name by resting the mouse pointer on the tool to display the tooltip.

6 Double-click the **Image** tool 🖼 in the toolbox. An empty rectangular box with sizing handles appears in the center of the form. This is the image control into which you will place the company's logo.

You place (or load) a picture into an image control by setting the control's **Picture property**.

7 If necessary, click **Picture** in the Properties list, then click **...** (ellipses) in the Settings box. The Load Picture dialog box appears.

8 Open the Tut01 folder on your Student Disk. A list of filenames appears.

9 Click **Inter** (inter.bmp) in the list, then click the **Open** button. The Interlocking Software logo appears in the image control.

Click inter.bmp in the list, then click the OK button. The Interlocking Software logo appears in the image control.

You will now give the image control a more meaningful name, and then position the control appropriately in the form.

To give the image control a more meaningful name, and then position the control in the form:

1 Set the image control's Name property to **imgLogo**. (The "img" identifies the object as an image control. Here again, this control will not be coded or used in code, so it does not need to be named. You are naming the control for practice only.)

2 Set the image control's Left property to **240** and its Top property to **700**. (Recall that you are given the values for the Left and Top properties in order for your screen to match the figure in the book. Instead of setting the Left and Top properties, you could simply drag the control into its proper location.)

3 Maximize the form, then drag the image control's right border to match Figure 1-21.

drag the right border to this position

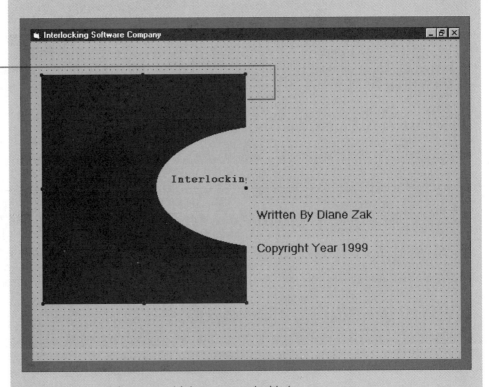

Figure 1-21: Copyright screen with image control added

Notice that the picture in the image control did not shrink along with the control itself. If you want the picture to be sized with the image control, you need to set the control's **Stretch property** to True. Do that now.

4 Press the **F4** key to display the Properties window, then set the image control's Stretch property to **True**. The picture in the image control shrinks to fit the current size of the control.

5 Restore the form to its standard size.

6 Click the **Save Project** button to save the form and the project under their current names, lcCopy.

According to the sketch (see Figure 1-1), the copyright screen is almost complete. All that remains is to add the Exit button.

Adding a Command Button to the Form

Every Windows application should give the user a way to exit the program. Most Windows applications provide either an Exit option on a File menu or an Exit button. As you saw earlier, the copyright application uses an Exit button. You create the Exit button by using the CommandButton tool.

In Windows applications, command buttons perform an immediate action when clicked. The OK and Cancel buttons are examples of command buttons found in many applications. In the copyright screen, the Exit command button will end the application when the button is clicked by the user.

To add a command button control to the form:

1 Double-click the **CommandButton** tool ☐ in the toolbox. A default-size button appears in the center of the form. The default name and caption of this control is Command1.

You will now set the Name, Caption, and Font properties for this control. You will also move the command button to the bottom right corner of the screen. Remember that you can position a control on the form either by dragging it or by setting its Left and Top properties.

2 Set the command button's Name property to **cmdExit**. The "cmd" identifies the control as a command button. The "Exit" identifies the purpose of this control.

3 Set the command button's Caption property to **Exit**.

4 Click **Font** in the Properties list. Set the font size to **10** points.

5 Maximize the form, then drag the command button to the lower right corner of the form, as shown in Figure 1-22.

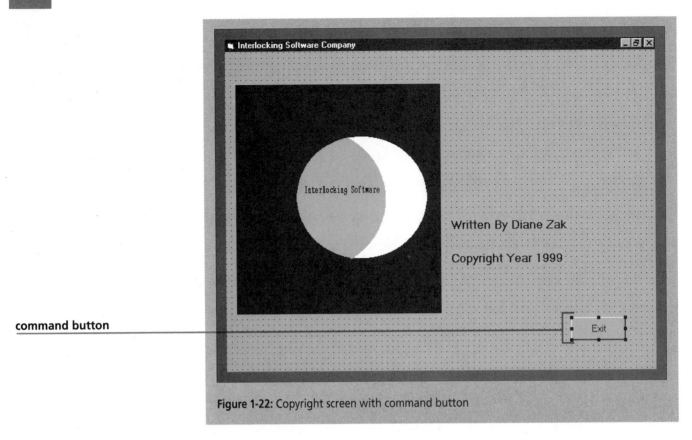

command button

Figure 1-22: Copyright screen with command button

Although the Exit button appears on the screen and its properties are set, you're not done with this control yet, as you'll see in the next section.

Writing Visual Basic Code

Think about the Windows environment for a moment. Did you ever wonder why the OK and Cancel buttons respond the way they do when you click them, or how the Exit option on the File menu knows to close the application? The answer to these questions is very simple: a programmer gave the buttons and menu option explicit instructions on how to respond to the actions of the user. Those actions—such as clicking, double-clicking, and scrolling—are called **events**. The Visual Basic instructions, or **code**, that tells an object how to respond to an event is called an **event procedure**.

At this point, the Exit button in the copyright screen does not know what it is supposed to do; you must tell it what to do by writing an event procedure for it. You write the event procedure in the object's Code window, which is a window you have not yet seen. Each object has its own set of Code windows—one window for each of the events the object can recognize. You open a Code window by double-clicking the object.

You will now open the Code window for the Exit button. Inside the Code window, you will enter instructions that tell the button to end the application when the button is clicked by the user.

To open the Exit button's Code window:

1   The form should still be maximized, so you just need to double-click the Exit command button on the form. The button's Code window opens.

The event procedure that appears when you open an object's Code window is typically the most commonly used procedure for that object. As Figure 1-23 shows, the most commonly used procedure for a command button is the Click event procedure.

Object box

input area

current event procedure

Figure 1-23: Open Code window for the Exit button

The Visual Basic Code window contains an Object box, a Proc (Procedure) box, and an input area. The **Object box** performs the same function as the Object box in the Properties window; both allow you to choose either the form or the controls on the form. You can also use the Object box to verify the name of a control while you are writing instructions in the Code window.

The **Proc (Procedure) box** in the Code window lists the event procedures to which the selected object is capable of responding. The Proc box shows that the current event procedure—the event procedure shown in the input area of the Code window—is Click. You can see what other event procedures an object can recognize by clicking the list arrow in the Proc box. Check out what other event procedures a command button can recognize.

To display the event procedures in the Proc box:

1   Click the **Proc box** list arrow located in the Code window. A list of event procedures appears. See Figure 1-24.

Figure 1-24: List of event procedures that a command button can recognize

The scroll bars on the list box indicate that not all of the event procedures are currently displayed. You would need to scroll down the list box to see the remaining event procedures. To change to another event procedure, simply click the one you want in the list.

2 Click **GotFocus** in the Proc list box. Notice that both the Private Sub statement and the Proc box now show that the GotFocus event procedure is the current one. See Figure 1-25.

current event procedure

Figure 1-25: GotFocus event procedure

Because you need to enter the instruction to end the application in the Click event, you will switch back to that procedure.

3 Click the **Proc box** list arrow to open the list of event procedures. Scroll the list, if necessary, then click **Click**. The Click event procedure shown in Figure 1-26 appears.

keywords

control name

current event

Figure 1-26: Click event procedure for the Exit button

You will notice that the input area of the Code window already contains some Visual Basic code (instructions). To help you follow the rules of its language, called **syntax**, Visual Basic provides you with a **code template** for every event procedure. The code template begins with the two keywords: Private Sub. A **keyword** is a word that has a special meaning in a programming language. The **Private** keyword tells Visual Basic that the event procedure can be used only within the form in which it is defined; it can't be used by any other form in the application. The **Sub** keyword is an abbreviation of the term **subprocedure** which, in programming terminology, refers to a block of code that performs a specific task. Following the Sub keyword is the name of the control (cmdExit), an underscore (_), the name of the current event (Click), and parentheses. The code template ends with the keywords "End Sub." You must enter your Visual Basic instructions between the Private Sub and End Sub lines. The instructions in the Code window tell the object (cmdExit) how to respond to the current event (Click).

If you are using a color monitor, notice that the keywords Private Sub and End Sub appear in a different color than both the object's name and the word "Click." Visual Basic displays keywords in a different color to help you quickly identify these elements in the Code window. In this case, the color coding helps you easily locate the beginning and end of the event procedure. Now enter the instruction that will tell the Exit button to end the application when clicked by the user.

The blinking insertion point located in the input area of the Code window means that Visual Basic is waiting for you to type something in the window. In this case you want to instruct the Exit button to end the application whenever the button is clicked. For this you will use the **End statement**, which has a very specific meaning in Visual Basic; it tells Visual Basic to terminate the current application. You'll indent the code in the Code window to make the instructions easier to read.

To enter the code into the open Code window for the Click event procedure, then save and run the application:

1 Press the **Tab** key to indent the line, then type **end** in the Code window, and then press the **Enter** key. See Figure 1-27.

Figure 1-27: End statement entered in the Exit button's Click event procedure

When the user clicks the Exit button, Visual Basic reads and processes the instructions entered in the Click event procedure's Code window. It is probably no surprise to you that Visual Basic processes the instructions, one after another, in the order in which the instructions are entered in the Code window. In programming, this is referred to as **sequential processing** or as the **sequence structure**. (You will learn about two other programming structures, selection and repetition, in future tutorials.) You're finished with the Code window, so you can close it.

2 Click the Code window's **Close** button ⊠ to close the Code window, then restore the form to its standard size.

Click the Code window's Control menu box ⊟, then click Close to close the Code window. Restore the form to its standard size.

3 Click the **Save Project** button 🖫 to save the form and the project.

Now that the files are saved, you can run the project to see if it is working correctly.

4 Click the **Start** button ▶ on the toolbar. The copyright screen appears. See Figure 1-28.

WINDOWS 3.1

It is a good practice to save both the form and project before running the application.

Minimize button

Maximize/Resize button

Close button

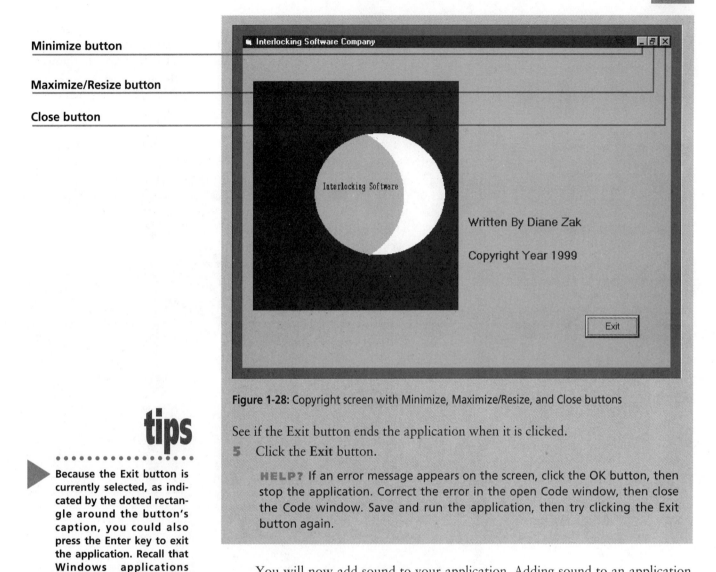

Figure 1-28: Copyright screen with Minimize, Maximize/Resize, and Close buttons

See if the Exit button ends the application when it is clicked.

5 Click the **Exit** button.

> **HELP?** If an error message appears on the screen, click the OK button, then stop the application. Correct the error in the open Code window, then close the Code window. Save and run the application, then try clicking the Exit button again.

You will now add sound to your application. Adding sound to an application adds interest and makes the application seem more professional and user-friendly. After adding sound to your application, the application will play some music when the copyright screen first appears.

Important Note: In order to complete the next section using the computer, you must be using the Professional Edition of Visual Basic 4.0. If you are using either the Standard Edition or the Working Model, you should still read the "Using the Multimedia Control to Add Sound to an Application" section. The next section you will be able to complete using the computer is the section titled "Setting the Visible Property."

Using the Multimedia Control to Add Sound to an Application

The Professional Edition of Visual Basic 4.0 includes many custom controls not included in the Standard Edition. (A custom control is an extension to the Visual Basic toolbox.) One of the custom controls, the **Multimedia MCI control**, allows you to add sound to your application. (In order to complete this section on the computer, you must be using the Professional Edition of Visual Basic 4.0. If you are using the Standard Edition or the Working Model, you should still read this section.) Before you can place a Multimedia MCI control on the form, you first need to insert the control into the current application's toolbox; for that you use the Custom Controls option on Visual Basic's Tools menu.

tips

▶ **To make a custom control a permanent member of the toolbox for all future applications, you simply open the Auto32ld project (Windows 95) or the Auto16ld project (Windows 3.1), which can be found in the main Visual Basic folder on either the hard drive or the local drive. You then select the custom controls that you want to see in the toolbox, and then click the Save button (the OK button in Windows 3.1).**

be sure this check box is checked

To insert the Multimedia MCI control into the toolbox for the current application:

1 Click **Tools** on the menu bar, then click **Custom Controls**. The Custom Controls dialog box, which lists the available custom controls, opens.

2 Scroll the Available Controls window until the Microsoft Multimedia Control option is visible, then click the **Microsoft Multimedia Control** check box to select this option, as shown in Figure 1-29.

Figure 1-29: Custom Controls dialog box with Microsoft Multimedia Control check box checked

3 Click the **OK** button. Visual Basic inserts the Microsoft Multimedia control (referred to as the MMControl) in the toolbox for the current application, as shown in Figure 1-30.

Microsoft Multimedia Control

Figure 1-30: Microsoft Multimedia Control inserted in the toolbox

Use Visual Basic Help to learn more about this custom control.

4   Click the **MMControl** tool in the toolbox, then press the **F1** key. Visual Basic displays the Multimedia MCI Control Help window, as shown in Figure 1-31.

> **HELP?** If a Windows Help dialog box appears with OK and Cancel buttons, click the Cancel button.

Figure 1-31: Multimedia MCI Control Help window

5   Read the Help window. If you'd like, scroll the Help window to see what information it contains. Don't worry if you don't understand everything; you're first learning the basics of Visual Basic. The Help windows will become more meaningful with time and practice.

As the Help window shows, the Multimedia control manages the recording and playback of multimedia files on MCI (Media Control Interface) devices. The Help window lists the various MCI devices with which the Multimedia control can communicate.

Notice that the Multimedia control contains the same nine buttons usually found on a CD (compact disc) player; these buttons control the playback of multimedia files. In some applications that include a Multimedia control, the user can manipulate the buttons by selecting them on the control; in other applications, the application itself manipulates the buttons through code. In the copyright application, you want the Multimedia control to play music automatically when the copyright screen appears. In other words, the music should play with no user intervention. Therefore, you will have to write the necessary code to play the multimedia file.

6   Close the Help window.

Now add a Microsoft Multimedia custom control to the form.

To add a Microsoft Multimedia (MMControl) custom control to the form:

1 Double-click the **MMControl** tool 🖾 in the toolbox. The MMControl appears on the form as shown in Figure 1-32.

MMControl

Figure 1-32: MMControl displayed on the form

2 Drag the MMControl to a location above the Image control. (Don't worry about the exact location.)

The Properties window shows that the default name for the MMControl is MMControl1. Change the name to a more meaningful one.

3 Set the MMControl's Name property to **mmcSound**. (The "mmc" indicates that the control is a Multimedia Control.)

To include sound in the copyright application, you will need to set three of the Multimedia control's properties: DeviceType, FileName, and Command. You'll begin with the DeviceType property; but first you will display its Help window.

4 The mmcSound control is already selected in the form, so you just need to click **DeviceType** in the Properties list, then press the **F1** key to display the Help window. The Help window for the DeviceType property opens as shown in Figure 1-33.

Figure 1-33: Help window for the DeviceType property

You use the **DeviceType property** to specify the type of MCI (Media Control Interface) device that you want the Multimedia control to open. Because the mmcSound control will play a sound file that has a .wav extension, you will set the device type to the WaveAudio MCI device. (The ".wav" stands for "waveform." Every sound has a waveform that describes its frequency, amplitude, and harmonic content. The digital representation of those waveforms are stored in .wav files.)

5 Close the Help window.

6 Click **DeviceType** in the Properties list, then type **WaveAudio** in the Settings text box and press the **Enter** key.

The next property you will set is the FileName property.

7 The mmcSound control is already selected in the form, so you just need to click **FileName** in the Properties list.

You use the **FileName property** to specify a file to be either opened or saved by the Multimedia control. In this case, you will use the FileName property to specify the file to be opened. The name of the file is CopySnd.wav; the file is located in the Tut01 folder on your Student Disk. The CopySnd file contains the sounds that the mmcSound control will play when the copyright screen first appears.

8 Depending on the location of your Student Disk, either type **a:\Tut01\CopySnd.wav** or **b:\Tut01\CopySnd.wav** in the FileName property's Settings text box, then press the **Enter** key. (Be sure to type the filename exactly as shown. Don't forget the \ after the drive letter and after the folder name, and don't include any spaces in the name.)

In addition to the FileName property, you also need to set the Command property for the Multimedia control. If you scan the Properties list, you will notice that the Command property does not appear in the list. Not all properties can be set at design time; some must be set at run time through code. The Command property is one of the properties that must be set while the program is running. Before setting the Multimedia control's Command property, open its Help window.

To open the Command property's Help window, then set the Command property:

1 Click the **mmcSound control** in the form, then press the **F1** key. Visual Basic displays the Help window for the Multimedia control. Click <u>**Properties**</u> at the top of the Help window, and then click *<u>**Command**</u>. Maximize the Help window. The maximized Help window for the Command property appears as shown in Figure 1-34. (You will need to scroll the Help window to see the remainder of its contents.)

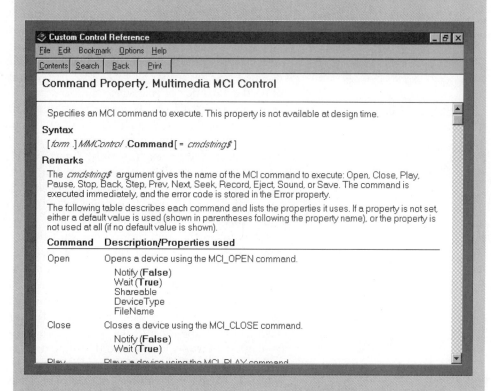

Figure 1-34: Help window for the Multimedia control's Command property

You use the **Command property** to specify the MCI command that you want the Multimedia control to execute. Notice the syntax section of the Help window. In programming terminology, the word **syntax** refers to the rules of the programming language. The Command property's syntax section, for example, shows [*form*.]*MMControl*.**Command**[= *cmdstring$*]. (Because this is your first look at the syntax of the Visual Basic language, the syntax may seem a bit overwhelming. Here again, be patient; everything new takes time to learn.) In the syntax, items appearing in square brackets ([]) are optional parts of the instruction. Words in bold, however, are required. Items in *italics* indicate where the programmer must supply information pertaining to the current application. In the Command property's syntax, [*form*] is the name of the form in which the control resides, *MMControl* is the name of the Multimedia control, and *cmdstring$* is one of the commands listed in the table of commands in the Help window. You will learn more about how to read and apply Visual Basic's syntax in future tutorials. For now, just notice how the instructions you will type in the next set of steps follow the Command property's syntax.

Before the application can play the sound file, the application must open the MCI device whose name you previously entered in the DeviceType property. According to the information in the Help window, you open the MCI device by setting the Command property to "Open". After opening the MCI device, you then need to set the Command property to "Play" in order to have the MCI device play the file you previously entered in the FileName property. Lastly, you set the Command property to "Close" to close the MCI device.

2 Close the Help window.

Because the Command property is not listed in the Properties list, you must set its value through code. The Visual Basic instruction you will use to open the MCI device is `mmcSound.Command = "Open"`. The Visual Basic instruction you will use to play the .wav file listed in the FileName property is `mmcSound.Command = "Play"`. The Visual Basic instruction you will use to close the MCI device is `mmcSound.Command = "Close"`. (These three instructions are referred to as assignment statements because they assign values to the properties of objects. You will learn about assignment statements in Tutorial 2.)

When programming in an object-oriented/event-driven language, such as Visual Basic, you must not only determine the proper instructions to get the objects to perform the way you want, but you must also determine where in the application to enter those instructions. In this case, for example, three instructions are needed to open the MCI device, play the .wav file, and close the MCI device. Now you need to decide where to enter those instructions—in other words at what point in the application you want those instructions to be processed. You must decide on the object that should perform the instructions and on which of the object's event procedures the instructions should be performed.

Because you want the Multimedia control to open the MCI device and then play the .wav file when the copyright screen first appears, you will need to enter both the `mmcSound.Command = "Open"` and the `mmcSound.Command = "Play"` instructions in the form's Load event. A **Load event** occurs when the application is run and the form is loaded into the computer's memory. Visual Basic automatically executes the instructions contained in the Load event procedure's Code window when the Load event occurs. You will close the MCI device when the user exits the application. That means that you will enter the `mmcSound.Command = "Close"` instruction in the Exit button's Click event procedure.

To enter the instructions in the form's Load event and in the Exit button's Click event, then save and run the application:

1 Double-click the **form** to open its Code window. Visual Basic displays the form's Load event procedure, which is the most commonly used procedure for a form.

   HELP? If the form's Load event procedure does not appear in the Code window, click the Object box list arrow in the Code window, then click Form in the list.

Now enter the two instructions that will open the MCI device and play the .wav file.

2 Press the **Tab** key to indent the first instruction, then type **mmcSound.command = "open"** and press the **Enter** key.

Notice that Visual Basic keeps the indentation for the next line. If you want to remove the indentation, you simply press the Backspace key. In this case, however, you want to keep the indentation.

3 Type **mmcSound.command = "play"** and press the **Enter** key.

4 Compare your code with the code shown in Figure 1-35. Make any needed corrections before going on to the next step.

opens the MCI device

plays the .wav file

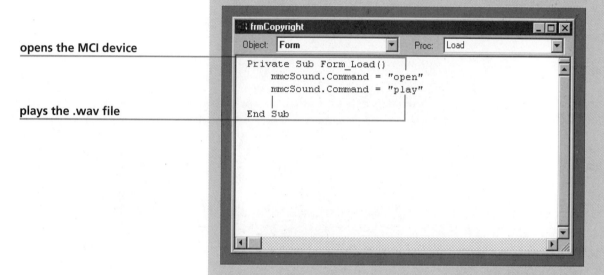

Figure 1-35: Form's Load event procedure

Now open the Exit button's Code window and set the mmcSound control's Command property to "Close".

5 Click the **Object box** list arrow. A list of objects included in the application appears. Click **cmdExit** in the list. The Click event procedure for the cmdExit control appears.

Notice that the blinking insertion point is at the left edge of the line containing the End instruction.

6 Press the **Enter** key to insert a line above the End instruction. Press ↑ on your keyboard to move the blinking insertion point to the new line, and then press the **Tab** key to indent the new line.

7 Type **mmcSound.command = "close"** and press the **Enter** key.

8 Close the Code window.

Before saving and running the application, review the steps required to use the Multimedia control. First you set the DeviceType property to the type of device you want the Multimedia control to open. You then set the FileName property to the name of the sound file to be opened. You then use three Visual Basic instructions to set the control's Command property appropriately. Typically, you enter two of the instructions in the form's Load event: *MMControl*.Command = "Open" and *MMControl*.Command = "Play". (Replace *MMControl* with the name of the Multimedia control in the user interface.) You usually enter the *MMControl*.Command = "Close" instruction in the Click event procedure of either an Exit command button or an Exit option on a menu.

Now save and run the application to see how the Multimedia control works.

To see how the Multimedia control works:

1 **Save** and **run** the application. If your computer has sound capability, you should hear some music when Visual Basic displays the copyright screen.

HELP? If an error message appears on the screen, click the OK button, then stop the application. Correct the error in the open Code window, then close the Code window and save and run the application again.

Notice that the Multimedia control shows in the user interface. If the application is giving the user the button capability mentioned in the Multimedia Control's Help window (Figure 1-31), the control should appear so that the user can click the buttons. In this application, however, the application, not the user, controls the playback of the sound file. End the application and learn how to hide an object in Visual Basic.

2 Click the **Exit** button to end the application.

Setting the Visible Property

Important Note: If you are using either the Standard Edition or the Working Model of Visual Basic, you do not have the mmcSound Multimedia control on your form; that control was added to the application in the previous section. You can still practice the Setting the Visible Property section by adding another command button to the form. Like Multimedia controls, command buttons also have a Visible property. After adding the command button to the form, change its name to mmcSound and drag it above the Image control. When the instructions in this section tell you to select the mmcSound control and set its properties, you should select the mmcSound command button. You will delete the command button at the end of this section.

An object's Visible property determines whether an object is visible or hidden at run time. The property has two predefined settings: the Boolean values True and False. If the property is set to True, the object appears when the application is run; if the property is set to False, the object is hidden from view during run time. You will set the Multimedia control's Visible property to False, which will hide the control from view when the application is run.

To hide the Multimedia control during run time:

1 Select the mmcSound control in the form, then set its Visible property to **False.**

2 Click the **Save Project** button, then click the **Start** button. As before, if your computer has sound capability, you should hear some music when the application is run. This time, however, the Multimedia control does not appear in the user interface.

3 Click the **Exit** button to end the application.

Important Note: If you are using either the Standard Edition or the Working Model, you can delete the mmcSound command button by clicking it in the form, and then pressing the Delete key.

Now that you know your application is working correctly, you can remove its Minimize, Maximize, and Close (*the Control menu box in Windows 3.1*) buttons. Removing those elements, called **border elements**, will prevent the user from sizing your copyright screen and from exiting without clicking the Exit button. You can remove the border elements by setting the form's BorderStyle property.

Setting the BorderStyle Property

The **BorderStyle property** determines the border style of an object. The default BorderStyle for a form is 2-Sizable, which means that the form can be sized while the application is running. If you want to prevent the user from sizing the user interface and from exiting using the Close button (*the Control menu box in Windows 3.1*), you can reset the BorderStyle property to 0-None.

To change the form's BorderStyle property, then save and run the project:

1 Click the **form's title bar** to select the form. The form's title bar is now highlighted.

2 Click **BorderStyle** in the Properties list, then click the **Settings box** list arrow.

You remove the border elements from a form by setting the BorderStyle property to 0-None.

3 Set the BorderStyle property to **0-None.**

4 Click the **Save Project** button 🖫 on the toolbar to save the form and the project under their current names, then click the **Start** button ▶ on the toolbar. Notice that the border elements are no longer displayed when you run the application. See Figure 1-36.

tips

You can also use both the Save File As and the Save Project As commands on the File menu to save the form and the project. Be sure to save the form before saving the project. You can press the F5 key or use the Start command on the Run menu to run an application.

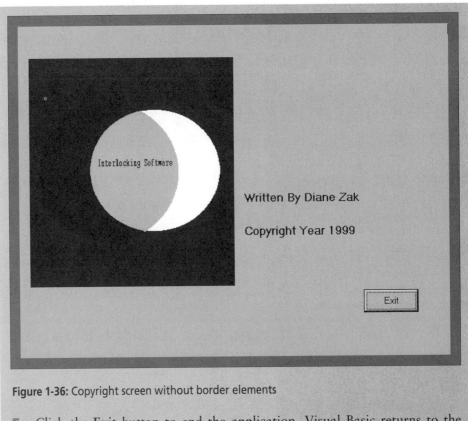

Figure 1-36: Copyright screen without border elements

5 Click the **Exit** button to end the application. Visual Basic returns to the design screen.

Be sure you do not change the BorderStyle property to 0-None until after you have tested your application and you are sure it is working correctly. Otherwise, you may not be able to end the application without losing data.

Your first application is finally complete. All that remains is to print the application, then make it into an executable (.exe) file that can be run directly from Windows, like the applications you previously ran in the Overview and in the beginning of this tutorial.

Printing a Visual Basic Application

You should always print a copy of the form, the properties of the objects included in the form, and the code you wrote. This information, called **documentation**, will help you understand and maintain the application in the future.

To print the documentation for the application:

1 Click **File** on the main menu.

The File menu contains an option called Print. If you choose that option to print the form, however, only the portion of the form currently showing on the screen will print. Notice that you can also print by using the Ctrl + P combination. (Ctrl + P means to press and hold down the Ctrl key as you type the letter p.) You can use the Ctrl + P combination to print the entire form, but first you need to maximize the form.

2 Click **File**, or press the **Esc** key, to close the File menu.

3 Maximize the Interlocking Software Company form. The form fills the entire screen.

4 Press **Ctrl + P**. (Press and hold down the Control key as you type the letter p.) The Print dialog box appears.

The Print What section of the dialog box shows that your three choices are Form Image, Form As Text, and Code. The Form Image option will print a copy of the form. (Be sure to have the form maximized.) The Form As Text option will print the properties of each object in the application. The Code option will print the Visual Basic instructions entered in the event procedures for each object.

5 Click the **Form Image** check box, then click the **Form As Text** check box, then click the **Code** check box. Check marks (*X's in Windows 3.1*) should appear next to each of the three selections. Click the **OK** button to begin printing.

6 When the printing stops, restore the form to its standard size.

The final task in this lesson is to make the copyright screen into an executable (.exe) file that can be run directly from Windows. (Recall that the Monthly Payment application in the Overview and the copyright screen you previewed in Tutorial 1 were run directly from Windows.)

Important Note: You will not be able to complete the next section if you are using the Working Model.

Making an Executable (.Exe) File

In the Overview you learned that high-level languages require either an interpreter or a compiler to convert the English-like instructions into machine code—the 0s and 1s the computer can understand. Recall that both interpreters and compilers are separate programs. An interpreter translates the high-level instructions into machine code, line by line, as the program is executing. For example, when you click the Start button to run the copyright screen application, Visual Basic's interpreter translates your application, line by line, into the machine code the computer can understand. Visual Basic's interpreter makes that translation each time you click the Start button.

Recall that a compiler translates the entire program into machine code before executing the program. Visual Basic's compiler saves the machine code in a separate file on your disk. The filename has an .exe extension; the .exe extension stands for "executable." Whenever you want to run your application, you simply tell the computer to execute the .exe file. Because the .exe file already contains the machine code version of your application, the computer does not need to retranslate the application, which means that your application will run faster.

Another reason for using Visual Basic's compiler to create an executable (.exe) file is that the .exe file can run on any computer system that is running Windows, even if the system does not have Visual Basic installed on it. You simply need to give the user a copy of the .exe file and a copy of the VB40032.DLL file (Windows 95) or the VB40016.DLL file (Windows 3.1). The VB40032.DLL and VB40016.DLL files come with Visual Basic, and Microsoft allows you to distribute these files with your applications without violating any licensing agreement. The .DLL files are in the Windows\System folder. You will make the copyright screen into an executable file and then try running it directly from Windows. (Recall that you cannot complete these steps if you are using the Working Model.)

tips

▶ You might also need to give the user additional files, such as data files, custom controls, other .DLL files, and initialization files. You can use Visual Basic's Setup Wizard to create the distribution disks that will contain the appropriate files. You will practice with the Setup Wizard in Discovery Exercise 5, which is at the end of Lesson C.

To make an executable (.exe) file and then run it from Windows:

1 Click **File**, then click **Make EXE File**. The Make EXE File dialog box opens.

2 Type **CopyExec** in the File name text box, then verify the entries in the Save in list box. You want to save the executable file in the Tut01 folder on your Student Disk.

Type CopyExec in the File name text box, then verify the entries in the Drives list box and in the Directories list box. You want to save the executable file in the Tut01 folder on your Student Disk.

3 Click the **OK** button. Visual Basic's compiler translates your application into machine code, which it saves in the CopyExec.exe file on your Student Disk. See Figure 1-37.

   HELP? If this is the second or subsequent time you are practicing this lesson, Visual Basic will display a dialog box that asks if you want to replace the existing file. Click the Yes button.

Figure 1-37: Visual Basic's compiler translates the project and form files into machine code

You will now save the project and exit Visual Basic before running the CopyExec.exe file from Windows.

4 Click the **Save Project** button ▣ to save the project.

5 Exit Visual Basic.

6 Click the **Start** button on the Windows 95 taskbar, then click **Run**. Click the **Browse** button in the Run dialog box, then locate the CopyExec file, which is saved in the Tut01 folder on your Student Disk. Click **CopyExec** (CopyExec.exe), then click the **Open** button. When the Run dialog box appears again, click the **OK** button. The copyright screen appears. If your computer has sound capability, you should hear some music when the copyright screen appears.

Restore Program Manager, if necessary. Click File on the Program Manager menu bar, then click Run. Click the Browse button, then locate the CopyExec.exe file, which is saved in the Tut01 folder on your Student Disk. Click copyexec.exe in the list of filenames, then click the OK button. When the Run dialog box appears again, click the OK button. The copyright screen appears. If your computer has sound capability, you should hear some music when the copyright screen appears.

7 Click the **Exit** button to end the application.

Now you can either exit Visual Basic and take a break, complete the end-of-lesson questions and exercises, or continue on to the Debugging section. The Debugging section may contain information that will help you to complete the end-of-lesson exercises. (If necessary, remember to redisplay the Windows 95 taskbar.)

S U M M A R Y

To open an object's Code window:

- ■ Double-click the object whose Code window you want to open.

To close an object's Code window:

- ■ Click the Code window's Close button ☒ (*or the Control menu box* ⊟ *in Windows 3.1*).

To print a Visual Basic form:

- ■ Maximize the form, then press Ctrl + P.
- ■ Click the Form Image check box to print the form, then click the OK button to start printing.

To print both the code and the properties of the objects in a Visual Basic application:

- ■ Click File, then click Print.
- ■ Click the Form As Text check box to print the properties of the objects, click the Code check box to print the contents of the Code windows.
- ■ Click the OK button to start printing.

To make an executable (.exe) file:

- ■ Click File, then click Make EXE File. The Make EXE File dialog box opens.
- ■ If necessary, enter a filename and select the appropriate drive and folder.
- ■ Click the OK button.

To display a picture in an image control:

- ■ Set the image control's Picture property.

To add a custom control to the current application's toolbox:

- ■ Click Tools on the menu bar, then click Custom Controls. Select the custom control(s) you want from the Available Controls window, then click the OK button.

To use the Multimedia Control to add sound to an application:

- ■ Set the control's DeviceType property appropriately. The DeviceType property specifies the type of MCI (Media Control Interface) device that you want the Multimedia control to open.
- ■ Set the control's FileName property appropriately. The FileName property specifies the name of the file to be either opened or saved.
- ■ In code, set the control's Command property appropriately. The Command property specifies the MCI command to execute. Typically you will enter two commands in the form's Load event: *MMControl*.Command = "Open" and *MMControl*.Command = "Play". (Replace *MMControl* with the name of the Multimedia control in the user interface.) You usually enter the *MMControl*.Command = "Close" command in the Click event procedure of either an Exit command button or an Exit option on a menu.

To hide an object:

■ Set the object's Visible property to False.

To remove a form's border elements (Minimize and Maximize buttons, and either the Close button in Windows 95 or the Control menu box in Windows 3.1):

■ Set the form's BorderStyle property to 0-None.

To have Visual Basic execute code when an application is run and the form is loaded into memory:

■ Enter the code in the form's Load event procedure.

To allow the user to end a running application:

■ One way of allowing the user to end a running application is to include the End command in the Click event procedure of a command button.

Q U E S T I O N S

1. If you want to print an entire form during design time, maximize the form on the screen and press _____ .
   a. Alt + P
   b. Ctrl + P
   c. Ctrl + F
   d. Shift + P
   e. Shift + F

2. You display a picture in an image control by setting the control's _____ property.
   a. ControlImage
   b. Icon
   c. Image
   d. Load
   e. Picture

3. The _____ instruction tells Visual Basic to end an application.
   a. Done
   b. End
   c. Finish
   d. Stop
   e. Timer

4. Printing the _____ will print the properties of the objects included in the form.
   a. Code
   b. Form As Text
   c. Form Image
   d. Properties
   e. Text

5. You tell an object what you want it to do by entering instructions in the object's
_____ window.
   a. Code
   b. Form
   c. Instruction
   d. Main
   e. Text

6. Actions such as clicking, double-clicking, and scrolling are called _____ .
   a. episodes
   b. events
   c. happenings
   d. procedures

7. The Visual Basic instructions that tell an object how to respond to an event are called
_____ .
   a. action procedures
   b. code procedures
   c. event procedures
   d. object procedures
   e. text procedures

8. The rules of a programming language are called its _____ .
   a. code
   b. events procedures
   c. guidelines
   d. regulations
   e. syntax

9. A(n) _____ is a word that has a special meaning in a programming
language.
   a. code word
   b. command
   c. event
   d. key
   e. keyword

10. The _____ control allows you to add sound to an application.
   a. CDPlayer
   b. Media
   c. Multimedia
   d. Player
   e. Sound

11. You use the _____ property to specify the type of MCI (Media Control
Interface) device that you want the Multimedia control to open.
   a. Command
   b. DeviceType
   c. FileName
   d. SoundDevice
   e. Type

12. You use the _____ property to specify the MCI (Media Control Interface)
command that you want the Multimedia control to execute.
   a. Command
   b. DeviceType
   c. FileName
   d. SoundDevice
   e. Type

13. You use the _____ property to specify the file to be either opened or saved by the Multimedia control.
    a. Command
    b. DeviceType
    c. FileName
    d. SoundDevice
    e. Type

14. The _____ property cannot be set in the Properties window; it must be set during run time.
    a. Command
    b. DeviceType
    c. FileName
    d. SoundDevice
    e. Type

15. If you want Visual Basic to execute a set of instructions when the application is run and the form is read into memory, place the instructions in the form's _____ event procedure.
    a. AutoLoad
    b. Click
    c. Initialize
    d. Load
    e. MemLoad

16. The _____ property determines if the form displays with Minimize, Maximize, and Close buttons.
    a. BorderStyle
    b. ButtonStyle
    c. ElementStyle
    d. TitleBar
    e. TitleStyle

17. Explain how to open an object's Code window.

18. Write a one-sentence definition of an event procedure.

19. Explain the purpose of the Code window's Object box and its Proc (Procedure) box.

20. Write a one-sentence definition of syntax.

21. Explain how to use the Multimedia control. Specifically, explain the use of the DeviceType, FileName, and Command properties. What values are assigned to the Command property, and where is the code usually entered?

22. Explain the purpose of the Make EXE File command. Why would you want to use it?

E X E R C I S E S

1. In this exercise, you will add a label control, a command button, and an image control to a form. You will also change the properties of the form and its objects.
    a. If necessary, start Visual Basic and open a new project. Size and arrange the windows so they do not overlap each other. Your Student Disk should be in the appropriate drive.
    b. Save the form and the project as lc1Done in the Tut01 folder on your Student Disk. Remember to save the form *before* saving the project.

c. Set the following properties for the form:

Caption:	Peoria Animal Shelter
BackColor:	white
Name:	frmAnimal
WindowState:	2-Maximized

d. Add a label control to the form. Set the following properties for the label control:

Caption:	Welcome to the Peoria Animal Shelter
Name:	lblTitle
Font:	12 points, bold
AutoSize:	True

e. Maximize the form, then drag the lblTitle control to the top, center of the form.

f. Add an image control to the form. Set the following properties for the image control:

Name:	imgLogo
Picture:	Set the Picture property to the logo file, which is in the Tut01 folder on your Student Disk
Stretch:	True

g. Maximize the form, then drag the image control to the center of the form. Make the image control larger than its current size.

h. Add a command button to the form. Maximize the form, then drag the command button to the lower-right corner of the form.

i. Set the following properties for the command button:

Name:	cmdExit
Caption:	Exit
Font:	12 points, bold

j. Open the command button's Code window for the Click event procedure. Enter the End instruction, then close the Code window.

k. Save and run the application, then use the Exit button to end the application. If necessary, correct any errors and repeat this step again.

l. Maximize the form, then press Ctrl + P. When the Print dialog box opens, click the Form Image and the Code check boxes, then click the OK button.

2. In this exercise, you will add sound to the application you created in Lesson C's Exercise 1. In order to do this exercise, you must be using the Professional Edition of Visual Basic 4.0.

a. If necessary, start Visual Basic. Your Student Disk should be in the appropriate drive.

b. Open the lc1Done project that you created in Lesson C's Exercise 1.

c. Use both the File menu's Save File As command and its Save Project As command to save the form and the project, respectively, as lc2Done in the Tut01 folder on your Student Disk.

d. Use Visual Basic's Tools menu to add the Microsoft Multimedia Control to the current project's toolbox.

e. Add an MMControl (Microsoft Multimedia Control) to the form. Set the following properties for the MMControl:

Name:	mmcSound
DeviceType:	WaveAudio
FileName:	Depending on the location of your Student Disk, use either a:\Tut01\Notes.wav or b:\Tut01\Notes.wav
Visible:	False

f. Maximize the form, then drag the Multimedia control to the bottom of the form.

g. Open the form's Load event procedure and enter the following two instructions:

```
mmcSound.Command = "Open"
mmcSound.Command = "Play"
```

    h. Open the Exit button's Click event procedure and enter the following instruction above the End instruction:

        mmcSound.Command = "Close"

    i. Save and run the application, then use the Exit button to end the application. If necessary, correct any errors and repeat this step again.

    j. Remove the border elements from the form, then make the file into an executable file and save the application again. Call the executable file lc2Exec.

    k. Open the File menu and click the Print command. When the Print dialog box opens, click the Code check box, then click the OK button.

    l. Try running the lcE2 Executable file from the Run command on the Windows 95 Start menu.

Exercises 3 through 5 are Discovery Exercises, which allow you to both "discover" the solutions to problems on your own and experiment with material that is not covered in the tutorial.

discovery ▶ **3.** In this exercise, you will design your own user interface.

    a. If necessary, start Visual Basic and open a new project. Your Student Disk should be in the appropriate drive.

    b. Save the form and the project as lc3Done in the Tut01 folder on your Student Disk.

    c. Design your own user interface according to the following specifications:

        1) Be sure to include an Exit button that will end the application.

        2) Use label controls and image controls as desired.

        3) You can either set the image control(s) Picture property to the Interlocking picture you used in the tutorial, or you can use one of Visual Basic's icons. The Visual Basic icons are located in the Microsoft Visual Basic\Icons folder on the local hard drive or on the network drive. (Verify the location of the icon files with your instructor. The icon files are not available with the Working Model.)

        4) Be sure to name the objects appropriately.

        5) Experiment with color and font types, styles, and sizes.

    d. Save and run the application. Then use the Exit button to end the application. If necessary, correct any errors and repeat this step again.

    e. If you are using the Professional Edition:

        1) Add the Microsoft Multimedia Control to the current project's toolbox.

        2) Add an MMControl to the user interface. Name it appropriately.

        3) Have the application play the CopySnd.wav sound file, which is located in the Tut01 folder on your Student Disk.

        4) Save and run the application. If necessary, correct any errors and repeat this step again.

    f. Print the Form Image, the Form As Text, and the Code.

discovery ▶ **4.** In this exercise, you will experiment with image controls and command buttons.

    a. If necessary, start Visual Basic and open a new project. Your Student Disk should be in the appropriate drive.

    b. Save the form and the project as lc4Done in the Tut01 folder on your Student Disk. Remember to save the form *before* saving the project.

    c. Add an image control and three command buttons to a form. The Captions for the three command buttons should be On, Off, and Exit.

    d. Name the form and the four controls appropriately. (Call the form frmLcE4.)

    e. Set the image control's Picture property to one of Visual Basic's icons, or, if you are using the Working Model, use the Interlocking picture you used in the tutorial. The Visual Basic icons are located in the \Icons folder, which is located in the Visual Basic main folder on the local hard drive or on the network drive. (Verify the location of the icon files with your instructor.)

    f. Make the image control larger than its current size. The picture should size along with the control.

    g. In the Exit button, enter the command to end the application.

h. In the On button's Click event procedure, include an instruction to display the image control. In the Off button's Click event procedure, include an instruction to hide the image control.

i. Save and run the application. Use the Off button to hide the image control, then use the On button to display the image control. Lastly, use the Exit button to end the application. If necessary, correct any errors and repeat this step again.

j. Print the Form Image and the Code.

discovery ▶ 5. In this exercise you will experiment with Visual Basic's Setup Wizard. You cannot do this exercise if you are using the Working Model.

a. Click the Start button, point to Programs, point to Visual Basic 4.0, then click Application Setup Wizard.

WINDOWS 3.1

Double-click the Visual Basic 4.0 (16-bit) icon in Program Manager, then double-click the Application Setup Wizard (16-bit) icon in the Visual Basic group window.

b. Use the Help windows (or the *Microsoft Visual Basic Programmer's Guide* if you have access to it) to make distribution disks for the lcCopy project. You will need three blank, formatted disks. Be sure to label the disks Setup 1, Setup 2, and Setup 3.

c. After making the setup disks, try to locate a computer that does not have Visual Basic on it. Place the Setup 1 disk in the drive, then run the setup.exe file and follow the directions on the screen.

d. Submit the setup disks.

D E B U G G I N G

Technique

The simplest technique a programmer uses for debugging an application is to print the application's properties (Form As Text) and code. In the printout of the properties, the programmer looks for a property that is set incorrectly. In the code printout, the programmer looks for an instruction that is either in the wrong object's Code window or in the wrong event procedure.

At the end of each tutorial you will find a Debugging Section. In programming, the term "debugging" refers to the process of finding the errors in a program. Each Debugging Section will include debugging techniques, from the simple to the more complex, as well as exercises designed to let you practice debugging applications.

Tutorial 1's Debugging Section contains three debugging exercises. In each exercise you will open and then run an application that is not working correctly. Your task is to find and correct the errors in the application—in other words, to debug the application—using this tutorial's debugging technique.

Exercises

1. Open the debug1 project, which is in the Tut01 folder on your Student Disk, then view the form.

a. Notice two problems. 1) The form's title bar does not say Glamour-Us (the name of the beauty salon). 2) The label control does not display all of its contents on one line.

b. Display the Print dialog box and select the Form As Text option to print the properties of the objects in the user interface.

c. Use the Form As Text printout to locate the errors.

d. Correct the errors, then run the application to make sure it works correctly. (You do not need to save this application.)

e. Stop the application, then display the Print dialog box and select the Form As Text option.

f. Circle your corrections on the Form As Text printout from step e. (You do not need to save this application.)

2. Open the debug2 project, which is in the Tut01 folder on your Student Disk, then view the form.
   a. Display the Print dialog box and select both the Form As Text and Code options.
   b. Run the application. (You do not need to save this application.)
   c. Click the command button. Notice two problems. 1) The command button should say Exit. 2) The command button does not work (it should end the application when clicked by the user).
   d. Stop the application, then use both the Form As Text and Code printouts to locate the errors.
   e. Correct the errors, then run the application to make sure it works correctly. (You do not need to save this application.)
   f. Display the Print dialog box and select both the Form As Text and Code options.
   g. Circle your corrections on the Form As Text and Code printouts from step f. (You do not need to save this application.)

3. Exercise 3 can be done only if you are using the Professional Edition of Visual Basic 4.0.
   a. Open the debug3 project, which is in the Tut01 folder on your Student Disk, then view the form.
   b. Display the Print dialog box and select both the Form As Text and Code options.
   c. Run the application. (You do not need to save this application.)
   d. Notice two problems. 1) The application should play the contents of the CopySnd.wav file, which is located in Tut01 on your Student Disk. The Multimedia control, however, is not working correctly. 2) The Multimedia control is visible in the user interface during run time; it should be hidden.
   e. Stop the application. Use the Form As Text and Code printouts to locate the errors.
   f. Correct the errors, then run the application to make sure it works correctly. (You do not need to save this application.)
   g. Display the Print dialog box and select both the Form As Text and Code options.
   h. Circle your corrections on the Form As Text and Code printouts from step g. (You do not need to save this application.)

TUTORIAL

2

Designing Applications

Creating an Order Screen

case ▶ During your second week at Interlocking Software, you and Chris Statton, the senior programmer, meet with the sales manager of Skate-Away Sales. The sales manager, Jacques Cousard, tells you that his company sells skateboards by phone. The skateboards are priced at $100 each and are available in two colors—yellow and blue. He further explains that Skate-Away Sales employs 20 salespeople to answer the phones. The salespeople record each order on a form that contains the customer's name, address, and the number of blue and yellow skateboards ordered. They then calculate the total number of skateboards ordered and the total price of the skateboards, including a 5% sales tax.

Mr. Cousard feels that having the salespeople manually perform the necessary calculations is much too time-consuming and prone to errors. Also, the company now wants to send confirmation notices to the customers, and the handwritten form the salespeople currently complete is too informal to send. Mr. Cousard wants Interlocking to create a computerized application that will solve the problems of the current order-taking system.

Solving the Problem Using a Procedure-Oriented Approach

As you learned in the Overview, procedure-oriented languages preceded OOED (object-oriented/event-driven) languages. Recall that in procedure-oriented languages, the emphasis of a program is on *how* to accomplish a task. The programmer must instruct the computer every step of the way, from the start of the task to the completion of the task. The procedure-oriented approach to problem solving requires a programmer to think in a step-by-step, top-to-bottom fashion. Planning tools such as flowcharts and pseudocode make this approach easier. A **flowchart** uses standardized symbols to show the steps needed to solve a problem. **Pseudocode** uses English-like phrases to represent the required steps. Some programmers prefer to use flowcharts, while others prefer pseudocode; it's really a matter of personal preference. (You will learn more about pseudocode in this tutorial, and about flowcharts in Tutorial 4, as these planning tools are also useful in object-oriented/event-driven programming.) Take a look at a procedure-oriented approach to solving Skate-Away's problem. Figure 2-1 shows the solution written in pseudocode.

1. Get customer name, street address, city, state, zip, number of blue skateboards, number of yellow skateboards

2. Calculate total skateboards = number of blue skateboards + number of yellow skateboards

3. Calculate total price = total skateboards * $100 * 105%

4. Print customer name, street address, city, state, zip, number of blue skateboards, number of yellow skateboards, total skateboards, total price

5. End

Figure 2-1: Pseudocode for the procedure-oriented solution

You will notice that the pseudocode indicates the sequence of steps the computer must take to process an order. Using the pseudocode as a guide, the programmer then translates the solution into a language that the computer can understand. Figure 2-2 shows the pseudocode translated into Microsoft's QuickBASIC language. QuickBASIC, a procedure-oriented language, is a predecessor of Visual Basic.

```
Ans$ = "Y"
While Ans$ = "Y" or Ans$ = "y"
        Input "Enter the customer's name", Names$
        Input "Enter the street address:", Address$
        Input "Enter the city:", City$
        Input "Enter the state:", State$
        Input "Enter the zip code:", Zip$
        Input "Enter the number of blue skateboards:", Blue
        Input "Enter the number of yellow skateboards:", Yellow
        Totboards = Blue + Yellow
        Totprice = Totboards * 100 * 1.05
        Print "Customer name:", Names$
        Print "Address:", Address$
        Print "City:", City$
        Print "State:", State$
        Print "Zip:", Zip$
        Print "Blue skateboards:", Blue
        Print "Yellow skateboards:", Yellow
        Print "Total skateboards:", Totboards
        Print "Total price: $", Totprice
        Input "Do you want to enter another order? Enter Y if you
        do, or N if you don't.", Ans$
Wend
End
```

Figure 2-2: Procedure-oriented solution written in QuickBASIC

You will now enter an order using this procedure-oriented application.

To use the procedure-oriented application to enter an order:

1 If necessary, start Windows, then place your Student Disk in the appropriate drive.

2 Use the Run command on the Start menu to run the **proc95** (proc95.exe) file, which is located in the Tut02 folder on your Student Disk. A prompt requesting the customer's name appears on the screen.

Use the Run command on the Program Manager's File menu to run the proc31.exe file, which is located in the Tut02 folder on your Student Disk. A prompt requesting the customer's name appears on the screen.

WINDOWS 3.1

Assume that Sport Warehouse wants to place an order for 10 blue skateboards and 20 yellow skateboards.

3 Type **Sport Warehouse** and press the **Enter** key. A prompt requesting the street address appears on the screen.

4 Type **123 Main** and press the **Enter** key, then type **Glendale** for the city and press the **Enter** key, then type **IL** for the state and press the **Enter** key, and then type **60134** for the zip code and press the **Enter** key. The program now prompts you to enter the number of blue skateboards ordered.

5   Type **10** as the number of blue skateboards ordered, then press the **Enter** key. A prompt requesting the number of yellow skateboards ordered appears next.

6   Type **20** as the number of yellow skateboards ordered, then press the **Enter** key. The program computes and displays the total skateboards ordered (30) and the total price of the order ($3,150.00). (Recall that skateboards are $100 each and there is a 5% sales tax.) See Figure 2-3.

Customer name: Sport Warehouse

Address: 123 Main

City: Glendale

State: IL   **Zip:**   60134

Blue skateboards: 10

Yellow skateboards: 20

Total skateboards: 30

Total price: $3,150.00

Do you want to enter another order?
Enter Y if you do, or N if you don't.

Figure 2-3: Results of procedure-oriented program

Notice that the screen also contains a prompt that asks if you want to enter another order. If you do, you simply type the letter "Y" (for "yes"); otherwise you type the letter "N" (for "No").

7   Type **n** and press the **Enter** key to end the program.

Although Skate-Away Sales could use this procedure-oriented program to record its phone orders, the program has one very important limitation that is inherent in all procedure-oriented programs: the user has little, if any, control over the processing of the program. Recall, for example, that you could not control the sequence in which the order information was entered. What if the customer wants to order the yellow skateboards before the blue skateboards? Also recall that you couldn't change the information once you entered it. What if the customer changes his or her mind about how many blue skateboards to order? And, last, recall that you had no control over when the program calculated the total order and the total price. What if the customer wants to know the total price of the blue skateboards before placing the yellow skateboard order?

Now look at the object-oriented/event-driven approach to programming.

Solving the Problem Using an Object-Oriented/Event-Driven (OOED) Approach

As you learned in the Overview, in object-oriented/event-driven languages, the emphasis of a program is on the *objects* included in the user interface (such as scroll bars or buttons) and the *events* that occur on those objects (such as scrolling or clicking). Unlike the procedure-oriented approach to problem solving, in the OOED approach the programmer does not view the solution as a step-by-step, top-to-bottom process; instead, the OOED programmer's goal is to give the user as much control over the program as possible.

When using the OOED approach to problem solving, the programmer begins by identifying the tasks the application needs to perform. Then the programmer decides on the appropriate objects to which those tasks will be assigned, and on the event(s) necessary to trigger those objects to perform their assigned task(s). For example, in Tutorial 1, the copyright screen had to provide the user with a way to end the application. Recall that you assigned that task to the Exit command button. The event that triggered the Exit button to perform its assigned task was the Click event. In this book, you will use a TOE (Task, Object, Event) chart to assist you in planning your object-oriented/event-driven programs.

Before we discuss planning OOED applications further, you will run an OOED application designed to solve Skate-Away's problem. The OOED application, which is written using Visual Basic, contains a new control, a text box. You use a **text box** to provide areas in the form where the user can enter information.

To run the OOED application:

1 Use the Run command on the Start menu to run the **ooed95** (ooed95.exe) file, which is located in the Tut02 folder on your Student Disk. The order screen shown in Figure 2-4 appears.

WINDOWS 3.1

Use the Run command on the Program Manager's File menu to run the ooed31.exe file, which is located in the Tut02 folder on your Student Disk. The order screen shown in Figure 2-4 appears.

text box

label control

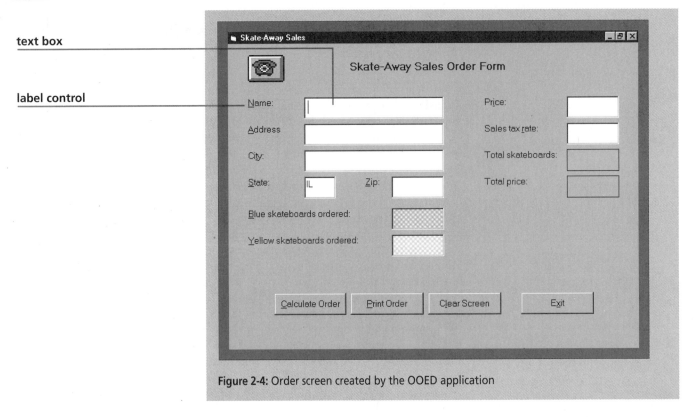

Figure 2-4: Order screen created by the OOED application

You will notice that Visual Basic displays a blinking insertion point in the first text box. The label control to the left of the text box identifies the information the user should enter—in this case, the customer's name. Enter Sport Warehouse's information.

tips

••••••••••••••

You can also click inside a text box to place the insertion point in the box.

To enter the order information using the OOED application:

1 Type **Sport Warehouse** as the customer's name, then press the **Tab** key twice. The blinking insertion point appears in the City text box.

2 Type **Glendale** as the city, then press **Shift + Tab** (press and hold down the Shift key as you press the Tab key) to move the insertion point to the Address text box.

Notice that the OOED application allows you to enter the order information in any order.

3 Type **123 Main** as the address, then press the **Tab** key twice. Because most of Skate-Away's customers reside in Illinois, the OOED application already contains IL in the State box.

4 Press the **Tab** key, then type **60134** as the zip code, and then press the **Tab** key. The blinking insertion point appears in the Blue skateboards text box.

5 Type **10** as the number of blue skateboards ordered and press the **Tab** key twice. Type **100** as the skateboard price and press the **Tab** key, then type **.05** as the sales tax rate and press the **Tab** key. Click the **Calculate Order** button. The Calculate Order button calculates the total skateboards (10) and the total price ($1,050.00). Notice that the OOED application allows you to tell the customer how much the blue skateboards will cost before the yellow skateboard order is placed.

6 Click the **Yellow skateboards ordered** text box, type **20**, then click the **Calculate Order** button. The application recalculates the total skateboards (30) and the total price ($3,150.00).

Now assume that Sport Warehouse wants to change its order to 20 blue skateboards.

7 Click to the **immediate left of** the 10 in the **Blue skateboards ordered** text box, press the **Delete** key to remove the 1, then type **2**. The number of blue skateboards ordered should now say 20. Click the **Calculate Order** button. The application recalculates the total skateboards ordered (40) and the total price ($4,200.00). See Figure 2-5.

Figure 2-5: Completed order using the OOED program

8 If your computer is connected to a printer, click the **Print Order** button. The confirmation notice prints on the printer.

Notice that each command button's caption, as well as most of the label controls, has an underlined letter, which is called an access key. An access key allows the user to select a control using the Alt key in combination with a letter. For example, when the salesperson is finished with an order, he or she can clear the screen either by clicking the Clear Screen button or by pressing the Alt key along with the letter l—the Clear Screen button's access key.

● Press **Alt + l** (the letter "l") to clear the screen for the next order. The previous customer's information (except the state, skateboard price, and sales tax rate) disappears, and the blinking insertion point is placed in the Name text box.

HELP? Pressing Alt + l means to press and hold down the Alt key as you type the letter l. Be sure to press the letter l, and not the number 1.

You will learn more about access keys in Lesson B.

10 Press **Alt + x** (or click the Exit button) to end the application.

Unlike the procedure-oriented program, the OOED application gives users a great deal of control over the program. Users can enter information in any order, change what they entered at any time, and calculate a subtotal whenever they like.

In Lesson A, you will learn how a Visual Basic programmer plans an OOED application. Then, in Lessons B and C, you will create the OOED application that you just viewed.

LESSON A
objectives

In this lesson you will learn how to:

- Plan an OOED application in Visual Basic
- Complete a TOE (Task, Object, Event) chart
- Follow the Windows standards regarding the layout and labeling of controls

Planning an OOED Application in Visual Basic

Creating an OOED Application

The process a programmer follows when creating an OOED application is similar to the process an architect follows when building a home. Both processes are shown in Figure 2-6.

An architect's process	A programmer's process
1. Plan the home (blueprint)	1. Plan the application (TOE chart)
2. Build the frame	2. Build the user interface
3. Complete the home	3. Code the application
4. Inspect the home and fix any problems	4. Test and debug the application
5. Assemble the documentation	5. Assemble the documentation

Figure 2-6: Processes used by an architect and a programmer

As Figure 2-6 shows, both the architect and the programmer first create a plan (blueprint) for the project. After the plan is approved by the customer, the architect builds the home's frame; likewise, the programmer builds the user interface, which is the application's frame. Once the frame is built, the architect completes the home by adding the electrical wiring, walls, and so on. Similarly, the programmer completes the application by adding the necessary code (instructions) to the user interface. When the home is complete, the architect makes a final inspection and corrects any problems before the customer moves in. Likewise, the completed application is tested by the programmer, and any problems, called **bugs**, are fixed before the application is given to the user. The final step in both processes is to assemble the project's documentation (paperwork), which is then given to the customer/user.

You will learn how to plan an OOED application in this lesson. The remaining four steps of the process are covered in Lessons B and C.

Planning an OOED Application

As any architect will tell you, the most important aspect of a home is not its beauty; rather, it is how closely the home matches the buyer's wants and needs. For example, a walk-in refrigerator may be appropriate for someone who frequently entertains. For someone who does not, it may be a waste of space and energy. The same is true for an OOED application. In order for an application to meet the user's needs, therefore, it is essential for the programmer to plan the application jointly with the user. It can't be stressed enough that the only way to guarantee the success of an application is to actively involve the user in the planning phase. Planning an OOED application in Visual Basic requires the following four steps:

1. Identify the tasks the application needs to perform.
2. Identify the objects to which you will assign those tasks.
3. Identify the events required to trigger an object into performing its assigned tasks.
4. Draw a sketch of the user interface.

You can use a TOE (Task, Object, Event) chart to plan your Visual Basic applications. The TOE chart lists the application's tasks, objects, and events. You will complete a TOE chart for the Skate-Away Sales application. Begin by identifying the tasks.

Identifying the Application's Tasks

Realizing that it is essential to involve the user when planning the application, you meet with the sales manager of Skate-Away Sales, Mr. Cousard, to determine his requirements. You ask Mr. Cousard to bring the form the salespeople use, currently, to record the orders. Viewing the current forms and procedures will help you gain a better understanding of the application. You can also use the current form as a guide when designing the user interface. The Skate-Away Sales company's current order-taking form is shown in Figure 2-7.

Figure 2-7: Current order-taking form used by Skate-Away Sales

When identifying the tasks an application needs to perform, it is helpful to ask the following questions:

■ What information, if any, will the user need to enter into the user interface?
■ What information, if any, will the application need to calculate?
■ What information, if any, will the application need to display on the screen and/or print on the printer?
■ How will the user end the application?
■ Will previous information need to be cleared from the screen before new information is entered?

The answers to these questions will help you identify the application's major tasks. Answer each question for the Skate-Away Sales application.

What information, if any, will the user need to enter into the user interface? In the Skate-Away Sales application, the salesperson (the user) must enter the customer's name, street address, city, state, zip code, skateboard price, sales tax rate, and the number of blue and yellow skateboards ordered.

What information, if any, will the application need to calculate? The Skate-Away Sales application needs to calculate the total number of skateboards ordered and the total price of the order.

What information, if any, will the application need to display on the screen and/or print on the printer? (Notice that "display" refers to the screen; "print" refers to the printer.) The application must display the order information entered by the user, as well as the total number of skateboards ordered and the total price of the order. Also recall that the sales manager wants the application to print a confirmation notice.

How will the user end the application? In Tutorial 1, you learned that all applications should give the user a way to exit the program. The Skate-Away Sales application needs to provide a way to end the application.

Will previous information need to be cleared from the screen before new information is entered? After Skate-Away's salesperson enters and prints an order, he or she will need to clear the previous order's information from the screen before the next order is entered.

Figure 2-8 shows the Skate-Away Sales application's tasks listed in a TOE chart. Unlike procedure-oriented planning, OOED planning does not require the TOE chart tasks to be in any particular order. In this case, they are listed in the order in which they were identified in this lesson.

Task	Object	Event

Get the following order information from the user:
  Customer's name
  Street address
  City
  State
  Zip code
  Price of a skateboard
  Sales tax rate
  Number of blue skateboards ordered
  Number of yellow skateboards ordered		

Calculate the total skateboards ordered and the total price		

Display the following information:
  Customer's name
  Street address
  City
  State
  Zip code
  Price of a skateboard
  Sales tax rate
  Number of blue skateboards ordered
  Number of yellow skateboards ordered
  Total skateboards ordered
  Total price		

Print a confirmation notice		
End the application		
Clear the screen for the next order		

Figure 2-8: Tasks entered in TOE chart

Identifying the Objects

After completing the Task column of the TOE chart, you then assign each task to an object in the user interface. For this application, the only objects you will use, besides the form itself, are the command button, the label control, and the text box. As you learned in Tutorial 1, you use a label control to display information that you don't want the user to change while your application is running, and you use a command button to perform an action immediately after it is clicked by the user. As you saw in the OOED application you ran earlier, you use a text box to give the user an area in which to enter data. Now assign each of the tasks in the TOE chart to an object.

The first task listed in Figure 2-8 is to get the order information from the user. For each order, the salesperson will need to enter the customer's name, address, city, state, and zip code, as well as the skateboard price, sales tax rate, and the number of blue and yellow skateboards ordered. Because you need to provide the salesperson with areas in which to enter that information, you will assign the first task to nine text boxes—one for each item of information. The names of the text boxes will be txtName, txtAddress, txtCity, txtState, txtZip, txtPrice, txtRate, txtBlue, and txtYellow. The "txt" prefix indicates that these objects are text boxes.

The second task listed in the TOE chart is to calculate the total skateboards ordered and the total price. So that the salesperson can calculate these amounts at any time, you will assign the task to a command button that will be named cmdCalc. As you learned in Tutorial 1, the "cmd" prefix indicates that the object is a command button.

The third task listed in the TOE chart is to display the order information, the total skateboards ordered, and the total price. The order information will be displayed automatically when the user enters that information in the nine text boxes. The total skateboards ordered and the total price, however, are not entered by the user; those amounts are calculated by the cmdCalc button. Because the user should not be allowed to change either amount, you will have the cmdCalc button display the total skateboards ordered and the total price in two label controls, which you will name lblTboards and lblTprice. Recall from Tutorial 1 that the "lbl" prefix indicates that a control is a label control, and that label controls do not allow the user to change their contents when the application is running. Notice that the task of displaying the total skateboards ordered involves two objects: cmdCalc and lblTboards; the task of displaying the total price also involves two objects: cmdCalc and lblTprice.

The last three tasks listed in the TOE chart are "Print a confirmation notice," "End the application," and "Clear the screen for the next order." You will assign these tasks to command buttons so that the user has control over when the tasks are performed. You will call the command buttons cmdPrint, cmdExit, and cmdClear. Figure 2-9 shows the TOE chart with the Task and Object columns completed.

Task	Object	Event
Get the following order information from the user:		
Customer's name	txtName	
Street address	txtAddress	
City	txtCity	
State	txtState	
Zip code	txtZip	
Price of a skateboard	txtPrice	
Sales tax rate	txtRate	
Number of blue skateboards ordered	txtBlue	
Number of yellow skateboards ordered	txtYellow	
Calculate the total skateboards ordered and the total price	cmdCalc	
Display the following information:		
Customer's name	txtName	
Street address	txtAddress	
City	txtCity	
State	txtState	
Zip code	txtZip	
Price of a skateboard	txtPrice	
Sales tax rate	txtRate	
Number of blue skateboards ordered	txtBlue	
Number of yellow skateboards ordered	txtYellow	
Total skateboards ordered	cmdCalc, lblTboards	
Total price	cmdCalc, lblTprice	
Print a confirmation notice	cmdPrint	
End the application	cmdExit	
Clear the screen for the next order	cmdClear	

Figure 2-9: Tasks and objects entered in TOE chart

> **tips**
> ••••••••••••••••••
> **Not all objects in a user interface will need an event to occur in order for the object to perform its assigned tasks.**

After defining the application's tasks and assigning those tasks to objects in the user interface, you must then determine which objects will need an event (such as clicking or double-clicking) to occur for the object to do its assigned task. Look at the tasks and the objects listed in Figure 2-9's TOE chart.

Identifying the Events

The nine text boxes listed in the TOE chart in Figure 2-9 are assigned the task of getting the order information. Text boxes accept information automatically from the user, so no special event is necessary for them to do their assigned task.

The two label controls listed in the TOE chart are assigned the task of displaying the total number of skateboards ordered and the total price of the order. Label controls automatically display their contents so, here again, no special event needs to occur. (Recall that the label controls will get their values from the cmdCalc button.)

The remaining objects listed in the TOE chart are the four command buttons: cmdCalc, cmdClear, cmdExit, cmdPrint. In this application you will have the command buttons perform their assigned tasks when they are clicked by the user. Figure 2-10 shows the TOE chart with the tasks, objects, and events necessary for the Skate-Away Sales application.

Task	Object	Event
Get the following order information from the user:		
Customer's name	txtName	None
Street address	txtAddress	None
City	txtCity	None
State	txtState	None
Zip code	txtZip	None
Price of a skateboard	txtPrice	None
Sales tax rate	txtRate	None
Number of blue skateboards ordered	txtBlue	None
Number of yellow skateboards ordered	txtYellow	None
Calculate the total skateboards ordered and the total price	cmdCalc	Click
Display the following information:		
Customer's name	txtName	None
Street address	txtAddress	None
City	txtCity	None
State	txtState	None
Zip code	txtZip	None
Price of a skateboard	txtPrice	None
Sales tax rate	txtRate	None
Number of blue skateboards ordered	txtBlue	None
Number of yellow skateboards ordered	txtYellow	None
Total skateboards ordered	cmdCalc, lblTboards	Click, None
Total price	cmdCalc, lblTprice	Click, None
Print a confirmation notice	cmdPrint	Click
End the application	cmdExit	Click
Clear the screen for the next order	cmdClear	Click

Figure 2-10: Completed TOE chart ordered by task

If the application you are creating is small, as is the Skate-Away Sales application, you can use the TOE chart in its current form to help you write the code. When the application you are creating is large, however, it is helpful to rearrange the TOE chart so that it is ordered by object instead of by task. To do so, you simply list all of your objects in the Object column, being sure to list each object only once. Then list the tasks you have assigned to each object in the Task column and the event in the Event column. Figure 2-11 shows the rearranged TOE chart, ordered by object rather than by task.

Task	Object	Event
1. Calculate the total skateboards ordered and the total price 2. Display the total skateboards ordered and the total price in the lblTboards and lblTprice objects	cmdCalc	Click
Clear the screen for the next order	cmdClear	Click
End the application	cmdExit	Click
Print the confirmation notice	cmdPrint	Click
Display the total skateboards ordered	lblTboards	None
Display the total price	lblTprice	None
Get and display the order information	txtName, txtAddress, txtCity, txtState, txtZip, txtPrice, txtRate, txtBlue, txtYellow	None

Figure 2-11: Completed TOE chart ordered by object

After completing the TOE chart, the next step is to draw a rough sketch of the user interface.

Drawing a Sketch of the User Interface

tips
. . . .
▶ Some companies have their own standards for user interfaces. A company's standards supersede the Windows standards.

Although the TOE chart lists the objects you need to include in the application's user interface, it does not tell you *where* to place those objects in the interface. While the design of an interface is open to creativity, there are some guidelines to which you should adhere so that your application is consistent with the Windows standards. This consistency will make your application easier to both learn and use because the user interface will have a familiar look to it.

In western countries, you should organize the user interface so that the information flows either vertically or horizontally, with the most important information always located in the upper-left corner of the screen. In a vertical arrangement the information flows from top to bottom; the essential information is located in the first column of the screen, while secondary information is placed in subsequent columns. In a horizontal arrangement, on the other hand, the information flows from left to right; the essential information is placed in the first row of the screen, with secondary information placed in subsequent rows. You can use either white space or a frame to group related controls together.

If command buttons appear in the interface, they should be either centered along the bottom of the screen or stacked in the upper-right corner. Limit, to six, the number of command buttons in the interface, and place the most commonly used button first—either on the left when the buttons are centered along the bottom of the screen, or on the top when the buttons are stacked in the upper-right corner.

Figures 2-12 and 2-13 show two different sketches of the Skate-Away Sales interface. In Figure 2-12, the information is arranged vertically; white space is used to group the related controls together and the command buttons are centered along the bottom of the screen. In Figure 2-13, the information is arranged horizontally; a frame is used to group the related controls together and the command buttons are stacked in the upper-right corner of the screen.

Figure 2-12: Vertical arrangement of the Skate-Away Sales application

Figure 2-13: Horizontal arrangement of the Skate-Away Sales application

Notice that each control in the user interface is labeled so the user knows the control's purpose. Labels should be left-aligned and positioned either above or to the left of the control, except in the case of command buttons. As you learned in

Tutorial 1, a command button's label, called its **caption**, appears *inside* the button. Labels, including captions, should be from one to three words only, and each should appear on one line. Labels and captions should be meaningful. Captions, for example, should tell the user what action the command button will perform when the button is clicked.

Except for the captions inside the command buttons, notice that each control's label ends with a colon (:). The colon distinguishes the label from other text in the user interface. The Windows standard is to use **sentence capitalization** for labels, which means you should capitalize only the first word and any words that are customarily capitalized. For command button captions, however, the Windows standard is to use book title capitalization. When using **book title capitalization**, you capitalize the first letter in each word, except for articles, conjunctions, and prepositions that do not occur at either the beginning or the end of the caption.

When laying out the controls in the user interface, try to minimize the number of different margins so that the user can more easily scan the information; you can do so by aligning the labels and controls wherever possible, as shown in both Figures 2-12 and 2-13.

In this section you learned some basic guidelines to follow when sketching a GUI (Graphical User Interface). You will learn more GUI guidelines as you progress through this book. For now, however, you have completed the first of the five steps involved in creating an application: plan the application. Recall that the planning step requires you to:

1. Identify the tasks the application needs to perform.
2. Identify the objects to which you will assign those tasks.
3. Identify the events required to trigger an object into performing its assigned tasks.
4. Draw a sketch of the user interface.

In Lesson B you will use the sketch shown in Figure 2-12 to build the interface for the Skate-Away Sales application. Recall that building the user interface is the second of the five steps involved in creating an OOED application. In Lesson C, you will complete the third (code the application), fourth (test and debug the application), and fifth (assemble the documentation) steps. For now, however, you can either take a break or complete the end-of-lesson questions and exercises.

Layout and Organization of Your Interface

- Organize the user interface so that the information flows either vertically or horizontally, with the most important information always located in the upper-left corner of the screen.

- Group related controls together using either white space or a frame.

- Either center the command buttons along the bottom of the screen or stack them in the upper-right corner. Use no more than six command buttons on a screen. Place the most commonly used command button first (either on the left or on the top).

- Use meaningful captions in command buttons. Place the caption on one line and use from one to three words only. Use book title capitalization for command button captions.

- Label each control in the user interface. The label should be from one to three words only, and entered on one line. Align each label on the left, and position each either above or to the left of the control. Follow the label with a colon (:) and use sentence capitalization. (Remember that the captions in command buttons have different guidelines.)

- Align the labels and controls in the user interface in order to minimize the number of different margins.

S U M M A R Y

To create an OOED application:

■ Follow these five steps:
   1 Plan the application.
   2 Build the user interface.
   3 Code the application.
   4 Test and debug the application.
   5 Assemble the documentation.

To plan an OOED application in Visual Basic:

■ Follow these four steps:
   1 Identify the tasks the application needs to perform.
   2 Identify the objects to which you will assign those tasks.
   3 Identify the events required to trigger an object into performing its assigned tasks.
   4 Draw a sketch of the user interface.

To assist you in identifying the tasks an application needs to perform, ask the following questions:

■ What information, if any, will the user need to enter?
■ What information, if any, will the application need to calculate?
■ What information, if any, will the application need to display or print?
■ How will the user end the application?
■ Will prior information need to be cleared from the screen before new information is entered.

Q U E S T I O N S

1. You use a _____ control to display information you don't want the user to change.
   a. command button
   b. form
   c. label
   d. text box
   e. user

2. You use a _____ control to accept or display information you will allow the user to change.
   a. changeable
   b. command button
   c. form
   d. label
   e. text box

3. You use a _____ control to perform an immediate action when it is clicked by the user.
   a. command button
   b. form
   c. label
   d. text box

4. You can use a _____ chart to plan your OOED applications.
   a. EOT
   b. ETO
   c. OET
   d. OTE
   e. TOE

5. When designing a user interface, you should organize the information _____ .
   a. either horizontally or vertically
   b. horizontally only
   c. vertically only

6. When designing a user interface, the most important information should be placed in the _____ of the screen.
   a. center
   b. lower-left corner
   c. lower-right corner
   d. upper-left corner
   e. upper-right corner

7. You can use _____ to group related controls together in an interface.
   a. a frame
   b. a label control
   c. a text box
   d. white space
   e. either a or d

8. Command buttons in an interface should be _____ .
   a. centered along the bottom of the screen
   b. stacked in the upper-left corner of the screen
   c. stacked in the upper-right corner of the screen
   d. either a or b
   e. either a or c

9. Use no more than _____ command buttons on a screen.
   a. five
   b. four
   c. seven
   d. six
   e. two

10. If more than one command button is used in an interface, the most commonly used command button should be placed _____ .
    a. first
    b. in the middle
    c. last
    d. either a or c

11. Which of the following statements is false?
    a. A command button's caption should appear on one line.
    b. A command button's caption should be from one to three words only.
    c. A command button's caption should be entered using book title capitalization.
    d. A command button's caption should end with a colon (:).

12. The labels for controls (other than command buttons) should be entered using

    _____ .
    a. book title capitalization
    b. sentence capitalization
    c. either a or b

13. Which of the following statements is false?
    a. Labels for controls (other than command buttons) should be aligned on the left.
    b. Labels for controls (other than command buttons) should be positioned either above or to the left of the control.
    c. Labels for controls (other than command buttons) should be entered using book title capitalization.
    d. Labels for controls (other than command buttons) should end with a colon (:).

14. Use _____ for labels, which means you capitalize only the first word and any words that are customarily capitalized.
    a. book title capitalization
    b. sentence capitalization

15. Use _____ command button captions, which means you capitalize the first letter in each word, except for articles, conjunctions, and prepositions that do not occur at either the beginning or the end.
    a. book title capitalization
    b. sentence capitalization

16. Listed below are the four steps you should follow when planning an OOED application. Put them in the proper order by placing a number (1 to 4) on the line to the left of the step.
    _____ Identify the objects to which you will assign those tasks.
    _____ Draw a sketch of the user interface.
    _____ Identify the tasks the application needs to perform.
    _____ Identify the events required to trigger an object into performing its assigned tasks.

17. Listed below are the five steps you should follow when creating an OOED application. Put them in the proper order by placing a number (1 to 5) on the line to the left of the step.
    _____ Test and debug the application.
    _____ Build the user interface.
    _____ Code the application.
    _____ Assemble the documentation.
    _____ Plan the application.

E X E R C I S E S

1. In this exercise, you will prepare a TOE chart and create two sketches of the application's user interface.

   Scenario: Sarah Brimley is the accountant at Paper Products. The salespeople at Paper Products are paid a commission, which is a percentage of the sales they make. The current commission rate is 10%. (In other words, if you have sales totalling $2,000, your commission is $200.) Sarah wants you to create an application that will compute the commission after she enters the salesperson's name, territory number, and sales. She also wants to print this information.

   a. Prepare a TOE chart ordered by task.

   b. Rearrange the TOE chart created in step a so that it is ordered by object.

   c. Draw two sketches of the user interface—one using a horizontal arrangement and the other using a vertical arrangement.

2. In this exercise, you will prepare a TOE chart and create two sketches of the application's user interface.

   Scenario: RM Sales divides its sales territory into four regions: North, South, East, and West. Robert Gonzales, the sales manager, wants an application in which he can enter the current year's sales for each region and the projected increase (expressed as a percentage) in sales for each region. He then wants the application to compute the following year's projected sales for each region. (For example, if Robert enters 10000 as the current sales for the South region, and then enters a 10% projected increase, the application should display 11000 as next year's projected sales.) He also wants to print the information.

   a. Prepare a TOE chart ordered by task.

   b. Rearrange the TOE chart created in step a so that it is ordered by object.

   c. Draw two sketches of the user interface—one using a horizontal arrangement and the other using a vertical arrangement.

In this lesson you will learn how to:

■ Build the user interface using your TOE chart and sketch

■ Follow the Windows standards regarding the use of graphics, color, and fonts

■ Apply the BackStyle, BorderStyle, and Appearance properties

■ Add a text box control to a form

■ Use the TabIndex property to control the focus

■ Lock the controls on the form

■ Assign access keys to the controls

Building the User Interface

Preparing to Build the User Interface

In Lesson A you completed the first of the five steps involved in creating an OOED application (plan the application). You are now ready to tackle the second step (build the user interface). You use the TOE chart and sketch you created in the planning step as guides when building the interface, which involves placing the appropriate controls on the form and setting the applicable properties of those controls. Recall that a property controls the appearance and behavior of the objects included in the interface, such as the object's font, size, and so on. Some programmers create the entire interface before setting the properties of each object; other programmers change the properties of each object as it is added to the form. Either way will work, so it's really just a matter of preference.

To save you time, your Student Disk contains a partially completed application for Skate-Away Sales. When you open the application, you will notice that most of the user interface has been created and most of the properties have been set. One control, however, is missing from the form: a text box control. You'll add the missing control later in this lesson. First open the project and save it under a different name so that the original files remain intact in case you want to practice this lesson again.

To open the partially completed project, then save the files under a new name:

1 Start Visual Basic, if necessary, and make sure your Student Disk is in the appropriate drive.

2 Open the **t2case** (t2case.vbp) file, which is located in the Tut02 folder on your Student Disk, then click the **View Form** button in the Project window to view the frmOrder form.

3 Use the Save File As option on the File menu to save the form as **lbOrder**, then use the Save Project As option on the File menu to save the project as **lbOrder**.

4 Maximize the form. Figure 2-14 identifies the controls already included in the application. (You won't see the names of the controls on your screen. The names are included in Figure 2-14 for your reference only.)

cmdCalc

cmdPrint
cmdClear
cmdExit

Figure 2-14: Partially completed Skate-Away Sales application

Notice that Figure 2-14 shows only the names of those controls whose names were changed from their default values. Only objects that will contain code or objects that will be referred to in code need to have their names changed to more meaningful ones.

The user interface shown in Figure 2-14 resembles the sketch shown in Lesson A's Figure 2-12. Recall that that sketch was created using the guidelines you learned in Lesson A. For example, the information is arranged vertically, with the most important information located in the upper-left corner of the screen. The command buttons are centered along the bottom of the screen, with the most commonly used button positioned first. The command buttons contain meaningful captions, which are entered using book title capitalization. Each caption appears on one line, and no caption exceeds the three-word limit. The labels identifying the controls other than the command buttons are left-aligned and positioned to the left of their respective controls; each uses sentence capitalization and each ends with a colon.

Notice that the labels and controls are aligned wherever possible to minimize the number of different margins appearing in the user interface. You can use the dots that Visual Basic displays on the form during design time to help you align the various controls in the interface. When positioning the controls, be sure to maintain a consistent margin from the edge of the window; two or three dots is recommended. As illustrated in Figure 2-14, related controls are typically placed on succeeding dots. For example, notice that the top of the txtAddress control is placed on the horizontal line of dots found immediately below the txtName control. Also notice that the left edge of the Print Order command button is placed on the vertical line of dots found to the immediate right of the Calculate Order command button. (If you are using the Visual Basic Working Model, you may see more dots between the controls.) Controls that are not part of any logical grouping, like the Exit button in this application, are typically positioned from two to four dots away from other controls.

Always size the command buttons in the interface relative to each other. When the command buttons are centered on the bottom of the screen, as they are in this interface, all the buttons should be the same height; their widths, however, may vary if necessary. If the command buttons are stacked in the upper-right corner of the screen, on the other hand, all the buttons should be the same height and the same width.

When building the user interface, keep in mind that you want to create a screen that no one notices. Snazzy interfaces may get "oohs" and "aahs" during their initial use, but they become tiresome after awhile. The most important point to remember is that the interface should not distract the user from doing his or her work. Unfortunately, it's difficult for many application developers to refrain from using the many different colors, fonts, and graphics available in Visual Basic; actually, using these elements isn't the problem—overusing them is. So that you don't overload your user interfaces with too much color, too many fonts, and too many graphics, the next three sections will give you some guidelines to follow regarding these elements. Consider the graphics first.

Placing and Sizing Design Elements

- Maintain a consistent margin of two or three dots from the edge of the window.
- Position related controls on succeeding dots. Controls that are not part of any logical grouping are typically positioned from two to four dots away from other controls.
- Command buttons in the user interface should be sized relative to each other. If the command buttons are centered on the bottom of the screen, then each button should be the same height; their widths, however, may vary. If the command buttons are stacked in the upper-right corner of the screen, then each should be the same height and the same width.
- Try to create a user interface that no one notices.

Including Graphics in the User Interface

The human eye is attracted to pictures before text, so include a graphic only if it is necessary to do so. You can use a graphic, for example, to either emphasize or clarify a portion of the screen. You can also use a graphic for aesthetic purposes, as long as the graphic is small and as long as it is placed in a location that does not distract the user. The small graphic in the Skate-Away Sales interface, for example, is included for aesthetics only. The graphic is purposely located in the upper-left corner of the interface, which is where you want the user's eye to be drawn first anyway. The graphic adds a personal touch to the Skate-Away Sales order form without being distracting to the user.

In the next section you will learn some guidelines pertaining to the use of different fonts in the interface.

Including Different Fonts in the User Interface

As you learned in Tutorial 1, you can change the type of font used to display the text in an object, as well as the style and size of the font. Recall that Courier and MS Sans Serif are examples of font types; regular, bold, and italic are examples of font styles; and 8, 10, and 18 points are examples of font sizes. The default font

GUI
Design Tips

Adding Graphics

- The human eye is attracted to pictures before text, so include a graphic only if it is necessary to do so. If the graphic is used solely for aesthetics, use a small graphic and place it in a location that will not distract the user.

used for interface elements in Windows is MS Sans Serif 8-point. A point, you may remember, is 1/72 of an inch; so each character in an 8-point font is 1/9 of an inch. You can use either 8, 10, or 12 point fonts for the elements in the user interface, but be sure to limit the number of font sizes used to either one or two. The Skate-Away Sales application uses two font sizes: 10 point and 12 point. The heading at the top of the interface is in 12 point; all of the other labels and captions are in 10 point.

Some fonts are serif and some are sans serif. A **serif** is a light cross stroke that appears at the top or bottom of a character. The characters in a serif font have the light strokes, whereas the characters in a sans serif font do not. ("Sans" is a French word meaning "without.") Books use serif fonts because those fonts are easier to read on the printed page. Sans serif fonts, on the other hand, are easier to read on the screen, so use a sans serif font for the text in the user interface. You should use only one font type for all of the text in the interface. Avoid using italics and underlining because both make text difficult to read. The Skate-Away Sales interface uses the default MS Sans Serif font.

Selecting Appropriate Font Style and Size

- Use either 8, 10, or 12 point fonts for the elements in the user interface.
- Limit the number of font sizes used to either one or two.
- Use a sans serif font for the text in the interface.
- Use only one font type for all of the text in the interface.
- Avoid using italics and underlining because both make text difficult to read.

GUI Design Tips

In addition to overusing graphics and fonts, many application developers make the mistake of using either too much color or too many different colors in the user interface. In the next section you will learn some guidelines pertaining to the use of color.

Including Color in the User Interface

Just as the human eye is attracted to graphics before text, it is also attracted to color before black and white, so use color sparingly. It is a good practice to build the interface using black, white, and gray first, then add color only if you have a good reason to do so. Keep the following four points in mind when deciding whether to include color in the interface:

1. Some users will be working on monochrome monitors.
2. Many people have some form of either color-blindness or color confusion, so they will have trouble distinguishing colors.
3. Color is very subjective; what's a pretty color to you may be hideous to someone else.
4. A color may have a different meaning in a different culture.

It is usually best to follow the Windows standard of using black text on either a white, off-white, or gray background. The Skate-Away Sales interface, for example, displays black text on a gray background. If you want to add some color to the interface, you can also use black text on either a pale blue or a pale yellow background. Because dark text on a light background is the easiest to read, never use a dark color for the background or a light color for the text; a dark background is hard on the eyes, and light-colored text can appear blurry.

If you are going to include color in the interface, limit the number of colors to three, not including white, black, and gray. Be sure that the colors you choose complement each other.

Although color can be used to identify an important element in the interface, you should never use it as the only means of identification. In the Skate-Away Sales application, for example, the colors blue and yellow help the salesperson quickly identify where to enter the order for blue skateboards and where to enter the order for yellow skateboards. Notice, however, that color is not the only means of identifying those areas in the interface; the labels to the left of the controls also tell the user where to enter the orders for blue and yellow skateboards.

Selecting Appropriate Colors

- The human eye is attracted to color before black and white. Build the interface using black, white, and gray first, then add color only if you have a good reason to do so.
- Use either white, off-white, or gray for an application's background, and black for the text. You can also use black text on either a pale blue or a pale yellow background. Dark text on a light background is the easiest to read.
- Never use a dark color for the background or a light color for the text; a dark background is hard on the eyes, and light-colored text can appear blurry.
- Limit the number of colors to three, not including white, black, and gray. The colors you choose should complement each other.
- Never use color as the only means of identification for an element in the user interface.

Now complete the user interface for the Skate-Away Sales application. First see what the interface looks like with a white background instead of a gray one.

To change the background color of the interface:

1 Press the **F4** key to display the Properties window, then set the form's BackColor property to white. The form's background color changes to white.

Notice that the background color of the label controls, however, is still gray. You can fix this problem in two ways. You can either set each label control's BackColor property to white, just as you did for the form, or you can set each label control's BackStyle property to 0-Transparent. For reasons you will learn in the next section, setting the BackStyle property is the preferred way.

The BackStyle Property

Recall from Tutorial 1 that the BackColor property determines an object's background color. The default background color for forms and label controls is gray. Because each form and each label control can have its own BackColor setting, changing the background color of the form does not change the background color of the label controls on that form. You can match the color of a label control to the background color of the form by setting the label control's BackStyle property.

A label control's **BackStyle property** determines whether the label is transparent or opaque. The default setting is 1-Opaque, which means that the color value stored in the control's BackColor property fills the control and obscures any color behind it—in this case, the gray in the label controls obscures the white background of the form. When a control's BackStyle property is set to 0-Transparent, Visual Basic ignores the setting in the control's BackColor property; instead, Visual Basic allows you to see through the control. In most cases it is more efficient to change the BackStyle property of the label controls, instead of their BackColor property; then, if you want to experiment with the background color of the form, you won't have to change the BackColor property of the label controls each time to match the form. Observe how this works by changing the BackStyle property for the label controls to 0-Transparent.

To change the BackStyle property:

1   The form should be maximized, so simply select all of the label controls except the lblTboards and lblTprice controls. (There are 12 label controls, not counting the lblTboards and lblTprice controls.) Gray handles appear around each selected control.

     HELP? Recall from Tutorial 1 that to select more than one control, you click the first control, then Ctrl-click the other controls.

2   Press the **F4** key to display the Properties window, then set the BackStyle property of the selected controls to **0-Transparent**. You can now see the form's white background through the label controls.

3   Click the **form** both to deselect the selected label controls and to remove the Properties window. (Be sure to click the form, and not one of the selected controls on the form.)

Suppose you decide that the user interface looked better with a gray background.

4   Press the **F4** key to display the Properties window, then set the BackColor property of the form to a light gray.

5   Click the **form** to both deselect the controls and remove the Properties window.

Notice that you can still see the form's background color, which is now gray, through the 12 label controls.

Before you set the BackStyle property for the lblTboards and lblTprice controls, you will change their BorderStyle property and their Appearance property.

The BorderStyle and Appearance Properties

As you learned in Tutorial 1, the BorderStyle property determines the style of the object's border. The **BorderStyle property** for a label control can be either 0-None, which is the default, or 1-Fixed Single. The 1-Fixed Single setting surrounds the label control with a thin line, so it looks similar in appearance to a text box. A control's **Appearance property**, on the other hand, determines if the control appears flat (0-Flat) or three-dimensional (1-3D) on the screen. Although the default setting of a label control's Appearance property is 1-3D, you will not see the three-dimensional effect unless you set the label control's BorderStyle property to 1-Fixed Single. You will change the BorderStyle property of the lblTboards and lblTprice controls to 1-Fixed Single, so that the label controls will have a border. You will then change their Appearance property to 0-Flat because, in Windows applications, controls that contain data that the user is not allowed to edit do not typically appear three-dimensional. The last change you will make to the lblTboards and lblTprice controls is to change their BackStyle property to 0-Transparent.

To change the properties of the lblTboards and lblTprice controls:

1   Select the lblTboards and lblTprice controls.

2   Press the **F4** key to display the Properties window. Set the selected controls' BorderStyle property to **1-Fixed Single**, then click the **form** to both deselect the controls and remove the Properties window. Notice that both label controls appear three-dimensional.

3   Now select the lblTboards and lblTprice controls again and set their Appearance property to **0-Flat**, then set their BackStyle property to **0-Transparent**.

4   Click the **form** to both deselect the controls and remove the Properties window. The two label controls appear as flat boxes on the screen.

Now continue building the interface.

Setting the Text Property

Recall that most of Skate-Away's customers are in Illinois. Instead of having the salesperson enter IL in the txtState control for each order, it would be more efficient to have IL appear, automatically, in the state text box when the application is run. If the user needs to change the state entry while the application is running, he or she can simply click the State text box, then delete the current entry and retype the new one. You can display IL in the txtState control by setting that control's Text property to IL. Do that now.

To set the txtState control's Text property:

1   The form should still be maximized. Click the **txtState control**, then press the **F4** key to display the Properties window. Click **Text** in the Properties list, then type **IL** and press the **Enter** key.

2   Click the **form** to remove the Properties window. IL appears in the txtState control.

3   Restore the form to its standard size.

Notice that the text box control in which the user enters the city is missing from the interface. You will add that control next.

Adding a Text Box Control to the Form

A **text box control** provides an area in the form where the user can enter data. Add the missing text box control to the form and then set its properties.

To add the text box control to the form, set its properties, and then save and run the application:

1   Double-click the **text box** tool [ab] in the toolbox. A default-sized text box control appears in the middle of the form.

The Text1 text you see inside the text box is the current setting of this control's Text property. The **Text property** for a text box is similar to the Caption property for a label control; both properties manage the text shown inside their respective controls. Because you don't want the Text1 text to appear when the application is run, you will delete the contents of this control's Text property.

2 Double-click **Text** in the Properties list, located in the Properties window. Visual Basic highlights the Text1 text in the Settings box, as shown in Figure 2-15.

double-click here to highlight Text1 text

Figure 2-15: Text property highlighted in Settings box

HELP? If the Text1 text is not highlighted in the Settings box, double-click the Text property again until the Text1 text is highlighted. You can also drag in the Settings box to highlight the Text1 text.

3 Press the **Delete** key, then press the **Enter** key to remove the highlighted text. The text box is now empty.

4 Set the following two properties for this text box control:

Name: **txtCity**   ("txt" stands for text box)
Font: **10** points

5 Drag the txtCity control to a location immediately below the txtAddress control, then drag the txtCity control's right border until the control is as wide as the txtAddress control. The correct location and size are shown in Figure 2-16.

correct size and placement of the txtCity control

Figure 2-16: Text box shown in its proper location and size

Now save and run the project to see if it is working correctly.

6   **Save and run** the project. A blinking insertion point appears in the txtName control.

The blinking insertion point indicates that this text box is the active control. In Windows terminology, the txtName control has the **focus**, which means that the control is ready to receive input from you. Try this next.

7   Type **Sport Warehouse** as the customer name. Notice that a text box displays the information it receives from you. The information is recorded in the text box's Text property. In this case, for example, the information is recorded in the Text property of the txtName control.

In Windows applications, you can move the focus from one control to another by pressing the Tab key.

8   Press the **Tab** key to move the focus to the txtAddress control, then type **123 Main**.

The city entry is next.

9   Press the **Tab** key to move the focus to the txtCity control. Notice that the focus skips the txtCity control and moves to the txtState control.

Stop the application and think about why this happened. The End statement has already been entered in the Exit button's Click event procedure.

10   Click the **Exit** button to end the application. The application ends, and Visual Basic returns to the design screen.

Controlling the Focus with the TabIndex Property

The **TabIndex property** determines the order in which a control receives the focus when the user is using the Tab key to tab through the application. Not all controls have a TabIndex property; Menu, Timer, CommonDialog, Data, Image, Line, and Shape controls do not. When you add a control that has a TabIndex property to a form, Visual Basic sets the control's TabIndex property to a number representing the order in which that control was added to the form. Keep in mind that when assigning these numbers Visual Basic starts counting at 0 (zero). In other words, the TabIndex property for the first control added to a form is 0 (zero), the TabIndex property for the second control is 1, and so on. Visual Basic uses the TabIndex property to determine the Tab order for the controls. To get a better idea of how this works, check the TabIndex property for the txtAddress, txtState, and txtCity controls.

To view the TabIndex property:

1 Click the **txtAddress control**, then click **TabIndex** in the Properties list. Notice that Visual Basic set the TabIndex property to 13. A TabIndex property of 13 means that this was the fourteenth control added to the form.

Now look at the TabIndex property for the txtState control.

> **HELP?** If the TabIndex property is not 13, you might have selected the Address: label control instead of the txtAddress text box. Click the txtAddress text box, then repeat Step 1.

2 Click the **txtState control**. Notice that the txtState control's TabIndex property is set to 14. A control with a TabIndex of 14 will receive the focus immediately after the control with a TabIndex of 13. In this case, for example, the txtState control will receive the focus immediately after the txtAddress control.

Now look at the TabIndex property for the txtCity control, which was the last control added to the form.

3 Click the **txtCity control**. Notice that the txtCity control's TabIndex property is set to 26, which means it's the 27th control added to the form.

To tell Visual Basic that you want the txtCity control to receive the focus immediately after the txtAddress control, you need to change the TabIndex property of the txtCity control to 14, which is one number greater than the TabIndex of the txtAddress control (13). Figure 2-17 shows the current TabIndex values for the txtAddress, txtCity, and txtState controls and what their TabIndex values should be.

Control Name	Current TabIndex Value	New TabIndex Value
txtAddress	13	13
txtCity	26	14
txtState	14	15

Figure 2-17: TabIndex values

The only TabIndex value you will need to change is the one for the txtCity control. Changing the txtCity control's TabIndex property to 14 will cause Visual Basic to renumber the controls on the form, beginning with the control that originally had a TabIndex of 14. For example, the TabIndex of the txtState control, which was originally 14, will be assigned a TabIndex of 15. The control that had a TabIndex of 15 will be assigned a TabIndex of 16, and so on. After you change the TabIndex for the txtCity control, you will verify the renumbering by selecting the txtState control and looking at its TabIndex value.

To change the txtCity control's TabIndex property, then save and run the project:

1 The TabIndex property for the txtCity control should already be selected in the Properties window, so just type **14** and press the **Enter** key.

Verify that the txtState control's TabIndex property is now 15.

2 Click the **txtState control**. The value of its TabIndex property should be 15.

3 **Save and run** the project.

4 Type **Sport Warehouse** as the customer name, then press the **Tab** key to move the focus to the txtAddress control.

5 Type **123 Main** as the address, then press the **Tab** key. Notice that the focus now moves to the txtCity control.

You can check the focus order of the remaining controls by simply pressing the Tab key.

6 Press the **Tab** key. The focus moves from the txtCity control to the txtState control, which is correct.

7 Press the **Tab** key, slowly, ten times. The focus correctly moves to the following controls: txtZip, txtBlue, txtYellow, txtPrice, txtRate, cmdCalc, cmdPrint, cmdClear, cmdExit, and finally back to the txtName control.

In Windows applications, the Tab key moves the focus forward, and the Shift+Tab key combination moves the focus backward. Try the Shift+Tab key combination.

8 Press **Shift + Tab**. The focus moves to the Exit button, as indicated by its highlighted border and the dotted rectangle around its caption.

> **HELP?** Press Shift + Tab means to press and hold down the Shift key as you press the Tab key.

9 Because the Exit button has the focus, you can simply press the **Enter** key to end the application. The application ends and Visual Basic returns to the design screen.

Now that all of the controls are on the user interface, you can lock them in place.

Locking the Controls on a Form

Once you have placed all of the controls in the desired locations on the form, it is a good idea to lock the controls in their current positions so you don't inadvertently move them. Once the controls are locked, you will not be able to move them until you unlock them; you can, however, delete them.

You can also lock and unlock the controls on a form by using the Lock Controls command on the Edit menu. If the controls are locked, the Lock Controls command will have a check mark next to it.

To lock the controls on the form:

1 Make sure the form is the active window, then click the **Lock Controls** button 🔒 on the Toolbar. The 🔒 now looks like 🔒, which indicates that the controls on the current form are locked.

2 Try moving one of the controls to a different location on the form. You won't be able to.

If you need to change the location of a control after you've locked the controls in place, you will need to click the Lock Controls button 🔒 again. The 🔒 button will then look like 🔒, which indicates that the controls are unlocked and can be repositioned.

The user interface is almost complete. The final task is to assign access keys to the controls.

Assigning Access Keys

An **access key** allows the user to select an object using the Alt key in combination with a letter. For example, you can use Alt + F to open Visual Basic's File menu because the letter "F" is the File menu's access key. Access keys are not case sensitive—in other words, you can open Visual Basic's File menu by pressing either Alt + F or Alt + f.

You should consider assigning access keys to each of the essential elements in the interface for the following three reasons. First, access keys allow a user to work with the application even if the mouse becomes inoperative. Second, access keys allow users who are fast typists to keep their hands on the keyboard. Third, and most important, access keys allow people with disabilities, which may prevent them from working with a mouse, to use the application.

You can assign an access key to any control that has a Caption property. You assign the access key by including an ampersand (&) in the control's caption. The ampersand is entered to the immediate left of the character you want to designate as the access key.

Each access key appearing in the interface must be unique. The first choice for an access key is the first letter of the caption, unless another letter provides a more meaningful association. For example, the letter X is typically the access key for an Exit button because the letter X provides a more meaningful association than does the letter E. If you can't use the first letter (perhaps because it is already used as the access key for another control) and no other letter provides a more meaningful association, then use a distinctive consonant in the caption. The last choice for an access key is a vowel in the caption.

In the Skate-Away Sales application, you will assign an access key to each of the four command buttons. Then, instead of clicking the command button, the user can simply press the Alt key along with its access key.

To assign an access key to each of the four command buttons:

1 Maximize the form, then select the **Calculate Order** button in the user interface. Press the **F4** key to display the Properties window. The Calculate Order caption should be highlighted in the Properties window's Settings box. Press the **Home** key to move the insertion point to the beginning of the Calculate Order caption.

tips

The ampersand in a label control's Caption property designates an access key only if the label control's UseMnemonic property is set to True, which is the default for that property. In the rare cases that you don't want the ampersand to designate an access key—for example, you want the label control's Caption property to say, literally, J & M Sales—then you need to set the label control's UseMnemonic property to False.

HELP? If the Calculate Order caption is not highlighted in the Settings box, then click Calculate Order in the Settings box, then press the Home key to move the insertion point to the beginning of the Calculate Order caption.

You'll use the letter C as the access key for the Calculate Order button.

2   Type & (ampersand), then press the **Enter** key. The Caption property should now say &Calculate Order. (You may not be able to read the entire Caption in the Settings box.)

Now assign the letter "P" as the access key for the Print Order button.

3   Use the Properties window's Object box to select the **cmdPrint** control, then change its Caption property to **&Print Order**.

Next, you'll assign an access key to the Clear Screen button. In this interface, you can't use the letter "C" for the access key because that is the access key for the Calculate Order button; remember, access keys must be unique. Assign the letter "L" as the access key for the Clear Screen control.

4   Use the Properties window's Object box to select the **cmdClear** control, then change its Caption property to **C&lear Screen**.

In Windows applications, the letter "X" is customarily the access key for an Exit button.

5   Use the Properties window's Object box to select the **cmdExit** control, then change its Caption property to **E&xit**.

6   Click the **form** to remove the Properties window.

The caption inside each of the command buttons should now have an underlined letter, which is that button's access key. But you are not finished assigning access keys yet. Recall that you should give users a way to access all of the important elements of the interface without using the mouse; that includes the text boxes in which the order information must be entered. But, you may be thinking, you can't assign an access key to a text box because text box controls do not have a Caption property. The answer to this dilemma is to assign an access key to the label control that identifies the text box; in this case, to the label control that appears to the left of each text box. Do that next.

To assign access keys to the label controls that identify the text boxes in the interface:

1   The form should still be maximized. Press the **F4** key to display the Properties window. Use the Object box to select the **Label2** control. Sizing handles appear around the Name: label in the user interface. Change the Label2 control's Caption to **&Name:**.

2   Use Figure 2-18 to assign access keys to the other label controls.

Control Name	Caption	Access Key
Label3	Address:	A
Label4	City:	T
Label5	State:	S
Label6	Zip:	Z
Label7	Blue skateboards ordered:	B
Label8	Yellow skateboards ordered:	Y
Label9	Price:	I
Label10	Sales tax rate:	R

Figure 2-18: Access keys for label controls

(You will not assign access keys to the Total skateboards: and Total price: label controls because the controls to their immediate right are label controls, not text boxes.)

In addition to assigning an access key to the label control that identifies the text box, you must also set the label control's TabIndex property so that its value is one number less than the TabIndex value of its corresponding text box. (In other words, the text box's TabIndex value should be one number greater than the label control's TabIndex value.) Since label controls cannot receive the focus, pressing the label control's access key will automatically send the focus to the next control in the tab order sequence—in other words, to the text box. For example, if the Name: label control has a TabIndex of 5 and its corresponding text box (txtName) has a TabIndex of 6, pressing Alt + N will move the focus to the txtName text box. You will now adjust the TabIndex values appropriately.

To set the TabIndex values, then save and run the application:

1 Use the information shown in Figure 2-19 to set the TabIndex values of the controls.

Control Name	Caption for Label Controls	TabIndex Value
Label2	Name:	0
txtName		1
Label3	Address:	2
txtAddress		3
Label4	City:	4
txtCity		5
Label5	State:	6
txtState		7
Label6	Zip:	8
txtZip		9
Label7	Blue skateboards ordered:	10
txtBlue		11
Label8	Yellow skateboards ordered:	12
txtYellow		13
Label9	Price:	14
txtPrice		15
Label10	Sales tax rate:	16
txtRate		17
cmdCalc		18
cmdPrint		19
cmdClear		20
cmdExit		21

Figure 2-19: TabIndex values for controls

2 Restore the form to its standard size, then **save and run** the application.

3 Press **Alt + b** to move the focus to the txtBlue control. Type **10** for the number of blue skateboards ordered.

4 Press **Alt + s** to move the focus to the txtState control. Press the **Delete** key on your keyboard two times to remove the IL, then type **CA**.

5 Press **Alt + x** to access the Exit button. The application ends, and Visual Basic returns to the design screen.

Design Tips

Rules for Assigning Access Keys

- When assigning an access key to a control, use the first letter of the caption, unless another letter provides a more meaningful association. If you can't use the first letter and no other letter provides a more meaningful association, then use a distinctive consonant in the caption. Lastly, use a vowel in the caption.

- Access keys must be unique.

- To give users keyboard access to text boxes, assign an access key to the text box control's identifying label. Set the TabIndex property of the label control so that its value is one number less than the value in the TabIndex property of the corresponding text box. (In other words, the TabIndex value of the text box should be one number greater than the TabIndex value of the label control.)

You have now finished two of the five steps involved in creating an OOED application: planning the application and building the user interface. You will complete the remaining three steps in Lesson C. For now, you can either take a break or complete the end-of-lesson questions and exercises.

S U M M A R Y

To set the tab order:

■ Set each control's TabIndex property to a number that represents the order in which you want that control to receive the focus. Remember to begin with 0 (zero).

To lock/unlock the controls on the form:

■ Click the Lock Controls button 🔓. When the controls are locked, the 🔓 button changes to 🔒. When the controls are unlocked, the 🔒 button changes to 🔓. You can also use the Lock Controls command on the Edit menu. If the controls on the form are locked, the Lock Controls command displays a check mark.

To assign an access key to a control:

■ In the control's Caption property, type an ampersand (&) to the immediate left of the letter you want to designate as the access key. (The ampersand in a label control's Caption property designates an access key only if the label control's UseMnemonic property is set to True, which is the default for that property.)

To give users keyboard access to a text box:

■ Assign an access key to the text box control's identifying label control. Set the label control's TabIndex property so that its value is one number less than the corresponding text box's TabIndex value.

To access a control that has an access key:

■ Press and hold down the Alt key as you press the control's access key.

To control the border around a label control:

■ Set the label control's BorderStyle property to 1-Fixed Single if you want the border; otherwise set the control's BorderStyle property to 0-None, which is the default.

To see through a label control:

■ Set the label control's BackStyle property to 0-Transparent. The default is 1-Opaque.

To view a control as either flat or three-dimensional:

■ Set the control's Appearance property to either 0-Flat or 1-3D; 1-3D is the default.

Q U E S T I O N S

1. The _____ property determines the order in which a control receives the focus when the user is tabbing.
   a. OrderTab
   b. SetOrder
   c. TabIndex
   d. TabOrder
   e. TabStop

2. When placing controls on a form, you should maintain a consistent margin of _____ dots from the edge of the window.
   a. one or two
   b. two or three
   c. two to five
   d. three to ten
   e. ten to twenty

3. If the command buttons are centered on the bottom of the screen, then each button should be _____ .
   a. the same height
   b. the same width
   c. the same height and the same width

4. If the command buttons are stacked in the upper-right corner of the screen, then each button should be _____ .
   a. the same height
   b. the same width
   c. the same height and the same width

5. The human eye is attracted to _____ . (Choose two answers.)
   a. black and white before color
   b. color before black and white
   c. graphics before text
   d. text before graphics

6. When building an interface, always use _____ .
   a. dark text on a dark background
   b. dark text on a light background
   c. light text on a dark background
   d. light text on a light background
   e. either b or c

7. Use either _____ fonts for the elements in the user interface.
   a. 6, 8, or 10 point
   b. 8, 10, or 12 point
   c. 10, 12, 14 point
   d. 12, 14, 16 point

8. Limit the number of font sizes used in an interface to _____ .
   a. one or two
   b. two or three
   c. three or four

9. Use a _____ font for the text in the user interface.
   a. sans serif
   b. serif

10. Limit the number of font types used in an interface to _____ .

    a. one

    b. two

    c. three

    d. four

11. You can lock the controls on a form by _____ .

    a. clicking the Lock Controls icon on the toolbar

    b. clicking the Lock Form icon on the toolbar

    c. using the Lock Controls command on the Edit menu

    d. using the Lock Controls command on the File menu

    e. either a or c

12. If you want to put a border around a label control, set the label control's _____ to 1-Fixed Single.

    a. Appearance

    b. BackStyle

    c. Border

    d. BorderStyle

    e. Caption

13. If you want a label control to appear flat on the screen, set the label control's _____ to 0-Flat.

    a. Appearance

    b. BackStyle

    c. Border

    d. BorderStyle

    e. Caption

14. If you want to see through a label control, set the label control's _____ to 0-Transparent.

    a. Appearance

    b. BackStyle

    c. Border

    d. BorderStyle

    e. Caption

15. Explain the procedure for choosing a control's access key.

16. Explain how you give users keyboard access to a text box.

E X E R C I S E S

1. In this exercise, you will finish building a user interface.
   a. Open the lb1 (lb1.vbp) project, which is located in the Tut02 folder on your Student Disk.
   b. Finish building the user interface shown in Figure 2-20 by adding a text box named txtName. Change the txtName control's font size to 10 points. Be sure to assign access keys to the text boxes and command buttons. Also adjust the TabIndex values appropriately.

add this text box

Figure 2-20

   c. Lock the controls on the form.
   d. Change the background color of the form to white.
   e. Change the BackStyle property of the label controls to 0-Transparent. Change the lblComm control's BorderStyle property to 1-Fixed Single. (Leave its appearance at 1-3D.)
   f. Save the form and the project as lb1Done in the Tut02 folder on your Student Disk.
   g. Run the application. The Print button and the Exit button have already been coded for you. (You will learn how to code a Print button in Lesson C.)
   h. Click the Print button to print the form on the printer.

i. Click the Exit button to end the application.

2. In this exercise, you will finish building a user interface.

    a. Open the lb2 (or lb2.vpb) project, which is located in the Tut02 folder on your Student Disk.

    b. Finish building the user interface shown in Figure 2-21 by adding a text box named txtNsales. Change the txtNsales control's font size to 10 points. Be sure to assign the access keys and adjust the TabIndex values appropriately.

add this text box

Figure 2-21

c. Lock the controls on the form.

d. Change the background color of the form to either white, pale blue, or pale yellow.

e. Change the properties of the label controls appropriately.

f. Save the form and the project as lb2Done in the Tut02 folder on your Student Disk.

g. Run the application. The Print button and the Exit button have already been coded for you. (You will learn how to code a Print button in Lesson C.)

h. Click the Print button to print the form on the printer.

i. Click the Exit button to end the application.

In this lesson you will learn how to:

- Use the TOE chart to code the application
- Use pseudocode to plan an object's code
- Use the SetFocus and PrintForm methods
- Write an assignment statement
- Include internal documentation in the code
- Write Visual Basic equations
- Use the Val and Format functions

Coding, Testing and Debugging, and Documenting the Application

Coding the Application

After planning the application and building the user interface, you can then write the Visual Basic instructions to tell the objects in the interface how to respond to events. The instructions are called **code**, and the process of writing the instructions is called **coding**. You will need to write code for each object that has an event listed in the third column of the TOE chart you created in Lesson A. For your reference while coding, the TOE chart is shown in Figure 2-22.

Task	Object	Event
1. Calculate the total skateboards ordered and the total price 2. Display the total skateboards ordered and the total price in the lblTboards and lblTprice objects	cmdCalc	Click
Clear the screen for the next order	cmdClear	Click
End the application	cmdExit	Click
Print a confirmation notice	cmdPrint	Click
Display the total skateboards ordered	lblTboards	None
Display the total price	lblTprice	None
Get and display the order information	txtName, txtAddress, txtCity, txtState, txtZip, txtPrice, txtRate, txtBlue, txtYellow	None

Figure 2-22: Completed TOE chart ordered by object

According to the TOE chart, you will need to write code for the four command buttons, as they are the only objects with an event listed in the third column of the chart. The Exit button has already been coded for you, so you need to write the code for only the Print Order, Clear Screen, and Calculate Order buttons. First, however, open the lbOrder project that you created in Lesson B.

To open the lbOrder project, then save the form and the project under a different name:

1 Start Visual Basic, if necessary, and make sure your Student Disk is in the appropriate drive.

2 Open the **lbOrder** (or lborder.vbp) file, which is located in the Tut02 folder on your Student Disk, then click the **View Form** button in the Project window to view the frmOrder form.

3 Use the Save File As option on the File menu to save the form as **lcOrder**, then use the Save Project As option on the File menu to save the project as **lcOrder**.

4 Maximize the form. Figure 2-23 identifies the controls included in the user interface. (You won't see the names of the controls on your screen. The names are included in Figure 2-23 for your reference only.)

Figure 2-23: Skate-Away Sales user interface

Recall that the controls are locked on the form. Also recall that only the controls that will be referred to in code need to have their names changed to more meaningful ones. You'll code the Print Order button first.

Coding the Print Order Button

According to the TOE chart, the Print Order button is assigned the task of printing the confirmation notice, which is basically the form itself, but without the command buttons showing. The Print Order button, therefore, must first hide the command buttons, then print the confirmation notice, and then redisplay the command buttons. Last, the Print Order button should send the focus to the Clear Screen button; after printing an order, the salesperson will typically need to clear the screen for the next order. Sending the focus to the Clear Screen button will allow the user to select that button by pressing the Enter key. (Remember, not everyone can, or wants to, use a mouse.) Figure 2-24 lists what you want the Print Order button to do.

Print Order button

1. Hide the 4 command buttons
2. Print the form
3. Display the 4 command buttons
4. Send the focus to the Clear Screen button

Figure 2-24: Steps for the Print Order button

Notice that the list shown in Figure 2-24 is composed of short statements in English. The statements represent the steps the Print Order button needs to follow in order to print the confirmation notice. In programming terms, the list of steps shown in Figure 2-24 is called pseudocode. **Pseudocode** is a tool programmers use to help them plan the steps that an object needs to take in order to perform its assigned task. Even though the word *pseudocode* might be unfamiliar to you, you've already written pseudocode without even realizing it. Think about the last time you gave directions to someone. You wrote each direction down on paper, in your own words; your directions were a form of pseudocode.

The programmer uses the pseudocode as a guide when coding the application. For example, you will use the pseudocode shown in Figure 2-24 to write the appropriate Visual Basic instructions for the Print Order button. The first step in that pseudocode is to hide the four command buttons. In Tutorial 1 you learned that you hide a control by setting its Visible property to False. You also learned that you can use an assignment statement to set the value of a property during run time. (Recall that, in Tutorial 1, you set the Command property of the mmcSound control to "Open", "Play", and "Close" while the Copyright application was running.)

Assigning a Value to a Property During Run Time

You can use an **assignment statement**, which is simply a Visual Basic instruction, to assign a value to the property of an object while the application is running. In this case you want to assign the False value to the Visible property of each of the four command buttons when the Print Order button is clicked. Assigning the False value to the Visible property will hide the command buttons. Then, after the form is printed, you want to assign the True value to the Visible property of each of the command buttons. Assigning the True value to the Visible property will display the buttons on the form.

An assignment statement that assigns a value to the property of an object must follow this syntax: [*form.*]*object.property* = *value*. *Form* is the name of the form in which the object is located, *object* is the name of the object, and *property* is the name of the property to which you want the value assigned. As you learned in Tutorial 1, items appearing in square brackets ([ ]) in an instruction's syntax are optional parts of the instruction, and items in *italics* indicate where the programmer must supply information pertaining to the current application. According to the syntax of an assignment statement, the name of the form is optional; if the object is in the current form, you can omit the form name and simply use the syntax: *object.property* = *value*. Notice that you use a period to separate the form's name, if used, from the object's name, and the object's name from the property name. You follow the *[form.]object.property* information with an equal sign (=) and the value you want to assign to the object's property. For example, the assignment statement to change the Calculate Order button's Visible property to False, which will hide the button from view, could be written as either `frmOrder.cmdCalc.Visible = False`, or simply as `cmdCalc.Visible = False`. Because the Calculate Order button is in the current form, both versions of the assignment statement will work correctly.

When Visual Basic sees an assignment statement in a Code window, Visual Basic assigns the value on the right side of the equal sign to the object and property appearing on the left side of the equal sign. For example, the `cmdCalc.Visible = False` assignment statement tells Visual Basic to assign the Boolean value of False to the Visible property of the cmdCalc control. You will now enter the code to tell the Print Order button to hide the four command buttons before printing the form.

To begin coding the Print Order command button:

1   The form should be maximized. Open the Print Order button's Code window. The Click event procedure for the cmdPrint control appears.

      HELP? Recall that you open a control's Code window by double-clicking the control.

2   Press the **Tab** key, then type **cmdCalc.visible = false** and press the **Enter** key. Visual Basic changes the instruction to cmdCalc.Visible = False. (Notice the capitalization.)

When entering code, you can type the names of commands and properties in lowercase letters. When you move to the next line, Visual Basic will automatically change your code to reflect the proper capitalization of those elements. This provides a quick way of verifying that you entered the code using the correct syntax; if the capitalization does not change, then Visual Basic does not recognize the command or property.

3   Type **cmdPrint.visible = false** and press the **Enter** key.

4   Type **cmdClear.visible = false** and press the **Enter** key.

5   Type **cmdExit.visible = false** and press the **Enter** key.

tips

You can also enter the object names in lowercase, and Visual Basic will change them to their proper capitalization. The steps in this book, however, use the correct capitalization for the object names so that the names are easier for you to identify. You can type the names in lowercase, if you prefer.

These four assignment statements will hide the four command buttons. Now enter the instructions that will print the form and redisplay the command buttons.

Using the PrintForm Method

You can use Visual Basic's PrintForm method to print the form. A **method** is a predefined Visual Basic procedure. The syntax of the PrintForm method is [*form.*]**PrintForm** where *form* is the name of the form you want to print and PrintForm is the name of the method. Recall from Tutorial 1 that items appearing in bold in the syntax are required—in this case, the method's name, PrintForm, is required. The name of the form, on the other hand, is optional; if specified, however, notice that you use a period to separate the form's name from the name of the method. If you omit the form's name from the instruction, Visual Basic prints the current form only—in this case, for example, the instruction `frmOrder.PrintForm` will print the current form, and so will the instruction `PrintForm`.

To finish coding the Print Order button, then save and run the application:

1   The Code window showing the cmdPrint control's Click event procedure should still be open. Type **printform** and press the **Enter** key.

After the form is printed, you need to display the four command buttons for the user. To do that you must enter four additional assignment statements into the Code window. These assignment statements will set the Visible property of the four command buttons to True. Instead of typing the four additional statements, you will copy the existing assignment statements to the clipboard, and then paste them into the Code window, below the PrintForm instruction. Then, in each of the copied statements, you can simply change the False to True.

2   Position the I-bar I at the beginning of the first assignment statement in the Code window. Press and hold down the left mouse button and drag until all four assignment statements are highlighted, then release the mouse button. See Figure 2-25.

drag to highlight these four assignment statements

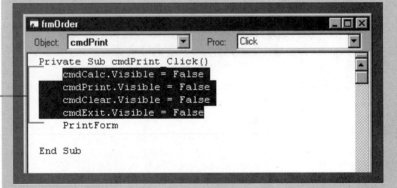

Figure 2-25: Four assignment statements highlighted in the Print Order button's Code window

3   Press **Ctrl + c** to copy the assignment statements to the clipboard.

4   Position the I-bar I in the empty line below the PrintForm instruction (immediately below the P), then click at that location. The blinking insertion point appears at that location.

5   Press **Ctrl + v** to paste the four assignment statements into the Code window, then press the **Enter** key.

6   In the four assignment statements you just copied, change the False to True. (You can look ahead to Figure 2-26 to see the end result.)

The last step in the Print Order button's pseudocode is to send the focus to the Clear Screen button. You can use Visual Basic's SetFocus method to do so.

Using the SetFocus Method

The SetFocus method allows you to move the focus to a specified control or form while the application is running. The syntax of the SetFocus method is *object*.**SetFocus** where *object* is the name of the object in which you want the focus, and SetFocus is the name of the method.

To enter the SetFocus method in the Print Order button's Click event:

1   The cmdPrint control's Click event procedure should still be open. Position the I-bar $\mathcal{I}$ in the blank line below the `cmdExit.Visible = True` instruction, immediately below the c, then click at that location. Type **cmdClear.setfocus** and press the **Enter** key. (You can look ahead to Figure 2-26 to see the end result.)

Internally Documenting the Program Code

It's a good practice to leave yourself some messages as reminders in the Code window; programmers refer to this as **internal documentation**. Visual Basic provides an easy way to document a program internally. You simply place an apostrophe (') before the statement you want Visual Basic to treat as a comment. Visual Basic ignores everything after the apostrophe on that line. Add some comments to the Print Order button's Code window.

To document the code in the Print Order button, then save and run the application:

1   Position the I-bar $\mathcal{I}$ at the end of the first line in the Code window (the line with the Private Sub instruction), then click at that location. The blinking insertion point appears at that location.

2   Press the **Enter** key to insert a new line, then type **'Hide Command buttons before printing the form**. Don't type the period, but be sure to type the apostrophe (').

3   Position $\mathcal{I}$ after the PrintForm instruction, then click at that location. Notice that the internal documentation changes to a different color when you move the insertion point to another line. Recall from Tutorial 1 that Visual Basic displays keywords and key symbols in a different color to help you quickly identify these elements in the Code window. In this case, the color coding helps you easily locate the internal documentation.

4   Press the **Enter** key, then press the **Backspace** key to cancel the indentation. Type **'Display Command buttons after the form is printed**. Don't type the period, but be sure to type the apostrophe ('). Figure 2-26 shows the completed Code window for the Print Order button's Click event.

Figure 2-26: The completed Code window for the Print Order button's Click event

5 Compare your code with the code shown in Figure 2-26 and make any necessary corrections, then close the Code window and restore the form to its standard size.

It is a good programming practice to write the code for one object at a time and then test and debug that object's code before coding the next object. This way, if something is wrong with the program, you know exactly where to look for the error.

6 **Save and run** the application.

HELP? If an error message appears in a dialog box, click the End button. Open the Print Order button's Code window and compare your code with Figure 2-26. Make the necessary corrections.

7 If your computer is connected to a printer, click the **Print Order** button to print the confirmation notice.

Following the instructions you entered in the Print Order button's Code window, Visual Basic hides the command buttons, prints the form, redisplays the command buttons, and sends the focus to the Clear Screen button. You can tell that the Clear Screen button has the focus because the button has a darkened border and a dotted rectangle around its caption.

8 Click the **Exit** button to end the application. Visual Basic returns to the design screen.

Code the Clear Screen button next.

Coding the Clear Screen Button

According to the TOE chart, the Clear Screen button is assigned the task of clearing the screen for the next order. Here again, you can use assignment statements to accomplish this task. To clear the prior customer information from the screen, you will need to remove the contents of seven of the nine text boxes. The two text boxes whose contents you won't need to remove are the txtPrice and txtRate controls;

after the user enters the price and tax rate for the first order, the user should not have to enter that information again. You will also need to remove the entries recorded in the Caption property of two of the label controls, lblTboards and lblTprice. After the screen is cleared, the Clear Screen button should place the focus in the txtName control so that the user will be ready to enter the next order. Figure 2-27 lists the steps—the pseudocode—you want the Clear Screen button to follow.

Clear Screen button

1. Clear the Text property of the Text box controls (except txtPrice and txtRate)
2. Clear the Caption property of the Label controls (lblTboards and lblTprice)
3. Send the focus to the txtName control

Figure 2-27: Pseudocode for the Clear Screen button

You are assigning IL to the txtState control in case the user changed the state.

You will use an assignment statement to assign the string "IL" to the txtState control, and a zero-length string to the remaining eight controls. A **string** is a group of characters enclosed in quotation marks. For example, the word "Jones" is considered a string. Likewise, "45" is a string, but 45 is not; 45 is a number. "Jones" is a string with a length of five because there are five characters between the quotation marks, and "45" is a string with a length of two because there are two characters between the quotation marks. Following this logic, a **zero-length string** is a set of quotation marks with nothing between them, like this: "". You will assign a zero-length string, also called an **empty string**, to the Text property of each of the text boxes (except the state, price, and sales tax rate text boxes) and to the Caption property of the two label controls, lblTboards and lblTprice. Assigning the zero-length string to the Text property and to the Caption property will clear the prior customer's information from the controls.

To code the Clear Screen button:

1 Maximize the form, then open the Clear Screen button's Code window. The cmdClear control's Click event procedure appears.

First, include some documentation in the Code window.

2 Maximize the Code window, then type **'Clear the screen for the next order** and press the **Enter** key. Be sure to type the apostrophe (').

Recall that the names of the text boxes are txtName, txtAddress, txtCity, txtState, txtZip, txtBlue, and txtYellow.

3 Press the **Tab** key, then type **txtName.text = ""** and press the **Enter** key. (Don't type any spaces between the quotation marks.)

4 Copy the `txtName.Text = ""` assignment statement to the clipboard, then paste the assignment statement into the Code window six times, between the original assignment statement and the End Sub instruction. Change the names of the controls in the assignment statement, as well as the value assigned to the txtState control, to match Figure 2-28.

Recall that the syntax of an assignment statement is *[form.]object.property = value*. In this case, you don't need the form name in the assignment statement because the txtName control is in the current form.

change the control
names as shown

change this value

Figure 2-28: Assignment statements entered in the Clear Screen button's Code window

HELP? To copy the txtName.Text = "" statement to the clipboard, highlight the statement, then press Ctrl + c. To paste the txtName.Text = "" statement into the Code window, first click at the location where you want to begin pasting, then press Ctrl + v.

The two label controls are next.

5 Position the blinking insertion point in the blank line immediately below the last assignment statement, as shown in Figure 2-28.

6 Type **lblTboards.caption = ""** and press the **Enter** key, then type **lblTprice.caption = ""** and press the **Enter** key. (Don't enter any spaces between the "".)

According to the pseudocode, you should set the focus to the txtName control next.

7 Type **txtName.setfocus** and press the **Enter** key. The completed Code window is shown in Figure 2-29.

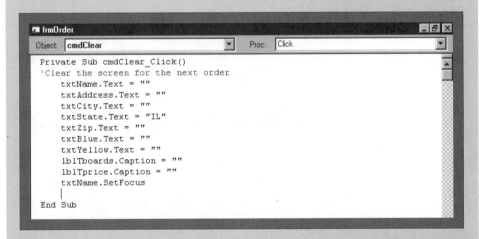

Figure 2-29: The completed Code window for the Clear Screen button's Click event

8 Close the Clear Screen button's Code window, restore the form to its standard size, and then **save** and **run** the application.

> **HELP?** If an error message appears in a dialog box, click the End button. Open the Clear Screen button's Code window and compare your code with Figure 2-29. Make the necessary corrections.
>
> 9 To test the application, enter your name and address information (including the city, state, and zip), then enter **10** for the number of blue skateboards and **10** for the number of yellow skateboards. Enter **100** for the skateboard price and **.05** for the sales tax rate. Click the **Clear Screen** button. The prior customer's information disappears from the screen, and the focus is in the txtName control. Notice that the txtState control still contains IL, the txtPrice control still contains 100, and the txtRate control still contains .05.
>
> 10 Click the **Exit** button to end the application. Visual Basic returns to the design screen.

The Calculate Order button is the only object that still needs to be coded. Before you can code that button, however, you will need to learn how to write mathematical equations in Visual Basic.

Writing Visual Basic Equations

Most applications require the computer to perform some calculations. You instruct the computer to perform a calculation by writing an arithmetic equation in an object's Code window. The mathematical operators you can use in your arithmetic equations, along with their precedence numbers, are listed in Figure 2-30. The precedence numbers represent the order in which Visual Basic performs the mathematical operations in an equation. You can, however, use parentheses to override the order of precedence. Operations within parentheses are always performed before operations outside of parentheses.

Operator	Operation	Precedence Number
^	exponentiation (raises a number to a power)	1
–	negation	2
*, /	multiplication and division	3
\	integer division	4
Mod	modulo arithmetic	5
+, –	addition and subtraction	6

Important Note: You can use parentheses to override the order of precedence. Operations within parentheses are always performed before operations outside of parentheses.

Figure 2-30: Mathematical operators and their order of precedence

When you create an arithmetic equation, keep in mind that Visual Basic follows the same order of precedence as you do when solving equations; that is, an operation with a lower precedence number is done before one with a higher precedence number. If the equation contains more than one operator having the same priority, those operators are evaluated from left to right. For example, in the equation 3+9/3*5, the division (/) would be done first, then the multiplication (*), and then the addition (+). In other words, Visual Basic would first divide 9 by 3, then multiply by 5, and then add 3. The equation evaluates to 18. You can use parentheses to change the order in which the operators will be evaluated. For example, the equation (3+9)/3*5 (notice the parentheses around the 3+9) evaluates to 20, not 18. That's because the parentheses tell Visual Basic to add 3 + 9 first, then divide by 3, and then multiply by 5.

Two of the mathematical operators listed in Figure 2-30 might be less familiar to you; these are the integer division operator (\) and the modulo arithmetic operator (Mod). The integer division operator (\), like the standard division operator (/), is used to divide two numbers. Unlike the standard division operator, however, the integer division operator returns an integer (whole number) result. For example, the expression 211\4 results in 52, whereas the expression 211/4 results in 52.75. The modulo arithmetic operator is also used to divide two numbers, but it results in the remainder of the division. For example, 211 Mod 4 equals 3 (the remainder of 211 divided by 4).

When entering equations in Visual Basic, you do not enter the dollar sign ($) or the percent sign (%). If you want to enter a percentage, you must convert the percentage to its decimal equivalent—for example, you would need to convert 5% to .05.

In addition to the mathematical operators, Visual Basic also allows you to use relational operators and logical operators in your equations. You will learn about those two types of operators in Tutorial 4. For now, you will need to know only the mathematical operators in order to code the Calculate Order button in the Skate-Away Sales application.

Coding the Calculate Order Button

According to your TOE chart for this application, the Calculate Order button is responsible for calculating both the total number of skateboards ordered and the total price of the order, as well as displaying those amounts in the two label controls. The instructions to accomplish the Calculate Order button's tasks must be placed in the button's Click event procedure. The Calculate Order button's pseudocode, which lists the steps the button will need to take in order to accomplish its tasks, is shown in Figure 2-31.

Calculate Order button

1. Calculate total skateboards = blue skateboards + yellow skateboards
2. Calculate total price = total skateboards * skateboard price *
   (1 + sales tax rate)
3. Display total skateboards and total price in lblTboards and lblTprice label controls
4. Send the focus to the Print Order button

Figure 2-31: Pseudocode for the Calculate Order button

The first step listed in the pseudocode shown in Figure 2-31 is to calculate the total number of skateboards. To do this, the Calculate Order button will need to add the number of blue skateboards to the number of yellow skateboards. Recall that the number of blue skateboards is recorded in the txtBlue control's Text property as the user enters that information. Likewise, the number of yellow skateboards is recorded in the txtYellow control's Text property. Recall from your TOE chart that the total number of skateboards should be displayed in the lblTboards control. You can use an assignment statement to add the two Text properties together and then assign the sum to the Caption property of the lblTboards control. This is illustrated in Figure 2-32.

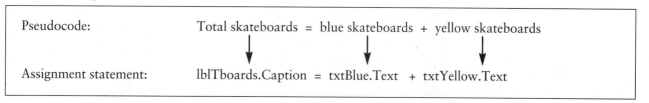

Figure 2-32: Illustration of the total skateboards calculation

The next step shown in the pseudocode is to compute the total price of the order. To do this, the application needs to multiply the total number of skateboards by the skateboard price ($100); it then must add a 5% sales tax to that amount. The total number of skateboards is recorded in the lblTboards control, the price is entered in the txtPrice control, and the sales tax rate is entered in the txtRate control. Recall from your TOE chart that the total price should be displayed in the lblTprice control. The total price equation is illustrated in Figure 2-33.

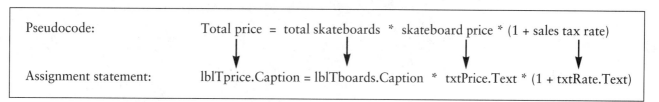

Figure 2-33: Illustration of the total price calculation

The last step in the Calculate Order button's pseudocode is to set the focus to the Print Order command button; after calculating an order, the salesperson will typically print the confirmation notice. Open the Calculate Order button's Code window and write the necessary code.

To code the Calculate Order button:

1 Maximize the form, then open the Calculate Order button's Code window. The current event procedure is Click, which is the event you want.

2 Maximize the Code window, then type **'Calculate total number of skateboards** and press the **Enter** key.

3 Press the **Tab** key, then type **lblTboards.caption = txtBlue.text + txtYellow.text** and press the **Enter** key.

4   Press the **Backspace** key to remove the indentation, then type **'Calculate total price** and press the **Enter** key.

5   Press the **Tab** key, then type **lblTprice.caption = lblTboards.caption * txtPrice.text * (1 + txtRate.text)** and press the **Enter** key.

6   Type **cmdPrint.setfocus** and press the **Enter** key. See Figure 2-34.

the code in the Code window was compressed so that you could read the entire line

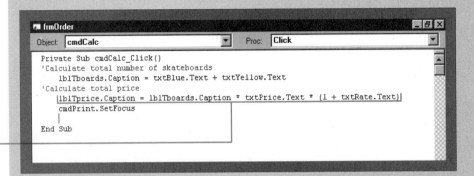

Figure 2-34: Calculate Order button's Click event

7   Compare your code with the code shown in Figure 2-34. Make any needed corrections before continuing to the next step. (The code in Figure 2-34 was compressed so that you could read the entire line. You may not be able to see the entire equation that calculates the total price without scrolling the Code window.)

8   Close the Calculate Order button's Code window, restore the form to its standard size, then **save and run** the application.

    HELP? If an error message appears in a dialog box, click the End button. Open the Calculate Order button's Code window and compare your code with Figure 2-34. Make the necessary corrections.

9   Press the **Tab** key five times to move the focus to the txtBlue control, type **5** and press the **Tab** key. Type **10** as the number of yellow skateboards ordered, then press the **Tab** key. Type **100** as the skateboard price and press the **Tab** key. Type **.05** as the sales tax rate, then click the **Calculate Order** button. The Calculate Order button calculates, incorrectly, the total skateboards and the total price, then moves the focus to the Print Order button, as shown in Figure 2-35.

these figures are incorrect

Figure 2-35: Screen showing incorrect figures calculated by the Calculate Order button

Notice that the application shows 510 as the total number of skateboards. Instead of mathematically adding the two order quantities together, which should have resulted in a total of 15, Visual Basic appended the second order quantity to the end of the first order quantity, giving 510. When the total skateboards figure is incorrect, it follows that the total price figure will also be incorrect, as the total skateboards figure is used in the total price equation. Exit the application and think about what went wrong.

10 Click the **Exit** button to end the application. Visual Basic returns to the design screen.

The `lblTboards.Caption = txtBlue.Text + txtYellow.Text` equation you entered in the Calculate Order button's Code window is supposed to calculate the total skateboards, but the equation is not working correctly. Instead of the plus sign (+) adding the blue skateboard quantity to the yellow skateboard quantity, the plus sign appends the latter quantity to the end of the first one. This occurs because the plus sign (+) in Visual Basic performs two roles: it adds numbers together and it concatenates (links together) strings. You will learn about string concatenation in Tutorial 3. (Recall that strings are groups of characters enclosed in quotation marks.)

In Visual Basic, values in both the Caption and Text properties of controls are treated as strings, not numbers, even though you don't see the quotation marks. Adding strings together will not give you the same result as adding numbers together. As you saw in the Skate-Away Sales application, adding the string "5" to the string "10" results in the string "510," whereas adding the number 5 to the number 10 results in the number 15. To fix this problem, you need to tell Visual Basic to treat the entries in the Text property of both the txtBlue and txtYellow controls as numbers, not as strings. For this, you need to use the Val function.

The Val Function

Like a method, a **function** is a predefined procedure that performs a specific task. Unlike a method, however, a function results in a value. For example, the **Val** function, which tells Visual Basic to treat a character string as a numeric value, results in a number. The syntax of the Val function is **Val**(*StringExpression*), where *StringExpression* is the character string you want treated as a number. Because Visual Basic must be able to interpret the *StringExpression* as a numeric value, the expression cannot include a letter or a special character, such as the dollar sign, comma, or the percent sign (%); it can, however, include the period. When Visual Basic encounters an invalid character in the Val function's *StringExpression*, Visual Basic stops converting the *StringExpression* to a number at that point. Figure 2-36 shows some examples of how the Val function would interpret various *StringExpressions*.

This Val function:	Would be converted to:
Val("456")	456
Val("24,500")	24
Val("123X")	123
Val("$56.88")	0
Val("Abc")	0
Val("")	0
Val("25%")	25

Figure 2-36: Examples of the Val function

Notice that the Val function converts the "$56.88", the "Abc", and the "" (empty string) to the number 0.

To fix the assignment statement entered in the Calculate Order button's Code window, you will use the Val function to tell Visual Basic to treat the Text property of both the txtBlue and txtYellow controls as numbers instead of strings.

To include the Val function in the Calculate Order button's Code window, then print the confirmation notice:

1   Maximize the form. Open the Calculate Order button's Code window, then maximize the Code window. The cmdCalc control's Click event procedure fills the screen.

2   Change the `lblTboards.Caption = txtBlue.Text + txtYellow.Text` assignment statement to **lblTboards.Caption = val(txtBlue.Text) + val(txtYellow.Text)**. Be sure to watch the placement of the parentheses.

3   Also change the `lblTprice.Caption = lblTboards.Caption * txtPrice.Text * (1 + txtRate)` to **lblTprice.caption = val(lblTboards.caption) * val(txtPrice.text) * (1 + val(txtRate.text))**. See Figure 2-37. Be sure to watch the placement of the parentheses; notice that there are two parentheses at the end of the equation. (The code in Figure 2-37 was compressed so that you could read more of each instruction. On your screen, you may need to scroll the Code window to see the instructions in their entirety.)

Figure 2-37: Calculate Order button's Code window showing Val function

the code in the Code
window was compressed
so that you could read the
entire line

tips

••••••••••••••••••

If you are thinking that
the instructions are get-
ting a bit unwieldy, you
are correct. In Tutorial 3
you will learn how to
write more compact
assignment statements.

4   Close the Code window, restore the form to its standard size, then **save and run** the project.

   HELP? If an error message appears in a dialog box, click the End button. Open the Calculate Order button's Code window and compare your code with Figure 2-37. Make the necessary corrections.

5   Click the **txtBlue control**, type **5** and press the **Tab** key. Type **10** as the number of yellow skateboards ordered, **100** as the skateboard price, and **.05** as the sales tax rate. Click the **Calculate Order** button. The application correctly calculates the total skateboards (15) and the total price (1575), then sends the focus to the Print Order button.

6   If your computer is connected to a printer, then press the **Enter** key to select the Print Order button. The confirmation notice prints on the printer, and the cmdClear button receives the focus.

7   If you printed the confirmation notice, then the Clear Screen button has the focus, so you can simply press the **Enter** key to clear the screen. If you did not print the confirmation notice because your computer was not connected to a printer, then click the **Clear Screen** button to clear the screen.

The information is cleared from the screen, and the focus moves to the txtName control.

8   Click the **Exit** button. Visual Basic returns to the design screen.

The final change you will make to this application is to display a dollar sign ($) and a comma in the lblTprice control.

Using the Format Function

You can use the **Format function** to improve the appearance of the numbers in your application. The syntax of the Format function is: **Format**(*expression, format*). *Expression* specifies the number, date, time, or string whose appearance you want to format. *Format* is either the name of a predefined Visual Basic format or, if you want more control over the appearance of the expression, a string containing special symbols that tell Visual Basic how you want the expression displayed. (You can display the Help window for the Format function to learn more about these special symbols.) In this case, you will use one of Visual Basic's predefined formats, some of which are explained in Figure 2-38.

Format Name	Description
Currency	Displays a number with a dollar sign and two decimal places; if appropriate, displays a number with a thousand separator; negative numbers are enclosed in parentheses
Fixed	Displays a number with at least one digit to the left and two digits to the right of the decimal point
Standard	Displays a number with at least one digit to the left and two digits to the right of the decimal point; if appropriate, displays a number with a thousand separator; negative numbers are enclosed in parentheses
Percent	Multiplies a number by 100 and displays the number with a percent sign (%); displays two digits to the right of the decimal point

Figure 2-38: Some of Visual Basic's predefined formats

Because you want a dollar sign and a comma to display in the lblTprice control, you will use the "Currency" format in the Format function. You will enter the Format function in the Calculate Order button's Code window.

tips

You could have added the Format function in the equation that calculates the total price, but then the equation would be so long that it would be hard to understand.

To enter the Format function in the Calculate Order button's Code window:

1   Maximize the form. Open the Calculate Order button's Code window, then maximize the Code window. The cmdCalc Click event procedure fills the screen.

2   Click at the beginning of the cmdPrint.SetFocus instruction and press the Enter key to insert a blank line above that instruction. Press ↑ on your keyboard. If necessary, position the blinking insertion point immediately above the c in the cmdPrint.SetFocus instruction.

3   Type **lblTprice.caption = format(lblTprice.caption, "currency")**, as shown in Figure 2-39.

enter this line of code

```
frmOrder                                                        _ □ ×
Object:  cmdCalc                           ▼    Proc:  Click                ▼
    Private Sub cmdCalc_Click()
    'Calculate total number of skateboards
        lblTboards.Caption = Val(txtBlue.Text) + Val(txtYellow.Text)
    'Calculate total price
        lblTprice.Caption = Val(lblTboards.Caption) * Val(txtPrice.Text) * (1 +
        lblTprice.Caption = Format(lblTprice.Caption, "currency")
        cmdPrint.SetFocus

    End Sub
```

Figure 2-39: Format function entered in Calculate Order button's Code window

4   Close the Code window. Restore the form to its standard size, then **save** and **run** the application.

5   Enter the following order:

Sport Warehouse, 123 Main, Glendale, IL, 60134, 100 blue skateboards, 150 yellow skateboards.

6 Enter **100** as the skateboard price and **.05** as the sales tax rate.

7 Click the **Calculate Order** button. The application calculates the total skateboards and total price, as shown in Figure 2-40.

total price appears with
a $ and two decimal places

Figure 2-40: Total price displayed using the Format function

8 Click the **Exit** button. Visual Basic returns to the design screen.

You have now completed the first three of the five steps involved in creating an OOED application: planning the application, building the user interface, and coding the application. The fourth step is to test and debug the application. You will do that next.

Testing and Debugging the Application

You test an application by running it and entering some sample data. You should use both valid and invalid test data. **Valid data** is data that the application is expecting—for example, the Skate-Away Sales application is expecting the user to enter a numeric value as the skateboard price. **Invalid data,** on the other hand, is data that the application is not expecting. In this application, for example, the application is not expecting the user to enter a letter for the number of either blue or yellow skateboards ordered. You should test the application as thoroughly as possible; you don't want to give the user an application that ends abruptly because invalid data was entered. (You will learn more about handling invalid data in later tutorials.)

Debugging refers to the process of locating errors in the program. Program errors can be either syntax errors or logic errors. When you enter an instruction incorrectly—for example, typing `Edn` instead of `End`—you create a syntax error.

Visual Basic can detect syntax errors for you, as you will learn in Tutorial 3. Also, because you typically test each object's code before coding another object, as you did in this lesson, the syntax errors will already have been corrected by the time you get to testing and debugging the entire application.

An example of a much more difficult type of error to find, and one that Visual Basic cannot find for you, is a logic error. When you enter an instruction that won't give you the results for which you are looking, you create a logic error. The instruction

```
lblAverage.Caption = Val(txtNum1.Text) + Val(txtNum2.Text) / 2,
```

which is supposed to calculate the average of two numbers, is an example of a logic error. Although the instruction is syntactically correct, it is logically incorrect. The instruction to calculate the average of two numbers, written correctly, should be

```
lblAverage.Caption =(Val(txtNum1.Text) + Val(txtNum2.Text)) / 2;
```

because division has a higher precedence number than does addition, you must place parentheses around the `Val(txtNum1.Text) + Val(txtNum2.Text)`.

To test and debug the current application with both valid and invalid data:

1 **Run** the application, then test the application by clicking the **Calculate Order** button without entering any data. The application displays 0 for the total number of skateboards, and $0.00 for the total price.

2 Try entering a letter (any letter) for the number of blue skateboards ordered and a letter for the number of yellow skateboards ordered. Enter 100 for the skateboard price and .05 for the sales tax rate. Click the **Calculate Order** button. The application displays 0 for the total number of skateboards, and $0.00 for the total price. (Recall that the Val function converts letters to the number 0.)

3 Click the **Clear Screen** button. Enter 10 as the number of blue skateboards ordered, and 10 as the number of yellow skateboards ordered. Now highlight the 100 in the txtPrice control, then type the letters **xyz**. Click the **Calculate Order** button. The application displays 20 as the total number of skateboards ordered, and $0.00 as the total price.

4 Click the **Clear Screen** button, then enter an order that is correct. Click the **Calculate Order** button.

5 Click the **Clear Screen** button, then practice with other entries to see how the application responds.

6 When you are finished, click the **Exit** button to end the application.

After you've tested the application to verify that it is working correctly, you can move on to the last step involved in creating an OOED application, which is to assemble the documentation.

Assembling the Documentation

Assembling the documentation refers to placing your planning tools and a printout of the application in a safe place, so you can refer to them if you need to change the application in the future. Your planning tools include the TOE chart, sketch of the user interface, and either the flowcharts or pseudocode. The printout of the application includes the form image, form as text, and code.

To print the Form Image, Form as Text, and Code:

1 Maximize the form, then press **Ctrl + p** to display the Print dialog box.

2 Click **Form Image**, then click **Form As Text**, then click **Code**. Check marks (*or Xs in Windows 3.1*) should appear next to each of the three selections. Click the **OK** button to begin printing.

3 When finished printing, restore the form to its standard size.

You have now completed the five steps involved in creating an application:
1. Planning the application.
2. Building the user interface.
3. Coding the application.
4. Testing and debugging the application.
5. Assembling the documentation.

You can either take a break, complete the end-of-lesson questions and exercises, or read and complete the Debugging section and exercises. The Debugging section may contain information that will help you complete the end-of-lesson exercises.

S U M M A R Y

To move the focus to an object while the program is running:

■ Use the SetFocus method. Its syntax is [*form.*]*object*.**SetFocus**.

To print a form:

■ Use the PrintForm method. Its syntax is [*form.*]**PrintForm**.

To assign a value to the property of an object:

■ Use an assignment statement. Its syntax is [*form.*]*object.property* = *value*.

To document Visual Basic code with comments:

■ Begin the comment with an apostrophe (').

To clear an object's Caption/Text property:

■ Use an assignment statement to assign a zero-length string (""), also called an empty string, to the object's Caption/Text property.

To tell Visual Basic to treat a character string as a numeric value:

■ Use the Val function. Its syntax is **Val**(*StringExpression*).

To improve the appearance of numbers in the user interface:

■ Use the Format function. Its syntax is **Format** (*expression, format*).

Q U E S T I O N S

1. The _____ method prints a form.
   a. Form
   b. FormPrint
   c. Print
   d. Printer
   e. PrintForm

2. Which of the following is a valid assignment statement?
   a. txtName.Caption = 'Jones'
   b. txtName.Caption = "Jones"
   c. txtName.Text = 'Jones'
   d. txtName.Text = "Jones"
   e. None of the above is valid

3. Which of the following is a valid assignment statement?
   a. lblName.Caption = Jones
   b. txtName.Caption = "Jones"
   c. txtName.Caption = 'Jones'
   d. CmdExit.Visible = "False"
   e. None of the above is valid

4. Which of the following assignment statements will not calculate correctly?
   a. txtTotal.Text = Val(txtSales1.Text) + Val(txtSales2.Text)
   b. txtTotal.Text = Val(lblSales1.Caption) + Val(lblSales2.Caption)
   c. txtTotal.Text = Val(txtRed.Text) * 2
   d. txtTotal.Text = Val(lblBlue.Caption) * 1.1
   e. All of the above are correct

5. You use the _____ character to assign an access key to a control.
   a. &
   b. *
   c. @
   d. $
   e. ^

6. You can assign an access key to any control that has a(n) _____ property.
   a. Access
   b. Caption
   c. Key
   d. KeyAccess
   e. Text

7. You use the _____ function to display dollar signs and commas in numbers.
   a. Focus
   b. Format
   c. PrintForm
   d. SetFocus
   e. Val

8. The _____ function tells Visual Basic to treat a string as a numeric value.
a. Focus
b. Format
c. PrintForm
d. SetFocus
e. Val

9. Listed below are the five steps you should follow when creating an OOED application. Put them in the proper order by placing a number (1 to 5) on the line to the left of the step.
_____ Assemble the documentation.
_____ Plan the application.
_____ Code the application.
_____ Build the user interface.
_____ Test and debug the application.

10. The instruction `txtTotal.Text = Val(txtNum.Text) / 2`, which should multiply the contents of the txtNum text box by 2 and assign the result to the txtTotal text box, is an example of _____ .
a. a logic error
b. a syntax error
c. a correct instruction

11. The instruction PrintFrm is an example of _____ .
a. a logic error
b. a syntax error
c. a correct instruction

E X E R C I S E S

NOTE: In each of the following exercises you will perform the five steps involved in creating an OOED application. Recall that those five steps are:
1. Plan the application. (Prepare a TOE chart, ordered by object, and draw a sketch of the user interface.)
2. Build the user interface. (To help you remember the names of the controls as you are coding, print the Form Image and write the names next to each object.)
3. Code the application. (Be sure to write pseudocode for each of the objects that will be coded.)
4. Test and debug the application. (Use the sample data provided in each of the exercises.)
5. Assemble the documentation. (TOE chart, sketch, printout of the form, form as text, and code)

1. Scenario: Recall that 1440 twips is equal to one inch. Create an application that allows you to enter the number of twips, convert the twips to inches, and print the user interface.
a. Perform the five steps involved in creating an OOED application.
b. Save the form and the project as lc1Done in the Tut02 folder on your Student Disk.
c. Test the application two times, with the following data. Print the application with the test data showing. Twips: 2880   Twips: abc
d. Assemble the documentation (TOE chart, pseudocode, 2 printouts of the form from step c, Form as Text, and Code).
e. Make an executable file. Name it lc1Done.exe. (You can't make an executable file if you are using the Visual Basic Working Model.)

2. Scenario: John Lee wants an application in which he can enter the following three pieces of information: his cash balance at the beginning of the month, the amount of money he earned during the month, and the amount of money he spent during the month. He wants the application to compute his ending balance, then print all of the information.

   a. Perform the five steps involved in creating an OOED application.
   b. Save the form and the project as lc2Done in the Tut02 folder on your Student Disk.
   c. Test the application twice using the following data. Print the application with the test data showing.

Beginning cash balance: 5000	Earnings: 2500	Expenses: 3000
Beginning cash balance: xyz	Earnings: xyz	Expenses: xyz

   d. Assemble the documentation (TOE chart, pseudocode, 2 printouts of the form from step c, Form as Text, and Code).

3. Scenario: Lana Jones wants an application that will compute and print the average of any three numbers she enters.

   a. Perform the five steps involved in creating an OOED application.
   b. Save the form and the project as lc3Done in the Tut02 folder on your Student Disk.
   c. Test the application twice using the following data. Print the application with the test data showing.

First Number: 27	Second Number: 9	Third Number: 18
First Number: A	Second Number: B	Third Number: C

   d. Assemble the documentation (TOE chart, pseudocode, 2 printouts of the form from step c, Form as Text, and Code).

4. Scenario: Martha Arito, manager of Bookworms Inc., needs an inventory application. Martha will enter the title of a book, the number of paperback versions of the book currently in inventory, the number of hardcover versions of the book currently in inventory, the cost of the paperback version, and the cost of the hardcover version. Martha wants the application to compute the value of the paperback versions of the book, the value of the hardcover versions of the book, the total number of paperback and hardcover versions, and the total value of the paperback and hardcover versions. Martha will need to print this information.

   a. Perform the five steps involved in creating an OOED application.
   b. Save the form and the project as lc4Done in the Tut02 folder on your Student Disk.
   c. Test the application twice using the following data. Print the application with the test data showing.

   Book Title: An Intro to Visual Basic

Paperback versions: 100	Paperback cost: 40
Hardcover versions: 50	Hardcover cost: 75

   Book Title: Advanced Visual Basic

Paperback versions: A	Paperback cost: B
Hardcover versions: C	Hardcover cost: D

   d. Assemble the documentation (TOE chart, pseudocode, 2 printouts of the form from step c, Form as Text, and Code).

5. Scenario: Jackets Unlimited is having a 25% off sale on all its merchandise. The store manager asks you to create an application that requires the clerk simply to enter the original price of a jacket. The application should then compute and print both the discount and the new price.

   a. Perform the five steps involved in creating an OOED application.
   b. Save the form and the project as lc5Done in the Tut02 folder on your Student Disk.

   c. Test the application twice using the following data. Print the application with the test data showing.

     Jacket's original price: 50

     Jacket's original price: ***

   d. Assemble the documentation (TOE chart, pseudocode, 2 printouts of the form from step c, Form as Text, and Code).

6. Scenario: Typing Salon charges $.10 per typed envelope and $.25 per typed page. The company accountant wants an application to help her prepare bills. She will enter the customer's name, the number of typed envelopes, and the number of typed pages. The application should compute and print the total bill.

   a. Perform the five steps involved in creating an OOED application.

   b. Save the form and the project as lc6Done in the Tut02 folder on your Student Disk.

   c. Test the application twice using the following data. Print the application with the test data showing.

     Customer's name: Alice Wong

     Number of typed envelopes: 250   Number of typed pages: 200

     Customer's name: Alice Wong

     Number of typed envelopes: $4   Number of typed pages: AB

   d. Assemble the documentation (TOE chart, pseudocode, 2 printouts of the form from step c, Form as Text, and Code).

7. Scenario: Management USA, a small training center, plans to run two full-day seminars on December 1. The seminars are called "How to Be an Effective Manager" and "How to Run a Small Business." Each seminar costs $200. Registration for the seminars will be done by phone. When a company calls to register its employees, the phone representative will ask for the following information: the company's name, address (including city, state, and zip), the number of employees registering for the "How to Be an Effective Manager" seminar, and the number of employees registering for the "How to Run a Small Business" seminar. Claire Jenkowski, the owner of Management USA, wants the application to calculate the total number of employees the company is registering and the total cost. Ms. Jenkowski also wants to print the company information.

   a. Perform the five steps involved in creating an OOED application.

   b. Save the form and the project as lc7Done in the Tut02 folder on your Student Disk.

   c. Test the application twice using the following data. Print the application with the test data showing.

     Company Name: ABC Company

     Address: 345 Main St.

     City, State, Zip: Glen, TX 70122

     "How to Be an Effective Manager" registrants: 10

     "How to Run a Small Business" registrants: 5

     Company Name: 1

     Address: 2

     City, State, Zip: 3

     "How to Be an Effective Manager" registrants: A

     "How to Run a Small Business" registrants: B

   d. Assemble the documentation (TOE chart, pseudocode, 2 printouts of the form from step c, Form as Text, and Code).

8. Scenario: Suman Gadhari, the payroll clerk at Sun Projects, wants an application that will compute net pay for each of the company's employees. Suman will enter the employee's name, hours worked, and rate of pay. For this application, you do not have to worry about overtime, as this company does not allow anyone to work more than 40 hours. Suman wants the application to compute the gross pay, the federal withholding tax (FWT), the social security tax (FICA), the state income tax, and the net pay. Suman also wants to print the payroll information on the printer. Use the following information when computing the three taxes:

   FWT: 20% of gross pay
   FICA: 8% of gross pay
   state income tax : 2% of gross pay

   a. Perform the five steps involved in creating an OOED application.
   b. Save the form and the project as lc8Done in the Tut02 folder on your Student Disk.
   c. Test the application twice using the following data. Print the application with the test data showing.

   Employee's name: Susan Reha
   Hours worked: 40
   Rate of pay: 12

   Employee's name: Susan Reha
   Hours worked: X
   Rate of pay: Y

   d. Assemble the documentation (TOE chart, pseudocode, 2 printouts of the form from step c, Form as Text, and Code).
   e. Make an executable (.EXE) file. Name it lc8Done.exe. (You can't make an executable file if you are using the Visual Basic Working Model).

Exercises 9 through 15 are Discovery Exercises, which allow you to "discover" the solutions to problems on your own. Discovery Exercises may include topics that are not covered in the tutorial.

discovery ▶ 9. Scenario: Colfax Industries needs an application that allows the shipping clerk to enter the quantity of an item in inventory and how many of the item can be packed in a box for shipping. When the shipping clerk clicks a command button, the application should compute and display the number of full boxes that can be packed and how many of the item are left over.

   a. Perform the five steps involved in creating an OOED application.
   b. Save the form and the project as lc9Done in the Tut02 folder on your Student Disk.
   c. Test the application using the following data, then print the application with the test data showing.   Colfax has 45 skateboards in inventory. If six skateboards can fit into a box for shipping, how many full boxes could the company ship, and how many skateboards will remain in inventory?
   d. Assemble the documentation (TOE chart, pseudocode, printout of the form from step c, Form as Text, and Code).

discovery ▶ 10. Scenario: Perry Brown needs an application that will allow him to enter the length of four sides of a polygon. When he clicks a command button, the application should compute and display the perimeter of the polygon.

   a. Perform the five steps involved in creating an OOED application.
   b. Save the form and the project as lc10Done in the Tut02 folder on your Student Disk.
   c. Test the application using the following data, then print the application with the test data showing.   Each day Perry rides his bike around a park that has side lengths of 1/2 mile, 1 mile, 1/2 mile, and 1 mile. How far does Perry ride his bike each day?
   d. Assemble the documentation (TOE chart, pseudocode, printout of the form from step c, Form as Text, and Code).

discovery ▶ **11.** Scenario: Builders Inc. needs an application that will allow their salesclerks to enter both the diameter of a circle and the price of railing material per foot. When the clerk clicks a command button, the application should compute and display the circumference of the circle and the total price of the railing material. (Use 3.14 as the value of pi.)

a. Perform the five steps involved in creating an OOED application.

b. Save the form and the project as lc11Done in the Tut02 folder on your Student Disk.

c. Test the application using the following data, then print the application with the test data showing.   Jack Jones, one of Builders Inc.'s customers, is building a railing around a circular deck having a diameter of 36 feet. The railing material costs $2 per foot. What is the circumference of the deck and the total price of the railing material?

d. Assemble the documentation (TOE chart, pseudocode, printout of the form from step c, Form as Text, and Code).

discovery ▶ **12.** Scenario: Temp Employers wants an application that will allow their employees to enter the number of hours worked. When the employee clicks a command button, the application will compute and display the number of weeks (assume a 40-hour week), days (assume an 8-hour day), and hours worked. For example, if the user enters the number 70, the application will display 1 week, 3 days, and 6 hours.

a. Perform the five steps involved in creating an OOED application.

b. Save the form and the project as lc12Done in the Tut02 folder on your Student Disk.

c. Test the application three times using the following data, then print the application with each of the test data showing.

    1) Hours worked: 88

    2) Hours worked: 111

    3) Hours worked: 12

d. Assemble the documentation (TOE chart, pseudocode, 3 printouts of the form from step c, Form as Text, and Code).

discovery ▶ **13.** Scenario: Tile Limited wants an application that will allow their salesclerks to enter the length and width, in feet, of a rectangle, and the price of a square foot of tile. When the clerk clicks a command button, the application will compute and display the area of the rectangle and the total price of the tile.

a. Perform the five steps involved in creating an OOED application.

b. Save the form and the project as lc13Done in the Tut02 folder on your Student Disk.

c. Test the application using the following data, then print the application with the test data showing.   Susan Caper, one of Tile Limited's customers, is tiling a floor in her home. The floor is 12 feet long and 14 feet wide. The price of a square foot of tile is $1.59. What is the area of the floor and how much will the tile cost?

d. Assemble the documentation (TOE chart, pseudocode, printout of the form from step c, Form as Text, and Code).

discovery ▶ **14.** Scenario: Willow Pools wants an application that will allow their salespeople to enter the length, width, and height of a rectangle. When the salesperson clicks a command button, the application will compute and display the volume of the rectangle.

a. Perform the five steps involved in creating an OOED application.

b. Save the form and the project as lc14Done in the Tut02 folder on your Student Disk.

c. Test the application using the following data, then print the application with the test data showing.   The swimming pool at a health club is 100 feet long, 30 feet wide, and 4 feet deep. How many cubic feet of water will the pool contain?

d. Assemble the documentation (TOE chart, pseudocode, printout of the form from step c, Form as Text, and Code).

discovery ▶ 15. Scenario: Quick Loans wants an application that will allow their clerks to enter the amount of a loan, the interest rate, and the term of the loan (in years). When the clerk clicks a command button, the application should compute and display the total amount of interest and the total amount to be repaid.

 a. Perform the five steps involved in creating an OOED application.

 b. Save the form and the project as lc15Done in the Tut02 folder on your Student Disk.

 c. Test the application using the following data, then print the application with the test data showing. You visit Quick Loans because you want to borrow $9000 in order to buy a new car. The loan is for three years at an annual interest rate of 12%. How much will you pay in interest over the three years, and what is the total amount you will repay?

 d. Assemble the documentation (TOE chart, pseudocode, printout of the form from step c, Form as Text, and Code).

D E B U G G I N G

Technique

As you saw in this tutorial, you may not get the expected results when a calculation includes either the Text property or the Caption property of a control; that's because both properties are treated as strings, not as numbers. Recall that you should use the Val function in equations to tell Visual Basic to treat the Text property and the Caption property as numbers instead of strings. Observe what happens when you don't use the Val function in the equations.

Exercises

To test an application without the Val function included:

1 Open the t2Db (or t2db.vbp) project, which is located in the Tut02 folder on your Student Disk, and view the form. The application allows you to enter a number; it then doubles the number and displays the result in the lblAnswer control.

2 Open the Double Number button's Code window and view the code. Notice that the equation does not contain the Val function.

3 Close the Code window. **Run**, but don't save, the application.

Now see what happens if the user forgets to enter a number.

4 Click the **Double Number** button without entering any data.

Visual Basic displays a dialog box informing you of an error in the application. The error is "Run-time error '13': Type mismatch." A "Type mismatch" error means that Visual Basic has encountered something that it wasn't expecting in an instruction—for example, a string where a number is required or a number where a string is needed. In this case, Visual Basic expected to find a number in the txtNum control's Text property, but it found the empty string there instead.

Notice the four buttons that appear in the dialog box: Continue (which is currently dimmed), End, Debug, and Help. You will have a lot more practice with this dialog box as you progress through this book. For now, however, let's simply end the application.

5 Click the **End** button to remove the dialog box and end the application.

Now observe what happens if the user enters a letter in the txtNum control.

6 **Run,** but don't save the application. Type **a** in the txtNum control, then click the **Double Number** button.

The "Type mismatch" error occurs again because Visual Basic found a string, instead of a number, in the txtNum control's Text property.

7 Click the **End** button to remove the dialog box and end the application.

You can prevent the "Type mismatch" error by including the Val function in the Double Number button's equation. Do that now and see how the application will handle both an empty txtNum control and a txtNum control that contains a letter.

To test the application with the Val function included:

1 Open the Double Number button's Code window, then include the Val function in the equation. The equation should now say
```
lblAnswer.Caption = Val(txtNum.Text) * 2.
```

2 Close the Code window, then **run,** but don't save, the application. Click the **Double Number** button without entering any data. A 0 (zero) appears in the lblAnswer control; that's because Visual Basic converts the empty string in the txtNum control's Text property to zero, and zero times two is zero.

3 Type **a** in the txtNum control, then click the **Double Number** button. A 0 (zero) appears in the lblAnswer control; that's because Visual Basic converts the letter in the txtNum control's Text property to zero, and zero times two is zero.

4 Click the **Exit** button to end the application.

As this debugging exercise shows, the Val function can prevent an application from ending in an error when the user enters invalid data.

TUTORIAL
3

Using Variables and Constants

Revising the Skate-Away Sales Application

case ▶ In Tutorial 2 you created an order screen for Skate-Away Sales. In order to complete the application, you just need to add the Interlocking Software copyright screen to the project. Before doing so, however, Mr. Cousard, the manager of Skate-Away Sales, calls to tell you that he wants to make a modification to the application. He now wants to include a message on each confirmation notice. The message should say "Thank you for your order. The sales tax was," followed by the sales tax amount and the name of the salesperson who recorded the order. You will need to modify the application's code to accommodate this change. Preview the completed application.

Previewing the Completed Application

To preview the completed application:

1   If necessary, start Windows, then place your Student Disk in the appropriate drive.

2   If you are running the Professional or Standard Edition of Visual Basic, then use the Run command on the Start menu to run the **Skate95** (Skate95.exe) file, which is located in the Tut03 folder on your Student Disk. If you are using the Visual Basic Working Model, use the Run command on the Start menu to run the Skate95x (Skate95x.exe) file, which is located in the Tut03 folder on your Student Disk. A copyright screen similar to the one that you created in Tutorial 1 appears first. Then, in a few seconds, a dialog box that requests the salesperson's name appears as shown in Figure 3-1. (Your dialog box will look different if you are using the Working Model.)

WINDOWS   **3.1**

Use the Run command on the Program Manager's File menu to run the skate31.exe file, which is located in the Tut03 folder on your Student Disk. A copyright screen similar to the one that you created in Tutorial 1 appears first. Then, in a few seconds, a dialog box that requests the salesperson's name appears as shown in Figure 3-1.

**your dialog box will
look different if
you are using the
Working Model**

Figure 3-1: The dialog box that requests the salesperson's name

The copyright form contains a Timer control that removes the form from the screen after a few seconds, then displays the dialog box. You will learn how to use a Timer control, as well as how to create a dialog box, in Lesson C.

3   Type your name in the Salesperson's name text box and press the **Enter** key. An order screen similar to the one that you created in Tutorial 2 appears.

4   Enter the following customer information: **Skaters Inc., 34 Plum Drive, Chicago, IL, 60654.**

5   Type 100 for the price and press the **Tab** key, then type .05 for the sales tax rate.

6 Click the **Blue skateboards ordered** text box, then type **25** as the number of blue skateboards ordered.

Although the Calculate Order button does not have the focus, you can still select it by pressing the Enter key; that's because the Calculate Order button is the default command button in the user interface. You will learn how to assign a default button in Lesson B.

7 Press the **Enter** key to calculate the order. The application calculates the order as shown in Figure 3-2.

your name will
appear here

sales tax is
calculated and
appears here

Figure 3-2: Completed order screen

Notice that a message, which contains the amount of sales tax and the salesperson's name (your name), appears in the confirmation notice. The application uses string concatenation, which you will learn about in Lesson B, to display the message.

8 Click the **Exit** button to end the application.

In Lesson A you will learn how to store information, temporarily, in memory locations inside the computer. You will modify the Skate-Away Sales application in Lessons B and C.

LESSON A
objectives

In this lesson you will learn how to:

■ Create a local, form-level, and global variable

■ Assign a data type to a variable

■ Control the scope of a variable

■ Use the Option Explicit statement

■ Create a symbolic constant

Creating Variables and Constants

Using Variables to Store Information

Recall that in the Skate-Away Sales application, all the skateboard information is temporarily stored in the properties of various controls on the form. For example, the number of blue skateboards ordered is stored in the Text property of the txtBlue control, and the number of yellow skateboards ordered is stored in the Text property of the txtYellow control. Also recall that the assignment statement `lblTboards.Caption = Val(txtBlue.Text) + Val(txtYellow.Text)`, which calculates the total skateboards ordered, adds the value stored in the txtBlue control's Text property to the value stored in the txtYellow control's Text property, and then assigns that sum to the Caption property of the lblTboards control. The total price equation, `lblTprice.Caption = Val(lblTboards.Caption) * Val(txtPrice.Text) * (1 + Val(txtRate.Text))`, calculates the total price of the order and assigns the result to the lblTprice control.

Besides storing data in the properties of controls, a programmer can also store data, temporarily, in memory locations inside the computer. These memory locations are called **variables** because the contents of the locations can change as the program is running. It may be helpful to picture a variable as a tiny box inside the computer. You can enter and store data in the box, but you can't actually see the box.

One use for a variable is to hold information that is not stored in a control on the user interface. For example, if the Skate-Away Sales application did not require you to display the total number of skateboards ordered, you could eliminate the lblTboards control from the form and store that information in a variable instead. You would then use the value stored in the variable, instead of the value stored in the Caption property of the lblTboards control, to compute the total price of the order.

You can also assign the properties of controls to variables. For example, you can assign the Text property of a text box to a variable; doing so allows you to control the preciseness of the numbers used in calculations, as you will see in the next section.

Data Types

Each variable (each tiny box in memory) must be assigned a data type by the programmer. The data type determines the type of data the variable (memory location) can store. Figure 3-3 describes the basic data types used in Visual Basic.

Type	Stores	Memory required	Range of values
Byte	Binary numbers	1 byte	0 to 255
Boolean	Logical values	2 bytes	True or False
Currency	Numbers with up to 15 digits to the left of the decimal and 4 digits to the right of the decimal	8 bytes	+/- 9E14
Date	Date and time information	8 bytes	January 1, 100 to December 31, 9999
Double	Floating-point numbers	8 bytes	+/- 5E-324 to 1.8E308
Integer	Integers	2 bytes	-32,768 to 32,767
Long	Integers	4 bytes	+/- 2 billion
Object	Any object reference	4 bytes	N/A
Single	Floating-point numbers	4 bytes	+/- 1E-45 to 3E38
String	Text information	Fixed-length: 1 byte per character Variable-length: 10 bytes + 1 byte per character	Fixed-length: 1 to 65,400 Variable-length: 0 to 2 billion for Windows 95, and 0 to 65,400 for Windows 3.1
Variant	Any of the other data types	With numbers: 16 bytes With characters: 22 bytes + 1 byte per character	Same range as for variable-length string

Figure 3-3: Basic data types in Visual Basic

Notice that Figure 3-3 shows the range of values that each data type can store and the amount of memory required to do so. For instance, variables assigned either the Integer or the Long data type can store **integers**, which are whole numbers—numbers without any decimal places. The differences between the two data types are in the range of numbers each type can store and the amount of memory each type needs to store the numbers. The memory requirement of a data type is an important consideration when coding an application; if you want to optimize an application's code, and thereby conserve system resources, you should use variables with smaller memory requirements wherever possible. For example, although a Long type variable can store numbers in the Integer type range of –32768 to 32767, the Long data type takes twice as much memory to do so. Therefore, it would be more efficient to store a person's age in an Integer variable. You would need to use a Long variable, however, to store the population of a large city.

Figure 3-3 also shows that both the Single type variable and the Double type variable can store a floating-point number. A **floating-point number** is a number that is expressed as a multiple of some power of 10. In Visual Basic, floating-point numbers are written in E (exponential) notation, which is similar to scientific notation. For example, the number 3,200,000 written in E (exponential) notation is 3.2E6; written in scientific notation it is 3.2×10^6. Notice that exponential notation simply replaces "$\times 10^6$" with the letter E followed by the power number—in this case, 6.

Another way of viewing the 3.2E6 is that the positive number after the E indicates how many places to the right to move the decimal point. In this case, E6 says to move the decimal point six places to the right; so 3.2E6 becomes 3,200,000. Moving the decimal point six places to the right is the same as multiplying the number by 10 to the sixth power.

Floating-point numbers can also have a negative number after the E. For example, 3.2E–6 means 3.2 divided by 10 to the sixth power, or .0000032. The negative number after the E tells you how many places to the left to move the decimal point. In this case, E–6 means to move the decimal point six places to the left.

Floating-point numbers, which can be stored in either a Single type variable or a Double type variable, are used to represent both extremely small and extremely large numbers. The differences between the Single type and the Double type are in the range of numbers each type can store and the amount of memory each type needs to store the numbers. Although the Double type can store numbers in the Single type's range, the Double type takes twice as much memory to do so.

The Currency data type listed in Figure 3-3 stores numbers with a fixed decimal point. Unlike floating-point numbers, fixed-point numbers are not expressed as a multiple of some power of 10. For example, the number 32000 expressed in the Single data type is 3.2E4, but that same number expressed in the Currency data type is simply 32000. Calculations involving fixed-point numbers are not subject to the small rounding errors that may occur when floating-point numbers are used. In most cases, these small rounding errors create no problems in the application. One exception, however, is when the application deals with money, where you need accuracy to the penny. In those cases, the Currency data type is the best type to use.

Also listed in Figure 3-3 is the String data type, which can store from one to approximately two billion characters.

WINDOWS 3.1 *The String data type can store 0 to 65,500 characters if you are using Windows 3.1.*

A string, you may remember from Tutorial 2, is a group of characters enclosed in quotation marks. "Desk" and "AB345" are two examples of strings.

Visual Basic Version 4.0 has four data types that are not available in previous versions: Boolean, Date, Object, and Byte. You use the Boolean data type to store the Boolean values True and False. You use the Date data type to store date and time information. The Object data type is used to store object references, and the Byte data type is used to store binary numbers.

The last data type listed in Figure 3-3 is Variant. If you don't assign a specific data type to a variable, Visual Basic assigns the Variant type to it. Unlike other variables, a Variant variable can store many different types of data, and it also can freely change the type of stored data while the program is running. For example, you can store the number 40 in a Variant variable at the beginning of the program and then, later on in the program, store the string "John Smith" in that same variable. Although the Variant data type is the most flexible, in many cases it is less efficient than the other data types. At times it uses more memory than necessary to store a value and, because the application has to determine which type of data is stored currently in the variable, your application will run more slowly.

Assigning an appropriate data type to the variables in a program will make the application run more efficiently. Here are some guidelines to follow when assigning the data type:

- Assign the Integer or Long data type when you are sure that a variable will always contain whole numbers—numbers without decimal places. Which type you choose, Integer or Long, will depend on the size of the numbers you expect to store in the variable.
- Assign either the Single, Double, or Currency data type when you need to store numbers with a decimal fraction. Here again, which type you choose will depend on the size of the numbers you expect to store in the variable and whether the variable will hold money values.
- Assign the String data type if the variable will always contain a string.
- Assign the Boolean data type if the variable will always contain Boolean values (True and False).
- Assign the Date data type if the variable will need to store date and time information.
- Assign the Object data type if the variable will contain a reference to an object.
- Assign the Variant data type if your variable needs to be flexible about the type of data it will store and if you are not concerned with speed and the amount of memory used.

In addition to assigning a data type to the variables used in an application, the programmer must also assign a name to each variable. (You will learn *how* to assign both the data type and name later in this lesson.)

Naming Variables

You should use a descriptive name for each variable; the name should help you remember both the data type and purpose of the variable. One popular naming convention is to have the first two characters in the name represent the data type, and the remainder of the name represent the variable's purpose. Figure 3-4 lists the two characters typically associated with the Visual Basic data types.

Type	ID
Byte	by
Boolean	bl
Currency	cr
Date	dt
Double	db
Integer	in
Long	lg
Object	ob
Single	sg
String	st
Variant	vr

Figure 3-4: Data types and their two-character IDs

It is a common practice to type the two-character ID in lowercase and capitalize the first letter in the part of the name that identifies the purpose. For example, a good name for a variable that contains sales amounts is crSales. Although S could also be used as the name for that variable, notice that it is not as descriptive as the name crSales. In the latter case, the name reminds you that the variable is a currency variable that stores sales amounts.

In addition to being descriptive, the name that a programmer assigns to a variable must follow several specific rules. These rules are listed in Figure 3-5, along with examples of valid and invalid variable names.

Rules for naming variables
1. The name must begin with a letter.
2. The name must contain only letters, numbers, and the underscore. No punctuation characters or spaces are allowed in the name.
3. The name cannot be more than 255 characters long.
4. The name cannot be a reserved word, such as Print, because reserved words have special meaning in Visual Basic.

Valid variable names:	Invalid variable names:	
cr94Sales	94SalesCr	(the name must begin with a letter)
inRegionWest	inRegion West	(the name cannot contain a space)
lgEastPopulation	lgEast.Population	(the name cannot contain punctuation)
stName	Name	(the name cannot be a reserved word)

Figure 3-5: Rules for variable names along with examples of valid and invalid names

In the next section you will learn how to declare (create) a variable in Visual Basic.

Declaring a Variable

You use either the **Dim statement** or the **Public statement** to create, or declare, a variable. (Dim comes from the word "dimension.") Which statement you use will depend on whether you want to create a local, form-level, or global variable. You will learn about local, form-level, and global variables later in this lesson.

Declaring a variable tells Visual Basic to create the variable in memory—in other words, to set aside a tiny section of the computer's internal memory. The syntax of both the Dim statement and the Public statement is identical, with the exception of the keywords Dim and Public—in other words, the Dim statement's syntax is **Dim** *variablename* [**As** *datatype*] and the Public statement's syntax is **Public** *variablename* [**As** *datatype*]. Notice that both statements allow you to assign the name and the data type to the variable you are creating. Although the "**As** *datatype*" part of both statements is optional, as indicated by the brackets in the syntax, you should always assign a specific data type to each variable. If you don't assign a data type, Visual Basic assigns the Variant type, which may not be the most efficient data type. Figure 3-6 shows examples of the Dim and Public statements used to declare (create) variables.

Statement	Explanation
Dim inHours as Integer	Creates an Integer variable named inHours
Dim sgDiscount as Single	Creates a Single variable named sgDiscount
Dim crPrice as Currency	Creates a Currency variable named crPrice
Public stFname as String	Creates a String variable named stFname

Figure 3-6: Examples of both Dim and Public statements

When you declare a variable using one of the numeric data types, Visual Basic automatically stores the number 0 (zero) in the variable. This is referred to as **initializing** the variable—in other words, giving the variable a beginning value. For example, the statement `Dim crSales as Currency` creates a Currency variable named crSales, which Visual Basic initializes to 0. Visual Basic initializes String and Variant variables by assigning a zero-length string to them. (Recall from Tutorial 2 that a zero-length string is called an empty string.) You can use an assignment statement to store other data in the variable, as you will see in the next section.

Storing Data in a Variable

An assignment statement is one way of storing data in a variable. In Tutorial 2 you learned that the format of an assignment statement that assigns a value to an object's property is [*form.*]*object.property* = *value*. Similarly, the format of an assignment statement that stores a value in a variable is *variablename* = *value*. The two instructions, `crSales = 500` and `stName = "Mary"`, are examples of assignment statements that assign values to variables. The `crSales = 500` assignment statement, for example, stores the number 500 in a currency variable named crSales. The `stName = "Mary"` assignment statement stores the string "Mary" (without the quotes) in the stName variable. The number 500 and the string "Mary" are called literal constants. A **literal constant** is simply an item of data whose value does not change while the program is running; 500 is a numeric literal constant and "Mary" is a string literal constant. Notice that you store literal constants in variables. Also notice that string literal constants are enclosed in quotation marks, but numeric literal constants and variable names are not. The quotation marks differentiate a string from both a number and a variable name. In other words, 500 is a number, but "500" is a string; "Mary" is a string, but Mary (without the quotes) would be interpreted by Visual Basic as the name of a variable.

It's easy to confuse literal constants with symbolic constants, which are also available in Visual Basic. **Symbolic constants** are memory locations whose contents cannot be changed while the program is running. To avoid confusing the two types of constants, simply remember that a literal constant is an item of data, whereas a symbolic constant is a memory location that stores an item of data. Unlike variables, which are memory locations whose contents *can* change while the program is running, the contents of a symbolic constant *cannot* change. You will learn more about symbolic constants at the end of this lesson.

It's important to remember that, like an object's property, a variable can store only one item of data at any one time. When you use an assignment statement to assign another item to the variable, the new data replaces the existing data. For example, assume that the Click event procedure for a command button contains the following three lines of code:

```
Dim crSales as Currency
crSales = 500
crSales = crSales * 2
```

When you run the application and click the command button, the three lines of code are processed as follows:

- The Dim statement creates the crSales variable in memory. Here again, you may want to picture the crSales variable as a tiny box inside the computer. Because the crSales variable is a numeric variable, Visual Basic initializes it to 0—in other words, Visual Basic places the number 0 inside the box.
- The crSales = 500 assignment statement removes the zero from the crSales variable and stores the number 500 there instead. The variable (box) now contains the number 500 only.
- The crSales = crSales * 2 assignment statement first multiplies the contents of the crSales variable (500) by the number 2, giving 1000. The assignment statement then removes the number 500 from the crSales variable and stores the number 1000 there instead. Notice that Visual Basic performs the calculation appearing on the right side of the equal sign before assigning the result to the variable whose name appears on the left side.

As you can see, after data is stored in a variable, you can use the data in calculations, just as you can with the data stored in the properties of controls. When you refer to a variable's name, the computer uses the value stored inside the variable.

You now know how to use the Dim and Public statements to declare a variable. Recall that the statements allow you to assign both a name and data type to the variable you are creating. You also know how to use an assignment statement to store data inside a variable. There's just one more thing about variables that you need to learn: in addition to a name and a data type, every variable also has a scope.

The Scope of a Variable

A variable's **scope** indicates which procedures in the application can use the variable. The scope, which can be either global, form-level, or local, is determined by *where* you declare the variable—in other words, where you enter either the Dim or Public statement. You can declare a variable in three places:

- an object's event procedure
- a form's General declarations section
- a code module's General declarations section

(You have not yet seen the General declarations section of either a form or a code module; you will see both in this lesson.)

You use the Dim statement, which you learned earlier, to declare a variable in an object's event procedure. When you declare a variable in an event procedure, only that event procedure can use the variable. For example, if you enter the Dim crSales as Currency statement in a command button's Click event procedure, only that command button's Click event procedure can use the crSales variable. A variable declared in an event procedure is called a **local variable** because its use is limited to only the procedure in which it is declared. No other procedures in the application are allowed to use the variable. Actually, no other procedure in the application will even know that the variable exists. When the event procedure ends, Visual Basic removes the local variable from the computer's memory. Most of the variables in your applications will be local variables.

You also use the Dim statement to declare a variable in a form's General declarations section. When you declare a variable in the General declarations section of a form, all procedures in that form, including the procedures of the controls contained on the form, can use the variable. For example, if you enter the `Dim crSales as Currency` statement in the form's General declarations section, every procedure in the form can use the crSales variable. A variable declared in a form's General declarations section is called a **form-level variable**. Form-level variables remain in memory until the application ends.

You use the Public statement to declare a variable in the General declarations section of a code module. If you declare a variable in a code module's General declarations section, all procedures in every form and control included in the application can use the variable. Variables declared in a code module's General declarations section are called **global variables**. Global variables, which are used in applications containing multiple forms, remain in memory until the application ends.

To recap, you use the Dim statement to declare both local and form-level variables. When creating a local variable, you enter the Dim statement in the event procedure of an object; only the procedure in which the local variable is declared can use the variable. When creating a form-level variable, on the other hand, you enter the Dim statement in the form's General declarations section; all of the procedures in that form, including the procedures of its controls, can use the form-level variable. Last, when creating a global variable, you enter the Public statement in the General declarations of a code module; every procedure in the application can use the global variable.

The difference between local, form-level, and global variables is best illustrated with a few examples. On your Student Disk are two project files that contain examples designed to help clarify the concept of scope. Before looking at those examples, however, you will need to learn about the `Option Explicit` statement.

The Option Explicit Statement

In the previous sections you learned that it is important to declare the variables used in an application; by doing so you have control over their data type. Unfortunately, in Visual Basic you can create variables "on the fly," which means that if your code contains the name of an undeclared variable—a variable that does not appear in either a Dim or a Public statement—Visual Basic creates one for you and assigns the Variant data type to it. Recall that the Variant type is many times not the most efficient data type. Because it is so easy to forget to declare a variable—and so easy to misspell a variable's name while coding, thereby inadvertently creating an undeclared variable—Visual Basic provides a way that will prevent you from using undeclared variables in your code. You simply enter the `Option Explicit` statement in the form's General declarations section. Then if your code contains the name of an undeclared variable, Visual Basic informs you of the error.

tips

▶ You can use the Static statement to create a local variable that retains its value when the procedure ends. You will learn more about the Static statement in Lesson A's Discovery Exercise.

tips

▶ In some instances you may want to create a variable in a code module that can be used by the code module only. In those cases you would use the Dim statement, instead of the Public statement, to declare the variable in the General declarations section of the code module.

tips

▶ If the application includes a code module or more than one form, the `Option Explicit` statement must be entered in the code module's General declarations section and in each form's General declarations section.

tips
. . . .
▶ To have Visual Basic enter the `Option Explicit` statement automatically in every new form and module, click Tools, then click Options. Click the Require Variable Declaration option, which is located on the Environment tab, to turn the option on.

In the next set of steps, you will open the first application designed to help illustrate the concept of scope. You will then enter the `Option Explicit` statement in the form's General declarations section. The `Option Explicit` statement will prevent you from using an undeclared variable in the code.

To enter the `Option Explicit` statement in an application:

1   Start Visual Basic, if necessary, then place your Student Disk in the appropriate drive. Open the **scope1** (scope1.vbp) file, which is located in the Tut03 folder on your Student Disk, then click the **View form** button in the Project window to view the frmSales form.

2   Use the Save File As option on the File menu to save the form as **laScope1**, then use the Save Project As option on the File menu to save the project as **laScope1**.

3   Maximize the form. Figure 3-7 identifies the controls already included in the application.

lblSales

lblCommission

cmd2Comm

cmdDisplay

cmd5Comm

cmdExit

Figure 3-7: The laScope1 user interface

4   Double-click the **Exit** button. The cmdExit control's Click event procedure appears.

Notice that the Exit button already contains the End statement. Before coding the other command buttons, you will enter the `Option Explicit` statement in the form's General declarations section. Recall that the `Option Explicit` statement tells Visual Basic to warn you if your code contains the name of an undeclared variable—a variable that does not appear in either a Dim or Public statement.

5   Click the **Object** list arrow, then scroll the list until you see (General), which is at the top of the list. Click (**General**) in the list. The form's General declarations section appears in the Code window. Type **option explicit** and press the **Enter** key. See Figure 3-8.

tips
. . . .
▶ Each form has its own general declarations section.

form name

**form's General
declarations section**

Figure 3-8: Option Explicit statement entered in the form's General declarations section

When an application is run, Visual Basic automatically processes the instructions entered in the form's General declarations section.

6   Close the Code window.

The current application will give you an opportunity to experiment with local and form-level variables only. Global variables will be shown in another application, which you will open later in this lesson. Begin by creating a local variable.

Creating a Local Variable

Recall that local variables are declared with the Dim statement in the event procedure of an object. In this case, you will create a local Currency variable, named crSales, in the Click event procedure of the Display Sales button (the cmdDisplay control). It is customary to enter the Dim statements at the beginning of the event procedure, immediately below the Private Sub instruction.

To experiment with a local variable:

1   Double-click the **Display Sales** button. The cmdDisplay control's Click event procedure appears in the Code window. Press the **Tab** key, type **dim crSales as currency** and press the **Enter** key. When the application is run, this statement will create and initialize (to zero) a local Currency variable named crSales.

You can now use an assignment statement to store data in the local crSales variable.

2   Type **crSales = 500** and press the **Enter** key. When the application is run, this instruction will assign the number 500 to the local crSales variable; in other words, it will store the literal constant 500 in the memory location named crSales.

Next, use an assignment statement to display the contents of the crSales variable in the lblSales control on the form.

3   Type **lblSales.caption = crSales** and press the **Enter** key. This assignment statement tells Visual Basic to assign the contents of the crSales variable to the Caption property of the lblSales control. See Figure 3-9.

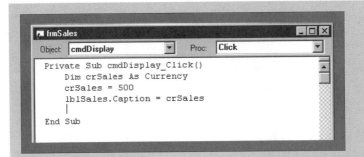

Figure 3-9: Code entered in Display Sales button's Click event procedure

You can now run the application and test the Display Sales button.

4   Close the Code window, restore the form to its standard size, then **save and run** the application.

First Visual Basic processes the `Option Explicit` statement found in the form's General declarations section. Recall that instructions in the form's General declarations section are processed automatically when the application is run.

5   Click the **Display Sales** button.

Following the instructions entered in the button's Click event procedure, Visual Basic first creates and initializes a local variable named crSales. Visual Basic then assigns the literal constant 500 to the crSales variable, and then displays the contents of the crSales variable (500) in the lblSales control. When the Click event procedure ends, which occurs when Visual Basic processes the `End Sub` statement in the procedure's Code window, the local crSales variable is removed from the computer's memory.

6   Click the **Exit** button to end the application. Visual Basic returns to the design screen.

As this example shows, a local variable can be used by the event procedure in which it is declared. Now see if another event procedure can use the local variable. You can do that by coding the Calc 2% Commission button (the cmd2Comm control). The Calc 2% Commission button should calculate a 2% commission on the sales entered in the crSales variable and then display the result in the lblCommission control.

To code the Calc 2% Commission button:

1   Click the **View Code** button in the Project window. Click the Code window's **Object** list arrow, then click **cmd2Comm** in the list. The Code window for the cmd2Comm control's Click event procedure appears.

2   Press the **Tab** key, type **lblCommission.caption = crSales * .02** and press the **Enter** key. This instruction tells Visual Basic to multiply the contents of the crSales variable by .02 (the decimal equivalent of 2%) and then assign the result to the Caption property of the lblCommission control.

   HELP? Recall from Tutorial 2 that, in Visual Basic, you must convert percentages in an equation to their decimal equivalent.

3   Close the Code window, then **save and run** the application. Click the **Display Sales** button, then click the **Calc 2% Commission** button. Visual Basic displays the warning message shown in Figure 3-10.

Figure 3-10: Warning message caused by an undeclared (undefined) variable

4   Click the **OK** button to remove the "Variable not defined" message from the screen. Visual Basic highlights the name of the undefined variable, crSales, in the Code window. (An undefined variable is the same as an undeclared variable.) Notice that the undefined variable is in the cmd2Comm control's Click event procedure. See Figure 3-11.

undefined variable

Figure 3-11: Undefined variable highlighted in the Code window

5   Close the Code window, restore the form to its standard size, then click the **End** button on the toolbar. The application ends and Visual Basic returns to the design screen.

Recall that the `Option Explicit` statement, which you entered in the form's General declarations section, tells Visual Basic to display a warning message if your code contains the name of an undeclared variable. In this case the undeclared variable is the crSales variable appearing in the cmd2Comm control's Click event procedure. At this point you may be thinking "But I did declare the crSales variable." Recall, however, that you declared the crSales variable in the cmdDisplay control's Click event procedure; only the cmdDisplay control's Click event procedure can use that variable. The cmd2Comm control's Click event procedure doesn't know about the crSales variable, so it treats it as an undefined variable. In other words, we have just shown that a local variable can be used only by the event procedure in which it is declared.

Now observe what happens if you declare the same variable in two event procedures. Specifically, you will declare a crSales variable in the cmdDisplay control's Click event procedure and a crSales variable in the cmd2Comm control's Click event procedure. The `Dim crSales as Currency` statement is already in the cmdDisplay control's Click event procedure, so you just need to enter the same statement in the cmd2Comm control's Click event procedure.

To declare a crSales variable in the cmd2Comm control's Click event procedure, then save and run the application:

1   Click the **View Code** button in the Project window, then click the **Object** list arrow. Click **cmd2Comm** in the list. The cmd2Comm control's Click event procedure appears.

2   Position the I-bar Ⅰ after the) in the `Private Sub cmd2Comm_Click ( )` instruction and click at that location, then press the **Enter** key to insert a blank line below the Private Sub instruction.

3   In the blank line below the Private Sub instruction, press the **Tab** key, type **dim crSales as currency** and then close the Code window.

4   **Save and run** the application, then click the **Display Sales** button. The contents of the cmdDisplay control's local crSales variable (500) appears in the lblSales control.

When the Click event procedure ends, the cmdDisplay control's crSales variable is removed from memory. Confirm that by clicking the Calc 2% Commission button, whose Click event procedure contains the `Dim crSales as Currency` instruction and the `lblCommission.Caption = crSales * .02` instruction.

5   Click the **Calc 2% Commission** button. A zero appears in the lblCommission control. The correct commission, however, should be 10 (2% of the $500 sales).

The zero appears because the `Dim crSales as Currency` instruction in the cmd2Comm control's Click event procedure creates and initializes (to zero) its own local crSales variable. The `lblCommission.Caption = crSales * .02` instruction multiplies the contents of the cmd2Comm control's local crSales variable (0) by .02, giving zero, and then assigns the zero to the Caption property of the lblCommission control. When the cmd2Comm control's Click event procedure ends, its local crSales variable is removed from the computer's memory.

6   Click the **Exit** button to end the application. Visual Basic returns to the design screen.

As this example shows, when you use the same name to declare a variable in more than one event procedure, each procedure creates its own local variable. Although the variables have the same name, each refers to a different location (box) in memory.

But what if you want both command buttons to use the same crSales variable? In that case you will need to declare the variable in the form's General declarations section.

Creating a Form-Level Variable

Recall that variables declared in the form's General declarations section are called form-level variables. Form-level variables can be used by every procedure in the form, and they remain in memory until the application ends. Observe what happens when you declare the crSales variable as a form-level variable.

To declare the crSales variable as a form-level variable:

1 Click the **View Code** button in the Project window. The form's General declarations section appears. All form-level variables must be declared in this section of the form.

2 Press ↓ on your keyboard to position the blinking insertion point in the blank line immediately below the Option Explicit statement, then type **dim crSales as currency** and press the **Enter** key.

You will need to remove the Dim crSales as Currency statement from both the cmdDisplay and cmd2Comm controls' Click event procedures, as those Dim statements tell Visual Basic to create two local crSales variables.

3 Use the Code window's Object list box to open the cmd2Comm control's Click event procedure. Highlight only the Dim crSales as Currency statement in the Code window, then press the **Delete** key to remove the highlighted statement from the Code window.

4 Use the Code window's Object list box to open the cmdDisplay control's Click event procedure. Highlight only the Dim crSales as Currency statement in the Code window, then press the **Delete** key to remove the highlighted statement from the Code window.

5 Close the Code window, then **save and run** the application.

Visual Basic processes both the Option Explicit and the Dim crSales as Currency statements, which are in the form's General declarations section. The Dim statement creates and initializes a form-level variable named crSales. Observe what happens when you click the Display Sales button.

6 Click the **Display Sales** button. Visual Basic processes the instructions in the button's Click event procedure. The crSales = 500 instruction stores the number 500 in the form-level crSales variable. The lblSales.Caption = crSales displays the contents of the form-level crSales variable (500) in the lblSales control.

Now see what happens when you click the Calc 2% Commission button.

7 Click the **Calc 2% Commission** button. Visual Basic processes the instructions in the button's Click event procedure. The lblCommission.Caption = crSales * .02 instruction multiplies the contents of the form-level crSales variable (500) by .02, giving 10. The instruction then displays the result (10) in the lblCommission control.

8 Click the **Exit** button to end the application. Visual Basic removes the form-level crSales variable from the computer's memory and then returns to the design screen.

As this example shows, when you declare a form-level variable, every procedure in the form can use the variable.

In this next example, you will see what happens when you declare a variable both as a form-level variable and as a local variable. The Dim crSales as Currency statement is already entered in the form's General declarations section, so you will simply enter the same instruction in the Calc 5% Commission button's Click event procedure.

To see what happens when you declare a variable both as a form-level variable and as a local variable:

1 Click the **View Code** button in the Project window, then use the Code window's Object list box to open the cmd5Comm control's Click event procedure.

2 In the cmd5Comm control's Click event procedure, press the **Tab** key, then type **dim crSales as currency** and press the **Enter** key.

The cmd5Comm control should calculate a 5% commission on the sales.

3 Type **lblCommission.caption = crSales * .05** and press the **Enter** key.

4 Close the Code window, then **save and run** the application.

Recall that when the application is run, the `Dim crSales as Currency` instruction in the form's General declarations section instructs Visual Basic to create and initialize a form-level variable named crSales. The form-level crSales variable remains in memory until the application ends.

5 Click the **Display Sales** button. The `crSales = 500` instruction stores the number 500 in the form-level crSales variable. The `lblSales.Caption = crSales` instruction displays the contents of the form-level crSales variable (500) in the lblSales control.

6 Click the **Calc 2% Commission** button. The `lblCommission.Caption = crSales * .02` instruction multiplies the contents of the form-level crSales variable (500) by .02, giving 10. The instruction then displays the result (10) in the lblCommission control.

7 Click the **Calc 5% Commission** button. A zero appears in the lblCommission control. The zero appears because the `Dim crSales as Currency` instruction in the cmd5Comm control's Click event procedure creates and initializes (to zero) a local variable named crSales. The local crSales variable is different from the form-level crSales variable. The next instruction in the cmd5Comm control's Click event procedure, `lblCommission.Caption = crSales * .05`, multiplies the contents of the local crSales variable (0) by .05, giving 0. The instruction then displays the result (0) in the lblCommission control. When the Click event procedure ends, Visual Basic removes the local crSales variable from the computer's memory. The form-level crSales variable, however, remains in memory, as you will see in the next step.

8 Click the **Calc 2% Commission** button. The number 10, which is the crSales variable multiplied by .02, appears in the lblCommission control.

9 Click the **Exit** button to end the application. Visual Basic removes the form-level crSales variable from the computer's memory and then returns to the design screen.

As this example shows, if you use the same name to declare both a form-level variable and a local variable, the event procedure in which the local variable is declared will use its local variable instead of the form-level variable.

The next example you will view deals with global variables.

Creating a Global Variable

You have probably seen computer programs where the first screen prompts the user to enter his or her name. The name is then used to create personalized messages that are displayed to the user during the program. That type of application typically uses two or more forms: one form simply requests the user to enter his or her name; the remaining forms constitute the program's user interface. The application program you will open in this section will work similarly. It will use one form to request the user's name, then display the name, along with a message, on a second form. When you open the application and look at the code, don't be concerned if you do not understand all of the instructions; you will be learning those instructions in Lessons B and C. For now, just pay attention to *how* and *where* you must declare a variable that will be used by procedures in more than one form.

Important Note: You cannot complete the following steps on the computer if you are using the Working Model. The next section you will be able to do on the computer is the section on Symbolic Constants.

To open the project that contains an example of a global variable, then save the project under a different name:

1 Open the **scope2** (scope2.vbp) file, which is located in the Tut03 folder on your Student Disk. The Project window shows that this application contains two forms, frmName and frmWelcome.

2 Click **FRMNAME.FRM** in the Project window, then use the Save File As option on the File menu to save the frmName form as **laName**.

3 Click **FRMWEL.FRM** in the Project window, then use the Save File As option on the File menu to save the frmWelcome form as **laWel**.

4 Use the Save Project As option on the File menu to save the project as **laScope2**.

5 Click **LANAME.FRM** in the Project window, then click the **View Form** button. The user interface for the frmName form appears.

The frmName user interface contains a text box (txtName) in which the user enters his or her name. The form also contains an OK command button (cmdOK). Look at the code in the OK command button.

6 Open the Code window for the OK button's Click event procedure. See Figure 3-12.

form name

assigns Text property to stName variable

displays frmWelcome form

removes frmName form

Figure 3-12: The OK button's Click event procedure

Don't be concerned that you don't recognize a couple of the instructions; you will learn them in Lesson C.

Basically, the code for the OK button assigns the Text property of the txtName text box to a variable named stName. The code then displays (shows) the frmWelcome form on the screen and removes (unloads) the frmName form from the screen and from memory.

7 Close the Code window, then close the frmName form.

Now look at the code in the frmWelcome form.

8 Click **LAWEL.FRM** in the Project window, then click the **View form** button to view the frmWelcome form. Maximize the frmWelcome form.

The frmWelcome form contains a label control (lblWelcome) that will display a message to the user. The form also contains an image control (imgLogo), as well as a command button (cmdExit) that will end the application. Look at the code in the frmWelcome form's Load event procedure.

9 Double-click the **frmWelcome form** to open its Load event procedure, then maximize the Code window. See Figure 3-13.

form name

string concatenation operator

displays the user's name

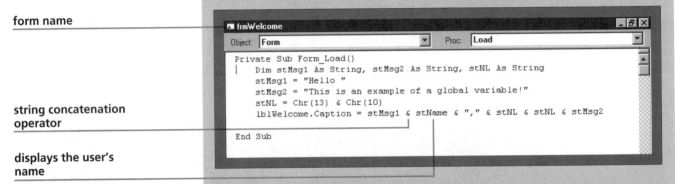

Figure 3-13: The frmWelcome's Load event procedure

The Load event's code uses string concatenation (linking) to display a message, along with the contents of the stName variable, in the lblWelcome control on the frmWelcome form. You will learn how to concatenate strings in Lesson B.

10 Close the Code window, then close the frmWelcome form.

When this application is run, the frmName form, which requests the user's name, will appear on the screen first. When the user enters his or her name and clicks the OK button, the OK button's Click event procedure will store the user's name in the stName variable. The Click event procedure will then both display the frmWelcome form on the screen and remove the frmName form from the screen. The frmWelcome form's Load event procedure will use the stName variable in the welcome message that it displays to the user. In order for both forms to use the stName variable, the variable's scope must be global; that means that you will need to use the Public statement to declare the stName variable in the General declarations of a code module. You will do that in the next section.

An application can contain more than one module, but that is rare.

Adding a Code Module to a Project

A **code module** is a separate file, added to your application, that contains only code; it does not contain any forms or controls. All variables that you want to make available to all forms in the application must be declared in the General declarations section of a code module. In this application, for example, you will declare the stName variable in a code module's General declarations section so that both the frmName and frmWelcome forms can use the variable.

tips

· · · · · · · · · · · · · · · · ·

▶ You can also add a code module to a project by using the Module command on the Insert menu. You can remove a file from a project by clicking the file's name in the Project window, then using the Remove File command on the File menu.

To add a code module to the current project:

1 Click the **Module** button [image] on the toolbar. Visual Basic adds the Module1 file name to the Project window, and the General declarations section of the Module1 module appears on the screen.

If an application contains more than one form and/or module, you must enter the `Option Explicit` statement in each form's General declarations section and in each module's General declarations section.

2 Type **option explicit** and press the **Enter** key.

HELP? If the Require Variable Declaration option is selected on the Environment tab in the Options dialog box, the `Option Explicit` statement may already be entered in the code module's General declarations section.

You can now enter the Public statement that will declare a global variable named stName.

3 Type **public stName as string** and press the **Enter** key. See Figure 3-14.

statement declares a
global variable ─────────────────

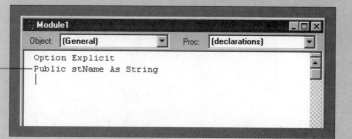

Figure 3-14: Option Explicit and Public statements entered in the code module

Now save the code module under a more descriptive name.

4 Use the Save File As command on the File menu to save the code module as **laModule**, then close the code module's Code window. As the Project window now shows, the code module is saved as LAMODULE.BAS. (The .BAS extension stands for "Basic.")

Whenever you make a change to the information in the Project window, you must be sure to save the project so that the change is saved.

5 Click the **Save Project** button [image] to save the project under its current name.

Now run the application.

6 **Run** the application. When the frmName form appears, type your first name, then press the **Enter** key. The frmWelcome form appears with your name included in the welcome message.

7 Click the **Exit** button to end the application. Visual Basic removes the global stName variable from memory, then returns to the design screen.

Lastly, confirm that the current application will not run properly if you declare the stName variable either as a form-level variable or as a local variable. You can do so by removing the laModule.bas file from the project, and then experiment by placing a `Dim stName as String` statement in an object's event procedure and in the form's General declarations section.

Removing and Adding a File

To remove a file from a project, you first select the file's name in the Project window, then use the Remove File command on the File menu.

tips
....
▶ The Remove File command removes the file from the project only; it does not remove the file from the disk.

To remove the laModule.bas file from the current project, then experiment by entering the Dim instruction in different locations:

1 Click **LAMODULE.BAS** in the Project window. The LAMODULE.BAS file is highlighted in the Project window. Click **File** on the menu bar, then click **Remove File**. Visual Basic removes the laModule.bas file from the Project window.

   HELP? If you inadvertently removed the wrong file, use the Add File command on the File menu to add the file to the project.

Remember, whenever you make a change to the information in the Project window, you must save the project.

2 Click the **Save Project** button 🖫 to save the project under its current name.

3 Click the **LANAME.FRM** name in the Project window, then click the **View Form** button.

First see what happens if you declare the stName variable as a local variable.

4 Open the OK button's Click event procedure, then type **dim stName as string** immediately below the Private Sub instruction. Close the Code window, then **run**, but don't save, the application. When the screen prompts you for your name, type your name and press the **Enter** key. When the "Variable not defined" warning message appears, click the **OK** button.

Notice that the frmWelcome form's Load event procedure does not recognize the local stName variable that you declared in the frmName form.

5 Close the Code window, then click the **End** button ▪ on the toolbar to end the application.

This example shows that the application will not work if the stName variable is declared as a local variable. Next observe what happens if you declare the stName variable as a form-level variable.

6 Open the OK button's Click event procedure and remove the
   `Dim stName as String` instruction.

7 Open the frmName form's General declarations section, then type **dim stName as string** immediately below the `Option Explicit` statement. Close the Code window, then **run**, but don't save, the application. When the screen prompts you for your name, type your name and press the **Enter** key. When the "Variable not defined" warning message appears, click the **OK** button. Notice that the frmWelcome form does not recognize the form-level stName variable that you declared in the frmName form's General declarations section.

8 Close the Code window, then click the **End** button ▪.

This example shows that the application will not work if the stName variable is declared as a form-level variable.

9 Open the frmName form's General declarations section and remove the
   `Dim stName as String` instruction, then close the Code window.

Now add the laModule.bas file, which you created earlier, to the project.

> To add the laModule.bas file to the project, then save and run the application again:
>
> **1** Click **File**, then click **Add File**. Click **laModule.bas** in the list of file names, then click the **Open** button.
>
> *Click File, then click Add File. Click laModule.bas in the list of file names, then click the OK button.*
>
> **2** **Save and run** the application When the screen prompts you for your name, type your name and press the **Enter** key. Your name appears in the message displayed in the lblMessage control. Notice that the application works only when the stName variable is declared as a global variable.
>
> **3** Click the **Exit** button.

Now review what you have learned about local, form-level, and global variables:

- Local variables are declared in an event procedure, and they can be used only by the event procedure in which they are declared. You use the Dim statement to declare local variables.
- If a variable with the same name is declared in more than one event procedure, each event procedure creates and uses its own variable with that name.
- Form-level variables are declared in a form's General declarations section, and they can be used by every event procedure in that form. You use the Dim statement to declare form-level variables. Each form has its own General declarations section.
- If a variable with the same name is declared as a local variable and as a form-level variable, the event procedure declaring the local variable uses the local variable. All other procedures use the form-level variable.
- Global variables are declared in the General declarations section of a code module, and every procedure in every form in the application can use the variable. You use the Public statement to declare global variables.
- If a variable with the same name is declared as a local, form-level, and global variable, the event procedure declaring the local variable uses the local variable; all other procedures in that form use the form-level variable. Procedures that are not affected by local or form-level variables use the global variable.

Next you will learn how to create a symbolic constant.

Symbolic Constants

Recall that Visual Basic has two types of constants, literal and symbolic. A literal constant is a specific value (such as 3) that does not change while a program is running. A **symbolic constant**, on the other hand, is a memory location whose *contents* cannot change while the program is running. Like variables, symbolic constants can be either local, form-level, or global. Local constants are declared in an object's event procedure, form-level constants are declared in a form's General declarations section, and global constants are declared in the General declarations section of a code module.

You create a symbolic constant with Visual Basic's Const statement, whose syntax is [**Public**] **Const** *constname* [**As** *datatype*] = *expression*. In the syntax, *constname* is the name of the symbolic constant and *expression* is the value you want assigned to the symbolic constant. The rules for naming a symbolic constant are the same as for variables, except you precede the symbolic constant's name with the three letters "con", which is short for "constant." Beginning the constant's name with "con" allows you to distinguish the symbolic constants from variables. The *expression* can be a literal constant or another symbolic constant; it can also contain arithmetic and logical operators. The *expression*, however, cannot contain variables or functions (such as Val).

Notice that both "**Public**" and "**As** *datatype*" are optional parts of the syntax. You use the Public keyword when declaring a global constant in the General declarations section of a code module. You use the **As** *datatype* clause to assign a data type to the symbolic constant. If you do not assign a data type, Visual Basic assigns the type that it feels is the most appropriate, which may not be the most efficient type. For example, if you create a symbolic constant for the number 45.6 and you don't assign a data type, Visual Basic assigns the Double data type to it, even though a Single data type is more efficient. Figure 3-15 shows some examples of the Const statement.

Const Statement	
Const conPi as Single = 3.141593	Creates a Single symbolic constant named conPi and assigns the literal constant 3.141593 to it.
Const conMsg as String = "Welcome!"	Creates a String symbolic constant named conMsg and assigns the literal constant "Welcome!" to it.
Const conPrice as Currency = 25	Creates a Currency symbolic constant named conPrice and assigns the literal constant 25 to it.
Public Const conMaxAge as Integer = 65	Creates a global Integer symbolic constant named conMaxAge and assigns the literal constant 65 to it.

Figure 3-15: Examples of the Const statement

Symbolic constants make your program more self-documenting and, therefore, easier to modify because they allow you to use meaningful words in place of values that are less clear. The symbolic constant conPi, for example, is much more meaningful than 3.141593, the numeric value of pi. Once you create the symbolic constant, you can then use the constant's name, instead of its value, in the code. Unlike variables, symbolic constants can't be inadvertently changed while your program is running.

The formula for the area of a circle, $A = \pi r^2$, points out the differences among literal constants, symbolic constants, and variables. Converted into Visual Basic code, the formula is: `sgArea = conPi * sgRadius ^ 2`. SgArea and sgRadius are Single variables, conPi is a symbolic constant, and 2 is a literal constant. The ^ symbol is the exponentiation operator that tells Visual Basic to raise the variable sgRadius to the second power. You will create a symbolic constant for pi in the next application.

To open the project in which you will create a symbolic constant:

1   Open the **symcon** (symcon.vbp) file, which is located in the Tut03 folder on your Student Disk, then click the **View Form** button. The frmArea form appears on the screen.

The frmArea user interface contains a text box (txtRadius), a label control (lblArea), and two command buttons (cmdCalc and cmdExit). The user can enter the radius of a circle in the txtRadius control, then click the Calculate the Area button to calculate and display the area of the circle. The Exit button will end the application.

2   Double-click the **Calculate the Area** button. The cmdCalc control's Click event appears.

3   Enter the Const statement and the assignment statement that calculates the area. Both statements are shown in Figure 3-16.

enter these statements

Figure 3-16: The Calculate the Area button's Click event procedure

The `Const conPi as Single = 3.141593` statement creates the symbolic constant in memory, and assigns the 3.141593 value to it. The `sgArea = conPi * sgRadius ^ 2` statement calculates the area of the circle.

4   Close the Code window. **Run**, but don't save, the application. Type **5** as the radius, then click the **Calculate the Area** button. Visual Basic displays 78.54 as the area of the circle.

5   Click the **Exit** button to end the application.

You have now completed Lesson A. You will use local, form-level, and global variables in the Skate-Away Sales application, which you will modify in Lessons B and C. You can either take a break or complete the end-of-lesson questions and exercises. (When you exit Visual Basic, or when you open another project, you do not need to save the modified symcom application.)

S U M M A R Y

To tell Visual Basic to check for undeclared variables:

- Enter the `Option Explicit` statement in the General declarations section of every form and module in the application.

To create a variable:

- See naming rules in Figure 3-5 and data types listed in Figure 3-3.
- To create a local variable, enter the Dim statement in the event procedure of an object. Its syntax is **Dim** *variablename* [**As** *datatype*].
- To create a form-level variable, enter the Dim statement in a form's General declarations section. Its syntax is **Dim** *variablename* [**As** *datatype*].
- To create a global variable, enter the Public statement in a code module's General declarations section. Its syntax is **Public** *variablename* [**As** *datatype*].

To use an assignment statement to assign data to a variable:

- Use the syntax *variablename* = *value*.

To create a symbolic constant:

- Use the Const statement. Its syntax is [**Public**] **Const** *constname* [**As** *datatype*] = *expression*.
- The rules for naming constants are the same as for variables, except you precede the constant's name with the three letters "con", which is short for "constant."
- Use the Const statement to declare local and form-level constants in an object's event procedure and form's General declarations section, respectively.
- Use the Public Const statement to declare a global constant in the General declarations section of a code module.

Q U E S T I O N S

1. _____ are memory locations in which you store information, temporarily.
   a. Boxes
   b. Forms
   c. Labels
   d. Variables
   e. Variances

2. Which of the following are valid variable names? (You can choose more than one.)
   a. cr94income
   b. crInc 94
   c. crIncome
   d. crInc_94
   e. crIncomeTax

3. Which of the following is the correct data type to use for a variable that will always contain whole numbers in the range 0 to 20,000?
   a. Currency
   b. Integer
   c. Long
   d. Single
   e. Variant

4. Which of the following is the only data type that can store numbers and strings?
   a. Currency
   b. Integer
   c. Long
   d. Single
   e. Variant

5. A variable known only to the procedure in which it is declared is called a(n) _____ variable.
   a. Event
   b. Form-level
   c. Local
   d. Procedure
   e. Protected

6. A data item whose value doesn't change while the program is running is called a _____ .
   a. literal constant
   b. literal variable
   c. symbolic constant
   d. symbolic variable
   e. variable

7. A memory location whose value can change while the program is running is called a _____ .
   a. literal constant
   b. literal variable
   c. symbolic constant
   d. symbolic variable
   e. variable

8. A memory location whose value cannot be changed while the program is running is called a _____ .
   a. literal constant
   b. literal variable
   c. symbolic constant
   d. symbolic variable
   e. variable

E X E R C I S E S

1. Assume your application needs to store an item's name and its price. On a piece of paper, write the appropriate Dim statements to create the necessary variables.

2. Assume your application needs to store the name of an item in inventory and its height and weight. The height may have decimal places; the weight will be whole numbers only. On a piece of paper, write the appropriate Dim statements to create the necessary variables.

3. Assume your application needs to store the name of an inventory item, the number of units in stock at the beginning of the current month, the number of units purchased during the current month, the number of units sold during the current month, and the number of units in stock at the end of the current month. (The number of units is always a whole number that will never be larger than 10000.) On a piece of paper, write the appropriate Dim statements to create the necessary variables.

4. Assume your application needs to store the name and the population of a city. (The population will never be more than 75000.) On a piece of paper, write the appropriate Dim statements to create the necessary variables.

5. Assume your application needs to store the part number of an item and its cost. (An example of a part number for this application is A103.) On a piece of paper, write the appropriate Dim statements to create the necessary variables.

6. Assume your application needs to store a person's name. On a piece of paper, write the appropriate Public statement to create the necessary variable.

7. Assume your application needs to store a person's age. On a piece of paper, write the appropriate Public statement to create the necessary variable.

8. On a piece of paper, write an assignment statement that assigns Miami to an existing variable named stCity.

9. On a piece of paper, write an assignment statement that assigns the part number AB103 to an existing variable named stPartno.

10. On a piece of paper, write the assignment statements that will assign the word Desk to an existing variable named stName, the number 40 to an existing variable named inInstock, and the number 20 to an existing variable named inOnorder.

11. On a piece of paper, write an assignment statement that will add the contents of the crReg1sales variable to the contents of the crReg2sales variable, then assign that sum to an existing variable named crTotalsales.

12. On a piece of paper, write an assignment statement that will multiply the contents of the crSalary variable by the number 1.5, then assign that result to the crSalary variable.

13. Assume a form contains two command buttons: cmdSalary and cmdBonus. Both buttons' Click event procedures need to use the stEmpName variable. On a piece of paper, write the appropriate statement to declare the stEmpName variable. Also write down where you will need to enter the statement and whether the variable is a local, form-level, or global variable.

14. Assume a form contains two command buttons: cmdWest and cmdSouth. The Click event procedure for the cmdWest button needs to use a variable named crWestsales. The Click event procedure for the cmdSouth button needs to use a variable named crSouthsales. Both buttons' Click event procedures need to use the crCompany variable. On a piece of paper, write the appropriate statements to declare the crWestsales variable, the crSouthsales variable, and the crCompany variable. Also write down where you will need to enter each statement and whether each variable is a local, form-level, or global variable.

15. Assume an application contains two forms: frmName and frmDisplay. Both forms need to use a variable named stEmployee. On a piece of paper, write the appropriate statement to declare the stEmployee variable. Also write down where you will need to enter the statement and whether the variable is a local, form-level, or global variable.

16. Assume an application contains two forms: frmRate and frmTax. The frmRate form's Load event procedure needs to use a variable named stState. The Click event procedure for the cmdDisplay control, which is on the frmRate form, also needs to use the stState variable. The Click event procedure for the cmdCalc control, which is on the frmTax form, needs to use a variable named crStateTax. Both the cmdDisplay and cmdCalc controls' Click event procedures need to use a variable named sgStateRate. (Remember that the cmdDisplay control is on the frmRate form and the cmdCalc control is on the frmTax form.) On a piece of paper, write the appropriate statements to declare the stState, crStateTax, sgStateRate variables. Also write down where you will need to enter each statement and whether each variable is a local, form-level, or global variable.

17. On a piece of paper, write the statement to declare a constant named conTaxRate whose value is .05.

18. Assume two procedures in a form need to use a constant named conAge whose value is 21. On a piece of paper, write the statement to declare the constant. Also write down where you will need to enter the statement and whether the constant is a local, form-level, or global constant.

19. Assume two procedures in two forms need to use a constant named conMessage whose value is "Welcome!". On a piece of paper, write the statement to declare the constant. Also write down where you will need to enter the statement and whether the constant is a local, form-level, or global constant.

Exercise 20 is a Discovery Exercise. Discovery Exercises, which may include topics that are not covered in the tutorial, allow you to "discover" the solutions to problems on your own.

discovery ▶

20. In this exercise you will see the effect of declaring a Static variable.
   a. Open the static (static.vbp) project, which is located in the Tut03 folder on your Student Disk. View the form. The project is supposed to count the number of times you press the Count button, but it is not working correctly.
   b. Run, but don't save, the project. Click the Count button. The message tells you that you have pressed the Count button 1 time, which is correct.
   c. Click the Count button again. Notice that the message still says that you have pressed the Count button 1 time; it should say that you have pressed the button 2 times.
   d. Click the Count button several more times. Notice that the number of times remains at 1.
   e. Click the Exit button to end the application.
   f. Open the Count button's Code window to view its Click event procedure. The procedure first declares a local variable named inCounter. It then adds 1 to the inCounter variable, and then displays the variable's value in the lblCounter control on the form.
   g. Change the `Dim inCounter as Integer` instruction to `Static inCounter as Integer`, then close the Code window.
   h. Run, but don't save, the application.
   i. Click the Count button several times. The message now tells you that you have pressed the Count button 1 time, 2 times, 3 times, and so on.
   j. Click the Exit button to end the application.
   k. Use the Help menu to display the Static statement's Help window. Then write a one-paragraph summary explaining the difference between using the Dim statement to declare a local variable and using the Static statement to declare a local variable. (You do not need to save the modified static application.)

In this lesson you will learn how to:

- Explore the Environment and Editor tabs on the Options dialog box
- Use local and form-level variables in an application
- Concatenate strings
- Use the InputBox function
- Define the Newline character
- Set the default button for a form

Modifying the Skate-Away Sales Application

Storing Information Using Local and Form-Level Variables

Recall that Mr. Cousard, the manager of Skate-Away Sales, called to tell you that the company now wants to include a message on each confirmation notice. The message should say "Thank you for your order. The sales tax was," followed by the sales tax amount and the name of the salesperson who recorded the order. You will need to modify the application's code to accommodate this change.

When making modifications to existing code, you should review the application's documentation and revise the necessary documents. In this case, you will need to revise the TOE chart and the pseudocode for the Calculate Order button, which is responsible for making the application's calculations. The revised TOE chart for the Skate-Away Sales application is shown in Figure 3-17. You will see the revised pseudocode for the Calculate Order button later on in this lesson.

Task	Object	Event
1. Calculate the total skateboards ordered and the total price 2. Display the total skateboards ordered and the total price in the lblTboards and lblTprice objects. 3. Calculate the sales tax. 4. Display the message, the sales tax, and the salesperson's name in the lblMsg object.	cmdCalc	Click
Clear the screen for the next order	cmdClear	Click
End the application	cmdExit	Click
Print the confirmation notice	cmdPrint	Click
Display the total skateboards ordered	lblTboards	None
Display the total price	lblTprice	None
Get and display the order information	txtName, txtAddress, txtCity, txtState, txtZip, txtPrice, txtRate, txtBlue, txtYellow	None
Get the salesperson's name	frmOrder	Load
Display the message, the sales tax, and the salesperson's name.	lblMsg	None

new tasks (pointing to tasks 3 and 4)

new tasks (pointing to "Get the salesperson's name" and "Display the message...")

Figure 3-17: Revised TOE chart for the Skate-Away Sales application

If you compare the revised TOE chart with the original TOE chart shown in Tutorial 2's Figure 2-11, you will notice that the cmdCalc control now has two more tasks. It must calculate the sales tax and also display the message, sales tax, and salesperson's name in the lblMsg control. Two additional objects and events are also included in the revised TOE chart. The frmOrder form's Load event is responsible for getting the salesperson's name when the application is run. The lblMsg control will display the message, sales tax, and salesperson's name. According to the revised TOE chart, you will need to change the code in the cmdCalc control's Click event procedure, and you will also need to code the form's Load event procedure. The lblMsg control, which shows None in the event procedure, does not need to be coded; the control will get its value from the cmdCalc control.

Before you can begin modifying the code, you will need to open the Skate-Away Sales application.

To open the Skate-Away Sales application, then save the files under a new name:

1 Start Visual Basic, if necessary, and make sure your Student Disk is in the appropriate drive.

2 Open the **t3case** (t3case.vbp) file, which is located in the Tut03 folder on your Student Disk, then click the **View form** button in the Project window to view the frmOrder form.

3 Use the Save File As option on the File menu to save the form as **lbOrder**, then use the Save Project As option on the File menu to save the project as **lbOrder**.

4 Maximize the form. Figure 3-18 identifies the controls already included in the application. (You won't see the names of the controls on your screen, except for the lblMsg control's name. The names are included in Figure 3-18 for your reference only.)

txtState

new control added to form

cmdPrint

cmdCalc

cmdClear

cmdExit

Figure 3-18: Skate-Away Sales user interface

You will notice that one minor modification was made to the user interface that you created in Tutorial 2. Specifically, the interface now contains a label control named lblMsg. You will use that control to display the "Thank you" message that contains both the sales tax amount and the name of the salesperson. The lblMsg control's font size is set to 10 points to match the other controls in the interface, and its BackStyle property is set to 0-Transparent.

5   Click the **lblMsg** control, then display the Properties window and delete the contents of its Caption property.

> **HELP?** To delete the contents of the Caption property, double-click Caption in the Properties list. Visual Basic highlights the contents of the Caption property in the Settings box. Press the Delete key to delete the highlighted caption.

6   Restore the form to its standard size.

Besides the minor modification to the user interface, one additional line of code was included in the Clear Screen button's Click event procedure. The Click event now contains an instruction that will remove the "Thank you" message from the lblMsg control when the user clicks the Clear Screen button. You will view this instruction in the next section.

The Options Dialog Box

Visual Basic provides two ways of viewing an application's code. You can view the code one procedure at a time in the Code window, as you have been doing, or you can view the code as a single scrollable listing. To view the code as a single scrollable listing, you will need to use the Tools menu to open the Options Dialog box.

To open the Options Dialog box:

1   Click **Tools** on the menu bar, then click **Options**. The Options dialog box appears.

2   The first tab in the dialog box is the Environment tab, as shown in Figure 3-19. (If you are using Windows 3.1, your Environment tab will look slightly different from Figure 3-19.)

> **HELP?** Don't be concerned if you have different options selected on your Environment tab.

Figure 3-19: Environment tab in the Options dialog box

You use the Environment tab to specify the characteristics of your Visual Basic design environment. For example, the Environment tab contains options that allow you to control the appearance of the form grid. The form grid refers to the dots that appear in the user interface during design time. In a typical Visual Basic environment, the "Show Grid" and "Align Controls to Grid" check boxes are checked, which means that the options are selected.

The Environment tab also allows you to control which windows, if any, you want displayed frontmost on the desktop when the window is visible. In the figure, the four check boxes are unchecked, which means that the options are not selected.

The Environment tab also provides three option buttons that determine whether Visual Basic automatically saves all files before running the application. In the figure the "Save Before Run, Prompt" option is selected, which means that Visual Basic will prompt you to save the application's files before the application is run; but only if the files have changed since the last time you saved them. If the "Don't Save Before Run" option is selected, then Visual Basic will run the files without saving them and without prompting you to save them. If the "Save Before Run, Don't Prompt" option is selected, then Visual Basic will automatically save the files, without prompting you, before running them; again, only if the files were changed since the last time you saved them.

The last three check boxes in the Environment tab are "Show ToolTips," "Require Variable Declaration," and "Auto Syntax Check." When the "Show ToolTips" check box is selected, as it is in Figure 3-19, ToolTips appear when the mouse rests on a button in either the toolbar or the toolbox. When the "Require Variable Declaration" check box is selected, Visual Basic automatically inserts the Option Explicit statement in the General declarations section of *new* forms and *new* modules; it does not, however, insert the Option Explicit statement in existing forms and modules. In Figure 3-19, the "Require Variable Declaration" option is unchecked, which is the default when you install Visual Basic. Last, when the "Auto Syntax Check" check box is selected, as it is in Figure 3-19, Visual Basic verifies, automatically, the syntax of each line of code immediately after it is entered.

Next look at the Editor tab's options.

To view the Editor tab's options:

1 Click the **Editor** tab in the Options dialog box. The Editor tab of the Options dialog box appears as shown in Figure 3-20. (If you are using Windows 3.1, your Editor tab will look slightly different from Figure 3-20.)

HELP? Don't be concerned if the options on your screen have different settings.

Figure 3-20: Editor tab in the Options dialog box

You can use the Editor tab to control the appearance of your Visual Basic code. For example, the tab contains a Font list box and a Size list box, which allow you to change the font type and font size, respectively, of the text used in the Code windows. The tab also contains a Code Colors list box that lists the various text elements found in a Code window—such as Code Window Text, Comment Text, Keyword Text, and Identifier Text. The Foreground and Background list boxes allow you to change the color of the text element selected in the Code Colors list box. A Sample box, which is located in the bottom right corner, displays a sample of the type, size, and color of the font you've chosen.

In the next set of steps, you will change the size of the font used in the Code windows to 8 points, which is slightly smaller than the current value of 10 points. You will also change the color of the Identifier Text, which is most of the code itself, to red.

To change both the size of the font and the color of the code used in the Code windows:

1 Click the **Size** list arrow, then scroll the list and click **8**. The text in the Sample box appears in the new size.

HELP? If you don't have a size 8, then select another size. Just be sure it is different from the default size.

2 Click **Identifier Text** in the Code Colors list box. If you have a color monitor, click the **Foreground** list arrow to display the color palette, then click a **red rectangle** in the color palette. The text in the Sample box appears in red.

The Editor tab also contains an Auto Indent check box. When selected, the Auto Indent check box allows you to tab the first line of code and have all subsequent lines start at that tab location. You can use the Tab Width text box, which is located immediately above the Auto Indent check box, to change the tab width from its default of 4 spaces.

Last, notice that the Editor tab also contains a Full Module View check box, which is unchecked, and a Procedure Separator check box, which is checked but dimmed. When the Full Module View check box is unchecked, as it is in Figure 3-20, Visual Basic displays each event procedure in a separate Code window. When the Full Module View is checked, on the other hand, the event procedures appear as a single scrollable listing. Selecting the Full Module View check box activates the Procedure Separator check box, as you will see in this next set of steps.

To view the code as a single scrollable listing:

1 Click **Full Module View** in the Editor tab. A check mark (*an X in Windows 3.1*) appears in the Full Module View check box, and the Procedure Separator check box darkens to indicate that it is now active. When the Procedure Separator check box is selected, which is the default, Visual Basic displays a line between each procedure in the listing. When the Procedure Separator check box is not selected, on the other hand, blank lines separate the procedures in the listing.

Now open the Code window and see how the changes you made in the Editor tab affect the code.

2 Click the **OK** button both to save the changes and to close the Options dialog box.

3 Click the **View Code** button in the Project window, then maximize the Code window. The application's code appears as a scrollable listing, as shown in Figure 3-21. Notice that a line separates one procedure from another.

   HELP? Don't be concerned if your screen does not match the figure exactly. The amount of code you see will depend on the font size you selected in the Editor tab and also on your monitor.

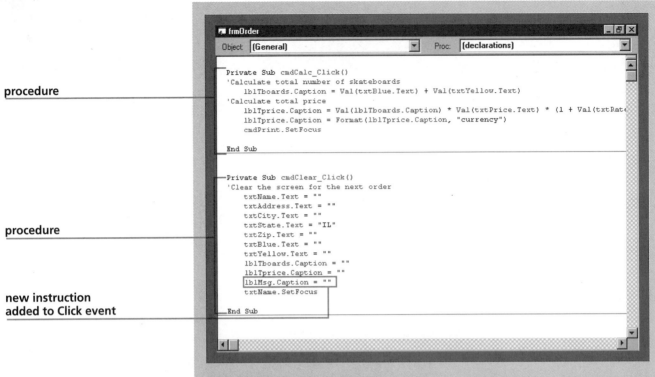

procedure

procedure

new instruction
added to Click event

Figure 3-21: Code shown in a scrollable listing

As Figure 3-21 shows, the new instruction in the Clear Screen button's Click event procedure is the `lblMsg.Caption = ""` instruction. This instruction, you may remember from Tutorial 2, tells Visual Basic to clear the contents of the lblMsg control by assigning the empty string to its Caption property.

4   Scroll the window until you reach the end of the listing. While scrolling, notice that only four procedures contain code: the Click event procedures for the cmdCalc, cmdClear, cmdExit, and cmdPrint controls.

5   Close the Code window.

Some programmers prefer to code the entire application using the Full Module View, while others prefer to use it only when editing the existing code; it's really a matter of preference. If you do use the Full Module View, you can use the Object and Proc list boxes, located at the top of the window, to select the appropriate object and event procedure. For most people, it is less confusing to write the code and perform the edits in the individual event procedure windows. By viewing each procedure in its own window, you will be less likely to enter instructions, inadvertently, in the wrong procedure; you also will be less likely to erase code inadvertently.

To set the Editor tab options to their original values:

1   Click **Tools** on the menu bar, then click **Options** to open the Options dialog box. Click the **Editor** tab, then click **Full Module View**. Visual Basic removes the check mark (*the X in Windows 3.1*) from the Full Module View check box and dims the Procedure Separator check box.

2   Change the font size back to its default value, **10** points.

3 Click **Identifier Text** in the Code Colors list box, then click the **Foreground** list arrow. Scroll the color palette until you see Automatic, which is at the top of the palette, then click **Automatic** in the color palette.

4 Click the **OK** button to both save the Editor tab changes and close the Options dialog box.

5 Click the **View Code** button in the Project window. The form's General declarations section appears in its own Code window.

Now begin modifying the Skate-Away Sales application so that it prints the sales tax amount on the order.

Modifying the Calculate Order Button's Code

Currently, the Calculate Order button calculates the sales tax in the total price equation. Recall that the total price equation from Tutorial 2 is `lblTprice.Caption = Val(lblTboards.Caption) * Val(txtPrice.Text) * (1 + Val(txtRate.Text))`. Because Skate-Away Sales now wants the sales tax amount to print on the order, you will need to include, in the Calculate Order button's code, a separate equation for the sales tax. In this lesson, you will remove the Calculate Order button's code, which you entered in Tutorial 2, and then recode the entire button—this time, however, you will use variables instead of control properties in the equations. As you learned in Lesson A, when an application uses variables, you should enter the `Option Explicit` statement in the form's General declarations section. Adding that statement to the application prevents you from inadvertently using an undeclared variable in the code.

To enter the `Option Explicit` statement in the form's General declarations section:

1 The form's General declarations section should be open. Type **option explicit** and press the **Enter** key.

Recall that before making changes to existing code, you should review the application's documentation and revise the necessary documents. You've already seen the revised TOE chart for the Skate-Away Sales application in Figure 3-17. Figure 3-22 shows the revised pseudocode for the Calculate Order button.

Calculate Order button
1. Declare variables
2. Assign values to variables
3. Calculate total skateboards = blue skateboards + yellow skateboards
4. Calculate subtotal = total skateboards * skateboard price
5. Calculate sales tax = subtotal * sales tax rate
6. Calculate total price = subtotal + sales tax
7. Display total skateboards and total price in lblTboards and lblTprice label controls
8. Display the "Thank you" message, sales tax, and salesperson's name in the lblMsg control
9. Send the focus to the Print Order button

Figure 3-22: Revised pseudocode for the Calculate Order button

If you compare the revised pseudocode with the original pseudocode shown in Tutorial 2's Figure 2-31, you will notice that the Calculate Order button will now make two additional calculations: a subtotal and the sales tax. The subtotal is computed by multiplying the total skateboards by the skateboard price. The sales tax is computed by multiplying the subtotal by the sales tax rate. The button will also display the "Thank you" message, the sales tax, and the salesperson's name in the lblMsg control.

First review, then remove, the code contained in the Calculate Order button's Click event procedure.

To review, then remove, the code in the Calculate Order button's Click event procedure:

1   Use the Code window's Object list box to open the cmdCalc control's Click event procedure, then maximize the Code window. The Click event procedure fills the screen.

The equations that calculate the total skateboards and the total price use the following six properties: txtBlue.Text, txtYellow.Text, lblTboards.Caption, txtPrice.Text, txtRate.Text, and lblTprice.Caption. The Val function in the equations is necessary because the Caption and Text properties of controls are treated as strings, not numbers. As you learned in Tutorial 2, the Val function returns the numeric equivalent of a string. What you didn't learn in Tutorial 2, however, is that the Val function returns a Double data type number. Therefore, the total skateboard equation first converts the contents of both the txtBlue.Text and txtYellow.Text properties to Double type numbers, then adds the Double numbers together and assigns the sum to the lblTboards control. Because a customer can order only a whole number of blue and yellow skateboards and, based on past sales, the number of skateboards ordered is typically under 1000 for each color, it would be more efficient to store the blue and yellow skateboard information in Integer variables. An Integer variable, you may remember, can store whole numbers between −32,768 and 32,767. As you learned in Lesson A, it is always more efficient to use a smaller data type wherever possible. By assigning the Text and Caption properties to variables, you can control the data type of the numbers used in the equations. In this case you will assign the Text and Caption properties of the controls to two Integer variables (inBlue and inYellow), one Currency variable (crPrice), and one Single variable (sgRate). You will assign the result of the total skateboard equation to an Integer variable (inTboards), and assign the result of the total price equation to a Currency variable (crTprice.) Additionally, you will store the subtotal and the sales tax in two Currency variables (crSubtotal and crStax). Figure 3-23 lists the variables and what you will assign to each.

Variable:	Assign:
inBlue	Value of txtBlue.Text
inYellow	Value of txtYellow.Text
inTboards	Sum of inBlue + inYellow
crPrice	Value of txtPrice.Text
sgRate	Value of txtRate.Text
crSubtotal	Product of inTboards * crPrice
crStax	Product of crSubtotal * sgRate
crTprice	Sum of crSubtotal + crTax

Figure 3-23: List of variables and what you will assign to each

Now remove the existing code from the Code window.

2　Highlight all of the instructions between the Private Sub and the End Sub instructions, as shown in Figure 3-24. Be sure that you don't highlight the Private Sub and End Sub instructions.

highlight only these instructions

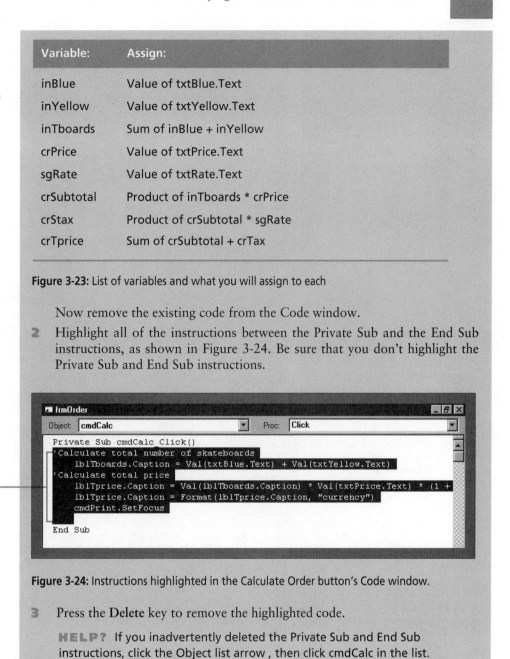

```
Private Sub cmdCalc Click()
'Calculate total number of skateboards
    lblTboards.Caption = Val(txtBlue.Text) + Val(txtYellow.Text)
'Calculate total price
    lblTprice.Caption = Val(lblTboards.Caption) * Val(txtPrice.Text) * (1 +
    lblTprice.Caption = Format(lblTprice.Caption, "currency")
    cmdPrint.SetFocus

End Sub
```

Figure 3-24: Instructions highlighted in the Calculate Order button's Code window.

3　Press the **Delete** key to remove the highlighted code.

HELP? If you inadvertently deleted the Private Sub and End Sub instructions, click the Object list arrow , then click cmdCalc in the list.

The first step listed in the pseudocode shown in Figure 3-22 is to declare the variables. Because only the Calculate Order button's Click event procedure will need to use the eight variables listed in Figure 3-23, you will declare all eight variables as local variables.

To begin coding the Calculate Order button's Click event procedure:

1   Enter the three Dim statements shown in Figure 3-25.

enter these
instructions

```
frmOrder                                                          _ 8 X
Object:  cmdCalc              ▼       Proc:  Click               ▼
Private Sub cmdCalc_Click()
    ┌ Dim inBlue As Integer, inYellow As Integer, inTboards As Integer
    │ Dim crPrice As Currency, sgRate As Single, crTprice As Currency
    └ Dim crSubtotal As Currency, crStax As Currency

End Sub
```

Figure 3-25: Dim statements entered in the Code window

tips

In the Dim statement, type the variable names using the exact capitalization you want. Then, any time you want to refer to the variables in the code, you can enter their names using any case and Visual Basic will adjust the name to match the case used in the Dim statement.

Notice that you can declare more than one variable in a Dim statement, but you must be sure to specify each variable's data type. If you leave a data type off of a variable's declaration, Visual Basic assigns the Variant data type to the variable.

The next step in the pseudocode is to assign values to the variables. The inBlue, inYellow, crPrice, and sgRate variables will get their values from the txtBlue, txtYellow, txtPrice, and txtRate text boxes. The remaining variables will get their values from the equations that calculate the total skateboards, subtotal, sales tax, and total price.

2   Enter the one line of documentation and the four assignment statements shown in Figure 3-26.

enter these instructions

```
frmOrder                                                          _ 8 X
Object:  cmdCalc              ▼       Proc:  Click               ▼
Private Sub cmdCalc_Click()
    Dim inBlue As Integer, inYellow As Integer, inTboards As Integer
    Dim crPrice As Currency, sgRate As Single, crTprice As Currency
    Dim crSubtotal As Currency, crStax As Currency
┌ 'Assign values to variables
│   inBlue = Val(txtBlue.Text)
│   inYellow = Val(txtYellow.Text)
│   crPrice = Val(txtPrice.Text)
└   sgRate = Val(txtRate.Text)

End Sub
```

Figure 3-26: Documentation and assignment statements in Code window

The `inBlue = Val(txtBlue.Text)` and `inYellow = Val(txtYellow.Text)` statements first convert the contents of the txtBlue and txtYellow text boxes to Double type numbers. The statements then store the numbers, as integers, in the inBlue and inYellow variables, respectively. Notice that Visual Basic changes the Double type numbers to integers before storing them in the Integer variables. Similarly, the `crPrice = Val(txtPrice.Text)` and `sgRate = Val(txtRate.Text)` statements first convert the values in the Text properties of the txtPrice and txtRate controls to Double type numbers. These statements then store the numbers in the crPrice and sgRate variables, respectively. The number in the crPrice variable is stored as a Currency data type; the number in the sgRate variable is stored as a Single data type.

The next step in the pseudocode is to calculate the total number of skateboards by adding the number of blue skateboards to the number of yellow skateboards. When entering the equation, you will use the variables instead of the control properties that you used in Tutorial 2's equation. In other words, you will enter `inTboards = inBlue + inYellow`, instead of `lblTboards.Caption = Val(txtBlue.Text) + Val(txtYellow.Text)`. Notice how, in addition to allowing you to control the preciseness of the numbers used in the calculations, variables also make the lines of code much shorter and easier to understand.

3 Press the **Backspace** key to remove the indentation in the Code window, then type **'Perform calculations** and press the **Enter** key. Press the **Tab** key, then type **inTboards = inBlue + inYellow** and press the **Enter** key.

The next steps in the pseudocode are to calculate the subtotal, sales tax, and total price. You calculate the subtotal by multiplying the number of skateboards ordered, which is stored in the inTboards variable, by the skateboard price, which is stored in the crPrice variable.

4 Type **crSubtotal = inTboards * crPrice** and press the **Enter** key.

You calculate the sales tax by multiplying the subtotal, which is stored in the crSubtotal variable, by the sales tax rate, which is stored in the sgRate variable.

5 Type **crStax = crSubtotal * sgRate** and press the **Enter** key.

To calculate the total price, you simply add the sales tax to the subtotal. The subtotal is stored in the crSubtotal variable, and the sales tax is stored in the crStax variable.

6 Type **crTprice = crSubtotal + crStax** and press the **Enter** key.

The next step in the pseudocode is to display the total skateboards and the total price, formatted as currency, in the appropriate label controls on the form. As you did in Tutorial 2, you will use the Format function to format the total price as currency, which will display a dollar sign ($) and two decimal places.

7 Press the **Backspace** key, then type **'Display variable values in controls** and press the **Enter** key.

8 Press the **Tab** key. Type **lblTboards.caption = inTboards** and press the **Enter** key, then type **lblTprice.caption = format(crTprice, "currency")** and press the **Enter** key.

The next step in the pseudocode is to display the "Thank you" message, sales tax, and salesperson's name in the lblMsg control. For now, just display the sales tax so you can verify that the sales tax equation is working correctly. You'll use the Format function to display the sales tax in the currency format—in other words, with a dollar sign and two decimal places.

9   Type **lblMsg.caption = format(crStax, "currency")** and press the **Enter** key.

The last step in the pseudocode is to send the focus to the Print Order button. You can use the SetFocus method to do so.

10   Type **cmdPrint.setfocus** and press the **Enter** key.

11   Compare your code to the code shown in Figure 3-27. Make any necessary corrections before continuing.

```
frmOrder                                                              _ □ ×
Object:  cmdCalc                      ▼        Proc:  Click                   ▼
    Private Sub cmdCalc_Click()
        Dim inBlue As Integer, inYellow As Integer, inTboards As Integer
        Dim crPrice As Currency, sgRate As Single, crTprice As Currency
        Dim crSubtotal As Currency, crStax As Currency
    'Assign values to variables
        inBlue = Val(txtBlue.Text)
        inYellow = Val(txtYellow.Text)
        crPrice = Val(txtPrice.Text)
        sgRate = Val(txtRate.Text)
    'Perform calculations
        inTboards = inBlue + inYellow
        crSubtotal = inTboards * crPrice
        crStax = crSubtotal * sgRate
        crTprice = crSubtotal + crStax
    'Display variable values in controls
        lblTboards.Caption = inTboards
        lblTprice.Caption = Format(crTprice, "currency")
        lblMsg.Caption = Format(crStax, "currency")
        cmdPrint.SetFocus

    End Sub
```

Figure 3-27: Calculate Order button's Click event procedure

Now save and run the application to test the code you've entered so far.

To test the code in the Calculate Order button's Click event:

1   Close the Code window, then **save and run** the application. Enter the following order:

blue skateboards ordered	10	skateboard price	100
yellow skateboards ordered	10	sales tax rate	.05

2   Click the **Calculate Order** button. Visual Basic displays the total number of skateboards ordered in the lblTboards control, the total price in the lblTprice control, the sales tax in the lblMsg control, then sends the focus to the Print Order button, as shown in Figure 3-28.

sales tax displayed in lblMsg control

focus is on Print Order button

Figure 3-28: Order screen showing sales tax

3   Click the **Exit** button. Visual Basic returns to the design screen.

In addition to displaying the sales tax, the lblMsg control must also display the message "Thank you for your order. Your sales tax was " and the name of the salesperson. To accomplish that task, you will need to learn how to concatenate (link together) strings.

Concatenating Strings

Connecting (or linking) strings together is called **concatenating**. In Visual Basic, you concatenate strings with the **concatenation operator**—the ampersand (&). Figure 3-29 shows some examples of string concatenation. Notice that you can also concatenate a number with a string. In those cases, Visual Basic treats the number as if it were a string.

Assume you have the following variables:		
Variables	**Data Type**	**Contents**
stFname	String	Sue
stLname	String	Chen
inAge	Integer	21

Using the above variables:	
This concatenated string:	**Would result in:**
stFname & stLname	SueChen
stFname & " " & stLname	Sue Chen
stLname & ", " & stFname	Chen, Sue
"She is " & inAge & "!"	She is 21!

Figure 3-29: Examples of string concatenation

tips

You can also use the plus sign (+) to concatenate strings. To avoid confusion, however, you should use the plus sign for addition and the ampersand for concatenation.

When concatenating strings, you must be sure to include a space before and after the concatenation operator—the ampersand (&). If you do not enter a space before and after the ampersand, Visual Basic will not recognize the ampersand as the concatenation operator.

You will use the concatenation operator to link the string "Thank you for your order. The sales tax was " to the sales tax stored in the crStax variable, and then concatenate the sales tax to a period, which will mark the end of the sentence. Using the examples shown in Figure 3-29 as a guide, the correct syntax for the lblMsg control's assignment statement would be `lblMsg.Caption = "Thank you for your order. The sales tax was " & Format(crStax, "currency") & ".".` However, to make that assignment statement shorter and easier to understand, you will first create a symbolic constant for the "Thank you" message, and then use that symbolic constant, instead of the long message, in the assignment statement.

You may be wondering why we are using a symbolic constant for the message instead of a variable, which would work just as well. Unlike the number of blue and yellow skateboards ordered, the "Thank you" message will never change as the program is running. Assigning the message to a constant reminds us of that fact in the future.

To create a symbolic constant, then concatenate that symbolic constant to the sales tax variable:

1 Click the **View Code** button in the Project window, then use the Object list box to open the cmdCalc control's Click event procedure.

2 Maximize the Code window. Insert a blank line below the last Dim statement, then type **const conMsg as string = "Thank you for your order. The sales tax was "** in the blank line. Be sure to include a space between the last letter s and the last quotation mark. You are including the space so that a space prints between the message and the sales tax amount. (You can look ahead to Figure 3-30 to see the end result.)

You can now concatenate the conMsg symbolic constant, the crStax variable, and a period to end the sentence.

3 Change the `lblMsg.Caption = Format(crStax, "currency")` assignment statement as shown in Figure 3-30.

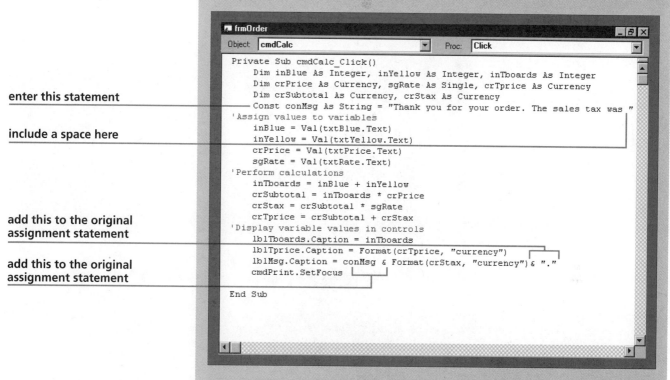

enter this statement

include a space here

add this to the original assignment statement

add this to the original assignment statement

```
frmOrder                                              _ 8 X
Object:  cmdCalc                    ▼    Proc:  Click                        ▼
Private Sub cmdCalc_Click()
    Dim inBlue As Integer, inYellow As Integer, inTboards As Integer
    Dim crPrice As Currency, sgRate As Single, crTprice As Currency
    Dim crSubtotal As Currency, crStax As Currency
    Const conMsg As String = "Thank you for your order. The sales tax was "
'Assign values to variables
    inBlue = Val(txtBlue.Text)
    inYellow = Val(txtYellow.Text)
    crPrice = Val(txtPrice.Text)
    sgRate = Val(txtRate.Text)
'Perform calculations
    inTboards = inBlue + inYellow
    crSubtotal = inTboards * crPrice
    crStax = crSubtotal * sgRate
    crTprice = crSubtotal + crStax
'Display variable values in controls
    lblTboards.Caption = inTboards
    lblTprice.Caption = Format(crTprice, "currency")
    lblMsg.Caption = conMsg & Format(crStax, "currency") & "."
    cmdPrint.SetFocus

End Sub
```

Figure 3-30: Const statement and modified assignment statement entered in the Code window

Now save and run the application to test the code you've entered so far.

4 Close the Code window, then **save and run** the application. Enter the following order:

blue skateboards ordered	10	skateboard price	100
yellow skateboards ordered	10	sales tax rate	.05

5 Click the **Calculate Order** button. Visual Basic displays the total number of skateboards ordered, the total price, and the message, including the sales tax, as shown in Figure 3-31.

message and sales tax
displayed in lblMsg
control

Skate-Away Sales

Skate-Away Sales Order Form

Name:

Address

City:

State: IL   Zip:

Blue skateboards ordered: 10

Yellow skateboards ordered: 10

Price: 100

Sales tax rate: .05

Total skateboards: 20

Total price: $2,100.00

Thank you for your order. The
sales tax was $100.00.

Calculate Order   Print Order   Clear Screen   Exit

Figure 3-31: Order screen showing message and sales tax.

6 Click the **Exit** button. Visual Basic returns to the design screen.

Now that you have the message and the sales tax displaying correctly in the lblMsg control, you just need to get the salesperson's name and then concatenate it to the end of the message. Recall from the revised TOE chart shown in Figure 3-17, the form's Load event procedure is responsible for getting the salesperson's name. You can use Visual Basic's InputBox function to prompt the user for his or her name at the beginning of the application. You can then concatenate the salesperson's name to the message displayed in the lblMsg control.

The InputBox Function

You can also assign the prompt and/or the title to either a variable or a constant. When using a variable or a constant in the InputBox function, you don't need the quotation marks.

The InputBox function displays one of Visual Basic's predefined dialog boxes. The dialog box contains a message, along with an OK button, a Cancel button, and an input area in which the user can enter information. The message that you display in the dialog box should prompt the user to enter the appropriate information in the input area of the dialog box. The user will then need to click either the OK button or the Cancel button in order to continue the application.

The format of the InputBox function is **InputBox**(*prompt, title*), where *prompt* is the message you want displayed inside the dialog box, and *title* is the text you want displayed in the dialog box's title bar. Both the *prompt* and *title* must be enclosed in quotation marks. Use sentence capitalization for the *prompt*, but book title capitalization for the *title*. (You learned about both sentence and book title capitalization in Tutorial 2's Lesson A.) If you omit the *prompt*, no message appears inside the dialog box. If you omit the *title*, the application's name appears in the title bar. Figure 3-32 shows some examples of the InputBox function used in assignment statements.

GUI
Design Tips

InputBox Function's Prompt and Title Capitalization

* In the InputBox function, use sentence capitalization for the *prompt*, and book title capitalization for the *title*.

Examples of the InputBox function
stName = InputBox("Enter your name:")
stCity = InputBox("Enter the capital:", "Capital Screen")
inAge = Val(InputBox("How old are you?", "Age"))

Figure 3-32: Examples of the InputBox function in assignment statements

Recall that a function is a predefined procedure that returns a value. In the case of the InputBox function, the value returned to the application is the value entered by the user in response to the prompt. In this application, you will use the InputBox function to prompt the salesperson to enter his or her name when he or she runs the application. You will store the user's response in a String variable named stSperson.

Now that you know that the InputBox function will require a variable in which to store the user's response, you must decide where to declare the variable. In other words, should the stSperson variable be a local, form-level, or global variable? When deciding, consider the fact that the form's Load event, which is responsible for getting the name, needs to use the variable; and so does the Calculate Order button's Click event procedure, which is responsible for concatenating the name to the message that displays in the lblMsg control. Recall from Lesson A that when two procedures in the *same* form need to use the *same* variable, you declare the variable as a form-level variable by entering the Dim statement in the form's General declarations section.

To continue coding the Skate-Away Sales application, then save and run the application:

1 Click the **View Code** button in the Project window. The form's General declarations section appears.

First declare the stSperson String variable as a form-level variable.

2 Press ↓ on your keyboard to position the blinking insertion point below the `Option Explicit` statement, then type **dim stSperson as string** and press the **Enter** key.

Now you will enter the InputBox function in the form's Load event procedure, so the function will be processed as soon as the salesperson runs the application. You'll use "Enter salesperson's name:" as the *prompt*, and "Name of Salesperson" as the *title*.

3 Open the form's Load event procedure, then maximize the Code window. Press the **Tab** key, then type **stSperson = inputbox("Enter salesperson's name:", "Name of Salesperson")** and press the **Enter** key.

HELP? To open the form's Load event procedure, click the Code window's Object list arrow, then click Form in the list.

This instruction will prompt the user to enter his or her name, and then store the response in the form-level stSperson variable. Recall that form-level variables remain in memory until the application ends.

You can now open the Calculate Order button's Click event procedure and concatenate the stSperson variable to the message assigned to the lblMsg control.

4   Open the Calculate Order button's Click event procedure. Modify the message assigned to the lblMsg control as shown in Figure 3-33.

add this to the assignment statement

```
frmOrder                                                          _ ☐ ×
Object: cmdCalc                    ▼    Proc: Click               ▼

Private Sub cmdCalc_Click()
    Dim inBlue As Integer, inYellow As Integer, inTboards As Integer
    Dim crPrice As Currency, sgRate As Single, crTprice As Currency
    Dim crSubtotal As Currency, crStax As Currency
    Const conMsg As String = "Thank you for your order. The sales tax was "
'Assign values to variables
    inBlue = Val(txtBlue.Text)
    inYellow = Val(txtYellow.Text)
    crPrice = Val(txtPrice.Text)
    sgRate = Val(txtRate.Text)
'Perform calculations
    inTboards = inBlue + inYellow
    crSubtotal = inTboards * crPrice
    crStax = crSubtotal * sgRate
    crTprice = crSubtotal + crStax
'Display variable values in controls
    lblTboards.Caption = inTboards
    lblTprice.Caption = Format(crTprice, "currency")
    lblMsg.Caption = conMsg & Format(crStax, "currency") & "." & stSperson
    cmdPrint.SetFocus

End Sub
```

Figure 3-33: Modified message assigned to lblMsg control

Next save and run the application to test the code you've entered so far.

5   Close the Code window, then **save and run** the application. The dialog box created by the InputBox function appears as shown in Figure 3-34.

Figure 3-34: Dialog box created by the InputBox function

6   Type your name in the input area of the dialog box, then click the **OK** button. The order screen appears.

7   Click the **Calculate Order** button. Your name now appears in the message.

In looking at the message, you decide that the name appears too close to the sales tax message. At this point you could modify the assignment statement in the cmdCalc control's Click event procedure so that it concatenates a period followed by two spaces (". "), instead of just a period ("."), as it does now. Or, you could display the salesperson's name on the next line. You decide to place the name on a separate line. You can use the newline character, which you will learn about in the next section, to do so.

8   Click the **Exit** button to end the application.

tips

▶ Chr, which stands for "character," is a function.

The Newline Character

The **newline character,** which is Chr(13) & Chr(10), instructs Visual Basic to issue a carriage return followed by a line feed. The combination of the carriage return followed by a line feed will advance the insertion point to the next line in the lblMsg control. Whenever you want Visual Basic to start a new line, you simply type the newline character at that location in your code. In this case, for example, you want Visual Basic to advance to a new line after displaying the sales tax message—in other words, before displaying the salesperson's name.

To include the newline character in the code:

1 Click the **View Code** button in the Project window.

2 Open the cmdCalc control's Click event procedure, then maximize the Code window.

First you will enter the instructions both to declare a local String variable named stNL and to assign a value to the stNL variable. Then you will concatenate the stNL variable to the message assigned to the lblMsg control.

3 Enter the two new instructions shown in Figure 3-35, then modify the assignment statement that assigns the message to the lblMsg control. See Figure 3-35. (The code in the figure was compressed so that you could read more of each line.)

enter these two statements

add this to the assignment statement

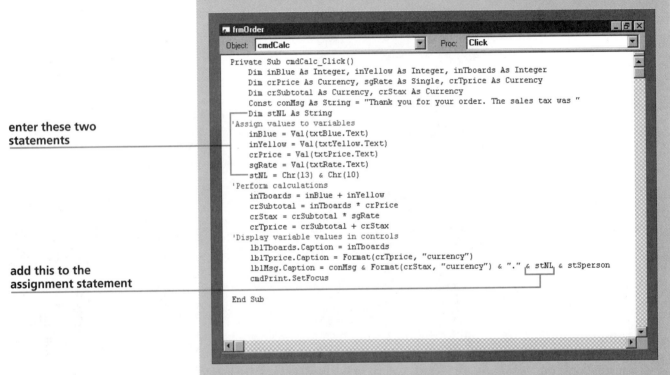

```
frmOrder                                                          _ 8 X
Object: cmdCalc                    ▼    Proc: Click                ▼
Private Sub cmdCalc_Click()
    Dim inBlue As Integer, inYellow As Integer, inTboards As Integer
    Dim crPrice As Currency, sgRate As Single, crTprice As Currency
    Dim crSubtotal As Currency, crStax As Currency
    Const conMsg As String = "Thank you for your order. The sales tax was "
    Dim stNL As String
'Assign values to variables
    inBlue = Val(txtBlue.Text)
    inYellow = Val(txtYellow.Text)
    crPrice = Val(txtPrice.Text)
    sgRate = Val(txtRate.Text)
    stNL = Chr(13) & Chr(10)
'Perform calculations
    inTboards = inBlue + inYellow
    crSubtotal = inTboards * crPrice
    crStax = crSubtotal * sgRate
    crTprice = crSubtotal + crStax
'Display variable values in controls
    lblTboards.Caption = inTboards
    lblTprice.Caption = Format(crTprice, "currency")
    lblMsg.Caption = conMsg & Format(crStax, "currency") & "." & stNL & stSperson
    cmdPrint.SetFocus

End Sub
```

Figure 3-35: Modified Click event procedure for the Calculate Order button

You may be wondering why we didn't create a symbolic constant for the new-line character; after all, its value will not change while the program is running. Recall from Lesson A, however, that you can't assign a function to a symbolic constant.

4 Close the Code window, then **save and run** the application. The dialog box created by the InputBox function appears.

Notice that the OK button in the dialog box has a darkened border, even though it does not have the focus; the text box has the focus. In Windows terminology, a command button that has a darkened border when it doesn't have the focus is called the default button. You can select a default button by pressing the Enter key at any time. In this case the user can select the OK button without taking his or her hands off the keyboard after typing the name. Try this.

5 Type your name in the InputBox function's dialog box. Then, instead of clicking the OK button, simply press the **Enter** key. The order screen appears.

6 Click the **Calculate Order** button. Your name now appears on a separate line in the lblMsg control.

7 Click the **Exit** button to end the application. Visual Basic returns to the design screen.

In this next section, you will learn how to create a default command button for the frmOrder form.

Making a Command Button the Default Button

As you already know from using Windows applications, you can choose a command button by pressing the Enter key when the button has the focus. If you make a command button the **default button**, however, you can choose it by pressing the Enter key even when the button does not have the focus. An interface's default button should be the button that represents the user's most likely action, except in cases where that action is both destructive and irreversible—for example, a command button that deletes information should not be designated as the default button. If you assign a default button in an interface, it is typically the first command button, which means that it is on the left when the buttons are centered along the bottom of the screen, and on the top when the buttons are stacked in the upper-right corner.

In the Skate-Away Sales interface, the command button that represents the user's most likely action is the Calculate Order button. Because that button's action is neither destructive nor irreversible, it is a safe choice for a default button. Assigning the Calculate Order button as the default command button will allow the user to calculate the order at any time by simply pressing the Enter key.

A command button's Default property determines which command button is the default button. When you create a command button, its Default property is initially set to False, which means that it is not the default button. If you want a command button to be the default button, you must set its Default property to True. Because only one command button on a form can be the default button, setting a command button's Default property to True sets the Default property of every other command button in the form to False. Make the Calculate Order button the default button for the order screen.

To make the Calculate Order button the default button, then save and run the application:

1 Use the Properties window's Object box, which is located below the Properties window's title bar, to select the cmdCalc control.

GUI
Design Tips

Rules for Assigning the Default Button

• The default button should be the command button that represents the user's most likely action, except in cases where that action is both destructive and irreversible. The default button is typically the first command button.

2 Set the cmdCalc control's Default property to **True**.

3 Save and run the application. When prompted for the salesperson's name, type your name and press the **Enter** key. When the order screen appears, press the **Enter** key to calculate the order. The order calculates and the message appears.

Now use the Exit button's access key to end the application.

4 Press **Alt + x** to select the Exit button. The application ends and Visual Basic returns to the design screen.

You have now completed Lesson B. In Lesson C you will learn ways to make the Skate-Away Sales application more professional-looking. For now, you can either take a break or complete the end-of-lesson questions and exercises.

S U M M A R Y

To specify the attributes of the Visual Basic environment:

■ Use one of the four tabs (Environment, Project, Editor, Advanced) in the Options dialog box. You can display the Options dialog box by clicking Tools, then Options.

To concatenate strings:

■ Use the concatenation operator—the ampersand (&). Be sure to put a space before and after the ampersand.

To display a dialog box containing a prompt, an input area, an OK button, and a Cancel button:

■ Use the InputBox function. Its syntax is **InputBox**(*prompt, title*). Both *prompt* and *title* must be enclosed in quotation marks unless they are either a variable or a constant. Use sentence capitalization for the *prompt*, and book title capitalization for the *title*.

To make a command button the default button:

■ Set its Default property to True. Only one of the command buttons on a form can be the default button.

To tell Visual Basic to advance to the next line:

■ Use the newline character. Its value is Chr(13) & Chr(10).

Q U E S T I O N S

1. Which tab in the Options dialog box allows you to control the appearance of the form grid during design time?
   a. Advanced
   b. Editor
   c. Environment
   d. Project

2. Which tab in the Options dialog box contains an option that tells Visual Basic to insert the Option Explicit statement automatically in every new form and module?
    a. Advanced
    b. Editor
    c. Environment
    d. Project

3. Which tab in the Options dialog box contains an option that tells Visual Basic to check the syntax of the code, automatically, as each line is entered into the Code window?
    a. Advanced
    b. Editor
    c. Environment
    d. Project

4. Which tab in the Options dialog box allows you to change the font type, size, and color of the text in the Code window?
    a. Advanced
    b. Editor
    c. Environment
    d. Project

5. The InputBox function displays a dialog box containing which of the following? (Choose more than one answer.)
    a. Cancel button
    b. Exit button
    c. input area
    d. OK button
    e. prompt

6. Which of the following is the concatenation operator?
    a. @
    b. #
    c. $
    d. &
    e. *

7. Assume the stReg1 variable contains the string "North" and the stReg2 variable contains the string "West". Which of the following will display the string "NorthWest" (one word) in the lblRegion control?
    a. lblRegion.Caption = stReg1 & stReg2
    b. lblRegion.Caption = "stReg1" & "stReg2"
    c. lblRegion.Caption = stReg1 $ stReg2
    d. lblRegion.Caption = stReg1 # stReg2
    e. lblRegion.Caption = stReg1 @ stReg2

8. Assume the stCity variable contains the string "Boston" and the stState variable contains the string "MA". Which of the following will display the string "Boston, MA" (the city, a comma, a space, and the state) in the lblAddress control?
    a. lblAddress.Caption = stCity # , & stState
    b. lblAddress.Caption = "stCity" & ", " & "stState"
    c. lblAddress.Caption = "stCity$", "&stState
    d. lblAddress.Caption = stCity & ", " & stState
    e. lblAddress.Caption = "stCity, " & "stState"

9. Which of the following is the newline character?
    a. Chr(10) & Chr(13)
    b. Chr(10) & Chr(12)
    c. Chr(13) & Chr(10)
    d. Str(10)$ Str(12)
    e. Str(10) & Str(13)

10. If you want to give the user the ability to select a specific command button when the button does not have the focus, set the command button's _____ property to True.
   a. Command
   b. Default
   c. Enter
   d. Focus
   e. SetFocus

E X E R C I S E S

NOTE: In the following exercises, be sure to enter the Option Explicit statement in the appropriate location. Also be sure to use variables.

1. In this exercise, you will modify the code in an existing application.

   Scenario: The existing application calculates the commission earned on a salesperson's sales. The commission rate is 10%.

   a. Open the lb1 (lb1.vbp) project, which is located in the Tut03 folder on your Student Disk. View the form.
   b. Save the form and the project as lb1Done in the Tut03 folder on your Student Disk.
   c. Make the Calculate Commission button the default button.
   d. Review the code in the Calculate Commission button's Click event procedure. Then recode the button's Click event procedure so that it uses variables, instead of control properties, in the equation that calculates the commission.
   e. Save and run the application.
   f. Enter Mary Smith as the name, 3405 as the territory number, and 7500 as the sales.
   g. Click the Calculate Commission button, then click the Print button, which has already been coded for you, to print the form on the printer.
   h. Click the Exit button, which has already been coded for you, to end the application.
   i. Print the code.
   j. Submit the printout from step g and the code from step i.

2. In this exercise, you will use variables to code an application.

   Scenario: Your math instructor has asked you to create an application that will calculate the square root of a number.

   a. Open the lb2 (lb2.vbp) project, which is located in the Tut03 folder on your Student Disk. View the form.
   b. Save the form and the project as lb2Done in the Tut03 folder on your Student Disk.
   c. Make the Square Root button the default button.
   d. Code the Square Root button so that it calculates and displays the square root of a whole number. Be sure to assign the numeric equivalent of the txtNumber.Text property to an Integer variable. Assign the square root to a Single variable. You can use Visual Basic's Sqr function to calculate the square root. Its syntax is Sqr(*number*).
   e. Save and run the application.
   f. Enter the number 144, then click the Square Root button. Click the Print button, which has already been coded for you, to print the form on the printer.
   g. Click the Exit button, which has already been coded for you, to end the application.
   h. Print the code.
   i. Submit the printout from step f and the code from step h.

3. In this exercise, you will use variables to code an application.

   Scenario: Mingo Sales needs an application in which they can enter the sales made in three states. The application should calculate the total sales and the commission.

a. Open the lb3 (lb3.vbp) project, which is located in the Tut03 folder on your Student Disk.
b. Save the form and the project as lb3Done in the Tut03 folder on your Student Disk.
c. Make the Calculate Commission button the default button.
d. Code the Exit button so that it ends the application when it is clicked.
e. Code the Clear Screen button so that it clears the screen when it is clicked. Send the focus to the New York sales text box.
f. Code the Print button so that it prints the form when it is clicked. Send the focus to the Clear Screen button.
g. Use the pseudocode shown in Figure 3-36 to code the Calculate Commission button. Format the sales and the commission to currency.

Calculate Commission button
1. Declare variables
2. Assign values to variables
3. Calculate total sales = New York sales + Maine sales + Florida sales
4. Calculate commission = total sales * 5%
5. Display total sales and commission in lblTsales and lblComm
6. Send the focus to the Print button

Figure 3-36: Pseudocode for the Calculate Commission button

h. Save and run the application. Enter the following information:

New York sales: 15000
Maine sales: 25000
Florida sales: 10500

i. Click the Calculate Commission button, then click the Print button to print the form with the test data showing, then click the Clear Screen button.
j. Click the Exit button to end the application.
k. Print the code.
l. Modify the code in the Calculate Commission button so that it uses the InputBox function to ask the user for the commission rate. (Use the InputBox function in the Calculate Commission button's Click event.) Store the commission rate in a variable and use the variable in the equation that calculates the commission.
m. Save and run the application. Enter the following information:

New York sales: 26000
Maine sales: 34000
Florida sales: 17000

n. Click the Calculate Commission button. Enter .1 (the decimal equivalent of 10%) as the commission rate, then click the OK button. Click the Print button to print the form with the test data showing.
o. Click the Exit button to end the application.
p. Print the code.
q. Submit the printouts from steps i and n, and the printed code from steps k and p.

4. In this exercise, you will build a user interface and use variables and string concatenation to code the application.

Scenario: IMY Industries needs an application that their personnel clerks can use to calculate the new hourly pay, given the current hourly pay for each of three job codes and the raise percentage (entered as a decimal). They also want to display the message "Raise percentage: XX" on the screen. The XX in the message should be replaced by the actual raise percentage, formatted to percent.

a. Create the user interface shown in Figure 3-37.

3 text boxes

3 label controls

lblMsg

Figure 3-37: User interface

b. Save the form and the project as lb4Done in the Tut03 folder on your Student Disk.
c. Make the New Hourly Pay button the default button.
d. Code the Exit button so that it ends the application when it is clicked.
e. Code the Print button so that it prints the form when it is clicked. Send the focus to the Job Code 1 text box.
f. Use the InputBox function to prompt the personnel clerk to enter the raise percentage at the beginning of the application; in other words, when he or she runs the application. The raise percentage will be used to calculate the new hourly pay for each job code.
g. Use the pseudocode shown in Figure 3-38 to code the New Hourly Pay button. Assign the "Raise percentage: " message to a constant. Format the new hourly pays to standard. Format the raise rate (in the message) to percent.

New Hourly Pay button

1. Declare variables and constant
2. Assign values to variables
3. Calculate new hourly pays = currently hourly pays *(1 + raise rate)
4. Display new hourly pays in appropriate label controls
5. Display message and raise rate in lblMsg control
6. Send the focus to the Print button

Figure 3-38: Pseudocode for the New Hourly Pay button

h. Save and run the application. Enter the following information. (Enter the raise percentage when prompted by the InputBox function. Enter the current hourly pay for each job code in the appropriate text boxes.)

Raise percentage (in decimal form):	.05
Job Code 1's current hourly pay:	5
Job Code 2's current hourly pay:	6.50
Job Code 3's current hourly pay:	8.75

i. Calculate the new hourly pays, then print the form with the test data showing.
j. Click the Exit button to end the application.
k. Print the code.
l. Modify the application's code so that it asks the personnel clerk to enter the raise for each job code separately. (You will need to use three InputBox functions.)

m. Change the message so that each rate appears on a separate line in the label control as follows:

Job Code 1: XX%
Job Code 2: XX%
Job Code 3: XX%

Assign each message to a constant.

n. Format the current hourly pays and the new hourly pays to currency.

o. Save and run the application. Enter the following information:

Job Code 1 raise percentage:	.03	(The decimal equivalent of 3%.)
Job Code 2 raise percentage:	.05	(The decimal equivalent of 5%.)
Job Code 3 raise percentage:	.045	(The decimal equivalent of 4.5%.)
Job Code 1's current hourly pay:	5	
Job Code 2's current hourly pay:	6.50	
Job Code 3's current hourly pay:	8.75	

p. Calculate the hourly pays, then print the form with the test data showing.

q. Click the Exit button to end the application.

r. Print the code.

s. Submit the printouts from steps i and p, and the code from steps k and r.

Use the following information to answer questions 5–7.

Variable/Constant Name	Contents
stCity	Madison
stState	WI
stZip	53711
conMessage	The capital of

5. On a piece of paper, write an assignment statement that will display the string "Madison, WI" in the lblAddress control. Be sure to use the information shown above.

6. On a piece of paper, write an assignment statement that will display the string "The capital of WI is Madison." in the lblAddress control. Be sure to use the information shown above.

7. On a piece of paper, write an assignment statement that will display the string "My zip code is 53711." in the lblAddress control. Be sure to use the information shown above.

In this lesson you will learn how to:

- Add a form to a project
- Create a Dialog Box
- Define the startup form
- Add a module to a project
- Use a global variable in an application
- Center a form on the screen
- Use the Load and Unload statements
- Use the Show and Hide methods
- Distinguish between a modal and a modeless form
- Use a Timer control

Improving the Appearance of the Skate-Away Sales Application

Using a Dialog Box

Although the InputBox function is a quick and easy way to create a dialog box, it has some limitations—for example, you can't control its appearance. Also, the user can enter only one item of data at a time; so if you wanted the user to enter both the salesperson's name and the date, you would need to use two InputBox functions. Instead of using the InputBox function, you can use a form to create more professional-looking dialog boxes that can request as much input as necessary. In this lesson you will replace the InputBox function's dialog box with a form that will resemble a dialog box. To save you time, the form that will act as a dialog box is already on your Student Disk. First open the Skate-Away Sales application that you modified in Lesson B.

To continue coding the Skate-Away Sales application:

1   Start Visual Basic, if necessary, and make sure your Student Disk is in the appropriate drive.

2   Open the **lbOrder** (lborder.vbp) file, which is located in the Tut03 folder on your Student Disk, then click the **View form** button in the Project window to view the frmOrder form. The Skate-Away Sales application from Lesson B appears on the screen.

3   Save the form and the project as **lcOrder**.

First remove the InputBox function from the form's Load event procedure.

4   Open the form's Load event procedure, then maximize the Code window. Highlight the `stSperson = InputBox("Enter salesperson's name:", "Name of Salesperson")` instruction, then press the **Delete** key. Visual Basic removes the instruction from the Code window.

5   Close the Code window, then close the frmOrder form.

Now add the input screen to the current application.

Adding an Existing File to the Application

You use the Add File command on the File menu to add an existing form to a project. In this case, you will add the t3input form file to the application.

> To add the t3input form file to the project:
>
> **1** Click **File**, then click **Add File**. Click **t3input** (t3input.frm) in the list of file names, then click the **Open** button (*the OK button in Windows 3.1*). Visual Basic adds the T3INPUT.FRM name to the Project window.
>
> **2** Size the Project window so that both file names are visible. You can drag either the top or the bottom border. You may then need to scroll the Project window to display both file names.
>
> **3** If necessary, click **T3INPUT.FRM** in the Project window to highlight the name in the Project window. Use the Save File As option on the File menu to save the t3input form as **lcInput**.
>
> **4** Click the **View Form** button. The frmInput form appears on the screen.
>
> The frmInput form is sized to resemble a dialog box. Its WindowState property is at the default setting of 0-Normal, so the form will appear in the size shown when the application is run. The form contains a text box (txtName) in which the salesperson enters his or her name, and an OK button (cmdOK) that will remove the dialog box (form) from the screen. The OK button's Default property is set to True, which makes the OK button the default button on the frmInput form.
>
> **5** Click the **View Code** button in the Project window. The frmInput form's General declarations section appears.
>
> **6** Type **option explicit** in the form's General declarations section and press the **Enter** key, then close the Code window.
>
> **7** Click the **form** to select it.

When a project includes more than one form, you must tell Visual Basic which of the forms you want automatically displayed when the application is run. You do that by specifying the startup form.

Specifying the Startup Form

When a multiform project is run, Visual Basic automatically loads and displays only one of the forms contained in the project; that form, called the **startup form**, can be any one of the forms in the project. You use the Options command on the Tools menu to specify which form you want Visual Basic to use as the startup form. In this case you want the frmInput form to be the startup form.

To specify the startup form:

1   Click **Tools**, then click **Options**. When the Options dialog box opens, click the **Project** tab. Click the **Startup Form** list arrow, then click **frmInput** in the list, and then click the **OK** button.

When you run this multiform application, Visual Basic will automatically load and display the frmInput form on the screen. You can then use the Show method, which you will learn in the next section, to both load and display the frmOrder form.

2   **Save and run** the application. The frmInput form appears on the screen.

Don't be concerned if the frmInput form does not appear centered on the screen. You will learn how to center the form later on in this lesson. You will also learn the Windows standards for dialog boxes.

3   Click the **End** button ▣ on the toolbar to end the application. Visual Basic returns to the design screen.

In the next section you will learn how to load, unload, show, and hide forms.

Loading and Displaying a Form

Visual Basic has two statements and two methods that control the loading and displaying, respectively, of forms. The two statements are Load and Unload, and the two methods are Show and Hide. The **Load statement** brings a form into memory, but it does not display the form on the screen. The **Unload statement**, on the other hand, removes a form from memory and from the screen. The syntax of the Load statement is **Load** *object*, and the syntax of the Unload statement is **Unload** *object*.

tips

· · · · · · · · · · · · · · ·

Don't confuse the Load statement with the form's Load event. The Load statement brings a form into memory, whereas the Load event occurs when the form is loaded into memory.

When you want to remove a form from the screen, but leave it in memory, you use the **Hide method** to do so. The syntax of the Hide method is *object*.**Hide**. Conversely, when you want to display a form on the screen, you use the **Show method** to do so. If the form is not already loaded, the Show method loads it before displaying it. The syntax of the Show method is *object*.**Show** [*style*]. *Style* is an integer, either 0 or 1, that determines if the form is modal or modeless. If *style* is either omitted or 0, the form is modeless; if *style* is 1, the form is modal. A **modeless form** is a form that does not require the user to take any action before the focus can switch to another form or dialog box, or before subsequent code is executed. Visual Basic's Help windows are examples of modeless forms. A **modal form**, on the other hand, is a form that requires the user to take some action before the focus can switch to another form or dialog box, or before any subsequent code can be executed. When the form is modal, no input from the keyboard or mouse can occur in the application until the current form is either hidden or unloaded. Although other forms in your application are disabled when a modal form is displayed, other applications are not; you can still access these other applications either using Alt-Tab or clicking the application in the Windows 95 taskbar. The Open Project dialog box in Visual Basic is an example of a modal form.

To help clarify the concept of modal and modeless, complete Lesson C's Exercise 1.

Figure 3-39 recaps the Load and Unload statements and the Show and Hide methods. Notice that the statement name always comes before the object name, but the method name always comes after.

Instruction:	Used To:	Syntax:
Load statement	Bring a form into memory.	**Load** *object*
Unload statement	Remove a form from memory.	**Unload** *object*
Show method	Display a form on the screen; if the form is not already loaded, the Show method loads it before displaying it.	*object*.**Show** [*style*]
Hide method	Hides a form from view, but leaves it in memory.	*object*.**Hide**

Figure 3-39: Recap of Load, Unload, Show, and Hide

Now that you know how to load, unload, hide, and show forms, you can continue coding the Skate-Away Sales application. You will code the frmInput form first.

To begin coding the frmInput form:

1 Double-click the **OK** button to open its Click event procedure.

When the user enters the salesperson's name and clicks the OK button, you want to assign the txtSperson control's Text property to the stSperson variable, then both load and display the frmOrder form. Last, you want to unload the frmInput form, as the frmInput form is no longer necessary.

2 Press the **Tab** key, then type **stSperson = txtSperson.text** and press the **Enter** key.

3 Type **frmOrder.show** and press the **Enter** key to both load and display the frmOrder form. Recall that the Show method will load an unloaded form before displaying it on the screen.

4 Type **unload frmInput** and press the **Enter** key to unload the frmInput form.

5 Close the Code window, then **save and run** the application.

6 When prompted for the salesperson's name, type your name and press the **Enter** key. Visual Basic displays the "Variable not defined" warning message.

7 Click the **OK** button to remove the warning message from the screen. Visual Basic highlights the problem variable in the Code window.

According to the Code window, the cmdOK control's Click event procedure, which is located in the frmInput form, does not recognize the stSperson variable. Stop the application and consider the problem.

8 Close the Code window, then click the **End** button ▣ on the toolbar to end the application. Visual Basic returns to the design screen.

In Lesson B you declared the stSperson variable as a form-level variable in the General declarations section of the frmOrder form. Recall that in Lesson B the stSperson variable was used by the frmOrder form's Load event procedure and the cmdCalc control's Click event procedure. Because both procedures were in the same form, you declared the stSperson variable as a form-level variable. Now that you've changed the application, however, a form-level variable will no longer work.

In the current application, the frmInput form's Load event procedure gets the salesperson's name, so the frmInput form needs to use the stSperson variable. The cmdCalc control on the frmOrder form, however, also needs to use that variable in order to include the name in the message displayed in the lblMsg control. As you learned in Lesson A, when two procedures in *different* forms need to use the *same* variable, you declare the variable as a global variable by entering the Public statement in the General declarations section of a code module. In the next section, you will add a code module to the current application and declare a global variable in its General declarations section.

Adding a Code Module to a Project

Important Note: If you are using the Visual Basic Working Model, you will not be able to use the computer to complete the steps in this section. Open the OK button's Click event and place an apostrophe (') before the stPerson=txtPerson.text instruction so that the application will not result in an error when it is run. The next section you will be able to complete on the computer is Making a Form Resemble a Standard Windows Dialog Box.

As you learned in Lesson A, a code module is a separate file, added to your application, that contains only code; it does not contain any forms or controls. All variables that you want to make available to all forms in the application must be declared in the General declarations section of a code module. In this application, you will declare the stSperson variable in a code module's General declarations section so that both the frmInput and frmOrder forms can use the variable.

tips

· · · · · · · · · · · · · · ·
You can also add a code module to a project by using the Module command on the Insert menu. You can remove a file from a project by clicking the file's name in the Project window, then using the Remove File command on the File menu.

To add a code module to the current project, then continue coding the application:

1   Click the **Module** button ▨ on the toolbar. Visual Basic adds the Module1 file to the Project window, and the General declarations section of the Module1 module appears.

2   Enter the two instructions shown in Figure 3-40.

declares a global
variable

Figure 3-40: Instructions entered in the code module's General declarations section

3   Use the File menu's Save File As option to save the code module as **lcModule**.

4   Close the code module's Code window.

5   Size and scroll the Project window, if necessary, until the three file names are visible in the window. The Project window shows that the code module is saved as **LCMODULE.BAS**. (The .BAS extension stands for "Basic.")

Whenever you make a change to the information in the Project window, you must be sure to save the project so that the change is saved.

6   Click the **Save Project** button 🖫 on the toolbar to save the project under its current name.

Before saving and running the application, you must first remove the Dim statement that declares the form-level variable in the frmOrder form's General declarations section.

To remove the form-level variable declaration, then save and run the application:

1   Click **LCORDER.FRM** in the Project window, then click the **View Code** button in the Project window. The frmOrder form's General declarations section appears.

2   Highlight the `Dim stSperson as String` instruction, then press the **Delete** key.

3   Close the Code window.

Now save and run the application.

4   **Save and run** the application. When the frmInput form appears, type your name, then press the **Enter** key. The frmOrder form appears. Press the **Enter** key to select the Calculate Order button.

Your name appears in the message in the lblMsg control.

5   Click the **Exit** button to end the application. Visual Basic returns to the design screen.

Now work on improving the appearance of the frmInput form so that it resembles a standard Windows dialog box.

Making a Form Resemble a Standard Windows Dialog Box

A standard Windows dialog box is centered on the screen, is not resizeable, and contains only a Close button ☒ (*Control Menu Box* ▭ *in Windows 3.1*) in its title bar; the Minimize and Maximize buttons do not appear in the title bar of a standard dialog box. In the Skate-Away Sales application, you will need to center the frmInput form on the screen, make it nonresizeable, and remove its Minimize and Maximize buttons so that the form resembles a standard dialog box. First, make the form nonresizeable and remove its Minimize and Maximize buttons.

You can remove a form's Minimize and Maximize buttons, as well as make the form nonresizeable, by changing the form's BorderStyle property to 3-Fixed Dialog.

tips

....

▶ **You learned about the BorderStyle property in Tutorial 1.**

To remove a form's Minimize and Maximize buttons and make the form non-resizeable:

1 If necessary, click **LCINPUT.FRM** in the Project window to highlight the file name in the Project window, then click the **View Form** button to view the frmInput form.

2 Set the frmInput form's BorderStyle property to **3-Fixed Dialog**.

Now make sure that the frmInput form, which is not maximized during run time, is centered when it appears on the screen. (Recall that the frmInput form's WindowState property is set to 0-Normal, so the form will appear in its current size.) To center a form, you will need to set both its Top and Left properties. What you set them to is based on both the height and width of the screen and the height and width of the form itself. The height and width of both the screen and the form is measured in twips. A twip, you may remember from Tutorial 1, is 1/1440 of an inch.

Suppose, for example, that the screen's height is 7000 twips and the form's height is 3900 twips. To center the form vertically, you simply subtract the form's height from the screen's height, then divide the remainder by two; the result will give you the value for the form's Top property. In this example, for instance, you subtract 3900 from 7000, giving 3100. You then divide the 3100 by 2, giving 1550. Setting the form's Top property to 1550 twips will center the form vertically on the screen.

To center the form horizontally, you subtract the form's width from the screen's width, then divide the remainder by two; the result will give you the value for the form's Left property. Suppose, for example, that the screen's width is 9000 twips and the form's width is 6500 twips. To calculate the value of the form's Left property, you subtract 6500 from 9000, then divide the remainder (2500) by 2. The result in this case is 1250. Setting the form's Left property to 1250 will center the form horizontally on the screen. Figure 3-41 shows an illustration of centering a form on the screen.

Figure 3-41: Illustration of a centered form

In Visual Basic the screen is considered an object; it is called the **Screen object.** You refer to the Screen object by using the keyword **Screen.** Therefore, the formula to center a form vertically on the screen is written as *formname*.Top = (Screen.Height - *formname*.Height)/2, where *formname* is the name of the form you want to center. The formula to center a form horizontally on the screen is written as *formname*.Left = (Screen.Width - *formname*.Width)/2.

Because you want the frmInput form centered as soon as it appears on the screen, you will need to place the formulas in the form's Load event procedure.

To center the form:

1 The frmInput form should be selected in the Project window, so just click the **View Code** button in the Project window to open the Code window. The General declarations section of the frmInput form appears.

2 Open the frmInput form's Load event procedure, then maximize the Code window.

3 Enter the three instructions shown in Figure 3-42.

enter these instructions

```
frmInput                                                    _ □ ×
Object: Form                          ▼   Proc: Load                    ▼
Private Sub Form_Load()
'Center the form
    frmInput.Top = (Screen.Height - frmInput.Height) / 2
    frmInput.Left = (Screen.Width - frmInput.Width) / 2

End Sub
```

Figure 3-42: Instructions to center the form

HELP? Remember that division has a higher precedence number than does subtraction, so you need to place parentheses around the subtraction part of the formula in order to change the order of precedence.

4 Close the Code window.

5 **Save and run** the application. The frmInput form appears in the center of the screen.

6 Click the **End** button ☐ on the toolbar to end the application. Visual Basic returns to the design screen.

Finish this tutorial by adding a copyright screen that is similar to the one you created in Tutorial 1 for the Skate-Away Sales application.

GUI
Design Tips

Dialog Box Standards

• The standard Windows dialog box is centered on the screen, is not resizeable, and contains only a Close button ☒ (*Control Menu Box* ☐ *in Windows 3.1*) in its title bar.

Adding the Copyright Form to the Project

Important Note: If you are using the Visual Basic Working Model, you will not be able to use the computer to complete the remaining sections in this lesson.

If you are using the Professional Edition of Visual Basic 4.0, the Copyright application that you created in Tutorial 1 contains the Microsoft Multimedia control, which plays a bit of music when the application first appears. Before adding the Copyright application's file to the Skate-Away Sales application, you will need to add the Microsoft Multimedia control to the toolbox for the current project. You will need to add the control only if you are using the Professional Edition of Visual Basic; if you are using the Standard Edition, you can skip Step 1 in the next set of steps, but be sure to do the remaining steps.

To add the Copyright application's file to the current project:

1   If you are using the Professional Edition of Visual Basic 4.0, click **Tools** on the menu bar, then click **Custom Controls**. Click the **Microsoft Multimedia Control** check box in the list of available controls. Be sure that a check mark (*an X in Windows 3.1*) appears in the check box. Click the **OK** button.

You will now add a Copyright screen that is similar to the one you created in Tutorial 1.

2   Click **File**, then click **Add File**.

3   If you are using the Professional Edition, click **copyprof** (copyprof.frm) in the list of file names, then click the **Open** button (*OK button in Windows 3.1*). If you are using the Standard Edition, click **copystan** (copystan.frm) in the list of file names, then click the **Open** button.

4   Click **File**, then click **Save File As**. Save the frmCopyright form as **lcCopy** in the Tut03 folder.

Recall that when you run a multiform project, Visual Basic loads, automatically, only one form—the startup form. Change the startup form to the frmCopyright form.

5   Click **Tools**, then click **Options**, and then click the **Project** tab.

6   Click the **Startup Form** list arrow, then click **frmCopyright** in the list, and then click the **OK** button.

7   Click the **Save Project** 🖫 button on the toolbar to save the project.

Now code the frmCopyright form so that it loads and displays both the frmInput and frmOrder forms. You'll load both forms in the frmCopyright form's Load event procedure, then display them when the user clicks the Exit button. Displaying the frmCopyright form will give the users something to look at while the other forms are being loaded. (Complex forms take time to load.)

To code the frmCopyright form:

1   Close the frmInput form.

2   Click **LCCOPY.FRM** in the Project window, then click the **View Form** button to view the frmCopyright form. Maximize the form. Change the Caption of the lblAuthor control to say "Written By" (without the quotes), followed by your name. Restore the form.

3 If your Student Disk is in the B drive and you are using the Professional Edition, click the **mmcSound control**, then change the FileName property from a:\Tut03\CopySnd.wav to **b:\Tut03\CopySnd.wav.**

4 Click the **View Code** button in the Project window, then open the form's Load event procedure.

Recall that you use the Load statement when you want to bring a form into memory without displaying it.

5 If you are using the Professional Edition, the form's Load event procedure contains two lines of code dealing with the multimedia control. Position the blinking insertion point in the line below both statements.

6 Press the **Tab** key, if necessary, then type **load frmInput** and press the **Enter** key, and then type **load frmOrder** and press the **Enter** key.

Now have the Exit button show the frmInput form and unload the frmCopyright form.

7 Open the cmdExit control's Click event procedure. Highlight the `End` statement, then press the **Delete** key to remove the statement from the Code window.

8 If you are using the Professional Edition, the Code window still contains the instruction that closes the multimedia control. Position the blinking insertion point in the line below that statement.

9 Press the **Tab** key, if necessary, then type **frmInput.show** and press the **Enter** key, and then type **unload frmCopyright** and press the **Enter** key.

10 Close the Code window, then **save and run** the application.

11 When the copyright screen appears, click the **Exit** button. When the input screen appears, type your name and press the **Enter** key. When the order screen appears, click the **Exit** button.

Most introductory screens wait a set period of time and then close on their own, without any user intervention. You can have the copyright screen show the frmInput form and then unload itself on its own by using a Timer control.

Using a Timer Control

You can use a Timer control to process code at regular time intervals. You simply need to set the control's Interval property to the length of the time interval, in milliseconds, and enter the code you want processed into the control's Timer event. The **Timer event** tells Visual Basic what to do after each time interval has elapsed. Add a Timer control to the current application.

tips

A millisecond is 1/1000 of a second. In other words, there are 1000 milliseconds in a second.

To add a Timer control:

1 Double-click the **Timer control** 🖾 in the toolbox, then drag the Timer control to the top of the form as shown in Figure 3-43. (If you are using the Standard Edition, you will not see the Microsoft Multimedia control in the interface.)

**Multimedia control
(Professional Edition)**

Timer control

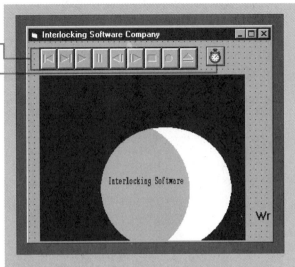

Figure 3-43: Timer control added to the user interface

You will now make the Copyright screen disappear after five seconds—in other words, after 5000 milliseconds.

2 Set the Timer control's Interval property to 5000.

Next you will move the code from the Exit button's Click event to the Timer control's Timer event.

3 Click the **View Code** button in the Project window. If necessary, open the cmdExit control's Click event procedure. The instructions in the Click event close the Multimedia control (if you are using the Professional Edition), show the frmInput form, and unload the frmCopyright form.

4 Highlight the instructions between the Private Sub and End Sub instructions, but do not highlight the Private Sub and End Sub instructions themselves. If you are using the Professional Edition, three instructions will be highlighted; if you are using the Standard Edition two instructions will be highlighted.

When moving important code from one Code window to another, it is often times safer to copy the data to the Clipboard, then paste the code in its proper place, and then go back and remove the code from its original location.

5 Press **Ctrl + c** to copy the instructions to the Clipboard. Open the Timer1 control's Timer event, then press **Ctrl + v** to paste the instructions into the window as shown in Figure 3-44. (Remember, if you are using the Standard Edition, your Code window will not contain the instruction to close the Multimedia control.)

tips

· · · · · · · · · · · · · · · · ·

▶ **You can also use the Edit menu to copy and paste instructions.**

you won't see this line
if you are using the
Standard Edition

you may have an empty
line above the End Sub
instruction

Figure 3-44: Instructions pasted in the Timer1 control's Timer event

6   Close the Code window.

In the next section you will learn the proper way of removing a coded control—in this case, the Exit button—from a form.

Removing a Coded Control from the Form

If a control does not contain any code, you can remove the control from the form by selecting the control and pressing the Delete key. If a control contains code, however, you should delete the code that you entered in its Code window(s) before deleting the control from the form; otherwise, Visual Basic retains the unnecessary code in your application, even though the control is gone.

You may want to use the scrollable listing view of the code to search for a control's coded procedures.

If you want to verify that the code from a deleted control was removed from the application, open the form's General declarations section and click the Proc list arrow. If the name of the deleted control appears in the list, then your application still contains the control's code. To remove the code, click the control's name in the list, then highlight the instructions in its Code window (including the Private Sub and End Sub instructions), and then press the Delete key.

To remove the Exit button from the frmCopyright form:

1   Maximize the form, then double-click the **Exit** button to open its Click event procedure.

The only procedure coded for the cmdExit control is the Click event procedure, so that is the only code you will need to delete before removing the control from the form. If other procedures were coded, you would also need to delete their code before deleting the control.

2   Highlight all of the instructions in the Code window, including the Private Sub and the End Sub instructions, then press the **Delete** key to delete the instructions in the Code window. Visual Basic removes the cmdExit control's Code window from the screen. The form's General declarations section appears.

3   Close the Code window. The Exit button should still be selected, so just press the **Delete** key to remove the control from the form. Visual Basic removes the Exit button from the form.

In the next step you will save and run the application. While the application is running, pay particular attention to the mouse pointer that appears when the copyright screen is showing.

4   Close the frmCopyright form, then **save and run** the application.

Recall that the copyright screen is on the screen for five seconds, which in computer time is a long time. It is a Windows standard that when a process will take a long period of time, the interface should display an hourglass. You can change the appearance of the mouse pointer by setting the form's MousePointer property.

5   Click the **End** button to end the application.

Changing the Appearance of the Mouse Pointer

The **MousePointer property** controls the type of mouse pointer Visual Basic displays when the mouse is over an object during run time. It is a Windows standard that when a process will take a long period of time, the interface should display an hourglass to indicate to the user that nothing will happen on the screen for awhile. You will change the mouse pointer to display the hourglass icon while the frmCopyright form is on the screen.

> The hourglass icon will appear only when the mouse pointer is on the form.

To change the form's mouse pointer to an hourglass:

1 Click **LCCOPY.FRM** in the Project window, then click the **View Form** button.

2 Click **MousePointer** in the Properties window, then click the **Settings** list arrow. Scroll the list until you see 11-Hourglass, then click **11-Hourglass** in the list.

3 **Save and run** the application. Notice that the hourglass appears while the copyright screen is running.

4 When the input screen appears, type your name and press the **Enter** key. When the order screen appears, enter an order, then press the **Enter** key to select the Calculate Order button.

5 If your computer is connected to a printer, click the **Print Order** button.

6 Click the **Clear Screen** button, then press **Alt + x** to select the Exit button.

The Skate-Away Sales application is finally complete. You can either take a break, complete the end-of-lesson questions and exercises, or read and complete the Debugging Section, which may contain information that will help you when completing the exercises.

GUI
Design Tips

Using the Hourglass Icon

- It is a Windows standard that when a process will take a long period of time, the interface should display an hourglass.

S U M M A R Y

To add an existing file to a project:

■ Use the Add File command on the File menu.

To specify the startup form:

■ Click Tools, then click Options. When the Options dialog box appears, click the Project tab. Click the Start up list arrow, then click the name of the startup form in the list.

To bring a form into memory, but not display it on the screen:

■ Use the Load statement. Its syntax is **Load** *object*.

To remove a form from both memory and the screen:

■ Use the Unload statement. Its syntax is **Unload** *object*.

To display a form on the screen:

■ Use the Show method. Its syntax is *object*.**Show** [*style*]. If the form is not already loaded, the Show method loads it before displaying it.

■ If style is either omitted or 0, the form is modeless. If style is 1, the form is modal.

To add a code module to a project:

■ Click the Module button ▦ on the toolbar. You can also add a code module to a project by using the Module command on the Insert menu.

To center a form on the screen:

■ Enter the following two lines of code in the form's Load event procedure:
formname.Top = (Screen.Height - *formname*.Height) /2
formname.Left = (Screen.Width - *formname*.Width) /2

To have the form resemble a standard dialog box:

■ Change the form's BorderStyle property to 3-Fixed Dialog.

To have Visual Basic perform code at specified intervals of time:

■ Include a Timer control on the form. Set the Timer controls Interval property to the number of milliseconds for each interval. Code the Timer control's Timer property.

To change the appearance of the mouse pointer while an application is running:

■ Set the form's MousePointer property.

To remove a coded control from the form:

■ Select the control you want to remove from the form.
■ Delete the code from the control's Code window(s), including the Private Sub and End Sub instructions.
■ Press the Delete key to remove the control from the form.

To verify that a deleted control's code was removed from the application:

■ Open the form's General declarations section and click the Proc list arrow. If the name of the deleted control appears in the list, click the control's name in the list, then highlight the instructions in its Code window (including the Private Sub and End Sub instructions), and then press the Delete key.

QUESTIONS

1. You use the _____ command on the File menu to add an existing file to a project.
   a. Add
   b. Add File
   c. Add Form
   d. Create

2. When you run a multiform project, Visual Basic automatically loads and displays
    _____ .
    a. all of the forms in the application
    b. the first form created
    c. the first form saved
    d. the initial form
    e. the startup form

3. The _____ brings a form into memory, but it does not display the form on
    the screen.
    a. Display statement
    b. Load method
    c. Load statement
    d. Show method
    e. Show statement

4. The _____ removes a form from memory and from the screen.
    a. Erase method
    b. Hide method
    c. Remove statement
    d. Unload method
    e. Unload statement

5. You use the _____ to display a form on the screen.
    a. Display statement
    b. Load method
    c. Load statement
    d. Show method
    e. Show statement

6. If a form is not already loaded into memory, the _____ loads it before dis-
    playing it.
    a. Display statement
    b. Load method
    c. Load statement
    d. Show method
    e. Show statement

7. The _____ removes a form from the screen, but leaves it in memory.
    a. Erase method
    b. Hide method
    c. Remove statement
    d. Unload method
    e. Unload statement

8. A _____ is a form that does not require the user to take any action before
    the focus can switch to another form or dialog box, or before subsequent code is
    executed.
    a. modal
    b. modeless

9. A _____ is a form that requires the user to take some action before the
    focus can switch to another form or dialog box, or before any subsequent code can be
    executed.
    a. modal
    b. modeless

10. When a form is _____ , you can still access other applications using Alt-Tab (or clicking the application in the Windows 95 taskbar.)
    a. modal
    b. modeless
    c. either modal or modeless

11. When two procedures in *different* forms need to use the *same* variable, you declare the variable as a _____ variable.
    a. form-level
    b. global
    c. local

12. You center a form by setting its _____ and _____ properties.
    a. Height
    b. Left
    c. Size
    d. Top
    e. Width

13. To make a form resemble a standard dialog box, change its _____ property to 3-Fixed Dialog.
    a. Border
    b. BorderSize
    c. BorderStyle
    d. Dialog
    e. Style

14. You can use a(n) _____ control to execute code at regular intervals.
    a. Clock
    b. Interval
    c. Time
    d. Timer

15. A form's _____ controls the appearance of the mouse pointer while the application is running.
    a. Button
    b. Mouse
    c. MouseButton
    d. MousePointer
    e. MouseStyle

EXERCISES

NOTE: When completing the exercises in this lesson, you should remember the following:
- If necessary, enter the Option Explicit statement in the appropriate locations.
- Use variables.
- Always assign access keys to the appropriate controls in the forms.
- Be sure to center the forms in the application.
- Assign a default command button to the form.
- If you are creating a dialog box, be sure to change the appropriate property so that the form resembles a standard dialog box.

1. In this exercise you will practice with both a modal and a modeless form.
    a. Click File, then click Open Project to view the Open Project dialog box. Try clicking other areas of the screen. Were you able to move the focus out of the Open Project dialog box? Does that mean the Open Project dialog box is modal or modeless?

b. Close the Open Project dialog box.

c. Click Help, then click Search for Help On. When the Help window appears, try clicking other areas of the screen. Were you able to move the focus out of the Help window? Does that mean that the Help window is modal or modeless?

d. Close the Help window.

e. On a piece of paper, answer the questions posed in steps a and c.

2. In this exercise, you will use two forms and string concatenation. You cannot complete this exercise if you are using the Visual Basic Working Model.

Scenario: RM Sales wants an application that will allow the user to enter the name of a salesperson. The salesperson's name will then be displayed in a label control that is located on another form, along with the following message "The award goes to ". For example, if the user enters Anu Patel, the message will say "The award goes to Anu Patel." (without the quotes, but with the period after the name).

a. Open the lc2 (lc2.vbp) project, which is located in the Tut03 folder on your Student Disk. View the frmAward form.

b. Read the Note at the beginning of the Exercise section.

c. Save the form and the project as lc2Done.

d. Add the t3Input (t3input.frm) file to the project, which is located in the Tut03 folder on your Student Disk, then save the t3Input form file as lc2input.

e. Add a code module to the form, then save the code module as lc2Mod.

f. Save the project using its current name (lc2Done).

g. Have the application display the frmInput form, which requests the salesperson's name, first. The frmInput form should be a standard dialog box. The frmInput form's OK button should assign the salesperson's name to a variable, then display the frmAward form and unload the frmInput form.

h. Code the frmAward form's Load event procedure so that it displays the message and the salesperson's name. Assign the message to a constant.

i. Save and run the application. Enter your name as the salesperson's name. Print the frmAward form with the test data showing, then exit the application.

j. Print the code for the entire project. (Click Project in the Range section of the Print dialog box.)

k. Submit the printouts and code from steps i and j.

3. In this exercise you will create a dialog box and add a form to it. You cannot complete this exercise if you are using the Visual Basic Working Model.

Scenario: RM Sales wants an application that allows the clerk to enter the current sales for four sales regions and the projected sales percentages for those regions. They want the application to calculate the projected sales.

a. Read the Note at the beginning of the Exercise section.

b. Open a new project, if necessary. Name the form frmRate, then save the form and the project as lc3Done.

c. Design the frmRate form so that it allows the user to enter the decimal equivalent of four percentage rates: the North region's rate, the South region's rate, the East region's rate, and the West region's rate. Include an OK button on the form. The form should resemble a standard dialog box.

d. Add the lc3 (lc3.frm) file, which is located in the Tut03 folder on your Student Disk, to the project. View the frmRMSales form, then save the form as lc3Sales.

e. Add a code module to the form, then save the code module as lc3Mod.

f. Have the application display the frmRate form first. The rates entered on the frmRate form will need to be used by the Projected Sales button, which is on the frmRMSales form. The Projected Sales button should display the rates, formatted to percent, in the appropriate label controls on the frmRMSales form. It should also calculate and display the projected sales, formatted to currency, in the appropriate label controls on the frmRMSales form.

g. The Projected Sales button should send the focus to the Print button. The Print button should send the focus to the North region's text box.

h. Save and run application. First enter the four rates in the frmRate form. When the frmRMSales form appears, enter the four sales. Calculate the projected sales, then print the form with the test data showing. Use the following rates and sales:

	Rates	Sales
North region:	.10	25000
South region:	.25	50000
East region:	.15	124000
West region:	.20	111000

i. Click the Exit button to end the application. Print the frmRate form's Form Image. Also print the code for the entire project. (Click Project in the Range section of the Print dialog box.)

j. Submit the printouts and code from steps h and i.

4. In this exercise you will create a dialog box and a form. You cannot complete this exercise if you are using the Visual Basic Working Model.

Scenario: The math teacher at the local high school has asked you to create an application that will display the square and square root of a number.

a. Read the Note at the beginning of the Exercise section. Although the design of the application is up to you, you must use two forms in the application. One of the forms should prompt the student for his or her name; that form should resemble a standard dialog box. You also must display the name on the main form when the main form is first run. The main form should include a Square/Square Root button, a Print button, and an Exit button. Use the InputBox function in the Square/Square Root button to prompt the user for the number. The application should display both the square and square root of the number. (Hint: You can use Visual Basic Sqr function, whose syntax is Sqr(*number*), to calculate the square root.)

b. The Print button should send the focus to the Square/Square Root button.

c. Save the main form and the project as lc4Done. Save the dialog box form as lc4Name. Save the code module as lc4Mod.

d. Follow the five steps involved in creating an application:
1) Plan the application. (Prepare a TOE chart, ordered by object, and draw a sketch of the user interface.)
2) Build the user interface.
3) Code the application. (Be sure to write pseudocode for each of the objects that will be coded.)
4) Test and debug the application. (Use the sample data provided in the exercise.)
5) Assemble the documentation.

e. Save and run the application. Enter your name, then print the application twice, using the following test data: 144 and 9.

f. Print the code for the entire project, and also print the Form Image for both forms. (Click Project in the Range section of the Print dialog box.)

g. Submit the TOE chart, sketch, pseudocode, printouts, and code from steps e and f.

5. In this exercise you will design and create an application on your own.

Scenario: Your friend Joe accumulates a lot of pennies in a jar, which he empties every month when he goes to the bank. As a favor, you decide to create an application that allows him to enter the number of pennies, and then calculates the number of dollars, quarters, dimes, nickels, and pennies he will receive when he trades the pennies in at the bank. (Hint: Review the mathematical operators listed in Figure 2-30 in Tutorial 2.)

a. Read the Note at the beginning of the Exercise section. Although the design of the application is up to you, you must include a Print button that will print the user interface, and an Exit button that will end the application.

b. Save the form and the project as lc5Done.

c. Follow the five steps involved in creating an application:
1) Plan the application. (Prepare a TOE chart, ordered by object, and draw a sketch of the user interface.)
2) Build the user interface.

3) Code the application. (Use variables. Be sure to write pseudocode for each of the objects that will be coded.)

4) Test and debug the application. (Use the sample data provided in the exercise.)

5) Assemble the documentation.

d. Save and run the application. Print the application twice, using the following test data: 2311 pennies and 7333 pennies.

e. Print the application's code.

f. Submit the TOE chart, sketch, pseudocode, printouts, and code from steps d and e.

6. In this exercise you will design and create an application on your own.

Scenario: The principal of Hinsbrook School would like you to create an application that will help her students, who are in grades 1 through 6, learn how to make change. The application should allow the student to enter the amount the customer owes and the amount of money the customer paid. The application should calculate the amount of change, as well as how many dollars, quarters, dimes, nickels, and pennies to return to the customer. For now, you do not have to worry about the situation where the price is greater than what the customer pays. You can always assume that the customer paid either the exact amount or more than the exact amount. (Hints: Review the mathematical operators listed in Figure 2-30 in Tutorial 2. Or, you can also display the Help window on the Int function.)

a. Read the Note at the beginning of the Exercise section. Although the design of the application is up to you, you must Include a Calculate Change button, which uses the InputBox function to prompt the user for the amount due and the amount paid. The Calculate Change button will display the amount due, amount paid, change, number of dollars, number of quarters, number of dimes, number of nickels, and number of pennies. Format the amount due, amount paid, and change to currency. You must also include a Print button that will print the user interface, a Clear button that will clear the user interface, and an Exit button that will end the application.

b. The Print button should send the focus to the Clear Screen button. The Clear Screen button should send the focus to the Calculate Change button.

c. Save the form and the project as lc6Done.

d. Follow the five steps involved in creating an application:

1) Plan the application. (Prepare a TOE chart, ordered by object, and draw a sketch of the user interface.)

2) Build the user interface.

3) Code the application. (Use variables. Be sure to write pseudocode for each of the objects that will be coded.)

4) Test and debug the application. (Use the sample data provided in the exercise.)

5) Assemble the documentation.

e. Save and run the application. Print the application three times, using the following test data:

75.33 as the amount due and 80.00 as the amount paid

39.67 as the amount due and 50.00 as the amount paid

45.55 as the amount due and 45.55 as the amount paid

f. Print the application's code.

g. Submit the TOE chart, sketch, pseudocode, printouts, and code from steps e and f.

Exercises 7 through 9 are Discovery Exercises. Discovery Exercises, which may include topics that are not covered in the tutorial, allow you to "discover" the solutions to problems on your own.

7. In this exercise, you will discover the difference between setting a form's BorderStyle property to 3-Fixed Dialog, and setting the form's MinButton and MaxButton properties to False.

a. Open a new project. Set the form's BorderStyle property to 3-Fixed Dialog. Run, but don't save the project. Notice the border. End the project.

b. Set the form's BorderStyle property back to its default, 2-Sizeable. Set the form's MinButton property to False and set its MaxButton property to False. Run, but don't save the project. Notice the border. End the project.

c. Although the borders in step a and step b look similar, they do not react to the user in the same way. Explain the difference between setting the BorderStyle property to 2-Sizeable and setting both the MinButton and MaxButton properties to False. You may find it helpful to display the Help windows for the BorderStyle, MinButton, and MaxButton properties.

8. In this exercise, you will discover the effect of setting the ClipControls property. You cannot complete this exercise if you are using the Visual Basic Working Model.

a. Use the Help menu to display the ClipControls property's Help window. You will notice that it mentions that complex forms usually load faster when the ClipControls property is set to False.

b. Open the lcOrder (lcorder.vbp) project that you created in Lesson C. Set the frmCopyright form's ClipControls property to False. Also set the frmOrder form's ClipControls property to False.

c. Save and run the project. You should notice that the forms load faster than they did when the ClipControls property was set to True.

9. In this exercise, you will discover the difference between the Val function and the CCur function.

a. Open a new project. Add a text box and a command button to the interface. Remove the Text property from the text box.

b. Open the Command1 button's Click event procedure, press the Tab key, then type `print val(text1.text) * 2` and press the Enter key. Close the Code window.

c. Run, but don't save the application.

d. Type 5000 in the text box, then click the Command1 button. The number 10000 appears in the upper-left corner of the form. Type 5,000 in the text box, then click the Command1 button. The number 10 appears on the form. Type $5000 in the text box, then click the Command1 button. A 0 (zero) appears on the form. On a piece of paper, summarize what this example shows you about the Val function.

e. Stop the application. Use the Help menu to search for the CCur function's Help window. Read the Help window, then close it.

f. Open the Command1 button's Click event procedure. Change the Val in the Print statement to CCur. The statement should now read `Print CCur(Text1.Text) * 2`. Close the Code window.

g. Run, but don't save the application.

h. Type 5000 in the text box, then click the Command1 button. The number 10000 appears in the upper-left corner of the form. Type 5,000 in the text box, then click the Command1 button. The number 10000 appears on the form. Type $5000 in the text box, then click the Command1 button. The number 10000 appears on the form. On a piece of paper, summarize what this example shows you about the CCur function.

i. Stop the application. Submit the summaries from steps d and h.

D E B U G G I N G

Technique

One of the most common errors made in writing code is mistyping the name of a variable. When you don't keep a variable's name consistent throughout the code, you create a bug in the program. You can have Visual Basic help you find this type of bug by entering the Option Explicit statement in the General declarations section of the form. Then if you use the name of a variable that has not been previously declared, Visual Basic will inform you of the error when you run the application.

If your application uses the InputBox function, remember that the user can:

- enter a valid response, then click the OK button
- enter an invalid response, then click the OK button
- click the OK button without entering a response
- click the Cancel button

You should test your application to see how it handles the various InputBox responses.

Remember that the Val function converts a string expression into a numeric value. Because Visual Basic must be able to interpret the string expression as a numeric value, the expression cannot include a letter or a special character, such as the dollar sign, comma, or the percent sign (%); it can, however, include the period. When Visual Basic encounters an invalid character in the Val function's string expression, Visual Basic stops converting the string expression to a number at that point.

Following are three debugging exercises that will allow you to practice your debugging skills.

Exercises

1. In this exercise, you will debug an application. Use the information in the debugging techniques section to help you.

   a. Start Visual Basic and open the t3db1 (t3db1.vbp) project, which is in the Tut03 folder on your Student disk. Click the **View Form** button, then **run**, but don't save, the project.

   b. Click the **Compute Average** button, type **300** as the first number and press the **Enter** key, then type **100** as the second number and press the **Enter** key. Notice that the application is not working correctly. Click the **Exit** button to end the application.

   c. Print the code.

   d. To help you find some of the errors in the code, type the **Option Explicit** statement in the form's General declarations section. (Note: The Option Explicit statement will not find all the errors.)

   e. **Run**, but don't save, the application. Click the **Compute Average** button, then correct the errors.

   f. After all of the errors are corrected, test the application with the following data:

      First number: 300
      Second number: 100

      The average should be 200.

   g. When the application is working correctly, print the code. You do not need to save the corrected application.

2. In this exercise, you will debug an application. Use the information in the debugging techniques section to help you.

   a. Start Visual Basic and open the t3db2 (t3db2.vbp) project, which is in the Tut03 folder on your Student disk. Click the **View Form** button, then **run**, but don't save, the project.

   b. Click the **Compute Sum** button, then click the **OK** button without entering a number. Click the **Debug** button. Notice the line of code that is not working correctly. Click the **End** button ▪ to end the application. Close the Code window.

   c. **Run**, but don't save, the application. Click the **Compute Sum** button, then click the **Cancel** button. Click the **Debug** button. Notice the line of code that is not working correctly. Click the **End** button ▪ to end the application. Close the Code window.

   d. Use the Help menu to display the InputBox function's Help window. Read the Help window, then close it.

   e. Correct the problem line(s) of code so that the application will not result in an error message when the user clicks the OK button without entering any data, and when the user clicks the Cancel button.

   f. **Run**, but don't save, the application. Click the **Compute Sum** button, then click the **Cancel** button when prompted for the first number. Also click the **Cancel** button when prompted for the second number. The application should not result in an error message. Click the **Compute Sum** button again. This time click the **OK** button when prompted for both the first and second numbers. The application should not result in an error message.

   g. When the application is working correctly, print the code. You do not need to save the corrected application.

3. In this exercise, you will debug an application. Use the information in the debugging techniques section to help you.

   a. Start Visual Basic and open the t3db3 (t3db3.vbp) project, which is in the Tut03 folder on your Student disk. Click the **View Form** button, then **run**, but don't save, the project.

   b. Type **10000** as the sales, then click the **Compute Commission** button. The application should calculate a 5% commission on the sales. Notice, however, that the application is not working correctly. Click the **Exit** button to end the application.

   c. Use the Help menu to display the Val function's Help window. Read the Help window, then close it.

   d. Correct the problem line(s) of code so that the application will work correctly.

   e. **Run**, but don't save, the application. Type **10000** as the sales, then click the **Compute Commission** button. The application should display a 5% commission ($500.00).

   f. When the application is working correctly, print the code. You do not need to save the corrected application.

TUTORIAL 4

The Selection Structure

Creating a Math Application

case ▶ On Monday you meet with Susan Chen, the principal of a local primary school. Ms. Chen needs an application that the first and second grade students can use to practice both adding and subtracting numbers. The application should display the addition or subtraction problem on the screen, then allow the student to enter the answer, and then verify that the answer is correct. If the student's answer is not correct, the application should give him or her as many chances as necessary to answer the problem correctly.

The problems displayed for the first grade students should use numbers from one through 10 only; the problems for the second grade students should use numbers from 10 through 100. Because the first and second grade students have not learned about negative numbers yet, the subtraction problems should never ask them to subtract a larger number from a smaller one.

Ms. Chen also wants the application to keep track of how many correct and incorrect responses the student makes; this information will help her assess the student's math ability. Because she doesn't want any additional pressure placed on the student while he or she is using the application, Ms. Chen wants to be able to control the display of this information.

Previewing the Completed Application

You'll begin by previewing the completed Math application.

To preview the completed application:

1 If necessary, start Windows, then place your Student Disk in the appropriate drive.

2 Use the Run command on the Start menu to run the **Math95** (math95.exe) file, which is located in the Tut04 folder on your Student Disk. The Math application's user interface appears on the screen. See Figure 4-1.

windows 3.1

Use the Run command on the Program Manager's File menu to run the math31.exe file, which is located in the Tut04 folder on your Student Disk. The Math application's user interface appears on the screen. See Figure 4-1.

your numbers may differ

enter the answer here

check box

option buttons

frame

Figure 4-1: Math application's user interface

Don't worry if the numbers on your screen do not match the ones in the figure. This application uses the Randomize statement and the Rnd and Int functions to display random numbers in the two label controls. You will learn how to use the Randomize statement and the Rnd and Int functions in Lesson B.

The Math application contains several new controls—option buttons, a check box, and frames. You will learn about these controls in Lesson B.

3 Click the **Display summary information** check box to select it. A check mark (*or an X if you are using Windows 3.1*) appears inside the check box, and a frame control, which will display the number of correct and incorrect responses, appears below the check box.

4 Type the correct answer to the addition problem appearing in the interface, then press the **Enter** key. (The Verify Answer button is the default command button.) The interface appears similar to Figure 4-2. Remember, your math problem may be different from the one shown in the figure.

enter the answer here

new problem appears

happy face icon appears with correct answer

number of correct responses

Figure 4-2: Interface showing that a correct response was made

When you answer the problem correctly, a happy face icon appears in the image control located to the left of the Verify Answer button. The number 1 appears as the number of correct responses, and a new problem appears in the interface.

5 Click the **Subtraction** option button. A black dot appears in the center of the Subtraction button, which indicates that the option button is selected. The math problem changes to one involving subtraction.

6 Click inside the text box in which you enter the answer. Type an incorrect answer to the subtraction problem appearing on the screen, then press the **Enter** key. The application removes the happy face from the image control and displays a dialog box that says "Try again."

7 Press the **Enter** key to remove the dialog box. The application highlights the incorrect answer in the text box and gives you another chance to enter a correct response. The interface shows that you have made one correct response and one incorrect response.

8 Type the correct answer to the subtraction problem, then press the **Enter** key. The happy face icon reappears, and the number of correct responses now says 2. The application displays a new math problem in the interface.

9 Click the **Display summary information** check box to deselect it. Visual Basic removes the check mark (*or the X if you are using Windows 3.1*) from the check box, and hides the frame control that contains the summary information.

10 Click the **Exit** button. The application ends.

Before you can begin coding the Math application, you will need to learn about the selection structure. You will learn that structure in Lesson A. In Lesson B you will complete the Math application's interface as you learn how to use three new controls: option buttons, check boxes, and frames. You will begin coding the application in Lesson B, and complete the application in Lesson C.

In this lesson you will learn how to:

- Write pseudocode for the selection structure
- Create a flowchart to help you plan an application's code
- Write an If...Then...Else statement
- Write code that uses relational operators and logical operators
- Write a nested selection structure
- Write the Select Case statement

The If...Then...Else and Select Case Statements

The Selection Structure

The applications you created in the previous three tutorials used the sequence programming structure only, where each of the program instructions was processed, one after another, in the order in which they appeared in the Code window. In many applications, however, the next instruction to be processed will depend on the result of a decision or a comparison that the program must make. For example, a payroll program might need to decide if an employee worked overtime. Assuming a 40-hour workweek, the program can make that determination by comparing the number of hours the employee worked with the number 40. Based on the result of that comparison, the program will then select either an instruction that computes regular pay or an instruction that computes overtime pay.

You use the **selection structure**, also called the **decision structure**, when you want a program to make a decision or comparison and then, based on the result of that decision or comparison, to select one of two paths. You can think of the selection structure as being a fork in the road. The selection structure, you might recall, is one of the three programming structures. The other two are sequence, which was covered in the previous tutorials, and repetition, which will be covered in Tutorial 5. You will need to use the selection structure to complete the Math application.

Each day you probably make hundreds of decisions, some so minor that you might not even realize you've made them. For example, every morning you have to decide if you are hungry and, if you are, what you are going to eat. Figure 4-3 shows other decisions you might have to make today.

Example 1	Example 2
If *it's raining* then	If *you have a test tomorrow* then
wear a rain coat	study tonight
bring an umbrella	Otherwise
	watch a movie

Figure 4-3: Decisions you might need to make today

In the examples shown in Figure 4-3, the portion in *italics*, called the **condition**, specifies the decision you are making and is phrased so that it results in either a true (yes) or a false (no) answer only. For example, either it's raining (true/yes) or it's not raining (false/no); either you have a test tomorrow (true/yes) or you don't have a test tomorrow (false/no).

If the condition is true, you perform a specific set of tasks. If the condition is false, however, you might or might not need to perform a different set of tasks. For instance, look at the first example shown in Figure 4-3. If it's raining (a true condition), then you will wear a raincoat and bring an umbrella. Notice, however, that you don't have anything in particular to do if it's not raining (a false condition). Compare this to the second example shown in Figure 4-3. If you have a test tomorrow (a true condition), then you will study tonight. If you don't have a test tomorrow (a false condition), however, then you will watch a movie.

Writing Pseudocode for the Selection Structure

Like you, the computer can also evaluate a condition and then select the appropriate tasks to perform based on that evaluation. The programmer must be sure to phrase the condition so that it results in either a true or a false answer only. The programmer must also specify the tasks to be performed when the condition is true and, if necessary, the tasks to be performed when the condition is false. Programmers refer to this as the **selection structure** (or the **decision structure**). Figure 4-4 shows two examples of the selection structure written in pseudocode.

Selection with a true path only	Selection with both true and false paths
If the part number is "AB203" then	If the sales > 1500 then
Assign "Desk" as the item name	Calculate commission = .02 * sales
Assign 56.60 as the item price	Else
End If	Calculate commission = .01 * sales
Display the part number in the lblPartno control	End If
	Display the commission in the lblComm control

Figure 4-4: Two examples of the If...Then...Else selection structure written in pseudocode

Although pseudocode is not standardized—every programmer has his or her own version—you will find some similarities among the various versions. For example, many programmers begin the selection structure with the word If and end the structure with the two words End If. The reason for the similarity in pseudocode is quite simple: the pseudocode written by many programmers greatly resembles the programming language they are using to code the program. Because many programming languages require the keywords If and End If in the selection structure code, those words generally appear in the programmer's pseudocode.

In the examples shown in Figure 4-4, the *italicized* portion of the instruction indicates the condition to be evaluated. Notice that each condition results in either a true or a false answer only. Either the part number is "AB203" or it isn't. Either the sales are greater than the number 1500, or they aren't.

When the condition is true, the set of instructions following the Then is selected for processing. The instructions following Then are referred to as the true path—the path you follow when the condition is true. The true path ends when you come to the Else or, if there is no Else, when you come to the end of the selection structure (the End If). After the true path instructions are processed, the instruction following the End If is processed. In the examples shown in Figure 4-4, the "Display" instructions would be processed after the true instructions.

The instructions selected for processing when the condition is false—the false path—depend on whether the selection structure contains an Else. When there is no Else, as in the first example shown in Figure 4-4, the instruction following the End If is processed when the condition is false. In the first example, for instance, the "Display the part number in the lblPartno control" is processed when the part number is not "AB203." In cases where the selection structure contains an Else, as in the second example shown in Figure 4-4, the set of instructions between the Else and the End If are processed first and then the instruction after the End If is processed. In the second example, the "Calculate commission = .01 * sales" is processed first, then the "Display the commission in the lblComm control" is processed.

In the next section you will learn how to show the selection structure in a flowchart.

Using a Flowchart

Besides using pseudocode, programmers also use flowcharts to help them plan each object's code. Unlike pseudocode, which is comprised of English-like statements, a flowchart uses standardized symbols to show the steps an object needs to take in order to accomplish its tasks. Figure 4-5 shows Figure 4-4's examples in flowchart form.

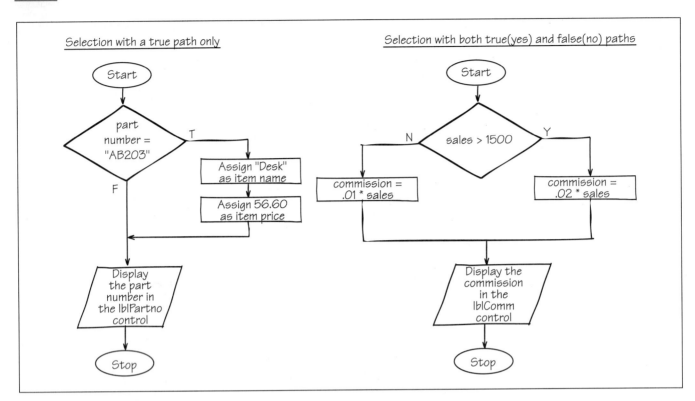

Figure 4-5: Two examples of the If...Then...Else selection structure drawn in flowchart form

You will notice that the flowcharts contain four different symbols—an oval, a rectangle, a parallelogram, and a diamond. The symbols are connected together with lines, called **flowlines**. The oval symbol is called the **start/stop symbol**. The start oval indicates the beginning of the flowchart, and the stop oval indicates the end of the flowchart. Between the start and the stop ovals are two rectangles, called **process symbols**. You use the process symbol to represent tasks such as declaring variables, assigning values to variables and to the properties of controls, setting the focus, and for calculations. In the first example, both rectangles represent assignment tasks. In the second example, both rectangles represent calculations.

The parallelogram is called the **input/output symbol**; it is used to represent input tasks, such as getting information from the user, and output tasks, such as displaying information. In both flowchart examples, the parallelograms represent output tasks.

The diamond in a flowchart is called the **selection/repetition symbol** because it is used to represent both selection and repetition. In Figure 4-5's flowcharts, the diamonds represent the selection structure. (You will learn how to use the diamond for repetition in Tutorial 5.) Notice that inside each diamond is a question that has a true (yes) or false (no) answer only. Each diamond also has one flowline entering the symbol and two flowlines leaving the symbol. The two flowlines leading out of the diamond should be marked so that anyone reading the flowchart can distinguish the true path from the false path. You can mark the flowlines either with a "T" and an "F" (for true and false) or a "Y" and an "N" (for yes and no).

To translate the flowchart into Visual Basic code, you simply start at the top of the flowchart and write the code for each symbol as you follow the flowlines down to the bottom of the flowchart. Some symbols in a flowchart may require more than one line of code. The only symbol that is not coded is the start oval. In the next section you will learn how to code the selection structure in Visual Basic.

Coding the Selection Structure in Visual Basic

You use the **If...Then...Else statement** to code the selection structure in Visual Basic. The syntax of the If...Then...Else statement is shown in Figure 4-6.

If *condition* **Then**

    [*instructions when the condition is true*]

[Else

    [*instructions when the condition is false*]**]**

End If

Figure 4-6: Syntax of If...Then...Else statement

In the syntax, the items in square brackets ([ ]) are optional. For example, the Else portion of the syntax, referred to as the Else clause, is optional; you don't need to include an Else clause in an If...Then...Else statement. Words in **bold**, however, are essential components of the If...Then...Else statement. The words If, Then, and End If, for instance, must be included in the statement. (The word Else must be included only if the statement uses the Else clause.) Items in *italics* indicate where the programmer must supply information pertaining to the current application. For instance, the programmer must supply the *condition* to be evaluated. The *condition* can contain variables, constants, properties, functions, mathematical operators, relational operators, and logical operators. You already know about variables, constants, properties, functions, and the mathematical operators. You will learn about the relational operators and the logical operators in the next two sections.

Relational Operators

Figure 4-7 lists the relational operators you can use in the If...Then...Else statement's *condition*.

Relational Operator	Meaning
=	Equal to
>	Greater than
>=	Greater than or equal to
<	Less than
<=	Less than or equal to
<>	Not equal to

Figure 4-7: Relational operators

Unlike the mathematical operators, the relational operators do not have an order of precedence. If an expression contains more than one relational operator, Visual Basic evaluates the relational operators from left to right in the expression. Keep in mind, however, that relational operators are evaluated after any mathematical operators in the expression. In other words, in the expression 5 − 2 > 1 + 2, the two mathematical operators (−, +) will be evaluated before the relational operator (>). The result of the expression is false, as shown in Figure 4-8.

Original Expression: 5 - 2 > 1 + 2

Evaluation steps:	Result:
5 - 2 is evaluated first	3 > 1 + 2
1 + 2 is evaluated second	3 > 3
3 > 3 is evaluated last	False

Figure 4-8: Evaluation steps for an expression containing mathematical and relational operators

All expressions containing a relational operator will result in either a true or false answer only. To illustrate this, your Student Disk contains a partially completed project, named "If." You will use this project to practice various If...Then...Else statements that contain relational operators in the *condition*.

To open the if project:

1 Start Visual Basic, if necessary, and open the **if** (if.vbp) project, which is in the Tut04 folder on your Student Disk.

2 Save the form and the project as **laIf**.

3 Click the **View Form** button in the Project window to view the frmIf form. The frmIf form appears on the screen. See Figure 4-9.

Figure 4-9: frmIf form

Example 1   **VB 245**

Some of the command buttons have been coded for you. For example, the Exit button contains the End instruction, which will end the application. The Clear button contains the following three instructions: `lblMsg.Caption = ""`, `txtData.Text = ""`, and `txtData.SetFocus`. These instructions clear the contents of the label control and the text box, then place the focus in the text box. You will now code the Click event procedure for the Example 1 command button.

Example 1

Assume you are creating a checkbook application. You will enter the amount of a transaction as a number in the text box on the screen. If the number entered in the text box is less than zero, you want to display the string "Withdrawal" in the label control. Figure 4-10 shows the flowchart, pseudocode, and Visual Basic code to accomplish this.

Figure 4-10: Flowchart, pseudocode, and Visual Basic code for Example 1

The Val(txtData.Text < 0) condition tells Visual Basic to compare the contents of the txtData control's Text property, converted to a number, with the number 0. If the condition is true, which means the number entered is less than 0, then the string "Withdrawal" will appear in the label control. If the condition is false, which means the number entered is not less than 0 (in other words, it's greater than or equal to 0), nothing will appear in the label control.

To code the Example 1 button:

1 Double-click the **Example 1** button to open its Code window. The button's Click event procedure appears.

2 Press **the Tab** key, then type **if val(txtData.text) < 0 then** and press the **Enter** key. Be sure to type the number 0, and not the letter O.

Now enter the true path instructions. Programmers usually indent these instructions for easier readability.

3   Press the **Tab** key, then type **lblMsg.caption = "Withdrawal"** and press the **Enter** key.

4   Press the **Backspace** key to cancel the indentation, then type **end if** and press the **Enter** key. Compare your instructions with Figure 4-11.

```
frmIf                                              _ □ ✕
Object:  cmdExam1          ▼    Proc:  Click              ▼

Private Sub cmdExam1_Click()                         ▲
    If Val(txtData.Text) < 0 Then
        lblMsg.Caption = "Withdrawal"
    End If
    |
End Sub
```

Figure 4-11: Code window for Example 1

5   Close the Code window, then **save and run** the application.

6   Type **−25** (be sure to type the minus sign) in the text box, then click the **Example 1** button to process the instructions in the Click event procedure. The string "Withdrawal" appears in the label control, then the Click event procedure ends. In this case, because the number entered in the text box is less than zero, Visual Basic processes the true path instruction before processing the instruction following the End If—in this case, the End Sub instruction.

7   Click the **Clear** button to clear the contents of the text box and the label control.

8   Type **500** in the text box, then click the **Example 1** button. This time nothing appears in the label control. Notice that when the number in the text box is not less than zero—a false condition—the instruction in the true path is not processed. Instead, Visual Basic processes the instruction following the End If—in this case, the End Sub instruction.

9   Click the **Exit** button. Visual Basic returns to the design screen.

Example 2

This time you will display the string "Withdrawal" when the number entered in the text box is less than zero and the string "Deposit" when the number is greater than or equal to zero. Figure 4-12 shows both the flowchart and the pseudocode to accomplish this.

Example 2   VB 247

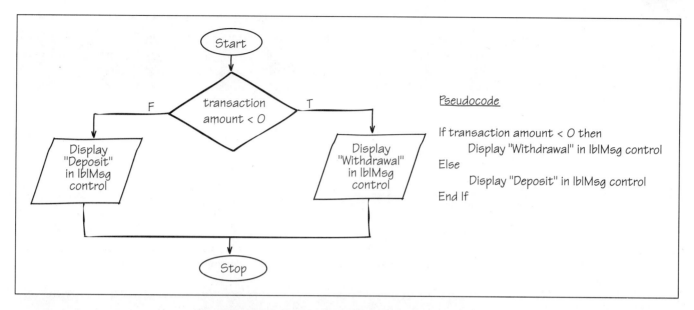

Pseudocode

If transaction amount < 0 then
  Display "Withdrawal" in lblMsg control
Else
  Display "Deposit" in lblMsg control
End If

Figure 4-12: Flowchart and pseudocode for Example 2

To save you time, the Visual Basic instructions have already been entered in the Example 2 button's Click event procedure.

To view the instructions in the Example 2 button's Click event procedure:

1 Double-click the **Example 2** button to open its Code window. The Click event procedure appears as shown in Figure 4-13.

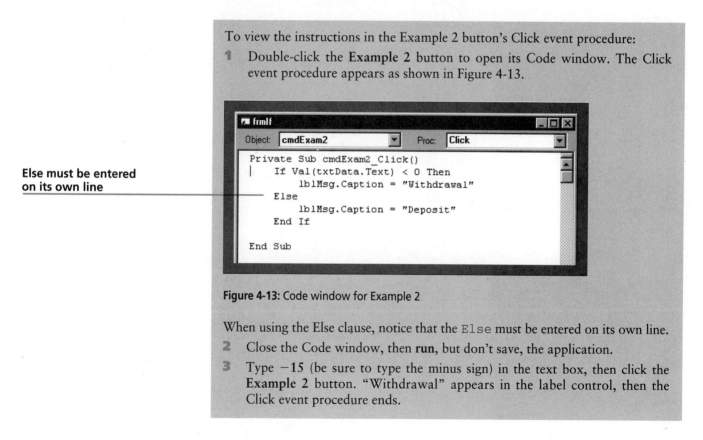

Else must be entered on its own line

```
Private Sub cmdExam2_Click()
    If Val(txtData.Text) < 0 Then
        lblMsg.Caption = "Withdrawal"
    Else
        lblMsg.Caption = "Deposit"
    End If

End Sub
```

Figure 4-13: Code window for Example 2

When using the Else clause, notice that the Else must be entered on its own line.

2 Close the Code window, then **run**, but don't save, the application.

3 Type **−15** (be sure to type the minus sign) in the text box, then click the **Example 2** button. "Withdrawal" appears in the label control, then the Click event procedure ends.

4 Click the **Clear** button, type 5 in the text box, then click the **Example 2** button. This time, "Deposit" appears in the label control, then the Click event procedure ends.

5 Click the **Exit** button. Visual Basic returns to the design screen.

Recall that you can also use logical operators to form the If...Then...Else statement's *condition*. Visual Basic has six logical operators—the most commonly used ones are Not, And, and Or.

Logical Operators

You can use the logical operators to combine several conditions into one compound condition. Figure 4-14 shows the three most commonly used logical operators, their meaning, and their order of precedence.

Logical Operator	Meaning	Precedence
Not	Reverses the value of the condition; True becomes False, False becomes True	1
And	All conditions connected by the And operator must be true for the compound condition to be true	2
Or	Only one of the conditions connected by the Or operator needs to be true for the compound condition to be true	3

Figure 4-14: Logical operators

The **truth tables** in Figure 4-15 summarize how Visual Basic evaluates the logical operators in an expression.

tips

If you want to see information about the other logical operators, use the Help menu to search for a Help window on logical operators.

Truth Table for NOT Operator

Value of A	Value of Not A
T	F
F	T

Truth Table for AND Operator

Value of A	Value of B	Value of A And B
T	T	T
T	F	F
F	T	F
F	F	F

Truth Table for OR Operator

Value of A	Value of B	Value of A Or B
T	T	T
T	F	T
F	T	T
F	F	F

Figure 4-15: Truth tables for the logical operators

As Figure 4-15 indicates, the Not operator reverses the truth value of the *condition*, which is referred to as A. If A (the *condition*) is true, then Not A is evaluated as false. Likewise, if A is false, then Not A is true. As you can see, the Not operator can be confusing; it's best to avoid using it if possible. In Tutorial 6, which covers sequential files, you will see a useful purpose for the Not operator. For now you don't need to worry about the Not operator; just be aware that it exists.

Now look at the truth tables for the And and Or operators. Notice that when you use the And operator to combine two conditions, A And B, the resulting compound condition is true only when both conditions are true. If either condition is false or if both conditions are false, then the compound condition is false. Compare that to the Or operator. When you combine conditions using the Or operator, A Or B, notice that the compound condition is false only when both conditions are false. If either condition is true or if both conditions are true, then the compound condition is true. Two examples might help to clarify the difference between the And and the Or operators.

Examples of the And and the Or Operators

Assume that you want to pay a bonus to the salespeople in Virginia whose sales total more than $10,000. To receive a bonus, the salesperson must live in the state of Virginia and he or she must sell more than $10,000 in product. Assuming the application uses the two variables, stState and crSales, you can phrase condition A as stState = "Virginia" and condition B as crSales > 10000. Now the question is "Should you use the And operator or the Or operator to combine both conditions into one compound condition?" To answer this question, you will need to look at the truth tables for the And and the Or operators.

To receive a bonus, remember that both condition A (stState = "Virginia") and condition B (crSales > 10000) must be true at the same time. If either condition is false, or if both conditions are false, then the compound condition should be false, and the salesperson should not receive a bonus. According to the truth tables, both the And and the Or operators will evaluate the compound condition as true when both conditions are true. Only the And operator, however, will evaluate the compound condition as false when either one or both of the conditions is false. The Or operator, you will notice, evaluates the compound condition as false only when *both* conditions are false. Therefore, the correct compound condition to use here is stState = "Virginia" And crSales > 10000.

Now assume that you want to send a letter to all customers living in Virginia and all customers living in Texas. Assuming the application uses the variable stState, you can phrase condition A as stState = "Virginia" and condition B as stState = "Texas". Now which operator do you use—And or Or?

At first it might appear that the And operator is the correct one to use. That's probably because the example says to send the letter to "all customers living in Virginia and all customers living in Texas." In our everyday conversations, you'll find that we sometimes use the word "and" when what we really mean is "or." Although both words do not mean the same thing, using "and" instead of "or" generally doesn't cause a problem because we are able to infer what another person means. Computers, however, cannot infer anything; they simply process the directions you give them, word for word. In this case, you actually want to send a letter to all customers living either in Virginia or in Texas, so you will need to use the Or operator. The Or operator is the only operator that will evaluate the compound condition as true if either one of the conditions is true. The correct compound condition to use here is stState = "Virginia" Or stState = "Texas".

Like expressions containing relational operators, expressions containing logical operators always result in either a true or false answer. The logical operators have an order of precedence as follows: the Not operator is evaluated first, then the And operator, and then the Or operator. Logical operators are evaluated after any mathematical operators or relational operators in the expression. In other words, in the expression, 12 > 0 And 12 < 10 * 2, the mathematical operator (*) is evaluated first, followed by the two relational operators (>, <), followed by the logical operator (And). The expression evaluates to true, as shown in Figure 4-16.

Example 3   **VB 251**

Original Expression: 12 > 0 And 12 < 10 * 2

Evaluation steps:	Result:
10 * 2 is evaluated first	12 > 0 And 12 < 20
12 > 0 is evaluated second	True And 12 < 20
12 < 20 is evaluated third	True And True
True And True is evaluated last	True

Figure 4-16: Evaluation steps for an expression containing mathematical, relational, and logical operators

Example 3

Assume you want the Example 3 button to display the string "In-range" when the number entered in the text box is greater than or equal to 1500, but less than 3000. If the number does not fall in that range, then you want to display the string "Out-of-range". Figure 4-17 shows both the flowchart and the pseudocode to accomplish this.

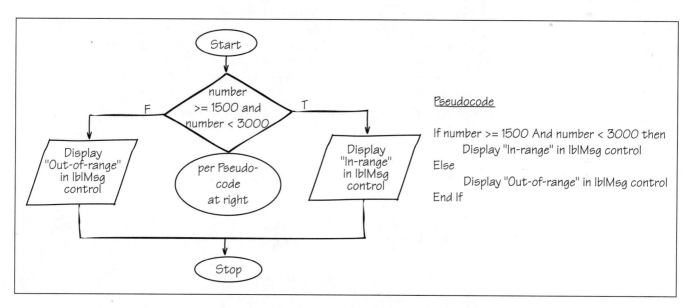

Figure 4-17: Flowchart and pseudocode for Example 3

The necessary Visual Basic instructions have already been entered into the Example 3 button's Code window.

To view Example 3's code, then run the application:

1   Double-click the **Example 3** button to open its Code window, then maximize the Code window. The Click event procedure appears as shown in Figure 4-18.

```
frmIf                                                              _ 8 X
Object:  cmdExam3                    ▼    Proc:  Click                ▼

Private Sub cmdExam3_Click()
    If Val(txtData.Text) >= 1500 And Val(txtData.Text) < 3000 Then
        lblMsg.Caption = "In-range"
    Else
        lblMsg.Caption = "Out-of-range"
    End If

End Sub
```

Figure 4-18: Code window for Example 3

2   Close the Code window, then **run**, but don't save, the application.

3   Type **2500** in the text box, then click the **Example 3** button. The string "In-range" appears in the label control because the number 2500 satisfies both of the conditions listed in the compound condition—it is greater than or equal to 1500 and it is less than 3000.

4   Click the **Clear** button, type **6500** in the text box, then click the **Example 3** button. The string "Out-of-range" appears in the label control because the number 6500 does not satisfy both of the conditions listed in the compound condition. Although 6500 is greater than or equal to 1500, it is not less than 3000.

5   Click the **Exit** button. Visual Basic returns to the design screen.

Now you'll modify Example 3's code to see what happens when you use the Or operator, instead of the And operator, in the If...Then...Else statement.

To modify the Example 3 button's code, then save and run the application:

1   Double-click the **Example 3** button to open its Code window. In the Click event procedure, change the And in the If statement's *condition* to an **Or**. The If statement should now say If Val(txtData.Text) >= 1500 Or Val(txtData.Text) < 3000 Then.

2   Close the Code window, then **save and run** the application.

3   Type **2500** in the text box, then click the **Example 3** button. The string "In-range" appears in the label control because the number 2500 satisfies both conditions listed in the compound condition.

4   Click the **Clear** button, type **6500** in the text box, then click the **Example 3** button. The string "In-range" appears in the label control because the number 6500 satisfies one of the conditions listed in the compound condition—specifically, the number 6500 is greater than or equal to the number 1500. Remember, when you use the Or operator, only one of the conditions needs to be true for the compound condition to be true.

Example 4   **VB 253**

5 Click the **Clear** button, type **3** in the text box, then click the **Example 3** button. The string "In-range" appears in the label control because the number 3 satisfies one of the conditions listed in the compound condition—specifically, the number 3 is less than the number 3000.

6 Click the **Exit** button. Visual Basic returns to the design screen.

By changing the And to an Or, the *condition* `Val(txtData.Text) >= 1500 Or Val(txtData.Text) < 3000`, will always evaluate as true; it will never evaluate as false because all numbers lie within this range.

7 Double-click the **Example 3** button to open its Code window, then change the Or back to an **And** in the If statement's *condition*.

8 Close the Code window, then **save** the application.

Next you'll learn how to include a string comparison in an If...Then...Else statement.

Example 4

Assume you want the Example 4 button to display the word "Pass" if the text box contains the letter P and the word "Fail" if the text box contains anything else. The Visual Basic instructions that would accomplish this have already been entered in the Example 4 button's Click event procedure, as shown in Figure 4-19. (You can open the Code window and view the code, if you want.)

```
frmIf                                          _ □ ×
Object:  cmdExam4          ▼    Proc:  Click           ▼

Private Sub cmdExam4_Click()
    If txtData.Text = "P" Then
        lblMsg.Caption = "Pass"
    Else
        lblMsg.Caption = "Fail"
    End If

End Sub
```

Figure 4-19: Code window for Example 4

To run the application to test the Example 4 button:

1 **Run** the application, type **P** (be sure to use an uppercase letter P) in the text box, then click the **Example 4** button. The string "Pass" appears in the label control.

Next you'll enter a letter other than the letter P.

2 Click the **Clear** button, type **K** in the text box, then click the **Example 4** button. The string "Fail" appears in the label control.

Now enter a lowercase letter p.

3 Click the **Clear** button, type **p** (be sure to type a lowercase letter p) in the text box, then click the **Example 4** button.

Although one might expect the word "Pass" to appear, the word "Fail" appears instead. We'll stop the application at this point and discuss why this happened.

4   Click the **Exit** button. Visual Basic returns to the design screen.

The UCase Function

As is true in many programming languages, string comparisons in Visual Basic are case sensitive. That means that the uppercase version of a letter is not the same as its lowercase counterpart. So, although a human recognizes "P" and "p" as being the same letter, a computer does not; to a computer, a "P" is different from a "p." As you saw in Example 4, a problem occurs when you need to include a string, entered by the user, in a comparison. The problem occurs because you can't control the case in which the user enters the string.

One way of handling the string comparison problem is to include the UCase (uppercase) function in your string comparisons. The syntax of the UCase function is **UCase**(*string*). The function temporarily converts the *string* to uppercase letters. The UCase function does not actually change the *string* to uppercase; the function just treats the *string* as though it contained uppercase letters. Figure 4-20 shows some examples of the UCase function.

UCase function:	Meaning:
If UCase(txtData.Text) = "YES" Then	Compares the uppercase version of the string entered in the text box to the string "YES"
If UCase(txtData.Text) > UCase(stItem)	Compares the uppercase version of the string entered in the text box to the uppercase version of the string contained in the stItem variable.
If "RENO" = UCase(lblCity.Caption)	Compares the string "RENO" to the uppercase version of the string contained in the label control.
txtName.Text = UCase(stEmpName)	Assigns the uppercase version of the string contained in the stEmpName variable to the Text property of the text box.

Figure 4-20: Examples of UCase function

In Example 4, you will need to change the If statement's *condition* from txtData.Text = "P" to UCase(txtData.Text) = "P". Then when Visual Basic processes the If statement, the UCase function will temporarily convert, to uppercase, the string entered in the text box. Visual Basic will then compare the uppercase version of the string to the uppercase letter P. If both are equal, Visual Basic will process the true path instructions; otherwise, it will process the false path instructions. By including the UCase function in the instruction, the user will be able to enter the letter P in any case and have the "Pass" message appear.

tips

· · · · · · · · · · · · · · · · · ·

▶ Visual Basic also has an **LCase** function that temporarily converts a string to lowercase. In order to produce the same results in Example 4, you could use the LCase function as follows: `LCase(txtData.Text) = "p"`.

When using the UCase function, be sure that everything you are comparing is in uppercase. In other words, `UCase(txtData.Text) = "p"` is incorrect because it tells Visual Basic to compare the uppercase version of a string with the lowercase letter p; this condition would always evaluate as false.

To modify the If instruction in Example 4's Click event procedure:

1 Double-click the **Example 4** button to open its Code window. Enter the UCase function as shown in Figure 4-21.

be sure to include the parentheses

```
frmIf                                              _ □ ✕
Object:  cmdExam4          ▾    Proc:   Click        ▾
  Private Sub cmdExam4_Click()
     If UCase(txtData.Text) = "P" Then
          lblMsg.Caption = "Pass"
     Else
          lblMsg.Caption = "Fail"
     End If

  End Sub
```

Figure 4-21: UCase function in Example 4's Code window

2 Close the Code window, then **save** and **run** the application.

3 Type **p** in the text box, then click the **Example 4** button. This time "Pass" appears in the label control.

4 Click the **Exit** button. Visual Basic returns to the design screen.

If...Then...Else statements can also be nested, which means you can place one If...Then...Else statement inside another If...Then...Else statement.

Nested If...Then...Else Statements

A nested If...Then...Else statement is one in which either the Then clause or the Else clause includes yet another If...Then...Else statement. Figures 4-22 and 4-23 show examples of writing a nested selection structure both in pseudocode and in a flow-chart. Figure 4-22 shows the nested If statement in the Then clause; Figure 4-23 shows the nested If statement in the Else clause. (The lines connecting the If, Else, and End If in the pseudocode are not necessary. They are included in the figures to help you see which clauses match up with each other.)

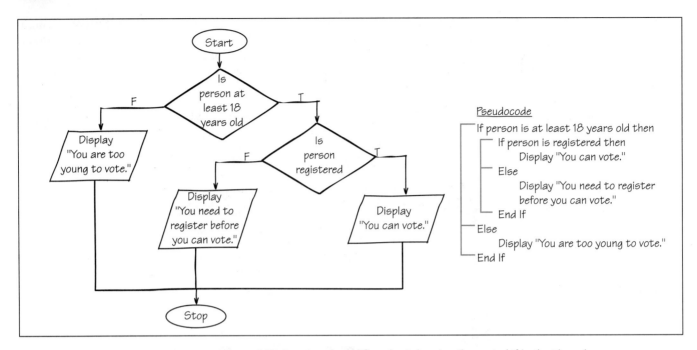

Figure 4-22: Pseudocode and flowchart showing the nested If in the Then clause

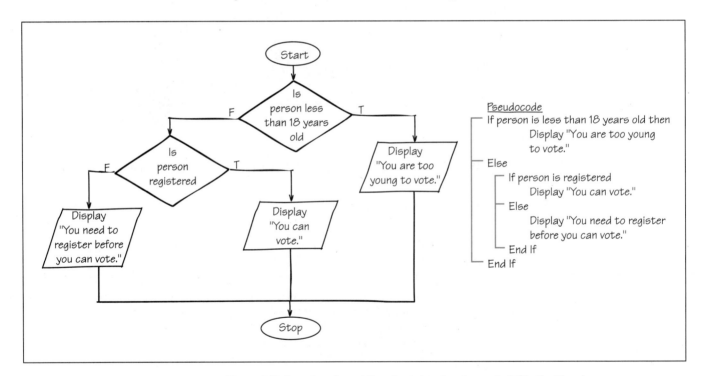

Figure 4-23: Pseudocode and flowchart showing the nested If in the Else clause

Figure 4-24 shows two ways of writing the syntax of the nested selection structure in Visual Basic—with the nested If statement on the Then clause and with the nested If statement on the Else clause.

Example 5   VB 257

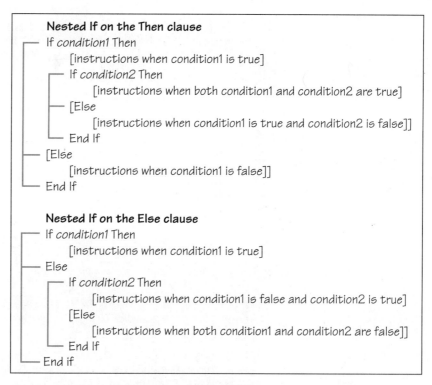

Figure 4-24: Syntax of Visual Basic's nested selection structure

Notice that each If...Then...Else statement is matched with an End If, which marks the end of that If...Then...Else statement. You will use a nested If...Then...Else statement in Example 5.

Example 5

The Example 5 button's Click event procedure contains a nested selection structure with the nested If on the Else clause.

To open Example 5's Code window:

1   Double-click the **Example 5** button to open its Code window, then maximize the Code window. The Click event procedure appears, as shown in Figure 4-25.

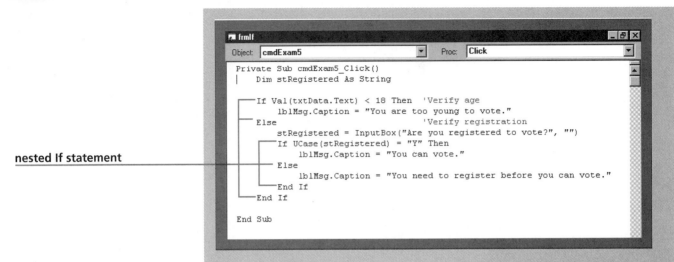

nested If statement

```
frmIf                                                    _ | 日 | X
Object: cmdExam5                ▼   Proc: Click                 ▼
Private Sub cmdExam5_Click()
    Dim stRegistered As String

    If Val(txtData.Text) < 18 Then   'Verify age
        lblMsg.Caption = "You are too young to vote."
    Else                             'Verify registration
        stRegistered = InputBox("Are you registered to vote?", "")
        If UCase(stRegistered) = "Y" Then
            lblMsg.Caption = "You can vote."
        Else
            lblMsg.Caption = "You need to register before you can vote."
        End If
    End If

End Sub
```

Figure 4-25: Code window for Example 5 showing nested If on the Else clause

The nested selection structure first compares the contents of the text box to the number 18. If the number entered in the text box is less than 18, then Visual Basic processes the instruction in the true path (the `lblMsg.Caption = "You are too young to vote."` instruction); otherwise, it processes the instructions in the false path. Notice that the false path contains an assignment statement that uses the InputBox function to ask the user if he or she is registered to vote, and then stores the response in the stRegistered variable. The false path also contains another If...Then...Else statement. This If...Then...Else statement compares the uppercase version of the user's response, stored in the stRegistered variable, to the letter "Y." If the stRegistered variable contains either "Y" or "y," then Visual Basic processes the instruction in the nested If statement's true path (the `lblMsg.Caption = "You can vote."` instruction); otherwise, it processes the instruction in the false path (the `lblMsg.Caption = "You need to register before you can vote."` instruction).

2 Close the Code window, then **run**, but don't save, the application.

First you will enter the number 17 in the text box. A person who is 17 years old is too young to vote.

3 Type **17** in the text box, then click the **Example 5** button. The "You are too young to vote." message appears in the label control.

Now you will enter the number 21. A person who is 21 years old can vote, but only if he or she is registered.

4 Click the **Clear** button, type **21** in the text box, then click the **Example 5** button. The InputBox function displays a dialog box containing the "Are you registered to vote?" prompt.

5 Type **y** and press the **Enter** key. The "You can vote." message appears in the label control.

Now you'll try answering "n" to the "Are you registered to vote?" prompt.

6 Click the **Example 5** button. Type **n** in answer to the "Are you registered to vote?" prompt and press the **Enter** key. The "You need to register before you can vote." message appears in the label control.

7 Click the **Exit** button to end the application. Visual Basic returns to the design screen.

In summary, the If...Then...Else statement first evaluates the condition specified in the If clause. Based on that evaluation, the statement then selects and processes the instructions in one of two paths—either the true path (the Then) or the false path (the Else).

In many applications, however, you might have more than two paths from which a selection structure must choose. When a selection structure has several paths from which to choose, it is most times simpler and clearer to use the Case form of the selection structure instead of the nested If form.

The Case Form of the Selection Structure

Suppose, for example, that your application needs to display a message based on a letter grade that the user enters in a text box. The letter grades and their corresponding messages are as follows:

Letter Grade	Message
A	Excellent
B	Above Average
C	Average
D, F	Below Average
I	Incomplete
W	Withdrawal
Other	Incorrect Grade

You could use a nested If...Then...Else statement to code this selection structure. However, when a selection structure has several paths from which to choose, it is usually clearer to use the Case form of the selection structure. The Case form is sometimes referred to as an **extended selection structure**. Figure 4-26 shows the flowchart and the pseudocode for the Case selection structure that would display a message based on the grade contained in a text box named txtInput.

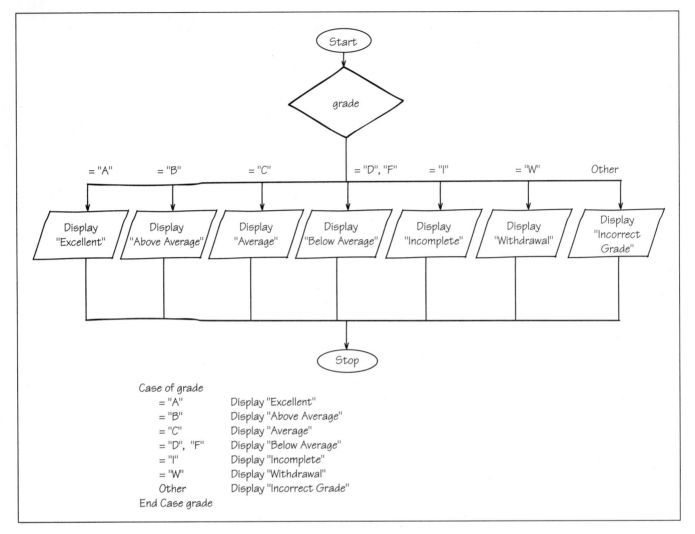

Figure 4-26: Flowchart and pseudocode of Case selection structure

Notice that the flowchart symbol for the Case selection structure is the same as the flowchart symbol for the If...Then...Else selection structure—a diamond. Unlike the If...Then...Else diamond, however, the Case diamond does not contain a condition requiring a true/false (yes/no) answer. Instead, the Case diamond contains an expression—in this case, grade—whose value will control which path is chosen.

Like the If...Then...Else diamond, the Case diamond has one flowline leading into the symbol. Unlike the If...Then...Else diamond, however, the Case diamond has many flowlines leading out of the symbol. Each flowline represents a possible path for the selection structure. The flowlines must be marked appropriately, indicating which value(s) are necessary for each path to be chosen. In Visual Basic, you use the Select Case statement to code the Case selection structure.

The Select Case Statement

You use Visual Basic's **Select Case statement** to code the Case selection structure. Figure 4-27 shows the syntax of the Select Case statement. It also shows the Select Case statement that will display a message based on the grade entered in the txtInput text box.

Select Case Syntax	Example
Select Case *testexpression*	Select Case txtInput.Text
[Case *expressionlist1*	Case "A"
[instructions for the first Case]]	lblMsg.Caption = "Excellent"
[Case *expressionlist2*	Case "B"
[instructions for the second Case]]	lblMsg.Caption = "Above Average"
[Case *expressionlistn*	Case "C"
[instructions for the nth Case]]	lblMsg.Caption = "Average"
[Case Else	Case "D", "F"
[instructions for when the *testexpression* does not match any of the *expressionlists*]]	lblMsg.Caption = "BelowAverage"
	Case "I"
End Select	lblMsg.Caption = "Incomplete"
	Case "W"
	lblMsg.Caption = "Withdrawal"
	Case Else
	lblMsg.Caption = "Incorrect Grade"
	End Select

Figure 4-27: The syntax and an example of the Case selection structure

The Select Case statement begins with the Select Case clause and ends with the two words End Select. Between the Select Case clause and the End Select are the individual Case clauses. Each Case clause represents a different path that the selection structure can follow. You can have as many Case clauses as necessary in a Select Case statement. If the Select Case statement includes a Case Else clause, the Case Else clause must be the last clause in the statement.

Notice that the Select Case clause must include a *testexpression*. The *testexpression* can be any numeric or string expression, which means it can contain a combination of variables, constants, functions, operators, and properties. In the example shown in Figure 4-27, the *testexpression* is txtInput.Text.

Each of the individual Case clauses, except the Case Else, must contain an *expressionlist*, which can include one or more numeric or string expressions. You include more than one expression in an *expressionlist* by simply separating each expression with a comma, as in Case "D", "F". The data type of the expressions must be compatible with the data type of the *testexpression*. In other words, if the *testexpression* is numeric, the expressions must be numeric. Likewise, if the *testexpression* is a string, the expressions must be strings. In the example shown in Figure 4-27, the *testexpression* (txtInput.Text) is a string, and so are the expressions—"A", "B", "C", "D", "F", "I", "W"—as the surrounding quotation marks indicate. (Recall from Tutorial 2 that the value in the Text property of a control is treated as a string, not as a number.)

When processing the Select Case statement, Visual Basic first compares the value of the *testexpression* with the values listed in *expressionlist1*. If a match is found, Visual Basic processes the instructions for the first Case and then skips to the instruction following the `End Select`. If a match is not found in *expressionlist1*, Visual Basic skips to the second Case clause, where it compares the *testexpression* with the values listed in *expressionlist2*. If a match is found, Visual Basic processes the instructions for the second Case clause and then skips to the instruction following the `End Select`. If a match is not found, Visual Basic skips to the third Case clause and so on. If the *testexpression* does not match any of the values listed in any of the *expressionlists*, Visual Basic then processes the instructions listed in the `Case Else` clause or if there is no `Case Else` clause, it processes the instruction following the `End Select`. Keep in mind that if the *testexpression* matches a value in more than one Case clause, only the instructions in the first match are processed.

The SelCase project on your Student Disk contains three examples of the Select Case statement.

To view the examples in the SelCase project:

1 Open the **SelCase** (selcase.vbp) project, which is in the Tut04 folder on your Student Disk. Click the **View Form** button. The frmSelCase form appears on the screen, as shown in Figure 4-28.

Figure 4-28: frmSelCase form

Each of the command buttons has been coded for you. You'll look at the code in the Example 1 button's Click event procedure first.

Example 1   **VB 263**

Example 1

Example 1 uses the Select Case statement to display a message based on the grade entered in the txtInput text box. The flowchart and pseudocode for this example are shown in Figure 4-26.

To view the code for Example 1, then test the Example 1 button:

1 Double-click the **Example 1** button to open its Code window, then maximize the Code window. The button's Click event procedure appears on the screen, as shown in Figure 4-29.

converts contents of text box to uppercase, temporarily

```
frmSelCase                                                    _ 8 X

Object:  cmdExam1              ▼   Proc:   Click                  ▼

Private Sub cmdExam1_Click()
    Select Case UCase(txtInput.Text)
        Case "A"
            lblMessage.Caption = "Excellent"
        Case "B"
            lblMessage.Caption = "Above Average"
        Case "C"
            lblMessage.Caption = "Average"
        Case "D", "F"
            lblMessage.Caption = "Below Average"
        Case "I"
            lblMessage.Caption = "Incomplete"
        Case "W"
            lblMessage.Caption = "Withdrawal"
        Case Else
            lblMessage.Caption = "Incorrect Grade"
    End Select
End Sub
```

Figure 4-29: Code window for Example 1

Notice that the code uses the UCase function to temporarily convert the contents of the text box to uppercase before comparing it to the uppercase letter grades. This way the user can enter the grade in either uppercase or lowercase.

2 Close the Code window, then **run**, but don't save, the application. Type **c** in the Enter Data here text box, then click the **Example 1** button. Visual Basic processes the instructions in the button's Click event procedure. "Average" appears in the label control.

So how does the Example 1 button work? (You may find it helpful to refer back to Figure 4-29 as you read the following explanation.) First, Visual Basic temporarily converts the contents of the txtInput control's Text property ("c") to uppercase, giving "C". It then compares the "C" with the value listed in the first Case's *expressionlist* ("A"). Because "C" does not match "A", Visual Basic skips to the second Case clause where it compares "C" with that Case's *expressionlist* ("B"). Because "C" does not match "B", Visual Basic skips to the third Case clause where it compares "C" with that Case's *expressionlist* ("C"). Here there is a match, so Visual Basic processes the lblMsg.Caption = "Average" instruction, which displays the string "Average" in the label control. Visual Basic then skips the remaining instructions in the Select Case statement and processes the instruction after the End Select—in this example, the End Sub instruction.

Now see what happens if you enter an incorrect grade in the text box.

3   Click the **Clear** button to clear the label control and the text box, type **t** in the text box, then click the **Example 1** button. Because the value in the text box does not match any of the values listed in any of the Case clauses, the `Case Else` instruction is processed and the string "Incorrect Grade" appears in the label control. Visual Basic then processes the instruction following the `End Select`—the `End Sub` instruction.

4   Click the **Exit** button to end the application. Visual Basic returns to the design screen.

In the next two examples, you will learn how to specify a range of values in an *expressionlist*—such as the values 1 through 4, and values greater than 10. You will also learn how to use numbers, instead of strings, in the *testexpression* and in the *expressionlists*.

Using To and Is in an *Expressionlist*

You can use either the keyword `To` or the keyword `Is` to specify a range of values in an *expressionlist*. The specified values can be either numeric or strings. You will use the keyword `To` in Example 2 and the keyword `Is` in Example 3.

Example 2

XYZ Corporation offers programming seminars to a variety of companies. The price per person depends on the number of people the company registers, as shown in the following chart.

Number of registrants	Charge
1 – 4	$ 100 per person
5 – 10	$ 80 per person
More than 10	$ 60 per person

Figure 4-30 shows the flowchart and the pseudocode for this example.

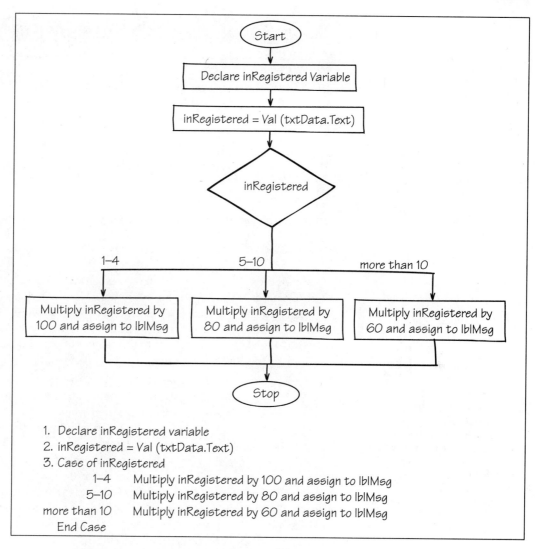

Figure 4-30: Example 2's flowchart and pseudocode

To view the code for Example 2, then test the Example 2 button:

1 Double-click the **Example 2** button to open its Code window, then maximize the Code window. The Example 2 button's Click event procedure appears on the screen, as shown in Figure 4-31.

```
frmSelCase                                                          _ 8 X
Object:  cmdExam2                    ▼    Proc:  Click              ▼

Private Sub cmdExam2_Click()
    Dim inRegistered As Integer
    inRegistered = Val(txtInput.Text)
    Select Case inRegistered
        Case 1 To 4
            lblMessage.Caption = Format(inRegistered * 100, "Currency")
        Case 5 To 10
            lblMessage.Caption = Format(inRegistered * 80, "Currency")
        Case Else
            lblMessage.Caption = Format(inRegistered * 60, "Currency")
    End Select

End Sub
```

Figure 4-31: Code window for Example 2

The code first declares an Integer variable named inRegistered. It then uses the Val function to assign the numeric equivalent of the txtInput control's Text property to the inRegistered variable. The inRegistered variable, instead of the txtInput's Text property, is then used as the *testexpression* in the Select Case clause. Because the inRegistered variable contains a number, the values listed in each *expressionlist* must be numeric.

tips

Visual Basic will not display an error message if the value preceding the `To` is greater than the value after the `To`; instead, the selection structure simply will not give the correct results. This is another reason why it is always important to test your code.

According to the XYZ Corporation's chart, the charge for one to four registrants is $100 each. You could, therefore, write the first Case clause as `Case 1, 2, 3, 4`. A more convenient way of writing that range of numbers, however, is to use the keyword `To`, but you must follow this syntax: *smallest value in the range* **To** *largest value in the range*. The expression `1 To 4` in the first Case clause, for example, specifies the range of numbers from 1 to 4, inclusive. The expression `5 To 10` in the second Case clause specifies the range of numbers from 5 to 10, inclusive. When you use the keyword `To`, the value preceding the `To` must always be smaller than the value after the `To`. In other words, `10 To 5` is not a correct expression. In Example 2, the Case Else clause will be processed when the number of registrants is greater than 10. (It will also be processed when the number of registrants is less than 1, as you will see in Step 5.)

2   Close the Code window, then **run**, but don't save, the application.

Assume a company registers seven people.

3   Type 7 in the text box, then click the **Example 2** button. $560.00, which is 7 times the $80 charge for 5 to 10 registrants, appears in the label control. That's because the number 7 matches a number in the range specified in the `Case 5 To 10` clause.

4   Click the **Clear** button. On your own, verify that 3 registrants will cost $300.00—3 times the $100 charge for 1 to 4 registrants. Also verify that 15 registrants will cost $900.00—15 times the $60 charge for more than 10 registrants. (The charge for the 15 registrants will be calculated by the Case Else clause.)

Always keep in mind that users will, at times, make mistakes when entering data. For example, the user might accidentally enter a negative number.

5 Click the **Clear** button, type –3 (be sure to type the minus sign) in the text box, then click the **Example 2** button. The negative number, ($180.00), appears in the label control. The parentheses indicate a negative currency value.

Because the –3 did not fall into either the 1 To 4 range or the 5 To 10 range, Visual Basic processed the lblMessage.Caption = Format(inRegistered * 60, "Currency") instruction in the Case Else clause, which multiplied the –3 times the $60 charge. It would be better if the application displayed a message alerting the user that an input error was made. You will learn how to display such a message in Example 3.

6 Click the **Exit** button to end the application. Visual Basic returns to the design screen.

Example 3

Example 3 is the same as Example 2, except that it requires the application to print an error message if the user enters an incorrect number of registrants. An incorrect number would include 0 (zero), a negative number, or a letter.

Number of registrants	Charge
1 – 4	$ 100 per person
5 – 10	$ 80 per person
More than 10	$ 60 per person
0, negative number, letter	"Incorrect Data"

Most of the code for Example 3 will be similar to the code for Example 2. Example 3, however, will include one additional Case clause, and its Case Else clause will be different.

To view the code for Example 3, then test the Example 3 button:

1 Double-click the **Example 3** button to open its Code window, then maximize the Code window. The button's Click event procedure appears on the screen, as shown in Figure 4-32.

```
frmSelCase                                                        _  B  X
Object:  cmdExam3                        ▼     Proc:  Click                    ▼
Private Sub cmdExam3_Click()
    Dim inRegistered As Integer
    inRegistered = Val(txtInput.Text)
    Select Case inRegistered
        Case 1 To 4
            lblMessage.Caption = Format(inRegistered * 100, "Currency")
        Case 5 To 10
            lblMessage.Caption = Format(inRegistered * 80, "Currency")
        Case Is > 10
            lblMessage.Caption = Format(inRegistered * 60, "Currency")
        Case Else
            lblMessage.Caption = "Incorrect Data"
    End Select

End Sub
```

Figure 4-32: Code window for Example 3

tips

▶ If you forget to type the Is in the expression, Visual Basic types it in for you. In other words, if you enter Case > 10, Visual Basic changes the clause to Case Is > 10. Because the inRegistered is declared as an Integer variable, you can also write the clause as Case Is >= 11.

tips

▶ You also could have written Example 3's Select Case statement with Case Is <= 0 as the first Case, Case 1 To 4 as the second Case, Case 5 To 10 as the third Case, and then let the Case Else clause handle the numbers greater than 10. The difference between both Select Case statements is the position of the error checking clause—the clause that catches the input errors. Unless you expect the user to enter mostly incorrect values, you can save computer time by putting the error checking at the end of the Case structure, as shown in Example 3, instead of at the beginning of the structure.

Notice the third Case clause, Case Is > 10, which was not included in Example 2's code. In addition to the keyword To, you can also use the keyword Is to specify a range of values. You use the Is keyword in combination with the relational operators, like this: **Is** relational operator *value*. Recall that the relational operators are =, <, <=, >, >=, and < >. The expression Is > 10, for example, specifies all numbers greater than the number 10.

Notice that, in this example, the Case Else clause is used to display an "Incorrect Data" message when the user enters something that is not included in any of the Case clauses—namely, a zero, a negative number, or a letter. (When using the Val function, you may remember, the numeric equivalent of a letter is zero.)

2 Close the Code window, then **run**, but don't save, the application.

Now enter a negative number.

3 Type –3 in the text box, then click the **Example 3** button. "Incorrect Data" appears in the label control.

4 Click the **Clear** button.

5 On your own, verify that the Example 3 button will display the "Incorrect Data" message when the user enters a letter.

6 Click the **Exit** button to end the application. You can now exit Visual Basic or open another project. You do not need to save the SelCase project.

You have now completed Lesson A. You can either take a break or complete the end-of-lesson questions and exercises.

S U M M A R Y

To evaluate an expression containing mathematical, relational, and logical operators:

■ Evaluate the mathematical operators first, then evaluate the relational operators, and then evaluate the logical operators.

To code a selection structure:

■ Use the If...Then...Else statement. Its syntax is:
　　If *condition* **Then**
　　　　[*instructions when condition is true*]
　　[Else
　　　　[*instructions when condition is false*]]
　　End If

To code a nested selection structure:

■ Use the nested If...Then...Else statement. Its syntax is shown in Figure 4-24.

To temporarily convert a string to uppercase:

■ Use the UCase function. The syntax is **UCase**(*string*).

To temporarily convert a string to lowercase:

■ Use the LCase function. The syntax is **LCase**(*string*).

To code a Case (an extended selection) structure:

■ Use the Select Case statement. Its syntax is:
> **Select Case** *testexpression*
>   [**Case** *expressionlist1*
>   [*instructions for the first Case*]]
>   [**Case** *expressionlist2*
>   [*instructions for the second Case*]]
>   [**Case** *expressionlistn*
>   [*instructions for the nth Case*]]
>   [**Case Else**
>   [*instructions when testexpression does not match any of the expressionlists*]]
> **End Select**

To specify a range of values in a Case clause's expressionlist:

■ Use the keyword `To` in the following syntax: *smallest value in the range* **To** *largest value in the range*. Examples: `1 To 4`,`"A" To "C"`.
■ Use the keyword `Is` in the following syntax: **Is** *relational operator value*. Examples: `Is > 10`, `Is <= "Jones"`.

To create a flowchart:

■ Use the start/stop oval to mark the beginning and the end of the flowchart.
■ Use the input/output parallelogram to represent steps that get data from the user and steps that display or print information.
■ Use the process rectangle to represent steps that declare variables, assign values to variables or properties, setting the focus, and for calculations.
■ Use the selection/repetition diamond to represent both selection and repetition.
■ Connect the flowchart symbols with flowlines

Q U E S T I O N S

1. Which of the following is a valid condition for an If...Then...Else statement? (Choose three.)
   a. Val(txtAge.Text) > 65
   b. Val(lblPrice.Caption <= 10)
   c. crSales > 500 And < 800
   d. crCost > 100 And crCost <= 1000
   e. UCase(stState) = "Alaska" and UCase(stState) = "Hawaii"

2. You can use the _____ function to temporarily convert a string to uppercase.
   a. Caseupper
   b. CaseU
   c. LCase
   d. UCase
   e. Upper

3. Assume you want to compare the string contained in the Text property of the txtName control with the name Bob. Which of the following conditions should you use in the If...Then...Else statement? (Be sure the condition will handle Bob, BOB, bob, and so on.)
   a. txtName.Text = "BOB"
   b. txtName.Text = UCase("BOB")
   c. txtName.Text = UCase("Bob")
   d. UCase(txtName.Text) = "Bob"
   e. UCase(txtName.Text) = "BOB"

4. Which of the following will change the contents of the txtName text box to uppercase?
   a. txtName.Text = UCase(txtName.Text)
   b. txtName.Text = TXTNAME.TEXT
   c. txtName.Text = "TXTNAME.TEXT"
   d. UCase(txtName.Text) = txtName.Text
   e. Upper(txtName.Text) = "txtName.Text"

5. The three logical operators are listed below. Indicate their order of precedence by placing a number (1, 2, or 3) on the line to the left of the operator.

   _____ And   _____ Not   _____ Or

6. An expression can contain mathematical, relational, and logical operators. Indicate the order of precedence for the three types of operators by placing a number (1, 2, or 3) on the line to the left.

   _____ Mathematical _____ Logical _____ Relational

7. Evaluate the following expression: 3 > 6 And 7 > 4
   a. True   b. False

8. Evaluate the following expression: 4 > 6 Or 10 < 2 * 6
   a. True   b. False

9. Evaluate the following expression: 7 >= 3 + 4 Or 6 < 4 And 2 < 5
   a. True   b. False

Use the following information to answer questions 10–16:
   X=5, Y=3, Z=2, A=True, B=False.

10. Evaluate the following expression: X – Y = Z
    a. True   b. False

11. Evaluate the following expression: X * Z > X * Y And A
    a. True   b. False

12. Evaluate the following expression: X * Z < X * Y Or A
    a. True   b. False

13. Evaluate the following expression: A And B
    a. True   b. False

14. Evaluate the following expression: A Or B
    a. True   b. False

15. Evaluate the following expression: X * Y > Y ^ Z
    a. True   b. False

16. Evaluate the following expression: X * Y > Y ^ Z And A Or B
    a. True   b. False

Use the following selection structure to answer questions 17–19.

```
If inNumber <= 100 Then
    inNumber = inNumber * 2
Else
    If inNumber > 500 Then
    inNumber = inNumber * 3
    End If
End If
```

17. Assume the inNumber variable contains the number 90. What value will be in the inNumber variable after the above selection structure is processed?
    a. 0
    b. 90
    c. 180
    d. 270
    e. null

18. Assume the inNumber variable contains the number 1000. What value will be in the inNumber variable after the above selection structure is processed?
    a. 0
    b. 1000
    c. 2000
    d. 3000
    e. null

19. Assume the inNumber variable contains the number 200. What value will be in the inNumber variable after the above selection structure is processed?
    a. 0
    b. 200
    c. 400
    d. 600
    e. null

20. Which of the following flowchart symbols represents the If...Then...Else selection structure?
    a. diamond
    b. hexagon
    c. oval
    d. parallelogram
    e. rectangle

21. Which of the following flowchart symbols represents the Case selection structure?
    a. diamond
    b. hexagon
    c. oval
    d. parallelogram
    e. rectangle

22. If the *testexpression* used in the Select Case clause is the numeric variable crSales, which of the following Case clauses are valid? (Choose two.)
    a. Case 2, 4, 6, 8
    b. Case "1" To "3"
    c. Case Is < "6"
    d. Case Is >= 8
    e. Case 4.5 Through 8.5

23. Assume the application uses a string variable named stState. If the *testexpression* used in the Select Case clause is UCase(stState), which of the following Case clauses are valid? (Choose three.)
    a. Case "TEXAS"
    b. Case "ALABAMA" And "ARKANSAS"
    c. Case Is > "Illinois"
    d. Case "COLORADO", "CALIFORNIA"
    e. Case "ALABAMA" To "ARKANSAS"

24. The _____ symbol is used in a flowchart to represent a calculation task.
    a. input
    b. output
    c. process
    d. start
    e. stop

25. The _____ symbol is used in a flowchart to represent a step that gets information from the user.
    a. input/output
    b. process
    c. selection/repetition
    d. start
    e. stop

26. The process symbol in a flowchart is the _____ .
    a. diamond
    b. oval
    c. parallelogram
    d. rectangle
    e. square

27. The input/output symbol in a flowchart is the _____ .
    a. diamond
    b. oval
    c. parallelogram
    d. rectangle
    e. square

28. The selection/repetition symbol in a flowchart is the _____ .
    a. diamond
    b. oval
    c. parallelogram
    d. rectangle
    e. square

29. Use the Help menu to search for a Help screen on the Select statement. Print the Help screen. How would you write an *expressionlist* that would match strings falling between the word "nuts" and the word "soup"? Assume you don't know the case of the strings.

E X E R C I S E S

1. Draw the flowchart that corresponds to the following Visual Basic code.

   ```
   If Hours > 40 Then
           lblMsg.Caption = "Overtime"
   Else
           lblMsg.Caption = "Regular"
   End If
   ```

2. Draw the flowchart that corresponds to the following Visual Basic code:

   ```
   Select Case Sales
        Case Is >= 10000
              Commission = .1 * Sales
        Case Is >= 5000
              Commission = .05 * Sales
        Case Else
              Commission = 0
   End Select
   ```

3. Draw the flowchart that corresponds to the following Visual Basic code:

   ```
   Select Case Hours
        Case Is > 40
              lblMsg.Caption = "Overtime"
        Case Else
              lblMsg.Caption = "Regular"
   End Select
   ```

4. Write the Visual Basic code that corresponds to the flowchart shown in Figure 4-33.

Figure 4-33

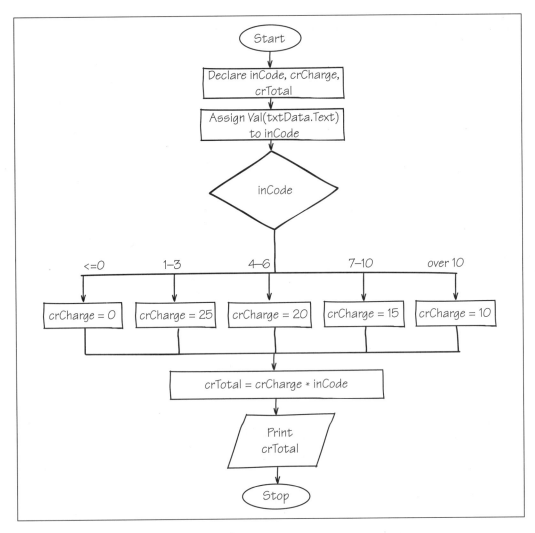

Figure 4-34

5. Write the Visual Basic code that corresponds to the flowchart shown in Figure 4-34.

6. Write an If...Then...Else statement that will display the string "Pontiac" in the lblType control if the txtCar control's Text property contains the string "Grand Am" (in any case).

7. Write an If...Then...Else statement that will display the string "Entry error" in the lblMsg control if the inUnits variable contains a number that is less than 0; otherwise, display the string "Valid Number". (Do not include the period.)

8. Write an If...Then...Else statement that will display the string "Reorder" in the lblMsg control if the crPrice variable contains a number that is less than 10; otherwise, display the string "OK". (Do not include the period.)

9. Write an If...Then...Else statement that will assign the number 10 to the crBonus variable if the crSales variable contains a number that is less than or equal to $250; otherwise, assign the number 15.

10. Write an If...Then...Else statement that will display the number 25 in the lblShipping control if the stState variable contains the string "Hawaii" (in any case); otherwise, display the number 50.

11. Assume you want to calculate a 3% sales tax if the stState variable contains the string "Colorado" (in any case); otherwise, you want to calculate a 4% sales tax. You can calculate the sales tax by multiplying the tax rate by the contents of the crSales variable. Display the sales tax in the lblStax control. Draw the flowchart, then write the Visual Basic code. Use the If...Then...Else selection structure.

12. Assume you want to calculate an employee's gross pay. Employees working more than 40 hours should receive overtime pay (time and one-half) for the hours over 40. Use the variables sgHours, crRate, sgGross. Display the contents of the sgGross variable in the lblGross control. Write the pseudocode, then write the Visual Basic code. Use the If...Then...Else selection structure.

13. Display the string "Dog" in the lblType control if the stAnimal variable contains the letter "D" (in any case); otherwise, display the string "Cat". (Do not include the period.) Draw the flowchart, then write the Visual Basic code. Use the If...Then...Else selection structure.

14. Assume you want to calculate a 10% discount on desks sold to customers in Colorado. Use the variables stItem, stState, and crSales. Format the discount to Currency and display it in the lblDisc control. (You don't know the case of either the stItem or the stState variables. In other words, the contents of those two variables can be in uppercase, lowercase, or a combination of uppercase and lowercase letters.) Write the pseudocode, then write the Visual Basic code. Use the If...Then...Else selection structure.

15. Assume you want to calculate a 10% discount on sales made to customers in California and in Texas. You can use the variables stState and crSales. Format the discount to Currency and display it in the lblDisc control. (You don't know the case of the stState variable. In other words, the contents of the variable can be in uppercase, lowercase, or a combination of uppercase and lowercase letters.) Write the Visual Basic code. Use the Case selection structure.

16. Display the string "Valid Entry" in the lblEntry control if the user enters either the number 1 or the number 2 in the txtEntry text box; otherwise, display the string "Entry Error". (Do not include the period.) Use the Case selection structure.

17. Assume you want to calculate a 2% price increase on all red shirts, but a 1% price increase on all other items. In addition to calculating the price increase, also calculate the new price. You can use the variables stColor, stItem, crOrigprice, crIncrease, and crNewprice. Format the original price to Currency and display it in the lblOrig control. Format the price increase to Standard and display it in the lblIncrease control. Format the new price to Currency and display it in the lblNew control. (You don't know the case of either the stColor variable or the stItem variable. In other words, the contents of those variables can be in uppercase, lowercase, or a combination of uppercase and lowercase letters.) Write the Visual Basic code. Use the If...Then...Else selection structure.

18. Display the string "Dog" in the lblAnimal control if the inAnimal variable contains the number 1. Display the string "Cat" if the inAnimal variable contains the number 2. Display the string "Bird" if the inAnimal variable contains anything other than the number 1 or the number 2. Write the Visual Basic code. Use the Case selection structure.

19. Assume you offer programming seminars to companies. Your price per person depends on the number of people the company registers. (For example, if the company registers 7 people, then the total amount owed by the company is $560.)

Number of registrants	Charge
1 – 4	$ 100 per person
5 – 10	$ 80 per person
11 or more	$ 60 per person

The number of people registered is stored in the Text property of the txtReg control. Calculate the total amount owed by the company. Store the amount in the crTotalDue variable. Write the Visual Basic code. Use the Case selection structure.

20. An application needs to display a shipping charge based on the state entered in the txtState control. Use the Case selection structure to display the shipping charge in the lblShip control. Use the chart below. (The state could be typed by the user in either uppercase or lowercase.)

State entered in txtState control	Shipping charge
Hawaii	$25.00
Oregon	$30.00
California	$32.50

(Any other state should result in an "Incorrect State" message.)
a. Write the pseudocode. Use the Case selection structure.
b. Write the Visual Basic code.

21. The price of a concert ticket depends on the seat location entered in a text box named txtSeat. Display the price in the lblPrice control. Use the chart below. (The seat location could be entered by the user in either uppercase or lowercase.)

Seat location	Concert ticket price
Box	$75.00
Pavilion	$30.00
Lawn	$21.00

(Any other seat location should result in an "Incorrect Seat Location" message.)
a. Write the Visual Basic code. Use the If...Then...Else selection structure.
b. Write the Visual Basic code. Use the Case selection structure.

22. In most companies the amount of vacation you receive depends on the number of years you've been with the company. The number of years is entered in a text box named txtYears. Store the numeric equivalent of the years in an Integer variable named inYears. Display the weeks of vacation in the lblWeeks control. Use the following chart:

Years with the company	Weeks of vacation
Less than 1	0
1 to 5	1
6 to 10	2
11 and over	3

a. Write the Visual Basic code. Use the If...Then...Else selection structure.
b. Write the Visual Basic code. Use the Case selection structure.

23. XYZ Corporation pays its salespeople a commission based on the amount of their sales. The sales amount is entered in a text box named txtSales. Store the numeric equivalent of the sales amount in a Currency variable named crSales. Use the following chart to calculate and display the commission.

Sales	Commission rate
$10,000.01 and over	10.0%
$5,000.01 – $10,000	7.5%
$1.00 – $5,000	5.0%
0 and under	Data Error

a. Write the Visual Basic code. Use the If...Then...Else selection structure.

b. Write the Visual Basic code. Use the Case selection structure.

24. Assume you want to calculate a 10% discount on sales made to customers in California and in Texas, a 7% discount on sales made to customers in Oregon and New Mexico, and a 6% discount on sales made to customers in all other states. The state is entered in the stState variable, and the sales amount is entered in the crSales control. Format the discount to Currency and display it in the lblDisc control. (You don't know the case of the stState variable. In other words, the contents of the variable might be in uppercase, lowercase, or a combination of uppercase and lowercase letters.)

a. Write the Visual Basic code. Use the If...Then...Else selection structure.

b. Write the Visual Basic code. Use the Case selection structure.

25. Recall that string comparisons in Visual Basic are case sensitive, which means that a "P" is different from a "p." In Lesson A you learned how to use the UCase function (and the LCase function) to handle the string comparison problem. Recall that the Example 4 button's Click event procedure contains the following code:

```
If UCase(txtData.Text) = "P" Then

        lblMsg.Caption = "Pass"

Else

        lblMsg.Caption = "Fail"

End If
```

Not all languages have a UCase function or an LCase function. Just for practice, assume that Visual Basic does not have either function. Without using either the UCase function or the LCase function, rewrite the If statement's condition so that it displays the "Pass" message when the user enters the letter "P" in either lowercase or uppercase.

LESSON B
objectives

In this lesson you will learn how to:

- Include Visual Basic's icons in an application
- Add an option button, frame control, and check box to a form
- Draw a control on the form and in a frame
- Use the Randomize statement, and the Rnd and Int functions
- Create a user-defined sub procedure
- Execute the Call statement
- Create a default option button

More Visual Basic Controls

The Math Application

Recall that Susan Chen, the principal of a local primary school, wants an application that the first and second grade students can use to practice both adding and subtracting numbers. The application should display the addition or subtraction problem on the screen, then allow the student to enter the answer, and then verify that the answer is correct. If the student's answer is not correct, the application should give him or her as many chances as necessary to answer the problem correctly.

The problems displayed for the first grade students should use numbers from one through ten, only; the problems for the second grade students should use numbers from ten through 100. Because the first and second grade students have not learned about negative numbers yet, the subtraction problems should never ask them to subtract a larger number from a smaller one.

Ms. Chen also wants the application to keep track of how many correct and incorrect responses the student makes; this information will help her assess the student's math ability. Recall that Ms. Chen wants to be able to control the display of this information. The sketch of the user interface is shown in Figure 4-35.

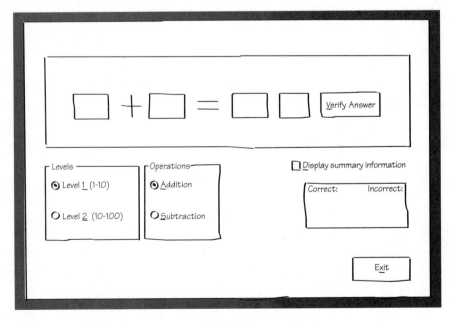

Figure 4-35: Sketch of the Math application's user interface

The math application's interface will contain one text box, four option buttons, one check box, three image controls, four frame controls, and various label controls. To save you time, your Student Disk contains a partially completed Math application. When you open the application, you will notice that most of the user interface has already been created and the properties of the existing objects have been set. You will finish creating the user interface in this lesson.

To open the partially completed application:

1 Start Visual Basic, if necessary, and open the **t4case** (t4case.vbp) project, which is in the Tut04 folder on your Student Disk.

2 Save the form and the project as **lbMath**.

3 Click the **View Form** button in the Project window to view the frmMath form. Figure 4-36 identifies the controls already included in the application. (To see the lblCorrect and lblIncorrect controls, you will need to click inside the fraInfo frame.)

HELP? If you are using the Visual Basic Working Model, you will not be able to see the icons imgHappy, imgPlus, and imgMinus.

cmdVerify
txtAnswer
imgEqual
lblNum2
imgOperator
lblNum1
fraData
fraInfo
optLevel1
optLevel2
optAdd
imgPlus
imgHappy
imgMinus
lblCorrect
cmdExit
lblIncorrect

Figure 4-36: Partially completed Math application

The Verify Answer button is the default command button. For now, don't worry about the three image controls at the bottom of the form. You will learn what they are for later on in this lesson.

Before adding the missing controls to the user interface, you will set the Picture property of the imgEqual control. (Although the imgEqual control will not be either coded or used in code, it was given a name to make it easier to refer to in this lesson.)

Using Visual Basic's Icons

Visual Basic comes with a collection of over 400 icons. You will find the icons in the icons folder, which is located in the main Visual Basic folder on either the local hard drive or on the network drive. In this application, you will display the equal sign icon in the imgEqual control.

> **Important Note: You will not be able to complete the following steps if you are using the Working Model.**

To display the equal sign icon in the imgEqual control:

1 Click the **imgEqual** control to select it. Sizing handles appear around the control.

2 Press the **F4** key to display the Properties window. Look in the Properties window's Object box to verify that the imgEqual control is selected.

3 If necessary, click **Picture** in the Properties list. Click **...** in the Settings box. The Load Picture dialog box appears.

4 The main Visual Basic folder—usually named Microsoft Visual Basic—should be open, so you just need to click the **icons** folder, then click the Open button. The icons folder opens.

The various Visual Basic icons are grouped by category. The icon you will use is in the misc (miscellaneous) folder.

5 Click the **misc** folder, then click the Open button to open the misc folder. Visual Basic displays each icon, as well as its file name, in the Look in list box. Scroll the list box until you locate the Misc22 icon—an equal sign. Click **Misc22** in the list box, then click the Open button. An equal sign appears in the imgEqual control.

The main Visual Basic folder—usually named vb—should be open, so you just need to click the icons folder, then click the OK button. The icons folder opens. The various Visual Basic icons are grouped by category. The icon you will use is in the misc (miscellaneous) folder. Scroll the Directories box until you see the misc folder. Click the misc folder, then click the OK button to open the misc folder. A list of icon files, which have a .ico filename extension, appears in the File name list box. Scroll the File name box until you locate the misc22.ico filename. Click misc22.ico in the list, then click the OK button. An equal sign appears in the imgEqual control.

WINDOWS 3.1

▶ If you are using Windows 3.1, pictures of the various icons can be found in the *Microsoft Visual Basic Programmer's Guide* manual.

The three image controls at the bottom of the interface also contain Visual Basic icons. The files for all three icons are in the misc folder. The plus sign file's name is misc18, the minus sign is misc19, and the happy face is face03. When you run the application in the next section, you will notice that the three icons do not appear in the interface; that's because their Visible property is set to False.

Now you can begin adding the missing controls. You'll start with the Subtraction option button.

Adding an Option Button Control to the Form

The option button tool draws an option button control. When option button controls are grouped together, only one of the buttons in the group can be selected at any one time. The **Option button** control is the control to use in situations where you want to limit the user to only one of two or more related and mutually exclusive choices. In the Math application, for example, you want to limit the mathematical operation to either addition or subtraction, and you want to limit the user's level to either Level 1 or Level 2.

The minimum number of option buttons in a user interface is two because the only way to deselect an option button is to select another option button. The recommended maximum number of option buttons in an interface is seven. (If you have more than seven choices from which the user can choose, you should consider using a list box control, which you will learn about in Tutorial 6.) You should always label each option button so that the user knows its purpose. You enter the label using sentence capitalization in the option button's Caption property. You should also assign an access key to each button.

Design Tips

GUI

Option Button Standards

- Use option buttons when you want to limit the user to one of two or more related and mutually exclusive choices.
- The minimum number of option buttons in an interface is two, and the recommended maximum is seven.
- The label in the option button's Caption property should be entered using sentence capitalization.
- Assign a unique access key to each option button.

To add an option button to the form:

1 Double-click the **Option button** tool ⬚ in the toolbox. An option button control appears on the form.

2 Press the **F4** key to display the Properties window. Set the option button's Name property to **optSub**, then set its Caption property to **&Subtraction**. "Opt" is the three-character ID for an option button control.

3 Drag the Subtraction button to a location immediately below the Addition button.

4 **Save and run** the application.

You select an option button by clicking it; you can click either its circle or its caption.

5 Click the **Addition** button. A black dot appears inside the circle. The black dot indicates that the option button is selected.

6 Click the **Subtraction** button. Visual Basic selects the Subtraction button as it deselects the Addition button.

7 Click the **Level 1** button. Visual Basic selects the Level 1 button as it deselects the Subtraction button.

Notice a problem with the way the option buttons are working: selecting the Level 1 button deselects the Subtraction button. That means the user will not be able to choose the level and the mathematical operation at the same time. You actually want Visual Basic to treat the Addition and Subtraction buttons as a separate group, independent of the Level 1 and Level 2 buttons. You create a separate group of option buttons by placing the buttons in a frame, which is another Visual Basic control.

8 Click the **Exit** button, which contains the End statement, to end the application. Visual Basic returns to the design screen.

Adding a Frame Control to the Form

You use the frame tool to draw a **frame control**, whose purpose is to be a container for other controls. You can use a frame control to visually separate related controls from other controls on the form. By placing related controls inside a frame, the controls and the frame are treated as one unit; moving the frame also moves all of the controls inside the frame, and deleting the frame also deletes all of the controls contained inside it.

You label a frame control by setting its Caption property. Labeling a frame control is optional; if you do include a label, the label should be entered using sentence capitalization.

You must use a frame control if you want more than one group of option buttons on a form. In this application, for example, you will group the Addition and Subtraction option buttons in one frame control, and the Level 1 and Level 2 option buttons in another frame control.

GUI Design Tips

Frame Control Standards

- You can use a frame control to visually separate controls from one another. You must use the frame control to create separate groups of option buttons.

- Use sentence capitalization for the optional label, which is entered in the frame's Caption property.

To add a frame control to the form:

1 Double-click the **Frame tool** ▣ in the toolbox. The Frame1 control appears on the form.

2 Press the **F4** key to display the Properties window. Set the Frame1 control's Name property to **fraLevel**, then set its Caption property to **Levels**. "Fra" is the three-character ID for a frame control.

You will now position the frame control and also make it larger.

3 Size and drag the frame control as shown in Figure 4-37. If you want to match the figure exactly, you can set the frame control's Height property to 1575, its Left property to 360, its Top property to 2400, and its Width property to 1935.

frame control

Figure 4-37: Frame control added to the form

The objects you add to a form belong to the form itself. Therefore, if you want to put the existing option buttons in a frame, you will need to detach the option buttons from the form first. In Windows terminology, you will cut the buttons from the form. That process will place the option buttons on the clipboard. You can then paste the option buttons from the clipboard into the frame control. Keep in mind that you can't just drag *existing* controls into a frame control. You must cut them from the form first, then paste them into the frame control.

tips

You can also use Ctrl + X to cut the selected controls from the form. Then, after selecting the frame control, you can use Ctrl + V to paste the controls into the frame.

To cut both the Level 1 and Level 2 option buttons from the form, then paste them into the Levels frame:

1 Click the **Level 1** button to select it, then press and hold down the **Ctrl** key as you click the **Level 2** button. Sizing handles appear around both option buttons.

Now cut the selected controls from the form, then paste them into the Levels frame.

2 Click **Edit** on the menu bar, then click **Cut** to cut the selected option buttons from the form. Visual Basic removes the two buttons from the form and places them on the clipboard.

Before you can paste the buttons into the frame control, you must first select the frame control.

3 Click the **Levels** frame to select it. Sizing handles appear around the frame control. Now click **Edit** on the menu bar, then click **Paste** to paste the option buttons into the selected frame.

4   Place the mouse pointer on one of the selected option buttons. With the mouse pointer on one of the selected option buttons, drag the option buttons further into the frame control, as shown in Figure 4-38.

drag buttons
into the frame

Figure 4-38: Option buttons positioned in the frame control

HELP? If you inadvertently deselected the option buttons, simply click one of the buttons and then press and hold down the Ctrl key as you click the other button.

5   Click the **form** to deselect the option buttons.

6   **Save and run** the application.

7   Click the **Addition** button to select it, then click the **Level 1** button to select it. Notice that selecting the Level 1 button does not deselect the Addition button.

8   On your own, try clicking the other option buttons. You should notice that when you select the Subtraction button, the Addition button is deselected; when you select the Addition button, the Subtraction button is deselected. The Addition and Subtraction buttons, however, have no effect on the Level buttons. Also notice that selecting one of the buttons in the Levels frame deselects the other button in the Levels frame, but it has no effect on the Addition and Subtraction buttons.

9   Click the **Exit** button. Visual Basic returns to the design screen.

Although you don't need to put the Addition and Subtraction option buttons in their own frame for the buttons to work, you will do so anyway. The frame will improve the appearance of the user interface by visually separating the option buttons from the other controls on the form.

To group the Addition and Subtraction option buttons in a frame control:

1   Double-click the **Frame** tool ▦ in the toolbox. The Frame1 control appears on the form.

2   Display the Properties window. Set the Frame1 control's Name property to **fraOperation**, then set its Caption property to **Operations**.

3   Size and drag the frame control as shown in Figure 4-39. If you want to match the figure exactly, you can set the frame control's Height property to 1575, its Left property to 2700, its Top property to 2400, and its Width property to 1575.

Figure 4-39: Operations frame in the user interface

4   Select the Addition and Subtraction buttons. Sizing handles appear around both buttons. Use Visual Basic's Edit menu to cut the selected buttons from the form. Click the **Operations** frame to select it, then use Visual Basic's Edit menu to paste the option buttons into the Operations frame.

5   With the mouse pointer on one of the selected option buttons, drag the option buttons further inside the frame.

6   Click the **form** to deselect the option buttons.

When you use a frame to group controls, Visual Basic treats the frame and the controls inside the frame as one unit. When you move or delete a frame control, Visual Basic moves or deletes the frame and the controls contained inside it.

7   Place the mouse pointer on the fraOperation control's caption (Operations), then drag the frame to match Figure 4-40. Notice that the controls inside the frame move along with the frame.

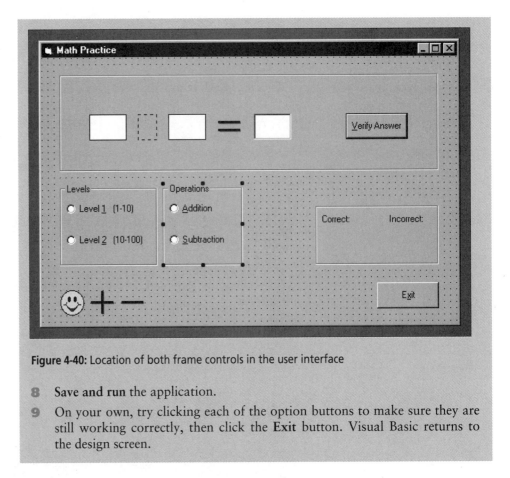

Figure 4-40: Location of both frame controls in the user interface

8 **Save and run** the application.

9 On your own, try clicking each of the option buttons to make sure they are still working correctly, then click the **Exit** button. Visual Basic returns to the design screen.

The next control you will add to the interface is the missing check box control.

Adding a Check Box Control to the Form

GUI
Design Tips

Check Box Standards

• Use check boxes to allow the user to select any number of choices from a group of one or more independent and nonexclusive choices.

• Enter the check box control's caption using sentence capitalization.

• Assign a unique access key to each check box.

Check boxes work similarly to option buttons in that they are either selected or deselected only; but that is where the similarity ends. You use option buttons when you want to limit the user to only one choice from a group of related and mutually exclusive choices. You use **check boxes**, on the other hand, to allow the user to select any number of choices from a group of one or more independent and nonexclusive choices. Unlike option buttons, where only one button in a group can be selected at any one time, any number of check boxes on a form can be selected at the same time.

You should always label each check box so that the user knows its purpose. You enter the label using sentence capitalization in the check box's Caption property. Be sure to assign an access key to each check box.

Besides double-clicking a tool in the toolbox, you can also draw a control on the user interface by first clicking the tool in the toolbox, then moving the mouse pointer onto the interface, and then dragging the mouse pointer until the control is the size you want. You will use this click and drag method to draw a check box on the form.

To draw a control on the form:

1 Click (don't double-click) the **Check box** tool ☑. When you move the mouse pointer onto the form, it becomes a crosshair +.

2 Place the crosshair + as shown in Figure 4-41.

place the crosshair here

Figure 4-41: Placement of crosshair

3 Drag the mouse down and to the right. When the check box control is about the same size shown in Figure 4-42, release the mouse button.

Figure 4-42: Check box control drawn on the form

HELP? If your check box is too small or too large, use its sizing handles to resize it.

4   Display the Properties window. Set the check box control's Name property to **chkDisplay**, then set its Caption property to **&Display summary information**. "Chk" is the three-character ID for a check box control.

5   Click the **form** to remove the Properties window.

6   **Save and run** the application.

You select a check box by clicking it. You can click either the square or the caption.

7   Click the **Display summary information** check box to select it. A check mark (*an X in Windows 3.1*) appears inside the check box. The check mark (*the X in Windows 3.1*) indicates that the check box is selected.

8   Click the **Display summary information** check box to deselect it. Visual Basic removes the check mark (*the X in Windows 3.1*) from the check box.

9   Click the **Exit** button. Visual Basic returns to the design screen.

The last control you will add to the interface is the image control that will display either a plus sign for addition or a minus sign for subtraction. That control should be placed inside the frame control at the top of the form.

Drawing a Control in a Frame

As you learned earlier in this lesson, in order to place *existing* controls inside a frame, you need to cut the controls from the form, then select the frame, and then paste the controls into the frame. If the control is not already on the form, however, you can use the click and drag method to draw the control right inside the frame.

To draw a control inside a frame:

1   Click the **Image** tool 🖼 in the toolbox. When you move the mouse pointer onto the form or into the frame, it becomes a crosshair +.

2   Position the crosshair + in the frame at the top of the form, then draw the image control to match Figure 4-43.

image control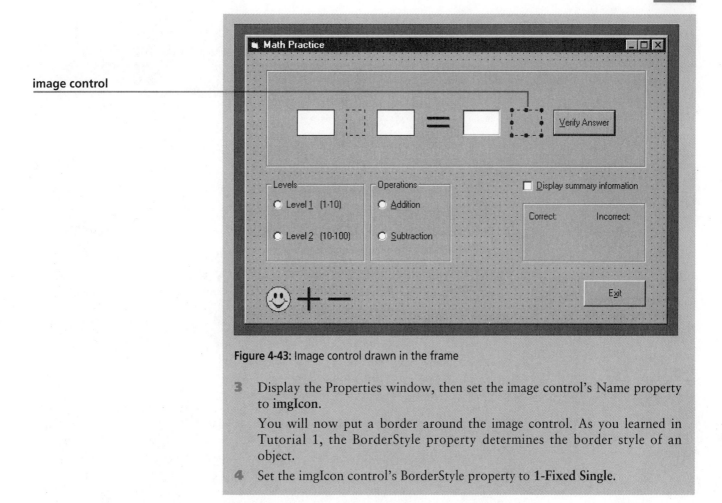

Figure 4-43: Image control drawn in the frame

3   Display the Properties window, then set the image control's Name property to **imgIcon**.

You will now put a border around the image control. As you learned in Tutorial 1, the BorderStyle property determines the border style of an object.

4   Set the imgIcon control's BorderStyle property to **1-Fixed Single**.

You have now completed the user interface, so you can lock the controls in place, then set each control's TabIndex property appropriately.

Locking the Controls and Setting the TabIndex Property

When you have completed a user interface, you should lock the controls in place, then set each control's TabIndex property appropriately. In this application, the first control to receive the focus should be the txtAnswer text box, so you will set its TabIndex property to 0. When the user presses the Tab key, the focus should move from the txtAnswer text box to the Level 1 option button, then to the Level 2 option button, the Addition option button, the Subtraction option button, the Display summary information check box, the Verify Answer command button, and lastly to the Exit button.

To lock the controls, then set each control's TabIndex property:

1   Click the **form** to select it, then click the **Lock Controls** button 🔒 on the toolbar.

2   Set the TabIndex property of the controls as follows:

txtAnswer	0	optSub	4
optLevel1	1	chkDisplay	5
optLevel2	2	cmdVerify	6
optAdd	3	cmdExit	7

3   **Save and run** the application.

4   Press the **Tab** key. The focus moves from the txtAnswer text box to the Level 1 option button. Notice the dotted rectangle around the button's caption.

5   Press the **Tab** key, slowly, five times. The focus moves to the Addition option button, the Display summary information check box, the Verify Answer command button, the Exit command button, and back to the txtAnswer text box.

Notice that the Tab key does not move the focus to either the Level 2 or the Subtraction option buttons. In Windows applications, only one option button in a group of option buttons receives the focus. When one of the option buttons in the group has the focus, the user can select the other option buttons in the group by pressing either the ↓ or the ↑ arrow keys on the keyboard.

6   The focus should be in the txtAnswer text box. Press the **Tab** key to move the focus to the Level 1 option button, then press the ↓ on your keyboard. The Level 2 option button is now selected. Press the ↑ on your keyboard; the Level 1 option is now selected. Press the **Tab** key two times to move the focus to the Display summary information check box. You can use the spacebar to select and deselect a check box when it has the focus. Press the **Spacebar** to select the check box, then press the **Spacebar** again to deselect it.

7   Click the **Exit** button to end the application. Visual Basic returns to the design screen.

You can now begin coding the application. The TOE chart for the Math application is shown in Figure 4-44.

Task	Object	Event
Display/hide number of correct and incorrect responses	chkDisplay	Click
End the application	cmdExit	Click
1. Calculate the correct answer to the math problem 2. Compare the correct answer to the user's answer 3. Display/remove a happy face icon 4. Add 1 to the number of either correct or incorrect responses 5. If the user's answer is incorrect, then prompt the user to "Try again"; otherwise display a new math problem 6. Display the number of correct and incorrect responses in the lblCorrect and lblIncorrect controls, respectively	cmdVerify	Click
Display the equal sign	imgEqual	None
Display the happy face icon	imgIcon	None
Display either the plus sign or the minus sign	imgOperator	None
Display the number of correct responses	lblCorrect	None
Display the number of incorrect responses	lblIncorrect	None
Display a random number	lblNum1	None
Display a random number	lblNum2	None
1. Display two random numbers in the lblNum1 and lblNum2 controls 2. Display the plus sign in the imgOperator control	optAdd	Click
Display two random numbers from 1 to 10 in the lblNum1 and lblNum2 controls	optLevel1	Click
Display two random numbers from 10 to 100 in the lblNum1 and lblNum2 controls	optLevel2	Click
1. Display two random numbers in the lblNum1 and lblNum2 controls 2. Display the minus sign in the imgOperator control	optSub	Click
Get and display the user's answer	txtAnswer	None

Figure 4-44: TOE chart for the Math application

To save you time, the `Option Explicit` statement has already been entered in the form's General declarations section, and the code to center the frmMath form on the screen has already been entered in the form's Load event procedure. You will begin by coding the Level 1 and Level 2 option buttons.

Coding the Level 1 and Level 2 Option Buttons

According to the TOE chart, the Level 1 and Level 2 buttons are responsible for displaying two random numbers—one in the lblNum1 control and the other in the lblNum2 control. In Visual Basic, you use both the Randomize statement and the Rnd function to generate random numbers. The **Randomize statement** initializes Visual Basic's random-number generator, and the **Rnd function** generates the random number. The Rnd function produces decimal numbers within the zero to one range, including zero but not including one. For example, the instruction `lblNum1.Caption = Rnd` would display, in the lblNum1 control, a decimal number that is greater than or equal to zero, but less than one.

You can use the following formula to generate random decimal numbers in a range other than zero to one: (*upperbound − lowerbound* + 1) * Rnd + *lowerbound*. In the formula, *lowerbound* is the lowest number in the range, and *upperbound* is the highest number in the range. For example, to produce decimal numbers from one through ten, you would use the formula `(10 − 1 + 1) * Rnd + 1`.

If you want to generate a range of integers, as you do in the Math application, you need to include the Int function (Int stands for Integer) in the random number formula, like this: Int((*upperbound − lowerbound* + 1) * Rnd + *lowerbound*). The **Int function**, whose syntax is **Int**(*number*), returns the integer portion of a number. Figure 4-45 shows some examples of formulas that generate random numbers.

This formula:	Generates these numbers:
(10 − 1 + 1) * Rnd + 1	decimal numbers from 1 through 10
(25 − 5 + 1) * Rnd + 5	decimal numbers from 5 through 25
Int((10 − 1 + 1) * Rnd + 1)	integers from 1 through 10
Int((25 − 5 + 1) * Rnd + 5)	integers from 5 through 25
Int((100 − 10 + 1) * Rnd + 10)	integers from 10 through 100

Figure 4-45: Examples of formulas that generate random numbers

In the Math application, you will need to generate two random numbers for each math problem. If the user selects the Level 1 option button, both numbers should be in the range of one through ten; otherwise the numbers should be in the ten to 100 range. You will store the random numbers in two Integer variables named inNum1 and inNum2. According to the TOE chart, the random numbers will be used by the Level 1 and Level 2 option buttons, the Addition and Subtraction option buttons, and the Verify Answer command button. Because more than one procedure in the form will need to use the variables, you will declare the variables in the form's General declarations section—in other words, you will make them form-level variables.

To declare the inNum1 and inNum2 variables as form-level variables:

1   Double-click the **form** to open its Code window. The code to center the form is already entered in the form's Load event procedure. Use the Code window's Object box to open the form's General declarations section.

The `Option Explicit` statement is already in the form's General declarations section.

2　Position the blinking insertion point below the `Option Explicit` statement, then type **dim inNum1 as integer, inNum2 as integer** and press the **Enter** key.

The flowchart for the Level 1 and Level 2 option buttons is shown in Figure 4-46.

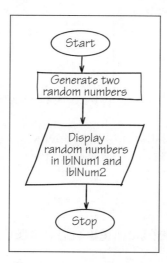

Figure 4-46: Flowchart for the Level 1 and Level 2 option buttons

As the flowchart indicates, the Level 1 and Level 2 controls must generate and display two random numbers in the appropriate label controls on the form. The code for both controls' Click event procedures is almost identical, as shown in Figure 4-47.

Level 1 button's code	Level 2 button's code
Randomize	Randomize
inNum1 = Int((10 − 1 + 1) * Rnd + 1)	inNum1 = Int((100 − 10 + 1) * Rnd + 10)
inNum2 = Int((10 − 1 + 1) * Rnd + 1)	inNum2 = Int((100 − 10 + 1) * Rnd + 10)

Figure 4-47: Code for the Level 1 and Level 2 buttons' Click event procedures

Notice that the only difference in the code for both procedures is in the random number formulas: the Level 1 button's formulas generate numbers from one through ten, and the Level 2 button's formulas generate numbers from ten through 100. Although you could enter the code shown in Figure 4-47 in both Click event procedures, that would be inefficient because several lines of code would be duplicated. A better approach is to place the code in a user-defined sub procedure and then have the Level 1 and Level 2 option buttons invoke (call) the sub procedure as needed.

Before learning how to create a user-defined sub procedure, you will change the flowchart for the Level 1 and Level 2 buttons to reflect the fact that the buttons will call a user-defined procedure. The procedure will be named RandomNumbers. The revised flowchart is shown in Figure 4-48.

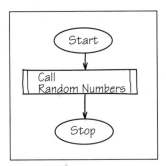

Figure 4-48: Revised flowchart for the Level 1 and Level 2 option buttons

Notice the symbol—a rectangle with side borders—used to represent a call to a sub procedure. The symbol is called the **sub procedure box**. You will now create the user-defined sub procedure that will both generate and display the random numbers.

Creating a User-Defined Sub Procedure

You are already familiar with procedures. Clicking a command button, for example, causes an event procedure to occur, provided you have added the appropriate code. A **user-defined sub procedure**, often just called a **user-defined procedure**, is a collection of code that can be invoked from one or more places in your program. When the code, or a portion of the code, for two or more objects is almost identical, it is more efficient to enter the code once, in a user-defined procedure, instead of duplicating the code in each event procedure.

The user-defined procedure you will create for the Math application will initialize the random number generator first. Next, it will determine which of the level option buttons—either Level 1 or Level 2—is selected, and then generate and display the appropriate random numbers in the lblNum1 and lblNum2 controls in the interface.

To create a user-defined sub procedure, you simply open any Code window, then click Insert on the menu bar, and then click Procedure from the Insert menu. The rules for naming a user-defined procedure are the same as those for naming variables and constants. You will name the user-defined procedure RandomNumbers.

To create the RandomNumbers procedure:

1 A Code window is already open, so you just need to click **Insert** on the menu bar, then click **Procedure**. The Insert Procedure dialog box appears as shown in Figure 4-49.

Figure 4-49: Insert Procedure dialog box

2 Type **RandomNumbers** in the Name box.

You want to create a sub procedure, so leave the Sub option button selected in the Type box. The user-defined procedure will be used only by the form in which it is created, so you will make its scope Private.

3 Click the **Private** option button in the Scope box, then click the **OK** button. The Insert Procedure dialog box closes and the Code window for the RandomNumbers procedure appears, as shown in Figure 4-50.

Figure 4-50: RandomNumbers procedure

A user-defined procedure can receive variables or constants, called **arguments**, that you send (pass) to it; the arguments, if any, are listed inside the parentheses following the procedure's name. You pass arguments when you want the procedure to process them in some way. For example, you might create a procedure that sorts a list of numbers. The arguments you pass would be the numbers themselves; the procedure would then sort, and perhaps display, those numbers. (You will learn how to pass arguments in Tutorial 8.) The RandomNumbers procedure does not receive any variables or constants, so you will not need to list any information inside the parentheses.

The first task the RandomNumbers procedure will perform is to initialize the random number generator. Recall that you use the Randomize statement to do so.

4   Press the **Tab** key, then type **randomize** and press the **Enter** key.

The procedure now needs to generate and display the random numbers. The range of random numbers depends on which of the level option buttons—either Level 1 or Level 2—is selected. If the Level 1 button is selected, then the application should generate random numbers from one through ten; otherwise it should generate numbers from ten through 100. You will use the selection structure, which you learned about in Lesson A, to determine which of the level option buttons is selected before generating the random numbers. You can tell if an option button is selected by looking at its Value property. When an option button is selected, its Value property contains the Boolean value True; otherwise it contains the Boolean value False. After generating the random numbers, you will display them in the lblNum1 and lblNum2 controls.

5   Enter the code shown in Figure 4-51.

Figure 4-51: Code entered in the RandomNumbers procedure

You invoke a user-defined procedure with Visual Basic's Call statement.

The Call Statement

You use Visual Basic's Call statement, whose syntax is **Call** *name* [(*argumentlist*)], to invoke a user-defined sub procedure. The brackets in the syntax indicate that the *argumentlist* is optional and, if included, must be enclosed in parentheses. If you have no information to pass to the sub procedure that you are calling, as is the case in the Math application, you do not need to enter anything inside the parentheses.

The Level 1 and Level 2 option buttons should call the RandomNumbers procedure when each is clicked by the user. You will therefore enter the Call statement in each button's Click event procedure.

To enter the Call statement in the Level 1 and Level 2 buttons' Click event procedures:

1 Use the Code window's Object box to open the optLevel1 control's Click event procedure, which is the most common event for an option button. Press the **Tab** key, then type **call RandomNumbers** and press the **Enter** key.

When the Call statement is processed, the program will leave the option button's Click event procedure, temporarily, in order to process the instructions in the RandomNumbers procedure. When the RandomNumbers procedure ends, the program will return to the option button's Click event procedure, to the line below the Call statement. In this application, the line below the Call statement will be the End Sub instruction, which will end the option button's Click event procedure. Figure 4-52 illustrates this concept.

leave Click event,
temporarily

return to Click event

Figure 4-52: Illustration of the Call statement

Now copy the Call instruction to the Level 2 button's Click event procedure.

2 Select the `Call RandomNumbers` instruction in the open Code window. Click **Edit**, then click **Copy**. Use the Code window's Object box to open the optLevel2 control's Click event procedure. Click **Edit**, then click **Paste**. (You then need to position the blinking insertion point at the beginning of the instruction and press the Tab key to indent the instruction.)

3 Close the Code window, then **save and run** the application.

4 Click the **Level 1** button. The program leaves the Level 1 button's Click event procedure, temporarily, in order to process the instructions in the RandomNumbers procedure. The RandomNumbers procedure generates and displays, in the label controls, two numbers between one and ten, inclusive. When the RandomNumbers procedure ends, the program returns to the Level1 button's Click event procedure to process its `End Sub` instruction, which ends the Click event.

5 Click the **Level 2** button. The program leaves the Level2 button's Click event procedure, temporarily, in order to process the instructions in the RandomNumbers procedure. The RandomNumbers procedure generates and displays, in the label controls, two numbers between ten and 100, inclusive. When the RandomNumbers procedure ends, the program returns to the Level2 button's Click event procedure to process its `End Sub` instruction, which ends the Click event.

6 Click the **Exit** button. Visual Basic returns to the design screen.

Next, code the Addition and Subtraction option buttons.

Coding the Addition and Subtraction Option Buttons

According to the TOE chart shown in Figure 4-44, the Addition and Subtraction option buttons should display two random numbers in the label controls, as well as display the appropriate operator, either a plus or a minus sign, in the imgOperator control. You can have the Addition and Subtraction buttons call the RandomNumbers procedure to display the random numbers. When the RandomNumbers procedure ends, each option button can then display the appropriate operator.

The Addition and Subtraction option buttons should perform their assigned tasks when they are clicked by the user, so you will need to code their Click event procedures.

To code the Click event procedures for the Addition and Subtraction option buttons:

1   Double-click the **Addition** button to open its Code window. The Click event procedure appears.

First have the Addition button call the RandomNumbers procedure.

2   Press the **Tab** key, then type **call RandomNumbers** and press the **Enter** key.

The Addition button must also display the plus sign icon in the imgOperator control. You can do this by assigning the Picture property of the imgPlus control, which is located at the bottom of the form, to the Picture property of the imgOperator control. In other words, you can use the assignment statement `imgOperator.Picture = imgPlus.Picture`.

3   Type **imgOperator.picture = imgPlus.picture** and press the **Enter** key.

Now copy the Addition button's code to the Subtraction button's Click event procedure.

4   Select both the `Call RandomNumbers` and `imgOperator.Picture = imgPlus.Picture` instructions. Click **Edit** on the menu bar, then click **Copy** to copy the instructions to the clipboard. Use the Code window's Object box to open the Click event procedure for the optSub control. Click **Edit** on the menu bar, then click **Paste** to paste the instructions into the optSub control's Code window.

You want the Subtraction button to display the minus sign, which is stored in the imgMinus control at the bottom of the form.

5   Change the Code window to match Figure 4-53.

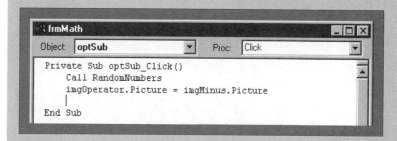

Figure 4-53: Code entered in the Level 2 button's Click event procedure

6   Close the Code window, then **save and run** the application.

Notice that none of the option buttons are selected in the interface. It is customary in Windows applications to have an option button selected in each group when the interface first appears. You'll learn how to select an option button, automatically, in the next section.

7   Click the **Addition** option button. The program leaves the Addition button's Click event procedure, temporarily, in order to process the instructions in the RandomNumbers procedure. The RandomNumbers procedure generates and displays the random numbers. When the RandomNumbers procedure ends, the program returns to the Addition button's Click event procedure to process the `imgOperator.Picture = imgPlus.Picture` instruction, which displays the plus sign in the imgOperator control, and the `End Sub` instruction, which ends the Click event.

8   Click the **Subtraction** option button. The program leaves the Subtraction button's Click event procedure, temporarily, in order to process the instructions in
the RandomNumbers procedure. The RandomNumbers procedure generates
and displays the random numbers. When the RandomNumbers procedure
ends, the program returns to the Subtraction button's Click event procedure to
process the `imgOperator.Picture = imgMinus.Picture` instruction,
which displays the minus sign in the imgOperator control, and the `End Sub`
instruction, which ends the Click event.

9   Click the **Exit** button. Visual Basic returns to the design screen.

In the next section you will learn how to have an option button automatically
selected when the interface first appears on the screen.

Creating a Default Option Button

It is customary in Windows applications to have an option button already selected
when the interface first appears. The selected button is called the **default option
button**. If an interface contains more than one group of option buttons, you
should select a default button in each group. In the Math application, for example, you will make the Level 1 button the default button in the Levels group, and
the Addition button the default button in the Operations group.

You make an option button the default button by assigning the Boolean value
True to the button's Value property; assigning True to the Value property selects
the option button and also triggers its Click event. Because you want the Level 1
and Addition option buttons selected when the user interface first appears on the
screen, you will need to place the appropriate assignment statements in the form's
Load event procedure. Recall that instructions in the form's Load event procedure
are processed when the application is run and the form is loaded into memory.

**GUI
Design Tips**

Default Option Button

• A default button should be
  selected in each group of
  option buttons.

To make the Level 1 and Addition option buttons the default buttons in their
respective groups:

1   Double-click the **form** to open its Load event procedure.

2   Position the blinking insertion point below the two instructions that center
the form. If necessary, press the **Tab** key to indent the instruction. Type
optLevel1.value = true and press the **Enter** key, then type **optAdd.value =
true** and press the **Enter** key.

These two instructions will select the Level 1 and Addition option buttons in the
interface, and also trigger their Click event procedures.

3   Close the Code window, then **save** and **run** the application.

Notice that the application selects, automatically, the Level 1 and Addition
option buttons. The first math problem appears in the interface.

4   Click the **Level 2** option button. Random numbers in the range of ten
through 100 appear in the label controls.

5   Click the **Subtraction** option button. A subtraction problem appears in the
interface.

The modified code creates an Integer variable named inTemp (short for "temporary"). The If statement contains two conditions that are combined with the And logical operator. The first condition, `optSub.Value = True`, checks to see if the Subtraction button is selected. The second condition, `inNum2 > inNum1`, checks to see if the second number is greater than the first number. Recall that when you combine conditions using the And operator, both conditions must be true for the entire condition to be true. In this case, the Subtraction button must be selected *and* the second number must be greater than the first number in order for the entire condition to be true. If the entire condition is true, you simply interchange (swap) the numbers in the inNum1 and inNum2 variables.

The three instructions that accomplish the swap are `inTemp = inNum1`, `inNum1 = inNum2`, and `inNum2 = inTemp`. First, the `inTemp = inNum1` instruction assigns the value in the inNum1 variable to the inTemp variable. Next, the `inNum1 = inNum2` instruction assigns the value in the inNum2 variable to the inNum1 variable. Lastly, the `inNum2 = inTemp` instruction assigns the value in the inTemp variable to the inNum2 variable. The inTemp variable is necessary to store the contents of the inNum1 variable temporarily so that the swap can be made. If you did not store the inNum1 value in the inTemp variable, the inNum2 value would write over the value in the inNum1 variable and the value in the inNum1 variable would be lost. Figure 4-55 illustrates the concept of "swapping."

Figure 4-55: Illustration of "swapping" concept

3   Close the Code window, then **save and run** the application.

4   Try clicking each of the option buttons. Notice that when the Subtraction button is selected, the number in lblNum2 is never greater than the number in lblNum1.

5   Click the **Exit** button to end the application.

You have now completed Lesson B. You can either take a break or complete the end-of-lesson questions and exercises. You will complete the Math application in Lesson C.

S U M M A R Y

To limit the user to only one of several related and mutually exclusive choices:

- Use the option button tool

To allow the user to select any number of choices from a group of independent and nonexclusive choices:

- Use the check box tool

To create separate groups of option buttons, or to visually separate areas of the form:

- Use the frame tool

To place an existing control into a frame:

- Cut the existing control from the form, then select the frame, and then paste the control into the frame.

To draw a control on a form or in a frame:

- Click (do not double-click) the appropriate tool in the toolbox. Position the crosshair $+$ on the form or inside the frame, then drag until the control is the desired size.

To generate random numbers:

- First use the Randomize statement to initialize the random number generator. You can then use the Rnd function to generate random decimal numbers between zero and 1, including zero but not including one. To generate decimal numbers within a specific range, use the formula (*upperbound* − *lowerbound* + 1) * **Rnd** + *lowerbound*. To generate integers within a specific range, use the formula **Int**((*upperbound* − *lowerbound* + 1) * **Rnd** + *lowerbound*).

To return the integer portion of a number:

- Use the Int function. (Int stands for Integer.) Its syntax is **Int**(*number*).

To create a collection of code that can be invoked from one or more places in your program:

- Create a user-defined sub procedure. First open any Code window, then click Insert in Visual Basic's menu bar, then click Procedure. Give the procedure a name, type, and scope. The rules for naming a user-defined procedure are the same as those for naming variables and constants.

To invoke a user-defined sub procedure:

- Use the Call statement. Its syntax is **Call** *name* [(*argumentlist*)].

To swap the values contained in two variables:

- Assign the value in the first variable to a temporary variable, then assign the value in the second variable to the first variable, and then assign the value in the temporary variable to the second variable.

Q U E S T I O N S

1. Which of the following controls allows the user to select only one choice?
   a. check box
   b. command button
   c. label
   d. option button
   e. shape

2. Which of the following controls allows the user to select one or more choices?
   a. check box
   b. command button
   c. label
   d. option button
   e. shape

3. If you want to create separate groups of option buttons, you will need to place each group in its own _____ control.
   a. check box
   b. circle
   c. container
   d. frame
   e. shape

4. Assume the form contains three option buttons. (The buttons are not in a frame control.) How many option buttons can be on at any one time?
   a. one
   b. two
   c. three
   d. four
   e. five

5. Assume the form contains two frame controls. Each frame control contains three option buttons. How many option buttons can be on at any time?
   a. one
   b. two
   c. three
   d. four
   e. five

6. Assume the form contains three check boxes. (The check boxes are not in a frame control.) How many check boxes can be on at any one time?
   a. one
   b. two
   c. three
   d. four
   e. five

7. Assume the form contains two frame controls. Each frame control contains two check boxes. How many check boxes can be on at any time?
   a. one
   b. two
   c. three
   d. four
   e. five

8. Assume the form contains two frame controls. One frame control contains two option buttons; the other frame control contains three check boxes. What is the total number of option buttons and check boxes that can be on at any one time?

   a. one
   b. two
   c. three
   d. four
   e. five

9. Which of the following initializes Visual Basic's random number generator?

   a. Generate
   b. Initialize
   c. Randomize
   d. RandomNumb
   e. Rnd

10. The `lblNumber.Caption = Rnd` instruction will generate random numbers _____.

    a. between 0 and 1, including 0 and 1
    b. between 0 and 1, including 0 but not including 1
    c. between 0 and 1, including 1 but not including 0
    d. greater than 0 but less than 1
    e. less than 0 and greater than 1

11. Which of the following will generate random decimal numbers from 5 through 30?

    a. (5 − 30 + 1) * Rnd + 30
    b. (30 − 5 + 1) * Rnd + 5
    c. (30 + 5 − 1) * Rnd + 1
    d. (30 + 5 − 1) * Rnd + 5
    e. (30 − 5 − 1) * Rnd + 30

12. Which of the following will generate random integers from 1 through 25?

    a. Int((1 − 25 + 1) * Rnd + 25)
    b. Int((25 − 1 + 1)) * Rnd + 1
    c. Int((25 + 1 − 1) * Rnd + 1)
    d. Int((25 + 1 − 1)) * Rnd + 1
    e. Int((25 − 1 + 1) * Rnd + 1)

13. A collection of code that can be invoked from one or more places in your program is called a _____.

    a. code collection
    b. code procedure
    c. procedure
    d. user-defined collection
    e. user-defined sub procedure

14. You use the _____ statement to invoke a user-defined sub procedure.

    a. Call
    b. DoProcedure
    c. Get
    d. Invoke
    e. ProcedureCall

15. Which of the following instructions will select the optInsured option button and trigger its Click event procedure?

a. optInsured.Button = on

b. optInsured.Button = true

c. optInsured.Status = on

d. optInsured.Value = on

e. optInsured.Value = true

16. Assume the form contains a command button named cmdExit. How could you place this control in a frame?

17. How do you draw a control in a frame?

18. Explain how to swap the values contained in two variables named crPrice1 and crPrice2.

E X E R C I S E S

1. In this exercise you will create an interface that contains option buttons and frames. You will then code the application using the If...Then...Else structure.

Scenario: Woodland School wants an application that the students can use to study the capitals of five states. After selecting a state and its corresponding capital, the user will click the Check Answer command button to verify that the capital he or she chose is correct. If the capital is correct, display the word "Correct" in the label control; otherwise display the word "Incorrect."

a. Create the user interface shown in Figure 4-56.

label control —————————

Figure 4-56

b. Save the form and the project as lb1Done.

c. Center the form on the screen.

d. Make the Check Answer button the default command button. Make the California and Denver buttons the default option buttons in their respective groups.

e. Code the Exit control so that it ends the application.

f. Code the Print control so that it prints the form with the command buttons showing.

g. Use the flowcharts shown in Figure 4-57 to code the state and capital option buttons and the Check Answer command button's Click event procedures.

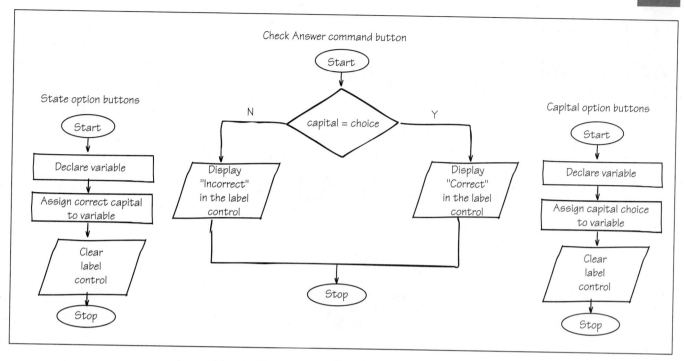

Figure 4-57

h. Save and run the application.

i. Test the application by selecting Illinois from the State group and Salem from the Capital group. Click the Check Answer button, then click the Print button.

j. Test the application again by selecting Wisconsin from the State group and Madison from the Capital group. Click the Check Answer button, then click the Print button.

k. Click the Exit button to end the application.

l. Print the application's code.

m. Submit the printouts from steps i and j, and the code from step l.

2. In this exercise you will open an application that contains check boxes and a frame control. You will use the If...Then...Else structure to code the application.

Scenario: Willow Health Club needs an application that they can use to calculate each member's monthly dues. The basic fee is $80. After the user selects the additional charges, if any, the user will click the Calculate Total button to calculate and display the total additional charge and the total due. The total due is calculated by adding the basic fee to the total additional charge. The individual additional charges are as follows: Tennis, $30 per month; Golf, $25 per month; Racquetball, $20 per month.

a. Open the lb2 project, which is located in the Tut04 folder on your Student Disk. View the form.

b. Save the form and the project as lb2Done in the Tut04 folder on your Student Disk.

c. Make the Calculate Total button the default command button.

d. Center the form on the screen.

e. Draw the flowcharts or write the pseudocode for the application, then code the application. (The Print button should print the form without the command buttons showing. The Exit button should end the application.)

f. Save and run the application.

g. Test the application by selecting Golf. Click the Calculate Total button, then click the Print button.

h. Test the application again by deselecting Golf, then selecting Tennis and Racquetball. Click the Calculate Total button, then click the Print button.

i. Exit the application, then print the application's code.

j. Submit the printouts from steps g and h, and the code from step i.

LESSON C
objectives

In this lesson you will learn how to:

- Create a static variable
- Use the LoadPicture, MsgBox, and Len functions
- Set the SelStart and SelLength properties

Completing the Math Application

Static Variables

You still need to code the Verify Answer button and the chkDisplay check box. Before doing so, however, you will learn about static variables. A **static variable** is a local variable that retains its value when a procedure ends.

To learn about static variables:

1 Start Visual Basic, if necessary, then open the **static** (static.vbp) project, which is located in Tut04 on your Student Disk.

2 View the form, then **run**, but don't save, the project.

The static application should count the number of times you press the Count button, but it is not working correctly, as you will see in the next step.

3 Click the **Count** button. The message tells you that you have pressed the Count button 1 time, which is correct. Now click the **Count** button several more times. Notice that the message still says that you pressed the Count button 1 time, which is incorrect.

4 Click the **Exit** button to end the application.

5 Double-click the **Count** button to open its Code window. The Count button's Click event procedure opens, as shown in Figure 4-58.

Figure 4-58: Code entered in the Count button's Click event procedure

Each time you click the Count button, the Dim statement in the button's Click event procedure declares and initializes a local variable named inCounter. The procedure then adds 1 to the inCounter variable, whose value it displays in the lblCounter control on the form. When Visual Basic processes the `End Sub` statement, the inCounter variable is removed from the computer's memory.

In order for this application to work correctly, you need the inCounter variable to remain in memory until the application ends. The way to accomplish this is to declare the local variable as a static variable. When you declare a variable as a static variable, Visual Basic does not remove the variable from memory when the procedure in which it is declared ends; instead, the variable and its value remain in memory until the application ends. You declare a static variable by using the keyword Static, instead of the keyword Dim.

6   Change the `Dim inCounter as Integer` instruction to **Static inCounter as Integer**, then close the Code window.

7   **Run**, but don't save, the application.

8   Click the **Count** button.

The Count button's Click event procedure declares and initializes a static variable named inCounter. It then adds one to the inCounter variable and displays a 1 in the lblCounter control on the form. When the `End Sub` instruction is processed, the Click event procedure ends, but the inCounter variable is not removed from the computer's memory; it remains in memory with its current value, 1.

9   Click the **Count** button again.

This time the Count button's Click event procedure does not declare and initialize the inCounter variable; rather, it simply adds one to the existing inCounter variable, giving two, and displays a 2 in the lblCounter control on the form. When the `End Sub` instruction is processed, the inCounter variable remains in memory with its current value of 2.

10   Click the **Count** button several times. The message now tells you that you pressed the Count button 3 times, 4 times, 5 times, and so on.

11   Click the **Exit** button to end the application.

Now that you know how to use a static variable, you can finish coding the Math application.

---

tips

● ● ● ● ● ● ● ● ● ● ● ● ● ●

▶ **Although you could also use the Dim statement to declare the inCounter variable as a form-level variable, which will maintain the variable and its value until the application ends, that is not the preferred way. The inCounter variable is not needed by more than one procedure in the form, so it should not be declared as a form-level variable.**

Coding the Verify Answer Button

To complete the Math application, you still need to code the Verify Answer button and the Display summary information check box. You will code the Verify Answer button first.

To finish coding the Math application:

1 Open the **lbMath** (lblMath.vbp) project that you created in Lesson B. The project is in the Tut04 folder on your Student Disk. You do not need to save the static application.

2 Save the form and the project as **lcMath**.

3 Click the **View Form** button in the Project window to view the frmMath form.

According to the TOE chart, shown earlier in Figure 4-44, the Verify Answer button has the following tasks:

- Calculate the correct answer to the math problem
- Compare the correct answer to the user's answer
- Display/remove a happy face icon
- Add 1 to the number of either correct or incorrect responses
- If the user's answer is incorrect, then prompt the user to "Try again"; otherwise display a new math problem.
- Display the number of correct and incorrect responses in the lblCorrect and lblIncorrect controls, respectively.

The flowchart for the Verify Answer button's Click event procedure is shown in Figure 4-59.

The Click event procedure will use the four local variables shown in Figure 4-60.

Variable's Name	Data Type	Use to store:
inUserAnswer	Integer	the user's answer to the math problem
inCorrectAnswer	Integer	the correct answer to the math problem
inNumCorrrect	Integer	the number of correct responses made by the user
inNumIncorrect	Integer	the number of incorrect responses made by the user

Figure 4-60: Four variables used by the Verify Answer button's Click event procedure

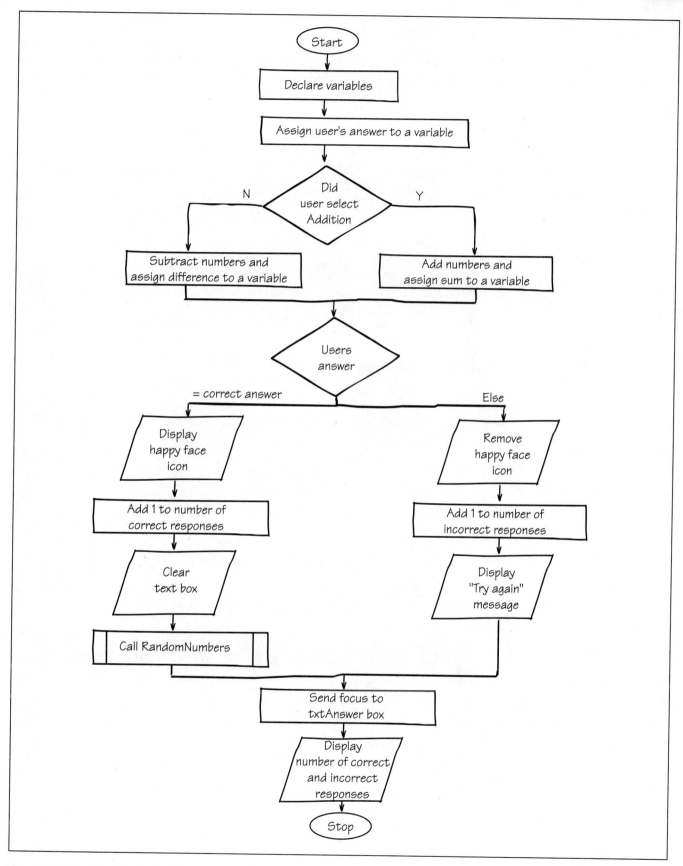

Figure 4-59: Flowchart for the Verify Answer button's Click event procedure

Each time the Verify Answer button is clicked, you want its Click event procedure to declare and initialize the inUserAnswer and inCorrectAnswer variables; you will declare those two variables with the Dim statement. You do not, however, want the Click event procedure to declare and initialize the inNumCorrect and inNumIncorrect variables each time the Verify Answer button is clicked; instead, you want the value of these variables to remain in memory until the application ends. Therefore, you will need to declare the inNumCorrect and inNumIncorrect variables as static variables.

To code the Verify Answer button's Click event procedure:

1   Double-click the **Verify Answer** button to open its Code window, then maximize the Code window. Enter the Dim and Static statements shown in Figure 4-61.

```
frmMath                                                      _ □ ×
Object: cmdVerify              ▼      Proc: Click             ▼
Private Sub cmdVerify_Click()
    Dim inUserAnswer As Integer, inCorrectAnswer As Integer
    Static inNumCorrect As Integer, inNumIncorrect As Integer
    |
End Sub
```

Figure 4-61: Dim and Static statements entered in the Verify Answer button's Click event procedure

Next you will assign the user's response, which he or she entered in the txtAnswer control, to the inUserAnswer variable.

2   Type **inUserAnswer = val(txtAnswer.text)** and press the **Enter** key.

You now need to determine which of the option buttons in the Operations frame is selected—the Addition button or the Subtraction button—in order to calculate the correct answer to the math problem appearing in the interface. You can determine if an option button is selected by looking at its Value property. If an option button is selected, then its Value property contains the Boolean value True; otherwise, its Value property contains the Boolean value False. You can use either the If...Then...Else selection structure or the Case selection structure to determine which option button is selected. You will use the If...Then...Else structure.

3   Enter the selection structure shown in Figure 4-62.

enter the selection structure

```
frmMath                                                      _ □ ×
Object: cmdVerify              ▼      Proc: Click             ▼
Private Sub cmdVerify_Click()
    Dim inUserAnswer As Integer, inCorrectAnswer As Integer
    Static inNumCorrect As Integer, inNumIncorrect As Integer
    inUserAnswer = Val(txtAnswer.Text)
    If optAdd.Value = True Then
        inCorrectAnswer = inNum1 + inNum2
    Else
        inCorrectAnswer = inNum1 - inNum2
    End If
    |
End Sub
```

Figure 4-62: Selection structure entered in the Verify Answer button's Click event procedure

The next step is to determine if the user entered the correct answer. You can use either the If...Then...Else selection structure or the Case selection structure to do so. Just for practice, this time you will use the Case selection structure.

The first possibility is that the user entered the correct answer—in other words, the value in the inUserAnswer variable is equal to the value in the inCorrectAnswer variable. According to the flowchart, when the user enters the correct answer, you should assign the happy face icon, which is located at the bottom of the form, to the imgIcon control. You then need to add one to the number of correct responses, which is stored in the inNumCorrect variable. Lastly, you need to clear the txtAnswer text box so the user can enter the answer to the next problem, then display a new problem for the user.

4   Enter the additional code shown in Figure 4-63, then position the blinking insertion point as shown in the figure.

enter this code

Figure 4-63: Current status of the Verify Answer button's Click event procedure

You can now code the Case Else part of the structure next.

5   With the blinking insertion point positioned as shown in Figure 4-63, press the **Backspace** key, then type **case else** and press the **Enter** key.

If the user's answer is incorrect, then you want to remove the happy face icon from the imgIcon control, add the number 1 to the number of incorrect responses, and display a "Try again" message. You can use Visual Basic's LoadPicture function to remove the happy face icon, and Visual Basic's MsgBox function to display the "Try again" message.

The LoadPicture Function

You can use the **LoadPicture function** to display a graphic in a form, picture box control, or image control; you can also use it to clear a graphic from those objects. The syntax of the LoadPicture function is **LoadPicture([*stringexpression*])**, where *stringexpression* represents the location and name of a graphics file; the *stringexpression* should be enclosed in quotation marks. For example, assume that the misc01.ico graphics file is located in the Microsoft Visual Basic\icons\misc (*vb\icons\misc in Windows 3.1*) folder on the local hard drive. You would use the following instruction to display the icon in the imgIcon control: `imgIcon.Picture = LoadPicture("c:\Microsoft Visual Basic\icons\misc\misc01.ico")`.

If you are using Windows 3.1, you would use the following instruction to display the icon in the imgIcon control:
`imgIcon.Picture = LoadPicture("c:\vb\icons\misc\misc01.ico)`.

If you omit the *stringexpression* from the LoadPicture function, the function clears the existing picture from the Image control. In this application, for example, you can use the `imgIcon.Picture = LoadPicture()` instruction to remove the happy face icon from the imgIcon Image control.

To continue coding the Verify Answer button:

1   Press the **Tab** key, then type **imgIcon.picture = loadpicture()** and press the **Enter** key.

Now add the number 1 to the number of incorrect responses. Recall that the number of incorrect responses is stored in the inNumIncorrect variable.

2   Type **inNumIncorrect = inNumIncorrect + 1** and press the **Enter** key.

Recall that the application should allow the student to answer the problem as many times as necessary. You can use Visual Basic's MsgBox function to prompt the user to answer the problem again. At this point you will close the Code window; you will return to complete the Verify Answer button's Click event procedure after learning about the MsgBox function.

3   Close the Code window.

The MsgBox Function

The **MsgBox function** displays one of Visual Basic's predefined dialog boxes. The dialog box contains a message, one or more command buttons, and an optional icon. After displaying the dialog box, the MsgBox function waits for the user to choose a button. It then returns a value that indicates which button the user chose. To learn more about the MsgBox function, you will display its Help window.

To learn about the MsgBox function:

1   Click **Help** on the menu bar, then click **Search For Help On**. Display the Help window for the MsgBox Function, then maximize the Help window. The maximized Help window is shown in Figure 4-64.

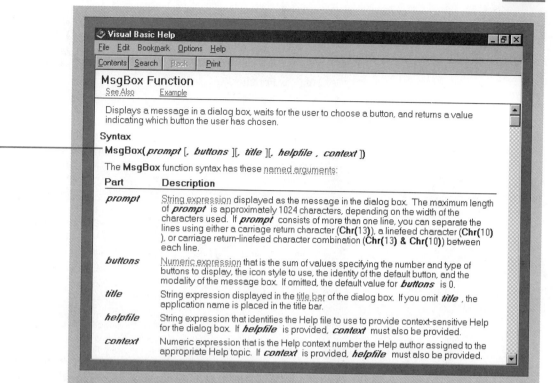

syntax

Figure 4-64: MsgBox function's Help window

The syntax of the MsgBox function is **MsgBox**(*prompt*[, *buttons*][, *title*]
[, *helpfile*, *context*]). *Prompt* is the message you want displayed in the dialog
box; the message should be enclosed in quotation marks and entered using sentence capitalization. *Buttons* is an optional numeric expression that represents
the sum of values specifying the number and type of buttons to display, the icon
style to use, the identity of the default button, and the dialog box's modality. If
you omit the *buttons* argument, the dialog box contains an OK button only.
Title is a string expression displayed in the title bar of the dialog box. It is customary in Windows applications to display the application's name in the title
bar; if you omit the *title* argument in the MsgBox function, the application's
name appears, automatically, in the title bar. If you want to use a different string
expression for the title argument, be sure to enter the string expression using
book title capitalization. You use the optional *helpfile* and *context* arguments to
provide context-sensitive help for the dialog box. Take a closer look at the *buttons* argument.

2   Scroll the Help window as shown in Figure 4-65.

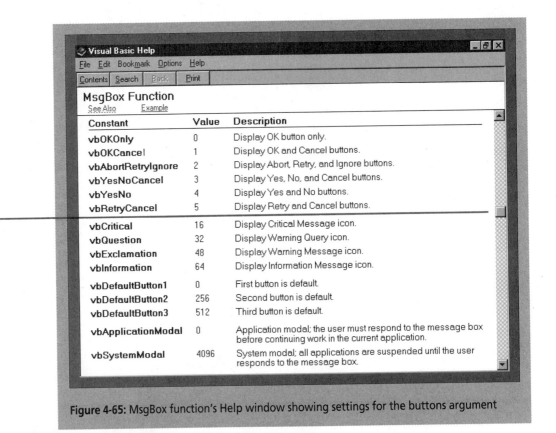

note location of scroll box

Figure 4-65: MsgBox function's Help window showing settings for the buttons argument

Notice that each argument setting has a constant and a numeric value associated with it. When entering the *buttons* argument in the MsgBox function, you can either use the setting's value or its constant. Using the constant makes the program more self-documenting, so it is the preferred way of entering the *buttons* argument.

The settings for the *buttons* argument are split into four groups. The first group controls the number and types of buttons displayed in the dialog box. The vbOKOnly setting, for example, displays one button, the OK button. The vbYesNoCancel setting, on the other hand, displays three buttons—Yes, No, and Cancel.

The second group of settings controls the style of the icon displayed in the dialog box. The vbCritical setting, for example, displays the Critical Message icon, which alerts the user of a serious problem that requires intervention or correction before the application can continue. You would use the Critical Message icon in a dialog box that alerts the user that the disk in the disk drive is write-protected.

The vbQuestion setting displays the Warning Query icon; you would use this icon in a Windows 3.1 dialog box that contains a message phrased as a question. The Warning Query icon is not used in Windows 95 applications.

The vbExclamation setting displays the Warning Message icon. You use the Warning Message icon to alert the user that he or she must first make a decision and then enter a response before the application can continue. The message to the user can be phrased as a question—for example, "Do you want to continue?"

The vbInformation setting displays the Information Message icon, which you use in a dialog box whose purpose is to display information only. The dialog box should display the OK button only; it should not offer the user any choices. The user acknowledges the informational message by clicking the OK button. This is the proper icon to use for the "Try again" message in the Math application.

The third group of settings for the buttons argument identifies the default button, which is the button that is chosen automatically when the user presses the Enter key. The default button is the one that represents the user's most likely action, as long as that instruction is not destructive.

The fourth group controls the dialog box's modality, which can be either application modal or system modal. **Application modal**, the default modality, means that the user must respond to the message in the dialog box before he or she can continue working in the current application; however, the user can still access other applications either using Alt-Tab or clicking the application button on the Windows 95 taskbar. When a dialog box is **system modal**, on the other hand, all applications are suspended until the user responds to the message.

The *buttons* argument is the sum of one of the numbers from each group. The default value for the *buttons* argument is 0 (vbOKOnly + vbDefaultButton1 + vbApplicationModal), which means that the dialog box will display an OK button only; it will not contain an icon. The OK button will be the default button and the dialog box will be application modal. Now say that you want the dialog box to display Yes and No buttons along with the Warning Query icon. Additionally, you want the No button to be the default button, and you want the dialog box to be application modal. To display a dialog box matching that description, you would enter, as the *buttons* argument, either the expression vbYesNo + vbQuestion + vbDefaultButton2 + vbApplicationModal, or the number 292 (4 + 32 + 256 + 0). To make your programs more self-documenting, it is a good practice to enter the expression that contains the constants instead of the numeric value.

Now here's one for you to try. Say that you want the Abort, Retry, and Ignore buttons, with the Critical Message icon, the second button as the default, and the dialog box to be system modal. What expression would you enter as the *buttons* argument? You should enter vbAbortRetryIgnore + vbCritical + vbDefaultButton2 + vbSystemModal. (The numeric value you could enter would be 4370, which is 2 + 16 + 256 + 4096.)

GUI Design Tips

MsgBox Function Standards

- Enter the dialog box message using sentence capitalization.
- Display the application's name in the dialog box's title bar. The title bar text should be entered using book title capitalization.
- Display the Critical Message icon when you want to alert the user of a serious problem that must be corrected before the application can continue.
- Display the Warning Query icon in a Windows 3.1 dialog box whose message is phrased as a question; don't use the Warning Query icon in a Windows 95 application.
- Display the Warning Message icon in a dialog box when you want to alert the user that he or she must first make a decision and then enter a response before the application can continue; you can phrase the message as a question.
- Display the Information Message icon in a dialog box that displays an informational message along with an OK button only. The dialog box should not offer any choices to the user.
- The default button in the dialog box should be the one that represents the user's most likely action, as long as that instruction is not destructive.

To continue viewing the MsgBox function's Help window:

1 Scroll the Help window as shown in Figure 4-66.

note location of scroll box

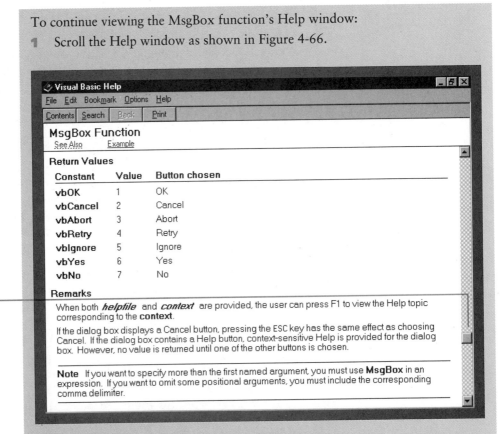

Figure 4-66: MsgBox function's Help window showing values returned by the MsgBox function

The Help window lists the constants and numeric values returned by the MsgBox function. The information returned by the MsgBox function indicates which button the user selected in the dialog box. For example, if the Yes button was selected, the MsgBox function returns the integer 6, which can be referred to as vbYes.

2 Close the Help window.

In this application the MsgBox function should display a dialog box that contains a "Try again" message, an OK button, and an Information Message icon, as well as the words "Math Application" in its title bar. The dialog box should be application modal and the first button, which is the only button in the dialog box, should be the default. The correct MsgBox function is MsgBox("Try again.", vbOKOnly + vbInformation + vbDefaultButton1 + vbApplicationModal, "Math Application"). To shorten the instruction, which will make it easier to read in the future, you will assign the *buttons* argument, vbOKOnly + vbInformation + vbDefaultButton1 + vbApplicationModal, to a constant named conBtns. ("Btns" is short for "buttons.") You will then use the constant instead of the long expression in the MsgBox function—in other words, you will enter the MsgBox function as MsgBox("Try again.", conBtns, "Math Application").

Because the MsgBox function returns a value—an integer that represents which button was selected—you will need to declare a variable in which to store the value. You will declare an Integer variable named inRetVal (for "Returned Value") for this purpose.

To continue coding the Verify Answer button's Click event procedure:

1 Open the Verify Answer button's Click event procedure. Maximize the Code window, then enter the code shown in Figure 4-67. Be sure to declare the inRetVal variable, and enter both the Const statement and the MsgBox function. (The code in the figure was compressed so that you could read the entire screen.)

declare this variable

enter this statement

enter this statement

```
frmMath                                                          _ 8 X
Object:  cmdVerify                    ▼    Proc:  Click                ▼
Private Sub cmdVerify_Click()
    Dim inUserAnswer As Integer, inCorrectAnswer As Integer, inRetVal As Integer
    Static inNumCorrect As Integer, inNumIncorrect As Integer
    Const conBtns = vbOKOnly + vbInformation + vbDefaultButton1 + vbApplicationModal
    inUserAnswer = Val(txtAnswer.Text)
    If optAdd.Value = True Then
        inCorrectAnswer = inNum1 + inNum2
    Else
        inCorrectAnswer = inNum1 - inNum2
    End If
    Select Case inUserAnswer
        Case Is = inCorrectAnswer
            imgIcon.Picture = imgHappy.Picture
            inNumCorrect = inNumCorrect + 1
            txtAnswer.Text = ""
            Call RandomNumbers
        Case Else
            imgIcon.Picture = LoadPicture()
            inNumIncorrect = inNumIncorrect + 1
            inRetVal = MsgBox("Try again.", conBtns, "Math Application")

End Sub
```

Figure 4-67: Current status of the Verify Answer button's Click event procedure

You can now end the Select Case statement, then send the focus to the txtAnswer control, and then display the number of correct and incorrect responses in lblCorrect and lblIncorrect controls, respectively.

2 Enter the additional code shown in Figure 4-68. (Recall that the code in the figure was compressed.)

```
frmMath                                                                    _ 8 X
Object: cmdVerify                          ▼   Proc: Click                       ▼
Private Sub cmdVerify_Click()
    Dim inUserAnswer As Integer, inCorrectAnswer As Integer, inRetVal As Integer
    Static inNumCorrect As Integer, inNumIncorrect As Integer
    Const conBtns = vbOKOnly + vbInformation + vbDefaultButton1 + vbApplicationModal
    inUserAnswer = Val(txtAnswer.Text)
    If optAdd.Value = True Then
        inCorrectAnswer = inNum1 + inNum2
    Else
        inCorrectAnswer = inNum1 - inNum2
    End If
    Select Case inUserAnswer
        Case Is = inCorrectAnswer
            imgIcon.Picture = imgHappy.Picture
            inNumCorrect = inNumCorrect + 1
            txtAnswer.Text = ""
            Call RandomNumbers
        Case Else
            imgIcon.Picture = LoadPicture()
            inNumIncorrect = inNumIncorrect + 1
            inRetVal = MsgBox("Try again.", conBtns, "Math Application")
    End Select
    txtAnswer.SetFocus
    lblCorrect.Caption = inNumCorrect
    lblIncorrect.Caption = inNumIncorrect
End Sub
```

enter this code

Figure 4-68: Additional code entered in the Verify Answer button's Click event procedure

3 Close the Code window, then **save and run** the application.

4 Enter a correct answer to the math problem that appears in the interface, then press the **Enter** key. (Recall that the Verify Answer button is the default command button in the interface.) The application displays the happy face icon in the imgIcon control. It also displays the number 1 in the lblCorrect control, clears the txtAnswer text box, and displays a new math problem.

5 Enter an incorrect answer to the math problem appearing in the interface, then press the **Enter** key. The MsgBox function displays the dialog box shown in Figure 4-69.

Figure 4-69: MsgBox function's dialog box

6 Press the **Enter** key to remove the dialog box from the screen. The application removes the happy face icon from the imgIcon control. It also displays the number 1 in the lblIncorrect control and places the focus in the txtAnswer text box.

Notice that the user will need to press the Backspace key to remove the text in the txtAnswer control before entering another answer. When the focus is sent to a text box that contains text, it is customary in Windows applications to highlight the existing text. By doing so, the new text entered by the user replaces, automatically, the highlighted text. You can use Visual Basic's SelStart and SelLength properties to highlight the existing text in a text box.

7 Click the **Exit** button to end the application. Visual Basic returns to the design screen.

The SelStart and SelLength Properties

You will need to use both the SelStart and the SelLength properties to highlight (select) the text in the txtAnswer text box. The **SelStart property** tells Visual Basic where in the text box to position the blinking insertion point—in other words, where to start the text selection; the **SelLength property** tells Visual Basic how many characters to select.

The syntax of the SelStart property is *object*.**SelStart** [= *index*]. *Object* is the name of the control in which the characters are to be selected and *index* is a number that indicates the position of the insertion point. The first position in the box is position 0, the second is position 1, and so on. The instruction, `txtAnswer.SelStart = 0`, for example, will place the blinking insertion point in position 0—the first position in the text box.

After positioning the blinking insertion point in its proper place, you can use the SelLength property to select (highlight) the text in the control. The format of the SelLength property is *object*.**SelLength** [= *number*], where *object* is the name of the control in which the text is to be selected and *number* indicates the number of characters to select. The `txtAnswer.SelLength = 5` instruction, for example, will select five characters, beginning with the character to the immediate right of the blinking insertion point.

But how do you select all of the text in a text box when you don't know precisely how many characters it contains? In those cases, you can use the Len function to determine the number of characters for you.

The Len Function

You can use the Len (short for "length") function to determine the number of characters contained in a text box. The syntax of the Len function is **Len**(*string*). The `Len(txtAnswer.Text)` instruction, for example, returns the number of characters contained in the Text property of the txtAnswer control—in other words, if the txtAnswer control contains two characters, the function returns the number 2. To select the number of characters contained in the txtAnswer Text box, you would use the instruction, `txtAnswer.SelLength = Len(txtAnswer.Text)`.

To continue coding the Verify Answer button's Click event procedure:

1 Open the Verify Answer button's Code window to view its Click event procedure, then maximize the Code window. Enter the two instructions shown in Figure 4-70. (The code in the figure was compressed so that you could read the entire screen.)

enter these two
instructions

```
frmMath
Object: cmdVerify                          Proc: Click

Private Sub cmdVerify_Click()
    Dim inUserAnswer As Integer, inCorrectAnswer As Integer, inRetVal As Integer
    Static inNumCorrect As Integer, inNumIncorrect As Integer
    Const conBtns = vbOKOnly + vbInformation + vbDefaultButton1 + vbApplicationModal
    inUserAnswer = Val(txtAnswer.Text)
    If optAdd.Value = True Then
        inCorrectAnswer = inNum1 + inNum2
    Else
        inCorrectAnswer = inNum1 - inNum2
    End If
    Select Case inUserAnswer
        Case Is = inCorrectAnswer
            imgIcon.Picture = imgHappy.Picture
            inNumCorrect = inNumCorrect + 1
            txtAnswer.Text = ""
            Call RandomNumbers
        Case Else
            imgIcon.Picture = LoadPicture()
            inNumIncorrect = inNumIncorrect + 1
            inRetVal = MsgBox("Try again.", conBtns, "Math Application")
            txtAnswer.SelStart = 0
            txtAnswer.SelLength = Len(txtAnswer.Text)
    End Select
    txtAnswer.SetFocus
    lblCorrect.Caption = inNumCorrect
    lblIncorrect.Caption = inNumIncorrect
End Sub
```

Figure 4-70: Values assigned to the SelStart and SelLength properties

2 Close the Code window, then **save and run** the application.

3 Enter an incorrect response to the math problem appearing in the interface, then press the **Enter** key. When the "Try again." message appears, press the **Enter** key to remove the dialog box.

The application places the focus in the txtAnswer control. This time, however, the existing text is highlighted.

4 Enter a correct response to the math problem appearing in the interface, then press the **Enter** key.

Notice that you did not need to remove the existing text before entering the new text; the new text replaces the highlighted text in the txtAnswer control.

5 Click the **Exit** button to end the application.

The next control you will code is the Display summary information check box.

Coding the Display Summary Information Check Box

When the interface first appears, the Display summary information check box should be unchecked (not selected) and the fraInfo frame control should not be visible in the user interface. When the user selects the Display summary information check box, the application should display the fraInfo frame control, then send the focus to the txtAnswer control. When the user deselects the Display summary information check box, the application should hide the fraInfo frame control, then send the focus to the txtAnswer control.

tips

Recall that option buttons also have a Value property. If an option button is selected, however, its Value property contains the Boolean value True; otherwise its Value property contains the Boolean value False.

To code the Display summary information check box:

1 Click the **Display summary information** check box. Display the Properties window, then click **Value** in the Properties list.

The Value property indicates the status of the check box. If the check box is selected (checked), then its Value property contains the number 1. If the check box is not selected (unchecked), which is the default, then its Value property contains the number 0. The Value property of the Display summary information check box is 0; that means that the Display summary information check box will be unchecked when the interface first appears.

2 Use the Object box, located in the Properties window, to select the **fraInfo** frame control. Sizing handles appear around the frame. Set the fraInfo control's Visible property to **False** so that the frame control will not be visible when the interface first appears.

3 Click the **form** to remove the Properties window, then double-click the **Display summary information** check box to open its Code window. The Click event procedure, which is the most common event for a check box, opens. Enter the code shown in Figure 4-71.

Figure 4-71: Code entered in the Display summary information box's Click event procedure

4   Close the Code window, then **save and run** the application.

When the interface appears, notice that the Display summary information check box is unchecked and the fraInfo control is not visible.

5   Click the **Display summary information** check box to select it. (You can click either the square or the Caption.) The check box's Click event procedure displays the fraInfo frame control.

6   Click the **Display summary information** check box to deselect it. The check box's Click event procedure hides the fraInfo frame control.

7   Click the **Exit** button to end the application.

You have now completed Lesson C. You can either take a break or complete the end-of-lesson questions and exercises, or read and complete the Debugging section, which may contain information that will help you when completing the exercises.

tips

You can also select and deselect a check box by pressing the Spacebar when the check box has the focus.

S U M M A R Y

To determine if a check box is checked (selected) or unchecked (not selected):

■   Look at the check box's Value property. If the Value property contains the number 1, then the check box is checked. If the Value property contains the number 0, then the check box is not selected.

To determine if an option button is selected or unselected:

■   Look at the option button's Value property. If the Value property contains the Boolean value True, then the option button is selected. If the Value property contains the Boolean value False, then the option button is not selected.

To retain a local variable's value when the procedure ends:

■   Declare a static variable in the object's event procedure. Its syntax is **Static** *variablename* [As *datatype*].

To display a graphic in a form, picture box, or image; or to clear a graphic from these objects:

■ Use the LoadPicture function. Its syntax is **LoadPicture**([*stringexpression*]), where *stringexpression* represents the location and name of a graphics file; the *stringexpression* should be enclosed in quotation marks. If you omit the stringexpression, the LoadPicture function clears the graphic from the object.

To display one of Visual Basic's predefined dialog boxes:

■ Use the MsgBox function. Its syntax is **MsgBox**(*prompt*[, *buttons*][, *title*][, *helpfile*, *context*]). The dialog box contains a message, one or more command buttons, and an optional icon. After displaying the dialog box, the MsgBox function waits for the user to choose a button. It then returns a value that indicates which button the user chose.

To select the existing text in a text box:

■ Use the SelStart and SelLength properties, and the Len function. Set the SelStart property to 0, then set the SelLength property to the length (Len) of the text in the text box.

Q U E S T I O N S

1. If a check box is checked, its Value property is set to _____ .
   a. 0 (zero)
   b. 1 (One)
   c. False
   d. True
   e. Yes

2. If an option button is not selected, its Value property is set to _____ .
   a. 0 (zero)
   b. 1 (One)
   c. False
   d. True
   e. Yes

3. A _____ is a local variable that retains its value when a procedure ends.
   a. consistent variable
   b. constant variable
   c. static variable
   d. stationary variable
   e. term variable

4. Which of the following instructions will clear the contents of the imgCalc image control?
   a. Clear.imgCalc
   b. imgCalc.Clear
   c. imgCalc.Picture = LoadPicture
   d. imgCalc.Picture = LoadPicture(Clear)
   e. imgCalc.Picture = LoadPicture()

5. The MsgBox function displays a dialog box that contains _____ .
   a. a message
   b. one or more command buttons
   c. an optional icon
   d. all of the above

6. The MsgBox function's *buttons* argument controls _____ .
   a. the number and types of buttons displayed in the dialog box
   b. the style of the optional icon displayed in the dialog box
   c. the default button
   d. the dialog box's modality
   e. all of the above

7. You use the _____ icon in the MsgBox function's dialog box to alert the user of a serious problem that requires intervention or correction before the application can continue.
   a. Critical Message
   b. Warning Message
   c. Information Message

8. You use the _____ icon in the MsgBox function's dialog box to alert the user that he or she must first make a decision and then enter a response before the application can continue.
   a. Critical Message
   b. Warning Message
   c. Information Message

9. You use the _____ icon in the MsgBox function's dialog box when the message in the dialog box is for informational purposes only.
   a. Critical Message
   b. Warning Message
   c. Information Message

10. When a dialog box is _____ , the user can still access other applications either using Alt + Tab or clicking the application button on the Windows 95 taskbar.
    a. application modal
    b. consistent modal
    c. system modal
    d. user modal

11. When a dialog box is _____ , the user cannot access other applications until he or she responds to the message in the dialog box.
    a. application modal
    b. consistent modal
    c. system modal
    d. user modal

12. Which of the following instructions will position the blinking insertion point at the beginning of a text box named txtName?
    a. txtName.SelBegin = 0
    b. txtName.SelBegin = 1
    c. txtName.SelLength = 0
    d. txtName.SelStart = 0
    e. txtName.SelStart = 1

13. Assume that the blinking insertion is positioned at the beginning of the txtName text box. Which of the following instructions will select the contents of the txtName text box?
    a. txtName.SelAll = txtName.Text
    b. txtName.SelAll = Len(txtName.Text)
    c. txtName.SelLen = Length(txtName.Text)
    d. txtName.SelLength = txtName.Text
    e. txtName.SelLength = Len(txtName.Text)

E X E R C I S E S

1. In this exercise you will use the Randomize statement, the Rnd function, and the Int function.

   Scenario: Jacques Cousard has been playing the lotto for four years and has yet to win any money. He wants an application that will select the six lotto numbers for him. Each lotto number can range from one to 54 only. (An example of six lotto numbers would be: 4, 8, 35, 15, 20, 3.)

   a. Create a user interface that will display the six lotto numbers. Place each lotto number in a separate label control. In the user interface, be sure to include a Print button, which will print the interface without the command buttons showing, and an Exit button.

   b. Save the form and the project as lc1Done in the Tut04 folder on your Student Disk.

   c. Run the application. Display the six lotto numbers, then click the Print button. Display another six lotto numbers, then click the Print button.

   d. Click the Exit button to end the application, then print the application's code.

   e. Submit the two printouts from step c and the code from step d.

2. In this exercise you will practice with the Case selection structure. (You will not be able to do step (c) if you are using the Working Model.)

   Scenario: Expand the Math application to include multiplication and division.

   a. Open the lcMath application that you created in Lesson C.

   b. Save the form and the project as lc2Done in the Tut04 folder on your Student Disk.

   c. Add two image controls to the interface. Position the image controls at the bottom of the form. Name the image controls imgMultiply and imgDivide. Set the Picture property of the imgMultiply control to display the misc20 icon (a multiplication sign), then set the Picture property of the imgDivide control to display the misc21 icon (a division sign). Recall that the icon files are in the icons\misc folder, which is located in the main Visual Basic folder on either the local hard drive or the network drive.

   d. Add two option buttons to the Operations frame. Name the option buttons optMultiply and optDivide. Set the optMultiply button's Caption property to Multiplication. Set the optDivide button's Caption property to Division. The new option buttons should call the RandomNumbers user-defined sub procedure, then display the appropriate icon in the imgOperator control.

   e. Open the Verify Answer button's Click event procedure. Currently, the Code window contains an If...Then...Else statement that determines which of the Operations buttons—either Addition or Subtraction—is selected, then calculates the correct answer to the math problem. Change the If...Then...Else statement to a Select Case...End Select statement that determines which of the Operations buttons—either Addition, Subtraction, Multiplication, or Division—is selected, then calculates the correct answer to the math problem.

   f. Open the RandomNumbers procedure. If the user selects the Division option button, then swap the inNum1 and inNum2 numbers when the inNum2 number is greater than the inNum1 number.

   g. Save and run the application. Test the application to be sure that it is working correctly, then print the application's code.

   h. Submit the code from step g.

3. In this exercise you will practice with option buttons, check boxes, and a frame control.

   Scenario: Ferris Seminars runs computer seminars. The owner of Ferris Seminars wants an application that the registration clerks can use to calculate the registration fee for each customer. Many of Ferris Seminars' customers are companies that register more than one person for a seminar. The registration clerk will need to enter the number registered for the seminar, then select either the Seminar 1 option button or the Seminar 2 option button. If a company is registering more than three people for a seminar, then the company is entitled to a 10% discount, so the clerk will need to click the 10% discount check box. After the selections are made, the clerk will click the Calculate Total Due command button to calculate the total registration fee. Seminar 1 is $100 per person and Seminar 2 is $120 per person.

a. Create the interface shown in Figure 4-72.

Figure 4-72

b. Save the form and the project as lc3Done in the Tut04 folder on your Student Disk.

c. Be sure to center the form on the screen, code the Exit button, and code the Print button. The Print button should print the interface without the command buttons and its surrounding frame showing. (Remember that the frame and its controls are treated as one unit.)

d. Draw the flowcharts or write the pseudocode for the option buttons, the check box, and the Calculate Total Due command button. Use your flowcharts or pseudocode to code the application. Also be sure to code the Print button and the Exit button.

e. Save and run the application.

f. To test the application, enter 3 as the number registered, then select the Seminar 2 button. Click the Calculate Total Due button, then click the Print button.

g. Test the application again by entering 5 in the text box. Select the Seminar 1 button and the 10% discount check box. Click the Calculate Total Due button, then click the Print button.

h. Exit the application, then print the application's code.

i. Submit the printouts from steps f and g, and the code from step h.

4. In this application you will practice with the If...Then...Else and Select Case...End Select statements.

Scenario: Jacob Heaters Inc. wants an application that the clerks can use to calculate the total amount due on an order. The clerk will need to enter the number of units ordered. The application should calculate the total amount due by multiplying the number of units by the price per unit. The price per unit depends on how many units are ordered, as follows:

Number of units	Price per unit
1 – 4	$ 10
5 – 10	9
11 and over	7

a. Create an appropriate user interface. Be sure to include a Print button, which will print the interface without any command buttons showing, and an Exit button. Also be sure to center the form on the screen.

b. Save the form and the project as lc4Done in the Tut04 folder on your Student Disk.

c. Code the application using the If...Then...Else statement.

d. Save and run the application.

e. To test the application, enter 10 as the number of units ordered, then calculate the total amount due, and then print the interface.

f. Test the application again by entering 15 as the number of units ordered. Calculate the total amount due, then print the interface.

g. Test the application again by entering 2 as the number of units ordered. Calculate the total amount due, then print the interface.

h. Click the Exit button to end the application, then print the application's code.

i. Change the If...Then...Else statement that calculates the price per unit to a Select Case...End Select statement.

j. Save and run the application. To test the application, enter 6 as the number of units ordered, then calculate the total amount due, and then print the interface.

k. Test the application again by entering 11 as the number of units ordered. Calculate the total amount due, then print the interface.

l. Test the application again by entering 4 as the number of units ordered. Calculate the total amount due, then print the interface.

m. Click the Exit button to end the application, then print the application's code.

n. Submit the printouts from steps e, f, g, j, k, and l. Also submit the code from steps h and m.

5. In this exercise you will practice with the Select Case...End Select statement.

Scenario: Flowers Forever wants an application that the clerks can use to calculate each salesperson's annual bonus. The clerk will need to enter the sales. The application should calculate the bonus based on the amount of sales, as follows:

Amount of sales	Bonus
0 – 3000.99	$ 0
3001 – 5000.99	50
5001 – 9999.99	100
10000 and over	250

a. Create an appropriate user interface. Be sure to include a Print button, which will print the interface without any command buttons showing, and an Exit button. Also be sure to center the form on the screen.

b. Save the form and the project as lc5Done in the Tut04 folder on your Student Disk.

c. Code the application using the Select Case statement.

d. Save and run the application.

e. To test the application, enter 900 as the sales, then calculate bonus, and then print the interface.

f. Test the application again by entering 3001 as the sales. Calculate the bonus, then print the interface.

g. Test the application again by entering 9000 as the sales. Calculate the bonus, then print the interface.

h. Test the application again by entering 20500 as the sales. Calculate the bonus, then print the interface.

i. Click the Exit button to end the application, then print the application's code.

j. Submit the printouts from steps e, f, g, and h. Also submit the code from step i.

Exercises 6 through 9 are Discovery Exercises, which allow you to both "discover" the solutions to problems on your own and to experiment with material that is not covered in the tutorial.

discovery ▶ 6. In this exercise you will practice with the Select Case...End Select statement and string data.

Scenario: Western Veterinarians wants an application that their receptionist can use to look up the doctor's fee for performing a specific medical procedure. The receptionist will need to enter a two-letter code that represents the procedure. The application should then display the doctor's fee. The two-letter codes are as follows:

Code	Procedure	Fee
TC	Teeth Cleaning	$50
RV	Rabies Vaccination	15
OS	Other Shots	5
HW	Heartworm Test	15
FC	Fecal Check	5
OV	Office Visit	15
Other Codes		Invalid Entry

a. Create an appropriate user interface. Be sure to include a Print button, which will print the user interface without the command buttons showing, and an Exit button.

b. Save the form and the project as lc6Done in the Tut04 folder on your Student Disk.

c. Plan the application's code using either a flowchart or pseudocode, then code the application using the Select Case...End Select statement.

d. Save and run the application.

e. Test the application by entering RV. Display the fee, then print the interface.

f. Test the application again by entering TC. Display the fee, then print the interface.

g. Test the application again by entering OS. Display the fee, then print interface.

h. Exit the application, then print the application's code.

i. Submit the printouts from steps e, f, and g, and the code from step h.

discovery ▶ 7. In this exercise you will practice with the selection structure.

Scenario: Marine Packing Company wants an application that the order department can use to calculate the price of an order. The order clerks will need to enter the number of units ordered, and whether the customer is a retailer or a wholesaler. The application should calculate the total due. The price per unit depends on both the customer type (wholesaler or retailer) and the number of units ordered, as follows:

Wholesaler:		Retailer:	
Number of units	Price per unit	Number of units	Price per unit
1 – 4	$ 10	1 – 3	$ 15
5 and over	9	4 – 8	14
		9 and over	12

a. Create an appropriate user interface. Be sure to include a Print button, which will print the user interface without the command buttons showing, and an Exit button.

b. Save the form and the project as lc7 Done in the Tut04 folder on your Student Disk.

c. Plan the application's code using either a flowchart or pseudocode, then code the application.

d. Save and run the application.

e. Test the application by calculating the total due for a retailer that orders 10 units. Print the interface.

f. Test the application by calculating the total due for a retailer that orders 2 units. Print the interface.

g. Test the application again by calculating the total due for a wholesaler that orders 10 units. Print the interface.

h. Test the application again by calculating the total due for a wholesaler ordering 2 units. Print the interface.

   i. Test the application again by calculating the total due for a wholesaler ordering 4 units. Print the interface.

   j. Exit the application, then print the application's code.

   k. Submit the printouts from steps e, f, g, h, and i, and the code from step j.

discovery ▶ 8. In this exercise, you will learn more about the SetFocus method.

   a. Open a new project, if necessary. Add a check box and a text box to the form. Remove the Text1 from the text box's Text property.

   b. Enter the `Check1.Value = 1` instruction in the form's Load event. This instruction will select the Check1 check box and trigger its Click event when the form is loaded.

   c. Enter the `Text1.SetFocus` instruction in the check box's Click event procedure. When the check box's Click event is triggered, it will send the focus to the Text1 text box.

   d. Run, but don't save the application. Visual Basic displays the error dialog box on the screen. Click the Debug button. Notice that the `Text1.SetFocus` instruction is causing the error.

   e. Stop the application, then close the Code window.

   f. Use the Help menu to display the SetFocus method's Help window. Use the information in the Help window to fix the application.

   g. Run, but don't save, the application. No error message should appear. The check box should be selected and the text box should have the focus.

   h. Stop the application. Print the application's code, which you will need to submit. You do not need to save this application.

discovery ▶ 9. In this exercise you will practice entering formulas.

Scenario: Your brother is currently taking a geometry class. He would like you to create an application that he can use to verify his calculations. Specifically, he wants the application to calculate the area of a square, rectangle, parallelogram, circle, and triangle.

   a. Create an appropriate interface.

   b. Save the form and the project as lc9Done in the Tut04 folder on your Student Disk.

   c. Save and run the application. Test the application with the following data: square side measurement of 4, rectangle length of 5 and width of 3, parallelogram base of 3 and height of 4, circle radius of 2, triangle base of 4 and height of 3.

   d. Write the answers to the calculations on a piece of paper.

   e. Exit the application, then print the form and the application's code.

   f. Submit the answers from step d and the printout and code from step e.

D E B U G G I N G

Technique Use Visual Basic's Print method to verify the contents of the variables in the application. The syntax of the Print method that prints information on a form is **Print** [*expressionlist*]. Notice that the *expressionlist* part of the instruction is optional, as indicated by the brackets; if you omit the *expressionlist*, the Print method prints a blank line. You can also include other information in the Print method. To learn more about the Print method, use the Help menu to search for its Help window.

Exercises

1. Open the debug1 (debug1.vbp) project, which is in the Tut04 folder on your Student Disk. Click the View Form button to view the form.

   a. Print the code, then **run**, but don't save, the application. This application calculates the total cost of the tapes, records, and CDs ordered by a customer.

   b. Enter 5 as the number of tapes, enter 5 as the number of records, enter 5 as the number of CDs, then click the **Calculate Total Price** button. (Be sure to enter all three numbers.) The application calculates and displays the total price of the order ($149.35). Notice that the application does not display the individual totals for the tapes, records, and CDs.

   c. Click the **Exit** button to end the application. You will now use the Print method to print the contents of the crTotTape, crTotRecord, and crTotCD variables on the form. The sum of these three variables should equal the total price of the order.

   d. Open the Calculate Total Price button's Code window, then maximize the Code window. In the blank line immediately above the End Sub instruction, type **print crTotTape, crTotRecord, crTotCD** and press the **Enter** key. Notice that you can include more than one item on a Print instruction. You can separate each item with either a comma (,) or a semicolon (;). Using the comma to separate the items allows you to take advantage of Visual Basic's preset tabs. The comma tells Visual Basic to tab to the next print zone before printing; each print zone is 14 columns wide. If you use a semicolon to separate one item from another, the second item prints immediately after the first item. (When printing positive numbers, Visual Basic prints the number with both a leading and a trailing space. When printing negative numbers, Visual Basic prints the number with a negative sign on the left and a trailing space on the right.)

   e. Close the Code window, then **run**, but don't save, the application.

   f. Enter 5 as the number of tapes, enter 5 as the number of records, enter 5 as the number of CDs, then click the **Calculate Total Price** button. The total price ($149.35) appears in the label control. The contents of the crTotTape variable ($49.95), the crTotRecord variable ($39.95), and the crTotCD variable ($59.45) appear in the upper-left corner of the form. If you add those three amounts together, you will get $149.35, which appears correctly as the total price. Click the **Exit** button to end the application, then print the code.

   g. You can now exit Visual Basic or open another project. You do not need to save the Debug1 project.

2. Open the debug2 (debug2.vbp) project, which is in the Tut04 folder on your Student Disk. Click the View Form button to view the form.

   a. Print the code, then **run**, but don't save, the application. Notice that the Wholesale button is selected when the application first appears.

   b. Type **10** as the quantity ordered, then click the **Calculate** button. Notice that the application does not calculate the total due correctly. Click the **Retail** button, then click the **Calculate** button. This time the application calculates the total due correctly. Click the **Wholesale** button, then click the **Calculate** button. Here again, the application calculates the total due correctly.

   c. Find and correct the problem with the application, then print the code. (Hint: Use the Print statement to print the contents of the crPrice variable. Enter the Print statement in the Calculate button's Click event procedure.)

   d. Explain the difference between setting an option button's Value property to True in the Properties window and setting its Value property to True in code.

TUTORIAL

5

The Repetition Structure

Creating a Grade Calculation Application

case ▶ Next Monday is Career Day at your alma mater. Professor Carver, one of your computer programming instructors, has asked you to be a guest speaker in his Introduction to Programming class. You gladly accept this speaking engagement and begin planning your presentation. You decide to show the students how to create an application that will calculate their grade in Professor Carver's class.

Previewing the Completed Application

First preview the completed grade application.

To preview the completed application:

1 If necessary, start Windows, then place your Student Disk in the appropriate drive.

2 If you are running the Professional Edition of Visual Basic using Windows 95, then use the Run command on the Start menu to run the **Grade95** (Grade95.exe) file, which is located in the Tut05 folder on your Student Disk. If you are using either the Standard Edition or the Working Model, then use the Run command on the Start menu to run the **Grade95X** (Grade95X.exe) file, which is located in the Tut05 folder on your Student Disk. The Grade application's user interface appears on the screen. See Figure 5-1.

Use the Run command on the Program Manager's File menu to run the grade31.exe file, which is located in the Tut05 folder on your Student Disk. The Grade application's user interface appears on the screen. See Figure 5-1.

WINDOWS 3.1

spin buttons

graph control (not available if you are using the Visual Basic Standard Edition or the Working Model)

Figure 5-1: Grade application's user interface

If you are using the Professional Edition of Visual Basic, you will notice that the grade application contains two new controls: spin buttons and a graph control. You will learn about these controls, which are available in the Professional Edition only, in Lesson C. (You will not be able to do most of Lesson C on the computer if you are using either the Standard Edition or the Working Model.)

3 Click the **Project 1** check box. The graph disappears. If you are using the Professional Edition, then click the **Project 1 spin button's up arrow** until the number 9 appears in the text box. If you are using either the Standard Edition or the Working Model, then type **9** in the **Project 1** text box.

4 Click the **Midterm** check box, then type **45** in the **Midterm** text box.

5 Click the **Display Grade** button. A grade of A appears in the Grade text box. If you are using the Professional Edition, a graph that compares the number of earned points with the number of possible points appears in the graph control. See Figure 5-2.

Figure 5-2: Grade application showing grade and graph

6 If your computer is connected to a printer, then click the **Print** button to print the form.

7 Click the **Exit** button, then click the Yes button to end the application.

In addition to the two new controls, the grade application also uses the repetition structure, a counter and an accumulator, and control arrays. You will learn about the repetition structure, as well as counters and accumulators, in Lesson A. Control arrays are covered in Lesson B. Recall that the two new controls, which are only available in the Professional Edition of Visual Basic, are covered in Lesson C.

LESSON A
objectives

In this lesson you will learn how to:

■ Create the For Next, Do While, and Do Until repetition structures

■ Move a control across the screen

■ Initialize and update counters and accumulators

The Repetition Structure (Looping)

The For Next Loop

Programmers use the **repetition structure**, also called **looping**, to tell the computer to repeat one or more instructions contained in a program. The three forms of the repetition structure are: For Next, Do While, and Do Until.

The For Next (Automatic Counter) Loop

The **For Next loop**, also called an **automatic counter loop**, repeats a block of statements a specified number of times. You use Visual Basic's **For...Next statement** to code the automatic counter loop. Figure 5-3 shows both the syntax and an example of the For...Next statement. The example repeats the Print method, which you learned about in Tutorial 4's Debugging section, three times.

Syntax	Example
For *counter* = *startvalue* **To** *endvalue* [**Step** *stepvalue*]	For inCount = 1 to 3 Step 1
[*instructions*]	Print inCount
Next *counter*	Next inCount

Figure 5-3: Syntax and an example of the For...Next statement

Notice that the syntax begins with the For statement and ends with the Next statement. Between those two statements, you enter the instructions you want the loop to repeat. In the syntax, *counter* is the name of a numeric variable, which is a variable that can store a number. Visual Basic uses the numeric variable to keep track of the number of times the loop instructions are processed. The name of the numeric variable in Figure 5-3's example is inCount.

The *startvalue*, *endvalue*, and *stepvalue* items control how many times to process the loop instructions. The *startvalue* tells the loop where to begin, the *endvalue* tells the loop when to stop, and the *stepvalue* tells the loop how much to add to (or subtract from) the *startvalue* each time the loop is processed. If you omit the *stepvalue*, Visual Basic uses a *stepvalue* of positive 1. In Figure 5-3's example, the *startvalue* is 1, the *endvalue* is 3, and the *stepvalue* is 1. Those values tell the loop to start counting at 1 and, counting by 1's, stop at 3—in other words, count 1, 2, and then 3.

Startvalue, *endvalue*, and *stepvalue* must be numeric and they can be either positive or negative, integer or non-integer. If *stepvalue* is positive, then *startvalue* must be less than or equal to *endvalue* for the loop instructions to be processed. In other words, the instruction `For inCount = 1 To 3 Step 1` is correct, but the instruction `For inCount = 3 To 1 Step 1` is not correct because you can't count from 3 (the *startvalue*) to 1 (the *endvalue*) by adding increments of 1 (the *stepvalue*). If, on the other hand, *stepvalue* is negative, then *startvalue* must be greater than or equal to *endvalue* for the loop instructions to be processed. For example, the instruction `For inCount = 3 To 1 Step -1` is correct, but the instruction `For inCount = 1 To 3 Step -1` is not correct because you can't count from 1 to 3 by subtracting increments of 1. The For Next loop performs the following three tasks:

1. The loop initializes the counter (the numeric variable) to the startvalue. This is done only once, at the beginning of the loop.

2. If the stepvalue is positive, the loop checks if the value in the counter is greater than the endvalue. (Or, if the stepvalue is negative, the loop checks if the value in the counter is less than the endvalue.) If it is, the loop stops; if it's not, the instructions within the loop are processed and task 3 (below) is performed.

3. The loop adds the stepvalue to the counter. It then repeats steps 2 and 3 until the counter is greater than (or less than, if the stepvalue is negative) the endvalue.

On your Student Disk is a project that contains two examples of the For Next loop. Before opening the project, however, you will look at the flowchart and the pseudocode for the For Next loop structure that will print the numbers 1 through 3 on the form. Both are shown in Figure 5-4.

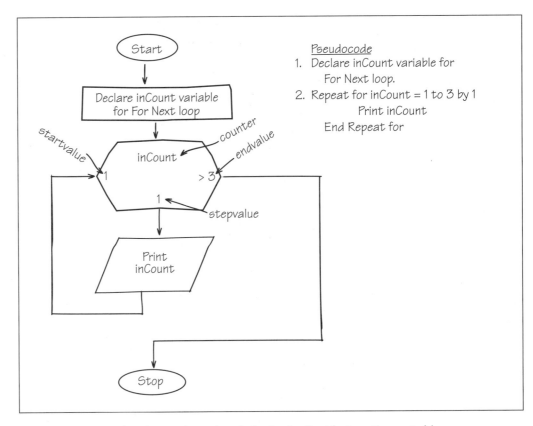

Figure 5-4: Flowchart and pseudocode for the For Next (automatic counter) loop

The For Next loop is represented in a flowchart by a hexagon—a six-sided symbol. Four values are recorded inside the hexagon: the name of the *counter*, the *startvalue*, the *stepvalue*, and the *endvalue*. Notice that the *endvalue* is preceded by a > (greater-than sign). That's to remind you that the loop will stop when the value in the *counter* is greater than the *endvalue*. (If the *stepvalue* is negative, however, a < (less-than sign) should precede the *endvalue*, as that loop will stop when the value in the *counter* is less than the *endvalue*.) Now open the project that contains the examples of the For Next loop.

To open the project that contains the For Next loop examples:

1   Start Visual Basic, if necessary, and open the **For** (for.vbp) project, which is located in the Tut05 folder on your Student Disk. View the form. The frmFor form appears on the screen, as shown in Figure 5-5.

Figure 5-5: frmFor interface

Each of the command buttons has been coded for you. First you will look at the code in the Example 1 button's Click event procedure.

Example 1

The Example 1 button's Click event procedure contains the code that will display the numbers 1 through 3 on the form.

To view the Example 1 button's code, then test the Example 1 button:

1 Double-click the **Example 1** button to open its Code window. The button's Click event procedure appears on the screen, as shown in Figure 5-6.

```
frmFor
Object: cmdExam1          Proc: Click

Private Sub cmdExam1_Click()
    Dim inCount As Integer
    For inCount = 1 To 3 Step 1
        Print inCount
    Next inCount

End Sub
```

Figure 5-6: Example 1 button's Click event procedure

The code first declares a numeric variable, inCount, which will be used as the *counter* in the For...Next statement. Because the *counter* will contain only whole numbers, the inCount variable is declared as an Integer variable. The For...Next statement then instructs Visual Basic to print the contents of the inCount variable on the form, three times.

2 Close the Code window, then **run**, but don't save, the application.

3 Click the **Example 1** button. Visual Basic processes the For...Next statement as shown in Figure 5-7, and the numbers 1, 2, and 3 appear in the upper-left corner of the form.

Steps in Processing Example 1's For...Next Statement

1. Loop initializes the *counter*, inCount, to 1 (*startvalue*).
2. Loop checks if value in inCount is greater than 3 (*endvalue*). It's not.
3. Visual Basic prints 1 (contents of inCount) on the form.
4. Loop adds 1 (*stepvalue*) to inCount, giving 2.
5. Loop checks if value in inCount is greater than 3 (*endvalue*). It's not.
6. Visual Basic prints 2 (contents of inCount) on the form.
7. Loop adds 1 (*stepvalue*) to inCount, giving 3.
8. Loop checks if value in inCount is greater than 3 (*endvalue*). It's not.
9. Visual Basic prints 3 (contents of inCount) on the form.
10. Loop adds 1 (*stepvalue*) to inCount, giving 4.
11. Loop checks if value in inCount is greater than 3 (*endvalue*). It is.
12. Loop stops.
13. End Sub statement ends the Click event procedure.

Figure 5-7: Processing steps for Example 1's For...Next statement

4 Click the **Exit** button to end the application. Visual Basic returns to the design screen.

In Example 2, you will use a For Next loop to move an object across the screen.

Example 2

You can move an object across the screen by setting its Left property within a For Next loop, as you will see when you open the Example 2 button's Click event procedure.

To view the Example 2 button's code, then test the Example 2 button:

1 Double-click the **Example 2** button to open its Code window. The button's Click event procedure appears on the screen, as shown in Figure 5-8.

Figure 5-8: Example 2 button's Click event procedure

Notice that the *counter* variable in the For...Next statement controls the value of the imgAirPlane control's Left property. When you run the application and click the Example 2 button, the loop will initialize the image control's Left property to 0 twips, which will place the image control at the left edge of the form. (Recall that the Left property is measured in twips from the left edge of the form.) It will then add 50 twips to the Left property each time the loop is processed—in other words, the Left property will be increased from 0 to 50, then to 100, and so on. As the value in the Left property increases, the image control will move farther away from the left edge of the form. When the Left property contains a number that is greater than 6,500 (the *endvalue*), the loop will stop and the image control will be positioned on the right side of the form. In this example, the loop will stop when the Left property reaches a value of 6,550, which is 50—the *stepvalue*—more than the *endvalue* of 6,500.

2   Close the Code window, then **run**, but don't save the application.

3   Click the **Example 2** button. The airplane icon moves from the left edge of the screen to the right edge of the screen.

4   Click the **Example 2** button again. The airplane icon again moves from left to right across the screen.

5   Click the **Exit** button to end the application. Visual Basic returns to the design screen.

Recall that the three forms of the repetition structure (loops) are: For Next, Do While, and Do Until. You can use any loop to repeat a set of instructions a specified number of times, although the For Next loop is usually used in those situations because it requires less coding. When you don't know precisely how many times the loop instructions should be repeated, which is the case in many applications, then you must use either the Do While loop or the Do Until loop.

The Do While and the Do Until Loops

The **Do While** loop repeats a block of instructions *while* a condition is true, whereas the **Do Until** loop repeats a block of instructions *until* a condition becomes true. You can use Visual Basic's **Do While...Loop statement** to code the Do While loop, and Visual Basic's **Do...Loop Until statement** to code the Do Until loop. Figure 5-9 shows the syntax for each loop. It also gives an example of how you could use either loop to display the numbers 1 through 3 on the form.

Do While Loop	Do Until Loop
<u>Syntax:</u>	<u>Syntax:</u>
Do While *condition*	**Do**
loop instructions	*loop instructions*
Loop	**Loop Until** *condition*
<u>Example:</u>	<u>Example:</u>
Dim inCount as Integer	Dim inCount as Integer
inCount = 1	inCount = 1
Do While inCount < = 3	Do
Print inCount	Print inCount
inCount = inCount + 1	inCount = inCount + 1
Loop	Loop Until inCount > 3

Figure 5-9: Syntax and examples of the Do While and the Do Until loops

The Do While loop begins with the Do While statement and ends with the Loop statement. The Do Until loop, on the other hand, begins with the Do statement and ends with the Loop Until statement. Between each loop's beginning and ending statements, you enter the instructions you want the loop to repeat.

Both loops require a *condition*, which is located at the top of the Do While loop and at the bottom of the Do Until loop. The *condition* can contain variables, constants, properties, functions, mathematical operators, relational operators, and logical operators. Like the *condition* used in the If...Then...Else statement, which you learned in Tutorial 4, the loop *condition* must also evaluate to either true or false. The *condition* determines if the loop instructions will be processed. In the Do While loop, the loop instructions are processed only if the *condition* evaluates to true; if the *condition* evaluates to false, the loop instructions are not processed. In the Do Until loop, the loop instructions are processed only if the *condition* evaluates to false; if the *condition* evaluates to true, the loop instructions are not processed.

Programmers call the Do While loop a **pretest loop** because the loop evaluates (tests) the *condition* before processing any of the instructions within the loop. (The For Next loop is also a pretest loop.) Depending on the *condition*, the instructions in a Do While loop may not be processed at all. For example, if the *condition* evaluates initially to false, Visual Basic skips the instructions within the loop; processing then continues with the instruction immediately following the end of the loop.

Programmers call the Do Until loop a **posttest loop** because the loop evaluates (tests) the *condition* after processing the instructions within the loop. The Do Until loop always processes the loop instructions at least once.

Take a closer look at the two examples shown in Figure 5-9. Begin with the example of the Do While loop, which will display the numbers 1 through 3 on the form. The example first declares and initializes, to 1, an Integer variable named inCount. The `Do While` statement then evaluates the *condition*, `inCount <= 3`, to determine if the instructions within the loop should be processed. If inCount contains a number that is less than or equal to 3, the loop instructions, which display the value of inCount on the form and also add 1 to inCount, are processed. Then the `Loop` statement, which marks the end of the loop, sends the program back to the beginning of the loop (the `Do While` statement), where the *condition* is tested again. If the value in inCount is still less than or equal to 3, the loop instructions are processed again, and so on.

If inCount does not contain a number that is less than or equal to 3 (in other words, if inCount is greater than 3), the loop stops—that is, the instructions within the loop are not processed. Processing then continues with the instruction following the `Loop` statement.

To summarize, the Do While loop repeats the loop instructions as long as the *condition* evaluates to true. When the *condition* evaluates to false, the Do While loop stops. Next, look at the Do Until example, which also displays the numbers 1 through 3 on the form.

The Do Until example first declares and initializes, to 1, an Integer variable named inCount. The `Do` statement, which simply marks the beginning of the loop, is processed next. Visual Basic then processes the loop instructions, which display the value of inCount on the form and also add 1 to inCount. The `Loop Until` statement then evaluates the *condition*, `inCount > 3`, to determine if the loop instructions should be processed again. Notice that the *condition* is not evaluated until after the loop instructions are processed the first time. If inCount contains a number that is greater than 3, the loop stops; processing then continues with the instruction following the `Loop Until` statement. If inCount contains a number that is not greater than 3 (in other words, if it's less than or equal to 3), the loop instructions are processed again.

To summarize, the Do Until loop repeats the loop instructions as long as the *condition* evaluates to false. When the *condition* evaluates to true, the Do Until loop stops. Now look at the flowchart and pseudocode for both loops.

Flowchart and Pseudocode for the Do While and the Do Until Loops

The flowcharts for the Do While and the Do Until loops that display the numbers 1 through 3 on the form are shown in Figure 5-10; the pseudocode is shown in Figure 5-11.

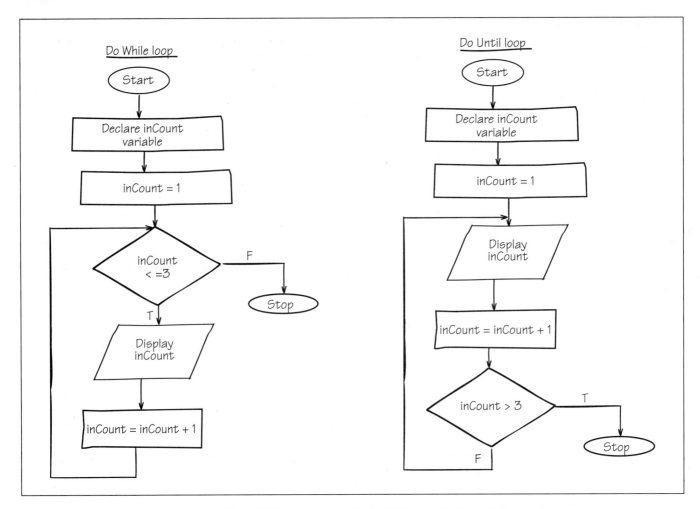

Figure 5-10: Flowchart for the Do While and the Do Until loops

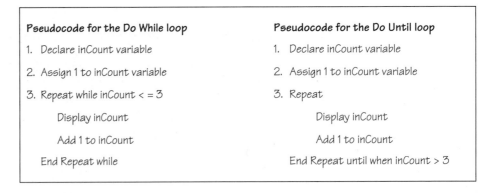

Figure 5-11: Pseudocode for the Do While and the Do Until loops

Both loops are represented in a flowchart by a diamond. Like the selection diamond you learned about in Tutorial 4, the repetition diamond contains a question that has a true (yes) or false (no) answer only. Also like the selection diamond, the repetition diamond has one flowline leading into the diamond and two flowlines leading out of the diamond.

On your Student Disk is a project that contains the code for the flowcharts and pseudocode shown in Figures 5-10 and 5-11.

To view the examples of the Do While and Do Until loops:

1   Open the **DoLoops** (doloops.vbp) project, which is in the Tut05 folder on your Student Disk. Click the **View Form** button to view the frmDo form. The interface contains three command buttons: Do While, Do Until, and Exit.

The command buttons have already been coded for you. The Exit button will end the application, and the Do While and Do Until buttons will each display the numbers 1 through 3 on the form. You will look at the code in the Do While button first.

Do While Example

The Do While command button uses the `Do While...Loop` statement to display the numbers 1 through 3 on the form.

To look at the code, then test the Do While button:

1   Double-click the **Do While** button to open its Code window. The button's Click event procedure appears on the screen, as shown in Figure 5-12.

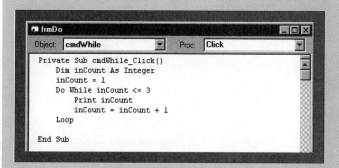

```
Private Sub cmdWhile_Click()
    Dim inCount As Integer
    inCount = 1
    Do While inCount <= 3
        Print inCount
        inCount = inCount + 1
    Loop

End Sub
```

Figure 5-12: Do While button's Click event procedure

2   Close the Code window, then **run**, but don't save, the application. Click the **Do While** button. Visual Basic processes the instructions as shown in Figure 5-13, and the numbers 1, 2, and 3 appear in the upper-left corner of the form.

Steps in processing Do While loop

1. inCount variable is declared as an integer.

2. inCount variable is assigned the number 1.

3. Do While statement checks if the value in inCount is less than or equal to 3. It is.

4. Visual Basic prints 1 (the contents of inCount) on the form.

5. Visual Basic adds 1 to inCount, giving 2.

6. Loop statement sends the program to the beginning of the loop (the Do While statement).

7. Do While statement checks if the value in inCount is less than or equal to 3. It is.

8. Visual Basic prints 2 (the contents of inCount) on the form.

9. Visual Basic adds 1 to inCount, giving 3.

10. Loop statement sends the program to the beginning of the loop (the Do While statement).

11. Do While statement checks if the value in inCount is less than or equal to 3. It is.

12. Visual Basic prints 3 (the contents of inCount) on the form.

13. Visual Basic adds 1 to inCount, giving 4.

14. Loop statement sends the program to the beginning of the loop (the Do While statement).

15. Do While statement checks if the value in inCount is less than or equal to 3. It's not.

16. Loop stops.

17. End Sub statement ends the Click event procedure.

Figure 5-13: Processing steps for Do While button

3   Click the **Exit** button to end the application. Visual Basic returns to the design screen.

Next, look at the code in the Do Until button's Click event procedure.

Do Until Example

The Do Until command button uses the `Do...Loop Until` statement to display the numbers 1 through 3 on the form.

To look at the code in the Do Until button's Click event procedure, then test the button:

1 Double-click the **Do Until** button to open its Code window. The button's Click event procedure appears on the screen, as shown in Figure 5-14.

```
frmDo
Object:  cmdUntil            Proc:  Click

Private Sub cmdUntil_Click()
    Dim inCount As Integer
    inCount = 1
    Do
        Print inCount
        inCount = inCount + 1
    Loop Until inCount > 3

End Sub
```

Figure 5-14: Do Until button's Click event procedure

2 Close the Code window, then **run**, but don't save, the application. Click the **Do Until** button. Visual Basic processes the instructions as shown in Figure 5-15, and the numbers 1, 2, and 3 appear in the upper-left corner of the form.

Steps in processing Do Until loop

1. inCount variable is declared as an integer.
2. inCount variable is assigned the number 1.
3. Do statement marks the beginning of the loop.
4. Visual Basic prints 1 (the contents of inCount) on the form.
5. Visual Basic adds 1 to inCount, giving 2.
6. Loop until statement checks if the value in inCount is greater than 3. It's not.
7. Loop Until statement sends the program to the beginning of the loop (the Do statement).
8. Visual Basic prints 2 (the contents of inCount) on the form.
9. Visual Basic adds 1 to inCount, giving 3.
10. Loop Until statement checks if the value in inCount is greater than 3. It's not.
11. Loop Until statement sends the program to the beginning of the loop (the Do statement).
12. Visual Basic prints 3 (the contents of inCount) on the form.
13. Visual Basic adds 1 to inCount, giving 4.
14. Loop Until statement checks if the value in inCount is greater than 3. It is.
15. Loop stops.
16. End Sub statement ends the Click event procedure.

Figure 5-15: Processing steps for the Do Until button

3   Click the **Exit** button to end the application. Visual Basic returns to the design screen.

Although it appears that the Do While loop and Do Until loop work identically—in this case, both loops displayed the numbers 1 through 3 on the form—that will not always be the case. In other words, the two loops are not always interchangeable. The difference between the Do While (pretest) loop and the Do Until (posttest) loop will be more apparent in the next set of steps.

To see the difference between the Do While and the Do Until loops:

1   Double-click the **Do While** button to open its Code window. The button's Click event procedure appears.

2   Change the inCount = 1 instruction to **inCount = 10**.

By setting the initial value of inCount to 10, the loop's *condition* (inCount <= 3) will evaluate to false, so Visual Basic will skip the loop instructions. See if that is, in fact, what happens.

3   Close the Code window, then **run**, but don't save, the application. Click the **Do While** button. As expected, the numbers 1 through 3 do not appear in the upper-left corner of the form. Because the Do While loop's *condition* (inCount <= 3) evaluated to false, the instructions within the loop were not processed. Figure 5-16 shows how Visual Basic processed the Do While command button's code.

Steps in processing modified Do While loop

1. inCount variable is declared as an integer.

2. inCount variable is assigned the number 10.

3. Do While statement checks if the value in inCount is less than or equal to 3. It's not.

4. Loop stops.

5. End Sub statement ends the Click event procedure.

Figure 5-16: Processing steps for the modified code in the Do While button

4   Click the **Exit** button. Visual Basic returns to the design screen.

Now make the same change to the Do Until button.

5   Double-click the **Do Until** button to open its Code window. Change the inCount = 1 instruction to **inCount = 10**.

See how the Do Until loop handles this change.

6   Close the Code window, then **run**, but don't save, the application. Click the **Do Until** button. This time the number 10 appears in the upper-left corner of the form. Because the Do Until loop instructions are processed before the *condition* (inCount > 3) is tested, the value in inCount, 10, appears on the form. Figure 5-17 shows how Visual Basic processed the Do Until command button's code.

Steps in processing modified Do Until loop

1. inCount variable is declared as an integer.
2. inCount variable is assigned the number 10.
3. Do statement marks the beginning of the loop.
4. Visual Basic prints 10 (the contents of inCount) on the form.
5. Visual Basic adds 1 to inCount, giving 11.
6. Loop until statement checks if the value in inCount is greater than 3. It is.
7. Loop stops.
8. End Sub statement ends the Click event procedure.

Figure 5-17: Processing steps for the modified code in the Do Until button

As this example shows, it is possible for the Do While and the Do Until loops to give different results. When deciding which loop to use, keep in mind that the Do Until loop will always process the loop instructions at least once, whereas the Do While loop might not process the instructions at all.

7 Click the **Exit** button. Visual Basic returns to the design screen.

You will now look at another example that uses the Do While loop.

Another Example of the Do While Loop

In this next example you will see how the Do While loop can be used to play a game that races two rocket ships against each other.

To look at the rocket ship game:

1 Open the **Rocket** (rocket.vbp) project, which is in the Tut05 folder on your Student Disk. You do not need to save the frmDo form.

2 Click the **View Form** button, then maximize the form. The user interface appears, as shown in Figure 5-18.

imgRocket2

imgRocket1

Figure 5-18: frmRocket user interface

The Start Race and Exit command buttons have already been coded for you. Look at the code in the Start Race button.

3   Double-click the **Start Race** button, then maximize the Code window. The maximized Code window appears as shown in Figure 5-19. The code in the figure was compressed so that you could read more of each line.

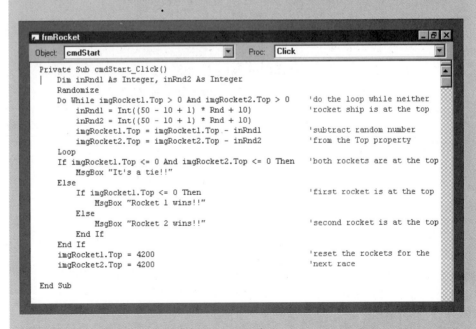

```
Private Sub cmdStart_Click()
    Dim inRnd1 As Integer, inRnd2 As Integer
    Randomize
    Do While imgRocket1.Top > 0 And imgRocket2.Top > 0    'do the loop while neither
        inRnd1 = Int((50 - 10 + 1) * Rnd + 10)            'rocket ship is at the top
        inRnd2 = Int((50 - 10 + 1) * Rnd + 10)
        imgRocket1.Top = imgRocket1.Top - inRnd1          'subtract random number
        imgRocket2.Top = imgRocket2.Top - inRnd2          'from the Top property
    Loop
    If imgRocket1.Top <= 0 And imgRocket2.Top <= 0 Then   'both rockets are at the top
        MsgBox "It's a tie!!"
    Else
        If imgRocket1.Top <= 0 Then                       'first rocket is at the top
            MsgBox "Rocket 1 wins!!"
        Else
            MsgBox "Rocket 2 wins!!"                      'second rocket is at the top
        End If
    End If
    imgRocket1.Top = 4200                                 'reset the rockets for the
    imgRocket2.Top = 4200                                 'next race

End Sub
```

Figure 5-19: Start Race button's Click event procedure

The Click event procedure first declares two Integer variables, inRnd1 and inRnd2, then uses the Randomize statement to initialize Visual Basic's random number generator. The instructions within the Do While loop generate two random numbers, which are stored in the inRnd1 and inRnd2 variables. The loop instructions then subtract the contents of the inRnd1 and inRnd2 variables from the Top property of the imgRocket1 and imgRocket2 controls, respectively. Visual Basic will process the Do While instructions as long as the Top property of both image controls is greater than zero, which indicates that neither control has reached the top of the form. (When a control is at the top of the form, its Top property has a value of 0.) The Do While loop will stop when the Top property of one, or both, of the image controls contains a value that is less then or equal to zero, which indicates that the control is at the top of the form. When the Do While loop stops, the selection structure that follows the loop uses the Top property to determine which control is at the top of the form. If the Top property of both image controls contains a value that is less than or equal to zero, then the application displays the "It's a tie!!" message. If, however, the Top property of only one of the controls is less than or equal to zero, the application displays the appropriate message—either "Rocket 1 wins!!" or "Rocket 2 wins!!". The code then resets the Top property of the image controls for the next race.

4   Close the Code window, then restore the form to its standard size. **Run,** but don't save the application, then click the **Start Race** button. A message box appears on the screen; the message box will either say "It's a tie!!", "Rocket 1 wins!!", or "Rocket 2 wins!!".

5   Press the **Enter** key to remove the dialog box. The application resets each rocket to its original location, ready for the next race.

6   Click the **Exit** button to end the application.

Now that you know how to use the Do While and the Do Until repetition structures, you can learn about counters and accumulators. You will often find either a counter or an accumulator, or both, within a repetition structure. Counters are used to answer the question "How many?"—for example, "How many salespeople live in Virginia?" Accumulators, on the other hand, are used to answer the question "How much?"—for example, "How much did the salespeople sell this quarter?"

Counters and Accumulators

Counters and accumulators are used within a repetition structure to calculate subtotals, totals, and averages. A **counter** is a numeric variable used for counting something—such as the number of employees paid in a week. An **accumulator** is a numeric variable used for accumulating (adding together) something—such as the total dollar amount of a week's payroll.

Two tasks are associated with counters and accumulators: initializing and updating. **Initializing** means to assign a beginning value to the counter or accumulator. Although that beginning value is usually zero, counters and accumulators can be initialized to any number.

Updating, also called **incrementing,** means adding a number to the value stored in the counter or the accumulator. A counter is always incremented by a constant value, whereas an accumulator is incremented by a value that varies. The assignment statement that updates a counter or an accumulator is placed within the repetition structure.

On your Student Disk is a project that contains examples of a counter and an accumulator. Both examples will show you how to use a counter and an accumulator to calculate the average of the sales amounts that are entered by the user. One example uses the Do While loop; the other uses the Do Until loop. Before opening the project, look at the flowcharts, shown in Figure 5-20, for each of the examples.

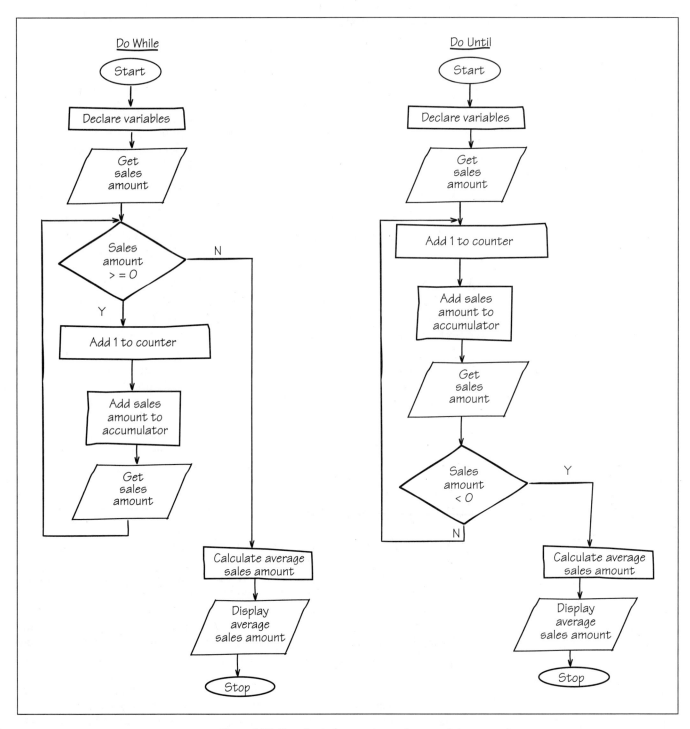

Figure 5-20: Flowcharts for counter and accumulator examples

The Do While loop first declares the necessary variables, then gets a sales amount from the user. The loop then tests if the sales amount that the user entered is greater than or equal to zero. If it is, the counter is incremented by one, the accumulator is incremented by the sales amount, and another sales amount is requested from the user. The program then returns to the beginning of the loop where the condition is tested again. If the user enters a sales amount that is not greater than or equal to zero, the loop stops and the average sales amount is calculated and displayed.

The Do Until loop also first declares the necessary variables and gets a sales amount from the user. The loop then increments both the counter by one and the accumulator by the sales amount before requesting another sales amount from the user. The loop then tests if the sales amount that the user entered is less than zero. If it's not, the program returns to the beginning of the loop and processes the loop instructions again; if it is, the loop stops and the average sales amount is then calculated and displayed.

To look at the counter and accumulator examples:

1　Open the **CtrAccum** (ctraccum.vbp) project, which is in the Tut05 folder on your Student Disk. You do not need to save the frmRocket form.

2　View the frmCtrAccum form. The frmCtrAccum form appears on the screen as shown in Figure 5-21.

Figure 5-21: frmCtrAccum user interface

The Do While and the Do Until command buttons have already been coded for you. Look at the code for the Do While button first.

3　Double-click the **Do While** button, then maximize the Code window. The maximized Code window appears, as shown in Figure 5-22.

Figure 5-22: Do While button's Click event procedure

The code begins by declaring four variables: crSales, inNumSales, crSumSales, and crAvgSales. Three of the variables—crSales, crSumSales, and crAvgSales—will store dollar amounts and are declared as Currency type variables. The crSales variable will store the sales amounts entered by the user, crSumSales (the accumulator variable) will store the total of the sales amounts, and crAvgSales will store the average sales amount. The remaining variable, inNumSales, is the counter variable that will count the number of sales amounts entered. InNumSales is declared as an Integer type variable because it will store whole numbers only.

Recall that counters and accumulators must be initialized, or given a beginning value. Because the Dim statement automatically assigns a zero to Integer and Currency variables when the variables are created, you do not need to enter any additional code to initialize the inNumSales counter or the crSumSales accumulator—in other words, the Dim statement initializes the variables for you. If you want to initialize a counter or an accumulator to a value other than zero, however, you would need to include the appropriate assignment statement in your code. For example, to initialize the inNumSales counter to 1, you would need to include the `inNumSales = 1` assignment statement in your code. The statements that initialize counters and accumulators to a value other than zero are entered after any Dim statements in the Code window. In this application, you want both the counter and the accumulator initialized to zero, so no assignment statements are necessary.

After the variables are declared, the Inputbox function, which you learned about in Tutorial 3, asks the user to enter a sales amount. The numeric equivalent of the user's response is stored in the crSales variable. The `Do While` statement then evaluates the *condition*, `crSales >= 0`, to determine if the loop instructions should be processed. If the sales amount entered by the user is greater than or equal to zero, the loop instructions are processed; if the sales amount is not greater than or equal to zero (in other words, if it's less than zero), the loop instructions are not processed. Now take a closer look at the instructions within the loop.

The `inNumSales = inNumSales + 1` instruction updates the counter by a constant value of one. Notice that the counter variable, inNumSales, appears on both sides of the assignment statement. The statement tells Visual Basic to add one to the contents of the inNumSales variable, then place the result back in the inNumSales variable. InNumSales will be incremented by one each time the loop is processed.

The `crSumSales = crSumSales + crSales` instruction updates the accumulator. Notice that the accumulator variable, crSumSales, also appears on both sides of the assignment statement. The statement tells Visual Basic to add the contents of the crSales variable to the contents of the crSumSales variable, then place the result back in the crSumSales variable. CrSumSales will be incremented by a sales amount, which will vary, each time the loop is processed.

After the counter and the accumulator are updated, the Inputbox function is used again to ask the user for another sales amount. Notice that the `crSales = Val(Inputbox("Enter a sales amount:"))` instruction appears twice in the code—before the Do While loop and within the Do While loop. You may be wondering why you need to repeat the same instruction. Recall that the `Loop` statement sends the program to the top of the loop—to the `Do While` statement. Because the first Inputbox instruction is located before the `Do While` statement, the program will never return to that instruction once the loop begins. (It may help to refer to the flowchart shown in Figure 5-20.) In other words, the `crSales = Val(Inputbox("Enter a sales amount:"))` instruction located above the loop gets only the first sales amount from the user. The `crSales = Val(Inputbox("Enter a sales amount:"))` instruction located within the loop gets each of the remaining sales amounts, if any, from the user.

After the user enters another sales amount, the `Loop` statement sends the program to the `Do While` statement where the *condition* is tested again. If the *condition* is true, the loop instructions are processed again. If the *condition* is false—in this case, if the user enters a sales amount that is less than zero—the loop stops and the instruction after the `Loop` statement is processed. That statement calculates the average sales amount by dividing the contents of the accumulator variable (crSumSales) by the contents of the counter variable (inNumSales). The next instruction displays the average sales amount, formatted as currency, in the lblMsg control.

You should always test your application with both correct and incorrect data. Incorrect data is data that the application is not expecting.

To test the Do While button:

1   Close the Code window, then **run**, but don't save, the application.

Recall that the Do While button will calculate the average of the sales amounts that are entered by the user.

2   Click the **Do While** button, type **3000** in the dialog box and press the **Enter** key. Because the sales amount is not less than zero, the loop instructions are processed. Those instructions add one to the inNumSales variable, giving 1, and also add 3000 to the crSumSales variable, giving 3000. The user is then prompted for another sales amount.

3   Type **4000** in the dialog box and press the **Enter** key. Because the sales amount is not less than zero, the loop instructions are processed again. Those instructions add one to the inNumSales variable, giving two, and also add 4000 to the crSumSales variable, giving 7000.

Now stop the loop. Recall that you stop the loop by entering a negative sales amount.

4   Type **–1** in the dialog box and press the **Enter** key. Because the sales amount is less than zero, the loop stops. The average sales amount, $3,500.00, is calculated and displayed in the lblMsg control, and the Click event procedure ends.

See what happens if the user clicks the Do While button and enters a negative value as the first sales amount.

5 Click the **Do While** button, type **–1** in the dialog box and press the **Enter** key. A dialog box containing the "Run-time error '6': Overflow" error message appears on the screen, as shown in Figure 5-23.

A dialog box containing the "Run-time error '11': Division by zero" error message appears on the screen.

The Windows 3.1 error message may be different

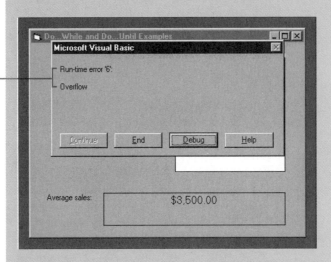

Figure 5-23: Dialog box showing Overflow error message

6 Click the **Debug** button to remove the dialog box, then maximize the Code window. Visual Basic highlights the crAvgSales = crSumSales / inNumSales instruction in the Code window.

When you enter a negative number as the first sales amount, the loop instructions are never processed. That means that the inNumSales variable is not updated from its initial value of zero. Because division by zero is not allowed, Visual Basic displays an error message when it attempts to process the crAvgSales = crSumSales / inNumSales assignment statement. Return to the design screen to fix this problem.

7 Close the Code window, then click the **End** button ■. Visual Basic returns to the design screen.

You can use a selection structure to correct the division-by-zero problem. Before calculating the average sales amount, you will first determine if the value in inNumSales is greater than zero. If it is, you will calculate and display the average sales amount; otherwise you will display a "No sales were entered." message in the lblMsg control.

8 Double-click the **Do While** button to open its Code window. Maximize the Code window and enter the selection structure shown in Figure 5-24.

enter this instruction

enter these instructions

```
frmCtrAccum                                                    _ 5 X
Object:  cmdWhile              ▼    Proc:  Click                      ▼

Private Sub cmdWhile_Click()
    Dim crSales As Currency
    Dim inNumSales As Integer            'counter
    Dim crSumSales As Currency           'accumulator
    Dim crAvgSales As Currency

    crSales = Val(InputBox("Enter a sales amount:"))
    Do While crSales >= 0
       inNumSales = inNumSales + 1           'update counter
       crSumSales = crSumSales + crSales    'update accumulator
       crSales = Val(InputBox("Enter a sales amount:"))
    Loop
    If inNumSales > 0 Then
       crAvgSales = crSumSales / inNumSales
       lblMsg.Caption = Format(crAvgSales, "currency")
    Else
       lblMsg.Caption = "No sales were entered."
    End If

End Sub
```

Figure 5-24: Selection structure entered in the Do While button's Click event procedure

9 Close the Code window, then **run**, but don't save, the application. Click the **Do While** button, then type **–1** and press the **Enter** key. This time an error does not occur; rather, the "No sales were entered." message appears in the lblAverage control.

10 Click the **Exit** button to end the application. Visual Basic returns to the design screen.

Now look at the same example written with the Do Until loop.

To view the code in the Do Until button:

1 Double-click the **Do Until** button, then maximize the Code window. The maximized Code window appears, as shown in Figure 5-25.

```
frmCtrAccum                                                    _ 5 X
Object:  cmdUntil              ▼    Proc:  Click                      ▼

Private Sub cmdUntil_Click()
    Dim crSales As Currency
    Dim inNumSales As Integer            'counter
    Dim crSumSales As Currency           'accumulator
    Dim crAvgSales As Currency

    crSales = Val(InputBox("Enter a sales amount:"))
    Do
       inNumSales = inNumSales + 1           'update counter
       crSumSales = crSumSales + crSales    'update accumulator
       crSales = Val(InputBox("Enter a sales amount:"))
    Loop Until crSales < 0

    crAvgSales = crSumSales / inNumSales
    lblMsg.Caption = Format(crAvgSales, "currency")


End Sub
```

Figure 5-25: Do Until button's Click event procedure

Notice that the condition, crSales < 0, appears at the bottom of the Do Until loop.

2   Close the Code window, then **run**, but don't save, the application.

Now enter the two sales amounts.

3   Click the **Do Until** button, then type **3000** in the dialog box and press the **Enter** key. The loop instructions add one to inNumSales, giving 1, and add 3000 to crSumSales, giving 3000. The user is then prompted to enter another sales amount.

4   Type **4000** in the dialog box and press the **Enter** key. Because the sales amount is not less than zero, the loop instructions are processed again. Those instructions add one to inNumSales, giving 2, and add 4000 to crSumSales, giving 7000. The user is then prompted to enter another sales amount.

Now stop the Do Until loop by entering a negative number.

5   Type **–1** in the dialog box and press the **Enter** key. Because the sales amount is less than zero, the loop stops and the average sales amount, $3,500.00, is calculated and displayed in the lblMsg control.

As you did with the Do While loop, see what happens if the user clicks the Do Until button and then enters a negative number as the first sales amount.

6   Click the **Do Until** button, then type **–1** in the dialog box and press the **Enter** key. The loop instructions add one to inNumSales and add a –1 to crSumSales. A dialog box requesting another sales amount appears.

Because the Do Until loop's *condition* (crSales < 0) is not tested until after the second sales amount is entered, you will need to enter another negative number to stop the loop.

7   Type **–1** and press the **Enter** key. The loop stops and ($1.00), which is probably not what you were expecting, appears in the lblAverage control. The ($1.00) is the result of dividing the contents of crSumSales (–1) by the contents of inNumSales (1).

Because you can never be sure what a user might do, it is usually safer to use the Do While loop instead of the Do Until loop. Use the Do Until loop only in situations where you know that the loop definitely can and will be processed at least once.

8   Click the **Exit** button to end the application. Visual Basic returns to the design screen.

9   Click **File** on the menu bar, then click **New Project**. When you are asked if you want to save the frmCtrAccum form, click the **No** button.

You have now completed Lesson A. You can either take a break or complete the end-of-lesson questions and exercises.

S U M M A R Y

To code the For Next (automatic counter) loop:

■ Use the For...Next statement. The syntax is:

For *counter* = *startvalue* To *endvalue* [Step *stepvalue*]

[*instructions*]

Next *counter*

■ The loop performs the following three tasks:
   1. The loop initializes the *counter* (the numeric variable) to the *startvalue*. This is done only once, at the beginning of the loop.
   2. If the *stepvalue* is positive (negative), the loop checks if the value in the *counter* is greater (less) than the *endvalue*. If it is, the loop stops; if it's not, the instructions within the loop are processed.
   3. The loop adds the *stepvalue* to the *counter*. It then repeats steps 2 and 3 until the *counter* is greater than the endvalue (or, if the *stepvalue* is negative, until the *counter* is less than the *endvalue*).

To move a control across the screen (from left to right or from right to left):

■ Use a For Next loop to set the control's Left property.

To code the Do While loop:

■ Use the Do While...Loop statement. Its syntax is:

Do While *condition*

[*instructions*]

Loop

To code the Do Until loop:

■ Use the Do...Loop Until statement. Its syntax is:

Do

[*instructions*]

Loop Until *condition*

To use a counter:

■ Initialize the counter, if necessary.
■ Use an assignment statement, within a repetition structure, to update the counter. You update a counter by incrementing (or decrementing) its value by a constant amount.

To use an accumulator:

■ Initialize the accumulator, if necessary.
■ Use an assignment statement, within a repetition structure, to update the accumulator. You update an accumulator by incrementing (or decrementing) its value by an amount that varies.

Q U E S T I O N S

1. Which of the following flowchart symbols represents the For Next loop?
   a. diamond
   b. hexagon
   c. oval
   d. parallelogram
   e. rectangle

2. Assuming inCount is a numeric variable, how many times will the Print inCount instruction be processed?

   ```
   For inCount = 1 to 6 Step 1
           Print inCount
   Next inCount
   ```
   a. 0
   b. 1
   c. 5
   d. 6
   e. 7

3. What is the value of inCount when the loop in question 2 stops?
   a. 1
   b. 5
   c. 6
   d. 7
   e. 8

4. Assuming inCount is a numeric variable, how many times will the Print inCount instruction be processed?

   ```
   For inCount = 4 to 10 Step 2
           Print inCount
   Next inCount
   ```
   a. 0
   b. 3
   c. 4
   d. 5
   e. 12

5. What is the value of inCount when the loop in question 4 stops?
   a. 4
   b. 6
   c. 10
   d. 11
   e. 12

6. When the *stepvalue* in a For Next loop is positive, the instructions within the loop are processed only when the *counter* is _____ the *endvalue*.
   a. equal to
   b. greater than
   c. greater than or equal to
   d. less than
   e. less than or equal to

7. When the *stepvalue* in a For Next loop is negative, the instructions within the loop are processed only when the *counter* is _____ the *endvalue*.
   a. equal to
   b. greater than
   c. greater than or equal to
   d. less than
   e. less than or equal to

8. Which two of the following are valid For instructions?
   a. For sgTemp = 1.5 To 5 Step .5
   b. For inTemp = 5 To 1 Step .25
   c. For inTemp = 1 To 3 Step −1
   d. For inTemp = 3 To 1
   e. For inTemp = 1 To 10

9. The For Next loop performs three tasks, as shown below. Put these tasks in their proper order by placing the numbers 1 through 3 on the line to the left of the task.

   _____ Adds the *stepvalue* to the *counter*.

   _____ Initializes the *counter* to the *startvalue*.

   _____ Checks if the value in the *counter* is greater (less) than the *endvalue*.

10. If you omit the *stepvalue* in a For...Next statement, Visual Basic uses a *stepvalue* of _____ .
    a. 0
    b. 1
    c. −1
    d. It results in an error message

11. The three forms of the repetition structure are:
    a. Do For
    b. Do Until
    c. Do While
    d. For Now
    e. For Next

12. You can use the _____ loop(s) when you don't know how many times the loop instructions should be processed.
    a. Do Until
    b. Do While
    c. For Next
    d. a or b
    e. a, b, or c

13. You can use the _____ loop(s) when you know precisely how many times the loop instructions should be processed.
    a. Do Until
    b. Do While
    c. For Next
    d. a or b
    e. a, b, or c

14. Programmers call the _____ loop a pretest loop because the condition is tested at the beginning of the loop.
    a. Do Until
    b. Do While
    c. For Next
    d. a and c
    e. b and c

15. Programmers call the _____ loop a posttest loop because the condition is tested at the end of the loop.
    a. Do Until
    b. Do While
    c. For Next
    d. a and c
    e. b and c

16. The _____ loop repeats the loop instructions as long as the condition is true. Once the condition becomes false, this loop stops.
    a. Do Until
    b. Do While

17. The _____ loop repeats the loop instructions as long as the condition is false. Once the condition becomes true, this loop stops.
    a. Do Until
    b. Do While

18. The _____ loop processes the loop instructions at least once, whereas the _____ loop instructions might not be processed at all.
    a. Do Until, Do While
    b. Do While, Do Until

19. A(n) _____ is a numeric variable used for counting something.
    a. accumulator
    b. adder
    c. constant
    d. counter
    e. integer

20. A(n) _____ is a numeric variable used for accumulating something.
    a. accumulator
    b. adder
    c. constant
    d. counter
    e. integer

21. The two tasks associated with counters and accumulators are:
    a. adding
    b. counting
    c. initializing
    d. printing
    e. updating

22. A(n) _____ is always incremented by a constant amount, whereas a(n) _____ is incremented by an amount that varies.
    a. accumulator, counter
    b. counter, accumulator

23. Which of the following will correctly update the counter variable named inNumber?
    a. inNumber = 0
    b. inNumber = 1
    c. inNumber = inNumber + inNumber
    d. inNumber = inNumber + crSales
    e. inNumber = inNumber + 1

24. Which of the following will correctly update the accumulator variable named crTotal?
    a. crTotal = 0
    b. crTotal = 1
    c. crTotal = crTotal + crTotal
    d. crTotal = crTotal + crSales
    e. crTotal = crTotal + 1

25. Counters and accumulators are automatically initialized to zero by _____.
    a. an assignment statement
    b. the Dim statement
    c. the Initialize statement
    d. the Update statement

E X E R C I S E S

1. Use the Help menu to search for a Help window on the For Next statement and a Help window on the Do Loop statement. Print both Help windows. Can you nest For Next loops? Can you nest Do loops?

2. Write the Visual Basic code that corresponds to the flowchart shown in Figure 5-26.

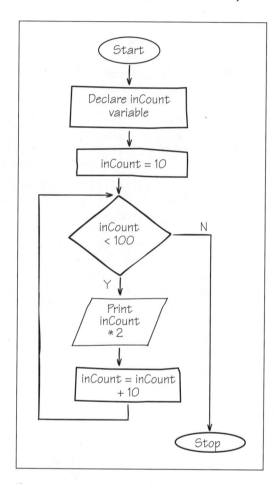

Figure 5-26

3. Draw the flowchart that corresponds to the following Visual Basic code.

    ```
    For inNumber = 1 To 10 Step 1
        Print "Hello"
    Next inNumber
    ```

4. In this exercise you will use the For Next loop to print numbers on the form.
    a. Open a new project. Add one command button to the form. In the command button's Click event procedure, enter a For Next loop that will print the numbers 0 through 117, in increments of 9, on the form. Use inTemp as the numeric variable in the For Next loop. What value will inTemp have when the loop stops?
    b. Run, but don't save the project. Click the command button to test your code. Mark down the value the inTemp variable has when the loop stops, then exit the application.
    c. Print the code. On the printout, mark the value inTemp has when the loop stops.

5. In this exercise, you will use the For Next loop to calculate and display the square of the even numbers from 2 to 12. Use the For Next loop and the Print method (which you learned about in Tutorial 4's Debugging section) to display the squares on the form.

   a. Open a new project. Add one command button to the form. Code the command button's Click event procedure appropriately.

   b. Run, but don't save, the project. Click the Command1 button to test your code. Mark down the squares of the even numbers from 2 through 12, then exit the application.

   c. Print the code. On the printout, mark the squares of the even numbers from 2 through 12.

6. In this exercise you will use the For Next loop to move an image control from right to left.

   a. Open the For (for.vbp) project located in the Tut05 folder on your Student Disk, then save the form and the project as la6Done.

   b. Open Example 2's Code window. Add another For Next statement that will move the image control from right to left. (Enter the additional For Next statement above the End Sub statement. Use 6500 as the *startvalue*, use –50 as the *stepvalue*, and use 0 as the *endvalue*.)

   c. Save, run, and test the Example 2 button. Then print the code.

7. In this exercise you will use the For Next loop to move an image control from top to bottom and diagonally from the upper-left corner to the lower-right corner of the form.

   a. Open the For (for.vbp) project, which is in the Tut05 folder on your Student Disk. Save the form and the project as la7Done.

   b. Add two command buttons to the form. Name one of the command buttons cmdExam3 and change its Caption to Example 3. Name the other command button cmdExam4 and change its Caption to Example 4.

   c. Open Example 3's Code window. In the Click event procedure, enter a For Next statement that will move the Image control from the top of the screen to the bottom of the screen.

   d. Open Example 4's Code window. In the Click event procedure, enter a For Next statement that will move the Image control diagonally from the upper-left corner of the screen to the lower-right corner of the screen.

   e. Save, run, and test the Example 3 and Example 4 command buttons. Print the form and the code.

8. In this exercise you will use the For Next loop to print the first 10 Fibonacci numbers.

   a. Create a user interface that contains three command buttons. Name one of the command buttons cmdDisplay and change its Caption to Display Fibonacci Numbers. Name another command button cmdExit and change its Caption to Exit. Name the remaining command button cmdPrint and change its Caption to Print.

   b. Save the form and the project as la8Done in the Tut05 folder on your Student Disk.

   c. Open the cmdDisplay control's Code window. In the Click event procedure, enter a For Next statement that will print the first 10 Fibonacci numbers (1, 1, 2, 3, 5, 8, 13, 21, 34, 55) on the form. (Hint: Notice that, beginning with the third number in the series, each Fibonacci number is the sum of the prior two numbers. In other words, two is the sum of one plus one, three is the sum of one plus two, five is the sum of two plus three, and so on.)

   d. Code the cmdPrint control's Click event procedure so that it will print the form on the printer.

   e. Code the cmdExit control's Click event procedure so that it will end the application.

   f. Save and run the application. Click the Display Fibonacci Numbers button, then click the Print button, and then click the Exit button.

   g. Print the code.

9. In this exercise you will use the Do While loop to display the word Hello on the form 10 times.

   a. Open a new project. Place a command button on the form. Code the command button's Click event procedure so that it prints the word Hello on the form 10 times. The partial code is shown below; you will need to complete the code.

```
Dim inCount as Integer
inCount = 1
Do _____
    Print "Hello"
    inCount = inCount + 1
Loop
```

   b. Run, but don't save, the application. Click the command button. Stop the application and print the code.

10. In this exercise you will use the Do Until loop to display the word Hello on the form 10 times.

   a. Open a new project. Place a command button on the form. Code the command button's Click event procedure so that it prints the word Hello on the form 10 times. The partial code is shown below; you will need to complete the code.

```
Dim inTemp as Integer
inTemp = 1
Do
    Print "Hello"
    inTemp = inTemp + 1
Loop _____
```

   b. Run, but don't save, the application. Click the command button. Stop the application and print the code.

11. Write a Do While statement that tells Visual Basic to stop the loop when the value in the crSales variable is equal to zero.

12. Write a Loop Until statement that tells Visual Basic to stop the loop when the value in the crSales variable is equal to zero.

13. Write a Do While statement that tells Visual Basic to stop the loop when the user enters the word "Done" (in either uppercase or lowercase letters) in the stFname variable.

14. Write a Loop Until statement that tells Visual Basic to stop the loop when the user enters the word "Done" (in either uppercase or lowercase letters) in the stFname variable.

15. What will print on the form when the following code is processed?

```
Dim inTemp as Integer
Do While inTemp < 5
    Print inTemp
    inTemp = inTemp + 1
Loop
```

16. What will print on the form when the following code is processed?

```
Dim inTemp as Integer
Do
    Print inTemp
    inTemp = inTemp + 1
Loop Until inTemp > 5
```

17. An instruction is missing from the following code. What is the missing instruction and where does it belong in the code?

```
Dim inNum as Integer
inNum = 1
Do While inNum < 5
    Print inNum
Loop
```

18. An instruction is missing from the following code. What is the missing instruction and where does it belong in the code?

```
Dim inNum as Integer
inNum = 10
Do
    Print inNum
Loop Until inNum = 0
```

19. The following code should print the commission (crSales * .1) for each sales amount that is entered. The code is not working properly because an instruction is missing. What is the missing instruction and where does it belong in the code?

```
Dim crSales as Currency
crSales = Val(Inputbox("Enter a sales amount"))
Do While crSales > 0
    Print crSales * .1
Loop
```

20. The following code should print the commission (crSales * .1) for each sales amount that is entered. The code is not working properly. What is wrong with the code and how will you fix it?

```
Dim crSales as Currency
crSales = Val(Inputbox("Enter a sales amount"))
Do
    crSales = Val(Inputbox("Enter a sales amount"))
    Print crSales * .1
Loop Until crSales <= 0
```

21. Write an assignment statement that updates a counter variable, named inNumStudents, by 1.

22. Write an assignment statement that updates a counter variable, named inQuantity, by 5.

23. Write an assignment statement that updates an accumulator variable, named crTotSales, by the value in the crSales variable.

24. Write an assignment statement that updates an accumulator variable, named crTotalGross, by the value in the crGross variable.

25. Write an assignment statement that initializes a counter variable, named inEmployees, to 1.

26. Look at the following two assignment statements. Which will correctly update a counter, and which will correctly update an accumulator? How do you know which one updates a counter and which one updates an accumulator?

```
inTotal = inTotal + 1
crTotal = crTotal + crSales
```

27. What will print when the following code is processed?

```
Dim inTotEmp as Integer
Do While inTotEmp <= 5
    Print inTotEmp
    inTotEmp = inTotEmp + 2
Loop
```

28. What will print when the following code is processed?

```
Dim inTotEmp as Integer
    inTotEmp = 1
Do
    Print inTotEmp
    inTotEmp = inTotEmp + 2
Loop Until inTotEmp >= 3
```

LESSON B
objectives

In this lesson you will learn how to:

- Create and code a control array
- Set the Enabled and Alignment properties
- Code the Change and GotFocus events

Using Control Arrays

The Grade Application

Recall that your task in this tutorial is to create an application that Professor Carver's students can use to calculate their grade during the semester. A student must complete three projects, worth 10 points each, and a midterm and final, worth 50 points each. If the student accumulates 90% of the points, a grade of A is assigned; 80% is a B; 70% is a C; 60% is a D; and below 60% is an F. The sketch of the user interface for the grade application is shown in Figure 5-27.

Figure 5-27: Sketch of user interface for grade application

The grade application will contain various label controls, check boxes, text boxes, and command buttons. If you are using the Professional Edition of Visual Basic, the application will also contain spin buttons and a graph control. To determine the grade, the student needs simply to click the appropriate check boxes, then enter the scores in the corresponding text boxes, and then click the Display Grade button. The Display Grade button will display the letter grade based on the work that has been completed so far. If you are using the Professional Edition, the Display Grade button will also display a bar graph that compares the number of points possible with the number of points earned by the student.

To save you time, your Student Disk contains a partially completed grade application. When you open the application you will notice that most of the user interface has already been created and most of the properties of the existing objects have been set. You will finish creating the user interface in this lesson. You will also begin coding the application.

To open the partially completed application:

1 Start Visual Basic, if necessary. Open the **t5Case** (t5case.vbp) project, which is in the Tut05 folder on your Student Disk.

2 Save the form and the project as **lbGrade**. View the frmGrade form. See Figure 5-28.

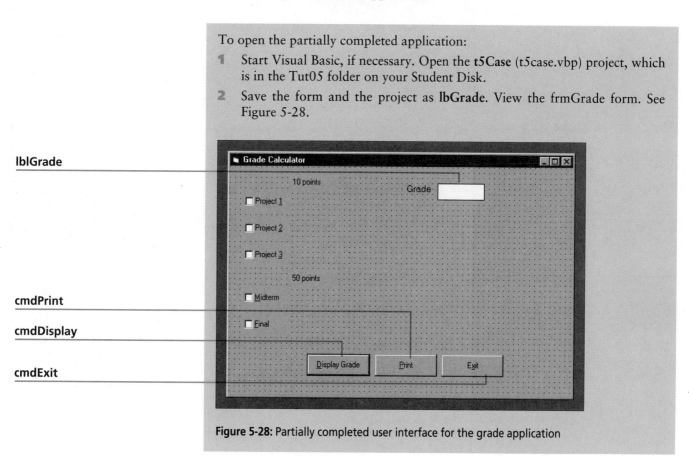

lblGrade

cmdPrint

cmdDisplay

cmdExit

Figure 5-28: Partially completed user interface for the grade application

Notice that the user interface is not complete; you still need to add the five text boxes, the five spin buttons (Professional Edition), and the graph control (Professional Edition) to it. You will add the five text boxes in this lesson, and the spin buttons and graph control in Lesson C.

The TOE chart for the grade application is shown in Figure 5-29.

Task	Object	Event
1. If the user selects a check box, then a. enter a zero in the corresponding text box b. send the focus to the corresponding text box 2. If the user deselects a check box, then clear the text from the corresponding text box	chkWork array	Click
1. For each selected check box, a. add the score found in its associated text box to the total student score accumulator b. if the check box is for a project, then add 10 to the total possible points accumulator; otherwise add 50 2. Calculate the ratio by dividing the value in the total student score accumulator by the value in the total possible points accumulator 3. Display the appropriate letter grade, based on the ratio, in the lblGrade control 4. Display the graph (Lesson C)	cmdDisplay	Click
End the application	cmdExit	Click
Print the interface	cmdPrint	Click
Center the form	frmGrade	Load
Display the letter grade	lblGrade	None
Display the project and test scores	txtScore array	None
Give the user a convenient way to enter the scores	spnScore array	SpinDown and SpinUp
Graph the earned and possible scores	graph control	None

Figure 5-29: TOE chart for the grade application

In this lesson, you will code the check box controls and the Display Grade command button. You will code the spin button controls in Lesson C. You will not need to code the Exit command button and the Print command button because both controls have been coded for you; the Exit button's Click event contains the End instruction, and the Print button contains the PrintForm instruction. Also, the instructions to center the form when it first appears on the screen have been entered in the form's Load event, and the Option Explicit statement has been entered in the form's General declarations section. In addition, the Display Grade button's Default property is set to True, which means that the button is the default command button on the form.

First you will add the five text boxes to the interface. While doing so, you will make the text boxes into a control array.

Creating a Control Array While Adding Controls to the Form

Many times an application will contain a group of controls, of the same type, that perform essentially the same task. In the grade application, for example, each of the five text boxes will get and display the score a student earned on either a project or a test. Instead of giving each of the related controls a different name, which can be difficult to remember, Visual Basic allows you to assign the same name to each of them. When you give the same name to more than one control, you create a **control array**—a group of controls of the same type that have the same name and share the same set of event procedures. All of the controls in an array must be of the same type—in other words, they must all be text boxes, or label controls, or check boxes, and so on.

Visual Basic assigns a unique number, called an **index**, to each of the controls in an array. It might help to picture a control array as a group of mailboxes on a street. The name of the array is the name of the street, and the index is the address on each mailbox. The index reflects the control's position in the array, just as the address reflects a mailbox's position on a street. The first control (mailbox) in an array has an index (address) of 0, the second control has an index of 1, and so on. You refer to each control in an array by the array's name (street name) and the control's index (address). The index is specified in a set of parentheses immediately following the name. For example, the first control in an array named txtScore is referred to as txtScore(0), the second control is txtScore(1), and so on. The name of the array is stored in each control's Name property; the index is stored in each control's Index property.

If the controls to be included in an array are not already on the form, you can use the copy and paste method to create the control array; you will use this method to create the txtScore control array, which will consist of five text boxes. Before you can use the copy and paste method, you need to add the first array control—in this case, a text box—to the form and then set its properties.

To add the first text box to the form, then use copy and paste to create the txtScore control array:

1   Double-click the **TextBox** tool ⬛ in the toolbox, then drag the text box until it is positioned to the right of the Project 1 check box, and immediately below the "10 points" label. (If you want to match the figures in this book exactly, you can set the text box's Left property to 1440 and its Top property to 600.)

2   Display the Properties window. Delete the contents of the text box's Text property, then set its Font size to 10, its Height property to 375, and its Width property to 975.

3   Scroll the Properties list, if necessary, until both the Name property and the Index property are visible.

Notice that the default name of the first text box is Text1, and the Index property is empty. When the Index property is empty, it means that the control is not a member of an array. You will set the Name property of this text box to txtScore; this will become the name of the control array when the array is created.

4 Click **Name** in the Properties list, then type **txtScore** and press the **Enter** key.

Now that the text box is on the form and its properties are set, you can use the copy and paste method to create the control array. First copy the text box to the clipboard.

5 Click the **txtScore** control to return to the form. Click **Edit** on the menu bar, then click **Copy** to copy the text box to the clipboard. Click the **form** to select it. Visual Basic highlights the form's title bar. Click **Edit**, then click **Paste** to paste a copy of the text box on the form. Visual Basic displays the message dialog box shown in Figure 5-30.

Figure 5-30: Message dialog box

HELP? If Copy is dimmed on the Edit menu, then repeat step 5. This time be sure to click the txtScore control in the form before opening the Edit menu.

The dialog box warns you that the form already contains a control named txtScore, and it asks if you want to create a control array.

6 Click the **Yes** button to create the control array. Another text box appears in the upper-left corner of the form. Press the **F4** key to display the Properties window. See Figure 5-31.

tips

· · · · · · · · · · · · · · · ·

You can also use Ctrl + C to copy the selected control to the clipboard, and Ctrl + V to paste the control on the form.

new text box

Index property

Name property

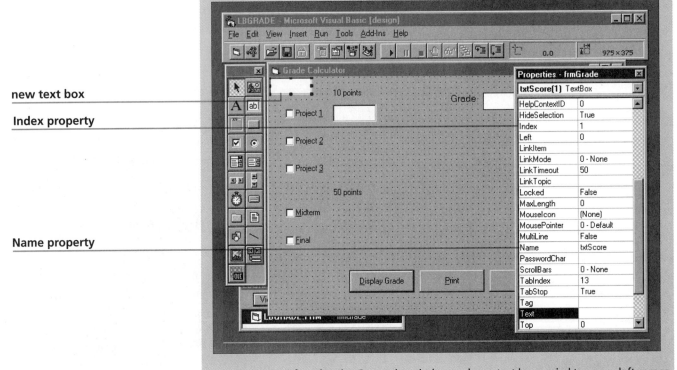

Figure 5-31: Interface showing Properties window and new text box copied to upper-left corner

HELP? If a copy of the text box does not appear on the form, repeat steps 5 and 6. This time, be sure to click the txtScore control in the form before copying the text box to the clipboard.

The Properties window shows txtScore (the name of the control array) in this control's Name property and the number 1 in its Index property. TxtScore(1)—the full reference to this control—appears in the Object box. Visual Basic also copies the font size, as well as the text, height, and width property values from the original text box to the new text box. (You can scroll the Properties window to verify that, if you want.)

7 Drag the **txtScore(1)** control until it is positioned to the immediate right of the Project 2 check box.

Now see what changes Visual Basic made to the properties of the first text box.

8 Click the **first text box**, then press the **F4** key to display the Properties window. The Name property says txtScore, as it did before. The Index property, however, now contains a zero, and the Object box now shows that the full name of the control is txtScore(0). Both the zero in the Index property and the (0) after the name in the Object box indicate that the control is the first control in an array.

The text box is still on the clipboard, so you just need to paste it into the form three more times.

9 Click the **form** to select it. Use the Edit menu to paste three more text boxes onto the form. Position each text box to the right of its corresponding check box as shown in Figure 5-32. (Be sure to position the txtScore(2) control next to the Project3 check box, the txtScore(3) control next to the Midterm check box, and the txtScore(4) control next to the Final check box.)

position text boxes here

Figure 5-32: Correct position of text boxes in the user interface

Now verify that the controls were named correctly.

10 Display the Properties window, then click the **Object box** list arrow. The names of the five text boxes in the txtScore array should appear as shown in Figure 5-33.

tips

• • • • • • • • • • • • • • • • • • •

▶ If the Object box does not contain the correct names for the text box controls, then close the Object box and rename the controls whose names are missing or incorrect.

5 text box names

Figure 5-33: Open Object box showing the names of the five text boxes in the txtScore array

You have now finished creating the txtScore text box array.

11 Close the Object box, then click the **form** to select it.

You can also make existing controls into a control array.

Making Existing Controls into a Control Array

According to the TOE chart, shown earlier in Figure 5-29, each of the five check boxes is responsible for assigning a value (either zero or the empty string) to its corresponding text box in the txtScore array. Each check box is also responsible for sending the focus to its corresponding text box when it is selected by the user. Because each check box has the same responsibilities, you will make them into a control array named chkWork. You make existing controls into a control array simply by giving them the same name—in other words, by setting their Name property to the same value.

To make the check boxes into a control array named chkWork:

1 Click the **Project 1** check box to select that control. Display the Properties window, then scroll the Properties list, if necessary, until both the Name property and the Index property are visible.

Notice that the default name of the first check box is Check1, and that the Index property is empty. Remember that when the Index property is empty, it means that the control is not a member of an array.

2   Click **Name** in the Properties list, type **chkWork** and press the **Enter** key. ChkWork appears both in the Name property and in the Object box, and the Index property is still empty. Be sure to verify, in the Properties window, that you have typed chkWork correctly.

3   Click the **Project 2** check box to select it, then display the Properties window. The Name property should be selected, so you just need to type **chkWork** and press the **Enter** key. When Visual Basic displays the dialog box that asks if you want to create a control array, click the **Yes** button. ChkWork appears in the Name property, 1 appears in the Index property, and chkWork(1) appears in the Object box. This control is the second control in the chkWork array.

   HELP? If the dialog box does not appear, repeat step 3. Be careful to type chkWork correctly. The Name property for this control must match the Name property of the first check box.

Now name the remaining three check boxes.

4   Click the **Project 3** check box, then display the Properties window. Type **chkWork** in the Name property and press the **Enter** key. Look in the Properties window to verify that chkWork appears in the Name property, 2 appears in the Index property, and chkWork(2) appears in the Object box. ChkWork(2) indicates that this is the third control in the array.

5   Click the **Midterm** check box, then display the Properties window. Type **chkWork** in the Name property and press the **Enter** key. Look in the Properties window to verify that chkWork appears in the Name property, 3 appears in the Index property, and chkWork(3) appears in the Object box. The chkWork(3) control is the fourth control in the array.

6   Click the **Final** check box, then display the Properties window. Type **chkWork** in the Name property and press the **Enter** key. Look in the Properties window to verify that chkWork appears in the Name property, 4 appears in the Index property, and chkWork(4) appears in the Object box. This control is the fifth control in the chkWork array.

7   Click the **form** to select it.

Now that you have completed the user interface, you can lock the controls and set their TabIndex properties appropriately.

To lock the controls, then set their TabIndex values:

1   Click the **Lock Controls** button 🔒 on the toolbar.

2   Set each object's TabIndex property according to Figure 5-34.

Control	TabIndex
chkWork(0)	0
txtScore(0)	1
chkWork(1)	2
txtScore(1)	3
chkWork(2)	4
txtScore(2)	5
chkWork(3)	6
txtScore(3)	7
chkWork(4)	8
txtScore(4)	9
cmdDisplay	10
cmdPrint	11
cmdExit	12

Figure 5-34: TabIndex values

3   **Save** and **run** the application. Press the **Tab** key several times to verify that the TabIndex properties are set correctly.

4   Click the **Exit** button to end the application.

Before coding the application, you will look at the code window for a control array.

Viewing the Code Window for a Control Array

The controls in an array not only share the same name, they also share the same event procedures. That means that the code you enter in an array's Code window applies to all of the controls in the array. In other words, when you code one of the controls in an array, you're actually coding all of the controls in the array. The Code window associated with a control array differs slightly from the Code windows you've seen so far—specifically, the Code window includes an additional item of information. Because the controls in an array share the same event procedures, you can open their Code window by double-clicking any one of the controls in the array.

To open the check box array's Code window:

1   Double-click **one of the check boxes**. The Code window opens as shown in Figure 5-35.

argument

Figure 5-35: Click event procedure for the chkWork array

In the Code windows you've seen so far, an empty set of parentheses followed the name of the event procedure. If a Code window belongs to a control array, however, `Index as Integer` will appear inside the parentheses. Items inside the parentheses are called **arguments**; they are used by Visual Basic to pass information to the event procedures. The information passed to the event procedures of control arrays is the value in the Index property of the control that is receiving the event. In this case, for example, if the user clicks the first check box, Visual Basic records the first check box's Index property value—0—in the Index argument. If the user clicks the second check box, Visual Basic records the second check box's Index property value—1—in the Index argument, and so on. You can prove this by entering a `Print Index` instruction, temporarily, in the Click event's Code window; when you click a check box, this instruction will print the value of the Index argument on the form.

tips

● ● ● ● ● ● ● ● ● ● ● ●

▶ You learned about the Print method in Tutorial 4's debugging section. The syntax of the Print method that prints information on a form is **Print** [*expressionlist*].

To enter the Print Index instruction in the Click event procedure, then save, run, and test the application:

1   The Code window for the chkWork array's Click event should still be open. Type **print index** in the open Code window, then press the **Enter** key.

Recall that the code in the Code window applies to each of the controls in the array. In other words, Visual Basic will process the `Print Index` instruction when any one of the check boxes is clicked.

2   Close the Code window, then **save** and **run** the application.

See what Visual Basic assigns to the Index argument when you click the first check box.

3   Click the **Project 1** check box. Visual Basic prints a 0, the first check box's index, in the upper-left corner of the form.

4   On your own, click each of the remaining four check boxes to select them. Visual Basic will print the numbers 1, 2, 3, and 4 when you click the second, third, fourth, and fifth check boxes, respectively.

5   On your own, click each of the five check boxes to deselect them. Visual Basic prints the corresponding index—either 0, 1, 2, 3, or 4—on the form.

Now that you know what values Visual Basic records in the Index argument when the Click event occurs, you can stop the application, open the chkWork array's Code window, and delete the `Print Index` instruction.

6 Click the **Exit** button to stop the application. Double-click **one of the check boxes** to open the chkWork array's Code window, delete the `Print Index` instruction from the Code window, then close the Code window.

You can now begin coding the application.

Coding the Check Box Array

The pseudocode for the check box array's Click event is shown in Figure 5-36.

Pseudocode for the check box array's Click event

If the check box is selected then

      assign 0 to the corresponding text box

      send the focus to the corresponding text box

Else

      clear the contents of the corresponding text box

End If

Figure 5-36: Pseudocode for the check box array's Click event

As you learned in Tutorial 4, you click a check box to select it; you also click a check box to deselect it. According to the pseudocode, if the user selects a check box, then the chkWork array's Click event should perform two tasks; it should perform a different task if the user deselects a check box. As you learned in Tutorial 4, when a check box is selected, its Value property contains the number 1; otherwise it contains the number 0. You can use an If...Then...Else selection structure to determine if the check box is selected; the If...Then...Else statement will compare the check box's Value property to the number one.

    If chkWork were the name of a check box that was not a member of a control array, the `If` statement to determine if the check box is selected would be written correctly as `If chkWork.Value = 1 then`. In this application, however, because chkWork is the name of a control array, the If statement to determine if the check box is selected is written correctly as `If chkWork(Index).Value = 1 then`. Notice how you use the Index argument to determine if the current check box—the check box that was just clicked—is selected.

tips

Recall that Visual Basic records, in the Index argument, the index of the control receiving the event—in this case, the index of the check box that the user clicked.

To code the chkWork array's Click event, then save and run the application:

1 Double-click **one of the check boxes** to open the chkWork array's Click event procedure. Press the **Tab** key, then type **if chkWork(index).value = 1 then** and press the **Enter** key.

If the user clicks a check box to select it, the Click event should place a zero in the corresponding text box in the txtScore array, then send the focus to that text box. In other words, the first check box should enter a zero in the first text box, then send the focus to the first text box; the second check box should enter a zero in the second text box, then send the focus to the second text box, and so on. Figure 5-37 shows the relationship between the check boxes and the text boxes.

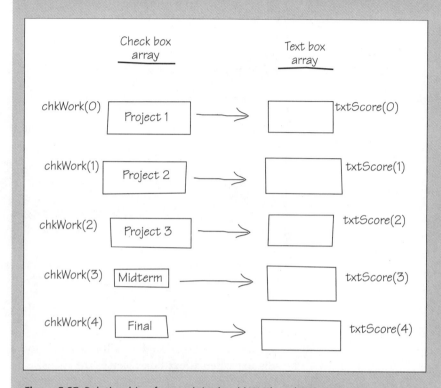

Figure 5-37: Relationship of controls in the chkWork and txtScore arrays

Notice that each check box has the same index as its corresponding text box, which is the text box located to its right. The first check box in the chkWork array and the first text box in the txtScore array, for example, both have an index of 0. Likewise, the second check box and its corresponding text box both have an index of 1. The same relationship is true for the remaining check boxes and text boxes contained in the two arrays. Arrays whose controls are related by their position in the arrays—in other words, by their index—are called **parallel arrays**.

You can use the `txtScore(Index).Text = 0` instruction to enter a zero in the appropriate text box. When the user clicks a check box, this instruction tells Visual Basic to assign a zero to the text box that has the same index as the check box. If the user clicks the first check box, for example, the Index argument will contain a 0 and Visual Basic will send the focus to the txtScore(0) control, which is the first text box in the txtScore array.

2   Press the **Tab** key. Type **txtScore(index).text = 0** and press the **Enter** key.

You can use the SetFocus method, along with the Index argument, to send the focus to the check box's corresponding text box.

3   Type **txtScore(index).setfocus** and press the **Enter** key.

If the user clicks the check box to deselect it, then the Click event should clear the text from the corresponding text box.

4   Enter the additional code shown in Figure 5-38.

**enter these three
lines of code**

```
frmGrade                                        _ □ ×
Object: chkWork              ▼    Proc: Click        ▼
    Private Sub chkWork_Click(Index As Integer)
        If chkWork(Index).Value = 1 Then
            txtScore(Index).Text = 0
            txtScore(Index).SetFocus
      ─ Else
            txtScore(Index).Text = ""
      ─ End If
        │
    End Sub
```

Figure 5-38: Else branch shown in the Code window

5 Close the Code window, then **save** and **run** the application.

6 Click the **Project 1** check box. The Click event enters a zero in the first text box, and sets the focus to that text box. Notice that the user will need to delete the zero from the text box before entering the score. It would be more efficient for the user if the application automatically highlighted the zero in the text box; then, when the user entered the score, the score would replace the highlighted text. You will make this modification in the next section.

7 Click the **Project 1** check box to deselect it. The Click event removes the zero from the text box.

8 Click the **Exit** button to end the application.

In the next section you will learn how to have Visual Basic highlight the existing text when a text box receives the focus.

The GotFocus Event

As you learned in Tutorial 4, when the focus is sent to a text box that contains text, it is customary in Windows applications to highlight the existing text. By doing so, the new text entered by the user automatically replaces the highlighted text. Recall that you use the SelStart and SelLength properties, as well as the Len function, to highlight, or select, the existing text. The SelStart property tells Visual Basic where in the text box to position the blinking insertion point—in other words, where to start the text selection. The SelLength property tells Visual Basic how many characters to select. You use the Len (short for "length") function to determine the number of characters contained in the text box.

In this application, you will have Visual Basic highlight the existing text when the text box receives the focus. In order to do that, you will need to place the appropriate code in the txtScore array's GotFocus event. As its name implies, the **GotFocus event** occurs when an object receives the focus, either by user action, such as tabbing to or clicking the object, or by changing the focus in code using the SetFocus method.

GUI
Design Tips

Highlighting Existing Text

• It is customary in Windows applications to highlight, or select, the existing text in a text box when the text box receives the focus.

To code the txtScore array's GotFocus event:

1　Double-click **one of the text boxes** in the txtScore array. The Change event appears.

2　Use the Proc box to open the GotFocus event. Maximize the Code window, then enter the code shown in Figure 5-39. The code in the figure was compressed so that you could read more of each line.

```
frmGrade                                                        _  8  X
Object:  txtScore                          ▼      Proc:  GotFocus        ▼
Private Sub txtScore_GotFocus(Index As Integer)
     txtScore(Index).SelStart = 0
     txtScore(Index).SelLength = Len(txtScore(Index).Text)

End Sub
```

Figure 5-39: Code entered in txtScore array's GotFocus event

3　Close the Code window, then **save** and **run** the application.

4　Click the **Project 1** check box. The check box's Click event enters a zero in the text box, then sends the focus to that text box. The text box's GotFocus event highlights the existing text in the text box.

5　Type **8** as the first project score and press the **Tab** key. The 8 replaces the highlighted text in the text box.

6　Press **Shift + Tab** to move the focus back to the Project 1 text box. The txtScore array's GotFocus method highlights the existing text in the text box.

7　Click the **Exit** button to end the application. Visual Basic returns to the design screen.

Next you will code the Display Grade command button.

Coding the Display Grade Command Button

The pseudocode for the Display Grade button's Click event is shown in Figure 5-40.

Pseudocode for the Display Grade command button

1. Declare variables

2. Repeat for each check box

   If the check box is selected then

   add the text box score to the earned points accumulator

   Case of check box's Index

   = 0, 1, 2   add 10 to the possible points accumulator

   Other   add 50 to the possible points accumulator

   End Case check box's Index

   End If

   End Repeat for each check box

3. Calculate ratio by dividing the earned points by the possible points

4. Case of ratio

   > = .9   Display "A" in label control

   > = .8   Display "B" in label control

   > = .7   Display "C" in label control

   > = .6   Display "D" in label control

   Other   Display "F" in label control

   End Case ratio

Figure 5-40: Pseudocode for the Display Grade button's Click event procedure

The Display Grade button's Click event procedure will use four local variables: inEarnAccum, inPosAccum, sgRatio, and inCount. Two of the variables, both Integer variables, will be accumulators. The inEarnAccum variable will accumulate the total points earned by the student, and the inPosAccum variable will accumulate the total possible points based on which check boxes are selected. SgRatio, a Single variable, will store the ratio found by dividing the number of points earned by the number of points possible—in other words, dividing the value in the inEarnAccum variable by the value in the inPosAccum variable. InCount, an Integer variable, will serve as the counter variable for a For Next loop.

To begin coding the Display Grade button:

1 Double-click the **Display Grade** button to open its Click event procedure, then maximize the Code window. Press the **Tab** key, then type **dim inEarnAccum as integer, inPosAccum as integer** and press the **Enter** key.

2 Type **dim sgRatio as single, inCount as integer** and press the **Enter** key.

For each selected check box, you want to add the score entered in the corresponding text box to the inEarnAccum variable, and add either 10 or 50 points to the inPosAccum variable. Whether you add 10 or 50 points to the inPosAccum variable depends on which check box is selected. Project check boxes are each worth 10 points; the midterm and final check boxes are each worth 50 points.

To code the Display Grade button's Click event procedure, you will need to use both a repetition structure and a selection structure to determine which of the five check boxes, if any, is selected, then update the inEarnAccum variable appropriately. You will then use a selection structure to determine how many points to add to the inPosAccum variable, 10 or 50.

Figure 5-41 shows two ways of writing the code to determine which check boxes, if any, are selected, then update the inEarnAccum and inPosAccum variables appropriately. The two examples show the code written with a For Next loop and a Do While loop. Either loop will work; however, when a programmer knows precisely how many times the loop instructions are to be processed, he or she will typically use the For Next loop.

HELP? Recall that the check boxes in the chkWork array have indexes of 0 through 4.

tips

The examples shown in Figure 5-41 use the Case selection structure to determine the number of points to add to the inPosAccum variable. You could have used an If...Then...Else selection structure instead.

Display Grade button's code using a For Next loop

```
For inCount = 0 to 4 Step 1
    If chkWork(inCount).Value = 1 then
        inEarnAccum = inEarnAccum + Val(txtScore(inCount).Text)
        Select Case inCount
            Case 0, 1, 2
                inPosAccum = inPosAccum + 10
            Case Else
                inPosAccum = inPosAccum + 50
        End Select
    End If
Next inCount
```

Display Grade button's code using a Do While loop

```
Do While inCount < = 4
    If chkWork(inCount).Value = 1 then
        inEarnAccum = inEarnAccum + Val(txtScore(inCount).Text)
        Select Case inCount
            Case 0, 1, 2
                inPosAccum = inPosAccum + 10
            Case Else
                inPosAccum = inPosAccum + 50
        End Select
    End If
    inCount = inCount + 1
Loop
```

Figure 5-41: Display Grade button's code using a For Next loop and a Do While loop

3   Enter the code shown in Figure 5-42.

```
frmGrade                                              _ 🗗 ✕
Object: cmdDisplay            ▼    Proc: Click             ▼

Private Sub cmdDisplay_Click()
    Dim inEarnAccum As Integer, inPosAccum As Integer
    Dim sgRatio As Single, inCount As Integer
 ┌─ For inCount = 0 To 4 Step 1
 │      If chkWork(inCount).Value = 1 Then
 │          inEarnAccum = inEarnAccum + Val(txtScore(inCount).Text)
 │          Select Case inCount
 │              Case 0, 1, 2
 │                  inPosAccum = inPosAccum + 10
 │              Case Else
 │                  inPosAccum = inPosAccum + 50
 │          End Select
 │      End If
 └─ Next inCount

End Sub
```

enter this code

Figure 5-42: Current status of Display Grade button's Click event procedure

After accumulating the number of points earned and the number of points possible in the inEarnAccum and inPosAccum variables, respectively, you will then divide the value in the inEarnAccum variable by the value in the inPosAccum variable, and assign the result to the sgRatio variable. You will then use a Case structure to determine if the student should receive a grade of A, B, C, D, or F. The appropriate grade is determined by the value in the sgRatio variable. If the sgRatio variable contains a value that is .9 or above, which means that the student has earned at least 90% of the possible points, then he or she should receive an A.

4   Enter the code shown in Figure 5-43. The code in the figure was compressed so you could read more of each line.

enter this code

```
frmGrade                                                        _ 5 X
Object:  cmdDisplay              ▼    Proc:  Click                ▼
Private Sub cmdDisplay_Click()
    Dim inEarnAccum As Integer, inPosAccum As Integer
    Dim sgRatio As Single, inCount As Integer
    For inCount = 0 To 4 Step 1
        If chkWork(inCount).Value = 1 Then
            inEarnAccum = inEarnAccum + Val(txtScore(inCount).Text)
            Select Case inCount
                Case 0, 1, 2
                    inPosAccum = inPosAccum + 10
                Case Else
                    inPosAccum = inPosAccum + 50
            End Select
        End If
    Next inCount
    sgRatio = inEarnAccum / inPosAccum
    Select Case sgRatio
        Case Is >= 0.9
            lblGrade.Caption = "A"
        Case Is >= 0.8
            lblGrade.Caption = "B"
        Case Is >= 0.7
            lblGrade.Caption = "C"
        Case Is >= 0.6
            lblGrade.Caption = "D"
        Case Else
            lblGrade.Caption = "F"
    End Select
End Sub
```

Figure 5-43: Calculation and Case structure in Display Grade button's Click event procedure

5 Close the Code window, then **save** and **run** the application.

6 Click the **Project 1** check box, then type **6** and press the **Enter** key to select the Display Grade button, which is the default command button on the form. A grade of D appears in the lblGrade control.

7 Press the **Tab** key two times. The Project 2 text box now has the focus, as the blinking insertion point indicates. Type **10** and press the **Enter** key. Although the student should receive a grade of B at this point, the D grade still appears in the lblGrade control.

HELP? The student should receive a grade of "B" because 6 + 10 = 16, which is 80% of the total possible points of 20.

HELP? If, when typing 10, the 0 replaces the 1, the SelStart and SelLength instructions were entered in the Change event instead of the GotFocus event. Remove the SelStart and SelLength instructions from the txtScore array's Change event, then enter both instructions in the txtScore array's GotFocus event.

Recall that the instruction to update the inPosAccum variable is in the chkWork array's Click event procedure. Because you did not select the Project 2 check box, the inPosAccum variable was not updated. You will fix this problem by disabling the text boxes when the interface first appears on the screen. When a text box is disabled, the user cannot enter information into it. You will enable the text box only when the user clicks its corresponding check box.

8 Click the **Exit** button to end the application.

In Visual Basic, you use the Enabled property to enable and disable an object.

The Enabled Property

The **Enabled property** determines whether an object can respond to user-generated events. You can set the Enabled property to the Boolean values of either True or False. When the Enabled property is set to its default value, True, the object can respond to a user-generated event. Setting the object's Enabled property to False prevents the object from responding to the user.

It is customary in Windows applications to disable objects that don't apply to the current state of the application. In this application, for example, a text box does not apply until the user selects the corresponding check box, which indicates that the work has been completed. Therefore, you will have all of the text boxes disabled when the interface first appears on the screen. When the user selects a check box, you will enable its corresponding text box so the user can enter his or her score. When the user deselects a check box, you will disable its corresponding text box.

GUI
Design Tips

Enabling and Disabling Controls

• It is customary in Windows applications to disable objects that don't apply to the current state of the application.

To enable and disable the text boxes:

1 Select the five txtScore text boxes. Display the Properties window, then set the Enabled property to **False.**

2 Double-click **one of the check boxes** to display the chkWork array's Click event. Enter the two instructions shown in Figure 5-44.

enter these two instructions

```
Private Sub chkWork_Click(Index As Integer)
    If chkWork(Index).Value = 1 Then
        txtScore(Index).Enabled = True
        txtScore(Index).Text = 0
        txtScore(Index).SetFocus
    Else
        txtScore(Index).Enabled = False
        txtScore(Index).Text = ""
    End If

End Sub
```

Figure 5-44: Current status of the chkWork array's Click event procedure

These instructions tell Visual Basic to enable the corresponding text box when the user selects a check box, and disable the text box when the user deselects the check box.

3 Close the Code window, then **save** and **run** the application.

4 Press the **Tab** key. The focus moves to the Project 2 check box rather than the first text box.

5   Try to click inside the Midterm text box. The Midterm text box cannot receive the focus because its Enabled property is set to False.

6   Click the **Midterm** check box to select it. The check box array's Click event enables the corresponding text box. Type **50** and press the **Enter** key. A grade of A appears in the lblGrade control.

7   Click the **Midterm** check box to deselect it. The check box array's Click event removes the 50 from the text box; it also disables the text box. You can prove that the text box is disabled by trying to click inside the Midterm text box.

Notice that the grade still appears in the lblGrade control, even though the interface shows that no project or tests are completed. You will fix this problem in the next section.

8   Click the **Exit** button to end the application.

In the next section you will learn how to have Visual Basic clear the contents of the lblGrade control when the contents of a text box change.

The Change Event

A text box's Change event occurs when the contents of the text box are changed. This can happen as a result of either the user entering data into the text box, or the program code changing the contents of the text box's Text property. In this application, you will code the txtScore array's Change event so that it clears the lblGrade control when the text in the text box changes.

To code the txtScore array's Change event:

1   Double-click **one of the text boxes**. The txtScore array's GotFocus event appears.

2   Use the Code window's Proc box to open the txtScore array's Change event.

3   Press the **Tab** key, then type **lblGrade.caption = ""** and press the **Enter** key. (Be sure to enter this code in the txtScore array's Change event.)

4   Close the Code window, then **save** and **run** the application.

5   Click the **Midterm** check box to select it, then type **50** and press the **Enter** key. A grade of A appears in the lblGrade control.

6   Click the **Midterm** check box to deselect it. Recall that the chkWork array's Click event procedure contains the `txtScore(Index).Text = ""` instruction, which removes the score from the text box. When the score is removed from the text box, the txtScore array's Change event occurs. That event clears the grade from the lblGrade control.

Now see what happens when the user clicks the Display Grade button without clicking any of the check boxes.

7   Click the **Display Grade** button. A dialog box containing the "Run-time error '6': Overflow" error message appears.

The dialog box message may say "Run-time error '11': Division by zero".

8 Click the **Debug** button in the dialog box. The Display Grade button's Click event procedure appears as shown in Figure 5-45. Notice that Visual Basic highlights the instruction that is causing the problem—the sgRatio = inEarnAccum / inPosAccum instruction. (The code in the figure was compressed so that you could read more of each line.)

this instruction is
causing error

```
frmGrade                                                    _  □  ×

Object:  cmdDisplay        ▼      Proc:  Click               ▼

  Private Sub cmdDisplay_Click()
      Dim inEarnAccum As Integer, inPosAccum As Integer
      Dim sgRatio As Single, inCount As Integer
      For inCount = 0 To 4 Step 1
          If chkWork(inCount).Value = 1 Then
              inEarnAccum = inEarnAccum + Val(txtScore(inCoun
              Select Case inCount
                  Case 0, 1, 2
                      inPosAccum = inPosAccum + 10
                  Case Else
                      inPosAccum = inPosAccum + 50
              End Select
          End If
      Next inCount
      sgRatio = inEarnAccum / inPosAccum
      Select Case sgRatio
```

Figure 5-45: Instruction highlighted in the Display Grade button's Click event procedure

You can stop the application at this point.

9 Click **Run** on the menu bar, then click **End** to stop the application. Close the Code window.

The sgRatio = inEarnAccum / inPosAccum instruction is causing the overflow problem (*division by zero in Windows 3.1 problem*) because the inPosAccum variable, which stores the number of possible points, is not updated from its initial value of zero until the user clicks a check box. Because division by zero is not allowed, Visual Basic displays the error message.

Like the txtScore text boxes, the Display Grade button also does not apply until a check box is selected. You will therefore disable the Display Grade command button when the interface first appears, then enable it when the user selects a check box.

To enable and disable the Display Grade button:

1 Click the **Display Grade** button. Display the Properties window, then set the button's Enabled property to **False**.

2 Double-click **one of the check boxes**. The chkWork array's Click event procedure appears. Maximize the Code window, then enter the cmdDisplay.Enabled = True statement as shown in Figure 5-46.

enter this instruction

```
frmGrade                                                        _ 5 X
Object: chkWork                  ▼    Proc: Click                ▼
Private Sub chkWork_Click(Index As Integer)
    If chkWork(Index).Value = 1 Then
        cmdDisplay.Enabled = True
        txtScore(Index).Enabled = True
        txtScore(Index).Text = 0
        txtScore(Index).SetFocus
    Else
        txtScore(Index).Enabled = False
        txtScore(Index).Text = ""
    End If

End Sub
```

Figure 5-46: Current status of the chkWork array's Click event procedure

This instruction will enable the Display Grade button when the user selects a check box.

When the user deselects a check box, the check box array's Click event will need to determine if any of the check boxes are selected. If no check boxes are selected, then the Click event will disable the Display Grade button.

3   Enter the additional code and documentation shown in Figure 5-47. The code in the figure was compressed so that you could read more of each line.

enter this Dim statement

enter these six instructions

enter this documentation

```
frmGrade                                                        _ 5 X
Object: chkWork                  ▼    Proc: Click                ▼
Private Sub chkWork_Click(Index As Integer)
    Dim inCount As Integer
    If chkWork(Index).Value = 1 Then        'if the check box is selected
        cmdDisplay.Enabled = True
        txtScore(Index).Enabled = True
        txtScore(Index).Text = 0
        txtScore(Index).SetFocus
    Else                                     'if the check box is deselected
        txtScore(Index).Enabled = False
        txtScore(Index).Text = ""
        For inCount = 0 To 4 Step 1          'determine if any check box is selected
            If chkWork(inCount).Value = 1 Then
                Exit Sub                     'leave the Click event if at least
            End If                           'one check box is selected
        Next inCount
        cmdDisplay.Enabled = False           'when none of the check boxes are
    End If                                   'selected, disable the Display Grade
                                             'button
End Sub
```

Figure 5-47: Additional code and documentation in the chkWork array's Click event procedure

The additional code declares an Integer variable named inCount, which serves as the *counter* variable for the For Next loop. As the loop is processed, the inCount variable will take on values of zero through four; these values correspond to the indexes of the controls in the chkWork array.

The selection structure within the For Next loop compares each check box's Value property to the number one, which indicates that the check box is selected. If the loop determines that one of the check boxes is selected, the Exit Sub statement is used to exit the event procedure immediately; no further code is processed in the chkWork array's Click event procedure. If, on the other hand, the loop determines that none of the five check boxes are selected, the instruction following the For Next loop—the `cmdDisplay.Enabled = False` instruction—disables the Display Grade button.

4   Close the Code window, then **save** and **run** the application. Notice that the Display Grade button appears dimmed, which indicates that it is disabled.

5   Click the **Display Grade** button. The button will not respond until you select a check box.

6   Click the **Project 1** check box. The Display Grade button darkens to indicate that it is now enabled. Type **9** as the number of points earned on the first project. Press the **Tab** key until the Midterm check box has the focus, then press the **Spacebar**. You can use the Spacebar to either select or deselect the check box that has the focus. Type **40** as the number of points earned on the midterm, then press the **Enter** key to select the Display Grade button. A grade of B appears in the lblGrade control.

7   Click the **Midterm** check box to deselect it, then click the **Display Grade** button. A grade of A appears in the lblGrade control.

8   Click the **Project 1** check box to deselect it. Notice that the Display Grade button now appears dimmed. Because none of the check boxes are currently selected, the check box array's Click event procedure disables the Display Grade button.

9   Click the **Exit** button to end the application.

You can improve the appearance of the user interface by centering the grade in the lblGrade control. This will be the final modification you will make to the application in this lesson.

Centering the Contents of a Label Control

The caption in a Label control aligns, automatically, on the left side of the control. You can change the alignment to either center or right-aligned by setting the label control's Alignment property.

To center the lblGrade control's caption, then save and run the application:

1   Click the **lblGrade** control. Display the Properties window, then set the label control's Alignment property to **2-Center**.

2   **Save** and **run** the application. Enter scores for the three projects, the midterm, and the final. Click the **Display Grade** button. Visual Basic centers the appropriate grade in the label control.

3   If your computer is connected to a printer, click the **Print** button to print the application.

4   Click the **Exit** button to end the application. Visual Basic returns to the design screen.

You have now completed Lesson B. You can either take a break or complete the questions and exercises at the end of the lesson. In Lesson C you will add the spin buttons and the graph control. (You will only be able to do this if you are using the Professional Edition of Visual Basic; you will not be able to complete Lesson C if you are using the Working Model.) You will also learn how to use the form's Unload event.

S U M M A R Y

To create a control array when the controls are already on the form:

■ Enter the same name in the Name property for each of the controls to be included in the array. When you are asked if you want to create a control array, click the Yes button.

To create a control array as you are entering the controls on the form:

■ Add the first control to the form and set its properties. Click Edit, then click Copy to copy the control to the clipboard. Click Edit, then click Paste to paste a copy of the control on the form. When you are asked if you want to create a control array, click the Yes button. Continue pasting copies of the control until the entire array is created.

To process code when an object receives the focus:

■ Place the code in the object's GotFocus event.

To control whether an object can or cannot respond to user-generated events:

■ If you want an object to respond to user-generated events, set the object's Enabled property to True (default). If you want to prevent an object from responding to user-generated events, set the object's Enabled property to False.

To process code when the contents of a control have changed:

■ Place the code in the control's Change event.

To align the contents of a label control:

■ Set the label control's Alignment property to either 0-Left, 1-Right, or 2-Center.

Q U E S T I O N S

1. When you give the same name to more than one control, you create a _____ .
   a. control array
   b. control group
   c. group
   d. name array
   e. name group

2. Visual Basic assigns a unique number, called a(n) _____ , to each of the controls in an array.
   a. address
   b. control number
   c. control value
   d. index
   e. value

3. Which of the following is the name of a control in an array?
   a. txtName.1
   b. txtName-1
   c. txtName[1]
   d. txtName_1
   e. txtName(1)

4. The index of the fourth control in an array is _____ .
   a. 3
   b. 4
   c. 5

5. Items appearing within the parentheses after an event procedure's name are called _____ .
   a. arguments
   b. controls
   c. indexes
   d. properties
   e. values

6. Arrays that have corresponding elements are called _____ arrays.
   a. associated
   b. coordinated
   c. matching
   d. parallel
   e. same

7. To select the existing text when a text box receives the focus, place the appropriate code in the text box's _____ event.
   a. Focus
   b. GotFocus
   c. ReceiveFocus
   d. Select
   e. SelectFocus

8. To prevent an object from responding to user-generated events, set the object's _____ property to False.
   a. Enabled
   b. Focus
   c. Prevent
   d. Response
   e. Select

9. The _____ event occurs when the contents of a control are modified.
   a. Change
   b. ControlChange
   c. Edited
   d. Modified
   e. SelChange

10. You can align the contents of a label control by setting the control's _____ property.
   a. Align
   b. Alignment
   c. Change
   d. Center
   e. LabelAlign

11. Which one of the following is an incorrect For instruction?
    a. For inX = 1 To 3 Step 1
    b. For inX = 3 To 1 Step 1
    c. For inX = 3 To 1 Step –1
    d. For inX = 100 To 200 Step 10
    e. For inX = 75 to 100

12. Assume the application contains a control array named txtSales. The txtSales array contains three text boxes. Which of the following loops will accumulate the contents of each text box in the array?
    a. For inX = 2 To 0 Step –1
           sgTotal = sgTotal + txtSales(inX).Text
       Next inX
    b. For inX = 3 To 1 Step –1
           sgTotal = sgTotal + txtSales(inX).Text
       Next inX
    c. For inX = 1 To 3 Step 1
           sgTotal = sgTotal + txtSales(inX).Text
       Next inX
    d. For inX = 0 To 2 Step 1
           sgTotal(inX) = sgTotal(inX) + txtSales.Text
       Next inX

13. In question 12, what will be the value of inX when the loop stops?
    a. –1
    b. 0
    c. 1
    d. 2
    e. 3

14. Assume the user interface contains four option buttons. Explain how to make these option buttons into a control array named optChoice. What values will be contained in each of the button's Index properties?

15. Assume you want to create a control array named chkChoice that contains three check boxes. The check boxes are not, as yet, on the form. Explain how to create the array at the same time as you add the controls to the form. What values will be contained in each of the check box's Index properties?

E X E R C I S E S

1. In this exercise you will create a control array. You will then code the application using the For Next, Do While, and Do Until loops.

   Scenario: Colfax Industries wants an application that they can use to sum the sales made in four regions: North, South, East, and West.
   a. Create the user interface shown in Figure 5-48. Make the text boxes into a control array named txtRegion. The name of the label control, lblTotal, was placed in the control's Caption property so that you could easily identify the location of the control in the interface. You should not enter lblTotal in the control's Caption property.

Figure 5-48

    b. Save the form and the project as lb1Done in the Tut05 folder on your Student Disk.

    c. Name the objects appropriately. Be sure to enter the `Option Explicit` statement in the form's General declarations section. Also be sure to enter the code to center the form on the screen.

    d. Center the contents of the lblTotal control.

    e. Code the Exit button so that it ends the application.

    f. Code the Print button so that it prints the form on the printer, without the frame and its controls showing.

    g. Code the txtRegion array so that the existing text is highlighted when a text box receives the focus.

    h. Code the txtRegion array so that it clears the lblTotal control when a change is made to the contents of a text box.

    i. Use the For Next loop to code the Add button. The Add button should add the four sales amounts together, and display the sum in the lblTotal control.

    j. Save and run the application. Test the application by entering the following four sales amounts: 1000, 2000, 3000, 4000. Click the Add button, then click the Print button. Click the Exit button to end the application.

    k. Print the code.

    l. Change the Add button's code so that it uses the Do While loop instead of the For Next loop.

    m. Save and run the application. Test the application by entering the following four sales amounts: 5000, 10000, 15000, 20000. Click the Add button, then click the Print button. Click the Exit button to end the application.

    n. Print the code.

    o. Change the Add button's code so that it uses the Do Until loop instead of the Do While loop.

    p. Save and run the application. Test the application by entering the following four sales amounts: 10, 20, 30, 40. Click the Add button, then click the Print button. Click the Exit button to end the application.

    q. Print the code.

    r. Submit the printouts from steps j, m, and p. Also submit the code from steps k, n, and q.

2. In this exercise, you will create two parallel control arrays.

Scenario: Your niece needs an application that she can use to practice for a test on state capitals.

a. Create the user interface shown in Figure 5-49. Make the State option buttons into a control array named optState. Make the Capital option buttons into a control array named optCapital. The name of the label control, lblAnswer, was placed in the control's Caption property so that you could easily identify the location of the control in the interface. You should not enter lblAnswer in the control's Caption property.

Figure 5-49

b. Save the form and the project as lb2Done in the Tut05 folder on your Student Disk.

c. Name the objects appropriately. Be sure to enter the `Option Explicit` statement in the form's General declarations section. Also be sure to enter the code to center the form on the screen.

d. Have the application select the first option button in the optState array and the first option button in the optCapital array when the form first appears on the screen.

e. Center the contents of the lblAnswer control.

f. Code the Exit button so that it ends the application.

g. Code the Print button so that it prints the form on the printer, without the command buttons showing.

h. Code the application so that the lblAnswer control is cleared when either a state or a capital option button is clicked.

i. To use the application, the user just needs to click both a state and a capital option button, then click the Verify button to verify that the capital is correct. Code the Verify command button so that it displays "Correct" in the lblAnswer control when the user selects the correct capital; otherwise display "Incorrect".

j. Save and run the application. Test the application by clicking Illinois, then clicking Denver. Click the Verify button, then click the Print button.

k. Test the application again by clicking California, then clicking Sacramento. Click the Verify button, then click the Print button. Click the Exit button to end the application.

l. Print the code.

m. Submit the printouts from steps j and k, and the code from step l.

Exercise 3 is a Discovery Exercise, which allows you to both "discover" the solutions to problems on your own and to experiment with material that is not covered in the tutorial.

discovery ▶ 3. In this exercise, you will use three parallel control arrays to create a Tic-Tac-Toe game.

Scenario: After studying for a big test, you and your friend like to relax by playing a few games of Tic-Tac-Toe. In this exercise, you will finish creating a Tic-Tac-Toe game that you and your friend can play.

a. Open the TicTacTo (tictacto.vbp) project, which is in Tut05 on your Student Disk. View the form. The interface contains option buttons, frame controls, label controls, and command buttons. The form's General declarations section contains the `Option Explicit` statement, and the form's Load event contains the code to center the form. The Exit button contains the `End` statement.

b. Create three parallel control arrays named optX, optO, and lblXO. The optX control array should contain the nine X option buttons. The optO control array should contain the nine O option buttons. The lblXO control array should contain the nine label controls.

c. Center the contents of the label controls.

d. The BorderStyle property of the label controls was set to 1-Fixed Single to help you identify the label controls in the user interface. You can improve the appearance of the interface by removing the border on the label controls. Set the label controls' BorderStyle property to 0-None.

e. When the user clicks an option button, the appropriate letter (X or O) should appear in the corresponding label control.

f. Display a message to the user indicating who won the game, either the Xs or the Os. You do not need to display a message if there is no winner. In order to win the game, you must have three Xs or Os placed either vertically, horizontally, or diagonally.

g. When the application is working correctly, print the form image, the form as text, and the code.

LESSON C
objectives

In this lesson you will learn how to:

- Communicate with the user using the MsgBox function
- Code a form's Unload event
- Add a spin button to the form
- Add a graph control to the form
- Code a spin button and a graph control

Completing the Grade Application

Adding More Controls to the Grade Application

The grade application is almost complete; you just need to add spin buttons and a graph control. You will also include a dialog box that asks the user to verify that he or she wants to end the grade application. First you need to open the lbGrade project that you created in Lesson B.

To open the lbGrade project:

1 Start Visual Basic, if necessary, then open the **lbGrade** (lbgrade.vbp) project, which is in the Tut05 folder on your Student Disk.

2 Save the form and the project as **lcGrade**.

3 View the frmGrade form.

Now you will use the MsgBox function to display a dialog box that allows the application to communicate with the user.

Using the MsgBox Function to Communicate with the User

In Tutorial 4 you learned that the MsgBox function displays one of Visual Basic's predefined dialog boxes. The dialog box contains a message, one or more command buttons, and an optional icon. The syntax of the MsgBox function, you may remember, is **MsgBox**(*prompt*[, *buttons*][, *title*][, *helpfile, context*]). *Prompt* is the message you want displayed in the dialog box. *Buttons* is an optional numeric expression that represents the sum of values specifying the number and type of buttons to display, the icon style to use, the identity of the default button, and the dialog box's modality. *Title* is a string expression, typically the application's name, displayed in the title bar of the dialog box. You use the optional *helpfile* and *context* arguments to provide context-sensitive help for the dialog box.

Recall that, after displaying the dialog box, the MsgBox function waits for the user to choose one of the buttons. The function then returns a value that indicates which button the user chose. If the Yes button is selected, for example, the MsgBox function returns the constant vbYes.

tips

Recall that the value returned by the MsgBox function can be referred to by either its numeric value or its constant.

When the user clicks the grade application's Exit button, you will use the MsgBox function to ask the user to verify that he or she wants to exit. The function's dialog box will be application modal and will include Yes and No buttons, as well as the Warning Message icon, which alerts the user that he or she must first make a decision and then enter a response before the application can continue.

As you learned in Tutorial 4, one of the buttons in the dialog box is the default button—the button that is selected when the user presses the Enter key. In Windows applications, the default button in a dialog box is typically the button that represents the most likely action, as long as that action is not destructive. In this case, the most likely action is that the user does want to quit the application, so the Yes button should be the default button. If the user selects the Yes button in error, he or she will simply need to reenter the five scores, which does not involve a lot of work. (If the user were to lose much more data by exiting in error, you should make the No button the default button.)

The correct MsgBox function to use in this application is `MsgBox("Do you want to exit?", vbYesNo + vbExclamation + vbDefaultButton1 + vbApplicationModal, "Grade Application")`. As you did in Tutorial 4, you will shorten the instruction by assigning the *buttons* argument, `vbYesNo + vbExclamation + vbDefaultButton1 + vbApplicationModal`, to a constant named conBtns. ("Btns" is short for "buttons.") You will then use the constant, instead of the long expression, in the MsgBox function. You will assign the user's response to an Integer variable named inUserResponse.

To modify the code in the Exit button:

1 Double-click the **Exit** button to open its Code window, then maximize the Code window. Press the **Enter** key to insert a blank line below the Private Sub statement. Press ↑ on your keyboard to move the insertion point to the blank line. Press the **Tab** key, type **dim inUserResponse as integer** and press the **Enter** key. Then type **const conBtns as integer = vbYesNo + vbExclamation + vbDefaultButton1 + vbApplicationModal** and press the Enter key.

2 Now enter the additional line of code shown in Figure 5-50. Also compare the code that you entered with the code in the figure. The code in the figure was compressed so that you could read more of each line.

enter this instruction

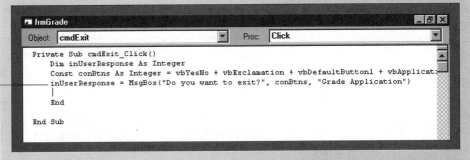

Figure 5-50: Current status of the Exit button's Click event procedure

If the user chooses the Yes button, then the application should end; otherwise, the user should be returned to the application.

3 Enter the additional code shown in Figure 5-51.

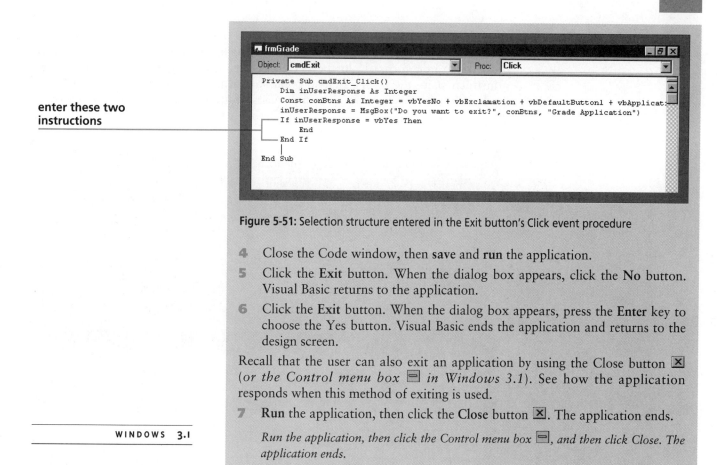

enter these two
instructions

Figure 5-51: Selection structure entered in the Exit button's Click event procedure

4 Close the Code window, then **save** and **run** the application.

5 Click the **Exit** button. When the dialog box appears, click the **No** button. Visual Basic returns to the application.

6 Click the **Exit** button. When the dialog box appears, press the **Enter** key to choose the Yes button. Visual Basic ends the application and returns to the design screen.

Recall that the user can also exit an application by using the Close button ⊠ (*or the Control menu box* ⊟ *in Windows 3.1*). See how the application responds when this method of exiting is used.

7 **Run** the application, then click the **Close** button ⊠. The application ends.

Run the application, then click the Control menu box ⊟, *and then click Close. The application ends.*

Notice that the application does not display the MsgBox function's dialog box; rather, the application simply ends. That's because the Exit button's Click event is only triggered when you click the Exit button; it is not triggered when the user clicks the Close button ⊠ (*or the Control menu box* ⊟ *in Windows 3.1*). To fix this problem, you will move the Exit button's code to the form's Unload event, which you will learn about in the next section. You will then enter Visual Basic's Unload statement in the Exit button's Click event. First learn about the Unload event.

The Unload Event

tips

- - - - - - - - - - - - - - - -

▶ You can also use the Unload event to specify other instructions that should be processed when the form is unloaded—for example, instructions that save data to a file. You will learn about files in Tutorials 6, 7, and 8.

The **Unload event**, which occurs when a form is about to be removed from the screen, is triggered when you use either the Close button ⊠ (*or the Control menu box* ⊟ *in Windows 3.1*) to close the form; it is also triggered when you use the Unload statement in code. If you want to verify that the user wants to exit the application, you should place the appropriate code in the form's Unload event.

In the grade application, most of the code that verifies that the user wants to exit is already entered in the Exit button's Click event procedure; you will move the code to the form's Unload event procedure. You are moving the Exit button's instructions to the form's Unload event so that the instructions will be processed when the user closes the form with the Close button ☒ (*the Control menu box* ⊟ *in Windows 3.1*).

To move the Exit button's code to the form's Unload event:

1   Open the **Exit** button's Click event procedure, then maximize the Code window.

2   Select the statements between the Private Sub and End Sub instructions. Press **Ctrl + x** to move the highlighted instructions to the clipboard.

3   Use the Code window's Object box to open the form's Code window. The form's Load event appears. Use the Code window's Proc box to open the form's Unload event. Press **Ctrl + v** to paste the instructions into the form's Unload event as shown in Figure 5-52:

```
Private Sub Form_Unload(Cancel As Integer)
    Dim inUserResponse As Integer
    Const conBtns As Integer = vbYesNo + vbExclamation + vbDefaultButton1 + vbApplicat
    inUserResponse = MsgBox("Do you want to exit?", conBtns, "Grade Application")
    If inUserResponse = vbYes Then
        End
    End If

End Sub
```

Figure 5-52: Instructions pasted into the form's Unload event procedure

Notice the `Cancel As Integer` between the parentheses following the procedure's name. When you close a form, Visual Basic passes the number 0 to the Cancel argument. If the Unload event does not contain an instruction that changes the value in the Cancel argument, Visual Basic removes the form from the screen. Setting the Cancel argument to any nonzero value stops Visual Basic from removing the form. In this application, if the user selects the Yes button in the MsgBox function's dialog box, then you will end the application and remove the form. If the user selects the No button, on the other hand, you will set the Cancel argument to the number 1, which tells Visual Basic that you do not want to remove the form from the screen.

4   Modify the selection structure in the Unload event procedure as shown in Figure 5-53.

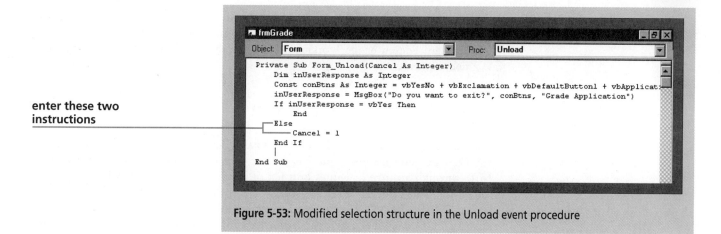

enter these two instructions

```
frmGrade
Object:  Form                              Proc:  Unload

Private Sub Form_Unload(Cancel As Integer)
    Dim inUserResponse As Integer
    Const conBtns As Integer = vbYesNo + vbExclamation + vbDefaultButton1 + vbApplicat
    inUserResponse = MsgBox("Do you want to exit?", conBtns, "Grade Application")
    If inUserResponse = vbYes Then
        End
    Else
        Cancel = 1
    End If

End Sub
```

Figure 5-53: Modified selection structure in the Unload event procedure

In the grade application, the Exit button also needs to display the MsgBox function's dialog box, and then either end the application or return the user to the application. For the Exit button to work appropriately, you simply need to enter the Unload statement in the button's Click event. Recall that the Unload statement triggers the form's Unload event.

To enter the Unload statement in the Exit button's Click event procedure, then save and run the application:

1 Use the Code window's Object box to open the cmdExit control's Code window. The Exit button's Click event procedure appears. Press the **Tab** key, then type **unload frmGrade** and press the **Enter** key.

2 Close the Code window, then **save** and **run** the application.

First see what happens when the user closes the form using the Close button ☒ (*the Control menu box ▭ in Windows 3.1*).

3 Click the **Close** button ☒ to end the application. This time the MsgBox function's dialog box appears. Click the **No** button. Visual Basic returns to the grade application.

WINDOWS 3.1

Click the Control menu box ▭, then click Close to end the application. This time the MsgBox function's dialog box appears. Click the No button. Visual Basic returns to the grade application.

4 Click the **Close** button ☒ to end the application. When the dialog box appears, click the **Yes** button. Visual Basic ends the application and returns to the design screen.

WINDOWS 3.1

Click the Control menu box ▭, then click Close to end the application. When the dialog box appears, click the Yes button. Visual Basic ends the application and returns to the design screen.

Now see how the application responds when the user clicks the Exit button.

5 **Run** the application again. Click the **Exit** button, then click the **No** button in the dialog box. Visual Basic returns to the grade application. Click the **Exit** button again, then click the **Yes** button. Visual Basic ends the application and returns to the design screen.

In the next section you will add spin buttons to the form.

Important note: In order to complete the remaining sections using the computer, you must be using the Professional Edition of Visual Basic 4.0. If you are using the Standard Edition or the Working Model, you should still read the remaining sections in this lesson.

Adding Spin Buttons to the Form

Included in the Professional Edition of Visual Basic 4.0 is a custom control called the **Outrider spin button**. You can use the spin button control to scroll back and forth through a range of values or a list of items. You can also use it to increment and decrement numbers that are stored in another control—typically a text box. Spin buttons offer another way of getting numeric information from the user. Instead of having the user type a number into a text box—a time-consuming process that can result in typing errors—you can use spin buttons instead.

You will add five spin buttons to the grade application's interface—one for each of the three project scores, one for the midterm score, and one for the final score. Then, rather than typing the score into the applicable text box, the student can use the spin button to enter the score in the txtScore text boxes. Because each of the five spin buttons has the same responsibility—each allows the user to enter a score—you will create a spin button control array named spnScore. The spnScore array, the txtScore array, and the chkWork array will be parallel arrays. The first control in each of the three arrays pertains to Project 1; the second control in each of the arrays pertains to Project 2, and so on.

To add the spin button tool to the toolbox, then create a spin button control array named spnScore:

1 Click **Tools** on the menu bar, then click **Custom Controls**. Scroll the Available Controls list box until you see Outrider SpinButton Control in the list, then click its check box. Be sure that a check mark (*an X in Windows 3.1*) appears in the check box. Click the **OK** button. The spin button tool appears in the toolbox as shown in Figure 5-54.

SpinButton tool

Figure 5-54: SpinButton tool in the toolbox

tips

● ● ● ● ● ● ● ● ● ● ● ● ●

▶ The spin button control's SpinOrientation property allows you to set the direction of the spin control arrows. The default is 0-Vertical (up and down arrows). You can change the default to 1-Horizontal (left and right arrows).

2 Double-click the **SpinButton tool** ▣ in the toolbox. A spin button control appears in the center of the form. Set the spin button's Height property to **375**, its Left property to **2520**, its Top property to **600**, and its Width property to **250**.

Similar to the way you handled the text boxes, you will disable the spin buttons when the user interface first appears, then enable the appropriate spin button when the user clicks a check box.

3 Set the spin button's Enabled property to **False**.

4 Set the spin button's Name property to **spnScore**.

5 Click the **spin button control** on the form to select it. Click **Edit** on the menu bar, then click **Copy** to copy the spin button control to the clipboard.

6 Click the **form** to select it. The form's title bar should be highlighted. Click **Edit** on the menu bar, then click **Paste**. When you are asked if you want to create a control array, click the **Yes** button.

7 Click the **Lock Controls** button ▣ to unlock the controls. Position the spin button to the right of the Project 2 text box.

8 Use the Paste option on the Edit menu to paste three more spin buttons on the form, then position them as shown in Figure 5-55.

position the spin buttons here

Figure 5-55: Spin buttons positioned on the form

9 Click the **Lock Controls** button ▣ to lock the controls.

When the user clicks the spin button's up arrow, the control's SpinUp event occurs. Likewise, when the user clicks the spin button's down arrow, the control's SpinDown event occurs. The SpinUp and SpinDown events are also triggered when the user presses and holds down either the up or down arrow; pressing and holding down the spin button's arrow keys allows you to cycle through the numbers more quickly. To use the spin button control, you simply need to enter the appropriate code in its SpinUp and SpinDown events. In this application, for example, you will code the spnScore array's SpinUp event so that it adds the number one to the score in the corresponding text box. You will code the spnScore array's SpinDown event so that it subtracts the number one from the score in the corresponding text box.

tips

You will see the effects of the Refresh method more clearly in Lesson C's Exercise 1.

To code the spnScore control array:

1 Double-click **one of the spin buttons** to open its Code window, then maximize the Code window. The spin button array's SpinDown event appears.

When the user clicks the spin button's down arrow, you want to subtract the number one from the contents of the corresponding text box.

2 Press the **Tab** key, then type **txtScore(index).text = val(txtScore(index).text) − 1** and press the **Enter** key. Each time the user clicks the spin button's down arrow, this instruction will decrement the number in the corresponding text box by one. The new number will appear in the text box as soon as the user releases the mouse button at the end of the click operation. If, however, the user presses and holds down the spin button's down arrow, he or she will not be able to tell how many times the number has been decremented until he or she releases the mouse button. In order for the user to see the change in the text box's number as it is being decremented, you simply need to include the Refresh method in the code. The syntax of the **Refresh** method is *object*.**Refresh**. The Refresh method tells Visual Basic to repaint (redraw) the control.

3 Type **txtScore(index).refresh** and press the **Enter** key.

Now enter the appropriate instructions in the spnScore array's SpinUp procedure. Those instructions should add the number one to the text box score, then refresh the text box. Because the instructions for the SpinUp procedure are almost identical to the SpinDown procedure's instructions, you can copy the SpinDown instructions to the clipboard, then paste them into the SpinUp event.

4 Highlight the instructions between the Private Sub and End Sub instructions in the SpinDown event. Press **Ctrl + c** to copy the instructions to the clipboard. Use the Code window's Proc box to open the spnScore array's SpinUp event. Press **Ctrl + v** to paste the instructions into the SpinUp event. Change the − (minus sign) in the assignment statement to a + (plus sign). The assignment statement should now say `txtScore(Index).Text = Val(txtScore(Index).Text) + 1`.

Now you need to modify the code in the chkWork array's Click event procedure. The modified code will enable the appropriate spin button when a check box is selected, then disable it when the check box is deselected.

To modify the code in the chkWork array's Click event procedure:

1 Use the Code window's Object box to open chkWork array's Click event procedure. Enter the additional code shown in Figure 5-56. The code in the figure was compressed so that you could read more of each line.

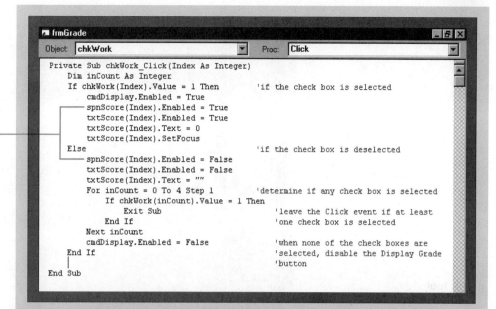

enter these two lines of code

```
frmGrade                                                    _ 8 X
Object:  chkWork                    ▼    Proc:  Click                    ▼

Private Sub chkWork_Click(Index As Integer)
    Dim inCount As Integer
    If chkWork(Index).Value = 1 Then        'if the check box is selected
        cmdDisplay.Enabled = True
        spnScore(Index).Enabled = True
        txtScore(Index).Enabled = True
        txtScore(Index).Text = 0
        txtScore(Index).SetFocus
    Else                                    'if the check box is deselected
        spnScore(Index).Enabled = False
        txtScore(Index).Enabled = False
        txtScore(Index).Text = ""
        For inCount = 0 To 4 Step 1          'determine if any check box is selected
            If chkWork(inCount).Value = 1 Then
                Exit Sub                     'leave the Click event if at least
            End If                           'one check box is selected
        Next inCount
        cmdDisplay.Enabled = False           'when none of the check boxes are
    End If                                   'selected, disable the Display Grade
                                             'button
End Sub
```

Figure 5-56: Additional code entered in the chkWork array's Click event procedure

2   Close the Code window, then **save** and **run** the application.

3   Click the **Project 1** check box, then click the **spin button's up arrow** two times. The text box now contains a 2. Notice that each time you click the up arrow, the spin button's SpinUp event increases the text box score by one.

4   Click the **spin button's down arrow** three times. The text box now contains a −1. Each time you click the down arrow, notice that the spin button's SpinDown event decreases the text box score by one.

5   Press and hold down the **spin button's up arrow** until 8 appears in the Project 1 text box. Click the **Display Grade** button. A grade of B appears in the lblGrade control.

6   Click the **Exit** button, then click the **Yes** button to end the application.

tips

In Lesson C's Exercise 2, you will modify the code in the SpinDown event so that the spin button will stop decrementing when the score reaches zero.

tips

A spin button's Delay property controls how quickly SpinUp and SpinDown events are generated—in other words, how quickly the button spins. The default value of the Delay property is 250, which is 1/4 of a second. Setting the Delay property to a number that is less than 250 makes the button spin faster; setting the Delay property to a number that is greater than 250 makes the button spin slower. You will experiment with the Delay property in Lesson C's Exercise 2.

In the next section you will add a graph control to the form.

Adding a Graph Control to the Form

The Professional Edition of Visual Basic includes a custom control, called the **Pinnacle-BPS Graph control,** that allows you to design graphs interactively on your forms. You will use the graph control to create a bar graph that compares the number of points earned to the number of points possible.

To add a graph control to the form:

1   Click **Tools** on the menu bar, then click **Custom Controls.** Scroll the Available Controls list box until you see Pinnacle-BPS Graph Control in the list, then click its check box. Be sure that a check mark (*an X in Windows 3.1*) appears in the check box. Click the **OK** button. The graph tool appears in the toolbox as shown in Figure 5-57.

graph tool

Figure 5-57: Graph tool in the toolbox

2   Double-click the **Graph tool** in the toolbox. The Graph1 graph control appears in the center of the form.

3   Set the graph control's Height property to **2700**, its Left property to **4100**, its Top property to **840**, and its Width property to **3500**.

4   Click the **form** to remove the Properties window. The graph control appears similar to Figure 5-58.

**graph control (your bars
may look different)**

Figure 5-58: Graph1 control in user interface

The graph on your screen may look different from the graph shown in Figure 5-58. That's because, as a design aid, the graph control automatically generates random data during design time to give you an idea of what the graph will look like.

Now use the GraphType property to tell Visual Basic which type of graph you want. Visual Basic has 11 different types of graphs from which to choose.

The GraphType Property

The **GraphType property** specifies the type of graph you want Visual Basic to display in the graph control. You can select from 11 types of graphs: 2D and 3D pie, 2D and 3D bar, Gantt, Line, Log/Lin, Area, Scatter, Polar, and High-Low-Close. The grade application will display a 3D bar graph.

To tell Visual Basic which type of graph to display in the graph control:

1   Click the **Graph1** control to select it, then set its GraphType property to **4-3D Bar**.

2   Click the **form** to remove the Properties window.

Because the graph control has an automatic redraw capability, each time you change one of the graph control's properties, the control redraws the graph so that you can see the effects of the change. Notice that the graph now appears as three-dimensional.

When a graph contains many bars and points, it is difficult to see where the bars and points intersect both the X and Y axes. You can assist the user in reading the graph by displaying a reference grid in the graph.

The GridStyle Property

You can use the **GridStyle property** to place either a horizontal or a vertical grid, or both, on the graph. A grid allows the user to more readily see where bars and points in the graph intersect both the X and Y axes. You will display a horizontal grid in the grade application's graph so the student will be able to identify where the top of each bar intersects the Y axis.

To display a horizontal grid in the graph:

1   Click the **Graph1** control to select it, then set its GridStyle property to **1-Horizontal**.

2   Click the **form** to both remove the Properties window and see the effect of setting the GridStyle property. A horizontal grid appears in the graph.

Every graph should include a title, which describes the contents of the graph. The title helps the user interpret the graph.

GUI
Design Tips

Including a Graph Title

- Always include a title on a graph. The title, which should describe the contents of the graph, will help the user interpret the graph.

▶ Be sure that the graph is sized large enough to display the title; otherwise the title simply will not display. If the title does not display, increase the size of the graph.

The GraphTitle Property

You can display a title for the graph by setting the graph control's **GraphTitle** property. The graph title, which cannot exceed 80 characters, displays above the graph. You will display the word "Points" as the title for the grade application's graph.

To display a graph title:

1. Click the **Graph1** control to select it, then set its GraphTitle property to **Points**.

2. Click the **form** to both remove the Properties window and see the effect of setting the GraphTitle property. "Points" appears above the graph.

You will set the NumSets and NumPoints properties next. These two properties tell Visual Basic the number of data sets and the number of data points that will be included in the graph.

The NumSets and NumPoints Properties

The **NumSets** property specifies the number of data sets to graph, and the **NumPoints** property specifies the number of data points in each set. In this application, you have one set of data—scores—and two data points—possible scores and earned scores.

To set the NumSets and NumPoints properties appropriately:

1. Click the **Graph1** control to select it. Look in the Properties window to verify that the graph control's NumSets property is set to **1**, which is that property's default value.

The default value of the NumPoints property is 5; you will need to change it to 2.

2. Set the graph control's NumPoints property to **2**.

3. Click the **form** to both remove the Properties window and see the effect of setting the NumSets and NumPoints properties. Instead of five bars, the graph now shows only two bars.

In addition to the graph title, which displays above the graph, you can also include titles on the X and Y axes. These titles, which are set with the Labels property, should assist the user in interpreting the graph.

The Labels Property

The **Labels property** determines whether labels are displayed along the graph's X and Y axes. An exception to this is for pie graphs, which do not have X and Y axes; for pie graphs, the Label property determines whether labels appear next to each pie slice. The labels should help the user to identify either the scale or the category of data being graphed. For example, you might use a label to inform the

GUI
Design Tips

Displaying Titles on the X and Y Axes or on a Pie Graph

• Display titles on either the X or Y axis, or both. For a pie graph, display titles next to each pie slice. The titles should identify either the scale or the category of data being graphed.

your numbers may be different

your bars may be different

user that the numbers along the Y axis represent sales in millions of dollars; or you might include labels on the X axis to inform the user that each set of bars represents the data for a particular year.

In the current graph, notice that numbers appear along the X and Y axes. You will change the graph so that the numbers display along the Y axis only. The numbers will represent the amount of either possible or earned points.

To display labels along the Y axis only, then save and run the application:

1 Click the **Graph1** control to select it, then set its Labels property to **3-Y axis labels only.** (You will not be able to see the entire value of the property in the Properties window.)

2 **Save** and **run** the application to see how the graph looks. The graph appears similar to Figure 5-59.

Figure 5-59: Current status of Graph1 control in the user interface

HELP? Remember that the graph control uses random data to draw the graph, so your graph may look different from the one shown in Figure 5-59.

3 Click the **Exit** button, then click the **Yes** button to end the application.

The automatic generation of data is useful when designing the graph. However, you do not want to have the application generate random data when the application is run. Rather, the graph needs to be generated by data the user enters, and this is accomplished through the GraphData property. Before setting the GraphData property, you need to deactivate the RandomData property that has been used during design time.

The RandomData Property

During design time, the graph control automatically generates random data, which it uses to draw the graph on the screen; this is done as an aid when designing graphs. After the graph is designed, you can cancel the automatic generation of random data by setting the graph control's **RandomData property** to 0-Off.

To set the RandomData property appropriately:

1 Click the **Graph1** control to select it, then set its RandomData property to **0-Off**.

2 Click the **form** to both remove the Properties window and see the effect of setting the RandomData property. Both bars display at their lowest point in the graph—0.

Next you will learn how to send your own data to the graph control. The graph control will then use your data, instead of the random data, to generate the graph.

The GraphData Property

At run time, you use the graph control's **GraphData property** to send data to the graph control. You need to set the GraphData property for each data point to be graphed. You determine the number of data points by multiplying the value in the graph control's NumSets property by the value in its NumPoints property. For example, if the NumSets property is set to 2 and the NumPoints property is set to 3, you would need to set the GraphData property six times (two sets of data points times three data points per set).

In the current graph, you will need to set the GraphData property two times because the Graph1 control's NumSets property is set to 1 and its NumPoints property is set to 2; two times one equals two. The two items you want to graph are the number of possible points, which is stored in the inPosAccum variable, and the number of earned points, which is stored in the inEarnAccum variable. You will use the `Graph1.GraphData = inPosAccum` instruction to send the Graph1 control the number of possible points, and the `Graph1.GraphData = inEarnAccum` instruction to send it the number of earned points. You will put both instructions in the Display Grade button's Click event procedure so that the graph will be displayed when the user clicks that button.

To send data to the graph control:

1 Open the Display Grade button's Click event procedure, then maximize the Code window.

2 Enter the two instructions shown in Figure 5-60, then position the blinking insertion point as shown in the figure. The code in the figure was compressed so that you could read more of each line.

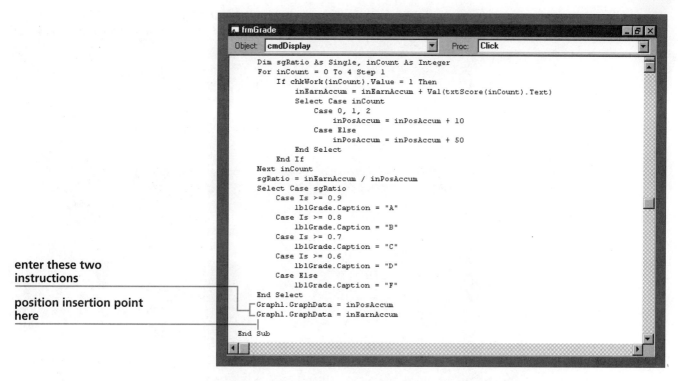

```
frmGrade
Object: cmdDisplay                          Proc: Click

    Dim sgRatio As Single, inCount As Integer
    For inCount = 0 To 4 Step 1
        If chkWork(inCount).Value = 1 Then
            inEarnAccum = inEarnAccum + Val(txtScore(inCount).Text)
            Select Case inCount
                Case 0, 1, 2
                    inPosAccum = inPosAccum + 10
                Case Else
                    inPosAccum = inPosAccum + 50
            End Select
        End If
    Next inCount
    sgRatio = inEarnAccum / inPosAccum
    Select Case sgRatio
        Case Is >= 0.9
            lblGrade.Caption = "A"
        Case Is >= 0.8
            lblGrade.Caption = "B"
        Case Is >= 0.7
            lblGrade.Caption = "C"
        Case Is >= 0.6
            lblGrade.Caption = "D"
        Case Else
            lblGrade.Caption = "F"
    End Select
    Graph1.GraphData = inPosAccum
    Graph1.GraphData = inEarnAccum

End Sub
```

enter these two instructions

position insertion point here

Figure 5-60: GraphData instructions in the Display Grade button's Click event procedure

After sending the appropriate data to the graph control, you need to tell Visual Basic to draw the graph in the control. You do so by setting the graph's DrawMode property.

The DrawMode Property

The **DrawMode property** defines the drawing mode for the graph control. During design time, the default value of the property is 2, which redraws the graph every time you change a property. If you want to redraw a graph during run time, you need to use an assignment statement to set the DrawMode property to 2. In the grade application, you will place the appropriate assignment statement in the Display Grade button's Click event procedure so that the graph will be redrawn each time the user clicks that button.

You clear a graph from a graph control by setting the control's DrawMode property to 1. In the grade application, you will set the DrawMode property to 1 in the txtScore array's Change event procedure so that the graph is removed when a score changes.

To set the DrawMode property:

1   The cmdDisplay control's Click event procedure should still be open, and the blinking insertion point should be located below the Graph1.GraphData = inEarnAccum instruction, as shown in Figure 5-60. Type **Graph1.drawmode = 2** and press the **Enter** key.

2   Use the Code window's Object box to open the txtScore array's Change event procedure. Below the lblGrade.Caption = " " instruction, type **Graph1.drawmode = 1** and press the **Enter** key.

> **HELP?** If you don't see the lblGrade.Caption = "" instruction, you do not have the correct event procedure open. Use the Object box and/or Proc box to open the txtScore array's Change event.

3   Close the Code window, then **save** and **run** the application.

4   Press the **spacebar** to select the Project 1 check box. The graph disappears from the graph control.

5   Type **6** in the text box and press the **Enter** key. The interface appears as shown in Figure 5-61.

Figure 5-61: Graph drawn on form

Notice that it is not readily obvious which bar represents the possible points and which represents the earned points. You can fix this problem by including a legend in the graph. You include a legend in a graph by setting the graph control's LegendText property.

6   Click the **Exit** button, then click the **Yes** button to end the application.

GUI
Design Tips

Including Legends in a Graph

- Include legends in a graph to help the user identify the various lines in a line graph, the bars in a bar graph, the segments in a stacked bar graph, and so on.

The LegendText Property

The **LegendText property** allows you to enter a legend for each data set. In the case of a pie graph or a bar graph that has only one set of data, you can enter a legend for each data point in the set. The legend text, which must be a string, cannot exceed 80 characters in length. In this application you will display the string "Possible: ", followed by the number of possible points, as the legend for the first bar in the graph. You will display the string "Earned: ", followed by the number of earned points, as the legend for the second bar in the graph. You will set the LegendText property in the Display Grade button's Click event procedure.

To set the LegendText property:

1 Open the Display Grade button's Code window, then maximize the Code window. The button's Click event procedure appears.

2 Enter the two instructions shown in Figure 5-62. Be sure to place the instructions above the `Graph1.DrawMode = 2` instruction, which redraws the graph.

enter these two instructions above the DrawMode instruction

```
frmGrade                                                              _ 8 X
Object:  cmdDisplay                      ▼   Proc:  Click                ▼
                inEarnAccum = inEarnAccum + Val(txtScore(inCount).Text)
                Select Case inCount
                    Case 0, 1, 2
                        inPosAccum = inPosAccum + 10
                    Case Else
                        inPosAccum = inPosAccum + 50
                End Select
            End If
    Next inCount
    sgRatio = inEarnAccum / inPosAccum
    Select Case sgRatio
        Case Is >= 0.9
            lblGrade.Caption = "A"
        Case Is >= 0.8
            lblGrade.Caption = "B"
        Case Is >= 0.7
            lblGrade.Caption = "C"
        Case Is >= 0.6
            lblGrade.Caption = "D"
        Case Else
            lblGrade.Caption = "F"
    End Select
    Graph1.GraphData = inPosAccum
    Graph1.GraphData = inEarnAccum
    Graph1.LegendText = "Possible: " & inPosAccum
    Graph1.LegendText = "Earned: " & inEarnAccum
    Graph1.DrawMode = 2

End Sub
```

Figure 5-62: LegendText instructions in the Display Grade button's Click event procedure

3 Close the Code window, then **save** and **run** the application.

4 Enter 8 as the Project 1 score, and 45 as the Midterm score. Click the **Display Grade** button to display both the grade and the graph. See Figure 5-63.

tips

Be sure that the graph is sized large enough to display the legend text; otherwise the legend text simply will not display. If the legend text does not display, increase the size of the graph.

legends

Figure 5-63: Graph control showing legends

5   Click the **Print** button to print the form. The graph control switches, temporarily, to black and white before the form prints.

Notice that the bars print with either a pattern or a solid color (probably black). You can use the graph control's PrintStyle property to tell Visual Basic to print the bars either in color, if you have a color printer, or in various shades of gray, if you don't have a color printer.

6   Click the **Exit** button, then click the **Yes** button to end the application.

GUI Design Tips

Printing a Graph

- If you are using a color printer, or have a printer capable of printing various shades of gray, it is best to set the graph control's PrintStyle property to either 1-Color or 3-Color with border.

The PrintStyle Property

You use the **PrintStyle property** to select the print style options for printing the graph control. The default setting is 0-Monochrome, which prints the graph using default patterns and symbols. If you are using a color printer, or have a printer capable of printing various shades of gray, it is best to set the PrintStyle property to either 1-Color or 3-Color with border. The 1-Color setting prints the graph in color (if you have a color printer) or in gray scales (if you don't have a color printer); the 3-Color with border setting does the same, but surrounds the graph control with a border. You will set the PrintStyle property to 1-Color in the Print button's Click event procedure. If you have a color printer, the graph will print in color; otherwise it will print in varying shades of gray.

To set the PrintStyle property, then save and run the application:

1 Open the Print button's Code window. The Click event procedure appears with the blinking insertion point at the beginning of the second line. Press the **Enter** key to insert a blank line above the `PrintForm` instruction. Press ↑ on your keyboard to move the blinking insertion point into the blank line, then press the **Tab** key. Type **Graph1.printstyle = 1** and press the **Enter** key.

2 Close the Code window, then **save** and **run** the application.

3 Enter any project and test scores, then click the **Display Grade** button to display both the grade and the graph. Click the **Print** button to print the graph. If you have a color printer, then each bar will print in a different color. If you don't have a color printer, then each bar will print in a different shade of gray.

4 Click the **Exit** button, then click the **Yes** button to end the application.

You have now completed Lesson C. You can either take a break, complete the questions and exercises at the end of the lesson, or read and complete the Debugging Section. The Debugging Section may contain information that will help you with problems you might encounter when doing the exercises at the end of the lesson.

S U M M A R Y

To display a dialog box that enables the application to communicate with the user:

■ Use the MsgBox function.

To process code before a form is removed from the screen:

■ Enter the code in the form's Unload event. The Unload event is triggered when you use either the Close button ☒ (*the Control menu box* ⊟ *in Windows 3.1*) to close the form; it is also triggered when you use the Unload statement in code.

To add spin buttons to the interface:

■ Use the Outrider SpinButton custom control. Spin buttons offer another way of getting numeric information from the user.

■ Enter the appropriate code in the spin button control's SpinUp and SpinDown events. If the code either increments or decrements numbers stored in a text box or label control, the new numbers will appear in the text box or label control when the user releases the mouse button at the end of the click operation. Use the Refresh method, whose syntax is *object*.**Refresh**, to allow the user to see the numbers change while pressing and holding down either the up or down arrow.

■ A spin button's Delay property controls how quickly the button spins. The default value of the Delay property is 250, which is 1/4 of a second. Setting the Delay property to a number that is less than 250 makes the button spin faster; setting the Delay property to a number that is greater than 250 makes the button spin slower.

■ The spin button control's SpinOrientation property allows you to set the direction of the spin control arrows to either 0-Vertical (up and down arrows) or 1-Horizontal (left and right arrows).

To display a graph in the interface:

■ Use the Pinnacle-BPS Graph custom control. Figure 5-64 recaps the graph control properties you learned in Lesson C.

Property	Use to
GraphType	specify the type of graph you want displayed in the graph control
GridStyle	place a horizontal or a vertical grid, or both, on the graph
GraphTitle	display a title for the graph
NumSets	specify the number of data sets to graph
NumPoints	specify the number of data points in each set
Labels	display labels along the graph's X and Y axes; or next to each slice in a pie graph
RandomData	specify whether random data is generated for the graph
GraphData	send data to the graph control
DrawMode	define the drawing mode for the graph control (for example, redraw and clear)
LegendText	enter a legend for each data set; or for each data point in the case of a pie graph or a bar graph that has only one set of data
PrintStyle	select the print style options for printing the graph control

Figure 5-64: Graph control properties

Q U E S T I O N S

1. You can use the _____ function to display a dialog box that enables the application to communicate with the user.
    a. Communicate
    b. DialogBox
    c. Message
    d. MsgBox
    e. UserMsg

2. The _____ event is triggered when you use the Close button ⊠ (*the Control menu box* ⊟ *in Windows 3.1*), or when you use the Unload statement in code.
    a. FormUnload
    b. FormRemove
    c. Remove
    d. RemoveForm
    e. Unload

3. A spin button's _____ and _____ events occur when the user clicks the spin button's up and down arrows.
    a. Down
    b. SpinDown
    c. SpinUp
    d. Up

4. Assume that an application uses a spin button to increment and decrement numbers. If you want the user to see the numbers change as he or she is pressing and holding down the spin button arrows, you need to include the _____ in the spin button's code.
    a. Click method
    b. Refresh event
    c. Refresh method
    d. Spin event
    e. Spin method

5. Which graph control property allows you to display a grid on a graph?
    a. GraphGrid
    b. Grid
    c. GridStyle
    d. StyleGrid
    e. Style

6. Which graph control property allows you to display a title above the graph?
    a. GraphStyle
    b. GraphTitle
    c. TitleGraph
    d. Title

7. Which graph control property allows you to specify the type of graph to display?
    a. Graph
    b. GraphStyle
    c. GraphType
    d. TypeGraph
    e. Type

8. Which graph control property allows you to display labels along the graph's X and Y axes, or next to each slice in a pie graph?
    a. AxisLabels
    b. DisplayLabels
    c. GraphLabels
    d. GraphLabelType
    e. Labels

9. Which graph control property specifies the number of data sets to graph?
    a. DataNumSets
    b. DataSets
    c. NumData
    d. NumSetDisplay
    e. NumSets

10. Which graph control property specifies the number of data points in each data set?
    a. DataNumPoints
    b. DataPoints
    c. NumPoints
    d. NumPointSet
    e. NumSetPoints

11. Which graph control property sends data to the graph control?
    a. DataGraph
    b. GraphData
    c. GraphPoint
    d. GraphSet
    e. PointData

12. Which graph control property specifies whether random data is generated for the graph?
    a. DataOffOn
    b. DataDraw
    c. DrawData
    d. Random
    e. RandomData

13. During run time, you need to set the _____ property when you want Visual Basic to redraw the graph.
    a. DrawMode
    b. Mode
    c. Redraw
    d. RedrawMode

14. Which graph control property allows you to enter a legend for each data set in the graph?
    a. DataLegend
    b. DataText
    c. Legend
    d. LegendData
    e. LegendText

15. The _____ property allows you to select the print style options when printing a graph control.
    a. Options
    b. PrintOptions
    c. PrintStyle
    d. Style
    e. StylePrint

E X E R C I S E S

NOTE: In the following exercises, you will not be reminded to enter the Option Explicit statement, center the form, assign access keys, highlight the existing text in a text box, and so on. When creating an application, think about all of the graphical user interface (GUI) design issues you've learned and include them in your application.

1. In this exercise you will experiment with the Refresh method.

    Scenario: This exercise will allow you to see the effect that the Refresh method has on spin button controls.
    a. Open a new project. Add a spin button control and a text box to the form.
    b. Remove the contents of the text box's Text property.
    c. Code the spin button's SpinDown event so that it decrements the number in the text box by one, then code the SpinUp event so that it increments the number in the text box by one. (Don't use the Refresh method in the code.)
    d. Run, but don't save the application.
    e. Click the spin button's up arrow, releasing the mouse button after each click. The number in the text box increases by one each time you click. Notice that the new number does not appear in the text box until you release the mouse button.
    f. Now press and hold down the spin button's up arrow for a few seconds, then release the mouse button. Notice that the number in the text box does not change until you release the mouse button.

g. Stop the application. Enter the Refresh method in both the SpinUp and SpinDown events, then run, but don't save the application. Press and hold down the spin button's up arrow for a few seconds. This time the number in the text box changes as you press and hold down the arrow.

h. Stop the application, then print the code. You do not need to save the application.

2. In this exercise you will stop a spin button from decrementing a value when the value reaches zero. You will also experiment with the Delay property.

Scenario: The spin buttons in the grade application that you created in Lesson C should stop decrementing when the text box score reaches zero. The user would also like the spin buttons to spin faster.

a. Open the lcGrade (lcgrade.vbp) project that you created in the tutorial's Lesson C. The project is located in the Tut05 folder on your Student Disk.

b. Set each spin button's Delay property to 150.

c. Open the spin button array's SpinDown event procedure. Modify the code so that it stops decrementing when the value in the corresponding text box reaches zero.

d. Save the form and the code as lcGrade in the Tut05 folder on your Student Disk.

e. Test the spin buttons to make sure that they stop at zero. Also notice the effect of setting the Delay property to 150.

f. Print the code.

3. In this exercise you will use spin buttons, a graph control, and the MsgBox function.

Scenario: Create an application that you can use to calculate and display your grade in one of the courses you are taking this semester. You can use the tutorial's application as a guide.

a. Create the interface for the application. Include a text box in which you can enter your name. Also include spin buttons and a graph control in the interface.

b. Save the form and the project as lc3Done in the Tut05 folder on your Student Disk.

c. The application should allow you to display the grade at any time during the semester. It should also allow you to print the interface, and exit the application. When exiting, the application should ask you to verify that you want to leave the application.

d. Test the application with your own data. Be sure to test it with both valid and invalid data.

e. Print the interface with the valid test data showing.

f. Print the form as text and the code.

g. Submit the printouts from steps e and f.

4. In this exercise you will use the graph control and the MsgBox function.

Scenario: Create an application that will allow you to track the number of kilowatt-hours of electricity used in each of the last 12 months. Display the 12-month data using a bar graph.

a. Create the interface for the application. Include a graph control in the interface.

b. Save the form and the project as lc4Done in the Tut05 folder on your Student Disk.

c. The application should allow you to print the interface. Also include an Exit button. When exiting, the application should verify that you want to leave the application.

d. Test the application with both valid and invalid data.

e. Test the application using the following data, then print the interface with this test data showing.

January	600 kWh	July	2400 kWh
February	600	Aug	1800
March	500	Sept	900
April	475	Oct	450
May	400	Nov	400
June	1200	Dec	500

f. Print the form as text and the code.

g. Submit the printouts from steps e and f.

5. In this exercise you will use the graph control and the MsgBox function.

Scenario: Georgia Industries' sales manager needs an application that he can use to compare the sales and expenses in each of four regions: North, South, East, and West.

a. Create the interface for the application. Provide eight text boxes in which the sales manager can enter the sales and expenses for the four regions. Include a graph control in the interface.

b. Save the form and the project as lc5Done in the Tut05 folder on your Student Disk.

c. The application should allow you to print the interface. Also include an Exit button. When exiting, the application should verify that you want to leave the application.

d. Use a bar graph to compare the sales and expenses in each of the four regions.

e. Test the application with both valid and invalid data.

f. Test the application using the following data, then print the interface with this test data showing.

Region	Sales	Expenses
North	25000	4000
South	30000	7000
East	45000	10000
West	40000	4000

g. Print the form as text and the code.

h. Submit the printouts from steps f and g.

Exercises 6 and 7 are Discovery Exercises, which allow you to both "discover" the solutions to problems on your own and to experiment with material that is not covered in the tutorial.

discovery ▶ 6. In this exercise you will use spin buttons.

Scenario: Mary Kayen needs to buy a new car, but she's not sure how much she can afford to pay for one. Create an application that Mary can use to calculate her monthly payment. She will provide you with the principal, the interest rate, and the term.

a. Create the user interface for the application. Provide a text box in which to enter the principal. Use a spin button, along with a label control, to enter the interest rate. The application should allow you to enter rates in increments and decrements of .25—for example, 8.00, 8.25, 8.50, and so on. Use options buttons for the terms, which should be 2 years, 3 years, 4 years, and 5 years only. Display the monthly payment in a label control. The interface should also include a Print button and an Exit button. When exiting, the application should verify that the user wants to leave the application.

b. Save the form and the project as lc6Done in the Tut05 folder on your Student Disk.

c. Use the Help menu to search for the Pmt function's Help window. (If you'd like, you can print the Help window.) In this application, the payments are due at the end of the month.

d. Display the monthly payment as a positive number, formatted to currency. The monthly payment should be centered in the label control

e. Test the application with both valid and invalid data.

f. Test the application with the following data, then print the interface with the test data showing.

Principal: $15,000
Interest (APR): 8.25%
Term: 3 years

g. Print the form as text and the code.

h. Submit the printouts from steps f and g.

7. In this exercise you will use the graph control.

Scenario: The Readers Club of Glenview recently sent out a survey asking the club members which types of books they prefer to read. The categories were Mystery, Romance, Nonfiction, and Other. The results of the survey are as follows:

Category	Number of Responses
Mystery	40
Romance	55
Nonfiction	25
Other	36

a. Graph this data using a pie graph. Be sure to put a title on the graph.

b. Save the form and the project as lc7Done in the Tut05 folder on your Student Disk.

c. Print the form, the form as text, and the code. Submit these printouts.

D E B U G G I N G

Technique

Users will, at times, make mistakes when entering data. For example, a user may enter a letter when a number is expected. In previous applications, you used the Val function to tell Visual Basic to treat a string as a number. In this Debugging section you will learn how to use the KeyPress event to prevent a user from entering anything other than a number in a text box.

The KeyPress event occurs when the user presses and releases a key that is a member of the ANSI (American National Standards Institute) character set. The ANSI character set contains 256 characters. The first 128 characters (0–127) correspond to the letters and symbols on a standard U.S. keyboard. For example, the ANSI characters 48 through 57 correspond to the numbers 0 through 9, respectively. The ANSI character 8 corresponds to the Backspace key. The remaining 128 characters (128–255) in the ANSI character set represent special characters, such as letters in international alphabets, accents, currency symbols, and fractions. To view the ANSI character set, use the Help menu to search for the topic "Character Sets."

Exercises

1. In the following Debugging exercise, you will use the KeyPress event, as well as the ANSI characters, to prevent the user from entering anything other than a number into a text box.

To prevent a user from entering a letter into a text box:

1 Open the **lcGrade** (lcgrade.vbp) project that you created in the tutorial's Lesson C (located in the Tut05 folder on your Student Disk), then view the form. **Run**, but don't save, the project.

2 Press the **Spacebar** to select the Project 1 check box, type the letter **a** into the text box, then press the **Enter** key.

Because you used the Val function in the equation that calculates the grade, the application does not end in an error. The application does, however, display the grade and the graph, which can be misleading. It would be better if the user were prevented from entering anything other than a number into the text box.

3 Click the **Exit** button, then click the **Yes** button to end the application.

4 Open the txtScore array's Code window. Use the Proc box to open the txtScore array's KeyPress event, then maximize the Code window.

Notice that the KeyPress event has two arguments: `Index as Integer and KeyAscii as Integer`. As you learned in Lesson B, the Index argument stores the index of the text box that is receiving the event. The KeyAscii argument stores the ANSI character that corresponds to the key pressed by the user. In this case you want to tell the KeyPress event to allow the user to press only the numbers 0 through 9, and the Backspace key. (The user may need to use the Backspace key to edit the contents of the text box.) Recall that the numbers 0 through 9 on the keyboard are represented in the ANSI character set by the characters 48 through 57, respectively. Also recall that the Backspace key is represented by the ANSI character 8.

5   Press the **Tab** key, then type **if (KeyAscii < 48 or KeyAscii > 57) and KeyAscii < > 8 then** and press the **Enter** key.

If the user presses an invalid key (a key other than the Backspace and the numbers 0 through 9), then you want the KeyPress event to cancel the key. You cancel the key by assigning the number 0 to the KeyAscii argument.

6   Press the **Tab** key, then type **KeyAscii = 0** and press the **Enter** key. (Be sure you type the number 0, and not the letter O.)

7   Press the Backspace key to cancel the indentation, then type **end if** and press the **Enter** key.

8   Close the Code window, then **save and run** the application.

9   Press the **Spacebar** to select the Project 1 check box. Try entering a letter into the text box; the text box will not allow you to do so. Enter a number, then use the Backspace key to remove the number. Notice that you can enter a number and also use the Backspace key.

10   Click the **Exit** button, then click the **Yes** button to end the application.

2.   In this Debugging exercise, you will need to find and correct the bug(s).
   a. Open a new project. Place two text boxes and a command button on the form. Name one of the text boxes txtFirst; name the other txtSecond. Name the command button cmdExit.
   b. Remove the contents of both text boxes' Text property. Set the command button's Caption property to E<u>x</u>it.
   c. Code the Exit button so that it ends the application.

   If the user presses the Enter key when the txtFirst text box has the focus, the txtFirst control's KeyPress event should move the focus to the txtSecond control. If the user presses the Enter key when the txtSecond text box has the focus, the txtSecond control's KeyPress event should move the focus to the cmdExit control.
   d. Open the txtFirst control's KeyPress event and enter the following selection structure:

   If KeyAscii = 12 then

      txtSecond.SetFocus

   End If
   e. Open the txtSecond control's KeyPress event and enter the following selection structure:

   If KeyAscii = 12 then

      cmdExit.SetFocus

   End If
   f. Close the Code window, then run, but don't save the project. Test the application to see if it is working properly, then stop the application and correct any errors.
   g. When the application is working correctly, print the code. You do not need to save the application.

TUTORIAL

6

Sequential Access Files and Menus

The PAO Application

case ▶ During July and August of each year the Political Awareness Organization (PAO) sends a questionnaire to the voters in their district. The questionnaire asks the voter to provide his or her political party (Democrat, Republican, Independent) and his or her age group (18–35, 36–50, 51–65, Over 65). From the returned questionnaires, the organization's secretary tabulates the number of Democrats, Republicans, and Independents in each of the four age groups—a time-consuming and tedious job. The secretary then sends a report summarizing the data to the organization's members and to various political offices in the district. The organization's president has asked for your help in simplifying this process.

In this tutorial you will create two applications for the PAO. One of the applications will tabulate the questionnaire data for the secretary, and the other can be used to write the summary report. As you've done in previous tutorials, you will preview the applications before creating them.

Previewing the Completed Applications

The first application you will preview is the one that will tabulate the questionnaire data for the secretary.

To preview the completed applications:

1 If necessary, start Windows, then place your Student Disk in the appropriate drive.

2 Use the Run command on the Start menu to run the **Pao95** (Pao95.exe) file, which is located in the Tut06 folder on your Student Disk. The PAO application's user interface appears on the screen. See Figure 6-1.

Use the Run command on the Program Manager's File menu to run the pao31.exe file, which is located in the Tut06 folder on your Student Disk. The PAO application's user interface appears on the screen. See Figure 6-1.

list boxes

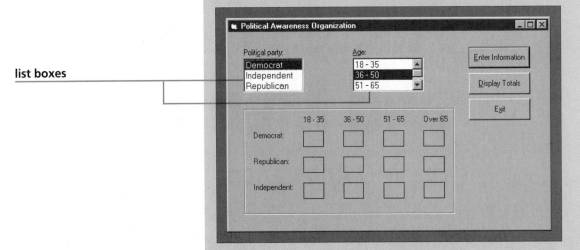

Figure 6-1: PAO application's user interface

This application contains a new control, a list box, which you will learn about in Lesson A. The organization's secretary will use the two list box controls to enter the respondent's political party and age group. Observe how the application works by entering some information.

3 Click **Republican** in the Political party list box, then click **18 - 35** in the Age list box.

When the user clicks the Enter Information button, the party and age information will be saved in a sequential access file on your Student Disk. You will learn about sequential access data files in Lessons A and C.

4 Click the **Enter Information** button to write the respondent's information to the data file.

5 Click **Independent** in the Political party list box. Scroll the Age list box, then click **Over 65** in the list. Click the **Enter Information** button to write the respondent's information to the data file.

When the organization wants to tabulate the responses, the secretary simply needs to click the Display Totals button.

6 Click the **Display Totals** button. The application counts and displays the total number of Democrats, Republicans, and Independents in each of the four age groups, as shown in Figure 6-2.

Figure 6-2: PAO application showing tabulated data

7 Click the **Exit** button to end the application.

Because this preview application is for demonstration only, it is coded so that it always displays the tabulated data shown in Figure 6-2. The application you will create in Lesson A will allow you to enter and tabulate other data.

WINDOWS   3.1

You will learn how to create this application in Lesson A. In Lessons B and C you will learn how to create a text editor that the organization's secretary can use to create the PAO's annual report. Take a look at this text editor now.

To preview the text editor application:

1 Use the Run command on the Start menu to run the **Edit95** (Edit95.exe) file, which is located in the Tut06 folder on your Student Disk. The text editor's user interface appears on the screen. See Figure 6-3.

Use the Run command on the Program Manager's File menu to run the edit31.exe file, which is located in the Tut06 folder on your Student Disk. The text editor's user interface appears on the screen. See Figure 6-3.

Figure 6-3: Text editor's user interface

2   Type **Text example editor** and press the **Enter** key.

3   Select the word **example** in the line that you just typed. Click **Edit**, then click **Cut**. Visual Basic removes the word "example" from the typed line, and places it on the clipboard.

4   Position the I-bar I at the end of the typed line, immediately after the word "editor," then click at that location. The blinking insertion point appears after the word "editor."

5   Press the **Spacebar** on your keyboard to insert a blank space. Click **Edit**, then click **Paste**. Visual Basic pastes the word "example" at the end of the typed line as shown in Figure 6-4.

Figure 6-4: Current status of the text editor

6   Click **File**, then click **Exit** to end the application.

In Lesson A you will learn about list boxes and sequential access data files as you code the first PAO application. You will learn about menus and string manipulation functions in Lesson B as you code the text editor application.

In this lesson you will learn how to:
- Add a List box control to the form
- Add items to a list box with the AddItem method
- Set the Sorted and the ListIndex properties
- Create, open, and close a sequential access data file
- Write records to and read records from a sequential access data file

Sequential Access Data Files

Creating the PAO Application

Recall that each year the Political Awareness Organization (PAO) sends a questionnaire to the voters in their district. When the questionnaires are returned, the organization's secretary tabulates the number of Democrats, Republicans, and Independents in each of the four age groups shown on the questionnaire. The president of the PAO wants you to create an application that will do this time-consuming task for the organization's secretary.

On your Student Disk is a partially completed application for the PAO organization.

To open the partially completed application:

1 Start Visual Basic, if necessary, and open the **t6Case** (t6case.vbp) file, which is in the Tut06 folder on your Student Disk. The `Option Explicit` statement has already been entered into the general Declarations section of the form.

2 Save the form and the project as **laPao**. Click the **View Form** button to view the frmPao form. The partially completed interface is shown in Figure 6-5.

cmdEnter

list box

cmdDisplay

cmdExit

lblDem array

lblRep array

lblInd array

frame control

Figure 6-5: Partially completed interface for the PAO

The frame control contains three parallel control arrays—lblDem, lblRep, and lblInd—and each control array consists of four label controls. The Enter Information button is the default button on the form.

Notice that the interface contains a new control, a list box named lstAge. To complete the interface, you will need to add another list box to the form.

Creating a List Box

Using the completed questionnaires, the organization's secretary will enter two items of information about each respondent into the interface: his or her political party and age group. The secretary will use two list boxes to record this information from the respondents. Like option buttons, which you learned about in Tutorial 4, a **list box control** also can be used to display a set of choices from which the user can select only one. Unlike option buttons, however, a list box does not require you to display all of the choices on the screen at the same time. You can make a list box any size you want, and if you have more items than will fit into the list box, Visual Basic will automatically supply scroll bars on the box, which you can use to view the undisplayed items. So if you have many possible choices, you can save space on the form by using a list box instead of option buttons.

List boxes should contain a minimum of three selections. If you have only two options to offer the user, you should use option buttons instead of a list box. The Windows standard is to display, in the list box, a minimum of three selections and a maximum of eight selections at a time.

tips

You can also create list boxes that allow the user to select more than one item in the list. You will learn how to create multi-selection list boxes in Lesson A's Discovery Exercise 9.

To add a list box control to the form, then lock the controls and set the TabIndex property:

1   Double-click the **ListBox tool** in the toolbox. The List1 list box appears in the center of the form.

   HELP? If your control says Combo1, you inadvertently double-clicked the ComboBox tool instead of the ListBox tool. Press the Delete key to remove the combo box from the form, then repeat Step 1.

2   Set the list box control's Name property to **lstParty**. ("Lst" is the three-character ID for the list box control.)

3   Set the list box control's Font size to **10** and its Width property to **1455**.

4   Drag the list box to the location shown in Figure 6-6, then size the list box as shown in the figure.

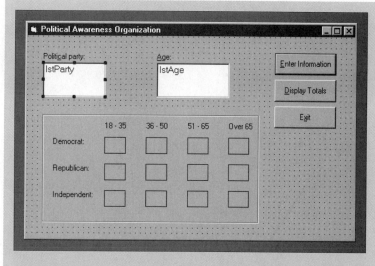

Figure 6-6: Correct location and size of the lstParty list box in the form

Don't be concerned that the list box's Name property, lstParty, appears inside the list box; the name won't appear when you run the application.

Now that the user interface is complete, you can lock the controls on the form.

5 If necessary, click the **form** to select it. Its title bar should be highlighted. Click the **Lock Controls** 🔒 button on the toolbar to lock the controls on the form.

Recall from Tutorial 2 that you should give keyboard access to the essential elements of the interface. In this interface, for example, you should give keyboard access to the three command buttons, which has already been done, and to the two list boxes. As with a text box, you give keyboard access to a list box by assigning an access key to the label control that identifies the list box. You must then set the label control's TabIndex value to a number that is one less than the list box's TabIndex value. In other words, if the "Political party:" label has a TabIndex of 0, as it does in this interface, then its corresponding list box (lstParty) should have a TabIndex value of 1. Likewise, if the "Age:" label has a TabIndex of 2, then its corresponding list box (lstAge) should have a TabIndex of 3. Figure 6-7 shows both the current and the new TabIndex values of the four controls.

Control	Current TabIndex Value	New TabIndex Value
Label1 (Political party:)	0	0
lstParty	26	1
Label2 (Age:)	1	2
lstAge	2	3

Figure 6-7: Current and new TabIndex values

In this case, you will simply need to set the TabIndex property of the lstParty list box to 1; Visual Basic will then renumber the TabIndex values of the Label2 and lstAge controls appropriately.

6   Click the **lstParty** list box, then set its TabIndex property to **1**.

Next you will use the AddItem method to tell Visual Basic what items you want displayed in each list box.

The AddItem Method

You use Visual Basic's **AddItem method** to specify the items you want displayed in a list box control. The syntax of the AddItem method is *control*.**AddItem** *item*. *Control* is the name of the control to which you want the item added, **AddItem** is the name of the method, and *item* is the string expression you want displayed in the control. If you want a number displayed in the list box, you must surround the number with quotation marks so that Visual Basic will treat the number as a string.

The lstParty list box should offer the user the following three selections: Republican, Democrat, Independent. That means you will need to enter three AddItem instructions—one for each of the selections. Because you want the lstParty list box to display its values when the form first appears on the screen, you will define the list box items in the form's Load event procedure. Recall from Tutorial 1 that the Load event occurs when the application is run and the form is loaded into the computer's memory. Visual Basic automatically executes the instructions contained in the Load event procedure's Code window when the Load event occurs.

To enter the AddItem instructions for the lstParty list box:

1   Double-click the **form** to open the form's Code window. The form's Load event, which already contains the instructions to center the form, as well as the AddItem instructions for the lstAge list box, appears.

2   Enter the additional AddItem instructions shown in Figure 6-8.

enter these three instructions

Figure 6-8: Additional AddItem instructions entered in the form's Load event procedure

When you run this application and the form is loaded into the computer's memory, Visual Basic will fill both list boxes with the values entered in the Load event procedure's Code window.

3 Close the Code window, then **save** and **run** the application. Visual Basic displays the form on the screen, as shown in Figure 6-9.

Figure 6-9: List boxes displayed in form

4 Click **Republican** in the Political party list box.

When you select an item in a list box, Visual Basic stores the item in the list box's Text property. In this case, "Republican" is stored in the lstParty control's Text property.

Because the Age list box is too small to display its four items at the same time, Visual Basic supplies scroll bars on the box. You can use those scroll bars to scroll through the various choices.

5 Scroll the Age list box until the **Over 65** option appears, then click **Over 65** to select it. Visual Basic stores the string "Over 65" in the lstAge control's Text property.

6 Click the **Exit** button, which already contains the Unload frmPao statement. The application ends and Visual Basic returns to the design screen.

In the next section you will learn how to put list box items in alphabetical order. Arranging information in either alphabetical, numerical, or chronological order is called **sorting**.

The Sorted Property

In Windows applications, list box items are either arranged by use, with the most used entries appearing first in the list, or the items are arranged (sorted) in ascending order either alphabetically, numerically, or chronologically. To arrange the list box items by use, you simply enter the AddItem instructions in the order in which you want the items to appear in the list. To arrange the items in ascending order, you can either add the items to the list box in the correct order or you can set the list box's Sorted property to True. Setting the list box's Sorted property to True automatically sorts the items as they are added to the list box. Use the Sorted property to sort the items in the lstParty list box.

To sort the items in the Political party list box:

1   Click the **lstParty** list box. Set the list box's Sorted property to **True**. Now Visual Basic will sort the items as they are added to the list box

It is customary in Windows applications to have one of the items in a list box selected when the interface appears; you can use a list box's ListIndex property to do so.

The ListIndex Property

Similar to the TabIndex property, which keeps track of the various objects in a form, the **ListIndex property** keeps track of the various items in a list box. The first item in a list box has a ListIndex of 0 (zero), the second item has a ListIndex of 1, and so on. When the user selects an item in a list box, Visual Basic records that item's index in the ListIndex property. For example, if the user selects the first item in the list box, the ListIndex property contains the number 0. You can use the ListIndex property to have the application, rather than the user, select an item in a list box. The `lstParty.ListIndex - 0` instruction, for instance, selects the first item in the lstParty list box.

tips

▶ If items are added to a list box during run time, the new items are placed in the correct sorted order if the list box's Sorted property is set to True; they are placed at the end of the list if the list box's Sorted property is set to False.

GUI
Design Tips

Order of List Box Items

• List box items are either arranged by use, with the most used entries appearing first in the list, or the items are sorted in ascending order either alphabetically, numerically, or chronologically.

When using a list box in an interface, it is customary to have a default item selected in the list when the application first appears. The default item should be either the most used selection or the first selection in the list. In this application, because most of the voters in the district are Democrats in the 36 to 50 age group, you will have Visual Basic select "Democrat" in the Political party list box and "36 - 50" in the Age list box. Because you want the list box items selected when the form first appears on the screen, you will need to set the ListIndex property in the form's Load event procedure.

GUI
Design Tips

Default Item Selected in a List Box

• A default item should be selected in a list box when the interface first appears. The default item should be either the most used selection or the first selection in the list.

To select a default item in each list box:

1 Double-click the **form** to open the Load event procedure's Code window.

When the application is run, "Democrat" will be the first item in the Political party list box, so its ListIndex value will be 0. (Recall that the 1st Party control's Sorted property is set to True.) "36 - 50" will be the second item in the Age list box, so its ListIndex value will be 1.

2 Enter the two instructions shown in Figure 6-10.

selects first item in the list box

enter these two instructions

selects second item in the list box

```
 frmPao

Object: Form              Proc: Load

Private Sub Form_Load()
    frmPao.Left = (Screen.Width - frmPao.Width) / 2
    frmPao.Top = (Screen.Height - frmPao.Height) / 2
    lstAge.AddItem "18 - 35"
    lstAge.AddItem "36 - 50"
    lstAge.AddItem "51 - 65"
    lstAge.AddItem "Over 65"
    lstParty.AddItem "Republican"
    lstParty.AddItem "Independent"
    lstParty.AddItem "Democrat"
    lstParty.ListIndex = 0
    lstAge.ListIndex = 1

End Sub
```

Figure 6-10: ListIndex instructions entered in the form's Load event procedure

3 Close the Code window, then **save** and **run** the application. Visual Basic displays the form on the screen.

Notice that the items in the Political party list box are in alphabetical order. Also notice that Visual Basic automatically selects the first item (Democrat) in the Political party list box, and the second item (36 - 50) in the Age list box.

4 Click the **Exit** button to end the application. Visual Basic returns to the design screen.

Before you can continue coding the application, you will need to learn about data files. The information pertaining to each respondent will be saved in a data file.

Data Files

In previous tutorials you saved the form and the project in separate files on your Student Disk. Those files, called **program files**, contain the instructions that create the user interface and tell the objects how to respond to events. Although the form and the project were saved, recall that the data entered into the user interface—for example, the student's scores in Tutorial 5's grade application—was not saved. That means you will need to enter the data (the student's scores) each time the grade application is run. So that the PAO's secretary will not have to enter the party and age information every time he or she runs the program, you will save that information in a file, called a **data file**, on your Student Disk.

The information in a data file is organized into fields and records. A field, also called a **data element**, is a single item of information about a person, place, or thing—for example, a social security number, a city, or a price. A **record** is a group of related fields that contain all of the necessary data about a specific person, place, or thing. For example, the college you are attending keeps a student record on you. Your student record contains the following fields: your social security number, name, address, phone number, credits earned, grades earned, grade point average, and so on. The place where you are employed also keeps a record on you. Your employee record contains your social security number, name, address, phone number, starting date, salary or hourly wage, and so on. A collection of related records is called a **data file**. The collection of records for each of the students in your class forms the class data file; the collection of employee records forms the employee data file. Figure 6-11 illustrates the concept of a field, a record, and a data file.

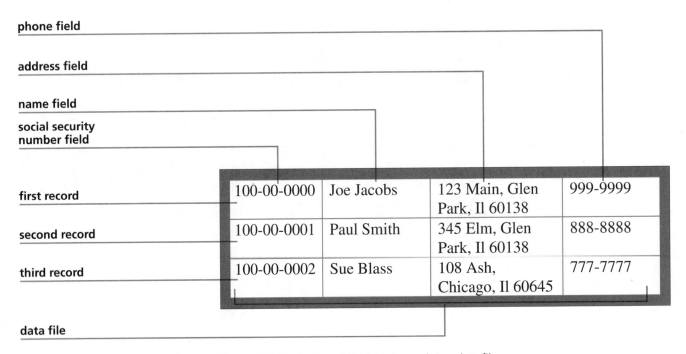

Figure 6-11: Illustration of fields and records in a data file

In the PAO application, only two elements of data are important—the respondent's political party and his or her age group. Together, those two fields form each respondent's record. The collection of respondents' records forms the PAO data file.

Visual Basic has three types of data files: sequential, random, and binary. The data file type refers to how the data is accessed. For example, the data in a sequential access file is always accessed sequentially—in other words, in consecutive order. The data in a random access file, on the other hand, can be accessed either in consecutive order or in random order. The data in a binary access file can be accessed by its byte location in the file. You will learn about sequential access files in this tutorial and random access files in Tutorial 8. Binary access files are beyond the scope of this book.

Sequential Access Data Files

Sequential access files are similar to cassette tapes in that each record in the file, like each song on a cassette tape, is both stored and retrieved in consecutive order (sequentially). Sequential access files have the advantage of being very easy to create. The drawback of this file type is the same drawback encountered with cassette tapes: the records in a sequential access file, like the songs on a cassette tape, can be processed only in the order in which they are stored. In other words, if you want to listen to the third song on a cassette tape, you must play (or fast-forward through) the first two songs. Likewise, if you want to read the third record in a sequential access file, you must first read the two records that precede it. Sequential access files work best when you want to process either a small file, like the one needed by the PAO, or a file consisting only of text, such as a file created with a typical text editor.

In this lesson you will learn how to create, open, and close a sequential access file, as well as write records to and read records from a sequential access file. The TOE chart for the PAO application is shown in Figure 6-12.

Task	Object	Event
Get the respondent's political party	lstParty	Click
Get the respondent's age group	lstAge	Click
Write the respondent's party and age group to a sequential access file	cmdEnter	Click
1. Read the data from the sequential access file. 2. Count the number of Democrats, Republicans, and Independents in each of the age groups 3. Display the results in the appropriate label controls in the lblDem, lblRep, and lblInd arrays	cmdDisplay	Click
End the application	cmdExit	Click
Center the form	frmPao	Load
Display the number of Democrats, Republicans, and Independents in each of the age groups	lblDem array lblRep array lblInd array	None

Figure 6-12: TOE chart for the PAO application

The PAO secretary will enter the respondent's party and age group in the lstParty and lstAge controls, respectively. After entering a respondent's information, the secretary will use the Enter Information button to write the information to the sequential file. The secretary will then need simply to click the Display Totals button to tabulate the responses and display the results. The Exit button will end the application.

You will need to code only two of the three command buttons shown in Figure 6-12 because the Exit button already contains the `Unload frmPao` statement. You don't need to code either of the list box's Click event procedures; when you click an item in a list box, Visual Basic assigns the item to the list box's Text property automatically. You will begin by coding the Enter Information button, which is responsible for saving each respondent's political party and age group in a sequential file on your Student Disk.

Coding the Enter Information Command Button

For each returned questionnaire, recall that the organization's secretary will enter the respondent's political party and age into the lstParty and lstAge controls, respectively. After entering a respondent's data into the user interface, the secretary will then click the Enter Information button to write the record to the data file. The pseudocode and flowchart for the Enter Information button are shown in Figure 6-13.

Pseudocode for the Enter Information button

1. Open the sequential access data file.
2. Write the respondent's record to the data file.
3. Close the data file.

Figure 6-13: Flowchart and pseudocode for the Enter Information button

The first step is to open the sequential access data file. You must open a data file before you can use it.

Opening a Data File

You open a data file with Visual Basic's **Open statement**. Its syntax is **Open** *filename* **For** *mode* **As #** *filenumber*. *Filename* is the name of the file you want to open; it should include the drive letter and path, and it must be enclosed in quotation marks. For sequential access files, *mode* can be Input, Output, or Append. You open a sequential access file for **Input** when you want to read its contents; if a file opened for Input does not exist, Visual Basic displays an error message when it attempts to open the file. You open the file for **Output** when you want to create a new sequential access file and then write data to it; if the file already exists, Visual Basic erases its contents before writing the new information. You open a file for **Append** when you want to add data to the end of an existing sequential access file; if the file does not already exist, Visual Basic creates it before adding the data to it. Figure 6-14 recaps the three modes used with sequential access files.

A file name can also be stored in a variable, and then the variable, instead of the file name, can be used in the Open statement. If the Open statement uses a variable for the file name, the variable is not enclosed in quotation marks.

Open statement mode	Use to:
Append	Add data to an existing sequential access data file. The file is created if it does not already exist.
Input	Read data from an existing sequential access data file. If the file does not exist, Visual Basic displays an error message when it attempts to open the file.
Output	Create a new sequential access data file and write data to it. If the file already exists, its contents are erased before the new data is written.

Figure 6-14: Summary of Open statement modes for sequential access files

Filenumber is a number that you assign to the file; it must be an integer between 1 and 511, inclusive. When the Open statement is processed, Visual Basic associates the *filenumber* with the file. You use the *filenumber* to refer to the file in other statements. The *filenumber* will be associated with the file as long as the file is open. Figure 6-15 shows examples of the Open statement.

Open statement	Result
Open "a:\tut06\Test.dat" for Append as #1	Opens a sequential access data file for append
Open "a:\tut06\Employee.dat" for Input as #1	Opens a sequential access data file for input
Open "a:\tut06\MyFile.dat" for Output as #2	Opens a sequential access data

Figure 6-15: Examples of the Open statement for sequential access files

Because the organization's secretary will be adding new records to the file as the questionnaires are returned, you will need to open the PAO file for Append; new records will then be added automatically to the end of the data file. You will name the data file Pao.dat and assign file number 1 to it. A .dat extension is commonly used in a file's name to indicate that the file is a data file.

To enter the Open statement:

1 Double-click the **Enter Information** button to open its Click event procedure, then press the **Tab** key.

2 Type one of the following Open statements into the Code window. Which statement you type will depend on the location of your Student Disk. Be sure to type the backslash (\), not the front slash (/) in the appropriate places.

> open "a:\tut06\Pao.dat" for append as #1
>
> open "b:\tut06\Pao.dat" for append as #1

3 Press the **Enter** key.

When the application is run and the user clicks the Enter Information button, the Open statement will open the sequential data file named Pao.dat. If the Pao.dat file does not exist, the Open statement will create the data file before opening it.

The next step shown in Figure 6-13 is to write the respondent's record to the data file—in other words, to enter the record in the file. Recall that a respondent's record consists of his or her political party and age group.

Writing to a Sequential Access File

You use Visual Basic's **Write # statement** to write a record to a sequential access file. The syntax of the Write # statement is **Write #** *filenumber* [, *expressionlist*]. *Filenumber* is the number used in the Open statement to open the sequential access file, and *expressionlist* is one or more numeric or string expressions, separated by commas. Figure 6-16 shows examples of the Write # statement.

Write statement	Result
Write #1, txtCity.Text	Writes the Text property of the txtCity control to the sequential access data file opened as file #1.
Write #2, stCity, crSales	Writes the contents of both the stCity and crSales variables to the sequential access data file opened as file #2.
Write #1, lstParty.Text, lstAge.ListIndex	Writes the contents of the lstParty control's Text property and the contents of the lstAge control's ListIndex property to the sequential access data file opened as file # 1.

Figure 6-16: Examples of the Write # statement for sequential access files

In this application you want to write the respondent's party and his or her age group to the data file. One method of doing so is to write each list box's Text property to the file; recall that when the user selects an item in a list box, Visual Basic stores the item in its Text property. Therefore, you could use the `Write #1, lstParty.Text, lstAge.Text` statement to write the respondent's record to the data file. If the user selects Democrat from the Political party list box and 36 - 50 from the Age list box, for example, the Write # statement would write `"Democrat","36 - 50"` to the data file.

You can also enter the respondent's information by writing each list box's ListIndex property, rather than its Text property, to the data file. Recall that the ListIndex property stores the index of the currently selected list box item. In other words, you could also use the `Write #1, lstParty.ListIndex, lstAge.ListIndex` statement to write the respondent's record to the data file. If the user selects Democrat from the Political party list box and 36 - 50 from the Age list box, for example, the Write # statement would write `0,1` to the data file. An advantage of writing the ListIndex property, rather than the Text property, is that it results in a smaller data file because fewer characters need to be stored for each record. In this case, instead of storing two strings (`"Democrat","36 - 50"`), the data file would store two numbers (`0,1`). The disadvantage of recording the ListIndex property in the file is that if the contents of the list box change, the value recorded in the file may no longer refer to the correct item in the list. For example, if you were to add a new party as the first item in the Political party list box, the 0 ListIndex value previously recorded in the Pao.dat file would not refer to Democrat; rather it would refer, incorrectly, to the new party.

In this application, you will not be adding any new items to either the Political party or the Age list boxes. So that you can observe the difference between recording the Text property and recording the ListIndex property, you will write the lstParty control's Text property and the lstAge control's ListIndex property to the sequential data file.

To add the Write # statement to the open Code window:

1　The cmdEnter control's Click event procedure should still be open. Type **write #1, lstParty.text, lstAge.listindex** and press the **Enter** key. This statement will write the lstParty control's Text property and the lstAge control's ListIndex property to the Pao.dat file on your Student Disk.

When you are finished with a data file, you should close it.

Closing a Sequential Access File

You use Visual Basic's **Close statement** to close a data file. Its syntax is **Close [# *filenumber*]**, where *filenumber* is the number used in the Open statement to open the file. A Close statement with no arguments closes all open files. When a file is closed, its *filenumber* is disassociated from the file. The *filenumber* can then be used by another file. In this case you want to close the file opened as #1.

To complete the Enter Information button's code, then save and run the application:

1 Maximize the Code window, then enter the Close statement and the documentation shown in Figure 6-17.

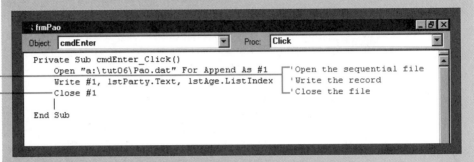

enter this documentation

enter this statement

```
: frmPao                                                    _ 8 X
Object: cmdEnter            ▼    Proc: Click               ▼
    Private Sub cmdEnter_Click()
        Open "a:\tut06\Pao.dat" For Append As #1    ┌'Open the sequential file
        Write #1, lstParty.Text, lstAge.ListIndex   │'Write the record
       ┌Close #1                                    └'Close the file

    End Sub
```

Figure 6-17: Enter Information button's Click event procedure

2 Compare your code with the code shown in Figure 6-17. Make any necessary corrections before continuing to the next step.

3 Close the Code window.

You will now test the Enter Information button by entering the data from three completed questionnaires.

4 Save and run the application.

The first questionnaire is from a Republican in the 18 - 35 age group.

5 Click **Republican** in the Political party list box, then click **18 - 35** in the Age list box. Click the **Enter Information** button. Because the Pao.dat file doesn't yet exist, Visual Basic creates the Pao.dat file on your Student Disk. Visual Basic writes the record to the file, then closes the file before the Click event procedure ends.

The second questionnaire is from a Democrat in the 36 - 50 age group.

6 Click **Democrat** in the Political Party list box, then click **36 - 50** in the Age list box. Click the **Enter Information** button. Visual Basic opens the existing Pao.dat file on your Student Disk, writes the second record to the file, and closes the file. The Click event procedure then ends.

The third questionnaire is from an Independent in the Over 65 age group.

7 Click **Independent** in the Political party list box, then click **Over 65** in the Age list box. Click the **Enter Information** button. Visual Basic opens the existing Pao.dat file on your Student Disk, writes the third record to the file, and closes the file. The Click event procedure then ends.

8 Click the **Exit** button. Visual Basic returns to the design screen.

tips

If you have already completed this lesson and are now practicing it again, you should use the method appropriate for your version of Windows to delete the Pao.dat from your Student Disk before running the PAO application; otherwise, the records will be added to the existing Pao.dat file.

You can use a basic word processor or text editor to verify that the records were written to the data file. For example, Windows 95 has a built-in word processor called WordPad, and Windows 3.1 has a built-in text editor called Notepad; you can use either one to view the contents of a data file. You can also make changes to the data file while you are using a word processor but you must be careful not to add any unnecessary characters—for example, don't leave any blank lines in the file by pressing the Enter key unnecessarily—or Visual Basic will have trouble reading the file. You also must be careful not to remove any needed punctuation. The Pao.dat file, shown in WordPad, would look similar to Figure 6-18.

Figure 6-18: Pao.dat file shown in WordPad

Each line in the data file represents a record and each record is composed of two fields: the respondent's party and his or her age. The two fields are separated by a comma. The party field is a string expression, as indicated by the surrounding quotation marks, and the age field is numeric. When you write a record to a sequential access file, Visual Basic automatically supplies the quotation marks around the string data and separates the data in each field by commas.

Next you will code the Display Totals button.

Coding the Display Totals Button

The pseudocode and flowchart for the Display Totals button's Click event procedure are shown in Figure 6-19. Before coding the Display Totals button, study the logic shown in this figure.

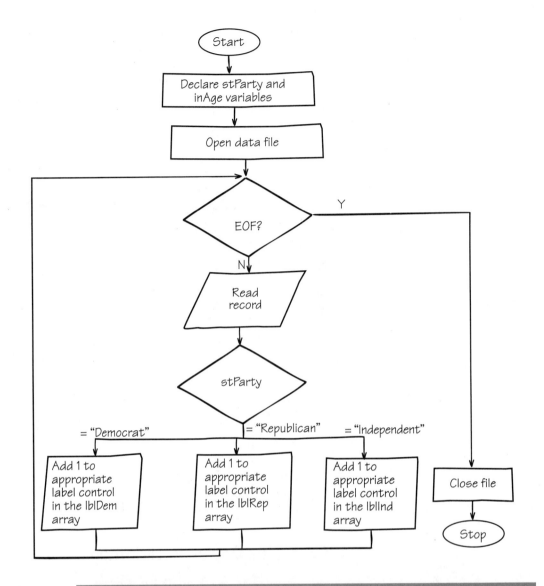

Figure 6-19: Flowchart and pseudocode for the Display Totals button's Click event procedure

After declaring the necessary variables, the Click event opens the sequential access data file, then uses a loop to read each record, one at a time. Recall that each record consists of the respondent's party and his or her age. As each record is read, a Case structure compares the party entry to "Democrat", "Republican", and "Independent". If the respondent is a Democrat, the appropriate label control in the lblDem control array is updated. If the respondent is a Republican, the appropriate label control in the lblRep control array is updated. Lastly, if the respondent is an Independent, the appropriate label control in the lblInd control array is updated. Notice that the loop will stop when there are no more records to read, a point referred to by programmers as "EOF" ("end of file"). When the loop stops, the data file is closed.

To begin coding the Display Totals button:

1   Double-click the **Display Totals** button. The cmdDisplay control's Click event procedure appears.

The Display Totals button's Click event procedure will need two local variables, stParty and inAge. Both variables will be used by the Input # statement to read a record from the data file. You will learn about the Input # statement later on in this lesson.

2   Press the **Tab** key, then type **dim stParty as string, inAge as integer** and press the **Enter** key.

Because you want to read from the file, you will open the file for input.

3   Type one of the following Open statements into the Code window. Which statement you type will depend on the location of your Student Disk. Be sure to type the backslash (\), not the front slash(/), in the appropriate places.

    open "a:\tut06\Pao.dat" for input as #1

    open "b:\tut06\Pao.dat" for input as #1

4   Press the **Enter** key.

The next step is to enter a Do While loop that tells Visual Basic to stop processing the loop instructions when the end of the file is reached.

The EOF Function

You may be wondering how Visual Basic will know when it has reached the end of the file. The answer is that Visual Basic uses a record pointer to keep track of which record it is looking at in the file. When you first open a sequential access file for input, Visual Basic sets the record pointer to the first record in the file. Each time you read a record, the record pointer moves to the next record in the file. (Recall that sequential access files are read sequentially—one record after another in the order in which they were written to the file.) You can use the **EOF function**, which stands for "end of file," along with the Not logical operator to test for the end of the file. The syntax of the EOF function is **EOF**(*filenumber*), where *filenumber* is the number of the file used in the Open statement. When the record pointer is at the end of the file, the EOF function returns the Boolean value True; otherwise, the function returns the Boolean value False. The instruction, `Do While Not EOF(1)`, tells Visual Basic to repeat the loop instructions while it is not the end of the file. When the end of the file is reached, the loop stops.

Recall from Tutorial 4 that the Not operator reverses the truth value of a *condition*.

To continue coding the Display Totals button:

1 The cmdDisplay control's Click event procedure should still be open. Type **do while not eof(1)** and press the **Enter** key. When the application is run, this instruction will tell Visual Basic to look in the Pao.dat file to see if the record pointer is at the end of the file.

According to the pseudocode, you now need to read a record from the open Pao.dat file.

Reading a Record from a Sequential Access File

You use Visual Basic's **Input # statement** to read a record from a sequential access file. The syntax of the Input # statement is **Input #** *filenumber, variablelist*, where *filenumber* is the number used in the Open statement to open the sequential file and *variablelist* is one or more numeric or string variables, separated by commas. Because each variable in the *variablelist* is associated with a field in the record, the number of variables listed in the Input # statement must be the same as the number of fields in the record, and the order of the variables in the *variablelist* must correspond to the order of the fields in the record. In this case, for example, because each record in the Pao.dat file contains two fields—a party and an age— the Input # statement's *variablelist* must contain two variables, stParty and inAge. The stParty variable must be listed first in the *variablelist* because the respondent's party is the first field in his or her record. (Recall that the Write # statement writes the party to the file before it writes the age.) When Visual Basic reads a record from the file, the value in each field is stored in the corresponding variable listed in the *variablelist*. Figure 6-20 illustrates the relationship between the *variablelist* and the fields in a record.

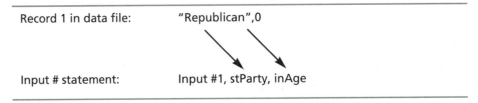

Record 1 in data file: "Republican",0

Input # statement: Input #1, stParty, inAge

Figure 6-20: Relationship between the Input # statement's *variablelist* and the fields in a record

Now add the Input # statement to the Display Totals button.

To continue coding the Display Totals button:

1 The cmdDisplay control's Click event procedure should still be open. Press the **Tab** key, then type **input #1, stParty, inAge** and press the **Enter** key.

The next step in the pseudocode is to use a Case selection structure to update the appropriate label control in one of the three control arrays.

Updating the Appropriate Label Control

For each respondent's record, you will need to add one to the appropriate label control in the interface. In order to understand how the application will determine the appropriate label control to update, you will need to look closely at the names of the label controls in the interface. The label controls and their names are shown in Figure 6-21.

index is 0

index is 1

index is 2

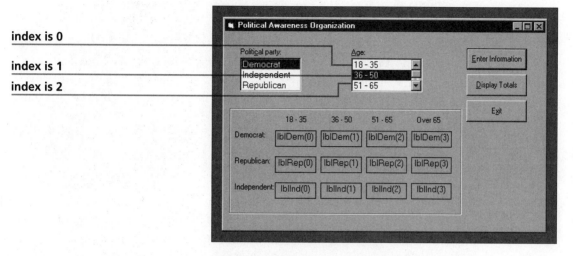

Figure 6-21: Label controls and their names

Notice that each row of label controls belongs to a control array, and each control array is associated with a political party. The four label controls in the first row belong to the lblDem control array, the four in the second row belong to the lblRep control array, and the four in the third row belong to the lblInd control array. You can use the respondent's party, which is stored in the stParty variable, to determine the row of label controls to update.

Also notice in Figure 6-21 that all of the label controls in the first column have an index of 0, the controls in the second column have an index of 1, the controls in the third column have an index of 2, and the controls in the fourth column have an index of 3. The PAO interface was designed so that the indexes of the label controls (0, 1, 2, and 3) in each of the three control arrays (lblDem, lblRep, and lblInd) correspond directly to the indexes of the items listed in the Age list box. For example, the index of the first item (18 - 35) in the Age list box is 0, and so are the indexes of the three label controls that correspond to this age group. Likewise, the index of the second item (36 - 50) in the Age list box is 1, and so are the indexes of its corresponding label controls.

Recall that the Write Information button writes the lstAge control's ListIndex property, which stores the index of the selected item, to the sequential data file. The Input # statement in the Display Totals button reads the index from the file and stores it in the inAge variable. Similar to the way you used the stParty variable to determine the proper array to update, you can use the inAge variable to determine the appropriate label control to update in the array. The statement `lblDem(inAge).Caption = Val(lblDem(inAge).Caption) + 1`, for example, will update the lblDem(0) control if the inAge variable contains the number 0; it will update the lblDem(1) control if inAge contains the number 1, and so on.

tips

Notice that you can also use a label control as a counter.

In summary, you can use the stParty variable to determine which row of label controls to update, and the inAge variable to determine which column.

According to the pseudocode, you will use a Case selection structure, along with the stParty variable, to determine which row to update. Do that now.

To complete the Display Totals button's Click event, then save and run the application:

1 The Display Totals button's Click event should still be open. Type **select case stParty** and press the **Enter** key.

One possibility is that the stParty variable contains "Democrat."

2 Press the **Tab** key, then type **case "Democrat"** and press the **Enter** key.

If the stParty variable contains "Democrat," then the application should update one of the four label controls in the lblDem control array. Which of the four label controls to update depends on the value in the inAge variable.

3 Maximize the Code window. Press the **Tab** key, then type **lblDem(inAge).caption = val(lblDem(inAge).caption) + 1** and press the **Enter** key.

This instruction tells Visual Basic to update the label control whose index matches the number in the inAge variable.

If the respondent is not a Democrat, he or she could be either a Republican or an Independent.

4 Complete the Case structure and the Do While loop as shown in Figure 6-22. Also enter the Close #1 statement to close the Pao.dat file, and the documentation.

enter these seven lines of code and the documentation

```
 frmPao                                                          _ □ X
Object: cmdDisplay          ▼     Proc: Click                        ▼

Private Sub cmdDisplay_Click()
    Dim stParty As String, inAge As Integer
    Open "a:\tut06\Pao.dat" For Input As #1          'open the sequential file
    Do While Not EOF(1)
        Input #1, stParty, inAge                     'read a record
        Select Case stParty                          'update label control
            Case "Democrat"
                lblDem(inAge).Caption = Val(lblDem(inAge).Caption) + 1
            Case "Republican"
                lblRep(inAge).Caption = Val(lblRep(inAge).Caption) + 1
            Case "Independent"
                lblInd(inAge).Caption = Val(lblInd(inAge).Caption) + 1
        End Select
    Loop
    Close #1                                          'close the file

End Sub
```

Figure 6-22: Completed Display Totals button's Click event procedure

5 Close the Code window, then **save** and **run** the application.

6 Click the **Display Totals** button. The interface appears as shown in Figure 6-23. (Recall that you wrote three records to the Pao.dat file when you tested the Enter Information button.)

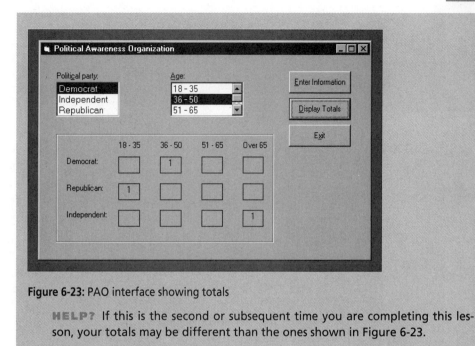

Figure 6-23: PAO interface showing totals

HELP? If this is the second or subsequent time you are completing this lesson, your totals may be different than the ones shown in Figure 6-23.

7 Click the **Exit** button to end the application.

You have now completed Lesson A. You can either take a break or complete the end-of-lesson questions and exercises.

S U M M A R Y

To add a list box to the form:

- Use the ListBox tool 📖.
- Use the AddItem method to specify the items you want to display in the list box. The syntax of the AddItem method is *Control*.**AddItem** *item*. Enter the AddItem instructions in the appropriate event procedure, which is usually the form's Load event procedure.
- Use the ListIndex property to refer to the location of an item in a list box.

To execute instructions automatically when a form is loaded into memory:

- Enter the instructions in the form's Load event procedure.

To open a sequential access data file:

- Use the Open statement. Its syntax is **Open** *filename* **For** *mode* **As** **#** *filenumber*.
- *Filename* is the name of the file, including the drive letter and path, and must be enclosed in quotation marks.
- *Mode* can be Input, Output, or Append. Use Input mode to open the file for reading. Use Output mode to create a new file and write information to it. Use Append mode to add records to an existing file.
- *Filenumber* is an integer expression with a value between 1 and 511, inclusive.

To write a record to an open sequential access file:

■ Use the Write # statement. Its syntax is **Write #** *filenumber* [, *expressionlist*].
■ *Filenumber* is the number used in the Open statement to open the sequential access file. *Expressionlist* is one or more numeric or string variables separated by a comma.

To close a file:

■ Use the Close statement. Its syntax is **Close** [# *filenumber*][, # *filenumber*]....
■ *Filenumber* is the number used in the Open statement to open the file. A Close statement with no arguments closes all open files.

To read a record from an open sequential access file:

■ Use the Input # statement. Its syntax is **Input #** *filenumber*, *variablelist*.
■ *Filenumber* is the number used in the Open statement to open the sequential access file. *Variablelist* is one or more numeric or string variables, separated by commas. Each variable in the list is associated with a field in the record.

To test for the end of the file:

■ Use the EOF function. Its syntax is **EOF**(*filenumber*). *Filenumber* is the number of the file used in the Open statement.

Q U E S T I O N S

1. You use this method to define the items in a list box control.
   a. AddItem
   b. Addlist
   c. ItemAdd
   d. ItemDefine
   e. ListAdd

2. The Windows standard for list boxes is to show a minimum of _____ selections, and a maximum of _____ selections at a time.
   a. three, eight
   b. three, seven
   c. two, eight
   d. two, seven
   e. two, six

3. When you select an item in a list box, Visual Basic stores the item in the list box's _____ property.
   a. AddItem
   b. Caption
   c. Item
   d. ListIndex
   e. Text

4. Sorting means arranging information in _____ order.
   a. alphabetical
   b. chronological
   c. numerical
   d. all of the above

5. To sort the list box items, set the list box's _____ property to True.
   a. Alignment
   b. Alphabetical
   c. Arrangement
   d. Sorted
   e. Text

6. The _____ property stores the index of the currently selected list box item.
   a. Caption
   b. Index
   c. List
   d. ListIndex
   e. ListNum

7. This event occurs when an application is run.
   a. Copy_Form
   b. Form_Run
   c. Load
   d. Run
   e. Run_Form

8. Which of the following will add the word DESK to a list box named lstOffice?
   a. AddItem.lstOffice DESK
   b. AddItem.lstOffice "DESK"
   c. ItemAdd.lstOffice "DESK"
   d. lstOffice.AddItem "DESK"
   e. lstOffice.ItemAdd DESK

9. Which of the following will display 1997 in a list box named lstYear?
   a. AddItem.lstYear 1997
   b. AddItem.lstYear "1997"
   c. ItemAdd.lstYear "1997"
   d. lstYear.AddItem "1997"
   e. lstYear.ItemAdd 1997

10. The second item in a list box has a ListIndex of _____ .
    a. 1
    b. 2
    c. 3

11. This assignment statement will select the first item in a list box named lstTerm.
    a. lstTerm.ItemList = 0
    b. lstTerm.ListIndex = 0
    c. lstTerm.ListIndex = 1
    d. lstTerm.ListItem = 1
    e. lstTerm.ListNum = 0

12. A _____ , also called a data element, is a single item of information about a person, place, or thing.
    a. data file
    b. field
    c. program file
    d. record

13. A group of related data elements that contain all of the data about a specific person, place, or thing is called a _____ .
    a. data file
    b. field
    c. program file
    d. record

14. A collection of related records is called a _____ .
    a. data file
    b. field
    c. program file
    d. record collection

15. You open a sequential file for _____ when you want to read its contents.
    a. Append
    b. Input
    c. Output
    d. Read
    e. Sequential

16. You open a sequential file for _____ when you want to create a new file and write information to it.
    a. Append
    b. Input
    c. Output
    d. Read
    e. Sequential

17. You open a sequential file for _____ when you want to add information to an existing file.
    a. Append
    b. Input
    c. Output
    d. Read
    e. Sequential

18. Which of the following is a valid Open statement?
    a. Open a:\data.dat for sequential as #1
    b. Open a:\data.dat for "append" as #1
    c. Open "a:\data.dat" for append as #1
    d. Open "a:\data.dat" for append
    e. Open "a:\data.dat" for sequential as #1

19. Which of the following is a valid Write statement?
    a. Write #1, Lname, Fname
    b. Write, Lname, Fname to #1
    c. Write to #1, Lname, Fname
    d. Write, #1, Lname, Fname
    e. Write Lname, Fname, to #1

20. Which of the following will close a file opened as file number #3?
   a. Close filenumber 3
   b. Close #3 file
   c. Close file #3
   d. Close #3
   e. Close file 3

21. Which of the following will correctly update a counter named inTotal?
   a. inTotal = inTotal + crAge
   b. inTotal = inTotal + 1
   c. inTotal + crAge = inTotal
   d. inTotal + 1 = inTotal
   e. inTotal = 1

22. Which two of the following will stop the loop when the record pointer is at the end of the file opened as #1?
   a. Do While EOF(1)
   b. Do Until EOF(1)
   c. Do While Not EOF(1)
   d. Do Until Not EOF(1)

23. The "EOF" in the EOF function stands for _____ .
   a. each open file
   b. end of file
   c. end of function
   d. every open file

24. Which of the following is a correct Input statement?
   a. Input #1, stName, inSalary
   b. Input stName, inSalary as #1
   c. Input into #1, stName, inSalary
   d. Input stName, inSalary into #1

25. Explain how you give keyboard access to a list box.

E X E R C I S E S

NOTE: When creating the user interfaces for the applications in this lesson, be sure to follow all GUI design rules. For example, assign access key to the essential components of the interface, center the form, highlight the existing text in a text box, create a default command button (if appropriate), and so on.

1. In this exercise you will use a list box and the Case selection structure.

Scenario: At work you typically call ten people. Rather than having to look up each person's telephone extension in the company's directory, create an application that will display the extension when you click the person's name in a list box. Use the following names and extensions:

Name	Extension	Name	Extension
Smith, Joe	3388	Patel, Orman	4566
Jones, Mary	3356	White, Pam	2993
Adkari, Joel	2487	Abram, Jill	3023
Lin, Sue	1111	Chen, Sue	2119
Li, Vicky	2222	Dune, Joe	2187

   a. Create the user interface. Include a list box and a label control. Also include Print and Exit buttons. (Include any other controls as necessary.)

   b. Save the form and the project as la1Done in the Tut06 folder on your Student Disk.

   c. Set the list box's Font property to 12 points. Set its Sorted property to True.

   d. Code the form's Load event so that it fills the list box with data, then selects the first item in the list. (The names are shown above.)

   e. Code the Exit button so that it unloads the form when clicked.

   f. Code the form's Unload event so that it asks the user if he or she wants to leave the application.

   g. Code the Print button so that it prints the form when clicked.

   h. Code the list box's Click event so that it displays the correct extension when a name is clicked in the list box. (The extensions are shown above.)

   i. Save and run the application. Test the application by selecting Sue Lin's entry in the list box. Print the form with the test data showing.

   j. Exit the application. Print the code.

   k. Submit the printout from step i and the code from step j.

2. In this exercise you will open, write, and close a sequential access file. You will also print the file in WordPad (*Notepad in Windows 3.1*).

Scenario: Consolidated Advertising, a new advertising firm, sends mail-order catalogs to businesses in many U.S. cities. They want an application that will record the various cities and their corresponding zip codes. Use the following information:

Darien	60561
Hinsdale	60544
Glen Ellyn	60137
Downers Grove	60135
Burr Ridge	60136

   a. Create the user interface. Include two text boxes: one for the user to enter the city and the other for the zip code. Also include two command buttons: Record Information and Exit. (Include any other controls as necessary.)

   b. Save the form and the project as la2Done in the Tut06 folder on your Student Disk.

   c. Code the Exit button so that it unloads the form when clicked.

   d. Code the form's Unload event so that it asks the user if he or she wants to leave the application.

   e. Code the Record Information button so that it writes the city and its zip code to a sequential access file named la2.dat in the Tut06 folder on your Student Disk.

   f. Save and run the application. Test the application by entering the cities and zip codes shown above.

   g. Exit the application. Print the form and the code.

   h. Switch to WordPad (*Notepad in Windows 3.1*). Open the la2.dat file, then print the data file.

   i. Submit the printout and code from step g, and the printout from step h.

3. In this exercise you will open, read, write, and close a sequential access file.

Scenario: Boggs Inc. wants an application that will calculate the average price of all of the items in inventory. The user will enter the item's inventory number, the quantity in stock, and the item's price. The application should record the inventory number, quantity, and price in a sequential access file. When the user clicks the Display Average button, the application should display the average price.

   a. Create the user interface. Include three text boxes: one for the user to enter the inventory number, another for the quantity, and another for the price. Also include a label control and four command buttons: Record Information, Display Average, Print, and Exit. (Include any other controls as necessary.)

   b. Save the form and the project as la3Done in the Tut06 folder on your Student Disk.

   c. Code the Exit button so that it unloads the form when clicked.

d. Code the form's Unload event so that it asks the user if he or she wants to leave the application.

e. Code the Record Information button so that it writes the item's inventory number, quantity, and price to a sequential access file named la3.dat in the Tut06 folder on your Student Disk.

f. Code the Display Average button so that it calculates and displays the average price of the inventory items.

g. Code the Print button so that it prints the form.

h. Save and run the application. Test the application by entering the following data. (Be sure to click the Record Information button after entering each record.)

Inventory Number	Quantity	Item Price
ABC12	100	10.50
XYZ35	50	15.99
KLK25	150	20.00

i. After entering the three records, click the Display Average button to display the average price in the label control, then click the Print button to print the interface.

j. Exit the application. Print the code.

k. Switch to WordPad (*Notepad in Windows 3.1*). Open the la3.dat file located in the Tut06 folder on your Student Disk, then print the data file.

l. Submit the printout from step i, the code from step j, and the printout from step k.

Exercises 4 through 10 are Discovery Exercises, which allow you to both "discover" the solutions to problems on your own and to experiment with material that is not covered in the tutorial.

discovery ▶ 4. In this exercise you will modify the la1Done project, which you created in Exercise 1, so that it loads information from a sequential access file into a list box.

Scenario: In Lesson A's Exercise 1, you created an application that displayed a telephone extension when you clicked a person's name in a list box. In that application you entered 10 AddItem instructions in the form's Load event procedure—one AddItem instruction for each of the 10 names. In this exercise, you will remove the 10 AddItem instructions from the form's Load event and replace them with code that reads the names from a sequential access file. The names shown in Exercise 1 have already been entered into a sequential access file for you. The file's name is la4.dat.

a. Open the la1Done (la1done.vbp) project that you created in Lesson A's Exercise 1.

b. Save the form and the project as la4Done in the Tut06 folder on your Student Disk.

c. Remove the 10 AddItem instructions from the form's Load event.

d. Code the form's Load event so that it reads the 10 names from the la4.dat file, which is located in the Tut06 folder on your Student Disk. As each name is read, the name should be entered into the list box.

e. Save and run the application. Test the application by selecting Pam White's entry in the list box. Click the Print button to print the interface.

f. Exit the application. Print the code.

g. Submit the printout from step e and the code from step f.

discovery ▶ 5. In this exercise you will search a sequential access file for a zip code, then display the corresponding city.

Scenario: Dr. Jonas, a dentist, has many patients under the age of 10. To encourage these patients to brush their teeth regularly, she mails them monthly reminder cards. Dr. Jonas wants an application that her receptionist can use to record the names, addresses, and birthdays of the patients that are under the age of 10. To make the information easier for the receptionist to enter, the application should display the appropriate city when the receptionist enters the zip code. The zip codes and cities have already been entered into a sequential access file for you. The name of the file is la5Zip.dat.

a. Create the user interface shown in Figure 6-24.

Figure 6-24

b. Save the form and the project as la5Done in the Tut06 folder on your Student Disk.
c. Use the Help menu to search for the LostFocus event's Help window. Notice that the LostFocus event occurs when a control loses the focus.
d. Use WordPad (*Notepad in Windows 3.1*) to print the la5Zip.dat file, which is located in the Tut06 folder on your Student Disk.
e. Code the txtZip control's LostFocus event so that it searches the la5Zip.dat file for the zip code entered in the txtZip control, then displays the corresponding city in the lblCity control. The la5Zip.dat file is located in the Tut06 folder on your Student Disk.
f. Code the Record Patient button so that it writes the patient's name, address, city, zip code, and birthday to a sequential access file named la5.dat.
g. Code the Exit button so that it unloads the form when clicked.
h. Code the form's Unload event so that it asks the user if he or she wants to leave the application.
i. Save and run the application. Test the application by entering the following patient information: Sally Bramas, 123 Main Street, 60137, 3/9/75. Click the Record Patient button. Glen Ellyn should appear in the lblCity control.
j. Exit the application. Print the code.
k. Open the la5.dat file in WordPad (*Notepad in Windows 3.1*). Print the file.
l. Submit the code from step j and the printouts from steps d and k.

discovery ▶ **6.** In this exercise you will use a list box and an image control array.

Important Note: You will not be able to complete this Discovery Exercise if you are using the Visual Basic Working Model. You will need to use either the Standard Edition or the Professional Edition.

Scenario: Create an application that displays an icon when the user makes a selection in a list box. The application should also print the form.

a. Create the user interface shown in Figure 6-25.

imgElement

imgIcons (4)

imgIcons (3)

imgIcons (2)

imgIcons (0)

imgIcons (1)

Figure 6-25

The icons are in the main Visual Basic folder, which is located on either the local hard drive or network drive. The main Visual Basic folder in Windows 95 is typically Microsoft Visual Basic; it is vb in Windows 3.1. The icons for the control array are as follows.

Image control	Icon file
imgIcons(0)	\icons\elements\cloud (or \icons\elements\cloud.ico)
imgIcons(1)	\icons\elements\litening (or \icons\elements\litening.ico)
imgIcons(2)	\icons\elements\rain (or \icons\elements\rain.ico)
imgIcons(3)	\icons\elements\snow (or \icons\elements\snow.ico)
imgIcons(4)	\icons\elements\sun (or \icons\elements\sun.ico)

b. Save the form and the project as la6Done in the Tut06 folder on your Student Disk.

c. Set the list box's Font property to 12 points. Set its Sorted property to True.

d. Code the form's Load event so that it fills the list box with the following data: Cloud, Rain, Snow, Sun, Lightning. When the interface appears on the screen, the first item in the list box should be selected and its corresponding icon from the imgIcons control array should be displayed in the imgElement control.

e. Set the imgElement control's BorderStyle property to 1-Fixed Single. Set its Stretch property to True.

f. Code the Exit button so that it ends the application when clicked.

g. Code the Print button so that it prints the form when clicked.

h. Code the list box's Click event so that it displays, in the imgElement control, the correct icon from the imgIcons control array.

i. Save and run the application. Test the application by selecting Snow in the list box. The appropriate icon should appear in the imgElement control. Click the Print button.

j. Exit the application. Print the code.

k. Submit the printout from step i and the code from step j.

discovery ▶ 7. In this exercise you will learn about the Printer object and the EndDoc method. You will use both to modify the laPao project that you created in Lesson A.

Scenario: As you learned in Tutorial 4's Debugging Section, you can use the Print method to print the contents of a variable on the form. Its syntax is Print [*expression-list*]. For example, `Print stName, stCity` will print the contents of both variables on the form. `Print "Hello"` will print the word Hello on the form. If you don't include an *expressionlist* in the Print method, Visual Basic prints a blank line.

To print information on the printer, simply include both the `Printer` keyword and a period before the Print method, like this: `Printer.Print stName, stCity`. The **Printer** keyword, which refers to the Printer object, tells Visual Basic to print the information on the printer instead of on the form.

In Visual Basic you use the EndDoc method to tell the printer that the end of the document has been reached, so the printer should print the page and then eject the paper to the next page. The syntax of the EndDoc method is simply **Printer.EndDoc**.

In this exercise you will modify the laPao project that you created in Lesson A to include a command button that will print the contents of the sequential access file.

a. Open the laPao (lapao.vbp) project that you created in Lesson A. The project is located in the Tut06 folder on your Student Disk.

b. Save the form and the project as la7Done in the Tut06 folder on your Student Disk.

c. Add a command button to the form. Set its Name property to cmdPrint, then set its caption to <u>P</u>rint File. Position the Print File button between the Display Totals and Exit buttons.

d. When printing the contents of a data file, programmers often include an "End of Print Job" message at the end of the data file so they can quickly verify that the entire file was printed. Code the Print File button so that it prompts the user to turn on the printer, then prints the contents of the laPao.dat file on the printer, followed by a blank line, and then a line that contains the "End of Print Job" message. The laPao.dat file is in the Tut06 folder on your Student Disk.

e. Save and run the application. Enter the following two records. Be sure to select the Write Information button after entering each one.

     Democrat   18 - 35
     Republican   Over 65

f. Click the Print File button to print the contents of the laPao.dat file on the printer.

g. Exit the application, then print the code.

h. Submit the printout from step f and the code from step g.

discovery ▶ 8. In this exercise you will learn about the Kill statement and the Dir function. You will use both to modify the laPao project that you created in Lesson A.

Scenario: Recall from Lesson A that you can't open a file for Input unless the file exists. If you try to open a file that doesn't exist, Visual Basic displays an error message. Currently, the laPao project's Display Totals button, which opens the laPao.dat file for Input, will result in an error if the data file does not exist in the Tut06 folder on your Student Disk. You can use the Dir function to verify that the file exists before you try opening it. You will modify the laPao project accordingly.

You will also make another modification to the laPao project. At the beginning of each year, the PAO secretary needs to erase the contents of the lbPao.dat file so he or she can begin entering the data for the new year. You will add a command button to the laPao project's interface that allows the secretary to do that. You will use the Kill statement in the command button's code.

a. Open the laPao (lapao.vbp) project that you created in Lesson A. The laPao project is located in the Tut06 folder on your Student Disk.

b. Save the form and the project as la8Done in the Tut06 folder on your Student Disk.

c. Use the Help menu to display the Dir function's Help window. Notice what the function returns when the file does not exist.

d. Open the Print Report button's code window. Use the Dir function to verify that the laPao.dat file exists. If it doesn't, display a message for the user, then return the user to the application.

e. Use the Help menu to display the Kill statement's Help window.

f. Add a command button to the form. Set its Name property to cmdNew, then set its caption to <u>N</u>ew File. Position the New File button above the Exit button.

g. Code the New File button so that it prompts the user to verify that he or she wants to erase the current file. Erase the current file from the disk only if the user wants to do so.

h. Save and run the application. Add the following two records. Be sure to select the Write Information button after entering each one.

     Republican 18 - 35
     Independent 51 - 65

i. Click the Display Report button to display the report. No error message should appear because the laPao.dat file does exist on the disk.

j. Use the New File button to erase the contents of the laPao.dat file.

k. Click the Display Report button to display the report. An error message should appear because the laPao.dat file does not exist on the disk. After removing the error message, the user should be returned to the application.

l. Exit the application, then print the code.

m. Submit the code from step l.

discovery ▶ 9. In this exercise you will create a multiselection list box. You will use three new list box properties: MultiSelect, Selected, and List.

Scenario: The list box control has a MultiSelect property that determines whether a user can make multiple selections in a list box control, and how the multiple selections can be made. When you create a list box control, Visual Basic also creates a List property array and a Selected property array.

a. Use the Help menu to research the list box's MultiSelect property.

b. Explain the difference between the three settings of the MultiSelect property.

c. Open a new project. Add a command button and a list box to the form. Set the list box's Sorted property to True. Leave the list box's MultiSelect property at its default value 0-None.

d. Save the form and the project as la9Done in the Tut06 folder on your Student Disk.

e. Code the form's Load event so that it fills the list box with the following five names: Ahmad, Jim, Debbie, Jeanne, Bill.

f. Code the command button so that it prints the selected item on the form. In other words, if the user clicks Debbie in the list box, and then clicks the command button, the name Debbie will print on the form.

g. Save and run the application. To test the application, click Debbie in the list box, then click the command button. The name Debbie should print on the form.

h. Exit the application and print the code.

i. Use the Help menu to research the list box control's Selected property and its List property.

j. Explain the purpose of a list box control's Selected and List properties.

k. Change the list box's MultiSelect property to 1-Simple. Change the code in the command button so that it prints the selected items on the form. In other words, if the user clicks Ahmad and Jeanne in the list box, the names Ahmad and Jeanne should print on the form.

l. Save and run the application. To test the application, click Ahmad, Debbie, and Jeanne to select the items in the list box. Click Debbie to deselect that item. Click the command button. The names Ahmad and Jeanne should print on the form.

m. Exit the application.

n. Change the list box's MultiSelect property to 2-Extended.

o. Save and run the application. To test the application, click Ahmad in the list box to select that item, then use Shift + Click to select Jim in the list box. All of the names should be highlighted in the list box. Use Ctrl + Click to deselect Debbie and Bill in the list. Use Ctrl + Click to select Bill in the list box. Click the command button. The names Ahmad, Bill, Jeanne, and Jim should print on the form.

p. Exit the application and print the code.

q. Submit the written explanations from steps b and j, and the code from steps h and p.

discovery ▶ 10. In this exercise you will move items from one list box to another. You will use one new list box control method (RemoveItem) and three new properties (MultiSelect, List, and Selected).

Scenario: ABC Corporation maintains two sequential access files. One of the files stores the active employees and the other stores the inactive employees. At the end of each year, the corporation's Personnel department reviews the names in the active file. Employees who are no longer active are removed from the active file and are added to the inactive file. Employees who are reactivated are removed from the inactive file and added to the active file. Employees who the personnel clerk knows will never be reactivated are removed permanently from the inactive file. ABC Corporation wants an application that they can use to handle this process for the personnel clerk.

a. Use the method appropriate for your version of Windows to make a copy of the la10act.ori and la10inac.ori files, which are located in the Tut06 folder on your Student Disk. Name the copied files la10act.dat and la10inac.dat, respectively, and place them in the Tut06 folder on your Student Disk. Remember that you can always recopy the .ori files if your .dat files get ruined while you are doing this exercise.

b. Use WordPad (*Notepad in Windows 3.1*) to print the la10act.dat and la10inac.dat files. Mark the printout "Step b."

c. Open a new project. Use the Help menu to research the list box control's RemoveItem method, and its MultiSelect, Selected, and List properties.

d. Create an appropriate interface. The interface must include two list boxes: one for the names of the active employees and the other for the names of the inactive employees.

e. Name one list box lstActive; name the other lstInactive. Set both list box controls' Sorted property to True. Set both list box controls' MultiSelect property to 1-Simple.

f. Save the form and the project as la10Done in the Tut06 folder on your Student Disk.

g. Code the form's Load event so that it adds the contents of the la10act.dat file to the lstActive list box, and adds the contents of the la10inac.dat file to the lstInactive list box.

h. Code the application so that it removes the selected items from the lstActive list box, and adds them to the lstInactive list box. The application should also allow the clerk to remove the selected items from the lstInactive list box and add them to the lstActive list box.

i. Save and run the application. Test the application to see if it is working correctly. Correct any errors before continuing to the next step.

j. Code the application so that it writes the contents of the lstActive control to the la10act.dat file, and writes the contents of the lstInactive control to the la10inac.dat file. The la10act.dat file should contain only active employees, and the la10inac.dat file should contain only inactive employees.

k. Save and run the application. To test the application, place Tom Willard and Jerry Krisen in the inactive list, then write the information to the files. Exit the application, then run the application again. The two names should appear in the lstInactive list box, and not in the lstActive list box. Exit the application.

l. Use WordPad (*Notepad in Windows 3.1*) to print the la10act.dat and la10inac.dat files. Mark the printouts "Step l."

m. Run the application again. To test the application, place Tom Willard back on the active list, then write the information to the files. Exit the application, then run the application again. Tom Willard's name should appear in the lstActive list box, and not in the lstInactive list box. Exit the application.

n. Use WordPad (*Notepad in Windows 3.1*) to print the la10act.dat and la10inac.dat files. Mark the printouts "Step n."

o. Code the application so that the personnel clerk can remove, permanently, the selected items from both the lstInactive list box and from the la10inac.dat file.

p. Save and run the application. To test the application, remove Jerry Krisen and Scotty Jones from the inactive list and from the file. Exit the application, then run the application again. The names Jerry Krisen and Scotty Jones should not appear in either list box. Exit the application.

q. Use WordPad (*Notepad in Windows 3.1*) to print the la10act.dat and la10inac.dat files. Mark the printouts "Step q."

r. Print the form and the code.

s. Submit the printouts from steps b, l, n, and q, and the form and code from step r.

In this lesson you will learn how to:

- Set a text box control's MultiLine and ScrollBars properties
- Code the Resize event
- Set the ScaleHeight and ScaleWidth properties
- Add a menu control to the form
- Access the Clipboard object using the Clear, GetText(), and SetText methods
- Select text with the SelText Property

Menus

Creating the Text Editor

In this lesson you will create a simple text editor that the PAO's secretary can use to type the PAO report, which is sent to the organization's members and to various political offices in the district. The sketch of the user interface is shown in Figure 6-26.

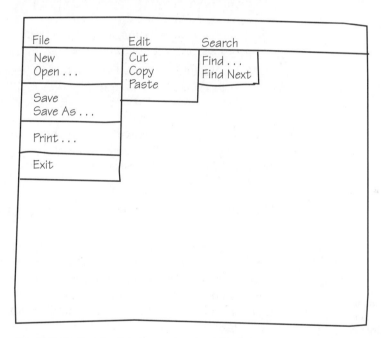

Figure 6-26: Sketch of the text editor's interface

First create the text editor's user interface.

To create the text editor's interface:

1 Start Visual Basic and open a new project, if necessary.

2 Display the Properties windows. Set the form's Name property to **frmEdit**, then set its Caption property to **Document - Text Editor**.

3 Set the form's WindowState property to **2-Maximized**. Recall that when the WindowState property is set to 2-Maximized, Visual Basic maximizes the form when the application is run.

The text editor's interface will contain one text box.

4   Double-click the **TextBox tool** [ab] in the toolbox. Display the Properties window. Remove the Text1 from the Text property. Set the text box's Name property to **txtEdit**. Drag the text box to the upper-left corner of the form. Verify, in the Properties window, that the text box's Left property is 0 and its Top property is 0.

5   Click the **form** to select it. The form's title bar should be highlighted. Click the **Lock Controls** button [icon] to lock the text box on the form.

6   Save the form and the project as **lbEdit** in the Tut06 folder on your Student Disk.

Now enter the instructions to center the form on the screen. Although the form will initially display maximized because its WindowState property is set to 2-Maximized, the user can still use the Restore button to restore it to its standard size. When the form is at its standard size, it should be centered on the screen.

7   Double-click the **form** to open its Code window. The Load event appears. Maximize the Code window. Press the **Tab** key, then type **frmEdit.top = (screen.height - frmEdit.height) / 2** and press the **Enter** key. Type **frmEdit.left = (screen.width - frmEdit.width) / 2** and press the **Enter** key.

8   Close the Code window, then **save** and **run** the application. The form should appear maximized on the screen. Restore the form to its standard size. The form should be centered on the screen.

9   Click the **End** button [icon] on the toolbar to end the application. Visual Basic returns to the design screen.

The txtEdit text box will need to both accept and display multiple lines of text entered by the user. To accomplish this, you will need to set the text box control's MultiLine and ScrollBars properties.

The MultiLine Property and the ScrollBars Property

The **MultiLine property** controls how many lines can appear in a text box. When the property is set at its default value of False, only one line of text can be entered in the text box. When the MultiLine property is set to True, on the other hand, the text box can both accept and display more than one line of text. Visual Basic automatically wraps the text in a multiline box if the text extends beyond the size of the box.

The **ScrollBars property** specifies whether a text box has no scroll bars (the default), horizontal scroll bars, vertical scroll bars, or both horizontal and vertical scroll bars. The scroll bars allow the user to scroll the text box in order to view all of the text. In this application, you will place a vertical scroll bar on the text box so that the user can scroll the text from top to bottom.

To set the MultiLine and ScrollBars properties:

1 Click the **txtEdit control**. Display the Properties window. Set the txtEdit control's MultiLine property to **True**, then set its ScrollBars property to **2-Vertical**.

2 Click the **form** to remove the Properties window. A scroll bar now appears along the right border of the txtEdit control.

In the next section you will learn how to change the size of a control when the size of the form changes. In this application, you will want the text box to size along with the form.

Sizing a Control Along with the Form

In Lesson B's Discovery Exercise 4 you will observe the difference between the Height, Width, ScaleHeight, and ScaleWidth properties.

In previous tutorials, you have had experience with an object's Height and Width properties. Those properties measure the size of the object from the center of one border to the center of the opposite border. A form also has a ScaleHeight property and a ScaleWidth property. The ScaleHeight and ScaleWidth properties measure the interior of the form—the area between the form's borders.

In order to size the txtEdit control so that it fits the interior of the form, you simply need to assign the form's ScaleHeight property to the txtEdit control's Height property, and assign the form's ScaleWidth property to the txtEdit control's Width property. Assigning the value in the form's ScaleHeight property to the text box's Height property tells Visual Basic to size the text box so that it fits within the form's top and bottom borders. Likewise, assigning the value in the form's ScaleWidth property to the text box's Width property tells Visual Basic to size the text box so that it fits within the form's left and right borders. You will place both assignment statements in the form's Resize event so that the statements are processed whenever the size of the form changes. A form's **Resize event** occurs when the form is first displayed on the screen; it also occurs when the user changes the size of the form either by minimizing, maximizing, or restoring it, or by using the form's borders to resize it.

To size the text box along with the form:

1 Double-click the **form** to open its Code window. Use the Proc box to open the form's Resize event. Enter the code shown in Figure 6-27.

```
frmEdit                                              _ □ ×
Object: Form            ▼      Proc: Resize              ▼
Private Sub Form_Resize()
    txtEdit.Height = frmEdit.ScaleHeight
    txtEdit.Width = frmEdit.ScaleWidth
    |
End Sub
```

Figure 6-27: Form's Resize event

2 Close the Code window. **Save** and **run** the application. The form's Resize event sizes the txtEdit control so that it fills the interior of the form.

3 Restore the form to its standard size. The code in the Resize event sizes the
txtEdit control accordingly.

4 Click the **End** button ▣ on the toolbar to stop the application.

In addition to a text box, the text editor's user interface will also contain a
menu control.

Adding a Menu Control to the Form

In Visual Basic, you create a menu in the **Menu Editor**. The menus you create can
contain the following elements: menu titles, menu items, submenu titles, and submenu items. Figure 6-28 identifies the location of these elements in a menu.

separator bar

Figure 6-28: Menu elements in a menu

As Figure 6-28 shows, menu titles appear on the menu bar at the top of the
form. When you click a menu title, its corresponding menu opens and displays a
list of options, called menu items. These menu items can be commands (such as
Open or Exit), separator bars, or submenu titles. As in all Windows applications,
clicking a command in a menu executes the command, and clicking a submenu
title opens an additional menu of options. The purpose of a separator bar is to
group related menu items together.

Although you can create up to four levels of submenus, it's best to use only
one level in your application. Too many layers of submenus can be confusing.
Create a menu for the text editor application.

tips

• • • • • • • • • • • • • •

**You can also open the
Menu Editor by clicking
Tools, then clicking Menu
Editor, or by pressing
Ctrl + E.**

To display the Menu Editor window:

1 Click the **Menu Editor** button ▣ on the toolbar. The Menu Editor appears
on the screen. See Figure 6-29.

HELP? If the Menu Editor button is dimmed, click the form to select it, then
repeat Step 1. Either the form or one of its controls must be selected in order
to open the Menu Editor.

properties

Menu Editor buttons

**list box that displays
created controls**

Figure 6-29: Menu Editor

The top portion of the Menu Editor contains the properties associated with menu controls. At the bottom of the Menu Editor is a list box that displays the menu controls as you are creating them. Visual Basic treats each entry in the list box as a separate menu control, so each entry can have its own properties and its own Visual Basic code.

Immediately above the list box are seven buttons. Figure 6-30 explains the purpose of each button.

Button	Purpose
Left arrow and right arrow	Changes the indentation level of a menu control
Up arrow and down arrow	Moves a menu control to another location in the list box
Next	Creates a new menu control or moves the highlight to the next menu control in the list
Insert	Inserts a new menu control above the highlighted menu control
Delete	Deletes the highlighted menu control

Figure 6-30: The Menu Editor's buttons

You must complete the Caption property and the Name property for each menu control in the list box. The Caption property controls the text appearing on the menu control, and the Name property gives the menu control a name to which you can refer when writing Visual Basic code.

Menu title captions, which appear in the title bar, should be one word only, with the first letter capitalized. Each menu title should have a unique access key. Menu item captions, on the other hand, can be from one to three words. Use book title capitalization for the menu item captions, and assign each menu item a

tips

You learned about access keys in Tutorial 2. A menu title's access key allows the user to open the menu by pressing the Alt key in combination with the access key. A menu item's access key, however, allows the user to select the item simply by pressing the access key when the menu is open.

unique access key. If a menu item requires additional information from the user, the Windows standard is to place an ellipsis (...) at the end of its caption. The ellipsis alerts the user that the command will require more information before it can be processed.

If a menu item is not applicable to the current state of the application—for example, the Cut command on an Edit menu is not applicable until the user makes a selection in the document—you can disable the item either by setting its Enabled property to False in code or by deselecting the Enabled property in the Menu Editor. A disabled menu item appears dimmed when the menu is open.

The Menu Editor also allows you to assign shortcut keys to menu items. **Shortcut keys**, which are displayed to the right of the menu items, allow you to select an item without opening the menu. For example, in Windows applications you can select the Open command when the File menu is closed by pressing Ctrl + O. You should assign shortcut keys to commonly used menu items.

Be sure that the menus you create follow the standard conventions used in other Windows programs. For example, the File menu is always the first menu title on the menu bar. The File menu typically contains commands for opening, saving, and printing files, as well as exiting the application. The text editor's File menu will contain six commands: New, Open, Save, Save As, Print, and Exit.

In addition to the File menu, the text editor will also include an Edit menu and a Search menu. The Edit menu will have three commands: Cut, Copy, and Paste. The Search menu will have two commands: Find and Find Next. You will begin by coding the Exit command on the File menu. As is customary in Windows applications, the letter "F" will be the File menu's access key. To stipulate this, you type an ampersand before the letter in the menu name that you want designated as an access key.

tips

The difference between a menu item's access key and its shortcut key is that the access key can be used only when the menu is open; the shortcut key can be used only when the menu is closed.

GUI Design Tips

Designing Menus

- Menu titles, which appear on the menu bar, should be one word, with the first letter capitalized. Each menu title should have a unique access key.

- Menu items, which appear on a menu, can be from one to three words. Use book title capatilization and assign a unique access key to each item. Assign shortcut keys to commonly used menu items.

- If a menu item requires additional information from the user, place an ellipsis (...) after the item's Caption.

- Follow the Windows standards for the placement of menu titles and items. For example, the File menu is always the first menu title, and it typically contains the New, Open, Save, Save As, Print, and Exit commands. The Edit menu is typically the second menu title, and it typically contains Cut, Copy, and Paste commands.

- Disable (dim) menu items that are not applicable to the current state of the application.

To begin creating the text editor's menu:

1 The Menu Editor should still be open. Type **&File** in the Caption text box, then press the **Tab** key. &File appears in the Caption text box and in the list box, and the insertion point is now located in the Name text box.

2 Type **mnuFile** in the Name text box, but don't press the Enter key yet. "Mnu" is the three-character ID for a menu control.

To enter the next menu control, you can either click the Next button or, because the Next button is the default button in the Menu Editor, you can press the Enter key.

3 Press the **Enter** key to select the Next button. The highlight moves down one line in the Menu Editor list box.

You want New to be the first item on the File menu. The New command will remove the existing document from the screen and allow the user to create a new one. The letter N is the standard access key for the New option.

4 Type **&New** in the Caption text box, press the **Tab** key, then type **mnuFileNew** in the Name text box. The mnuFileNew name will help you remember that New is a menu item on the File menu. &New appears as a menu control in the Menu Editor list box.

See what the menu looks like so far.

5 Click the **OK** button both to save the menu information and to close the Menu Editor. Visual Basic displays the menu in the form.

Notice that both File and New appear, incorrectly, as menu titles on the menu bar. You actually want File to be the menu title, and New to be a menu item on the File menu. Use the Menu Editor to make this modification.

Creating Menu Items

You control the placement of menu titles, menu items, and submenu items by indenting the entries in the Menu Editor list box. As you just saw, entries appearing flush left in the Menu Editor list box are displayed as menu titles on the menu bar. If you want a control to be an item on a menu, you must indent the entry once in the Menu Editor list box. Entries indented even further in the Menu Editor list box become submenu items. Figure 6-31 illustrates the placement of menu titles, menu items, and submenu items in the Menu Editor list box.

menu title

item on the Colors menu

items on the Backcolor submenu

Figure 6-31: Menu elements in the Menu Editor list box

You can now open the Menu Editor and designate New as a item on the File menu.

To continue creating the text editor's menu:

1   Click the **Menu Editor** button on the toolbar. The Menu Editor opens.

Click **&New** in the list box, then click the **right arrow** button above the list box to indent &New. Four dots (....) appear before &New in the list box. Visual Basic will now display New as an item on the File menu, instead of as a separate menu title on the menu bar.

Now assign a shortcut key to the New command.

2   Click the **Shortcut** list arrow in the Menu Editor. A list of shortcut keys appears.

The standard shortcut key for the New command is Ctrl + N.

3   Scroll the list until Ctrl+N appears, then click **Ctrl+N** in the list. Ctrl+N appears in the Shortcut combo box and to the right of the ...&New item in the Menu Editor list box.

Next you will include an Open command in the File menu. Because the Open command will need the user to enter the name of the file to open, you will place an ellipsis after its Caption. Recall that the ellipsis indicates that the command will require the user to enter some additional information before the command can be processed.

4   Click the **Next** button, then use the information shown in Figure 6-32 to add the Open command to the File menu.

Figure 6-32: Open command entered in the Menu Editor

You also need to include the Save and Save As commands on the File menu. Because both commands will perform a task that is entirely different from the tasks performed by the New and Open commands, you will use a horizontal line, called a **separator bar**, to separate the two groups of menu items.

Creating a Separator Bar

Using a separator bar to divide menu items into logical groups is another Windows convention. In Visual Basic, you create a separator bar by placing one hyphen (-) in the Caption text box of a menu control. (You must also give the separator bar a name.) Add a separator bar to this menu and then complete the File menu.

GUI
Design Tips

Using Separator Bar

• Use a separator bar to separate groups of related menu items.

To enter a separator bar in the File menu:

1 If necessary, click **&Open** in the Menu Editor list box. Click the **Next** button to enter a new menu control below the &Open item. Visual Basic assumes that this new entry will be another menu item, so it indents the entry for you.

2 Type - (a hyphen) in the Caption text box, then press the **Tab** key. Recall that you must complete the Name box for each menu control. Type **Hyphen1** in the Name text box. Be sure you don't include a space between Hyphen and 1. When the application is run, the File menu will display a separator bar below the Open command.

3 Press the **Enter** key to add a new menu control. The highlight moves down one line in the Menu Editor list box.

4 Use Figure 6-33 to finish creating the File menu. The names of the menu controls are shown next to each item in the figure.

mnuFileSave

mnuFileSaveAs

Hyphen2

mnuFilePrint

Hyphen3

mnuFileExit

Figure 6-33: Completed File menu for the text editor application

5 When you have finished creating the File menu, click the **OK** button both to save the menu information and to close the Menu Editor.

6 Click the **Save Project** button 🖫 on the toolbar to save the form and the project.

7 Click **File** on the form's menu bar to open the File menu. The open File menu appears as shown in Figure 6-34.

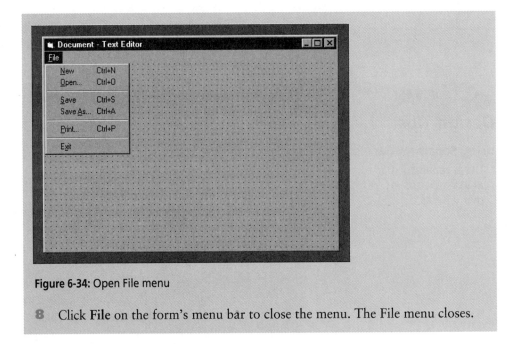

Figure 6-34: Open File menu

8   Click **File** on the form's menu bar to close the menu. The File menu closes.

You still need to add the Edit and Search menus to the application.

Creating the Edit and Search Menus

In Windows applications the Edit menu is typically the second menu listed on the menu bar. Three commands found on the Edit menu are Cut, Copy, and Paste. Cut is listed first, followed by Copy, and then Paste. The standard access keys for these commands are the letters T, C, and P, respectively; the standard shortcut keys are Ctrl+X, Ctrl+C, and Ctrl+V, respectively. You will include these three commands in the text editor's Edit menu.

To add the Edit menu to the application:

1   Click the **Menu Editor** button ▣ on the toolbar. Use Figure 6-35 to add the Edit menu to the application. The names of the menu controls are shown next to each item in the figure.

mnuEdit

mnuEditCut

mnuEditCopy

mnuEditPaste

Figure 6-35: Completed Edit menu for the text editor application

2 When you have finished creating the Edit menu, click the **OK** button both to save the menu information and to close the Menu Editor.

3 Click the **Save Project** button 🖫 on the toolbar to save the form and the project.

4 Click **Edit** on the form's menu bar to open the Edit menu. The open Edit menu appears as shown in Figure 6-36.

Figure 6-36: Open Edit menu

5 Click **Edit** on the form's menu bar to close the Edit menu.

Lastly add the Search menu to the application. The Search menu will contain the Find and Find Next commands. You will use the letter F as the access key for the Find command, and the letter N as the access key for the Find Next command. The shortcut keys will be Ctrl+F for the Find command, and F3 for the Find Next command.

To add the Search menu to the application:

1   Click the **Menu Editor** button 🗔 on the toolbar. Use Figure 6-37 to add the Search menu to the application. The names of the menu controls are shown next to each item in the figure.

mnuSearch

mnuSearchFind

mnuSearchFindNext

Figure 6-37: Completed Search menu for the text editor application

2   When you have finished creating the Search menu, click the **OK** button both to save the menu information and to close the Menu Editor.

3   Click the **Save Project** button 🖬 on the toolbar to save the form and the project.

4   Click **Search** on the form's menu bar to open the Search menu. The open Search menu appears as shown in Figure 6-38.

Figure 6-38: Open Search menu

5   Click **Search** on the form's menu bar to close the Search menu.

Now that you've created the menu, you can begin coding the application.

Coding Menu Items

The TOE chart for the text editor application is shown in Figure 6-39. Notice that you will need to code the Click event for each of the menu items and for each of the menu titles.

Task	Object	Event
Accept and display text entered by the user	txtEdit	None
Open a new document	mnuFileNew	Click
Open an existing document	mnuFileOpen	Click
Save the document using its current name	mnuFileSave	Click
Save the document using a new name	mnuFileSaveAs	Click
Print the document	mnuFilePrint	Click
Exit the application	mnuFileExit	Click
Enable/disable the Cut, Copy, and Paste commands	mnuEdit	Click
Remove selected text from the txtEdit control and place it on the clipboard	mnuEditCut	Click
Copy the text selected in the txtEdit control to the clipboard	mnuEditCopy	Click
Paste the text from the clipboard into the txtEdit control	mnuEditPaste	Click
1. Ask the user for the search string 2. Search the txtEdit control for the first occurrence of the search string	mnuSearchFind	Click
Search for subsequent occurrences of the search string	mnuSearchFindNext	Click

Figure 6-39: TOE chart for the text editor application

You will begin by coding the File menu's Exit option. When the user clicks this option, the application should use the Unload statement to unload the form.

To code the Exit option, then save and run the application:

1   Click **File** on the form's menu bar to open the File menu. (Be sure to open the form's File menu, not Visual Basic's File menu.)

You open a menu item's Code window by clicking the menu item, not double-clicking as you do with other controls.

2   Click **Exit** to open the mnuFileExit control's Code window. The Code window opens and displays the Click event procedure, which is the only event procedure a menu control recognizes.

Recall that you unload a form with the Unload statement.

3   Press the **Tab** key, type **unload frmEdit** and press the **Enter** key.

As you learned in Tutorial 5, the Unload statement triggers the form's Unload event.

4   Use the Code window's Object and Proc boxes to open the form's Unload event. Press the **Tab** key, then type **end** and press the **Enter** key.

5   Close the Code window.

See if the Exit command works correctly.

6   **Save** and **run** the application. Click **File** to open the File menu, then click **Exit** to end the application. Visual Basic unloads the frmEdit form and returns to the design screen.

You will code the remainder of the File menu in Tutorial 7. In this tutorial, you will code only the Edit and Search menus. Before you can begin coding the Edit menu, you need to learn about the Clipboard object.

The Clipboard Object

In addition to the Screen object that you learned about in Tutorial 3, Visual Basic also has a **Clipboard object**, which provides access to the Windows clipboard. The Clipboard object allows you to include cut, copy, and paste features in your application. In order to use the Clipboard object in the text editor application, you will need to learn three methods of the Clipboard object, as well as one new text box property. The three methods of the Clipboard object are SetText, GetText( ), and Clear. The new text box property is SelText. Begin with the three methods.

The SetText, GetText( ), and Clear Methods

You use the **SetText method** to send text to the clipboard. The syntax of the SetText method is **Clipboard.SetText** *data*, where *data* is the text you want placed on the clipboard. When you want to retrieve text from the clipboard, you use the **GetText( ) method** to do so. The syntax of the GetText( ) method is **Clipboard.GetText( )**. If no text is on the clipboard, the GetText( ) method returns the empty string (""). You use the **Clear method**, with the syntax *object*.**Clear**, to clear the contents of the clipboard. Figure 6-40 recaps these methods.

Method	Purpose
SetText	Places text on the clipboard
GetText( )	Retrieves text from the clipboard
Clear	Clears the clipboard

Figure 6-40: Recap of SetText, GetText( ), and Clear methods

In addition to the three methods of the Clipboard object, you will also need to use a text box control's SelText property when coding the Edit menu.

tips

It is not actually necessary to put the **End** statement in the form's Unload event, although, for documentation purposes, it is good programming practice to do so. Recall from Tutorial 5 that when the Unload event is triggered, Visual Basic passes the number 0 to the event's Cancel argument. If the Unload event does not contain an instruction that changes the value in the Cancel argument to a non-zero number, Visual Basic removes the form from the screen.

tips

In the Clear method's syntax, *object* can be a list box, combo box (which you will learn about in Tutorial 9), or the Clipboard object.

The SelText Property

When a user selects text in a text box, Visual Basic records the selected text in the text box's **SelText property**. For example, if the user selects the word "and" in a text box, Visual Basic records "and" in the text box's SelText property. If no text is selected in the text box, the SelText property contains the empty string (""). Figure 6-41 shows examples of how to use the methods of the Clipboard object, as well as the SelText property of a text box.

Instruction	Result
Clipboard.SetText "Have a nice day"	Places the string "Have a nice day" on the clipboard.
Clipboard.SetText txtEdit.Text	Places a copy of the txtEdit control's contents on the clipboard.
Clipboard.SetText txtEdit.SelText	Places a copy of the text currently selected in the txtEdit control on the clipboard.
txtEdit.Text = Clipboard.GetText( )	Retrieves the text from the clipboard and places a copy of it in the txtEdit control; the text replaces the entire contents of the text box.
txtEdit.SelText = Clipboard.GetText( )	Retrieves the text from the clipboard and places a copy of it in the txtEdit control; the text replaces the selected text in the txtEdit control
txtEdit.SelText = ""	Removes the selected text from the txtEdit control
Clipboard.Clear	Clears the contents of the clipboard

Figure 6-41: Examples of the Clipboard object's SetText, GetText( ), and Clear methods and the text box's SelText property.

You can now begin coding the Edit menu.

Coding the Edit Menu

Not every menu title's Click event will need to be coded. You only code a menu title's Click event when you need to set the properties of its commands, and the proper setting is based on some condition that must be evaluated during run time.

In Windows applications, recall that the Edit menu's Cut and Copy commands are not available until the user selects either some text or a graphic in the document, and the Paste command is not available until something, either text or graphics, is placed on the clipboard. You can enable and disable the Cut, Copy, and Paste commands at the appropriate times by coding the Edit menu title's Click event procedure.

When the user clicks Edit on the text editor's menu bar, the menu title's Click event procedure will verify that the user selected some text in the document. If no text is selected in the document, then the Click event will disable the Cut and Copy commands; otherwise—which means that some text is selected in the document—the Click event will enable the Cut and Copy commands. The Click event will also check if any text resides currently on the clipboard. If the clipboard does not contain any text, then the Edit menu's Click event will disable the Paste command; otherwise it will enable the Paste command.

tips

The text editor will not contain any graphics, so you do not need to check if any are selected in the txtEdit control, or if any reside on the clipboard. To learn more about sending and retrieving graphics to and from the clipboard, search Help for information on the GetData and SetData methods.

To code the Edit menu title, then save and run the application:

1 Click **Edit** on the form's menu bar. The Edit menu opens. Notice that clicking a menu title does not open the menu title's Code window.

To code a menu title's Click event, you need simply to open any Code window, then use the Object box to open the menu title's Code window.

2 Click **Cut**. The mnuEditCut command's Click event procedure appears. Use the Object box to open the mnuEdit Code window. The mnuEdit Click event procedure appears.

First you will use a selection structure, along with the txtEdit control's SelText property, to determine if any text is selected in the document. (Recall that the SelText property contains the empty string if no text is currently selected.) If the user did not select any text, then you will disable the Cut and Copy commands; otherwise you will enable the Cut and Copy commands.

3 Maximize the Code window, then enter the code and documentation shown in Figure 6-42.

be sure you are entering the code in the mnuEdit control's Click event

enter these lines of code and documentation

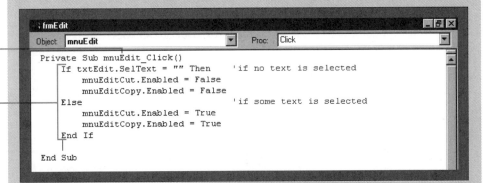

```
frmEdit                                                              _ 8 X
Object:  mnuEdit                  ▼        Proc:  Click              ▼

Private Sub mnuEdit_Click()
    If txtEdit.SelText = "" Then        'if no text is selected
        mnuEditCut.Enabled = False
        mnuEditCopy.Enabled = False
    Else                                'if some text is selected
        mnuEditCut.Enabled = True
        mnuEditCopy.Enabled = True
    End If

End Sub
```

Figure 6-42: Selection structure that enables and disables the Cut and Copy commands

tips

You can also use a text box's SelLength property to determine if any text is selected in the text box. The SelLength property contains a 0 (zero) when no text is selected.

Now you will use the GetText( ) method to determine if any text exists currently on the clipboard. If the clipboard does not contain any text, then you will disable the Paste command; otherwise you will enable it.

4 Complete the mnuEdit control's Click event by entering the code shown in Figure 6-43.

enter these lines of code and documentation

```
frmEdit                                                              _ 8 X
Object:  mnuEdit                  ▼        Proc:  Click              ▼

Private Sub mnuEdit_Click()
    If txtEdit.SelText = "" Then        'if no text is selected
        mnuEditCut.Enabled = False
        mnuEditCopy.Enabled = False
    Else                                'if some text is selected
        mnuEditCut.Enabled = True
        mnuEditCopy.Enabled = True
    End If
    If Clipboard.GetText() = "" Then        'if no text is on the clipboard
        mnuEditPaste.Enabled = False
    Else                                'if some text is on the clipboard
        mnuEditPaste.Enabled = True
    End If

End Sub
```

Figure 6-43: Additional selection structure that enables and disables the Paste command

5 Close the Code window, then **save** and **run** the application.

6 Type **Visual Basic** in the Text Editor window, then click **Edit** on the menu bar. Notice that the Cut and Copy commands are dimmed, which indicates that they are not available at the present time. The Paste command may or may not be dimmed; it depends on whether you have cut or copied any text to the clipboard prior to running the application.

7 Click **Edit** on the menu bar to close the Edit menu.

8 Select the word "Visual" in the text box, then click **Edit** on the menu bar. Notice that the Cut and Copy commands are no longer dimmed, which indicates that they are now available.

9 Click **Edit** on the menu bar to close the Edit menu.

10 Click **File**, then click **Exit**. Visual Basic returns to the design screen.

Next you will code the Edit menu's Copy command.

Coding the Edit Menu's Copy Command

When the user clicks Copy on the Edit menu, its Click event should clear the clipboard of its current contents, then place a copy of the selected text on the clipboard.

To code the Copy command:

1 Click **Edit** on the form's menu bar, then click **Copy**. The mnuEditCopy control's Click event procedure appears.

2 Maximize the Code window, then enter the code and documentation shown in Figure 6-44.

be sure you are entering the code in the mnuEditCopy control's Click event

```
frmEdit
Object:  mnuEditCopy          Proc:  Click
Private Sub mnuEditCopy_Click()
    Clipboard.Clear                    'clear clipboard
    Clipboard.SetText txtEdit.SelText  'send text to clipboard

End Sub
```

Figure 6-44: Copy command's Click event procedure

The `Clipboard.Clear` instruction will clear the contents of the clipboard. The `Clipboard.SetText txtEdit.SelText` instruction will send a copy of the selected text from the txtEdit control to the clipboard.

Next code the Cut command.

Coding the Edit Menu's Cut Command

When the user selects the Cut command, its Click event procedure should clear the clipboard; here again, you can use the Clipboard object's Clear method to do so. After clearing the clipboard, the Cut command's Click event should place the selected text on the clipboard, then remove the selected text from its location in the document. As you did in the Copy command's code, you can use the Clipboard object's SetText method and the txtEdit control's SelText property to place the selected text on the clipboard. After the text is on the clipboard, you can use the `txtEdit.SelText = ""` to replace the selected text in the txtEdit control with the empty string.

To code the Cut command:

1   The mnuEditCopy control's Code window should be open. Use the Proc box to open the mnuEditCut control's Click event procedure, then enter the code and documentation shown in Figure 6-45.

be sure you are entering the code in the mnuEditCut control's Click event

enter these lines of code and documentation

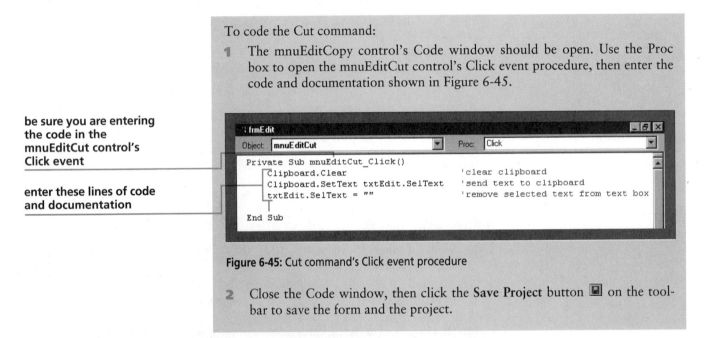

```
Private Sub mnuEditCut_Click()
    Clipboard.Clear                        'clear clipboard
    Clipboard.SetText txtEdit.SelText      'send text to clipboard
    txtEdit.SelText = ""                   'remove selected text from text box

End Sub
```

Figure 6-45: Cut command's Click event procedure

2   Close the Code window, then click the **Save Project** button 🖫 on the toolbar to save the form and the project.

Lastly, code the Paste command.

Coding the Edit Menu's Paste Command

The Paste command needs to retrieve the text from the clipboard and place it in the Text Editor document window beginning at the current location of the blinking insertion point. The instruction `txtEdit.SelText = Clipboard.GetText()` will accomplish this task. If no text is currently selected in the text box, this instruction will paste the retrieved text at the current location of the insertion point. If some text is currently selected in the document window, this instruction will replace the selected text with the retrieved text.

To code the Paste command, then save and run the application:

1   Click **Edit**, then click **Paste**. The mnuEditPaste control's Click event procedure appears.

2   Maximize the Code window, then enter the code and documentation shown in Figure 6-46.

be sure you are entering
the code in the
mnuEditPaste control's
Click event

Figure 6-46: Paste command's Click event procedure

3 Close the Code window, then **save** and **run** the application.

4 Type **Visual Basic** and press the **Enter** key.

5 Select the word **Visual** in the Text Editor document window. Click **Edit**, then click **Cut**. Visual Basic removes the word Visual from the document window and places it on the clipboard.

6 Click in the line below the word Basic in the document window. Click **Edit**, then click **Paste**. Visual Basic pastes the word "Visual" at that location in the document.

7 Select the word **Basic** in the document. Click **Edit**, then click **Copy**. Visual Basic places a copy of the word "Basic" on the clipboard.

8 Click after the word Visual in the Text Editor document window. Click **Edit**, then click **Paste**. Visual Basic pastes the word "Basic" at that location in the document.

9 On your own, enter some text in the document window, then practice cutting, copying, and pasting.

10 When you are finished practicing with the Cut, Copy, and Paste commands, click **File**, then click **Exit** to end the application. Visual Basic returns to the design screen.

You have now finished Lesson B. You can either take a break or complete the end-of-lesson questions and exercises. You will code the Search menu in Lesson C. Then, you will code the remainder of the File menu in Tutorial 7.

SUMMARY

To adjust the size of a control when the size of the form changes:

■ In the form's Resize event, assign the form's ScaleHeight property to the control's Height property, and assign the form's ScaleWidth property to the control's Width property.

To determine the size of an object from the center of one border to the center of the opposite border:

■ Use the Height and Width properties.

To determine the measurements of the interior of an object, which is the part of the object that lies within the borders:

■ Use the ScaleHeight and ScaleWidth properties.

To allow a text box to accept and display more than one line of text:

■ Set the text box control's MultiLine property to True.

To control whether a text box contains scroll bars:

■ Set the text box control's ScrollBars property to either 0-None (the default), 1-Horizontal, 2-Vertical, or 3-Both.

■ For a text box to display scroll bars, you must set the MultiLine property to True.

To create a menu control:

■ Click the Menu Editor button 📧 on the toolbar. You can also click Tools, then click Menu Editor; you can also press Ctrl + E.

■ Complete the Caption property and the Name property for each menu control. Complete other properties as necessary. Click the OK button to close the Menu Editor.

To create a separator bar in a menu:

■ Type - (one hyphen) in the Caption property of the menu control. Also type a name in the Name property of the menu control.

To assign a shortcut key to a menu control:

■ Open the Menu Editor, then click the appropriate menu control in the list box. Click the Shortcut list arrow, then click the desired shortcut key in the list. Click the OK button to close the Menu Editor.

To assign an access key to a menu control:

■ Open the Menu Editor, then click the appropriate menu control in the list box. In the Caption property of the control, type an ampersand (&) to the immediate left of the letter you want to designate as the access key.

To open the Code window for a menu control:

■ If the menu control is a menu title, open any Code window, then use the Code window's Object box to open the menu title's Code window.

■ If the menu control is a menu item, click the menu item on the menu to open its Code window.

To enable/disable menu controls:

■ To enable a menu control, set its Enabled property to True. To disable a menu control, set its Enabled property to False.

To access the Windows clipboard:

■ Use the Clipboard object.

■ Use the Clear method to clear the contents of the Clipboard object. The syntax of the Clear method is *object*.**Clear**, where *object* can be a list box, combo box, or the Clipboard object.

■ Use the SetText method to place text on the Clipboard object. The syntax of the SetText method is **Clipboard.SetText** *data*, where data is the text you want to put on the Clipboard object.

■ Use the GetText( ) method to retrieve text from the clipboard. The syntax of the GetText method is **Clipboard.GetText( )**. If no text is on the clipboard, this method returns the empty string (" ").

To determine the text selected in a text box:

■ Use the SelText property. If no text is selected in the text box, the SelText property contains the empty string (" ").

Q U E S T I O N S

1. The _____ event occurs when a form is first displayed on the screen, and when the user changes the size of the form.
   a. Caption
   b. Change
   c. FormSize
   d. Resize
   e. Size

2. To change the width of a control when the width of the form changes, assign the form's _____ property to the control's _____ property.
   a. Change, Size
   b. Resize, Size
   c. ScaleWidth, Width
   d. Size, Resize
   e. Width, ScaleWidth

3. To change the size of a control when the size of the form changes, place the appropriate instructions in the _____ event.
   a. control's Resize
   b. control's Size
   c. form's Resize
   d. form's Size
   e. form's SizeForm

4. The _____ properties measure the size of an object from the center of one border to the center of the opposite border. (Choose two answers.)
   a. Height
   b. ScaleHeight
   c. ScaleWidth
   d. Width

5. The _____ properties measure the interior of an object, which is the part of the object that lies between the borders. (Choose two answers.)
   a. Height
   b. ScaleHeight
   c. ScaleWidth
   d. Width

6. You must complete two of these properties for each menu control.
   a. Caption
   b. Menu
   c. Name
   d. Shortcut
   e. Text

7. Which of the following is the only event to which a menu control can react?
   a. Change
   b. Click
   c. Double-click
   d. Load
   e. Show

8. Entries that are flush left in the list box of the Menu Editor will appear as
   _____ .
   a. menu items
   b. menu titles
   c. submenu items
   d. submenu titles

9. The horizontal line in a menu is called a(n) _____ .
   a. dashed line
   b. hyphen line
   c. item separator
   d. menu bar
   e. separator bar

10. You create the horizontal line in a menu by typing a(n) _____ in the Caption property of a menu control.
    a. asterisk
    b. dash
    c. hyphen
    d. underscore

11. The underlined letter in a menu title, menu item, submenu title, or submenu item is called a(n) _____ key.
    a. access
    b. dash
    c. menu
    d. open
    e. shortcut

12. A(n) _____ key allows you to access a menu item without opening the menu.
    a. access
    b. dash
    c. menu item
    d. open
    e. shortcut

13. You create an access key for a control by entering a(n) _____ to the immediate left of the appropriate character in the Caption property.
    a. ampersand (&)
    b. asterisk (*)
    c. dash (–)
    d. plus sign (+)
    e. underscore (_)

14. Which of the following is NOT true about menus?
    a. Menu titles appear on the menu bar.
    b. Menu titles should be one word only.
    c. Each menu title should have a unique access key.
    d. You can code a menu title's event procedure.
    e. If a menu title requires additional information from the user, follow the menu title's name with an ellipsis (...).

15. Which of the following is NOT true about menus?
    a. Menu items, which can be from one to three words, should be entered using sentence capitalization.
    b. You should disable menu items that are not applicable to the current state of the application.
    c. You should use a separator bar to separate groups of related menu items.
    d. You should assign a unique access key to each menu item.
    e. You should assign shortcut keys to commonly used menu items.

16. Which of the following instructions will remove the contents of the Clipboard object?
    a. Clipboard.Clear
    b. Clipboard.Erase
    c. Clipboard.Null
    d. Clipboard.Remove

17. Which of the following instructions will place the word "Hello" on the Clipboard object?
    a. Clipboard.Get ("Hello")
    b. Clipboard.GetText ("Hello")
    c. Clipboard.Set "Hello"
    d. Clipboard.SetText "Hello"
    e. Clipboard.Text "Hello"

18. Which of the following instructions will display the contents of the Clipboard object in a label control named lblMsg?
    a. lblMsg.Caption = Clipboard.Get( )
    b. lblMsg.Caption = Clipboard.GetText( )
    c. lblMsg.Caption = Clipboard.Set
    d. lblMsg.Caption = Clipboard.SetText
    e. lblMsg.Caption = Clipboard.Text

19. When you select text in a text box, Visual Basic records the selected text in the text box's _____ property.
    a. Selected
    b. SelText
    c. SetText
    d. Text
    e. TextSel

20. If the Clipboard object does not contain any text, the _____ method returns the empty string.
    a. GetText( )
    b. SelText( )
    c. SetText( )
    d. TextGet( )
    e. TextSel( )

21. You enable/disable a menu control by setting its _____ property.
    a. Change
    b. Disabled
    c. Enabled
    d. Use

22. When set to True, the _____ property allows a text box to accept and display more than one line of code.
    a. DisplayMultiple
    b. MultiLine
    c. MultiText
    d. Text

23. This property controls the type of scroll bars displayed on a text box.
a. Bars
b. Scroll
c. ScrollBars
d. VerticalBars

24. For a text box to display scroll bars, this property must be set to True.
a. Bars
b. MultiLine
c. MultiText
d. Scroll
e. ScrollBars

E X E R C I S E S

NOTE: When creating the user interfaces for the applications in this lesson, be sure to follow all GUI design rules. For example, assign access keys to the essential components of the interface, center the form, highlight the existing text in a text box, create a default command button (if appropriate), and so on.

1. In this exercise you will create and code a menu.

Scenario: Mr. Barrows, an elementary school teacher, wants an application that he can use to calculate and display a student's grade. Mr. Barrows will enter the student's name and his or her scores on two projects, as well as the scores on the midterm and final. The projects are worth 50 points each, and the midterm and final are worth 100 points each. Mr. Barrows also wants to be able to print the interface.

a. Create an appropriate user interface. Use a command button to calculate and display the grade. Use a File menu that contains Print and Exit options. Be sure to include a separator bar. Also be sure to assign access keys to the menu and its options. Assign the appropriate shortcut key to the Print option.

b. Save the form and the project as lb1Done in the Tut06 folder on your Student Disk.

c. Code the command button's Click event procedure so that it sums the project and test scores and then assigns the appropriate grade according to the following chart.

Total Points	Grade
270 – 300	A
240 – 269	B
210 – 239	C
180 – 209	D
Less than 180	F

d. Code the Print option so that it prints the form. Code the Exit option so that it unloads the form.

e. Save and run the application. Test the application by entering the following data: Jill Strait, 50, 45, 75, 80. Calculate and display the grade, then open the File menu and click Print.

f. Use the File menu's Exit option to exit the application.

g. Print the form and the code. Submit both the form and the code.

2. In this exercise you will create and code a menu.

Scenario: Venus Motors, a car dealer, wants an application that the salespeople can use to calculate price quotes. The salesperson will need to enter the customer's name, the value of any trade-in, the car model, and the package type. The application should calculate the price before sales tax, the sales tax, and the total price including the sales tax.

a. Create the user interface shown in Figure 6-47. The car model option buttons should be a control array. The package type option buttons should also be a control array. Set the imgLogo control's Picture property so that it displays the \icons\industry\cars (or \icons\industry\cars.ico) icon. This icon file should be in Visual Basic's main folder on either the local hard drive or on the network drive. Recall that Visual Basic's main folder in Windows 95 is typically named Microsoft Visual Basic; its main folder in Windows 3.1 is typically named vb.

optModel array

imgLogo (you will not be able to create this control using the Working Model)

txtName

lblBase

lblPkg

txtTrade

lblSub

lblTax

lblTotal

optPkg array

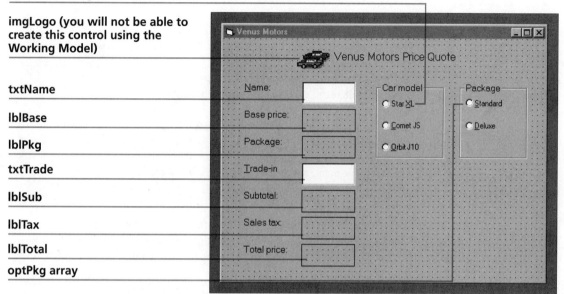

Figure 6-47

b. Save the form and the project as lb2Done in the Tut06 folder on your Student Disk.

c. Code the car model option button array so that it displays the appropriate base price in the lblBase control. The base prices are as follows:

Car Model	Base Price
Star XL	10500
Comet JS	21000
Orbit J10	15500

d. Code the package option button array so that it displays the appropriate package price in the lblPkg control. The Standard package costs $2000, and the Deluxe package costs $3000.

e. Add a File menu to the application. The File menu should contain a Clear option, a Print option, and an Exit option. Include a separator bar between each option. Assign access keys to the menu and to the Clear and Print options.

f. The Print option should have two submenu options, With Logo and No Logo. Code the With Logo option so that it prints the form. Code the With Logo option so that it prints the form with the imgLogo control showing. (Recall that you hide/display a control by setting its Visible property.)

g. Code the Clear option so that it removes the data from the Name and Trade-in Text boxes. It should also remove the data from the Subtotal, Sales tax, and Total price label controls.

h. Code the Exit option so that it unloads the form.

i. Add a Compute menu to the application. The Compute menu should contain a Rate – 5% option and a Rate – 7% option. Assign access keys to the menu and its options.

j. Code the Rate – 5% option so that it calculates and displays the subtotal, the sales tax, and the total price. To calculate the subtotal, add the base price to the package price, then subtract the trade-in value. Display the subtotal in the lblSub control. To calculate the sales tax, multiply the subtotal by .05. Display the sales tax in the lblTax control. To calculate the total price, add the subtotal to the sales tax. Display the total price in the lblTotal control.

k. Code the Rate – 7% option so that it calculates and displays the subtotal, the sales tax, and the total price. Use the same calculations shown in step j above, except use a 7% sales tax rate.

l. Save and run the application. Test the application as follows:

   1) Enter Darlene Zimmer as the name and 2000 as the trade-in value. Click Comet JS and Deluxe.
   2) Open the Compute menu and click Rate – 7%.
   3) Open the File menu and click Print, then click No Logo.
   4) Open the File menu and click Clear.
   5) Enter Dana Chou as the name and 1500 as the trade-in value. Click Orbit J10 and Standard.
   6) Open the Compute menu and click Rate – 5%.
   7) Open the File menu and click Print, then click With Logo.
   8) Open the File menu and click Exit.

m. Print the code.

n. Submit the printouts from steps l(3) and l(7), and the code from step m.

Exercises 3 and 4 are Discovery Exercises, which allow you to both "discover" the solutions to problems on your own and to experiment with material that is not covered in the tutorial.

discovery ▶ **3.** In this exercise you will use a menu control's Checked property.

Important Note: You will not be able to complete this Discovery Exercise if you are using the Visual Basic Working Model. You will need to use either the Standard Edition or the Professional Edition.

Scenario: In Windows applications, a check mark in a menu control indicates that the menu item is active. For example, in Microsoft Word's Window menu, a check mark indicates which of several open documents is currently displayed on the screen. You will use a check mark in this exercise to control which of two label and image controls are displayed in the interface.

a. Open a new project, if necessary. Add a label control and an image control to the form. Name the label control lblHead1 and the image control imgRocket. The image control should display a picture of a rocket. The rocket icon is in the \icons\industry\rocket.ico file, which is located in the main Visual Basic folder on either the local hard drive or the network drive. Set the label control's Caption property to Rocket Company.

b. Save the form and the project as lb3Done in the Tut06 folder on your Student Disk.

c. Click the lblHead1 control to select it. Press Ctrl + C to copy the control to the Windows clipboard, then press Ctrl + V to paste the control onto the form. When Visual Basic asks if you want to create a control array, click the No button.

d. Change the new Label control's Name property to lblHead2. Change its Caption to Bicycle Company. Set its Visible property to False. Drag the lblHead2 control directly on top of the lblHead1 control.

e. Click the imgRocket control to select it. Press Ctrl + C to copy the control to the Windows clipboard, then press Ctrl + V to paste the control onto the form. When Visual Basic asks if you want to create a control array, click the No button.

f. Change the new Image control's Name property to imgBicycle. Change its Picture property to display the \icons\industry\bicycle.ico icon, which is located in the main Visual Basic folder on either the local hard drive or the network drive. Change its Visible property to False. Drag the imgBicycle control directly on top of the imgRocket control.

g. You will use this application to switch between the two different headings and two different icons included in the interface. Add a Display menu to the application. The Display menu should have two options, Rocket and Bicycle. Assign access keys to the menu and its options. Assign Ctrl+R as the shortcut key for the Rocket option and Ctrl+B as the shortcut key for the Bicycle option.

h. Use the Help screens to research the menu control's Checked property.

i. Code the Rocket and Bicycle menu commands appropriately. The Rocket command should display the lblHead1 and imgRocket controls, and hide the lblHead2 and imgBicycle controls. When the lblHead1 and imgRocket controls are displayed in the interface, the Rocket command should be checked in the Display menu. Similarly, the Bicycle command should display the lblHead2 and imgBicycle controls, and hide the lblHead1 and imgRocket controls. When the lblHead2 and imgBicycle controls are displayed in the interface, the Bicycle command should be checked in the Display menu.

j. Save and run the application. The Rocket Company heading and the rocket logo should appear in the interface.

k. Open the Display menu. The Rocket option should be checked; the Bicycle option should be unchecked. Click Bicycle in the menu. The Bicycle Company heading and the bicycle logo should appear.

l. Open the Display menu again. The Bicycle option should be checked. The Rocket option should be unchecked. Click Rocket in the menu. The Rocket Company heading and rocket logo should appear.

m. Exit the application and print the code.

discovery ▶ 4. In this exercise you will discover the difference between a form's Height, Width, ScaleHeight, and ScaleWidth properties.

a. Open a new project. Place one text box in the upper left corner of the form. Change the text box's MultiLine property to True, and the ScrollBars property to 2-Vertical.

b. Open the form's Resize event. Enter the following two instructions.

    Text1.Height = Form1.Height
    Text1.Width = Form1.Width

c. Close the Code window. Run, but don't save, the application. Notice the size of the scroll bar along the right border of the text box.

d. Maximize the form. Again, notice the size of the scroll bar along the right border of the text box.

e. Stop the application. Open the form's Resize event. Change the two instructions to:

    Text1.Height = Form1.ScaleHeight
    Text1.Width = Form1.ScaleWidth

f. Close the Code window. Run, but don't save, the application. Notice the size of the scroll bar along the right border of the text box.

g. Maximize the form. Again, notice the size of the scroll bar along the right border of the text box.

h. Stop the application. On a piece of paper, explain the difference between the Height and Width and the ScaleHeight and ScaleWidth properties.

String Manipulation

Visual Basic's String Manipulation Functions

In many applications, your code will need to manipulate (process) string data. For example, the code may need to verify that an inventory part number begins with a specific letter; or the code may need to determine if the last three characters in the part number are valid. You may also need to locate a string contained within another string. Visual Basic provides a set of functions that makes string manipulation an easy task. In this lesson you will learn how to use four of Visual Basic's string manipulation functions: Left, Right, Mid, and Instr. You will use the Instr function in the code for the text editor application's Find and Find Next commands.

The Left and Right Functions

As you learned in Tutorial 2, functions always return a value. The Left and Right string functions, for example, return one or more characters from a string. Figure 6-48 shows the syntax and the purpose of both functions, as well as some examples of each.

Syntax	Purpose
Left(*stringexpression, n*)	Returns the leftmost *n* characters of the *stringexpression*
Right(*stringexpression, n*)	Returns the rightmost *n* characters of the *stringexpression*

Examples:

Assume that the stProgName variable contains "Visual Basic."

Function	Resulting String
Left("January", 3)	Jan
Right("January", 2)	ry
Left(stProgName, 6)	Visual
Right(stProgName, 5)	Basic

Figure 6-48: Syntax and examples of the Left and Right functions

In the first two examples, the Left and Right functions are used to return one or more characters from the *stringexpression* "January". In the first example, the Left function returns the leftmost three characters in the *stringexpression*—Jan. In the second example, the Right function returns the rightmost two characters in the *stringexpression*—ry.

In the last two examples shown in Figure 6-48, a string variable is used as the *stringexpression*. When the *stringexpression* is a string variable, the Left and Right functions use the contents of the variable, not the variable name itself. In other words, the leftmost six characters in the string contained in the stProgName variable are "Visual"; the rightmost five characters in the string are "Basic".

Your Student Disk contains an application that uses the Left and Right functions.

To view the application that contains examples of the Left and Right functions:

1 Start Visual Basic, if necessary, and open the **LftRgt** (lftrgt.vbp) project, which is located in the Tut06 folder on your Student Disk. View the frmSweatshirts form. The interface is shown in Figure 6-49.

txtCode
lblSize
imgDesign

imgEarth
imgSnow
imgSun

Figure 6-49: User interface for the LftRgt application

The Environmental Sweatshirts application will display a sweatshirt's design and its size based on the product code entered in the txtCode control. The product code consists of five characters. The first three characters—which can be 100, 200, or 300—indicate the type of design. The last two characters—which can be XS, SM, MD, LG, or XL—indicate the size. Design 100 is a picture of the earth, Design 200 is a picture of a snowflake, and Design 300 is a picture of the sun. XS stands for "extra small," SM for "small," MD for "medium," LG for "large," and XL for "extra large." View the code in the Display button's Click event procedure.

To view the Display button's code, then run the application:

1 Double-click the **Display** button to open its Code window, then maximize the Code window. The cmdDisplay control's Click event procedure opens as shown in Figure 6-50.

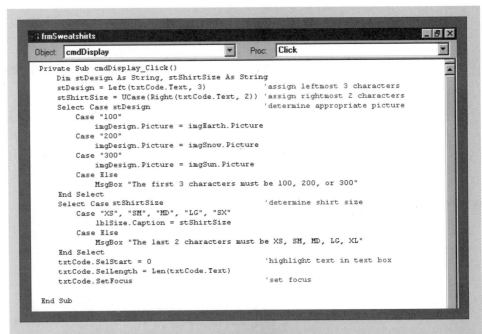

```
frmSweatshirts                                                    _ | 8 | X
Object:  cmdDisplay                      ▼    Proc:  Click                  ▼

 Private Sub cmdDisplay_Click()
     Dim stDesign As String, stShirtSize As String
     stDesign = Left(txtCode.Text, 3)           'assign leftmost 3 characters
     stShirtSize = UCase(Right(txtCode.Text, 2)) 'assign rightmost 2 characters
     Select Case stDesign                        'determine appropriate picture
         Case "100"
             imgDesign.Picture = imgEarth.Picture
         Case "200"
             imgDesign.Picture = imgSnow.Picture
         Case "300"
             imgDesign.Picture = imgSun.Picture
         Case Else
             MsgBox "The first 3 characters must be 100, 200, or 300"
     End Select
     Select Case stShirtSize                     'determine shirt size
         Case "XS", "SM", "MD", "LG", "SX"
             lblSize.Caption = stShirtSize
         Case Else
             MsgBox "The last 2 characters must be XS, SM, MD, LG, XL"
     End Select
     txtCode.SelStart = 0                         'highlight text in text box
     txtCode.SelLength = Len(txtCode.Text)
     txtCode.SetFocus                             'set focus

 End Sub
```

Figure 6-50: Display button's Click event procedure

The procedure begins by declaring two string variables, stDesign and stShirtSize. The `stDesign = Left(txtCode.Text, 3)` instruction assigns the product code's leftmost three characters to the stDesign variable. The `stShirtSize = UCase(Right(txtCode.Text, 2))` instruction assigns the product code's rightmost two characters to the stShirtSize variable. Two Case structures are then used to assign the appropriate picture and caption to the imgDesign and lblSize controls, respectively. Before the procedure ends, the code highlights the existing text in the txtCode control and sends the focus to that control.

2 Close the code window, then **run**, but don't save, the application. Notice that the earth, snowflake, and sun icons do not appear on the form during design time; that's because their Visible properties are set to False.

First enter a correct product code.

3 Type **200sm** in the Product code text box and press the **Enter** key to select the Display button, which is the default button on the form. The Display button's Click event assigns the leftmost three characters (200) to the stDesign variable, and assigns the rightmost two characters (sm), in upper-case, to the stShirtSize variable. The two Case structures then display the appropriate picture (the snowflake icon) and caption (SM) in the imgDesign and lblSize controls, respectively.

Now enter a product code that has an incorrect design type. As you enter the product code, you will notice that the application removes the contents of the imgDesign and lblSize controls; that's because the txtCode control's Change event contains the `imgDesign.Picture = LoadPicture()` and `lblSize.Caption = ""` instructions.

4 Type **500xs** in the Product code text box and press the **Enter** key. The MsgBox function's dialog box displays the message "The first 3 characters must be 100, 200, or 300." Click the **OK** button to remove the dialog box.

Now enter a product code that has an incorrect size.

5 Type **100ss** and press the **Enter** key. The MsgBox function's dialog box displays the message "The last 2 characters must be XS, SM, MD, LG, XL." Click the **OK** button to remove the dialog box.

6 Click the **Exit** button to end the application. Visual Basic returns to the design screen.

The Left and Right functions allow you to access the characters in a string, beginning from either the first character or the last character. The Mid function, which you will learn about in the next section, allows you to access the characters in a string, beginning with any of the characters in the string.

The Mid Function

The Mid function, whose syntax is Mid(*stringexpression*, *start*[, *n*]), returns *n* characters from a *stringexpression*, beginning with the *start* character. Figure 6-51 shows the syntax, purpose, and examples of the Mid function.

Syntax	Purpose
Mid(*stringexpression*, *start* [, *n*])	Returns *n* characters of the *stringexpression* beginning at position *start*. If *n* is omitted, the function returns all characters from the *start* position through the end of the *stringexpression*.

Examples:

Assume that the stProgName variable contains "Visual Basic."

Function	Resulting String
Mid("January", 2, 1)	a
Mid("January", 4, 2)	ua
Mid(stProgName, 8, 1)	B
Mid(stProgName, 8)	Basic

Figure 6-51: Syntax and examples of the Mid function

In the first two examples, the Mid function is used to return one or more characters from the *stringexpression* "January". The first example, `Mid("January", 2, 1)`, returns one character, beginning with the second character, in the *stringexpression*—the letter a. In the second example, the Mid function returns two characters, beginning with the fourth character, in the *stringexpression*—the letters "ua."

In the last two examples shown in Figure 6-51, the stProgName variable is used as the *stringexpression*. As the `Mid(stProgName, 8, 1)` example shows, the one character, beginning with the eighth character in the string contained in the stProgName variable, is the letter B. Notice that the `Mid(stProgName, 8)` instruction returns the word "Basic"; because the *n* is omitted from the instruction, Visual Basic returns all of the characters from the *start* position (8) through the end of the *stringexpression*.

Your Student Disk contains an application that uses the Mid function.

To view the application that contains an example of the Mid function:

1 Open the **Mid** (mid.vbp) project, which is located in the Tut06 folder on your Student Disk. If Visual Basic asks if you want to save the LftRgt form, click the No button.

2 View the frmConsolidated form. The interface is shown in Figure 6-52.

txtCode

lblStatus

Figure 6-52: User interface for the Mid application

All products at Consolidated Machinery have either the letter A or the letter C as the third character in the product code. When the user enters the product code in the txtCode control and clicks the Verify button, the application will display the message "The product code is valid." if the third character in the code is either an A or a C (entered in any case); otherwise it will display the message "The product code is not valid." View the code in the Verify button's Click event procedure.

To view the Verify button's code, then run the application:

1 Double-click the **Verify** button to open its Code window, then maximize the Code window. The cmdVerify Click event procedure opens as shown in Figure 6-53.

assign the third
character to the stCode
variable

assigns appropriate
caption

highlights text and sets
focus

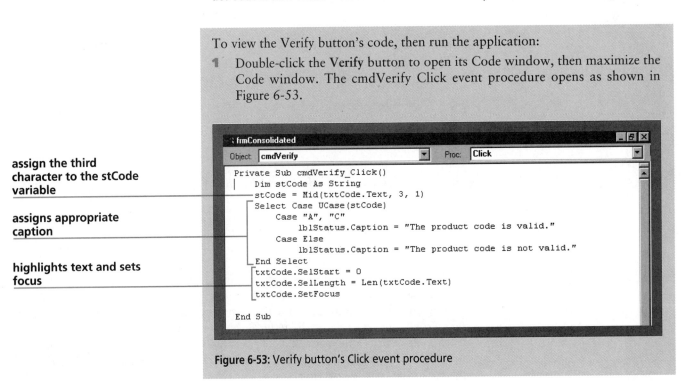

Figure 6-53: Verify button's Click event procedure

The procedure begins by declaring a string variable named stCode. The `stCode = Mid(txtCode.Text, 3, 1)` instruction assigns the one character, beginning with the third character in the txtCode control, to the stCode variable. A Case structure is then used to assign the appropriate message to the lblStatus control. Before the procedure ends, the code highlights the existing text in the txtCode control and sends the focus to that control.

2   Close the code window, then **run**, but don't save, the application.

First enter an incorrect product code.

3   Type **xyz5** in the Product code text box and press the **Enter** key to select the Verify button, which is the default button on the form. The message "The product code is not valid." appears in the Status text box.

Now enter a correct product code. As you enter the product code, you will notice that the message in the Status text box will disappear; that's because the txtCode control's Change event contains the `lblStatus.Caption = " "` instruction.

4   Type **abc5** in the Product code text box and press the **Enter** key. The message "The product code is valid." appears in the Status text box.

5   Click the **Exit** button to end the application. Visual Basic returns to the design screen

In the next section you will learn how to use the Instr function to determine if a specific string is contained within another string. You will use the Instr function in the text editor application's Find and Find Next commands.

The Instr Function

You can use the Instr function to search a string to determine if it contains another string. For example, you can use the Instr function to determine if the string "nice" appears in the string "Have a nice day". The syntax of the Instr function is **Instr**(*start, string1, string2*[, *compare*]), where *start* is a numeric expression that sets the starting position for the search—in other words, the character at which the search will begin. *String1* is the string expression being searched and *string2* is the string expression being sought. In the example, "Have a nice day" is *string1* and "nice" is *string 2*.

In the syntax, *compare* is either the number 0 or the number 1. If *compare* is set to its default value of 0, Visual Basic performs a case sensitive search; otherwise it performs a case insensitive search. For example, if *string2* is the word "nice" (entered in lowercase) and *compare* is set to 0, Visual Basic searches *string1* for the word "nice" entered in lowercase only. If *compare* is set to 1, on the other hand, Visual Basic searches *string1* for the word "nice" entered in either lowercase, uppercase, or a combination of both cases.

If *string2* is not contained within *string1*, then the Instr function returns the number 0. If *string2* is contained within *string1*, then the Instr function returns the starting position of *string2*. Figure 6-54 shows the syntax and some examples of the Instr function.

Function	Result (starting position of *string2* within *string1*)
Instr(1, "Have a nice day", "nice", 0)	8
Instr(1, "Have a nice day", "NICE", 0)	0
Instr(1, "Have a nice day", "NICE", 1)	8
Instr(9, "This is an Instr function example", "instr")	0
Instr(9, "This is an Instr function example", "instr", 1)	12

Figure 6-54: Syntax and examples of the Instr function

To complete the text editor's Search menu, you will need to use the Instr function only. You will code the Search menu's Find command first.

To open the text editor application:

1   Open the **lbEdit** (lbedit.vbp) project that you created in Lesson B. The project is located in the Tut06 folder on your Student Disk. If Visual Basic asks if you want to save the Mid form, click the No button.

2   View the frmEdit form. Save the form and the project as **lcEdit**.

Coding the Search Menu's Find Command

The Search menu's Find command will allow the user to locate a specific string within the text box. The pseudocode and flowchart for the Find command's Click event are shown in Figure 6-55.

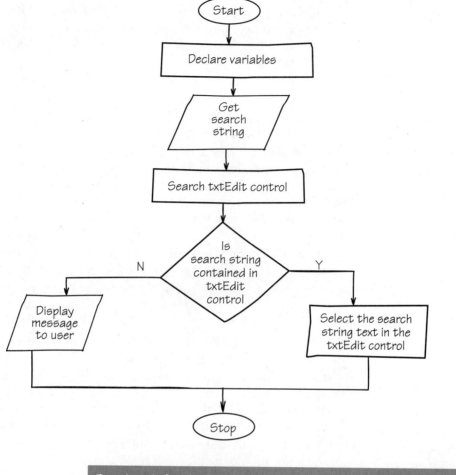

Pseudocode for the Search menu's Find command

1. Declare the variables.

2. Get the search string from the user.

3. Search the txtEdit control for the search string.

4. If the search string is not found in the txtEdit control then

> display a message to the user

Else

> select the search string text in the txtEdit control

End If

Figure 6-55: Flowchart and pseudocode for the Search menu's Find command

According to Figure 6-55, the first step is to declare the necessary variables. The Find command's Click event procedure will use a form-level variable named stSearchFor and a local variable named inFoundPos. The stSearchFor variable will store the search string—the string the user wants to find. You will declare stSearchFor as a form-level variable because it will also need to be used by the Find Next command's Click event procedure. The inFoundPos variable will store either the number 0, if the search string is not found in the txtEdit control, or it will store the starting position of the search string if the search string is found in the txtEdit control.

To begin coding the Find command's Click event:

1   Double-click the **form** to open its Code window. Use the Object box to open the form's General declarations section. If the `Option Explicit` statement does not appear in the Code window, then type **option explicit** and press the **Enter** key.

2   Type **dim stSearchFor as string** and press the **Enter** key.

3   Use the Code window's Object box to open the mnuSearchFind control's Click event procedure. Press the **Tab** key, then type **dim inFoundPos as integer** and press the **Enter** key.

After declaring the necessary variables, the Click event procedure will prompt the user for the search string—the string the user wants to find. You can use the InputBox function, which you learned about in Tutorial 3, to display a dialog box that contains a prompt and an input area in which the user can enter the search string. You will assign the user's response to the form-level stSearchFor variable.

4   Type **stSearchFor = inputbox("Find what:", "Find")** and press the **Enter** key.

You can now use the Instr function to search the txtEdit control for the string stored in the stSearchFor variable. You will perform a case insensitive search, beginning with the first character in the txtEdit control. You will assign the result of the Instr function to the local inFoundPos variable.

5   Maximize the Code window, then type **inFoundPos = instr(1, txtEdit.text, stSearchFor, 1)** and press the **Enter** key.

If the inFoundPos variable contains the number 0, then the Instr function did not find the search string in the txtEdit text box, so you should display an appropriate message to the user. You can use the MsgBox function, which you learned about in both Tutorials 4 and 5, to display the message in a dialog box.

6   Enter the additional instructions shown in Figure 6-56, then position the blinking insertion point as shown in the figure. (The instructions in the figure were compressed so that you could read more of each line.)

enter these instructions

position insertion point here

```
frmEdit                                                           _ 日 X
Object:  mnuSearchFind              ▼   Proc:  Click            ▼
Private Sub mnuSearchFind_Click()
    Dim inFoundPos As Integer, inUserResponse As Integer
    Const conBtns = vbOKOnly + vbInformation + vbDefaultButton1 + vbApplicationModal
    stSearchFor = InputBox("Find what:", "Find")
    inFoundPos = InStr(1, txtEdit.Text, stSearchFor, 1)
    If inFoundPos = 0 Then
        inUserResponse = MsgBox("The search string was not found.", conBtns, "Editor")
    Else

End Sub
```

Figure 6-56: Current status of the Find command's Click event procedure

If the inFoundPos variable does not contain the number 0, then the Instr function found the search string in the txtEdit text box. The Instr function, remember, returns the starting position of *string2* (the stSearchFor variable) within *string1* (the txtEdit control). You can use the number stored in the inFoundPos variable, along with the SelStart and SelLength properties, to highlight the text found in the txtEdit control.

As you learned in Tutorial 4, the SelStart property tells Visual Basic where in the text box to position the blinking insertion point—in other words, where to start the text selection. The first position in the text box, you may remember, is position 0. The SelLength property, on the other hand, tells Visual Basic the number of characters to select. Recall that the SelLength property begins the selection with the character to the immediate right of the blinking insertion point. Therefore, in order to highlight all of the characters in a text box, beginning with the first character, you must set the SelStart property to 0. Likewise, if you want to highlight a group of characters beginning with the fifth character, you must set the SelStart property to 4. Notice that, when selecting text, the SelStart value must always be one less than the position of the first character you want to select. Figure 6-57 illustrates this concept.

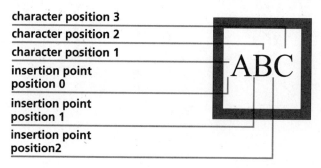

character position 3
character position 2
character position 1
insertion point position 0
insertion point position 1
insertion point position2

Figure 6-57: Illustration of insertion point positions and character positions

In the text editor application, recall that the inFoundPos variable contains a number that represents the position of the first character you want to select. In order to begin the selection with that character, you will need to position the insertion point to its immediate left. You can do so by subtracting one from the contents of the inFoundPos variable. After positioning the insertion point, you can use the SelLength property to tell Visual Basic to highlight the remaining characters that correspond to the search string.

To complete the Find command's Click event procedure, then save and run the application:

1   Enter the additional instructions and documentation shown in Figure 6-58. Also compare your code with the code shown in the figure. Correct any errors before continuing to the next step.

enter these lines of code and documentation

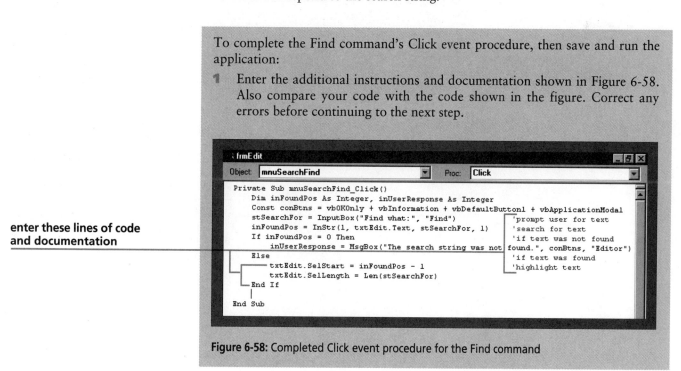

```
Private Sub mnuSearchFind_Click()
    Dim inFoundPos As Integer, inUserResponse As Integer
    Const conBtns = vbOKOnly + vbInformation + vbDefaultButton1 + vbApplicationModal
    stSearchFor = InputBox("Find what:", "Find")          'prompt user for text
    inFoundPos = InStr(1, txtEdit.Text, stSearchFor, 1)   'search for text
    If inFoundPos = 0 Then                                 'if text was not found
        inUserResponse = MsgBox("The search string was not found.", conBtns, "Editor")
    Else                                                  'if text was found
        txtEdit.SelStart = inFoundPos - 1                 'highlight text
        txtEdit.SelLength = Len(stSearchFor)
    End If

End Sub
```

Figure 6-58: Completed Click event procedure for the Find command

2 Close the Code window, then **save** and **run** the application.

3 Type **Have a nice day** and press the **Enter** key.

4 Click **Search**, then click **Find**. When the Find dialog box appears, type **nice** and press the **Enter** key. Visual Basic selects the word "nice" in the text editor, as shown in Figure 6-59.

Figure 6-59: The word "nice" highlighted in the txtEdit control

5 Click **Search**, then click **Find**. When the Find dialog box appears, type **Basic** and press the **Enter** key. The MsgBox function's dialog box informs you that the search string was not found.

6 Press the **Enter** key to remove the dialog box. Click **File**, then click **Exit** to end the application. Visual Basic returns to the design screen.

The Find command will search only for the first occurrence of the search string in the text box. If the user wants to find subsequent occurrences of the search string, he or she will need to use the Search menu's Find Next command.

Coding the Search Menu's Find Next Command

The pseudocode for the Search menu's Find Next command is shown in Figure 6-60.

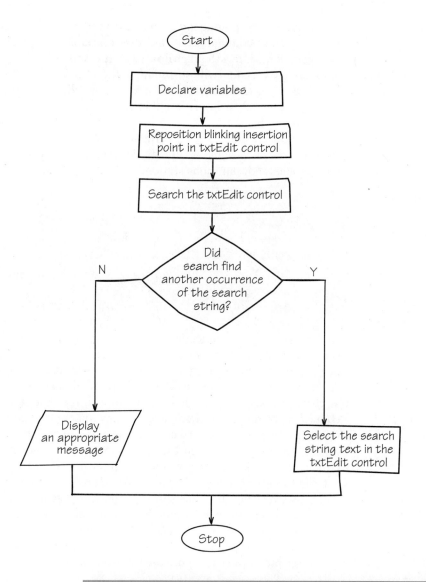

1. Declare variables.

2. Reposition the blinking insertion point in the txtEdit control.

3. Search the txtEdit control for another occurrence of the search string.

4. If another occurrence of the search string is not found in the txtEdit control then

      display an appropriate message to the user

  Else

      select the search string text in the txtEdit control

  Endif

Figure 6-60: Flowchart and pseudocode for the Search menu's Find Next command

According to the pseudocode, you first need to declare the necessary variables. The Find Next command will use three variables: stSearchFor, inFoundPos, and inBegSearch. The stSearchFor variable will store the search string. The inFoundPos variable will store either the number 0, if the search string is not found in the txtEdit control, or it will store the starting position of the search string if the search string is found in the txtEdit control. The inBegSearch variable will store the beginning position for the search. You will need only to declare the inFoundPos and inBegSearch variables in the Find Next command's Click event; the stSearchFor variable is already declared as a form-level string variable in the form's General declarations section.

To begin coding the Search menu's Find Next command:

1   Click **Search** on the form's menu bar, then click **Find Next**. The mnuSearchFindNext Click event procedure opens.

2   Press the **Tab** key, then type **dim inFoundPos as integer, inBegSearch as integer** and press the **Enter** key.

According to the pseudocode, you must reposition the blinking insertion point in the txtEdit control before continuing with the search. The new search should begin with the character that is located to the immediate right of where the search string was last found. For example, if the previous search found the search string at character position 8 in the txtEdit control, then the next search should start at character position 9. At first glance, it may appear that all you need to do to position the insertion point correctly is to add one to the text box's SelStart property. Recall, however, that when the search string is located in the text box, the Find command's Click event repositions the insertion point to the left of the first character in the search string; it repositions the insertion point in order to highlight the entire search string. In other words, if the search string is found at character position 8 in the txtEdit control, the Find command repositions the insertion point to insertion point position 7. (It may help to refer to Figure 6-57.) Therefore, to position the insertion point to the right of the search string, you will need to add two to the SelStart property. Figure 6-61 illustrates this concept.

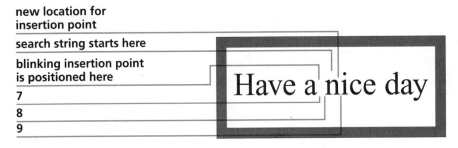

Figure 6-61: Illustration of the SelStart property

To continue coding the Search menu's Find Next command, then save and run the application:

1   Type **inBegSearch = txtEdit.SelStart + 2** and press the **Enter** key.

Now use the Instr function to search the txtEdit control for the search string, which is stored in the form-level stSearchFor variable. If the Instr function does not find the search string, then display an appropriate message; otherwise, position the insertion point appropriately and highlight the search string in the txtEdit control.

2   Maximize the Code window, then enter the code shown in Figure 6-62. Be sure to enter the Const instruction and declare the UserResponse variable. The code in the figure was compressed so that you could read more of each line.

add these lines of code

Figure 6-62: Completed Code window for the Find Next command

3   Close the Code window, then **save** and **run** the application.

4   Test the application by entering a few sentences in the text box, then using the Find and Find Next commands to search for one or more words in those sentences.

5   When you are finished testing the application, click **File**, then click **Exit** to end the application.

You have now completed Lesson C. You will finish coding the text editor application in Tutorial 7. For now, you can either take a break, complete the questions and exercises at the end of the lesson, or continue to the Debugging Section. The Debugging Section may contain information that will help you with problems you might encounter when doing the exercises at the end of the lesson.

S U M M A R Y

To manipulate strings:

- Use the Left, Right, or Mid functions.
- The Left function returns the leftmost *n* characters from the *stringexpression*. The syntax of the Left function is **Left**(*stringexpression*, *n*).
- The Right function returns the rightmost *n* characters from the *stringexpression*. The syntax of the Right function is **Right**(*stringexpression*, *n*).
- The Mid function returns *n* characters of the *stringexpression* beginning at position *start*. The syntax of the Mid function is **Mid**(*stringexpression*, *start*[,*n*]).

To search a string to determine if it contains another string:

- Use the Instr function. The syntax of the Instr function is **Instr**(*start*, *string1*, *string2*[, *compare*]).
- *Start* is a numeric expression that sets the starting position for the search.
- *String1* is the string expression being searched and *string2* is the string expression being sought.
- *Compare* is either the number 0 or the number 1. If *compare* is set to its default value of 0, Visual Basic performs a case sensitive search. If compare is set to 1, Visual Basic performs a case insensitive search.
- If *string2* is not contained within *string1*, then the Instr function returns the number 0. If *string2* is contained within *string1*, then the Instr function returns the starting position of *string2*.

Q U E S T I O N S

1. Which two functions can you use to manipulate one or more characters from the left side of a string?
   a. IsNumeric
   b. Left
   c. Mid
   d. Right
   e. Xtract

2. Which two functions can you use to manipulate one or more characters from the right side of a string?
   a. IsNumeric
   b. Left
   c. Mid
   d. Right
   e. Xtract

3. The _____ function allows you to extract *n* characters from a *stringexpression*, beginning with the *start* character.
   a. IsNumeric
   b. Left
   c. Mid
   d. Right
   e. Xtract

4. Assuming that the stMsg variable contained the string "Have a great day", the Left(stMsg, 2) function would return _____ .
   a. a
   b. av
   c. ay
   d. Ha
   e. v

5. Assuming that the stMsg variable contained the string "Have a great day", the Right(stMsg, 2) function would return _____ .
   a. a
   b. av
   c. ay
   d. d
   e. Ha

6. Assuming that the stMsg variable contained the string "Welcome home", the Mid(stMsg, 3, 4) function would return _____ .
   a. com
   b. come
   c. lcom
   d. ome

7. The Left(stName, 3) function is equivalent to which of the following?
   a. Mid(StName, 3, 1)
   b. Mid(StName, 1, 3)
   c. Mid(StName, 3, 0)
   d. Mid(StName, 0, 3)
   e. Mid(StName, 3, 3)

8. Assuming the StName variable contains the name "John Jeffries", the Right(StName, 3) function is equivalent to which of the following?
   a. Mid(StName, 3, 10)
   b. Mid(StName, 10, 3)
   c. Mid(StName, 3, 11)
   d. Mid(StName, 11, 3)

9. Assuming the stMsg variable contains the string "Don't forget to VOTE for your favorite candidate", the Instr(1, stMsg, "vote", 0) function would return

   _____ .
   a. 0
   b. 16
   c. 17

10. Assuming the stMsg variable contains the string "Don't forget to VOTE for your favorite candidate", the Instr(1, stMsg, "vote", 1) function would return

   _____ .
   a. 0
   b. 16
   c. 17

11. Assuming the stMsg variable contains the string "Don't forget to VOTE for your favorite candidate", the Instr(10, stMsg, "vote", 1) function would return

   _____ .
   a. 0
   b. 16
   c. 17

12. Assuming the stMsg variable contains the string "Don't forget to VOTE for your favorite candidate" , the Instr(10, stMsg, "vote", 0) function would return _____ .

a. 0
b. 16
c. 17

13. You use the _____ property to position the blinking insertion point in a text box.

a. Position
b. SelLength
c. SelPos
d. SelStart
e. SelText

14. In order to highlight a group of characters in a text box, beginning with character 10, you would need to set the SelStart property to _____ .

a. 9
b. 10
c. 11

E X E R C I S E S

NOTE: When creating the user interfaces for the applications in this lesson, be sure to follow all GUI design rules. For example, assign access keys to the essential components of the interface, center the form, highlight the existing text in a text box, create a default command button (if appropriate), and so on.

1. Evaluate the following:

Function	Resulting String
Left("Mary Jones", 4)	
Right("Sam Smith", 2)	
Mid("Bobby Day", 1, 1)	
Mid("Jack Li", 3, 2)	

Figure 6-63

2. Assuming that the stStateName variable contains "California", evaluate the following:

Function	Resulting String
Mid(stStateName, 8, 1)	
Left(stStateName, 6)	
Right(stStateName, 5)	
Mid(stStateName, 3, 5)	

Figure 6-64

3. In this exercise you will manipulate strings.

Scenario: Each salesperson at BobCat Motors is assigned an ID number, which consists of four characters. The first character is either the letter F or the letter P. The letter F indicates that the salesperson is a full-time employee; the letter P indicates that he or she is a part-time employee. The middle two characters are the salesperson's initials, and the last character is either a 1 or a 2. A 1 indicates that the salesperson sells new cars, and a 2 indicates that the salesperson sells used cars. The manager wants an application that will allow him or her to enter the salesperson's number. The application should display the salesperson's employment status (either full-time or part-time), the salesperson's initials, and which type of cars the salesperson sells (either new or used). Use label controls to display the information.

a. Create an appropriate user interface. Be sure to include either a Print command button or a Print item on a File menu. The Print button or menu item should print the form.

b. Save the form and the project as lc3Done in the Tut06 folder on your Student Disk.

c. Code the application according to the information supplied in the scenario. Be sure to display appropriate messages to the user if they enter something other than an F or a P as the first character, or if they enter something other than a 1 or a 2 as the last character.

d. Save and run the application. Test the application with the following correct ID numbers: FRJ2, PMM1. Print the interface after entering each employee number.

e. Now test the application with the following incorrect ID numbers: TLL1, FJJ5. On the printouts from step d, write down the error messages that appear after entering each of these incorrect employee numbers.

f. Exit the application, then print the code.

g. Submit the printouts from step d, which contains the error messages recorded in step e, and the code from step f.

4. In this exercise you will manipulate strings.

Scenario: Each employee at Acme Wares is assigned an employee number, which consists of three characters. If the employee is salaried, the second digit in the employee number is a 1—for example, employee number 117 would indicate a salaried employee. If the employee is hourly, the second digit in the number is a 2—for example, employee number 127 would indicate an hourly employee. The manager wants an application that will allow him or her to enter the employee's number. The application should display the employee's employment status, either salaried or hourly. Use label controls to display the information.

a. Create an appropriate user interface. Be sure to include either a Print command button or a Print item on a File menu. The Print button or menu item should print the form.

b. Save the form and the project as lc4Done in the Tut06 folder on your Student Disk.

c. Code the application according to the information supplied in the scenario. Be sure to display appropriate messages to the user if they enter something either than a 1 or a 2 as the second character.

d. Save and run the application. Test the application with the following correct employee numbers: 312, 421. Print the interface after entering each employee number.

e. Now test the application with the following incorrect employee numbers: 1A3, 267. On the printouts from step d, write down the error messages that appear after entering each of these incorrect employee numbers.

f. Exit the application, then print the code.

g. Submit the printouts from step d, which contains the error messages recorded in step e, and the code from step f.

5. In this exercise you will use a sequential access file and a menu control.

Scenario: Computer Warehouse wants an application that will calculate both the total number of items sold and the total number sold by item. The application should allow the user to print the interface.

a. Create the user interface shown in Figure 6-65.

Figure 6-65

b. Save the form and the project as lc5Done in the Tut06 folder on your Student Disk.

c. Set the list box's Font property to 12 points. Set its Sorted property to True. After filling the list box with data, have the application automatically select the first item in the list.

d. Set the Font property of both the lblTotal and the txtSold controls to 18 points. Set the label control's Alignment property to 2-Center.

e. Add a File menu to the application. Include Print and Exit options. Code the Exit button so that it unloads the form. Code the Print button so that it prints the form. Assign the appropriate access keys and the appropriate shortcut key.

f. Code the Enter Item button so that, when clicked, it writes the record (item number and number sold) to a sequential access data file named lc5.dat.

g. Add a Statistics menu to the application. Include two options: Calculate Total and Calculate by Item. Assign access and shortcut keys to both options.

h. Code the Calculate Total option so that it calculates the total number sold for all of the items in the file. Display an appropriate message along with the total number sold in the lblTotal control. (For example: Display the message "The total number sold is 300." in the lblTotal control.)

i. Code the Calculate by Item option so that it calculates the total sold for only the item the user chooses in the list box. (In other words, if the user clicks the ABC11 item in the list box, the Calculate by Item option will calculate and display only the total sold for the ABC11 item.) Display an appropriate message along with the total number sold for that item in the lblTotal control. (For example: Display the message "The total number sold for item ABC11 is 50." in the lblTotal control.)

j. Save and run the application. Test the application by entering each of the following records. After entering each record, be sure to click the Enter Item button to write the record to the file.

Item	Sold
BDX22	100
ABC11	150
BDX22	250
CVA33	100
ABC11	300

k. After entering the records, use the Statistics menu's Calculate Total option to calculate the total number sold. Use the File menu's Print option to print the interface.

l. Click the BDX22 item in the list box. Use the Statistics menu's Calculate by Item option to calculate the number of item BDX22 sold. Use the File menu's Print option to print the interface.

m. Exit the application. Print the code.

n. Submit the printouts from steps k and l, and the code from step m.

Exercises 6 through 8 are Discovery Exercises, which allow you to both "discover" the solutions to problems on your own and to experiment with material that is not covered in the tutorial.

discovery ▶ **6.** In this exercise you will create a text editor and use the HideSelection property of a text box.

Scenario: In Windows applications, the Find command is customarily found on the Edit menu. In this exercise you will create a text editor that has the Find command on the Edit menu instead of on a Search menu.

a. Open the lcEdit application that you created in Lesson C.

b. Save the form and the project as lc6Done in the Tut06 folder on your Student Disk.

c. Use the Help menu to search for information on a text box's HideSelection property.

d. In the lc6Done application, put the Find command in the Edit menu instead of in the Search menu. Include a separator bar between the Paste command and the Find command.

e. The Find command's Click event uses the InputBox function to ask the user for the search string. Replace the InputBox function with a form that resembles a dialog box. (Recall that you learned about creating dialog boxes in Tutorial 3.) The dialog box that you create should include a text box in which the user enters the search string, a Find Next button, and a Cancel button. You do not need to include a Replace button.

f. Move the code from the Find Next command on the Search menu to the Find Next button's Click event procedure.

g. Remove the Search menu from the application, including its Find and Find Next commands.

h. Modify the Edit menu's Find and Find Next code appropriately.

i. Save and run the application. Type a sentence in the text box, then use the Edit menu's Find command to search for a word in that sentence. When you click the Find Next button, the application should either find the next occurrence of the word, or display a message that the search is complete. The dialog box should remain on the screen when the word is found, and the word should be highlighted in the text box.

j. Exit the application. Print the application's code.

discovery ▶ **7.** In this exercise you will manipulate strings.

Scenario: Credit card companies typically assign a special digit, called a check digit, to the end of each customer's credit card number. Many methods for creating the check digit have been developed. One simple method is to multiply every other number in the credit card number by 2, then add the products to the remaining numbers to get the total. You would then take the last digit in the total and add it to the end of the number, as illustrated in Figure 6-66.

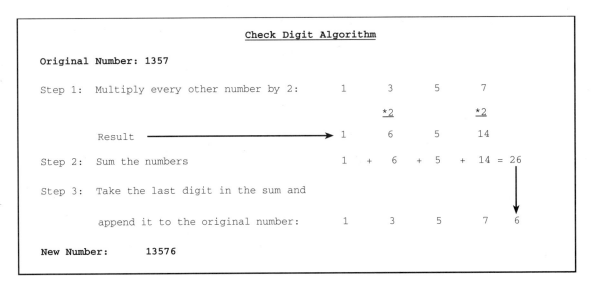

Figure 6-66

a. Based on the check digit algorithm shown in Figure 6-66, manually calculate the check digits for the following numbers, then write the new numbers with their check digits. The first example has been completed for you.

Number	Number with Check Digit
1357	13576
4273	42731
3907	39075
4621	46210

b. Open a new project, if necessary. Add a text box, a label control, and a command button to the interface.

c. Save the form and the project as lc7Done in the Tut06 folder on your Student Disk.

d. The application should allow the user to enter the number, including the check digit. When the user clicks the command button, the application should display "Correct" in the label control if the check digit is correct; it should display "Incorrect" in the label control if the check digit is incorrect. In other words, if the user enters 13576 in the text box, the application should display "Correct." However, if the user enters 13579 in the text box, then the application should display "Incorrect."

e. Save and run the application. Use the application to verify the check digits for the numbers shown in Step a.

f. Print the code

discovery ▶ 8. In this exercise you will manipulate strings and use a sequential access file and a list box.

Scenario: Each salesperson at BobCat Motors is assigned a code that consists of two characters. The first character is either the letter F or the letter P. The letter F indicates that the salesperson is a full-time employee; the letter P indicates that he or she is a part-time employee. The second character is either a 1 or a 2. A 1 indicates that the salesperson sells new cars, and a 2 indicates that the salesperson sells used cars. The manager wants an application that he or she can use to display one of the following listings in a list box:

1) the names of full-time salespeople
2) the names of part-time salespeople
3) the names of salespeople who sell new cars
4) the names of salespeople who sell used cars
5) the names of full-time salespeople who sell new cars
6) the names of full-time salespeople who sell used cars
7) the names of part-time salespeople who sell new cars
8) the names of part-time salespeople who sell used cars

a. Create an appropriate user interface. Display the desired listing in a list box whose Sorted property is set to true. Be sure to include either a Print command button or a Print item on a File menu. The Print button or menu item should print the form.

b. Save the form and the project as lc8Done in the Tut06 folder on your Student Disk.

c. Code the application according to the information supplied in the Scenario.

d. Use WordPad (*Notepad in Windows 3.1*) to create a sequential access data file that contains both the code number and names of 25 salespeople. Name the data file lc8.dat. (Recall that each code number should contain two characters. The first character must be either an F or a P. The second character must be either a 1 or a 2.) Print the contents of the lc8.dat file.

e. Save and run the lc8Done application. Test the application by displaying each listing. When you display the listing for the full-time salespeople who sell new cars, print the interface.

f. Exit the application, then print the code.

g. Submit the printout from steps d and e, and the code from step f.

D E B U G G I N G

Technique   Visual Basic's Edit menu provides two commands that you can use to edit the code in an application quickly. These commands are Find and Replace.

Following are two debugging exercises that will allow you to practice this tutorial's debugging technique.

> To debug the first application:
>
> **1**   Start Visual Basic, if necessary, and open the **Debug1** (debug1.vbp) project, which is located in the Tut06 folder on your Student Disk.
>
> **2**   View the frmDebug1 form. The user interface contains three label controls, one text box, and three command buttons.
>
> **3**   **Run** (but don't save) the application. Type **10** in the Old price text box, then click the **Calc 5%** button. The "Variable not defined" message appears. Click the **OK** button to remove the message. Visual Basic highlights the error in the cmd5 control's Click event procedure; the application does not recognize the Text1 entry.
>
> **4**   Click the **Object** list arrow in the Code window to display a list of the object names. The correct name of the text box in the interface is txtOld. You will use Visual Basic's Edit menu to correct the name in the Code windows.
>
> **5**   Click the **Object** list arrow to close the list of object names. Click **Edit**, then click **Replace**. The Replace dialog box appears as shown in Figure 6-67.

Figure 6-67: Replace dialog box

The Replace dialog box contains a Find What text box and a Replace With text box. You enter the search text—the text you want to search for—in the Find What box and you enter the replacement text—the new text—in the Replace With box. In this case, you want to replace Text1 with txtOld.

6 If necessary, type **Text1** in the Find What box. Press the **Tab** key, then type **txtOld** in the Replace With box.

Notice the four option buttons (Current Procedure, Current Module, Current Project, Selected Text) in the Search section of the dialog box. Selecting the Current Procedure option tells Visual Basic to look for the search text in the current procedure only. Selecting the Current Module option tells Visual Basic to perform the search in the current module only; the current module includes all of the procedures in the current form. If you select the Current Project option, every procedure in the entire application is searched. Lastly, if you select the Selected Text option, only the selected text is searched.

In this case, you will select the Current Module option, which will search all of the procedures in the current form.

7 If necessary, click the **Current Module** option button to select it. A black dot should appear inside the option button.

The Replace dialog box also contains three check boxes (Find Whole Word Only, Match Case, Use Pattern Matching). Selecting the Find Whole Word Only check box tells Visual Basic to search for the full word by itself, not as part of another word. In other words, if the search text is "the", Visual Basic should look for "the" as a whole word; it should not find "there", "them", and so on.

If the Match Case check box is selected, Visual Basic performs a case sensitive search; otherwise it performs a case insensitive search.

If the Use Pattern Matching check box is selected, you can use Visual Basic's pattern matching characters in the Find What text box. For example, you could search for all controls whose name begins with txt by entering txt* in the Find What text box; the asterisk (*) is one of Visual Basic's pattern matching characters. To learn more about the pattern matching characters, use the Help menu to display a Help window on the topic "pattern matching."

In this case you will not need to select any of the three check boxes.

8 Click the **Direction** list arrow. Notice that you can set the direction of the search to either Down, Up, or All. Click **All** in the list.

Now begin the search.

tips

· · · · · · · · · · · · · · · · ·

If no text is highlighted in the Code window when the Replace dialog box appears, the Selected Text option will be dimmed.

9 Click the **Find Next** button. Visual Basic highlights the Text1 entry in the cmd5_Click event. Click the **Replace** button to replace the Text1 entry in the cmd5_Click event with txtOld. Visual Basic then highlights the Text1 entry in the cmd8_Click event. Click the **Replace** button to replace the Text1 entry in the cmd8_Click event. The message "The specified region has been searched" appears. Click the **OK** button to remove the message, then click the **Cancel** button to remove the Replace dialog box.

10 Close the Code window, then click the **Continue** 🔳 button on the toolbar. The "Variable not defined" message appears. Click the **OK** button to remove the message. Visual Basic highlights the Label3 entry in the cmd5_Click event.

11 Click the **Object** list arrow. The correct name for the label control is lblNew. Click the Object list arrow to close the list.

12 Click **Edit**, then click **Replace**. Type **Label3** in the Find What box, then type **lblNew** in the Replace With box. This time click the **Replace All** button, which will automatically replace all occurrences of Label3 with lblNew. Visual Basic informs you that two replacements were made.

13 Click the **OK** button to remove the message, then click the **Cancel** button to remove the Replace dialog box.

14 Click the **Continue** button 🔳 on the toolbar. The interface appears with 10 in the Old price text box and 0.5 in the New price text label control. Click the **Calc 8%** button. The New price label control now shows 0.8.

15 Click the **Exit** button to exit the application. Correct the application so that it calculates the new price instead of the increase. **Run**, but do not save, the application. Test the application to verify that it is working correctly, then click the **Exit** button. You do not need to save the correct application.

To debug the second application:

1 Open the **Debug2** (debug2.vbp) project, which is located in the Tut06 folder on your Student Disk.

2 View the frmDebug2 form. The user interface contains three label controls, one text box, and three command buttons.

3 **Run** (but don't save) the application. Use the Edit menu's Replace command to correct the errors. Be sure that the application will work if the user mistakenly enters a letter instead of a number in the text box.

4 When the application is working correctly, print the application's code.

TUTORIAL

7

Dialog Boxes and Error Trapping

Completing the Text Editor Application

case ▶ In Tutorial 6 you began creating the Text Editor application for the PAO (Political Awareness Organization). Recall that the PAO sends a questionnaire to the voters in their district. The questionnaire asks the voter to provide his or her political party and age group. The data provided from the returned questionnaires is tabulated by the organization's secretary, who then sends a summary report to the organization's members and to various political offices in the district. In this tutorial, you will finish creating the Text Editor application.

Recall that you coded the application's Edit and Search menus, but you did not code its File menu. You will code the File menu in this tutorial.

Previewing the Completed Application

Begin by opening and previewing the completed Text Editor application for the PAO.

To preview the completed Text Editor application:

1   If necessary, start Windows, then place your Student Disk in the appropriate drive.

2   Use the Run command on the Start menu to run the **Edit95** (Edit95.exe) file, which is located in the Tut07 folder on your Student Disk. The Text Editor application's user interface appears on the screen. See Figure 7-1.

Use the Run command on the Program Manager's File menu to run the edit31.exe file, which is located in the Tut07 folder on your Student Disk. The Text Editor application's user interface appears on the screen. See Figure 7-1.

Figure 7-1: Text Editor application's user interface

3   Type your first name in the document, then press the **Enter** key.

In Tutorial 6 you previewed the Edit and Search menus; in this tutorial, you will preview the commands on the File menu. Begin with the Save As command.

4   Click **File**, then click **Save As**. When the Save As dialog box appears, open the Tut07 folder on your Student Disk, then type **Preview** in the File name text box. See Figure 7-2.

Figure 7-2: Save As dialog box created by the Common Dialog control

The Save As dialog box shown in Figure 7-2 was created with the Common Dialog control, which you will learn about in Lesson A.

5   Click the **Save** button to save the document.

WINDOWS **3.1**

Click the OK button to save the document.

HELP? If this is the second or subsequent time you are saving the Preview file, a message asking if you want to replace the existing Preview.txt file will appear. Click the Yes button.

6   Type your last name in the document, then press the **Enter** key.

Observe how the New command works.

7   Click **File**, then click **New**. Because the current document was changed since the last time it was saved, a message asking if you want to save the current document appears. Click the **Yes** button.

8   When the Save As dialog box appears, click the **Save** button. A message asking if you want to replace the existing Preview.txt file appears. Click the **Yes** button. The application saves the current document, then displays a new document.

WINDOWS **3.1**

When the Save As dialog box appears, click the OK button. A message asking if you want to replace the existing Preview.txt file appears. Click the Yes button.   The application saves the current document, then displays a new document.

Next observe how the Open command works.

9   Click **File**, then click **Open**. Open the Tut07 folder on your Student Disk, then click **Preview.txt** in the File name list box. See Figure 7-3.

Figure 7-3: Open dialog box created by the Common Dialog control

The Open dialog box shown in Figure 7-3 also was created with the Common Dialog control.

10 Click the **Open** button to open the file. The application opens the Preview.txt file and displays its contents (your first and last name) in the interface.

Click the OK button to open the file. The application opens the Preview.txt file and displays its contents (your first and last name) in the interface.

Now make a change to the document and use the Save command to save the document under its current name.

11 Delete your last name from the document. Click **File**, then click **Save**. The application saves the document on your Student Disk without asking if you want to replace the existing file.

Lastly, use the File menu's Print command.

12 If your computer is connected to a printer, click **File**, then click **Print**. When the Print dialog box appears, click the **OK** button. The application prints the document. A message box appears on the screen while the document is printing.

13 Click **File**, then click **Exit** to end the application.

WINDOWS 3.1

In Lesson A you will learn about the Common Dialog control, which will be used in the Text Editor application to display the Save As, Open, and Print dialog boxes. In Lesson B, you will learn how to trap any errors encountered when using the Common Dialog control. You will complete the Text Editor application in Lessons B and C.

Important Note: You will not be able to complete Lessons A, B, or C using the Visual Basic Working Model. You will need to use the Standard or Professional Edition of Visual Basic.

LESSON A
objectives

In this lesson you will learn how to:
- Display standard dialog boxes using the Common Dialog control
- Set the Common Dialog control's Filter and Filename properties
- Set the Common Dialog control's Flags property

Dialog Boxes

Important Note: You will not be able to complete Lesson A using the Visual Basic Working Model. You will need to use either the Standard or Professional Edition of Visual Basic.

The Common Dialog Control

The Common Dialog control provides a standard set of dialog boxes for operations such as opening, saving, and printing files, as well as selecting colors and fonts. You will use the Common Dialog control in the Text Editor application, which you will finish coding in this tutorial, to allow the user to open and save the documents that he or she creates. Recall that the PAO's (Political Awareness Organization) secretary will use the text editor to send a report to the organization's members and to various political offices in the district. Before opening the Text Editor application, however, you will open an application that will allow you to practice with each of the standard dialog boxes created by the Common Dialog control.

To open the application that contains examples of the Common Dialog control:

1. Start Visual Basic, if necessary, and open the **Common** (common.vbp) project, which is in the Tut07 folder on your Student Disk.

2. Save the form and the project as **laCommon**.

3. Click the **View Form** button to view the frmCommon form. The user interface appears as shown in Figure 7-4.

txtEdit

Figure 7-4: frmCommon user interface

This application will allow you to view the Open, Save As, Print, Font, and Color dialog boxes created by the Common Dialog control. First add the CommonDialog tool to the toolbox. Although the Common Dialog control is a custom control, it is one of the controls available in both the Standard and Professional Editions of Visual Basic.

4   Click **Tools** on the menu bar, then click **Custom Controls** to open the Custom Controls dialog box. Click the **Microsoft Common Dialog Control** check box. Be sure an X appears in the check box. Click the **OK** button to close the Custom Controls dialog box. The CommonDialog tool appears in the toolbox as shown in Figure 7-5.

CommonDialog tool

Figure 7-5: CommonDialog tool in the toolbox

5   Double-click the **CommonDialog tool** in the toolbox. The Common Dialog control, which appears as an icon, displays on the form. Set the control's Name property to **cdlCommon**. "Cdl" is the three-character ID for the Common Dialog control. Drag the icon to the position shown in Figure 7-6.

Common Dialog control

Figure 7-6: Common Dialog control added to the form.

6   Click the **Lock Controls** button 🔒 on the toolbar to lock the controls in place on the form.

7 Click the **Save Project** button 🔲 on the toolbar to save the form and the project.

During design time, the Common Dialog control displays as an icon on the form; you can't size the icon and it doesn't matter where the icon is positioned on the form. During run time, Visual Basic will display an appropriately sized dialog box, instead of the icon, in a default position in the interface. You tell Visual Basic which type of dialog box to display, as well as when to display the dialog box, by including one of the Common Dialog control's methods in an event procedure. The Common Dialog control's methods along with an explanation of each are shown in Figure 7-7.

Method	Purpose
ShowOpen	Displays a standard Open dialog box
ShowSave	Displays a standard Save As dialog box
ShowPrinter	Displays a standard Print dialog box
ShowColor	Displays a standard Color dialog box
ShowFont	Displays a standard Font dialog box

Figure 7-7: Common Dialog control's methods

You need to put only one Common Dialog control on the form. You can then use that one control to display one or more different dialog boxes. In the current application, for example, you will use the cdlCommon control to display the Open, Save As, Print, Font, and Color dialog boxes at different times while the application is running. Begin by coding the Open Dialog command button, which should display an Open dialog box that allows the user to open a file.

Displaying an Open Dialog Box

The Open Dialog command button should display the standard Open dialog box available in Windows applications. First, observe how a standard Open dialog box appears.

To view a standard Open dialog box, then begin coding the Open Dialog command button:

1 Click **File** on the menu bar, then click **Open Project.**

2 Open the Tut07 folder on your Student Disk. See Figure 7-8.

HELP? *If you are using Windows 3.1, your dialog box will differ from the one shown in Figure 7-8.*

HELP? If a dialog box asking if you want to save the changes to the frmCommon form appears, click the Yes button.

name of the current
folder

list of file names

empty when dialog box
appears

type of files
displayed in list

Figure 7-8: Visual Basic's Open Project dialog box

The Open dialog box shows that the name of the current folder is Tut07; it also displays a list of filenames in the File name list box. The filenames listed in the File name list box depend on the entry in the Files of type (*List files of type in Windows 3.1*) list box. In the Open dialog box shown in Figure 7-8, for example, the Files of type list box contains Project Files (*.Vbp;*.Mak); that entry describes the type of files to display in the File name list box—in this case, Project Files—and the filter—in this case, *.Vbp;*.Mak—that determines whether a file is a project file. The filter refers to the extension on the file's name. (Project filenames in Versions 2.0 and 3.0 of Visual Basic end in .Mak, rather than the .Vbp used in Version 4.0.) The *.Vbp;*.Mak filter tells Windows that only files with names ending in either .Vbp or .Mak are project files, so only files ending in .Vbp or .Mak should be displayed in the File name list box. Notice that the File name text box is empty when the Open dialog box appears. (*The File name text box displays the filter in Windows 3.1.*)

Many applications allow the user to select from a list of predefined descriptions and filters. For example, Visual Basic's Open Project dialog box allows you to display all of the files contained in the current folder. Observe that now.

3   Click the **Files of type** list arrow.

  Click the List files of type list arrow.

The standard description and filter for displaying all files in the current folder is All Files(*.*).

4   Click **All Files(*.*)**. Windows displays the names of all files in the current folder.

5   Click the **Cancel** button to close the Open Project dialog box.

Now code the Open Dialog button in the frmCommon form. You will need to use the Common Dialog control's ShowOpen method to display the standard Open dialog box.

6   Double-click the **Open Dialog** button to open its Click event procedure. Press the **Tab** key, then type **cdlCommon.showopen** and press the **Enter** key.

7   Close the Code window, then **save** and **run** the application.

8   Click the **Open Dialog** button. A standard Open dialog box appears.

9   Open the Tut07 folder on your Student Disk. See Figure 7-9.

tips

The asterisk (*) in the *filter* is known as a wildcard character because, similar to a wild card in a game of poker, you can use it to represent anything you want. In this case, the *.vbp;*.mak *filter* tells Windows to display all file names ending in either .vbp or .mak. The * indicates that you are not concerned with the beginning of the file name.

W I N D O W S   3 . 1

HELP? *If you are using Windows 3.1, your dialog box will look different from the one shown in Figure 7-9.*

current folder

list of filenames

this should contain a
description and filter

Figure 7-9: Open dialog box created by the Common Dialog control's ShowOpen method

The dialog box shows that the Tut07 folder is the current folder; it also displays a list of filenames in the File name list box. (*In Windows 3.1 the File name list box is empty.*) Notice that the File name text box is empty when the Open dialog box appears. The Files of type list box (*List files of type list box in Windows 3.1*) is also empty, which is not correct; it should contain the description and filter for the type of files to be displayed in the File name list box. You enter both a description and a filter in the Open dialog box by setting the Common Dialog control's Filter property.

10   Click the **Cancel** button to close the Open dialog box, then click the **Exit** button to end the application. Visual Basic returns to the design screen.

In Windows 95, when the Files of type box is empty, the File name list box displays the names of all files contained in the current folder.

The Filter Property

The **Filter property** stores a string that represents both the description and the filter for the files displayed in the File name list box when either the Open or the Save As dialog box appears. The string, which appears in the Files of type list box (*List files of type list box in Windows 3.1*) during run time, can contain any characters that are valid for a file name, including the * (asterisk).

The syntax of the instruction used to assign the description and filter to the Filter property is *object*.**Filter** = d*escription1*|*filter1*|*description2*|*filter2*..., where both *description* and *filter* are string expressions that specify the type of files to display. As the syntax shows, the Filter property can contain the descriptions and filters for multiple file types. Notice that you use the pipe symbol (|) to separate a *description* from its corresponding *filter*, and to separate one file type's *description* and *filter* from the next file type's *description* and *filter*. When typing the *filter*, be sure you don't include spaces before or after the pipe symbol; if you do, the spaces will be displayed, incorrectly, with the *description* and *filter* values. Figure 7-10 shows examples of Filter property settings.

Filter	Result
"All Files(*.*)l*.*"	Displays the names of all files contained in the current folder.
"Text Files(*.txt)l*.txtlAll Files(*.*)l*.*"	Displays the names of either the text files contained in the current folder or all files contained in the current folder.
"Project Files(*.vbp;*.mak)l*.vbp;*.mak"	Displays the names of project files contained in the current folder. Note: If a file type has more than one filename extension, notice that you separate the extensions with a semicolon (;).

Figure 7-10: Examples of Filter property settings

In this application, you want the Open dialog box to allow the user either to display the names of only text files in the current folder or to display the names of all files in the current folder.

To set the Filter property in the Open Dialog button's Click event procedure:

1 Double-click the **Open Dialog** button to open its Click event procedure, then maximize the Code window. The Filter property must be set before the Open dialog box is displayed. Enter the Filter property instruction shown in Figure 7-11.

enter this instruction

display text filenames

display all filenames

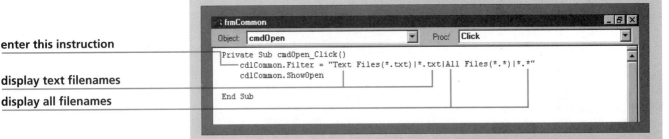

```
frmCommon
Object: cmdOpen          Proc: Click

Private Sub cmdOpen_Click()
    cdlCommon.Filter = "Text Files(*.txt)|*.txt|All Files(*.*)|*.*"
    cdlCommon.ShowOpen

End Sub
```

Figure 7-11: Instruction to set the Filter property entered in Code window

2 Close the Code window, then **save** and **run** the application.

3 Click the **Open Dialog** button. The Tut07 folder on your Student Disk should be open. Notice that Visual Basic uses the first filter listed in the Filter property as the default filter in the Files of type list box (*List files of type list box in Windows 3.1*); in this case the *.txt filter displays only the text files contained in the current folder.

In Windows 3.1, notice that the filter also appears in the File name text box.

If the user wants to view all of the files in the Tut07 folder, he or she can simply click the Files of type list arrow (*List files of type list arrow in Windows 3.1*), then select the All Files(*.*) entry in the list. Display all of the files in the current folder.

4 Click the **Files of type** list arrow.

Click the List files of type list arrow.

5 Click **All Files(*.*)** in the list. The names of all the files contained in the Tut07 folder appear in the File name list box.

WINDOWS 3.1

In Windows 3.1, notice that the new filter appears in the File name text box.

6 Click a filename in the list. The file's name appears in the File name text box. When the user either selects a file from the File name list box, or enters a name in the File name text box, the file's name is stored in the Common Dialog control's Filename property.

7 Click the **Open** button in the dialog box.

WINDOWS 3.1

Click the OK button in the dialog box.

The dialog box closes, but the file does not open. This is because the Open Dialog button's Click event contains only the code to create the Open dialog box; it does not include the code to actually open a file. You will learn how to use the Open dialog box to open a file in Lesson B.

See what happens when you click the Open Dialog button again.

8 Click the **Open Dialog** button. Notice that the File name text box contains the name of the file that you selected earlier. In Windows applications, the File name text box is typically empty when the Open dialog box appears. (*In Windows 3.1, the File name text box contains the filter when the Open dialog box appears.*) You can remove the filename from the File name text box by setting the Common Dialog control's Filename property to the empty string.

9 Click the **Cancel** button to close the Open dialog box, then click the **Exit** button to end the application. Visual Basic returns to the design screen.

The Filename Property

The **Filename property** stores the name of the file that appears in the File name text box. To remove the contents of the File name text box, you simply need to assign the empty string ("") to the Common Dialog control's Filename property before displaying the Open dialog box. Assigning the empty string to the Filename property will clear the contents of the File name text box. (*In Windows 3.1, assigning the empty string to the Filename property will display the appropriate filter in the File name text box.*)

To complete the Open Dialog button's Click event procedure:

1 Double-click the **Open Dialog** button to open its Click event procedure. Maximize the Code window, then enter the additional line of code shown in Figure 7-12.

enter this instruction

```
Private Sub cmdOpen_Click()
    cdlCommon.Filter = "Text Files(*.txt)|*.txt|All Files(*.*)|*.*"
    cdlCommon.filename = ""
    cdlCommon.ShowOpen

End Sub
```

Figure 7-12: Instruction to set the Filename property entered in Code window

2   Close the Code window, then **save** and **run** the application.

3   Click the **Open Dialog** button.

Now display the names of all the files in the Tut07 folder on your Student Disk.

4   Click the **Files of type** list arrow, then click **All Files(*.*)** in the list.

Click the List files of type list arrow, then click All Files(.*) in the list.*

5   Select a filename, then click the **Open** button.

Select a filename, then click the OK button.

The dialog box closes.

Now see what happens when you click the Open Dialog button again.

6   Click the **Open Dialog** button. Note the File name text box is empty.

If you are using Windows 3.1, the File name text box will display the filter.

7   Click the **Cancel** button to close the Open dialog box, then click the **Exit** button to end the application. Visual Basic returns to the design screen.

Now code the Save As command button, which will display a standard Save As dialog box.

Displaying a Save As Dialog Box

The Save As command button should display a standard Save As dialog box. Observe what a standard Save As dialog box looks like.

To view a standard Save As dialog box, then begin coding the Save As command button:

1   Click **File** on the menu bar, then click **Save File As**. Open the Tut07 folder on your Student Disk. See Figure 7-13.

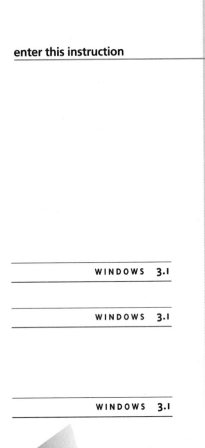

WINDOWS 3.1

WINDOWS 3.1

WINDOWS 3.1

GUI
Design Tips

Open Dialog Box Guidelines

• The Files of type list box (*List files of type list box in Windows 3.1*) should contain the descriptions and filters that control the display of the filenames in the File name list box.

• In Windows 95, the File name text box should be empty when the Open dialog box appears. (*In Windows 3.1, the File name text box should contain the default filter when the Open dialog box appears.*)

current folder

File name list box

current file's name

filter

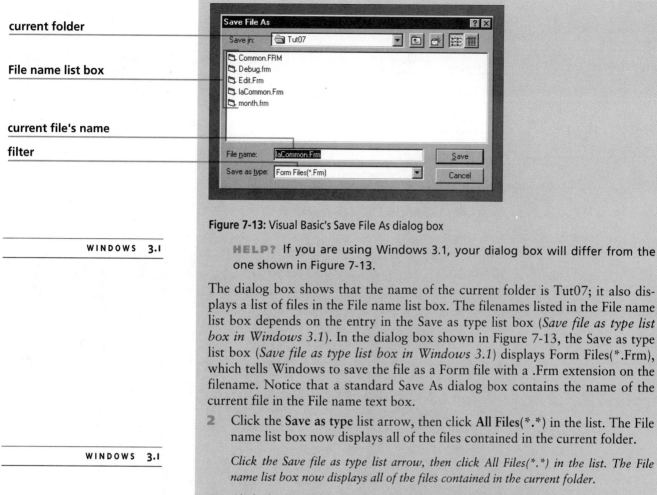

Figure 7-13: Visual Basic's Save File As dialog box

WINDOWS   **3.1**

HELP? If you are using Windows 3.1, your dialog box will differ from the one shown in Figure 7-13.

The dialog box shows that the name of the current folder is Tut07; it also displays a list of files in the File name list box. The filenames listed in the File name list box depends on the entry in the Save as type list box (*Save file as type list box in Windows 3.1*). In the dialog box shown in Figure 7-13, the Save as type list box (*Save file as type list box in Windows 3.1*) displays Form Files(*.Frm), which tells Windows to save the file as a Form file with a .Frm extension on the filename. Notice that a standard Save As dialog box contains the name of the current file in the File name text box.

2   Click the **Save as type** list arrow, then click **All Files(*.*)** in the list. The File name list box now displays all of the files contained in the current folder.

WINDOWS   **3.1**

Click the Save file as type list arrow, then click All Files(*.*) in the list. The File name list box now displays all of the files contained in the current folder.

3   Click the **Cancel** button to close the Save File As dialog box.

Now use the ShowSave method to code the Save As command button in the frmCommon form. In this example, you will use the Common Dialog control's Filter property to display only files that end in .txt.

4   Double-click the **Save As Dialog** button to open its Click event procedure. Enter the code shown in Figure 7-14.

enter these two instructions

Figure 7-14: Save As command button's Click event procedure

5   Close the Code window, then **save** and **run** the application.

6   Click the **Save As Dialog** button. See Figure 7-15.

list of filenames
matching filter

current folder

File name text box is
empty

filter

Figure 7-15: Save As dialog box created by the Common Dialog control's ShowSave method

The Save As dialog box shows that the name of the current folder is Tut07. The File name list box shows a list of filenames matching the filter specified in the Save as type list box. The File name text box is empty.

7 Type **Example** in the File name text box.

8 Click the **Save** button. The file name, Example, is recorded in the Common Dialog control's Filename property. (Remember, you have not coded the button to actually save the file. At this point, the dialog box merely treats the file as though it has been saved.)

Click the OK button. The filename, Example, is recorded in the Common Dialog control's Filename property. (Remember, you have not coded the button to actually save the file. At this point, the dialog box merely treats the file as though it has been saved.)

Observe what happens when you click the Save As Dialog button again.

9 Click the **Save As Dialog** button. Example.txt appears in the File name text box. *(If you are using Windows 3.1, either a:\Tut07\Example or b:\Tut07\Example appears in the File name text box.)* Notice that the name of the saved file appears in the Filename text box when the Save As dialog box appears. Also notice that the Save As dialog box automatically appends the .txt extension to the end of the filename when the file is saved. *(If you are using Windows 3.1, the Save As dialog box does not append the .txt extension to the end of the filename when the file is saved.)*

10 Click the **Cancel** button in the dialog box, then click the **Exit** button to end the application. Visual Basic returns to the design screen.

In the next example, you will use the ShowPrinter method to display a standard Print dialog box.

Displaying a Print Dialog Box

The Print Dialog command button should display a standard Print dialog box. In Windows applications, the Print dialog box allows the user to select the printer, as well as the print range, number of copies, paper orientation (portrait or landscape), and so on.

WINDOWS 3.1

GUI
Design Tips

Save As Dialog Box Guidelines

- The Save as type list box *(Save files as type list box in Windows 3.1)* should contain the descriptions and filters that control the display of the file names in the File name list box.

- If the current file is saved, its name should appear in the File name text box when the Save As dialog box appears.

To begin coding the Print Dialog command button:

1 Double-click the **Print Dialog** button to open its Click event procedure.

The method for displaying the Print dialog box is ShowPrinter.

2 Press the **Tab** key, then type **cdlCommon.showprinter** and press the **Enter** key.

3 Close the Code window, then **save** and **run** the application. Click the **Print Dialog** button. See Figure 7-16.

your Print dialog box will look different if you are using Windows 3.1

Figure 7-16: Print dialog box created by the Common Dialog control's ShowPrinter method

Notice that the Print dialog box contains options that allow you to select the print range (All, Pages, and Selection), as well as the number of copies to print. You can also choose to print to a file rather than to the printer.

WINDOWS   3.1

The Print Dialog box in Windows 3.1 will contain other options as well.

4 Click the **Properties** button. The Properties dialog box appears and displays the Paper, Graphics, Fonts, and Device Options tabs. On your own, click each of these tabs to view their contents, then click the **Cancel** button twice to return to the application.

WINDOWS   3.1

Click the Setup button in the Print dialog box. The Setup dialog box appears with options for selecting the printer, as well as the orientation, size, and source of the paper. Click the Cancel button twice to return to the application.

5 Click the **Exit** button to end the application. Visual Basic returns to the design screen.

Each of the dialog boxes discussed in this lesson has a Flags property that is used to either return or set the options for the dialog box. For example, in the next section, you will use the Flags property both to disable the Selection option button and to hide the Print to file check box in the Print dialog box. (Refer to Figure 7-16.) When you disable the Selection option button, you prevent the user from printing the selected text in the document. When you hide the Print to file check box, you prevent the user from printing to a file. Unless the user requires that these Print dialog elements be available, it is best to disable them; the code necessary to print a selected area and also print to a file can be complex.

The Flags Property

The Common Dialog control's **Flags property** is used either to return or to set the options for the dialog box. Each of the different dialog boxes has its own settings for the Flags property. View the Flags property settings for the Print dialog box.

tips

The Flags Property (File Dialog) gives information for both the Open and Save As dialog boxes.

WINDOWS 3.1

WINDOWS 3.1

To view the information on the Flags property settings:

1 Click **Help** on the menu bar, then click **Search for Help On**. Type **flags**, then click the **Display** button. The Topics Found dialog box appears with four entries—Flags Property (Color Dialog), Flags Property (File Dialog), Flags Property (Font Dialog), and Flags Property (Print Dialog). View the information about the Print dialog box's Flags property.

Click Help on the menu bar, then click Search for Help On. Type flags, then click the Show Topics button. Four topics appear in the lower list box: Flags Property (Color Dialog), Flags Property (File Dialog), Flags Property (Font Dialog), and Flags Property (Print Dialog). View the information about the Print dialog box's Flags property.

2 Click **Flags Property (Print Dialog)**, then click the **Display** button in the Topics Found dialog box. The Help window opens.

Click Flags Property (Print Dialog), then click the Display button in the Topics Found dialog box. The Help window opens.

Notice that the syntax to set the Flags property is *object*.**Flags** [= *value*], where *object* is the Common Dialog control, and *value* is one of the constants or values shown in the Help window's Settings table.

3 Maximize the Help window, then scroll the window as shown in Figure 7-17.

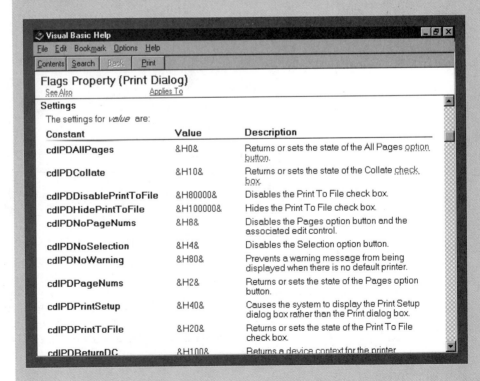

Figure 7-17: Flags Property (Print Dialog) Help window

Notice that each of the constants listed in the Help window begins with "cdl"; the cdl stands for Common Dialog control. According to the Help window, you disable the Selection option button, which will prevent the user from printing the selected text in a document, by setting the Flags property to the constant `cdlPDNoSelection`. You hide the Print to file check box by setting the Flags property to `cdlPDHidePrintToFile`; hiding the Print to file check box prevents the user from printing to a file. To set more than one flag for a dialog box, you simply add the constants together, then assign the sum to the Flags property. In other words, to display the Print dialog box with the Selection option button disabled and the Print to File check box hidden, you would use the instruction `cdlCommon.Flags = cdlPDNoSelection + cdlPDHidePrintToFile`.

To modify the code in the Print Dialog button:

1 Close the Help window, then double-click the **Print Dialog** button to open its Click event procedure. The Flags property must be set before you display the Print dialog box.

2 Maximize the Code window, then add the instruction to set the Flags property, as shown in Figure 7-18.

enter this instruction

disables Selection option button

hides Print to file check box

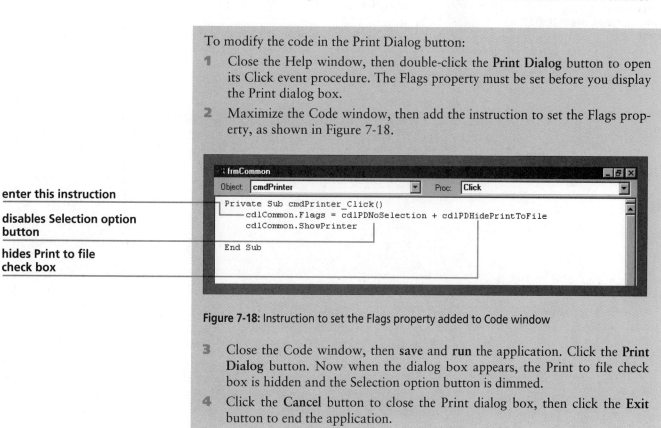

Figure 7-18: Instruction to set the Flags property added to Code window

3 Close the Code window, then **save** and **run** the application. Click the **Print Dialog** button. Now when the dialog box appears, the Print to file check box is hidden and the Selection option button is dimmed.

4 Click the **Cancel** button to close the Print dialog box, then click the **Exit** button to end the application.

In some applications, you may want to allow the user to select the name, type, and size of the font used to display the text in the document; you can use the Font dialog box to do so.

Displaying a Font Dialog Box

The Font dialog box created by the Common Dialog control allows the user to select from a list of fonts, types, and sizes. You will use the Font dialog box to control the name, type, and size of the font used to display the text in the txtEdit text box on the current form. Most of the code for the Font Dialog button is already entered in its Click event procedure.

To view the code in the Font Dialog command button:

1   Double-click the **Font Dialog** command button to open its Click event procedure. See Figure 7-19.

assign the current
values of the txtEdit
control to the Common
Dialog control

assign current selections
from Font dialog box to
the corresponding
properties of the txtEdit
control

```
frmCommon

Object: cmdFont          Proc: Click

Private Sub cmdFont_Click()

        cdlCommon.FontName = txtEdit.FontName
        cdlCommon.FontBold = txtEdit.FontBold
        cdlCommon.FontItalic = txtEdit.FontItalic
        cdlCommon.FontSize = txtEdit.FontSize

        txtEdit.FontName = cdlCommon.FontName
        txtEdit.FontBold = cdlCommon.FontBold
        txtEdit.FontItalic = cdlCommon.FontItalic
        txtEdit.FontSize = cdlCommon.FontSize

End Sub
```

Figure 7-19: Partially completed Click event procedure for the Font Dialog button

Before you can display the Font dialog box, you must set its Flags property to either `cdlCFScreenFonts`, `cdlCFPrinterFonts`, or `cdlCFBoth`. If you don't set the Font dialog box's Flags property to one of these settings, Visual Basic will display the "No fonts exist" error message. The `cdlCFScreenFonts` setting displays, in the Font dialog box, only the screen fonts available on your system, and the `cdlCFPrinterFonts` setting displays only fonts supported by your printer. The `cdlCFBoth` setting displays both the available screen and printer fonts. In this example, because you want the user to be able to change the font used in the text box on the screen only, you will have the Font dialog box display only your system's available screen fonts.

2   Press the **Tab** key, then type **cdlCommon.flags = cdlCFScreenFonts**.

The four instructions immediately below the instruction that you just entered assign the current value of the txtEdit control's FontName, FontBold, FontItalic, and FontSize properties to the Common Dialog control. By doing so, these values will be selected in the Font dialog box when the dialog box first appears; this will allow the user to identify how the text is displayed currently.

Now use the ShowFont method to display the Font dialog box.

3   Enter the ShowFont method as shown in Figure 7-20.

enter this instruction

Figure 7-20: ShowFont method entered in Font Dialog button's Click event

The four instructions below the ShowFont instruction assign the current selections from the Font dialog box to the corresponding properties of the txtEdit control; this will display the txtEdit control's text using the font name, type, and size chosen by the user.

4 Close the Code window, then **save** and **run** the application. Click the **Font Dialog** button. A standard Font dialog box appears as shown in Figure 7-21.

Figure 7-21: Font dialog box created by the Common Dialog control's ShowFont method

HELP? Your listing of Font names, styles, and sizes may be different from those shown in Figure 7-21, depending on the screen fonts available on your system.

5 On your own, select a different font name, type, and size. Click the **OK** button to close the Font dialog box. The text in the text box displays in the new font.

6 Click the **Exit** button the end the application. Visual Basic returns to the design screen.

As mentioned in Tutorial 2, color is very subjective; what is a pleasing color to you may not be to someone else. In many applications, you may want to allow your user to select the colors used in the interface. You can use a standard Color dialog box to do so.

Displaying a Color Dialog Box

The Color Dialog button in the current form will use the Color dialog box created by the Common Dialog control to allow the user to change the color of the text displayed in the txtEdit text box. The color of the text displayed in a text box is controlled by the text box's ForeColor property.

To code the Color Dialog button:

1 Double-click the **Color Dialog** button to open its Click event procedure.

First set the Flags property to the constant `cdlCCRGBInit`, which causes Visual Basic to select the black color square when the Color dialog box appears the first time. If the user selects another color square from the Color dialog box, the `cdlCCRGBInit` setting will select the corresponding color square when the Color dialog box appears again.

2 Press the Tab key, then type **cdlCommon.flags = cdlCCRGBInit** and press the **Enter** key.

Now use the ShowColor method to display the Color Dialog box.

3 Type **cdlCommon.showcolor** and press the **Enter** key.

All that remains is to assign the color that the user selected from the Color dialog box to the ForeColor property of the txtEdit control. When the user selects a color square from the Color dialog box, the color is stored in the Common Dialog control's Color property. Therefore, in this example, you simply need to assign the cdlCommon control's Color property to the txtEdit control's ForeColor property.

4 Type **txtEdit.forecolor = cdlCommon.color** and press the **Enter** key.

5 Compare your code with the code shown in Figure 7-22, and make any needed corrections before continuing.

```
frmCommon
Object: cmdColor          Proc: Click

Private Sub cmdColor_Click()
    cdlCommon.Flags = cdlCCRGBInit
    cdlCommon.ShowColor
    txtEdit.ForeColor = cdlCommon.Color

End Sub
```

Figure 7-22: Completed Click event procedure for the Color Dialog button

6 Close the Code window, then **save** and **run** the application. Click the **Color Dialog** button. The Color dialog box displays with the black square selected in the color palette, as shown in Figure 7-23.

black square is selected

Figure 7-23: Color dialog box created by the Common Dialog control's ShowColor method

7 Select a different color from the Color dialog box, then click the **OK** button. The text in the txtEdit control appears in the new color.

8 On your own, experiment with the Color dialog box. Try using the Define Custom Colors button to create a personalized color. When you are finished experimenting with the Color dialog box, click the **Exit** button to end the application. Visual Basic returns to the design screen.

You have now completed Lesson A. You can either take a break or complete the end-of-lesson questions and exercises. In Lessons B and C, you will finish coding the Text Editor application from Tutorial 6, and learn about error trapping.

S U M M A R Y

To display a standard set of dialog boxes for operations such as opening, saving, and printing files, as well as selecting colors and fonts:

■ Use the Common Dialog control.

■ The ShowOpen method displays a standard Open dialog box. The ShowSave method displays a standard Save As dialog box. The ShowPrinter method displays a standard Print dialog box. The ShowFont method displays a standard Font dialog box. The ShowColor method displays a standard Color dialog box.

To specify both a description and filter for the Open and Save As dialog boxes:

■ Set the Common Dialog control's Filter property. The syntax is *object*.**Filter** = *description1|filter1|description2|filter2...*, where both *description* and *filter* are string expressions that specify the type of files to display. The *filter* can contain the asterisk (*) character.

■ Use the pipe (|) symbol to separate a *description* from its corresponding *filter*, and to separate one file type's *description* and *filter* from the next file type's *description* and *filter*. Don't include spaces before or after the pipe symbol. If a file type has more than one file name extension, separate the extensions with a semicolon (;).

To set or return the name of the file in the Common dialog control's File name text box:

■ Use the Common Dialog control's Filename property.

To set or return the options for a Common Dialog control:

■ Set the Common Dialog control's Flags property. Each of the different dialog boxes has its own settings for the Flags property.

Q U E S T I O N S

1. The _____ control provides a standard set of dialog boxes for operations such as opening, saving, and printing files, as well as selecting colors and fonts.
   a. Box Dialog
   b. Common
   c. Common Dialog
   d. Dialog box
   e. Standard Dialog

2. You use the _____ method to display a standard Open dialog box.
   a. Open
   b. OpenDialog
   c. OpenShowDialog
   d. ShowDialog
   e. ShowOpen

3. You use the _____ method to display a standard Print dialog box.
   a. OpenPrint
   b. PrintDialog
   c. PrintShowDialog
   d. ShowPrint
   e. ShowPrinter

4. The ShowSave method displays a standard _____ dialog box.
   a. Open
   b. Save
   c. Save As
   d. None of the above

5. You use the _____ method to display a standard Color dialog box.
   a. Color
   b. ColorDialog
   c. ColorOpen
   d. ShowColor
   e. ShowColorDialog

6. You use the _____ method to display a standard Font dialog box.
   a. Font
   b. FontDialog
   c. FontOpen
   d. ShowFont
   e. ShowFontDialog

7. The _____ property stores a string that represents both the description and the filter for the files displayed in the File name list box when either the Open or the Save As dialog box appears.
   a. Description
   b. Filename
   c. Filter
   d. Text

8. Which of the following descriptions and filters tells Windows to display only file names ending in .pic?

a. `"Picture Files(*.pic)|*.pic"`

b. `"Picture Files(*.pic"|"*.pic"`

c. `"Picture Files(*.pic);*.pic"`

d. `"Picture Files|*.pic|(*.pic)"`

9. Which of the following descriptions and filters tells Windows to display only project file names—those ending in either .vbp or .mak?

a. `"Project Files(*.vbp;*.mak)|*.vbp;*.mak"`

b. `"Project Files("*.vbp;*.mak")|*.vbp|*.mak"`

c. `"Project Files(*.vbp|*.mak);*.vbp;*.mak"`

d. `"Project Files|*.vbp;*.mak|(*.vbp;*.mak)"`

10. When the user selects a file name from an Open dialog box, the file name is stored in the Common Dialog control's _____ property.

a. Description

b. File

c. Filename

d. Filter

11. Each of the dialog boxes created by the Common Dialog control has a(n) _____ property that is used to either return or set the options for the dialog box.

a. Filter

b. Flag

c. Flags

d. Option

e. Options

12. Before you can display the Font dialog box, you must set the Common Dialog control's _____ property to either cdlCFScreenFonts, cdlCFPrinterFonts, or cdlCFBoth.

a. Filter

b. Flag

c. Flags

d. Option

e. Options

E X E R C I S E S

1. a. View the Help window on the Flags Property (Color Dialog). Explain the purpose of the following two settings: `cdlCCFullOpen` and `cdlCCPreventFullOpen`. (*Note:* The Help window contains an error. The first constant should be `cdlCCFullOpen`, not `cdCCLFullOpen`.)

b. Create an application that contains a Common Dialog control and two command buttons. Change the caption for one of the command buttons to Full; change the other's caption to Partial. Code the Full button so that it sets the Common Dialog control's Flags property to `cdlCCFullOpen` before displaying the Color dialog box. Code the Partial button so that it sets the Common Dialog control's Flags property to `cdlCCPreventFullOpen` before displaying the Color dialog box.

c. Run, but don't save, the application. Observe the difference between the two Flags property settings by clicking each of the command buttons.

d. Stop the application, then print the code. You do not need to save this application.

2. a. View the Help window on the Flags Property (File Dialog). Explain the purpose of each of the following two settings: `cdlOFNCreatePrompt` and `cdlOFNOverwritePrompt`.

b. Create an application that contains a Common Dialog control and two command buttons. Change the caption of one of the command buttons to Open. Change the other's caption to Save. Code the Open button so that it sets the Common Dialog control's Filter property to display all of the files in the current folder, and sets the control's Flags property to `cdlOFNCreatePrompt` before displaying the Open dialog box. Code the Save button so that it sets the Common Dialog control's Filter property to display all of the files in the current folder, and sets the control's Flags property to `cdlOFNOverwritePrompt` before displaying the Save As dialog box.

c. Run, but don't save, the application. Click the Open command button. When the Open dialog box appears, type X in the File name box, then click the Open button *(the OK button in Windows 3.1)* On a piece of paper, write down the message that appears in the message box, then click the No button to remove the message box, and then click the Cancel button to remove the Open dialog box.

d. Click the Save command button. When the Save As dialog box appears, click any file name in the File name list box, then click the Save button *(the OK button in Windows 3.1)*. On a piece of paper, write down the message that appears in the message box, then click the No button to remove the message box, and then click the Cancel button to remove the Save As dialog box.

e. Stop the application, then print the code. You do not need to save this application.

3. a. View the Help window on the Flags Property (Font Dialog). Explain the purpose of each of the following three settings: `cdlCFEffects`, `cdlCFTTOnly`, and `cdlCFWYSIWYG`.

b. Create an application that contains a Common Dialog control and three command buttons. Change the caption of one of the command buttons to Effects. Change the second command button's caption to True Type. Change the third command button's caption to Flags:WYSIWYG. Code the Effects button so that it sets the Common Dialog control's Flags property to `cdlCFBoth + cdlCFEffects` before displaying the Font dialog box. Code the True Type button so that it sets the Common Dialog control's Flags property to `cdlCFBoth + cdlCFTTOnly` before displaying the Font dialog box. Code the WYSIWYG button so that it sets the Common Dialog control's Flags property to `cdlCFBoth + cdlCFWYSIWYG` before displaying the Font dialog box.

c. Run, but don't save, the application. Click the Effects command button to see the result of setting the Flags property to `cdlCFBoth + cdlCFEffects`. Click the Cancel button to remove the Font dialog box.

d. Click the True Type button to see the result of setting the Flags property to `cdlCFBoth + cdlCFTTOnly`. Click the Cancel button to remove the Font dialog box.

e. Click the WYSIWYG button to see the result of setting the Flags property to `cdlCFBoth + cdlCFWYSIWYG`. Click the Cancel button to remove the Font dialog box.

f. Stop the application, then print the code. You do not need to save this application.

4. a. View the Help window on the Flags Property (Print Dialog). Explain the purpose of each of the following two settings: `cdlPDDisablePrintToFile` and `cdlPDNoPageNums`.

b. Create an application that contains a Common Dialog control and one command button. Change the caption of the command button to Print. Code the Print button so that it sets the Common Dialog control's Flags property to `cdlPDDisablePrintToFile + cdlPDNoSelection + cdlPDNoPageNums`.

c. Run, but don't save, the application. Click the Print button to see the result of setting the Flags property to `cdlPDDisablePrintToFile + cdlPDNoSelection + cdlPDNoPageNums`. Click the Cancel button to remove the Print dialog box.

d. Stop the application, then print the code. You do not need to save this application.

In this lesson you will learn how to:

- Open a file using the Open dialog box
- Save a file using the Save As dialog box
- Write a string of characters to a sequential file using the Print # statement
- Set the Common Dialog control's CancelError property
- Include an error handling routine in code
- Code the Save As dialog box

Coding the Text Editor's File Menu

Important Note: You will not be able to complete Lesson B using the Visual Basic Working Model. You will need to use either the Standard or Professional Edition of Visual Basic.

Opening the Text Editor Application

In order to complete the Text Editor application that you created in Tutorial 6, you still need to code the File menu's New, Open, Save, Save As, and Print commands. Begin by opening the Text Editor application.

To open the Text Editor application, then add a Common Dialog control to the form:

1 Start Visual Basic, if necessary, and open the **Edit** (edit.vbp) project, which is located in the Tut07 folder on your Student Disk.

2 Save the form and the project as **lbEdit**.

3 Click the **View Form** button to view the frmEdit form. See Figure 7-24.

txtEdit

frmEdit

Figure 7-24: Text Editor application's user interface

The application's File menu will use the Common Dialog control, which you learned about in Lesson A, to display the Open, Print, and Save As dialog boxes. Add the Common Dialog control to the interface.

4   Click **Tools** on the menu bar, then click **Custom Controls** to open the Custom Controls dialog box. Click the **Microsoft Common Dialog Control** check box. Be sure an X appears in the check box. Click the **OK** button to remove the Custom Controls dialog box. The Common Dialog tool appears in the toolbox.

5   Double-click the **CommonDialog tool** in the toolbox. The Common Dialog control, which appears as an icon, displays on the form.

6   Click the **Lock Controls** button 🔓 on the toolbar to unlock the controls. Drag the Common Dialog control icon to the upper-left corner of the form, immediately below the txtEdit text box.

7   Set the Common Dialog control's Name property to **cdlEdit**.

8   Click the **form** to select it. The form's title bar should be highlighted. Click the **Lock Controls** button 🔒 on the toolbar to lock the controls in place on the form.

You can now continue coding the Text Editor application. The TOE chart for the application is shown in Figure 7-25.

Task	Object	Event
Accept and display text entered by the user	txtEdit	None
Open a new document	mnuFileNew	Click
Open an existing document	mnuFileOpen	Click
Save the document using its current name	mnuFileSave	Click
Save the document using a new name	mnuFileSaveAs	Click
Print the document	mnuFilePrint	Click
Exit the application	mnuFileExit	Click
Enable/disable the Cut, Copy, and Paste commands	mnuEdit	Click
Remove selected text from the txtEdit control and place it on the clipboard	mnuEditCut	Click
Copy the text selected in the txtEdit control to the clipboard	mnuEditCopy	Click
Paste the text from the clipboard into the txtEdit control	mnuEditPaste	Click
1. Ask the user for the search string 2. Search the txtEdit control for the first occurrence of the search string	mnuSearchFind	Click
Search for subsequent occurrences of the search string	mnuSearchFindNext	Click
Center the form	frmEdit	Load

Figure 7-25: TOE chart for the Text Editor application

Coding the Text Editor Application

The Text Editor application will use two form-level variables. One of the variables will keep track of whether the contents of the document—in this case, the contents of the txtEdit text box—has changed since the last time the document was saved. The other form-level variable will keep track of whether the user selected the Cancel button in the Save As dialog box; if the user selects the Cancel button in the Save As dialog box, the document will not be saved. If the current document is not saved after a change is made to it, then the File menu's Open and New commands, as well as the form's Unload event, will prompt the user to save the document before either a new or an existing document is displayed, or before the application ends.

Both of the form-level variables used in this application will be declared as Boolean variables. As you learned in Tutorial 3, Boolean variables can contain only the Boolean values True and False. You will name one of the variables blChange and the other blCancelSave.

tips

You also could have declared the form-level variables as String variables, and then assigned, for example, the values "Y" and "N" or "T" and "F" to each. When a variable's values will either be Yes/No or True/False, programmers typically use a Boolean variable rather than a String variable to store those values. When you use a Boolean value, you don't need to worry about the quotation marks surrounding the value, and you don't need to worry if the value is typed in uppercase, lowercase, or a combination of uppercase and lowercase.

To declare the two form-level variables:

1 Open the form's General declarations section. The `Option Explicit` statement and the `Dim stSearchFor as String` statement appear in the Code window. (Recall that you entered the `Option Explicit` and `dim stSearchFor as String` instructions in Tutorial 6.)

2 Position the insertion point below the Dim statement, then type **dim blChange as boolean, blCancelSave as boolean** and press the **Enter** key.

When the Text Editor application is run, the form's Load event will initialize the blChange variable to False. (The blCancelSave variable will be initialized in the File menu's Save As command.)

3 Open the form's Load event procedure, which contains the instructions to center the form. Maximize the Code window, then position the insertion point below the instruction that sets the form's Left property. Type **blChange = false** and press the **Enter** key.

If a change is subsequently made to the text box, the text box's Change event procedure will set the blChange variable to True.

4 Open the txtEdit control's Change event. Press the **Tab** key, then type **blChange = true** and press the **Enter** key.

5 Close the Code window, then click the **Save Project** button 🖫 on the toolbar.

tips

As you learned in Tutorial 5, a text box's Change event occurs when either the user or the program code changes the contents of the control.

The first command you will code is the File menu's Save As command.

Coding the File Menu's Save As Command

In Windows applications, the Save As command allows the user either to save a new file or to save an existing file under a new name. In this application, the Save As command will allow the user to save the document—in this case, the contents of the txtEdit control—in a sequential access file. The flowchart for the Save As command is shown in Figure 7-26.

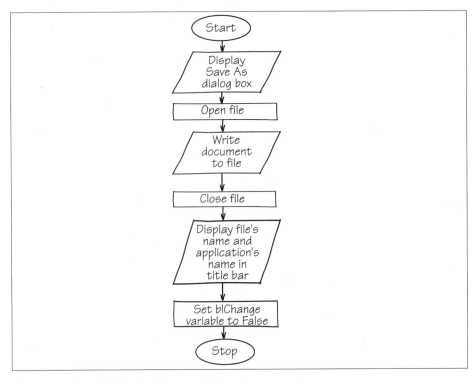

Figure 7-26: Flowchart for the File menu's Save As command

Design Tips

Save As Command

- In Windows applications, the Save As command allows the user either to save a new file or to save an existing file under a new name.

GUI
Design Tips

Title Bar Information

- When the current document has been saved, the document's name and the application's name appears in the application's title bar. If the current document has not been saved, then the type of document the application creates, along with the application's name, appears in the title bar.

Look briefly at the logic shown in the flowchart. The Save As command's Click event begins by displaying the Save As dialog box on the screen. When the user enters the name of the file to save, the file's name is stored in the Common Dialog control's Filename property. The file is then opened and the document (the text the user entered in the txtEdit control) is written to the file. The file is then closed. Before the procedure ends, the name of the saved file, followed by the name of the application (Text Editor), is displayed in the application's title bar, and the blChange variable is set to False.

Some of the code for the Save As command has already been entered in its Click event procedure for you.

To view the code in the Save As command's Click event:

1   Click **File** on the frmEdit form's menu bar, then click **Save As**. Maximize the Code window. Notice that the mnuFileSaveAs control's Click event procedure contains the instructions to set the cdlEdit control's Flags and Filter properties.

The `cdlEdit.Flags = cdlOFNOverwritePrompt + cdlOFNPathMustExist` instruction sets the Flags property for the Save As dialog box. The `cdlOFNOverwritePrompt` setting causes the Save As dialog box to generate a warning message if the user attempts to save a file using an existing name; the user will need to confirm whether he or she wants to overwrite the existing file. The `cdlOFNPathMustExist` setting causes the Save As dialog box to generate a warning message if the user enters a path that does not exist. (The **path** is a string expression that specifies the directory location for the file. The path may or may not include a drive letter specification.) The `cdlEdit.Filter = "Text`

`Files(*.txt)|*.txt"` instruction specifies the description and filter for the files to be displayed in the dialog box's File name list box; in this case, only text files are to be displayed.

Now enter the instruction to display the Save As dialog box.

2 Position the insertion point below the instruction that sets the Filter property, then type **cdlEdit.showsave** and press the **Enter** key.

Position the insertion point below the instruction that sets the Filter property, then type cdlEdit.DefaultExt = "txt" and press the Enter key, and then type cdlEdit.showsave and press the Enter key. Important note: Unlike Windows 95, Windows 3.1 does not automatically append an extension to the file name when the file is saved. You can, however, use the Common Dialog control's DefaultExt property to append an extension if one is not entered by the user. The syntax of the DefaultExt property is object.DefaultExt = string, where object is the name of the Common Dialog control and string is a string that specifies the file name extension. The cdlEdit.DefaultExt = "txt" instruction will append a .txt extension to the end of the file name when the file is saved, but only if the file name does not have an extension. (Notice that you do not include the period (.) in the string that specifies the extension.)

When the user either enters the name of the file to save in the File name text box, or selects an existing name from the File name list box, the file's name is stored in the cdlEdit control's Filename property. Use the Open statement and the Filename property to open a sequential file for Output.

3 Type **open cdlEdit.filename for output as #1** and press the **Enter** key.

According to the flowchart, the next step is to write the document (the contents of the txtEdit control) to the sequential file. For that you will need to learn about Visual Basic's Print # statement.

The Print # Statement

In Tutorial 6 you learned how to write records to a sequential file; recall that you use the Write # statement to do so. In the Text Editor application, however, you do not need to write any records to the file; rather, you need to write the contents of a text box. Unlike a record, the contents of a text box are not composed of related fields that identify a person, place, or thing; it is simply a string of characters. When writing a string of characters to a sequential file, you use the Print # statement, instead of the Write # statement. The syntax of the Print # statement is **Print** #*filenumber*, [*outputlist*], where *outputlist* is one or more expressions.

To continue coding the Save As command, then test the Save As command:

1 The Code window for the mnuFileSaveAs control's Click event should be open. With the insertion point positioned below the Open statement, type **print #1, txtEdit.text** and press the **Enter** key.

Next, use the Close statement to close the sequential file.

2 Type **close #1** and press the **Enter** key.

tips

The `cdlOFNPathMustExist` setting will display a warning message if the user attempts to save a file either on a nonexistent drive or in a nonexistent folder. It will also display a warning message if the disk drive is not ready—for example, if the drive does not contain a disk. The warning message displayed by the `cdlOFNPathMustExist` setting will vary depending on which error has occurred.

Now display the name of the saved file, along with the name of the application, in the form's title bar.

3   Type **frmEdit.caption = cdlEdit.filename & " - Text Editor"** and press the **Enter** key. (Be sure to enter a space before and after the hyphen.)

Next, set the blChange variable to False to indicate that no change has occurred in the txtEdit text box since the file was saved.

4   Type **blChange = false** and press the **Enter** key.

5   Compare your code with the code shown in Figure 7-27. (*If you are using Windows 3.1, your code will include the* `cdlEdit.DefaultExt = "txt"` *instruction.*)

If you are using Windows 3.1, your Code window will contain the `cdlEdit.DefaultExt = "txt"` **instructions above the ShowSave method.**

```
frmEdit                                                              _ ☐ ✕
Object:  mnuFileSaveAs            ▼      Proc:  Click                    ▼

Private Sub mnuFileSaveAs_Click()
    cdlEdit.Flags = cdlOFNOverwritePrompt + cdlOFNPathMustExist
    cdlEdit.Filter = "Text Files(*.txt)|*.txt"
    cdlEdit.ShowSave
    Open cdlEdit.filename For Output As #1
    Print #1, txtEdit.Text
    Close #1
    frmEdit.Caption = cdlEdit.filename & " - Text Editor"
    blChange = False

End Sub
```

Figure 7-27: Click event procedure for the File menu's Save As command

6   Close the Code window, then **save** and **run** the application.

Now test the Save As command.

7   Click **File**, then click **Save As**. If necessary, open the Tut07 folder on your Student Disk. Type **Test** in the File name box, then click the **Save** button (*the OK button in Windows 3.1*). The application saves the Test file as Test.txt in the Tut07 folder on your Student Disk. The form's title bar now shows the path and name of the saved file (either A:\Tut07\Test.txt or B:\Tut07\Test.txt), followed by the name of the application (Text Editor).

Observe the warning message displayed by the `cdlOFNOverwritePrompt` setting in the Flags property.

8   Click **File**, then click **Save As**. Notice that the name of the current file, Test.txt, appears in the File name text box. Click the **Save** button (*the OK button in Windows 3.1*). When the warning message appears asking if you want to replace the existing Test.txt file, click the **Yes** button.

Observe what happens if the user enters an incorrect path. Recall that the `cdlOFNPathMustExist` setting will display an appropriate message.

9   Click **File**, then click **Save As**. Type one of the following in the File name text box, depending on the location of your Student Disk.

   a:\tut\test.txt

   b:\tut\test.txt

10   Click the **Save** button (*the OK button in Windows 3.1*). A warning message appears informing you that the path does not exist. Click the **OK** button to remove the warning message.

When you click the Cancel button in the next step, you will notice that the application incorrectly saves the document under its current name. (You can tell that the file is being saved because the light on the drive that contains your Student Disk will flicker momentarily, and you will hear the drive spinning.)

11 The Save As dialog box should still be open. Click the **Cancel** button to remove the dialog box.

> **HELP?** If the Save As dialog box is not open, click File on the frmEdit form's menu bar, then click Save As.

Although the application should cancel the save, it saves the document under its current name instead. You will correct this problem in the next section.

12 Click **File**, then click **Exit** to end the application. Visual Basic returns to the design screen.

When the user clicks the Cancel button in the Save As dialog box, the application should cancel the save and return the user to the current document. In order to determine if the Cancel button was selected, you need to set the Common Dialog control's CancelError property to True.

Setting the CancelError Property

When the user selects the Cancel button in the Save As dialog box, the save should be canceled and the user should be returned to the current document. You can determine if the Cancel button was selected during run-time by telling Visual Basic to treat that selection as an error; you do so by setting the Common Dialog control's CancelError property to True. The **CancelError property**, which can be set to either True or False, specifies whether choosing the Cancel button is treated as an error. The default value of this property is False, which means that no error occurs when the user selects the Cancel button; setting the property to True tells Visual Basic to treat the selection as an error. The CancelError property is usually set at the beginning of the procedure, below the Dim and Const statements (if any).

To set the Common Dialog control's CancelError property:

1 Click **File** on the frmEdit form's menu bar, then click **Save As**. The mnuFileSaveAs control's Click event procedure appears. Maximize the Code window, then enter the instruction to set the CancelError property as shown in Figure 7-28. Also enter the documentation on that line.

enter this instruction and documentation

If you are using Windows 3.1, your Code window will contain the `cdlEdit.DefaultExt = "txt"` **instruction above the ShowSave method.**

```
frmEdit                                                                _ 8 X
Object:  mnuFileSaveAs                    ▼      Proc:   Click                        ▼
   Private Sub mnuFileSaveAs_Click()
       cdlEdit.CancelError = True                 'treat Cancel button as an error
       cdlEdit.Flags = cdlOFNOverwritePrompt + cdlOFNPathMustExist
       cdlEdit.Filter = "Text Files(*.txt)|*.txt"
       cdlEdit.ShowSave
       Open cdlEdit.filename For Output As #1
       Print #1, txtEdit.Text
       Close #1
       frmEdit.Caption = cdlEdit.filename & " - Text Editor"
       blChange = False

   End Sub
```

Figure 7-28: Instruction to set the CancelError property entered in the Code window

After setting the CancelError property to True, which will generate an error when the user selects the Cancel button during run-time, you then need both to intercept the error and to instruct the application on how to handle the error. The process of intercepting and handling a run-time error is called **error trapping**. The set of instructions that tells the application how to handle the error is called the **error-handling routine**, or **error handler**. In this application, the error handling routine will include the instructions that direct the application to cancel the save and return the user to the current document.

You use Visual Basic's On Error statement to include error trapping in your code.

The On Error Statement and the Error-Handling Routine

The **On Error statement** turns the error trapping process on. The syntax of the On Error statement is **On Error GoTo** *line*, where *line* is either a label or a number that identifies the position of the procedure's error handler—the set of instructions that tells the application how to handle the trapped errors. For the proper error trapping to occur, the On Error statement must be processed before the error occurs. Therefore, most programmers place the On Error statement at the beginning of the procedure in which the errors they are trying to trap may occur. The On Error statement alerts Visual Basic to watch for any run-time errors in the code listed below the On Error statement. If an error occurs, the On Error statement sends program control to the error-handling routine to determine how to handle the error. How the error is handled depends on the type of error that occurred.

A procedure that includes error trapping will typically follow the structure shown in Figure 7-29.

Structure of a procedure that includes error trapping

Private Sub statement

 [Dim statements, etc.]

 On Error GoTo *line*

 [statements]

 Exit Sub

line:

 [error-handling instructions]

End Sub

Figure 7-29: Structure of a procedure that includes error trapping

Notice the `Exit Sub` statement, which is placed immediately above the error handler in the code. The `Exit Sub` statement does exactly what it implies: it exits the sub procedure immediately. The `Exit Sub` statement prevents the error-handling routine from being processed when no error has occurred. Also notice that *line* located immediately above the error-handling instructions has a colon at the end, but *line* used in the `On Error` statement does not.

In the Text Editor application, you will include the On Error statement in the Save As command's Click event procedure, which will alert Visual Basic to watch for any errors that occur in that procedure. You will name the error handler ErrHandler. Because you set the Common Dialog control's CancelError property to True, Visual Basic will generate an error when the user selects the Cancel button in the Save As dialog box. The On Error statement will trap this error and will send program control to the ErrHandler routine. Before discussing the ErrHandler routine, enter the appropriate On Error statement in the mnuFileSaveAs control's Click event.

To enter the On Error statement in the mnuFileSaveAs control's Click event:

1 The mnuFileSaveAs control's Click event procedure should be open and maximized. Insert a blank line below the `Private Sub mnuFileSaveAs_Click()` instruction. In the blank line, type **on error goto ErrHandler** and press the **Tab** key four times, then type **'turn error trapping on.**

The error-handling routine, which is named ErrHandler, will need to set the form-level variable named blCancelSave to True, then simply exit the mnuFileSaveAs Click event without opening the sequential file and writing any information to it. (The form level blCancelSave variable, you may recall, keeps track of whether the user selected the Cancel button in the Save As dialog box. The variable will be used by the File menu's New and Open commands, as well as the form's Unload event.)

To complete the Save As command's Click event procedure:

1 The mnuFileSaveAs control's Click event procedure should be open and maximized. Enter the error-handling routine shown in Figure 7-30. Be sure to enter the `Exit Sub` statement before the error-handling routine.

If you are using Windows 3.1, your Code window will contain the `cdlEdit.DefaultExt = "txt"` **instruction above the ShowSave method.**

enter these four instructions

enter this documentation

```
frmEdit                                                          _ | □ | ×
Object:  mnuFileSaveAs          ▼    Proc:  Click                       ▼
Private Sub mnuFileSaveAs_Click()
    On Error GoTo ErrHandler                    'turn error trapping on
    cdlEdit.CancelError = True                  'treat Cancel button as an error
    cdlEdit.Flags = cdlOFNOverwritePrompt + cdlOFNPathMustExist
    cdlEdit.Filter = "Text Files(*.txt)|*.txt"
    cdlEdit.ShowSave
    Open cdlEdit.filename For Output As #1
    Print #1, txtEdit.Text
    Close #1
    frmEdit.Caption = cdlEdit.filename & " - Text Editor"
    blChange = False
    Exit Sub

ErrHandler:
    blCancelSave = True                         'Cancel button was selected
    Exit Sub

End Sub
```

Figure 7-30: Error-handling routine entered in the Save As command's Click event

2 Compare your code with the code shown in Figure 7-30. Make any needed corrections before continuing.

You need to add only one more instruction to the Save As command's Click event; that instruction will initialize the blCancelSave variable to False. (Recall that you initialized the blChange variable in the form's Load event, but you never initialized the blCancelSave variable.) The blCancelSave variable will contain the False value as long as the user does not click the Cancel button. Only if the user clicks the Cancel button will the variable's value be changed to True.

3 Insert a blank line below the `On Error GoTo ErrHandler` instruction. In the blank line, type **blCancelSave = false** and press the **Tab** key five times, then type **'initialize variable.**

4 Close the Code window, then **save** and **run** the application.

5 Click **File**, then click **Save As**. Click **Test.txt** in the File name list box, then click the **Cancel** button. The Cancel button generates an error that is trapped by the ErrHandler routine, which sets the blCancelSave variable to True and exits the Click event without opening or saving the document.

6 Click **File**, then click **Exit** to end the application. Visual Basic returns to the design screen.

The last procedure you will code in this lesson is the File menu's New command, which should remove the current document, if any, from the screen and from memory, then display a new document.

Coding the File Menu's New Command

In the Text Editor application, the New command on the File menu should remove the current document from both the screen and memory, then display a new document. If the current document has been changed since the last time it was saved, the application should prompt the user to save the current document before it is removed. The flowchart for the File menu's New command is shown in Figure 7-31.

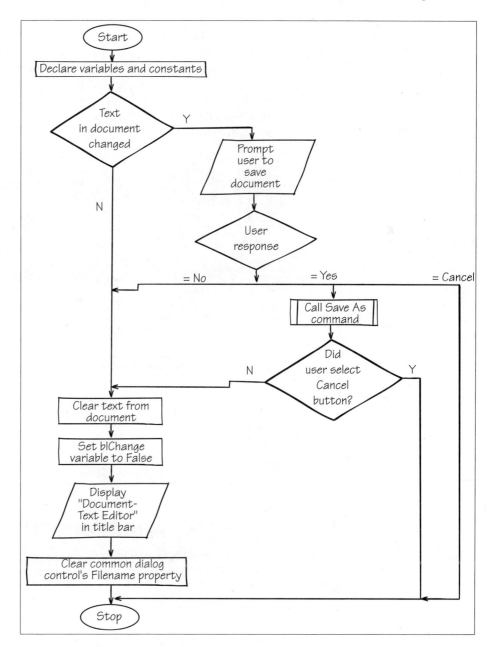

Figure 7-31: Flowchart for the File menu's New command

Briefly study the logic shown in the flowchart. The New command begins by determining if the text in the document was changed since the last time it was saved. If the document has not been changed since the last time it was saved, then a new document is displayed. If, on the other hand, the document has changed since the last time it was saved, the user is asked if he or she wants to save the document. At this point, the user can either choose to display a new document without saving the current document, choose to save the current document before a new document is displayed, or cancel the New command.

If the user chooses to cancel the New command, he or she is simply returned to the current document. If, on the other hand, the user chooses not to save the current file, then a new document is displayed. Lastly, if the user chooses to save the current document before a new document is displayed, then the New command calls the Save As command's Click event to save the document. Notice in the flowchart that when the Save As command's Click event procedure ends, the New command's Click event needs to determine if the user selected the Cancel button in the Save As dialog box. If the user selected the Cancel button in the Save As dialog box, the document was not saved. If the save was canceled, then the New command should return the user to the current document rather than display a new document.

To begin coding the New command:

1 Click **File** on the frmEdit form's menu bar, then click **New**. Maximize the Code window. The mnuFileNew control's Click event procedure appears as shown in Figure 7-32.

```
frmEdit                                                                _ 8 X

Object:  mnuFileNew              ▼     Proc:  Click                        ▼

Private Sub mnuFileNew_Click()
    Dim inUserResponse As Integer
    Const conBtns = vbYesNoCancel + vbExclamation + vbDefaultButton3 + vbApplicationMoc
    Const conMsg = "Do you want to save the current document?"
    If blChange = True Then        'text box was changed since last save
        inUserResponse = MsgBox(conMsg, conBtns, "Editor")
        Select Case inUserResponse
            Case vbYes             'user wants to save current file

            Case vbNo              'user does not want to save current file

            Case vbCancel          'user wants to cancel New command

        End Select
    End If
    txtEdit.Text = ""              'clear text box
    blChange = False               'reset variable
    frmEdit.Caption = "Document - Text Editor"
    cdlEdit.filename = ""

End Sub
```

Figure 7-32: Code entered in the New command's Click event procedure

The New command's code begins by declaring an Integer variable named inUserResponse and two constants named conBtns and conMsg; the variable and the constants are used by the MsgBox function. A selection structure then compares the contents of the blChange variable to the Boolean value True. If the blChange variable does not contain the True value, then no change was made to the document since the last time it was saved; when that is the case, the New command's Click event clears the contents of the txtEdit control, sets the blChange variable to False, assigns the string "Document - Text Editor" to the form's Caption property, and sets the Common Dialog control's Filename property to the empty string before ending the procedure.

If, on the other hand, the blChange variable contains the Boolean value True, then a change was made to the document since the last time it was saved. At this point the New command uses the MsgBox function to display a message asking the user if he or she wants to save the current document. The user can select either the Yes, No, or Cancel button in response to the message. A Case selection structure is used to determine the user's response and take the appropriate action. You will need to complete what the appropriate action is for each of the three responses. Begin with the Cancel button response.

If the user clicks the Cancel button in the MsgBox function's dialog box, it means that he or she has decided not to open a new document; rather, the user wants to continue working in the current document. In that case, the New command's Click event procedure should simply end; you can use Visual Basic's `Exit Sub` statement to do so.

tips

························

▶ Keep in mind that you clear a text box by assigning the empty string to it. Assigning the empty string to the text box will cause the Change event to occur. Because simply displaying a new document should not invoke the prompt to save the file, you need to set the blChange to False to indicate that the document does not need to be saved at this point.

To continue coding the New command's Click event procedure, then save and run the application:

1 Click in the blank line below the `Case vbCancel` statement. If necessary, press the **Tab** key until the insertion point is indented below that statement. Type **exit sub**, which will end the procedure when the user clicks the Cancel button.

Now code the No button response. If the user clicks the No button in response to the MsgBox function's message, it means that he or she does not want to save the current document before a new document is displayed. In that case, you simply need to process the instructions found below the `End If` statement. Those instructions display a new document by removing the contents of the txtEdit control, setting the blChange variable to False, resetting the form's caption, and assigning the empty string to the Common Dialog control's Filename property. For documentation purposes only, you will enter the comment "Process instructions below End If" in the `Case vbNo` clause. That is the only code you will need to enter for that case.

2 Click in the blank line below the `Case vbNo` statement. If necessary, press the **Tab** key until the insertion point is indented below that statement. Type **'Process instructions below End If**.

Now code the Yes button response. If the user clicks the Yes button in response to the MsgBox function's message, it means that he or she wants to save the current document before a new document is displayed. In that case the New command will call the Save As command's Click event procedure to save the file.

As you learned in Tutorial 4, you use the Call statement to call a user-defined procedure. You can also use the Call statement to call an event procedure. Recall that the syntax of the Call statement is **Call** *name* [(*argumentlist*)]. *Name* can be a user-defined sub procedure, as it was in Tutorial 4, or the name of an event procedure. In this case you will use the instruction `Call mnuFileSaveAs_Click` to call the Save As command's Click event procedure; that procedure will display the Save As dialog box, which will allow the user to save the current file before it is removed from the screen and from the computer's memory.

3 Click in the blank line below the `Case vbYes` statement. If necessary, press the **Tab** key until the insertion point is indented below that statement. Type **call mnuFileSaveAs_click** and press the **Enter** key.

When the Save As command's Click event is completed, the program will return to the New command's Click event. At that point, the New command's Click event must determine if the Cancel button was selected in the Save As dialog box. If the Cancel button was selected, then the current document was not saved, so the New command's Click event should end immediately. You can use the form-level blCancelSave variable to determine if the Cancel button was selected. Recall that the variable will contain the Boolean value True if the Cancel button was selected; otherwise it will contain the Boolean value False.

4   Enter the selection structure and documentation shown in Figure 7-33. Also compare your code with the code in the figure and make any needed corrections before continuing.

enter this selection structure and documentation

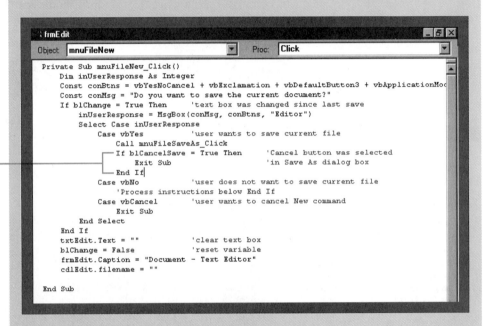

```
frmEdit                                                                    _ 5 X
Object:  mnuFileNew                        ▼   Proc:  Click                  ▼

Private Sub mnuFileNew_Click()
    Dim inUserResponse As Integer
    Const conBtns = vbYesNoCancel + vbExclamation + vbDefaultButton3 + vbApplicationMod
    Const conMsg = "Do you want to save the current document?"
    If blChange = True Then      'text box was changed since last save
        inUserResponse = MsgBox(conMsg, conBtns, "Editor")
        Select Case inUserResponse
            Case vbYes           'user wants to save current file
                Call mnuFileSaveAs_Click
                If blCancelSave = True Then      'Cancel button was selected
                    Exit Sub                     'in Save As dialog box
                End If
            Case vbNo            'user does not want to save current file
                'Process instructions below End If
            Case vbCancel        'user wants to cancel New command
                Exit Sub
        End Select
    End If
    txtEdit.Text = ""                    'clear text box
    blChange = False                     'reset variable
    frmEdit.Caption = "Document - Text Editor"
    cdlEdit.filename = ""

End Sub
```

Figure 7-33: Completed Click event for the File menu's New command

Now test the application's code.

To test the application's code:

1   Close the Code window, then **save** and **run** the application. Recall that the Load event sets the blChange variable to False.

2   Type your first name in the document, then press the **Enter** key. The txtEdit control's Change event sets the blChange variable to True to indicate that a change was made to the document.

3   Click **File**, then click **Save As**. Save the file as **Test2** in the Tut07 folder on your Student Disk.

4   Type your last name below your first name in the document, then press the **Enter** key.

Now test the File menu's New command.

5   Click **File**, then click **New**. A message appears asking if you want to save the current document. Notice that the Cancel button is the default button in the dialog box. Recall that the Cancel button should end the New command's Click event procedure and return the user to the current document.

Click the **Cancel** button. The New command's Click event procedure ends, and you are returned to the current document.

6   Click **File**, then click **New**. Recall that the Yes button in the dialog box should call the Save As command before displaying a new document. Click the **Yes** button. When the Save As dialog box appears, click the **Save** button (*the OK button in Windows 3.1*) to save the file under its current name. When the message asking if you want to replace the existing file appears, click the **Yes** button. Recall that the Save As command sets the blChange variable to False after the file has been saved.

7   Type your first name in the document. The blChange variable is set to True.

Now verify that the ErrHandler routine is correctly handling the error caused by the user selecting the Cancel button in the Save As dialog box.

8   Click **File**, then click **New**. Click the **Yes** button. When the Save As dialog appears, click the **Cancel** button. The New command's Click event procedure ends, and you are returned to the current document.

9   Click **File**, then click **New**. Now test the No button, which should simply display a new document. Click the **No** button. A new document appears on the screen.

10   Click **File**, then click **Exit** to end the application. Visual Basic returns to the design screen.

You have now completed Lesson B. You can either take a break or complete the end-of-lesson questions and exercises. You will complete the Text Editor application in Lesson C.

S U M M A R Y

To generate a warning message if the user attempts to save a file using an existing name:

- Set the Common Dialog control's Flags property to `cdlOFNOverwritePrompt`. The user will need to confirm whether he or she wants to overwrite the existing file.

To generate a warning message if the user enters a path that does not exist:

- Set the Common Dialog control's Flags property to `cdlOFNPathMustExist`.

To determine the name of the file either selected or entered in a Save As or Open dialog box:

- Use the Common Dialog control's Filename property.

To write a string of characters to a sequential file:

- Use the Print # statement. Its syntax is **Print #***filenumber*, [*outputlist*], where *outputlist* is one or more expressions.

To treat the selection of the Cancel button in a Common Dialog control's dialog box as an error:

- Set the Common Dialog control's CancelError property to True.

To turn the error trapping process on:

■   Use the On Error GoTo statement. Its syntax is **On Error GoTo** *line*, where *line* is either a label or a number that identifies the position of the procedure's error handler—the set of instructions that tells the application how to handle the trapped errors.

To include an error-handling routine in your code:

■   Use the structure shown in Figure 7-29.

To invoke (call) an event procedure:

■   Use the Call statement. Its syntax is **Call** *name* [*(argumentlist)*], where *name*, in this case, is the name of the event procedure you want to invoke. Any information that you want passed to the event procedure must be included in the *argumentlist*.

Q U E S T I O N S

1. In Windows applications, the File menu's Save As command allows the user to
   _____ .
   a. save a new file
   b. save an existing file under a new name
   c. both a and b

2. If the current document has been saved, what typically appears in the application's title bar?
   a. the document's name
   b. the application's name
   c. the type of document the application creates
   d. both a and b
   e. both b and c

3. If the current document has not been saved, what typically appears in the application's title bar?
   a. the document's name
   b. the application's name
   c. the type of document the application creates
   d. both a and b
   e. both b and c

4. When the Flags property is set to _____ , the Save As dialog box generates a warning message if the user attempts to save a file using an existing name; the user will need to confirm whether he or she wants to overwrite the existing file.
   a. `cdlOFNOverwritePrompt`
   b. `OverWritePrompt`
   c. `PromptCdlOverWrite`
   d. `WarningOverWrite`

5. When the Flags property is set to _____ , the Save As dialog box generates a warning message if the user enters a path that does not exist.
   a. `cdlOFNPath`
   b. `cdlOFNPathMustExist`
   c. `PathExist`
   d. `PathMustExist`
   e. `WarningPath`

6. Which of the following will display only the names of the Document files (those ending in .doc) in the Common Dialog control's File name list box?
   a. `cdlEdit.Filename = "Document Files(*.doc)|*.doc"`
   b. `cdlEdit.Filename = "Document Files(*.doc)/*.doc"`
   c. `cdlEdit.Filter = "Document Files(*.doc)|*.doc"`
   d. `cdlEdit.Filter = "Document Files(*.doc)/*.doc"`
   e. `cdlEdit.Filter = "Document Files(*.doc);*.doc"`

7. When the user either enters the name of the file to save in the File name text box of a Save As dialog box, or selects an existing name from the File name list box, the file's name is stored in the Common Dialog control's _____ property.
   a. CommonFile
   b. CommonFileName
   c. DialogFilename
   d. File
   e. Filename

8. Use the _____ statement to write records to a sequential file.
   a. Output #
   b. Print #
   c. Record #
   d. Write #

9. Use the _____ statement to write a string of characters to a sequential file.
   a. Output #
   b. Print #
   c. Record #
   d. Write #

10. The _____ property, which can be set to either True or False, specifies whether choosing the Cancel button is treated as an error by Visual Basic.
    a. Button
    b. ButtonCancel
    c. CancelButton
    d. CancelError
    e. ErrorCancel

11. The process of intercepting and handling a run-time error is called _____ .
    a. error interception
    b. error timing
    c. error trapping
    d. run-time interception

12. The set of instructions that tells the application how to handle a trapped run-time error is called an _____ .
    a. event procedure
    b. error processor
    c. error-handling routine or error handler
    d. function
    e. sub procedure

13. In Visual Basic, the _____ statement turns the error trapping process on.
    a. Error
    b. On Error GoTo
    c. On Error Process
    d. Process Error
    e. Trap Error

14. Always enter the _____ statement immediately above the error handler in the code.
   a. End
   b. Exit Error
   c. Exit Handler
   d. Exit Sub

15. The name of the error-handling routine ends with a _____ .
   a. colon (:)
   b. comma (,)
   c. period (.)
   d. semicolon (;)

16. Which of the following will call the mnuFileSaveAs command's Click event procedure?
   a. Call mnuFileSaveAs Click
   b. Call mnuFileSaveAs (Click)
   c. Call (mnuFileSaveAs)
   d. Call mnuFileSaveAs_Click

17. Boolean variables can contain the values _____ only.
   a. True and False
   b. Yes and No
   c. 0 and 1
   d. Boolean variables can contain any values.

E X E R C I S E S

1. In this exercise you will use the Common Dialog control to display the Color and Font dialog boxes.

   Scenario: CDA Car Sales wants an application that they can use to calculate the monthly payment on a car loan. The application you will code in this exercise is almost identical to the Month95 (Month31) application that you viewed in the Overview section; the only difference is that the application you create in this exercise will include a Format menu instead of a Color menu.

   a. Use the method appropriate for your version of Windows to run the Month95.Exe (Month31.Exe) file, which is located in the Overview folder on your Student Disk. When the interface appears, notice that the text in the Principal text box is selected. Both the 9.00% rate in the list box and the 5 years option button are also selected when the interface appears. The interest rates in the list box range from 7.00% to 12.00% in increments of .25%. Experiment with this application by calculating the monthly payment using various principals, interest rates, and terms. Also experiment with the File and Color menus. When you feel that you have a good idea of how the application works, exit the application.

   b. Open the Month (Month.vbp) project, which is located in the Tut07 folder on your Student Disk.

   c. Click the View Form button to view the form.

   d. Save the form and the project as lb1Done in the Tut07 folder on your Student Disk.

   e. Include the appropriate code to center the form on the screen.

   f. Code the form's Unload event so that it ends the application.

   g. Code the File menu's commands appropriately. (The Print command should use the PrintForm method to print the form.)

   h. Code the Format menu's commands appropriately. The Background Color command should allow the user to select a color for the form. The Information Box Color command should allow the user to select a color for the frame control. The Font command should allow the user to control the font name, type, and size of the text appearing in the lblPayment control.

    i. Code the Calculate button so that it calculates the monthly payment. (Hint: View the Help window on the Pmt function.)

    j. Include any additional code as necessary.

    k. Save and run the application. Test the application to verify that it is working correctly.

    l. Stop the application, then print the code.

2.   In this exercise you will use the Common Dialog control to display the Color and Font dialog boxes.

Scenario: In this exercise you will modify the lbEdit project that you created in Lesson B so that it includes a Format menu with Color and Font commands.

    a. Open the lbEdit (lbedit.vbp) project that you created in Lesson B. The file is located in the Tut07 folder on your Student Disk.

    b. Click the View Form button to view the form.

    c. Save the form and the project as lb2Done in the Tut07 folder on your Student Disk.

    d. Include a Format menu in the application. Position the Format menu between the Edit menu and the Search menu.

    e. Include two commands on the Format menu: Color and Font. (Remember that both commands will display a dialog box that requires the user to enter additional information. Refer to Tutorial 6 for the GUI design rules for menu commands.)

    f. Code the Color command so that it allows the user to select the background color of the txtEdit text box.

    g. Code the Font command so that it allows the user to select the font used to display the text in the txtEdit text box.

    h. Save and run the application. Test the Format menu's commands to see if they are working correctly.

    i. Exit the application, then print the code for only the Format menu's commands.

LESSON C
objectives

In this lesson you will learn how to:

■ Read a string of characters from a sequential file using the Input function

■ Return the number of characters in a sequential file using the LOF function

■ Code the Print and Open dialog boxes

Completing the Text Editor Application

Important Note: You will not be able to complete Lesson C using the Visual Basic Working Model. You will need to use either the Standard or Professional Edition of Visual Basic

Coding the File Menu's Save Command

To complete the Text Editor application, you need to code the File menu's Save, Open, and Print commands, as well as the form's Unload event procedure. Begin with the Save command.

In Windows applications, the Save command allows the user to automatically save the current document using its current name. If the current document has not been previously saved, then the Save command displays the Save As dialog box, which allows the user to give the document a name before it is saved. The flowchart for the File menu's Save command is shown in Figure 7-34.

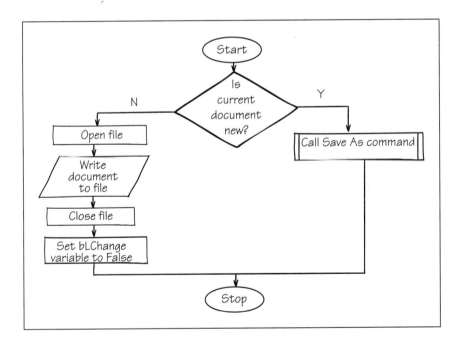

Figure 7-34: Flowchart for the File menu's Save command

According to the flowchart, the Save command first must determine if the current document is a new document—one that doesn't have a name because it hasn't been saved. You can make that determination by looking at the entry in the

GUI
Design Tips

Save Command

- In Windows applications, the Save command automatically saves the current document if the document already has a name; otherwise it displays the Save As dialog box.

application's title bar. Recall that if the document hasn't been saved, the application's title bar displays "Document - Text Editor"; otherwise the title bar displays the name of the saved document along with the name of the application.

If the document is new, then the Save command will call the Save As command's Click event; that event will display the Save As dialog box, which allows the user to enter a name for the document before it is saved. If, on the other hand, the current document is not a new document—it has been saved previously—then the Save command should automatically save the file under its current name.

The code for the Save command is already entered in its Click event procedure.

To view the code in the Save command's Click event procedure:

1 Start Visual Basic, if necessary, and open the **lbEdit** (lbedit.vbp) project, which is located in the Tut07 folder on your Student Disk.

2 Click the **View Form** button to view the frmEdit form. Save the form and the project as **lcEdit**.

3 Click **File** on the form's menu bar, then click **Save**. Maximize the Code window. The Save command's Click event appears as shown in Figure 7-35.

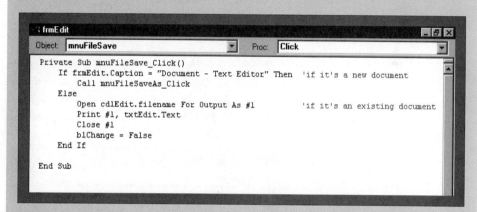

```
Private Sub mnuFileSave_Click()
    If frmEdit.Caption = "Document - Text Editor" Then    'if it's a new document
        Call mnuFileSaveAs_Click
    Else
        Open cdlEdit.filename For Output As #1              'if it's an existing document
        Print #1, txtEdit.Text
        Close #1
        blChange = False
    End If

End Sub
```

Figure 7-35: Save command's Click event procedure

The selection structure compares the value in the form's Caption property to the string "Document - Text Editor". If the Caption property contains that string, then the Save command calls the mnuFileSaveAs_Click event to save the document. If, on the other hand, the Caption property contains a value other than "Document - Text Editor", the current sequential file is opened and the txtEdit control's Text property is written to the file. The sequential file is then closed and the blChange variable is set to False.

4 Close the Code window, then **run** the application.

5 Type your first name in the document, then press the **Enter** key.

Observe how the Save command works when you use it to save a new document.

6 Click **File**, then click **Save**. Because the current document is new, the Save command calls the Save As command's Click event, which displays the Save As dialog box.

7 Save the file as **Test3** in the Tut07 folder on your Student Disk.

> **HELP?** If this is the second or subsequent time you are practicing this lesson, a prompt asking if you want to replace the existing Test3.txt file appears. Click the Yes button.

tips

> Recall that the blChange variable keeps track of whether a change has been made to the txtEdit control since the last time the document was saved. Now that the document is saved, you need to set the variable to False. If the user subsequently makes a change to the document, the text box control's Change event will set the blChange variable to True.

8 Type your last name in the document, then press the **Enter** key.

Now observe how the Save command works when you use it to save a document that has already been saved.

9 Click **File**, then click **Save**. Because the current document was saved previously, the Save command automatically saves the file using its current name and location.

10 Click **File**, then click **Exit** to end the application. Visual Basic returns to the design screen.

You will code the File menu's Print command next.

Coding the File Menu's Print Command

In this application, the File menu's Print command will simply print the document on the printer. You will use Visual Basic's PrintForm instruction to code the Print command. Most of the code for the Print command is already entered in its Click event procedure; you will need to enter only the PrintForm instruction.

To code the File menu's Print command, then save and run the application:

1 Click **File** on the form's menu bar, then click **Print**. Maximize the Code window. The mnuFilePrint control's Click event procedure appears.

2 Enter the PrintForm instruction as shown in Figure 7-36.

enter this instruction ────────────

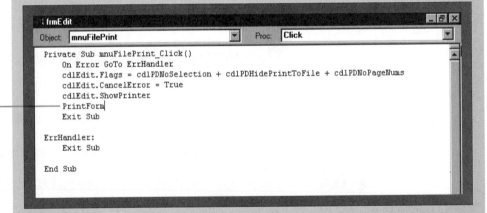

```
Private Sub mnuFilePrint_Click()
    On Error GoTo ErrHandler
    cdlEdit.Flags = cdlPDNoSelection + cdlPDHidePrintToFile + cdlPDNoPageNums
    cdlEdit.CancelError = True
    cdlEdit.ShowPrinter
    PrintForm
    Exit Sub

ErrHandler:
    Exit Sub

End Sub
```

Figure 7-36: PrintForm instruction entered in Print command's Click event procedure

After turning error trapping on, the code sets the Flags property. The `cdlPDNoSelection` setting disables the Selection option button. The `cdlPDHidePrintToFile` setting hides the Print to file check box. The `cdlPDNoPageNums` setting disables the Pages option button. The `cdlEdit.CancelError = True` instruction tells Visual Basic to treat the selection of the Cancel button as an error. The `cdlEdit.ShowPrinter` instruction displays the Print dialog box. The `PrintForm` instruction prints the form. The `Exit Sub` instruction exits the mnuFilePrint Click event before the ErrHandler code is processed. The ErrHandler code is only processed when an error occurs in the procedure.

3 Close the Code window, then **save** and **run** the application.

4 Type a few words in the document, then press the **Enter** key.

5 Click **File**, then click **Print**. Notice that the Selection and Pages option buttons are disabled; the user can choose to print only the entire document. Also notice that the Print to file check box does not appear in the dialog box. If your computer is connected to a printer, click the **OK** button in the Print dialog box; otherwise click the Cancel button. A message box appears, indicating that the document is printing. Notice that Visual Basic does not include the menu when it prints the form.

6 Click **File**, then click **Exit** to end the application. Visual Basic returns to the design screen.

The last menu command you will code is the File menu's Open command. The Open command will allow the user to open an existing document.

Coding the File Menu's Open Command

The File menu's Open command will allow the user to open an existing document so that he or she can continue working in that document. The Open command will display the document in the txtEdit control on the form.

The flowchart for the File menu's Open command is shown in Figure 7-37.

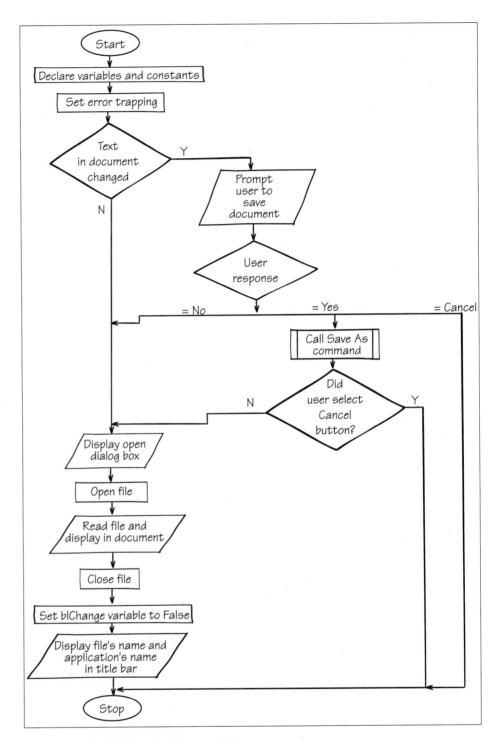

Figure 7-37: Flowchart for the File menu's Open command

After declaring the variables and constants and setting the error trapping, the Open command's Click event first must determine if the current document was changed since the last time it was saved. If it wasn't, then the procedure displays the Open dialog box, which allows the user to select the name of the file to open. The selected file is then opened and its contents are displayed in the txtEdit control. The file is then closed, the blChange variable is set to False, and the names of both the opened file and the application are displayed in the application's title bar before the procedure ends.

If, on the other hand, the document was changed since the last time it was saved, the Open command prompts the user to save the document. At this point the user can choose either to save the current document before another document is opened, or to open another document without saving the current one, or to cancel the Open operation. If the user chooses to cancel the Open command, he or she is simply returned to the current document. If the user chooses not to save the current document, then the Open command displays the Open dialog box; the selected file is then opened and its contents displayed in the txtEdit control before the file is closed. The blChange variable is set to False and the names of both the opened file and the application are displayed in the application's title bar before the procedure ends. Lastly, if the user chooses to save the current document before another document is opened, then the Open command calls the Save As command's Click event to save the file. As the flowchart shows, when the Save As command's Click event procedure ends, the Open command must determine if the user selected the Cancel button in the Save As dialog box. If the user selected the Cancel button in the Save As dialog box, then the current document was not saved; in that case the Open command should return the user to the current document rather than open a new one. If the user did not select the Cancel button in the Save As dialog box, then the Open dialog box is displayed; the selected file is then opened and its contents displayed in the txtEdit control before the file is closed. The blChange variable is then set to False and the names of both the opened file and the application are displayed in the application's title bar before the procedure ends.

In order to code the Open command, you will need to learn two new functions: Input and LOF.

The Input and LOF Functions

You use the **Input function** to read a string of characters from an open sequential file. The syntax of the Input function is **Input**(*number*, *filenumber*), where *number* specifies the number of characters in the file, and *filenumber* specifies the number used in the Open statement to open the file.

You can use Visual Basic's LOF function to determine the number of characters in the open file. The **LOF function**, which stands for "length of file," returns the number of characters contained in an opened file. The syntax of the LOF function is **LOF**(*filenumber*), where *filenumber* is the number used in the Open statement to open the file.

Most of the code for the Open command is already entered in its Click event procedure. You will need to enter only two additional lines of code.

▶ Unlike the Input # statement, which you used in Tutorial 6 to read the records from a sequential file, the Input function returns all of the characters it reads, including commas, carriage returns, linefeeds, quotation marks, and leading spaces.

▶ You use the FileLen function, instead of the LOF function, to obtain the length of an unopened file. Its syntax is FileLen(*pathname*), where *pathname* is a string expression that specifies the path and name of the unopened file.

To code the Open command's Click event:

1 Click **File** on the form's menu bar, then click **Open**. Maximize the Code window. The Open command's Click event appears. (You may need to scroll to see all of the code.)

To complete the Open command's Click event procedure, you will need to enter two additional instructions. The first instruction will use the Open statement to open the file the user selected in the Open dialog box. The second instruction will use the Input and LOF functions to read the contents of the opened file. The Input function will assign the contents of the file to the txtEdit control in the interface.

2   Enter the two additional instructions, as well as the documentation, shown in Figure 7-38.

enter these two instructions

Figure 7-38: Instructions to open and read the file entered in the Code window

3   Close the Code window, then **save** and **run** the application.
     Use the Open command to open a file.

4   Click **File**, then click **Open**. Use the Open dialog box to open the **Test3.txt** file, which is located in the Tut07 folder on your Student Disk. The Test3.txt file appears in the interface. The application's title bar should display the document's name and the application's name.

5   Click **File**, then click **Exit** to end the application. Visual Basic returns to the design screen.

The last procedure you will view is the form's Unload event. The code for the Unload event has already been entered in its Code window for you; you will only need to make one modification to the existing code.

Coding the Form's Unload Event

The flowchart for the form's Unload event is shown in Figure 7-39.

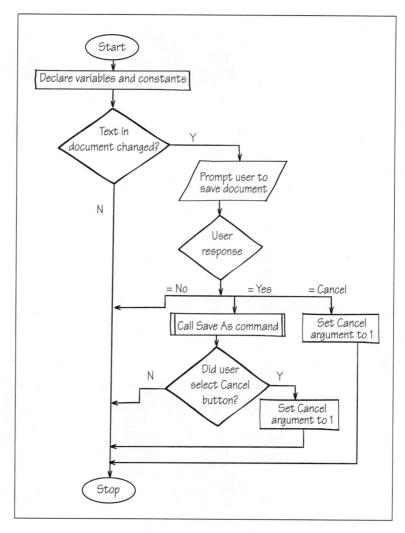

Figure 7-39: Flowchart for the form's Unload event procedure

After declaring the variables and constants, the Unload event first must determine if the current document was changed since the last time it was saved. If it wasn't, the Unload event simply unloads the form and the application ends. If, however, the current document was changed since the last time it was saved, the user is prompted to save the document. At this point the user can choose either to save the document before the application ends, or to end the application without saving the document, or to cancel the Unload event. If the user selects the Cancel button, he or she is returned to the current document; that is accomplished by setting the Unload event's Cancel argument to the number 1. If, however, the user wants to end the application without saving the current document, then the form is unloaded and the application ends. Lastly, if the user wants to save the current document before the application ends, then the Unload event calls the Save As command's Click event, which will display the Save As dialog box. As the flowchart shows, when the Save As command's Click event procedure ends, the Unload event must determine if the user selected the Cancel button in the Save As dialog box. If the user selected the Cancel button, then the Unload event's Cancel argument is set to the number 1, which will return the user to the current document; otherwise the form is unloaded and the application ends.

As mentioned earlier, the Unload event's code is already entered in the Code window. You will need to make only one modification to that code.

tips

Recall from Tutorial 5 that setting the Cancel argument to a nonzero value cancels the Unload event, which prevents the form from being unloaded.

To modify the code in the form's Unload event, then save and run the application:

1 Open the form's Unload event, then maximize the Code window.

2 Select the End statement and the documentation located below the Private Sub statement, then press the **Backspace** key to remove that line of code and documentation. See Figure 7-40.

End statement and documentation removed from procedure

```
frmEdit                                                               _ B X
Object:  Form                    ▼     Proc:  Unload                    ▼
    Private Sub Form_Unload(Cancel As Integer)

        Dim inUserResponse As Integer
        Const conBtns = vbYesNoCancel + vbExclamation + vbDefaultButton3 + vbApplicationMod
        Const conMsg = "Do you want to save the current document?"
        If blChange = True Then                   'text box was changed since last save
            inUserResponse = MsgBox(conMsg, conBtns, "Editor")
            Select Case inUserResponse
                Case vbYes                        'user wants to save current file
                    Call mnuFileSaveAs_Click
                    If blCancelSave = True Then    'user canceled save
                        Cancel = 1                 'return to document - don't unload form
                    End If
                Case vbNo                          'user does not want to save current file
                    'unload form and exit
                Case vbCancel                      'user wants to cancel New command
                    Cancel = 1                     'return to document - don't unload form
            End Select
        End If

    End Sub
```

Figure 7-40: Form's Unload event procedure

After declaring the necessary variables and constants, the code compares the value in the blChange variable, which keeps track of whether a change was made to the document, to the Boolean value True. If the blChange variable does not contain True, the form is unloaded and the application ends. If, however, the blChange variable contains the True value, then the MsgBox function prompts the user to save the current document. At this point the user can select either the Yes button, the No button, or the Cancel button. If the user selects the Cancel button, the Unload event's Cancel argument is set to the number 1 to prevent the form from being unloaded, then the Unload event procedure ends. If, on the other hand, the user selects the No button, the form is unloaded and the application ends. Lastly, if the user clicks the Yes button, the Unload event calls the Save As command's Click event. When that Click event ends, the Unload event uses the blCancelSave variable to determine if the user selected the Cancel button in the Save As dialog box. If the user selected the Cancel button, then the Cancel argument is set to the number 1 to prevent the form from being unloaded, then the Unload event procedure ends; otherwise the form is unloaded and the application ends.

3 Close the Code window, then **save** and **run** the application.

Now test the application to see if the Unload event works correctly.

4 Type your first name in the document. Click **File**, then click **Exit**. When the dialog box prompts you to save the current document, click the **Cancel** button. You are returned to the current document.

5 Click **File**, then click **Exit**. When the MsgBox function prompts you to save the current file, click the **No** button. The application ends.

6 **Run** the application. Type your first name in the document. Click **File**, then click **Exit**. When the dialog box prompts you to save the current document, click the **Yes** button. When the Save As dialog box appears, click the **Cancel** button. The application returns to the current document.

7 Click **File**, then click **Exit**. When the dialog box prompts you to save the current document, click the **Yes** button. When the Save As dialog box appears, save the document as **Test3** in the Tut07 folder on your Student Disk. When the message asking if you want to replace the existing Test3.txt file appears, click the **Yes** button. The application saves the document before the application ends.

You have now completed Lesson C and the Text Editor application. You can either take a break, complete the end-of-lesson questions and exercises, or read and complete the Debugging section. The Debugging section may contain information that will help you when completing the exercises.

S U M M A R Y

To read all of the characters in a sequential file, including commas, carriage returns, linefeeds, quotation marks, and leading spaces:

■ Use the Input function. Its syntax is **Input**(*number*, *filenumber*), where *number* specifies the number of characters in the file, and *filenumber* specifies the number used in the Open statement to open the file.

To determine the number of bytes contained in an opened file:

■ Use the LOF function. Its syntax is **LOF**(*filenumber*), where *filenumber* specifies the number used in the Open statement to open the file.

Q U E S T I O N S

1. In Windows applications, the Save command allows the user to _____ .
   a. automatically save the current document using its current name
   b. automatically save the current document using a new name
   c. give the file a name if it has not been previously saved
   d. both a and c
   e. both b and c

2. You use the _____ to read a string of characters from an open sequential file.
   a. Get # statement
   b. Get function
   c. Input # statement
   d. Input function
   e. Read function

3. The _____ returns all of the characters it reads from a sequential file, including commas, carriage returns, linefeeds, quotation marks, and leading spaces.
   a. Get # statement
   b. Get function
   c. Input # statement
   d. Input function
   e. Read function

4. The _____ function returns the number of bytes contained in an opened file.
   a. FileLen
   b. Len
   c. LFO
   d. LOF
   e. Num

5. The _____ function returns the number of bytes contained in an unopened file.
   a. FileLen
   b. Len
   c. LFO
   d. LOF
   e. Num

E X E R C I S E S

1. In this exercise you will modify the lcEdit application that you created in Lesson C.
   Scenario: Recall that the Open and New commands, as well as the form's Unload event, prompt the user to save the current document if a change was made to it since the last time it was saved; they do so by using the MsgBox function to display a dialog box with Yes, No, and Cancel buttons. If the user selects the Yes button, which indicates that he or she wants to save the current document, the application currently calls the mnuFileSaveAs command's Click event, which displays the Save As dialog box. In most Windows applications, however, if the user selects the Yes button in response to a "Do you want to save the current document?", the application automatically saves the document if the document already has a name; the Save As dialog box is only displayed if the document does not have a name.
   a. Open the lcEdit (lcedit.vbp) project, which is located in the Tut07 folder on your Student Disk.
   b. Click the View Form button to view the form.
   c. Save the form and the project as lc1Done in the Tut07 folder on your Student Disk.
   d. Modify the code in the Open and New commands, as well as in the form's Unload event, appropriately. In other words, if the user selects the Yes button in response to the "Do you want to save the current document?", have the application automatically save the document if the document already has a name; otherwise display the Save As dialog box so that the user can enter a name for the document.
   e. Save and run the application. Test the application to verify that it is working correctly.
   f. Print the code for the Open and New commands, as well as the form's Unload event.

2. In this exercise you will create a text editor that will allow you to view data files similar to the ones you created in Tutorial 6.
   Scenario: You learned how to create sequential data files in Tutorial 6. Recall that the files you created had a .dat extension. Also recall that you can use either a word processor or a text editor to view the contents of the data files. (For example, you could use WordPad in Windows 95 or Notepad in Windows 3.1.) In this exercise you will create a simple text editor that will allow you to open and view sequential data files. The text editor will also allow you to print the form.
   a. Open a new project, if necessary.
   b. Include one text box on the form.
   c. Save the form and the project as lc2Done in the Tut07 folder on your Student Disk.
   d. Create a simple text editor that contains a File menu with the following commands: Open, Print, and Exit. The Open command should display the Open dialog box and allow the user to view either data files (those whose file names end in .dat) or all files. The Print command should use the PrintForm method to print the form.

e. Save and run the application. Test the application by opening and printing the following four files, which are located in the Tut07 folder on your Student Disk: lcData1.dat, lcData2.dat, lcData3.dat, lcData4.dat.

f. End the application. Print the application's code.

g. Submit the printouts from step e and the code from step f.

3. In this exercise you will use the text editor that you created in this tutorial to create a sequential access data file. You will also use a menu control.

Scenario: Instead of using the Write # statement to create a sequential file that contains records, you can use the text editor that you created in this tutorial.

a. Open the lcEdit (lcedit.vbp) project that you finished coding in Lesson C. The project is located in the Tut07 folder on your Student Disk.

b. Run the application.

c. Enter the following six records. Each record contains a name, sex, and age. Press the Enter key only when indicated to do so. Be sure to include the quotation marks and commas as shown. Also be sure not to press the Spacebar on your keyboard.

"Mary","Female",21 <press the Enter key>
"Terri","Female",18 <press the Enter key>
"Jim","Male",33   <press the Enter key>
"George","Male",45 <press the Enter key>
"Paula","Female",53 <press the Enter key>
"Fred","Male",25   (DO NOT PRESS THE ENTER KEY)

d. Use the File menu's Save As option to save the file as lc3.txt in the Tut07 folder on your Student Disk.

e. Use the File menu's Print command to print the document.

f. Use the File menu's Exit command to exit the text editor.

g. Create an application that will read the records in the lc3.txt file. Save the form and the project as lc3Done in the Tut07 folder on your Student Disk.

The application should contain a File menu that includes Print and Exit options. (Be sure to assign the appropriate access keys and shortcut key.) The application should also contain a Display Information button that opens and reads the lc3.txt file that you saved in step d. The button should display the total number of males and the total number of females, as well as the average age of the males and the average age of the females. Display the information in label controls on the form.

h. Code the Print command so that it prints the form. Code the Exit option so that it unloads the form. Code the Unload event so that it ends the application.

i. Save and run the application. Click the Display Information button, then use the File menu's Print command to print the interface.

j. Exit the application, then print the application's code.

k. Submit the printouts from steps e and i, and the code from step j.

Exercises 4 through 6 are Discovery Exercises, which allow you to both "discover" the solutions to problems on your own and to experiment with material that is not covered in the tutorial.

discovery ▶ **4.** In this exercise you will learn about the FreeFile function.

a. View the Help window on the FreeFile function. What is the purpose of the FreeFile function?

b. Open the lcEdit (lcedit.vbp) project that you created in Lesson C. The file is located in the Tut07 folder on your Student Disk.

c. View the form.

d. Save the form and the project as lc4Done in the Tut07 folder on your Student Disk.

e. Modify the code so that it uses the FreeFile function appropriately.

f. Save and run the application. Test the application to verify that it is still working correctly.

g. Exit the application.

h. Print the code for the File menu's New, Open, Save, and Save As commands, as well as the code for the form's Unload event. Circle the sections of the code you needed to modify in order to include the FreeFile function in the application.

discovery ▶ 5. In this exercise you will learn about the Common Dialog control's FilterIndex property.

    a. View the Help window on the Common Dialog control's FilterIndex property. What is the purpose of the FilterIndex property?

    b. Open a new project, if necessary. Add the CommonDialog tool to the toolbox. Add a command button and a Common Dialog control to the form.

    c. Code the command button's Click event so that it sets the Common Dialog control's Filter property to display all text files (file names ending in .txt), all picture files (file names ending in .pic), and all files. After setting the Filter property, the Click event should show the Open dialog box.

    d. Save the form and the project as lc5Done in the Tut07 folder on your Student Disk.

    e. Run the application, then click the command button. Notice that the first filter listed in the Filter property is the default filter that appears in the dialog box.

    f. Stop the application. Open the command button's Click event. Before displaying the Open dialog box, set the Common Dialog control's FilterIndex property to 2.

    g. Save and run the application, then click the command button. Notice that the second filter listed in the Filter property is now the default filter in the dialog box.

    h. Stop the application. Open the command button's Click event. Modify the code so that the default filter is the third filter listed in the Filter property.

    i. Save and run the application, then click the command button to see if the modified code is working correctly.

    j. Stop the application. Print the command button's code.

discovery ▶ 6. In this exercise you will learn about the Resume statement.

Scenario: You use the Resume statement, whose syntax is **Resume [Next | line]**, to resume program execution after an error-handling routine is finished. (In the Visual Basic syntax, the pipe (|) symbol means either/or. In other words, you can choose either **Next** or *line*, but not both.) Resume, by itself, causes program execution to resume with the statement that caused the error. For example, let's assume that, when attempting to process a print instruction, an application determines that the printer is not online. When the On Error statement traps this error, it sends program control to the error handler. The error handler instructions can prompt the user to turn the printer on, wait until he or she does, and then use the Resume statement to resume program execution with the print instruction that caused the error.

The Resume Next instruction, on the other hand, causes program execution to resume with the statement immediately following the one that caused the error. If, for example, an instruction causes an "Internal error" (error code 51), the error handler instructions can prompt the user to copy the error message down on paper, wait for the user to do so, and then use the Resume Next statement to resume program execution with the instruction immediately following the one that caused the error.

You use the Resume *line* instructions in cases where the application cannot resume execution either with the instruction that caused the error or with the one immediately below that instruction. Resume *line* allows the error handler to resume program execution at *line*, which is either a label or a number that identifies an instruction located somewhere in the procedure.

    a. Create a simple application that makes use of the Resume statement. Print the application's code. You do not need to save the application.

    b. Create a simple application that makes use of the Resume Next instruction. Print the application's code. You do not need to save the application.

    c. Create a simple application that makes use of the Resume *line* instruction. Print the application's code. You do not need to save the application.

    d. Submit the code from steps a, b, and c.

D E B U G G I N G

Technique

As you learned in previous tutorials, it is important to test an application with both valid and invalid data. The application should be able to handle the invalid data appropriately; in other words, the application should not "crash"—end unexpectedly—because the user entered invalid data. Once you have determined which types of errors may occur in the application, you can use error trapping, along with the Err and Error functions, to instruct the application to take the appropriate action that will prevent the application from "crashing."

To practice this tutorial's Debugging technique:

1 Open the **Debug** (debug.vbp) project, which is located in the Tut07 folder on your Student Disk.

2 Click the **View Form** button to view the form. See Figure 7-41.

Figure 7-41: Debugging example's user interface

3 Save the form and the project as **DebDone** in the Tut07 folder on your Student Disk.

4 Open the Divide button's Code window and view the one line of code in its Click event procedure. The code simply divides the contents of the txtNum1 text box by the contents of the txtNum2 text box, then displays the result in the lblQuotient label control.

5 Close the Code window.

Now display a Help window that shows the types of errors that Visual Basic allows you to trap.

6 Use the Help menu to display the Help window on the Trappable Errors topic. When the Help window appears, maximize the Help window, then click **Miscellaneous Messages**. See Figure 7-42.

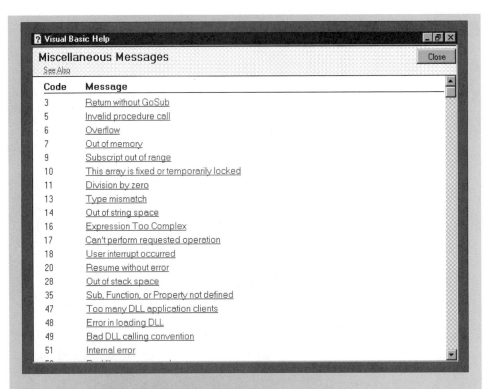

Figure 7-42: Miscellaneous Messages Help window

Notice that each error is identified by a code and a message. When an error occurs, Visual Basic assigns the error's code to a function named Err; it assigns the error's message to a function named Error. For example, if an application attempts to divide an expression by zero, Visual Basic assigns the number 11 (the error code corresponding to a "Division by zero" error) to the Err function and it assigns the string "Division by zero" to the Error function.

7 Scroll the Help window to view the various trappable errors, then close the Help window.

Recall that the current application divides the number entered in the Number 1 text box by the number entered in the Number 2 text box, then displays the quotient in the Quotient label control. Although the application is quite simple, it can still "crash" because of errors. You can determine the expected errors in an application by simply running the application and using it improperly—in other words, in a manner that the programmer did not intend. Observe how the application responds when the user clicks the Divide button without entering any numbers in the interface.

8 **Run** the application, then click the **Divide** button. Visual Basic displays error message number 6 ("Overflow") in a dialog box. Click the **End** button in the dialog box to end the application.

Now observe how the application responds when the user enters a string for the second number.

9 **Run** the application again, type **100** in the Number 1 text box, then type **S** in the Number 2 text box. Press the **Enter** key to select the Divide button. Visual Basic displays error message number 11 ("Division by zero") in a dialog box. Click the **End** button in the dialog box to end the application.

You can use error trapping, along with either the Err or Error functions, to trap both the Overflow and the Division by zero errors, and then take the appropriate action so that the application does not "crash" when these errors occur.

To include error trapping in the Divide button's Click event procedure:

1 Open the Divide button's Click event procedure. Maximize the Code window, then enter the code shown in Figure 7-43.

enter these five instructions

enter these nine instructions

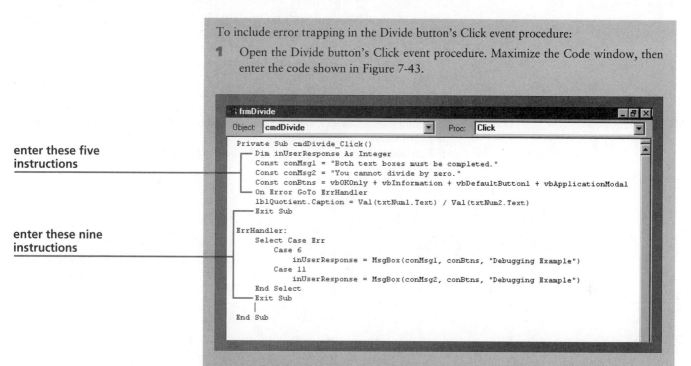

```
frmDivide

Object: cmdDivide          Proc: Click

Private Sub cmdDivide_Click()
    Dim inUserResponse As Integer
    Const conMsg1 = "Both text boxes must be completed."
    Const conMsg2 = "You cannot divide by zero."
    Const conBtns = vbOKOnly + vbInformation + vbDefaultButton1 + vbApplicationModal
    On Error GoTo ErrHandler
    lblQuotient.Caption = Val(txtNum1.Text) / Val(txtNum2.Text)
    Exit Sub

ErrHandler:
    Select Case Err
        Case 6
            inUserResponse = MsgBox(conMsg1, conBtns, "Debugging Example")
        Case 11
            inUserResponse = MsgBox(conMsg2, conBtns, "Debugging Example")
    End Select
    Exit Sub

End Sub
```

Figure 7-43: Error trapping code included in Divide button's Click event procedure

2 Close the Code window, then **save and run** the application.

Observe how the application responds when the user clicks the Divide button without entering any numbers in the interface.

3 Click the **Divide** button. The application displays the "Both text boxes must be completed." message in a dialog box. Click the **OK** button. Instead of "crashing," as it did when error trapping was not included, the application returns the user to the interface.

Now observe how the application responds when the user enters a string for the second number.

4 Type **100** in the Number 1 text box, then type **S** in the Number 2 text box. Press the **Enter** key to select the Divide button. The application displays the "You cannot divide by zero." message in a dialog box. Click the **OK** button. The application returns the user to the interface.

5 Click the **Exit** button to end the application. Visual Basic returns to the design screen.

Following is a Debugging Exercise for you to try.

Exercise   1. If necessary, open the DebDone (debdone.vbp) project that you created in this Debugging Section. The project is located in the Tut07 folder on your Student Disk.

a. Save the form and the project as DebDone2 in the Tut07 folder on your Student Disk.

b. Open the Divide button's Click event procedure. Modify the Case structure so that it uses the Error function, instead of the Err function, to determine which error occurred.

c. Save and run the application. Test the application by clicking the Divide button without entering any numbers. Also test the application by entering a string for the second number. Both errors should display the appropriate error message, then return the user to the interface.

d. End the application, then print the application's code.

TUTORIAL

8

Random Access Files

The Cole's Playhouse Application

case ▶ Every Sunday afternoon, Cole's Playhouse, a small community theater, performs plays featuring local talent. The theater holds only 48 seats, which must be reserved in advance of the performance. No tickets are sold at the door. The manager of the playhouse, Max Phillips, asks you to create an application that will keep track of each patron's name and phone number.

Previewing the Application

As you've done in previous tutorials, you will preview the application before creating it.

> Important Note: You will not be able to preview the application using the Working Model.

To preview the application:

1   If necessary, start Windows, then place your Student Disk in the appropriate drive.

2   Use the Run command on the Start menu to run the **Cole95** (cole95.exe) file, which is located in the Tut08 folder on your Student Disk. The application's user interface appears on the screen. Mr. Phillips can use this application to record the ticket reservations for each play, but first he needs to open either a new or an existing file.

WINDOWS 3.1

Use the Run command on the Program Manager's File menu to run the cole31.exe file, which is located in the Tut08 folder on your Student Disk. The application's user interface appears on the screen. Mr. Phillips can use this application to record the ticket reservations for each play, but first he needs to open either a new or an existing file.

First open an existing file named Preview.dat.

3   Click **File**, then click **Open**. An Open dialog box appears. Use the Open dialog box to open the **Preview.dat** file, which is located in the Tut08 folder on your Student Disk. Visual Basic displays the interface shown in Figure 8-1.

Figure 8-1: User interface for the Cole's Playhouse application

The form uses label controls to represent the 48 seats in the Cole's Playhouse theater. Notice that some of the label controls are red and some are white. A red label control indicates that the seat is reserved; a white label control indicates that the seat is not reserved. To reserve a seat, you simply click the corresponding label control. Reserve seat number 8.

4   Click seat number 8. The dialog box shown in Figure 8-2 opens.

Figure 8-2: Dialog box shown in the user interface

This dialog box is used to enter or cancel a reservation, as well as to return to the screen that displays the theater seats. Reserve seat number 8 for Sue Marlin.

5   Type **Sue Marlin** in the Patron name text box, press the **Tab** key, then type **111–1111** in the Phone text box. Press the **Enter** key to select the Enter Ticket button. The application saves Sue Marlin's name and phone number in a random access file on your Student Disk; it also closes the dialog box and changes the color of seat number 8 to red.

Observe how you cancel a reservation.

6   Click seat number 8. Sue Marlin's information appears in the form on the screen. Click the **Cancel Ticket** button. The application removes Sue Marlin's name and phone number from the random access file, then closes the dialog box and changes the color of seat number 8 to white.

You can also use the application to create a new file.

7   Click **File**, then click **New**. When the Save As dialog box appears, save the new file as **Prev2** in the Tut08 folder on your Student Disk. The form showing the 48 seats, each colored white to indicate that they are not reserved, appears.

HELP? If this is the second or subsequent time you are creating the Prev2 data file, the application will display a dialog box asking if you want to replace the existing file. Click the Yes button.

8   Experiment by reserving and canceling seats of your choosing.

9   When you are finished experimenting, click **File**, then click **Exit** to end the application.

In Lesson A you will learn how to use random access files in an application. You will code the Cole's Playhouse application in Lessons B and C as you learn how to refer to a control in another form and also use Visual Basic's color constants.

LESSON A
objectives

In this lesson you will learn how to:
- Create a user-defined data type
- Open and close a random access file
- Write data to a random access file
- Read data from a random access file
- Initialize a random access file

Random Access Files

Random Access Files Versus Sequential Access Files

As you learned in Tutorial 6, you can save the data that the user enters, such as the student scores from Tutorial 5 or the questionnaire responses from Tutorial 6, in a data file. A data file, you may remember, is organized into fields and records. A **field** is a single item of information about a person, place, or thing—for example, a social security number, a city, or a price. A **record** is a group of related fields that contain all of the necessary data about a specific person, place, or thing. A collection of related records is called a **data file**.

Recall that Visual Basic has three types of data files—sequential access, random access, and binary access. (Binary access files are beyond the scope of this book.) A sequential access file is similar to a cassette tape in that each record in the file, like each song on a cassette tape, is both stored and retrieved in consecutive order from the beginning of the file to the end of the file. A random access file, on the other hand, is similar to a compact disc (CD) in that each record in the file, like each song on a CD, can be stored and retrieved in any order. That means, for example, that you can read or write the third record in a random access file without first reading or writing the two records that precede it.

As you may know, each song on a CD is associated with a unique number. The number indicates the position of the song on the CD; it allows you to access the song directly. Each record in a random access file also has a unique number, called a **record number**, that indicates its position in the file. The first record in the file is record number 1, the second record is number 2, and so on. You can directly access a record in a random access file by its record number. For this reason, random access files are also referred to as **direct access files**.

The ability to directly access a record allows quick retrieval of information, which accounts for the extensive use of random access files for on-line activities, such as making airline reservations, looking up the prices of items at a store, and approving credit card purchases. In a random access file, you can access record number 500 just as quickly as record number 1. Accessing record number 500 in a sequential access file would take much longer because the program would have to read the previous 499 records first.

You may be wondering why programmers use sequential files at all if random access files are so much faster for retrieving data. Sequential access files are generally used when you are dealing with records that do not all have the same number of fields, or when you want to store text created with a typical text editor, as you did in Tutorial 7.

Before looking at a sample application involving a random access file, you will compare the way records are stored in a sequential access file with the way records are stored in a random access file. This will give you a better insight into how the computer accesses the records in each of the two file types, and why the records in a random access file can be processed so much faster than the records in a sequential access file.

Sequential Access vs. Random Access File Storage

Recall that you can use a simple text editor or word processor to view the records in a data file. Figure 8-3, for example, shows a sequential access file, displayed in WordPad, that contains three records. (WordPad is the text editor that is available with Windows 95.)

record
name field
price field

Figure 8-3: Sequential access file displayed in WordPad

Notice that each record appears on a separate line; that is because Visual Basic appends a carriage return character to the end of each record as it writes the record to the file. Each record in the file contains two fields: a name field and a price field. The name field stores strings, as indicated by the quotation marks around the data. The price field stores numbers. The comma, which separates the fields in a sequential access file, indicates where the name field ends and the price field begins.

In a sequential access file, the number of characters contained in a field usually varies from record to record. In Figure 8-3, for example, notice that each of the names stored in the name field is a different length. Because the field lengths are not the same in each record, the length of each record in a sequential access file will vary. That is why records in a sequential access file are referred to as **variable-length records.** Now look at these same three records in a random access file. Figure 8-4 shows a random access file, displayed in WordPad, containing the same three records shown in Figure 8-3.

binary representation of
price field

Figure 8-4: Random access file displayed in WordPad

Although the records are the same, notice that the random access file (Figure 8-4) looks different from the sequential access file (Figure 8-3). In the random access file, the three records appear on the same line with no commas separating the fields. The string field in the random access file does not contain quotation marks and the numbers in the price field display as strange-looking characters. The unusual characters appear because the numeric fields in a random access file are stored in a compressed format, called binary, which allows random access files to use less disk space than sequential access files when storing numbers. Because a text editor interprets all data it reads as text, most of the numbers display as unusual characters because their binary codes are not associated with standard keyboard characters.

Unlike sequential access files, in random access files the number of characters contained in a field must be identical from record to record. When creating a random access file, the programmer first assigns a specific length, in bytes, to each field in the record. A **byte** is the amount of storage needed to hold one character, so you can think of a byte as being equivalent to a character. In the random access file shown in Figure 8-4, the name field has a length of seven bytes (characters) and the price field has a length of two bytes.

If the data in a field is shorter than the length of the field, Visual Basic pads the unused space with blanks (spaces). In Figure 8-4, for example, the four-character string "Hats" is padded with three blanks before being stored in the seven-character name field. If, on the other hand, the data in the field is longer than the length of the field, Visual Basic crops (truncates) the data to fit the field. The eight-character string "Sweaters" would be cropped to a seven-character string ("Sweater") before being stored in the name field. Care must be taken to select the proper field length for string data. You don't want to have a string field so large that it wastes disk space, but you also don't want the field to be so small that it crops most of the strings.

Because the length of the fields in a random access file is identical from record to record, the length of each record in a random access file is also identical. That is why the records in a random access file are referred to as **fixed-length records**.

To summarize, sequential access files store variable-length records, whereas random access files store fixed-length records. The difference in the way the records are stored accounts for the difference in access time. Look at an illustration of this.

Example A in Figure 8-5 on the following page depicts five records stored in a sequential access file on a disk. Example B depicts the same five records in a random access file. The <cr> in the sequential access file stands for carriage return, which Visual Basic appends to the end of each record as the record is written to the sequential access file. To make the random access file illustration easier to understand, numbers are shown in place of the binary characters.

Figure 8-5: Examples of a sequential access and a random access file on disk

Notice that the length of each record in the sequential access file varies. The length of each record in the random access file, however, is nine bytes. Now assume that you want the computer to read the fourth record in the sequential access file. Because the records in a sequential access file are of variable lengths, the fourth record might begin with the sixth character in the file, the 123rd character in the file, or the 179th character in the file; it all depends on the lengths of the first three records. Although the computer does not know the exact location of the fourth record in the file, it does know that the fourth record begins immediately after the third carriage return in the file. (You can verify that by looking at Example A in Figure 8-5.) So, to locate the fourth record, the computer starts at the beginning of the file and reads every character until it finds the third carriage return. The character immediately following the third carriage return is the beginning of the fourth record.

Now assume that you want the computer to read the fourth record in the random access file shown in Figure 8-5's Example B. Recall that each record in the file is nine bytes (characters) long; so the fourth record in the file has to begin with the 28th character. Characters one through nine are record 1, characters 10 through 18 are record 2, and characters 19 through 27 are record 3. To read the fourth record in the file, the computer simply skips over the first 27 bytes (characters) in the file and begins reading with the 28th character.

It may help to picture a file as a book and each record as a chapter in the book. Now assume that you want to find Chapter 4 in a book that does not have a table of contents. If each chapter has a different length, similar to the records in a sequential access file, you would need to start at the beginning of the book and look at each page until you found the heading "Chapter 4." If, however, each chapter contains exactly the same number of pages, similar to the records in a random access file, you would know precisely where Chapter 4 begins and could turn to that page immediately. For example, if each chapter is 20 pages long, Chapter 4 would begin on page 61.

Although this section discussed the difference in reading the records from both file types, the same concepts hold true for writing the records to the file. Because the records in a sequential access file are of variable length, the computer can't write the fourth record before it writes the first three records because it wouldn't know where to start writing. Therefore, the records in a sequential access file must be written to the file in consecutive order from the beginning of the file to the end of the file. The records in a random access file, however, can be written to the file in any order. Because the records in a random access file are all the same length, writing the fourth record before the first three is simple. If each record is 10 bytes long, the computer simply skips over the first 30 bytes in the file and begins writing the fourth record with the 31st byte.

In the next section you will learn how to assign the field lengths to the fields in a random access file.

The Type Statement

Before you can create a random access file, you need to define its **record structure**—the names, data types, and lengths of the fields in the record. You define the record structure with the **Type statement**. Figure 8-6 shows the syntax and an example of the Type statement.

Syntax	Example
Type *structurename*	Type ItemStruc
fieldname1 **As** *datatype*	stName as String * 7
[*fieldname2* **As** *datatype*]	inPrice as Integer
[*fieldnameN* **As** *datatype*]	End Type
End Type	

Figure 8-6: Syntax and an example of Type statement

The Type statement begins with the keyword `Type` followed by the name of the record structure; the statement ends with the keywords `End Type`. Between the `Type` and the `End Type` keywords, you place the name of each field in the record. The name of the record structure and the names of the fields must follow the same naming rules as for variables. In Figure 8-6's example, the name of the record structure is ItemStruc and the names of the fields are stName and inPrice.

tips

· · · · · · · · · · · · · ·

The rules for naming variables are listed in Tutorial 3's Figure 3-5. The standard data types are listed in Tutorial 3's Figure 3-4.

Each field in the record structure must have a *datatype*, which defines the type of data the field will contain. The *datatype* can be any of the standard Visual Basic data types; it can also be another previously defined record structure. For all but the String data type, the length of the field is fixed by the data type you choose. If a field's data type is either Integer or Boolean, for example, Visual Basic automatically assigns a length of two bytes to the field. Visual Basic assigns a length of four bytes to both Long and Single fields; Double, Currency, and Date fields are assigned a length of eight bytes. In the example shown in Figure 8-6, the inPrice field is automatically set to two bytes because its data type is Integer.

If a field's data type is String, as is the stName field in Figure 8-6's example, you must specify the length of the field. You do so by appending both an asterisk (*) and a number, which represents the length of the field, to the data type. The `stName As String * 7` instruction in Figure 8-6, for example, tells Visual Basic to allocate seven bytes (characters) for the stName field.

The Type statement groups several related fields together into one unit—the record structure. The record structure itself actually becomes a data type, called a **user-defined data type**, which is separate and distinct from Visual Basic's standard data types. Figure 8-6's example groups together two fields, stName and inPrice, into a record structure (a user-defined data type) named ItemStruc.

Once the user-defined data type (record structure) is created, you can declare a variable of that data type in your code, just as you can with Visual Basic's standard data types. For example, the `Dim ItemRec as ItemStruc` instruction creates an ItemStruc variable named ItemRec, similar to the way the `Dim inAge as Integer` instruction creates an Integer variable named inAge. The difference, however, is that the variable declared as a user-defined data type, called a **record variable**, will itself contain one or more variables, called **field variables**. The `Dim ItemRec as ItemStruc` instruction, for example, creates a record variable named ItemRec and two field variables, stName and inPrice. When coding, you refer to the entire record variable by its name—in this case, ItemRec. To refer to the individual field variables, however, you must precede the field variable's name with the name of the record variable in which it is defined. You separate the record variable's name from the field variable's name with a period. The names of the field variables within the ItemRec record variable, for example, are ItemRec.stName and ItemRec.inPrice.

Your Student Disk contains a partially completed application that uses a random access file. You will finish coding the application in this lesson.

To open the random access file application:

1   Start Visual Basic, if necessary, then open the **Random** (random.vbp) file, which is located in the Tut08 folder on your Student Disk. The `Option Explicit` statement has already been entered in the General declarations section of the form.

2   Save the form and the project as **laRand**.

3   View the frmRandom form. See Figure 8-7.

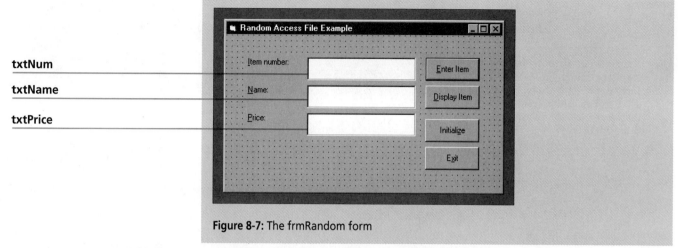

txtNum

txtName

txtPrice

Figure 8-7: The frmRandom form

To keep the current application simple, the item number used to identify each item will be a small integer that corresponds directly to its record number in the random access file. In other words, item number 1 will be record number one in the file, item number 2 will be record number 2, and so on. However, not all applications use small integers to identify the items, employees, and so on in a file. For example, a social security number, referred to as a key field, is usually used to identify an employee.

A store owner can use this application to both save and display information about the items he or she sells. To save the item's information, for example, the user simply enters the item's number, name, and price into the appropriate text boxes, then clicks the Enter Item button. The Enter Item button will save the item's name and price in a random access file. The user can display the item's name and price by entering the item's number in the Item number text box, then clicking the Display Item button. Visual Basic will use the item's number to locate the appropriate record in the random access file, and will display the item's name and its price in the Name and Price text boxes, respectively. Now begin coding this application.

Coding the Code Module

The first step in coding this application is to enter the Type statement that defines the record structure for the item records. The record structure indicates the information that you want to save to the random access file. In this case the record structure will contain two fields: the item's name and its price. You will name the record structure, ItemStruc, and the two fields, stName and inPrice.

You enter the Type statement in the General declarations section of a code module, which you learned about in Tutorial 3. A code module, you may remember, is a separate file, added to your application, that contains only code; it does not contain any forms or controls. When you declare a variable using a data type other than a standard one, Visual Basic searches the code module for a matching Type statement before creating the variable.

You can also add a code module to a project by using the Module command on the Insert menu.

To add a code module to the current project, then enter the Type statement:

1   Click the **Module** button on the toolbar. Visual Basic adds the Module1 file name to the Project window, and the General declarations section of the Module1 module appears on the screen.

2 Enter the instructions shown in Figure 8-8. (Recall that you should enter the `Option Explicit` statement in each module's General declarations section.)

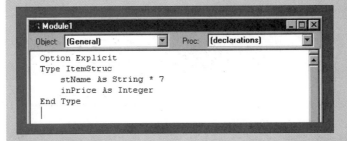

Figure 8-8: Type statement in code module

Each form and module in an application must be saved as a separate file. Because of this, an application can use forms and modules created for another application, often with few or no modifications. Save the current module under a more descriptive name.

3 Click **File**, then click **Save File As**. Save the file as RandMod in the Tut08 folder on your Student Disk. The Project window now shows that the module is saved as RandMod.Bas.

4 Close the module's Code window.

Recall that when you make any changes to the Project window, you must save the project in order for the changes to be saved.

5 Click the **Save Project** ▣ button on the toolbar.

The form's Load event, which is processed when the form is loaded into memory, is the next procedure to code. In the Load event you will include instructions that tell Visual Basic to open the random access file that contains each item's name and price. Before writing this code, however, you will learn how to use the Open statement both to create a new random access file and to open an existing one.

Creating and Opening a Random Access File

As with sequential access files, the **Open statement** either creates a new random access file, if the file doesn't exist, or opens an existing random access file. The syntax of the Open statement used with random access files is **Open** *filename* [**For** *mode*] **As #** *filenumber* **Len** = *reclength*. Notice that the syntax is very similar to the one used for sequential access files. *Filename* is the name of the file you want to open and *filenumber* is the number assigned to the file. Unlike sequential access files, however, where the mode is Input, Output, or Append, the mode for random access files is always Random. Opening a file for Random allows you to both read and write to the file.

The Open statement for a random access file must include the record length (*reclength*) for each record in the file. *Reclength* must be a positive integer between 1 and 32767, inclusive. You calculate the record length by adding together the length of each field in the record variable. Because making that calculation by hand is time-consuming and prone to errors, it is much better to let Visual

Basic calculate the record length for you. You do so by including the Len function, which you learned about in Tutorial 4, in the Open instruction. The syntax of the Len function to determine the length of a string, you may remember, is **Len**(*string*). Similarly, the syntax of the Len function to determine the length of a variable is **Len**(*variablename*). When using the Len function in the Open statement, *variablename* refers to the record variable's name. Assuming the record variable's name is ItemRec and the record length is 9 bytes, the two instructions `Open "a:\Tut08\Item.dat" for Random as #1 Len = 9` and `Open "a:\Tut08\Item.dat" for Random as #1 Len = Len(ItemRec)` are identical.

In the current application, you will place the Open statement in the form's Load event procedure so that the random access file will be opened as soon as the application is run.

Coding the Form's Load Event Procedure

The form's Load event procedure should declare the necessary variables, then open the random access file. In this application the Load event needs one variable—a record variable—that the Len function will use to calculate the record length for the Open statement. You will name the record variable ItemRec and declare it as a variable of the user-defined type ItemStruc, which is the name of the record structure created with the Type statement.

To code the form's Load event procedure:

1. Double-click the **form** to open its Code window. The Load event procedure appears. Notice that the instructions to center the form have already been entered in the Code window.

2. Maximize the Code window, then enter the Dim statement and the Open statement shown in Figure 8-9. If your Student Disk is in the B: drive, be sure to change the a: to b: in the Open statement.

enter these two lines of code

if your Student Disk is in drive B:, then change the drive letter to b:

```
frmRand
Object: Form                              Proc: Load

Private Sub Form_Load()
    Dim ItemRec As ItemStruc
    frmRand.Left = (Screen.Width - frmRand.Width) / 2
    frmRand.Top = (Screen.Height - frmRand.Height) / 2
    Open "a:\Tut08\Item.dat" For Random As #1 Len = Len(ItemRec)

End Sub
```

Figure 8-9: Code entered in the Load event procedure

While the random access file is open, the program can both read records from the file and write records to the file.

3. Close the Code window.

Remember that all open files should be closed before the application ends. Because it's so easy to forget to close the files, you should enter the Close instruction as soon after entering the Open instruction as possible.

Closing a Random Access File

The **Close statement** closes both sequential access files and random access files. Recall that the syntax of the Close statement is **Close**(*filenumber*), where *filenumber* is the number used in the Open statement to open the file you now want to close. In the current application you will have the form's Unload event close the Item.dat file, and then end the application. You will also enter the `Unload frmRand` instruction in the Exit button's Click event procedure so that it will trigger the form's Unload event.

To continue coding the application:

1   Double-click the **Exit** button to open its Click event procedure. Press the **Tab** key, then type **unload frmRand** and press the **Enter** key.

2   Open the form's Unload event. Press the **Tab** key, then type **close #1** and press the **Enter** key. Type **End** and press the **Enter** key.

3   Close the Code window.

Next you will learn how to write a record (store data) to a random access file on disk.

Writing Records to a Random Access File

You use the **Put statement** to write a record to a random access file. The syntax of the Put statement is **Put #** *filenumber*, [*recordnumber*], *variablename*. *Filenumber* is the number used in the Open statement to open the file, *recordnumber* is the number of the record to be written, and *variablename* is the name of the record variable. You will use the Put statement in the Enter Item button's Click event procedure to write the item information to the Item.dat file.

Coding the Enter Item Button

The pseudocode for the Enter Item button is shown in Figure 8-10.

Pseudocode for the Enter Item Button

1. Declare variables and constants

2. Assign the item number to the inItemNum variable

3. If inItemNum > 0 then

    Assign the name and the price to the ItemRec variable

    Write the ItemRec variable to the random access file

    Else

    Display message to user

    End If

4. Clear the text boxes

5. Set the focus to the txtNum text box

Figure 8-10: Pseudocode for the Enter Item button

To code the Enter Item button, then save and run the application:

1. Double-click the **Enter Item** button to open its Code window. The button's Click event procedure, which declares two constants and a variable, appears.

The Click event procedure requires two additional variables, which you will call inItemNum and ItemRec. InItemNum, an Integer variable, will store the item's number, which in this application corresponds to the record number. ItemRec, an ItemStruc variable, will store the record, which consists of an item's name and price. Both variables will be used in the Put statement to write each item's record to the Item.dat file.

2. Maximize the Code window. In the blank line below the existing Dim statement, type **dim inItemNum as integer, ItemRec as ItemStruc**.

Now assign the item number, which the user entered in the txtNum text box, to the inItemNum variable.

3. In the blank line below the last Const statement, type **inItemNum = val(txtNum.text)** and press the **Enter** key.

According to the pseudocode, you must now determine if the inItemNum variable contains a number that is greater than zero. The number stored in the inItemNum variable, remember, represents the record number in the file. Because the first record in a random access file is record number 1, any record number that is not greater than zero is invalid.

4. Type **if inItemNum > 0 then** and press the **Enter** key.

If the inItemNum variable contains a number that is greater than zero, then you will assign the values in the other two text boxes (txtName and txtPrice) to the ItemRec record variable. You do so by assigning the value in the txtName control to the ItemRec.stName field variable, and assigning the value in the txtPrice control to the ItemRec.inPrice field variable.

5. Press the **Tab** key, then type **ItemRec.stName = txtName.text** and press the **Enter** key. Then type **ItemRec.inPrice = val(txtPrice.text)** and press the **Enter** key.

Now write the item's record to the random access file. Recall that the syntax of the Put statement is **Put #** *filenumber*, [*recordnumber*], *variablename*. In this case the *filenumber* is 1, the *recordnumber* is the item number stored in the inItemNum variable, and the *variablename* is ItemRec.

6   Type **put #1, inItemNum, ItemRec** and press the **Enter** key. When Visual Basic writes the record variable to the file, it writes the information stored in each of the field variables. In this case, for example, Visual Basic will write the information stored in both the ItemRec.stName and ItemRec.inPrice field variables to the file.

If the inItemNum variable contains a number that is not greater than zero, then you will use the MsgBox function to display an appropriate message to the user.

7   Press the **Backspace** key, then type **else** and press the **Enter** key. Press the **Tab** key, then type **inAnswer = msgbox(conMsg, conBtns, "Random")** and press the **Enter** key. Press the **Backspace** key, then type **end if** and press the **Enter** key.

All that remains is to clear the text boxes and set the focus.

8   Enter the remaining code and documentation shown in Figure 8-11. The code in the figure was compressed so you could read more of each line.

enter these four lines
of code

enter this
documentation

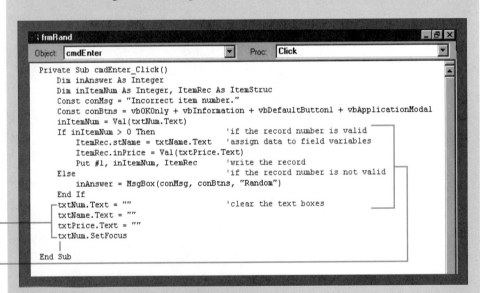

```
frmRand                                                          _ 8 X
Object: cmdEnter              ▼   Proc: Click                    ▼
Private Sub cmdEnter_Click()
    Dim inAnswer As Integer
    Dim inItemNum As Integer, ItemRec As ItemStruc
    Const conMsg = "Incorrect item number."
    Const conBtns = vbOKOnly + vbInformation + vbDefaultButton1 + vbApplicationModal
    inItemNum = Val(txtNum.Text)
    If inItemNum > 0 Then            'if the record number is valid
        ItemRec.stName = txtName.Text    'assign data to field variables
        ItemRec.inPrice = Val(txtPrice.Text)
        Put #1, inItemNum, ItemRec       'write the record
    Else                             'if the record number is not valid
        inAnswer = MsgBox(conMsg, conBtns, "Random")
    End If
    txtNum.Text = ""                     'clear the text boxes
    txtName.Text = ""
    txtPrice.Text = ""
    txtNum.SetFocus

End Sub
```

Figure 8-11: Completed Click event procedure for the Enter Item button

9   Compare your code with Figure 8-11 and make any needed corrections before continuing.

Now save and run the application to make sure the code you've entered is working correctly.

To test the application:

1   Close the Code window. **Save** and **run** the application. Visual Basic executes the instructions in the form's Load event procedure. Because the Item.dat file does not yet exist, the Open statement in the Load event first creates and then opens the random access file. The user interface appears on the screen.

In a random access file, you can enter the items in any order. Enter item number 2 first.

2 Type **2** as the item number and press the **Tab** key. Type **Hats** as the item name and press the **Tab** key. Type **15** as the price, then press the **Enter** key to select the Enter Item button. Visual Basic writes the information to the random access file.

Enter the fifth record next.

3 Type **5** as the item number, **Coats** as the item name, and **95** as the price. Press the **Enter** key to select the Enter Item button.

4 Click the **Exit** button to end the application.

If you view the Item.dat file in a text editor or word processor, you may find that the data file contains some extra characters, as shown in Figure 8-12. (You can verify this by opening the Item.dat file in either a text editor or a word processor. You don't need to be concerned if your data file does not look identical to Figure 8-12, or if your file does not contain any extra characters.)

record 2

garbage

garbage

record 5

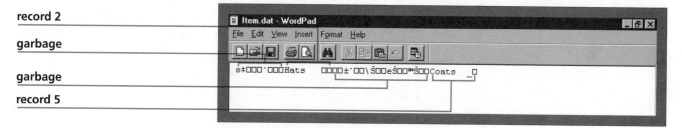

Figure 8-12: Item.dat random access file displayed in WordPad

You may find that a random access file contains "garbage"—useless characters in places on the disk where records have not been written. Notice, for example, that the space reserved for record 1 in the Item.dat file contains garbage. (Recall that you did not write any information to records 1, 3, and 4—only to records 2 and 5.) This is due to the way your computer's operating system saves and deletes files from a disk. When you save a file to a disk, the sectors that contain the file are marked as "in use." When you delete a file, the regions (sectors) on the disk that contain the file are marked as "available," but the file is not really erased from the disk. Those sectors will contain the remains of old files until you write over that information. When you don't write information to each record in a random access file, the space reserved for the unwritten records can contain anything. The solution to this problem is to initialize—in other words, to clear the disk space for the file.

Initializing a Random Access File

You initialize a random access file by writing spaces to the string fields and a zero to the numeric fields. A random access file should be initialized before any records are written to it; otherwise the existing records will be overwritten with the spaces and zeros. A user may also wish to initialize an existing data file so it can be reused for new data. If so, a confirmation message should appear that lets the user confirm his or her intent.

Before you can initialize a data file, you must estimate the maximum number of records the file will contain. It doesn't hurt to overestimate. Figure 8-13 shows the pseudocode to initialize a data file that will contain a maximum of 10 records.

Pseudocode for the Initialize Button

1. Declare variables and constants

2. Assign 7 spaces to the name field in the ItemRec variable

3. Assign a zero to the price field in the ItemRec variable

4. Verify that user wants to initialize the file

5. If the user wants to initialize the file then

     Repeat for inItemNum = 1 to 10 by 1

         Write the ItemRec record to the random access file

     End Repeat For

     Display "File was initialized" message to the user

   Else

     Display "File was not initialized" message to the user

   End If

6. Set the focus to the txtNum text box

Figure 8-13: Pseudocode for the Initialize button

The code to initialize the Item.dat has already been entered in the Initialize button. View that code now.

To view the code in the Initialize button, then save and run the application:

1 Double-click the **Initialize** button to open its Click event procedure, then maximize the Code window. See Figure 8-14.

```
frmRand                                                            _ 8 X
Object: cmdInit                    ▼      Proc: Click              ▼
Private Sub cmdInit_Click()
    Dim inUserResponse As Integer, inItemNum As Integer, ItemRec As ItemStruc
    Const conMsg = "Do you want to initialize the file?"
    Const conBtns1 = vbYesNo + vbExclamation + vbDefaultButton2 + vbApplicationModal
    Const conBtns2 = vbOKOnly + vbInformation + vbDefaultButton1 + vbApplicationModal
    ItemRec.stName = Space(7)
    ItemRec.inPrice = 0
    inUserResponse = MsgBox(conMsg, conBtns1, "Random")
    If inUserResponse = vbYes Then
        For inItemNum = 1 To 10
            Put #1, inItemNum, ItemRec
        Next inItemNum
        inUserResponse = MsgBox("File was initialized.", conBtns2, "Random")
    Else
        inUserResponse = MsgBox("File was not initialized.", conBtns2, "Random")
    End If
    txtNum.SetFocus

End Sub
```

assigns values to field variables in record variable

writes record variable 10 times

Figure 8-14: Code entered in the Initialize button

GUI
Design Tips

Communicating With the User

- If an operation is destructive, prompt the user to verify that he or she wants to proceed with the operation.
- Display messages to inform the user of the status of important events.

If you want to verify that the file no longer contains "garbage," open the Item.dat file in a text editor or word processor. Any "garbage" that was visible in the file before initialization will now be gone. When you're finished looking at the file, exit the text editor or word processor without saving the file.

Recall that you use the Input # statement to read a record from a sequential access file.

The code begins by declaring three variables—inUserResponse, inItemNum, ItemRec—and three constants. The inUserResponse variable and the three constants will be used by the MsgBox functions. The inItemNum variable will store the item number, and the ItemRec variable will store the record—the item's name and price. After the variables and constants are declared, the code uses the Space function to assign seven spaces to the ItemRec.stName field variable. The syntax of the **Space function** is Space(*number*), where *number* is the number of spaces you want. The code also assigns a zero to the ItemRec.inPrice field variable.

Initializing a data file destroys all data in it; therefore, before initializing a file, you should always present a warning message to the user and give him or her an opportunity to cancel the operation. In this procedure, the MsgBox function verifies that the user wants to initialize the data file. If he or she does, then a For Next loop initializes the file by writing the record variable to the file, 10 times. The record variable, remember, contains seven spaces for the stName field and a zero for the inPrice field. The MsgBox function then displays a message telling the user that the file was initialized, and the SetFocus method sets the focus to the Item number text box.

If, on the other hand, the user does not want to initialize the file, then the MsgBox function displays a message informing the user that the file was not initialized, and the SetFocus method sets the focus to the Item number text box.

2   Close the Code window.

Now initialize the Item.dat data file.

3   **Save** and **run** the application. Click the **Initialize** button, then click the **Yes** button to initialize the Item.dat file. Click the **OK** button to remove the message informing the user that the file was initialized.

Because the Initialize button destroyed the existing records in the Item.dat file, you will need to reenter records 2 and 5.

4   Type **2** as the item number, **Hats** as the item name, and **15** as the price. Press the **Enter** key to select the Enter Item button.

5   Type **5** as the item number, **Coats** as the item name, and **95** as the price. Press the **Enter** key to select the Enter Item button.

6   Click the **Exit** button to end the application.

Before coding the Display Item button, you will learn how to read a record from a random access file.

Reading Records from a Random Access File

You use the **Get statement** to read a record from a random access file. The syntax of the Get statement is **Get #** *filenumber*, [*recordnumber*], *variablename*. *Filenumber* is the number used in the Open statement to open the file, *recordnumber* is the number of the record to be read, and *variablename* is the name of the record variable. You will use the Get statement in the Display Item button's Click event procedure to read a record from the Item.dat file.

Coding the Display Item Button

To display the name and price of an existing item in the file, the user first needs to enter the item number in the Item number text box, then click the Display Item button. The pseudocode for the Display Item button is shown in Figure 8-15.

Pseudocode for the Display Item Button

1. Declare variables and constants

2. Assign the item number to the inItemNum variable

3. If inItemNum > 0 then

   Read the record corresponding to the item number

   Assign the name from the ItemRec variable to the Name text box

   Assign the price from the ItemRec variable to the Price text box

   Else

   Display "Incorrect item number" message to the user

   End If

4. Set the focus to the txtNum text box

Figure 8-15: Pseudocode for the Display Item button

Most of the code for this button has already been entered in the Code window for you; only three of the instructions are missing.

To view the code in the Display Item button's Code window, then save and run the application:

1. Double-click the **Display Item** button to open its Click event procedure, then maximize the Code window. Position the blinking insertion point as shown in Figure 8-16.

position insertion point here ⟶

```
frmRand
Object:  cmdDisplay                          Proc:  Click

Private Sub cmdDisplay_Click()
    Dim inUserResponse As Integer, inItemNum As Integer, ItemRec As ItemStruc
    Const conMsg = "Incorrect item number."
    Const conBtns = vbOKOnly + vbInformation + vbDefaultButton1 + vbApplicationModal
    inItemNum = Val(txtNum.Text)
    If inItemNum > 0 Then

    Else
        inUserResponse = MsgBox(conMsg, conBtns, "Random")
    End If
    txtNum.SetFocus

End Sub
```

Figure 8-16: Partially completed Code window for the Display Item button

The code begins by declaring three variables and two constants. The inUserResponse variable and both constants will be used by the MsgBox function. The inItemNum variable will store the item number, and the ItemRec variable will store the record. After the variables and constants are declared, the code assigns the item number, which is entered in the txtNum text box, to the inItemNum variable. If the inItemNum variable contains a number that is greater than 0, then the procedure should read the record from the random access file. Recall that the syntax of the Get statement is **Get #** *filenumber*, [*recordnumber*], *variablename*. In this case the *filenumber* is 1, the *recordnumber* is the item number stored in the inItemNum variable, and the *variablename* is ItemRec.

2   In the blank line below the If statement, type **get #1, inItemNum, ItemRec** and press the **Enter** key. This statement tells Visual Basic to read the record whose record number is stored in the inItemNum variable. As it reads the record, Visual Basic stores the first seven bytes of the record in the ItemRec.stName field variable and the last two bytes in the ItemRec.inPrice field variable.

Now display the contents of both field variables, ItemRec.stName and ItemRec.inPrice, in the appropriate text boxes.

3   In the blank line below the Get statement, type **txtName.text = ItemRec.stName** and press the **Enter** key. Then type **txtPrice.text = ItemRec.inPrice**.

The Else, MsgBox, End If, and SetFocus instructions are already entered in the Code window for you.

4   Compare your code with the code shown in Figure 8-17. Make any needed corrections before continuing to the next step.

be sure that you entered these three instructions

Figure 8-17: Completed Code window for the Display Item button

5 Close the Code window, then **save** and **run** the application.

First display the name and price of an existing item—item 5, for example.

6 Type 5 as the item number, then click the **Display Item** button. Item 5's name (Coats) and price (95) appear in the appropriate text boxes.

Now display the name and price of an item that does not exist—item 1, for example.

7 Type 1 as the item number, then click the **Display Item** button. Nothing appears in the txtName text box, and a zero appears in the txtPrice text box; that's because you initialized the name field to spaces and the price field to zero.

8 Click the **Exit** button to end the application. Visual Basic returns to the design screen.

You have now completed Lesson A. You can either take a break or complete the questions and exercises at the end of the lesson.

S U M M A R Y

To determine sequential access versus random access:

■ A sequential access file is similar to a cassette tape. Each song on a cassette tape, like each record in a sequential access file, is both stored and retrieved in consecutive order from beginning to end.

■ A random access file is similar to a CD. Each song on a CD, like each record in a random access file, can be played in any order by accessing its track (record) number.

To create a user-defined data type:

■ Enter the Type statement in the General declarations section of a code module. Its syntax is:

> **Type** *structurename*
> > *fieldname1* **As** *datatype*
> > [*fieldname2* **As** *datatype*]
> > [*fieldnameN* **As** *datatype*]
> **End Type**

To add a code module to an application:

■ Click the Module button ⬛ on the toolbar, or click Insert, then click Module.

To create or open a random access file:

■ Use the Open statement. Its syntax is **Open** *filename* [**For** *mode*] **As #** *filenumber* **Len =** *reclength*.

■ *Filename* is the name of the file, including the drive letter and path, and must be enclosed in quotation marks. If the *filename* is stored in a variable or a property, you do not need quotation marks.

■ *Mode* is Random. Random mode opens the file for reading and writing.

■ *Filenumber* is an integer expression with a value between 1 and 511, inclusive.

■ *Reclength* is the length of each record in the file and must be an integer in the range of 1 through 32767, inclusive.

To determine the size of a record:

■ Use the Len function. Its syntax is **Len**(*variablename*).

To close a file:

■ Use the Close statement. Its syntax is **Close** [# *filenumber*][, # *filenumber*].... *Filenumber* is the number used in the Open statement to open the file. A Close statement with no arguments closes all open files.

To write a record to an open random access file:

■ Use the Put statement. Its syntax is **Put #** *filenumber*, [*recordnumber*], *variablename*. *Filenumber* is the number used in the Open statement to open the random access file. *Recordnumber* is the number of the record to write. *Variablename* is the name of the record variable.

To initialize a string to spaces:

■ Use the Space function. Its syntax is **Space**(*number*), where *number* represents the number of spaces.

To read a record from an open random access file:

■ Use the Get statement. Its syntax is **Get #** *filenumber*, [*recordnumber*], *variablename*. *Filenumber* is the number used in the Open statement to open the random access file. *Recordnumber* is the number of the record to read. *Variablename* is the name of the record variable.

QUESTIONS

1. You use the _____ statement to define the structure of a record.
   a. Declare
   b. Define
   c. Record
   d. Structure
   e. Type

2. Records in a random access file can be accessed _____ .
   a. randomly
   b. sequentially
   c. either randomly or sequentially

3. The Type statement must be declared in the _____ .
   a. event procedure of an object
   b. General declarations section of a code module
   c. General declarations section of a form

4. Which of the following will define a 15-character string field named stCity?
   a. stCity as String
   b. stCity as String(15)
   c. stCity as String X 15
   d. stCity as String by 15
   e. stCity as String * 15

5. If you store the string "Chicago" (without the quotes) in a 15-character field named stCity, what will Visual Basic actually store in the stCity field?
   a. The string "Chicago" (with the quotes).
   b. The string "Chicago".
   c. The string "Chicago" followed by six blank spaces.
   d. The string "Chicago" followed by eight blank spaces.
   e. Eight blank spaces followed by the string "Chicago".

6. A _____ is equivalent to a character.
   a. bit
   b. byte
   c. integer
   d. number
   e. string

7. A field defined as Currency is stored in _____ bytes.
   a. 2
   b. 4
   c. 6
   d. 8
   e. 10

8. You create a random access file with the _____ statement.
   a. Create
   b. Declare
   c. Define
   d. Open
   e. Random

9. You open a random access file with the _____ statement.
   a. Create
   b. Declare
   c. Define
   d. Open
   e. Random

10. You use the _____ statement to write a record to a random access file.
    a. Define
    b. Get
    c. Put
    d. Record
    e. Write

11. You use the _____ statement to read a record from a random access file.
    a. Define
    b. Get
    c. Put
    d. Record
    e. Write

12. Which two of the following Open statements are valid? (The name of the record variable is Employee. Each record is 100 bytes.)
    a. Open a:\data.dat for random as #1 Len = Len(Employee)
    b. Open a:\data.dat for "random" as #1 Len = Len(Employee)
    c. Open "a:\data.dat" for random as #1 Len = Len(Employee)
    d. Open "a:\data.dat" for random Len = Len(Employee)
    e. Open "a:\data.dat" for random as #1 Len = 100

13. Which of the following will write the Employee record, which consists of a last name and a first name, to a random access file?
    a. Put #1, inRecNum, stLast, stFirst
    b. Put stLast, stFirst to #1
    c. Put inRecNum, stLast, stFirst to #1
    d. Put #1, inRecNum, Employee
    e. Put inRecNum, Employee to #1

14. Which of the following will close a random access file opened as file number 3?
    a. Close filenumber 3
    b. Close random #3
    c. Close file #3
    d. Close #3
    e. Close file 3

15. Which of the following will return the length of the Student record?
    a. Len(Student)
    b. Length(Student)
    c. Recordlength(Student)
    d. Student(Len)
    e. Student(Length)

16. Unless specified otherwise, an open random access file can be _____ .
    a. read from only
    b. written to only
    c. either read from or written to

17. Which of the following will assign 10 spaces to a variable named stFirstName?
    a. stFirstName = Blank(10)
    b. stFirstName = Blank$(10)
    c. stFirstName = Space&(10)
    d. stFirstName = Space(10)
    e. stFirstName = (10)Space

Use the following information to answer Questions 18 through 26.

```
Type CustStruc
        stName as String * 25
        stPhone as String * 12
        crSalary as Currency
End Type
Dim Customer as CustStruc
```

18. The name of the record structure is _____ .
    a. stName
    b. stPhone
    c. Customer
    d. crSalary
    e. CustStruc

19. The name of the record variable is _____.
   a. stName
   b. stPhone
   c. Customer
   d. crSalary
   e. CustStruc

20. The names of the three field variables are _____.
   a. stName
   b. stPhone
   c. Customer
   d. crSalary
   e. CustStruc

21. The length of the stName field variable is _____.
   a. 8
   b. 12
   c. 25
   d. 45
   e. unknown

22. The length of the crSalary field variable is _____.
   a. 8
   b. 12
   c. 25
   d. 45
   e. unknown

23. The length of the Customer record is _____.
   a. 8
   b. 12
   c. 25
   d. 45
   e. unknown

24. When coding, you would refer to the stPhone field variable as _____.
   a. stPhone
   b. stPhone.Customer
   c. stPhone.CustStruc
   d. Customer.stPhone
   e. CustStruc.stPhone

25. When coding, you would refer to the record variable as _____.
   a. stName
   b. stPhone
   c. Customer
   d. crSalary
   e. CustStruc

26. Assume that the inNum variable contains the number 2. Which two of the following will read the second customer record from a file opened as #1?
   a. Get #1, 2, Customer
   b. Get #1, 2, stName, stPhone
   c. Get #1 , inNum, Customer
   d. Get #1, inNum, stName, stPhone
   e. Get #1, inNum, Customer.stName, Customer.stPhone

EXERCISES

1. Write a Type statement that defines a record structure named BookStruc. The record structure contains three fields: stTitle, stAuthor, crCost. StTitle is a 20-character String field, stAuthor is a 20-character String field, and crCost is a Currency field.

2. Write a Type statement that defines a record structure named TapeStruc. The record structure contains four fields: stName, stArtist, inSong, and stLength. StName is a 25-character String field, stArtist is a 20-character String field, inSong is an Integer field, and stLength is a 6-character String field.

3. Write a Dim statement that declares a BookStruc variable named BookRec.

4. Write a Dim statement that declares a TapeStruc variable named TapeRec.

5. Write an Open statement that opens a random access file named "Books.dat" on your Student Disk. Open the file as #1. The contents of the BookRec record variable will be written to the file.

6. Write an Open statement that opens a random access file named "Tapes.dat" on your Student Disk. Open the file as #1. The contents of the TapeRec record variable will be written to the file.

7. Assume that the inRecNum variable contains the number 5 and the random access file was opened as #1. Write a Put statement that will write the contents of the BookRec record variable as the fifth record in the file.

8. Assume that the inRecNum variable contains the number 2 and the random access file was opened as #1. Write a Put statement that will write the contents of the TapeRec record variable as the second record in the file.

9. Assume that the inRecNum variable contains the number 3 and the random access file was opened as #1. Write a Get statement that will read the third record in the file. The name of the record variable is BookRec.

10. Assume that the inRecNum variable contains the number 5 and the random access file was opened as #1. Write a Get statement that will read the fifth record in the file. The name of the record variable is TapeRec.

11. Write the statement that will close the file opened as # 1.

Use the following record structure for Exercise 12.

```
Type ComputerStruc
      stName as String * 5
      crCost as Currency
End Type
```

12. a. Write a Dim statement that declares a ComputerStruc variable named CompRec.
    b. Write an Open statement that opens a random access file named "Computer.dat" on your Student Disk. Open the file as #1.
    c. Write the For...Next loop that will initialize the Computer.dat file for 10 records.
    d. Write an assignment statement that will assign the name "IB-50" to the stName field variable.
    e. Write an assignment statement that will assign the number 2400 to the crCost field variable.
    f. Assuming that the inRecNum variable contains the number 5, write the Put statement that will write the CompRec record as the fifth record in the random access file.
    g. Assuming that the inRecNum variable contains the number 5, write the Get statement that will read the fifth record in the random access file.

h. Write the assignment statements that will assign the value in the stName field variable to the lblName control, and the value in the crCost field variable to the lblCost control.

i. Write the statement that will close the random access file.

Use the following record structure for Exercise 13.

```
Type FriendStruc
      stLast as String * 10
      stFirst as String * 10
End Type
```

13. a. Write a Dim statement that declares a FriendStruc variable named FriendRec.
   b. Write an Open statement that opens a random access file named "Friends.dat" on your Student Disk. Open the file as #1.
   c. Write the For...Next loop that will initialize the Friends.dat file for five records.
   d. Write an assignment statement that will assign the value in the txtFirst control to the stFirst field variable.
   e. Write an assignment statement that will assign the value in the txtLast control to the stLast field variable.
   f. Assuming that the inRecNum variable contains the number 3, write the Put statement that will write the FriendRec record as the third record in the random access file.
   g. Assuming that the inRecNum variable contains the number 3, write the Get statement that will read the third record in the random access file.
   h. Write the assignment statement that will assign the value in the stFirst field variable and the value in the stLast field variable to the lblName control. (You will need to use string concatenation, which you learned about in Tutorial 3.)
   i. Write the statement that will close the random access file.

14. a. Write a Type statement that defines a record structure named CustStruc. The record structure contains three fields: stName, stPhone, crSales. StName is a 25-character String field, stPhone is an 8-character String field, and crSales is a Currency field.
   b. Write a Dim statement that declares a CustStruc variable named CustRec.
   c. Write an Open statement that opens a random access file named "Customer.dat" on your Student Disk. Open the file as #1.
   d. Write the For...Next loop that will initialize the Customer.dat file for five records.
   e. Write an assignment statement that will assign the value in the txtName control to the stName field variable.
   f. Write an assignment statement that will assign the value in the txtPhone control to the stPhone field variable.
   g. Write an assignment statement that will assign the value in the txtSales control to the crSales field variable.
   h. Assuming that the inRecNum variable contains the number 3, write the Put statement that will write the CustRec record as the third record in the random access file.
   i. Assuming that the inRecNum variable contains the number 3, write the Get statement that will read the third record in the random access file.
   j. Write the assignment statement that will assign the value in the stName field variable to the txtName control.
   k. Write the assignment statement that will assign the value in the stPhone field variable to the txtPhone control.
   l. Write the assignment statement that will assign the value in the crSales field variable to the txtSales control.
   m. Write the statement that will close the random access file.

15. In this exercise you will use a random access file to store data.

Scenario: Over the last several years Martha Martin has purchased a great number of compact disks (CDs). She would like an application that will allow her to keep track of the CDs she owns.

a. Open the la15 (la15.vbp) project, which is located in the Tut08 folder on your Student Disk.

b. Save the form and the project as la15Done in the Tut08 folder on your Student Disk.

c. Add a code module to the project. Define a record structure named CDStruc in the code module. The record structure should contain two fields: stName and stArtist. Define both fields as 20-character String fields.

d. Save the code module as la15Done in the Tut08 folder on your Student Disk.

e. In the form's Load event procedure, define a CDStruc variable named CDRec and open a random access file named CDs.dat.

f. Code the Exit button so that it unloads the form. Code the form's Unload event so that it closes the data file and ends the application.

g. Code the Initialize button so that it initializes the CDs.dat. To save space on your Student Disk, initialize the file for five records only. Be sure to include a prompt that verifies that the user wants to initialize the file. (You can use the pseudocode shown in Figure 8-13 as a guide.)

h. Code the Enter CD button so that it writes the CDRec record variable to the file. Be sure to verify that the CD number is greater than zero. (You can use the pseudocode shown in Figure 8-10 as a guide.)

i. Code the Display CD button so that it displays the CD information (name and artist) that corresponds to the CD number entered by the user. Be sure to verify that the CD number is greater than zero. (You can use the pseudocode shown in Figure 8-15 as a guide.)

j. Save and run the application.

k. To test the application:
   1) Initialize the CDs.dat file.
   2) Use the Enter CD button to enter the following three records, shown as CD number, CD name, and artist name:
      4, Western Way, Mingo Colfax
      2, Country For All, Barbara Mender
      1, Line Dancing, Helen Starks
   3) Enter CD number 2 and click the Display CD button. The Country For All CD by Barbara Mender should appear in the form.
   4) Click the Exit button to end the application.

l. Print the form and the application's code. Also, print the CDs.dat file in WordPad. (*If you are using Windows 3.1, use Notepad*).

Exercise 16 is a Discovery Exercise, which allows you to "discover" the solutions to problems on your own. Discovery Exercises may include topics that are not covered in the tutorial.

discovery ▶ **16.** In this exercise you will learn about the Printer object and the EndDoc method.

Scenario: ABC Company ranks cars according to customer satisfaction surveys sent out each year to new car buyers. The company wants you to create an application that will allow the clerk to enter each car model and price into a random access file. The car information should be stored in the file in order of customer satisfaction; in other words, the car with the highest satisfaction rating should be stored first, the second highest should be stored second, and so on. The application should also allow the clerk to enter the ranking number and display its corresponding car model and price. The company also wants to be able to print the contents of the random access file.

a. Create an appropriate user interface.

b. Save the form, the module, and the project as la16Done in the Tut08 folder on your Student Disk.

c. Use the Help menu to display the Help windows on the Print method, the Printer object, and the EndDoc method.

d. Code the application appropriately. Allow for up to 5 records in the random access file. Name the random access file Cars.dat.

e. Save and run the application.

f. To test the application:

   1) Initialize the Cars.dat file.

   2) Enter the following three records, shown as ranking number, model, and price:

      1, Firebird, 22000

      2, Camaro, 22500

      3, Stealth, 30000

   3) Display the model and price that correspond to each of the ranking numbers from 1 to 5.

   4) Print the contents of the random access file on the printer.

   5) Exit the application.

g. Print the form and the application's code.

h. Submit the printout from step f4), and the form and code from step g.

In this lesson you will learn how to:

- Utilize a control array and a random access file in an application
- Include Visual Basic's color constants in code
- Pass information to a sub procedure

The Cole's Playhouse Application

Important Note: You will not be able to complete Lesson B or Lesson C if you are using the Working Model. You will need to use either the Standard or Professional Edition of Visual Basic.

Coding the Cole's Playhouse Application

Recall that Cole's Playhouse performs plays featuring local talent. The theater holds only 48 seats, which must be reserved in advance of the performance. No tickets are sold at the door. The manager, Max Phillips, wants an application that will keep track of the reserved seating for each play. Specifically, Mr. Phillips wants to record each patron's name and phone number.

The Cole's Playhouse application will contain two forms, frmPatron and frmSeat. The sketch of the user interface for both forms is shown in Figure 8-18.

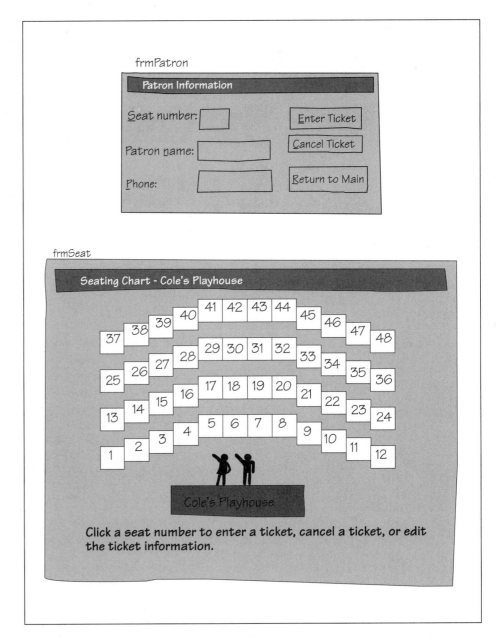

Figure 8-18: Sketches of the forms for the Cole's Playhouse application

Your Student Disk contains a partially completed application for Cole's Playhouse. Open that project now.

To open the partially completed Cole's Playhouse application:

1   Start Visual Basic, if necessary. Open the **Cole** (cole.vbp) project, which is in the Tut08 folder on your Student Disk.

2   Open Visual Basic's File menu, then use the Save Project As command to save the project as **lbCole**. (You do not need to save the frmPatron form under a different name because you will not be making any changes to it in this lesson.)

Currently the project contains only one form, the frmPatron form.

3 View the frmPatron form. See Figure 8-19.

Figure 8-19: frmPatron user interface

You learned how to add existing forms to a project in Tutorial 3.

The manager can use this form to enter the ticket information, cancel the ticket information, or return to the main screen—the frmSeat form. Now close the frmPatron form, then add the frmSeat form to the current project.

4 Click the frmPatron form's **Close** button ☒ to close the frmPatron form. Click **File**, then click **Add File**. Click **Seat** (seat.frm) in the list of file names, then click the **Open** button. Visual Basic adds the Seat.frm name to the Project window.

Click the frmPatron form's Control menu box ▬, then click Close to close the frmPatron form. Click File, then click Add File. Click Seat (seat.frm) in the list of file names, then click the OK button. Visual Basic adds the Seat.frm name to the Project window.

WINDOWS 3.1

5 Click **Seat.frm** in the Project window to select it. Use the File menu's Save File As command to save the file as **lbSeat**.

Recall that you should always save the project file whenever you make a change to the Project window.

6 Click the **Save Project** button 🖫 on the toolbar to save the project.

7 View the frmSeat form, then maximize it. The frmSeat form appears on the screen, as shown in Figure 8-20.

Figure 8-20: frmSeat user interface

As you learned in Tutorial 3, when a project includes more than one form, you must tell Visual Basic which of the forms you want automatically displayed when the application is run. That form, called the **startup form**, can be any one of the forms in the project. In this application, the frmSeat form will be the startup form. When the user wants to enter or cancel a ticket, he or she will need simply to click the appropriate seat number to display the frmPatron form, which contains both the Enter Ticket and the Cancel Ticket buttons. Specify the frmSeat form as the startup form.

8   Press the **Alt** key to display Visual Basic's main window, which includes the menu bar. Click **Tools** on the menu bar, then click **Options**. When the Options dialog box appears, click the **Project** tab. Click the **Startup Form** list arrow, then click **frmScat** in the list, and then click the **OK** button.

The label controls whose captions display the numbers 1 through 48 represent the 48 seats in the theater. Because each of those 48 controls will perform the same function, they were placed in a control array named lblSeat.

To verify that the 48 label controls belong to the lblSeat control array:

1   Click seat number **1**. Press the **F4** key to display the Properties window. If necessary, scroll the Properties window until both the Index and Name properties are visible. See Figure 8-21.

full reference to control

selected seat

Index property

Name property

Figure 8-21: Properties window showing Index and Name properties

The full reference to this control—lblSeat(0)—appears in the Object box in the Properties window. Recall that the name of the control array (lblSeat) is stored in the control's Name property; its index (0) is stored in its Index property. The lblSeat(0) control, which is the first control in the lblSeat control array, corresponds to seat number 1 in the theater.

2 Click seat number **29**. Display the Properties window. The name of the selected control is also lblSeat; its index is 28. Notice that the value stored in the Index property is always one less than the seat number. In other words, the control with index number 28 actually refers to seat number 29.

3 Restore the form to its standard size.

The label controls in the lblSeat array have their Visible property set to False, so they will not appear in the interface when the application is run. Verify this by running the application.

4 **Save** and **run** the application. Notice that the lblSeat controls are not visible in the form. If the user wants to record a reservation, he or she will have to use the File menu to open either a new or an existing file. When a new or existing file is opened, the application will display the lblSeat controls in the interface by setting their Visible property to True.

Now use the File menu's Exit command to end the application. (The Exit command already contains the Unload frmSeat instruction. The frmSeat form's Unload event contains the Close instruction, which will close any open data files, and the End instruction, which will end the application.)

5 Click **File**, then click **Exit** to end the application.

You can now begin coding the Cole's Playhouse application.

Coding the Cole's Playhouse Application

The TOE chart for the Cole's Playhouse application is shown in Figure 8-22.

Task	Object	Event
1. Create a new random access file. 2. Initialize a new or existing random access file. 3. Change seats to white.	frmSeat.mnuFileNew	Click
1. Open an existing random access file. 2. Change reserved seats to red and available seats to white.	frmSeat.mnuFileOpen	Click
Unload the frmSeat form.	frmSeat.mnuFileExit	Click
Display frmPatron form with patron information showing.	frmSeat.lblSeat control array	Click
Close the random access file.	frmSeat	Unload
1. Get patron's name and phone number from the user. 2. Write patron's name and phone number to a random access file. 3. Change the BackColor property of the reserved seat to red.	frmPatron.cmdEnter	Click
1. Write spaces to the patron's record in the random access file. 2. Change the BackColor property of the canceled seat to white.	frmPatron.cmdCancel	Click
Hide the frmPatron form	frmPatron.cmdReturn	Click
Center the frmPatron form	frmPatron	Load

Figure 8-22: TOE chart for the Cole's Playhouse application

For each play, the application will save the reservation information—each patron's name and phone number—in a separate data file. Because the application will need to read and write the patron records in any order, you will store the records for each play in a random access file. Before you can use a random access file, recall that you need to define the record structure for the records; you do so by entering the Type statement in a code module (often just called a module).

To add a module to the project, and then define the record structure:

1 Click the **Module** button 🔳 on the toolbar. The General declarations section of the Module1 module appears.

Each record in the data file will contain a patron's name and his or her phone number. You will name the record structure (the user-defined data type), PatronStruc, and the fields, stName and stPhone. StName will be a 20-character String variable and stPhone will be an eight-character String variable.

2 Enter the `Option Explicit` and Type statements shown in Figure 8-23.

Figure 8-23: Option Explicit and Type statements entered in code module

Now save the code module using a more descriptive name.

3 Module1 should be highlighted in the Project window. Use the File menu's Save File As command to save the module as **Cole**. Cole.Bas appears in the Project window.

4 Close the Code window.

5 Click the **Save Project** button on the toolbar to save the project.

Code the File menu's New command first.

Coding the File Menu's New Command

The New command should allow the user to either create a new file or initialize an existing file. The pseudocode for the New command is shown in Figure 8-24.

Pseudocode for the File menu's New command

1. Declare the variables and constants.
2. Begin error trapping.
3. Show the Save As dialog box to get the name of the file from the user.
4. If the file name does not end in .dat then

    append .dat to the end of the file name

    End If

    If the file does not exist then

    call the Initialize procedure to initialize the file. Pass the file name to the procedure.

    Else

    ask the user if he or she wants to replace the existing file

    If the user wants to replace the existing file then

    call the Initialize procedure to initialize the file. Pass the file name to the procedure.

    End If

    End If
5. Exit the Click event.

Figure 8-24: Pseudocode for the File menu's New command

Some of the code for the New command has already been entered in its Click event procedure for you.

To view the code in the New command's Click event procedure:

1   Click **File** on the form's menu bar, then click **New**. Maximize the Code window. The New command's Click event procedure appears as shown in Figure 8-25.

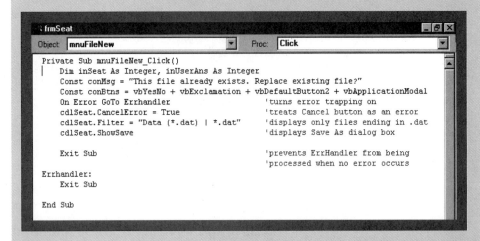

Figure 8-25: New command's Click event procedure

After declaring two variables, as well as two constants for the MsgBox function, the procedure turns error trapping on, sets the properties of the cdlSeat common dialog control, and displays the Save As dialog box. Notice that the error handling routine, which simply exits the Click event when an error occurs, is already entered in the Code window.

According to the pseudocode, you now need to determine if the filename that the user entered in the Save As dialog box ends in .dat. Recall from Tutorial 7 that the filename is stored in the common dialog control's Filename property. If the filename does not end in .dat, then the New command's Click event will append the .dat to the name.

2   Enter the code shown in Figure 8-26, then position the blinking insertion point as shown in the figure.

enter these three lines of code

position insertion point here

```
frmSeat                                                                    _ 8 X
Object:  mnuFileNew                      ▾     Proc:   Click                    ▾
    Private Sub mnuFileNew_Click()
        Dim inSeat As Integer, inUserAns As Integer
        Const conMsg = "This file already exists. Replace existing file?"
        Const conBtns = vbYesNo + vbExclamation + vbDefaultButton2 + vbApplicationModal
        On Error GoTo Errhandler                    'turns error trapping on
        cdlSeat.CancelError = True                  'treats Cancel button as an error
        cdlSeat.Filter = "Data (*.dat) | *.dat"     'displays only files ending in .dat
        cdlSeat.ShowSave                            'displays Save As dialog box
        If UCase(Right(cdlSeat.filename, 4)) <> ".DAT" Then
            cdlSeat.filename = cdlSeat.filename & ".dat"
        End If
    
        Exit Sub                                    'prevents ErrHandler from being
                                                    'processed when no error occurs
    
    Errhandler:
        Exit Sub
    
    End Sub
```

Figure 8-26: Additional code entered in the New command's Click event procedure

The next step in the pseudocode is to determine if the file name already exists on the disk; you can use the Dir function, which you learned about in Tutorial 7, to do so. Recall that the Dir function returns the file's name if the file exists; it returns the empty string ("") if the file does not exist. Compare the cdlSeat control's Filename property to the empty string.

3 With the blinking insertion point positioned as shown in Figure 8-26, type **if dir(cdlSeat.filename) = "" then** and press the **Enter** key.

tips

▶ You can also use the common dialog control's DefaultExt property to append a default extension of .dat to the end of a filename. The selection structure shown in Figure 8-26 is simply another method of appending the extension. The UCase function was covered in Tutorial 4. The Right function was covered in Tutorial 6.

According to the pseudocode, if the file does not exist, then you will call a user-defined sub procedure, which you will name Initialize, to create the file and initialize it for 48 records. In order for the user-defined procedure to know the name of the file to create and initialize, you will need to send (pass) it the contents of the common dialog control's Filename property.

Passing Information to a Sub Procedure

Recall from Tutorial 4 that you use Visual Basic's Call statement, whose syntax is **Call** *name* [(*argumentlist*)], to invoke a user-defined sub procedure. The brackets in the syntax indicate that the *argumentlist* is optional; not all procedures will require information to be passed to it. The RandomNumbers procedure that you created in Tutorial 4, for example, did not need any information to be passed to it. However, in situations where you do have information to send to the sub procedure, you simply include the information in a set of parentheses following the name of the procedure.

The procedure that sends data to another procedure is called the **passing procedure**, and the procedure that receives the data is called the **receiving procedure**. In this case, the New command's Click event (the passing procedure) will pass the contents of the cdlSeat control's Filename property to the Initialize sub procedure (the receiving procedure).

To continue coding the File menu's New command:

1 The mnuFileNew control's Click event procedure should still be open, and the blinking insertion point should be located below the `If Dir(cdlSeat.filename) = "" Then` instruction. If the file does not exist, the Click event should call the Initialize procedure, passing it the name of the file that the user wants to create; then the Click event should end. Press the **Tab** key, then type **call Initialize(cdlSeat.filename)** and press the **Enter** key.

If, however, the file does exist, then you should prompt the user to verify that he or she wants to replace the existing file. When a play is over, the manager may want to initialize the file so that he or she can reuse the file to record information about another play.

Use the conMsg and conBtns constants to display a message box that contains the "This file already exists. Replace existing file?" message, as well as the Warning Message icon (the exclamation point) and Yes and No buttons.

2 Press the **Backspace** key, then type **else** and press the **Enter** key. Press the **Tab** key, then type **inUserAns = msgbox(conMsg, conBtns, "Cole's Playhouse")** and press the **Enter** key.

If the user selects the Yes button, then you will call the Initialize procedure to both open and initialize the existing file; otherwise you will simply exit the Click event procedure.

3 Complete the Click event by entering the remaining code and documentation shown in Figure 8-27.

tips

Notice that the `If inUserAns = vbYes` selection structure does not need an Else clause to handle the possible vbNo answer. If the user selects the No button in the MsgBox dialog box, the code will fall through to the `Exit Sub` statement that appears before the ErrHandler, and the Click event will end.

enter these four lines of code

enter these three lines of documentation

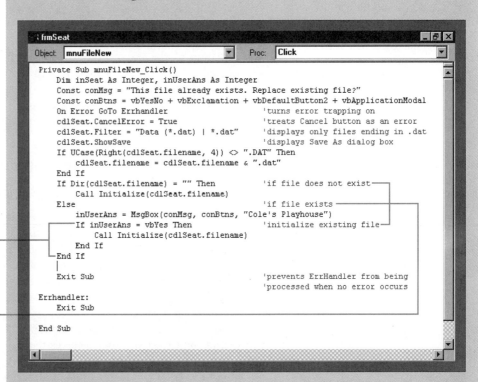

```
frmSeat
Object: mnuFileNew                        Proc: Click

Private Sub mnuFileNew_Click()
    Dim inSeat As Integer, inUserAns As Integer
    Const conMsg = "This file already exists. Replace existing file?"
    Const conBtns = vbYesNo + vbExclamation + vbDefaultButton2 + vbApplicationModal
    On Error GoTo Errhandler               'turns error trapping on
    cdlSeat.CancelError = True             'treats Cancel button as an error
    cdlSeat.Filter = "Data (*.dat) | *.dat"   'displays only files ending in .dat
    cdlSeat.ShowSave                       'displays Save As dialog box
    If UCase(Right(cdlSeat.filename, 4)) <> ".DAT" Then
        cdlSeat.filename = cdlSeat.filename & ".dat"
    End If
    If Dir(cdlSeat.filename) = "" Then     'if file does not exist
        Call Initialize(cdlSeat.filename)
    Else                                   'if file exists
        inUserAns = MsgBox(conMsg, conBtns, "Cole's Playhouse")
        If inUserAns = vbYes Then          'initialize existing file
            Call Initialize(cdlSeat.filename)
        End If
    End If

    Exit Sub                               'prevents ErrHandler from being
                                           'processed when no error occurs
Errhandler:
    Exit Sub

End Sub
```

Figure 8-27: Completed Click event procedure for the File menu's New command

4 Compare your code to the code shown in Figure 8-27. Make any needed corrections before continuing to the next step.

> **5**   Close the Code window, then click the **Save Project** button to save the application.

In order to test the New command's code, you first need to create the Initialize procedure. Before doing so, however, you will learn how to use Visual Basic's color constants in your code. You will need to use one of the color constants in the Initialize procedure.

Using Visual Basic's Color Constants

In Tutorial 3 you learned how to create a user-defined symbolic constant. Symbolic constants, you may remember, make your program more self-documenting and, therefore, easier to modify because they allow you to use meaningful words in place of values that are less clear. Because constants play such an important role in creating a well-written program, Visual Basic provides many **intrinsic** (built-in) constants that you can use in your code. You can view these built-in constants by displaying the Object Browser. Use the Object Browser to view the color constants.

To use the Object Browser to view Visual Basic's color constants:

1   Click the **Object Browser** button 🔲 on the toolbar. The Object Browser dialog box appears.

2   Click the **Libraries/Projects** list arrow, then click **VB - Visual Basic objects and procedures** in the drop-down list, and then click **ColorConstants** in the Classes/Modules list box. The Visual Basic color constants appear in the Methods/Properties list box. See Figure 8-28.

Figure 8-28: Object Browser dialog box showing color constants

Notice that the name of the color constant for red is vbRed, and the name for white is vbWhite. You can use the color constants in your code to refer to the various colors. For example, the `lblSeat(0).BackColor = vbWhite` instruction tells Visual Basic to change the BackColor property of the lblSeat(0) control to white.

3 Close the Object Browser dialog box.

You will use the vbWhite color constant in the Initialize procedure, which you will create in the next section.

Creating a User-Defined Procedure That Receives Data

Recall from Tutorial 4 that a user-defined sub procedure is a collection of code that can be invoked from one or more places in your program. When the code, or a portion of the code, for two or more objects is almost identical, it is more efficient to enter the code once, in a user-defined procedure, instead of duplicating the code in each event procedure. The procedure you will create for the Cole application will open and initialize a random access data file. As you observed in the File menu's New command, the Initialize procedure will be called when the file that the user wants to open doesn't exist; it will also be called in cases where the file exists and the user has chosen to initialize the existing file.

The pseudocode for the Initialize procedure is shown in Figure 8-29.

Pseudocode for the Initialize procedure

1. Receive a String variable named stFileName, which will store the name of the file passed to it by the File menu's New command.

2. Declare an Integer variable named inSeat and a PatronStruc variable named PatronRec.

3. Assign 20 spaces to the stName field variable in the PatronRec variable.

4. Assign 8 spaces to the stPhone field variable in the PatronRec variable.

5. Close the currently open file, if any.

6. Open the random access file whose name is stored in the stFileName variable.

7. Repeat for each seat in the lblSeat control array

    a. Write the record to the file. The record number should be one more than the contents of the inSeat variable.

    b. Change the BackColor property of the corresponding label in the lblSeat control array to white.

    c. Display the corresponding label in the lblSeat control array on the form.

  End Repeat for

8. Display the file name and application name in the form's title bar.

Figure 8-29: Pseudocode for the Initialize procedure

Now create the Initialize procedure.

To create the Initialize procedure:

1 Open any Code window, then click **Insert** on the menu bar, then click **Procedure**. The Insert Procedure dialog box appears.

2 Type **Initialize** in the Name box.

You want to create a sub procedure, so leave the Sub option button selected in the Type box. The user-defined procedure will be used only by the form in which it is created, so you will make its scope Private.

3 Click the **Private** option button in the Scope box, then click the **OK** button. The Insert Procedure dialog box closes and the Code window for the Initialize procedure appears.

As you learned in Tutorial 4, a user-defined procedure can receive variables or constants, called **arguments**, that you send (pass) to it; the arguments, if any, are listed inside the parentheses following the procedure's name. You pass arguments when you want the procedure to process them in some way. For example, you might create a procedure that sorts a list of numbers. The arguments you pass would be the numbers themselves; the procedure would then sort, and perhaps display, those numbers. In this application, the Call statements in the New command's Click event pass the contents of the cdlSeat control's Filename property. The Initialize procedure, which is the receiving procedure, will use that information to create/open and initialize the file.

The names of the receiving procedure's variables do not need to be identical to the names of the variables listed in the Call statement. The receiving procedure's variables, however, must be the same type as the passing variables, and they must be listed in the same order as the passing variables. In other words, if the passing procedure sends a String variable first and a Single variable second, then the receiving procedure must receive a String variable first and a Single variable second. In this application the Call statements pass a String (the cdlSeat control's Filename property); the Initialize procedure, therefore, will need to list a String variable as its argument.

Variables can be passed either by value or by reference. You control which way they are passed by including the keywords ByVal or ByRef before the variable's name in the receiving procedure arguments. When you pass a variable **by value**, Visual Basic creates a copy of the variable in memory, and only the copy is passed to the receiving procedure. Although the receiving procedure can change the contents of the copy, it cannot change the contents of the original variable.

If, on the other hand, you pass a variable **by reference**, Visual Basic passes the variable's actual address in memory. Because the actual address is passed to the receiving procedure, the contents of the variable can be permanently changed by the receiving procedure. Unless specified otherwise, all variables are passed by reference. Figure 8-30 shows some examples of passing information from one procedure to another. The Call statements would be entered in the passing procedure; the Private Sub statements represent the receiving procedure.

tips

▶ Because passing a variable by value creates another copy of the variable, the application will use more memory than if you pass the variables by reference. Lesson B's Exercise 1 will help clarify the difference between passing by value and passing by reference.

Call statement entered in the passing procedure	Private Sub statement in the receiving procedure
Call DoubleNumber(inNum) Calls the DoubleNumber procedure, passing it the inNum variable.	**Private Sub DoubleNumber(inNum as Integer)** Receives the inNum variable, which was passed by reference. Refers to the inNum variable as inNum.
Call Display(stName, inAge) Calls the Display procedure, passing it in the stName and inAge variables.	**Private Sub Display(stStudent as String, inNum as Integer)** Receives the stName and inAge variables, which were passed by reference. Refers to the stName variable as stStudent. Refers to the inAge variable as inNum.
Call Update(inNum) Calls the Update procedure, passing it the inNum variable.	**Private Sub Update(ByVal inNumber as Integer)** Receives the inNum variable, which was passed by value. The copy of the variable is named inNumber.

Figure 8-30: Examples of passing information from one procedure to another

In this application, you will name the receiving variable stFileName and declare it as a String variable. You will pass it by reference, which is the default.

To code the Initialize procedure:

1 Enter the receiving variable as shown in Figure 8-31.

receiving variable's name

Figure 8-31: Receiving variable shown in Initialize procedure

According to the pseudocode, the Initialize procedure will need to declare an Integer variable named inSeat and a PatronStruc variable named PatronRec. Recall that the PatronStruc data type contains two fields, stName and stPhone. To initialize the random access file, the Initialize procedure will assign 20 spaces to the stName field variable and eight spaces to the stPhone field variable. It will then close the currently open file, if any, and open the random access file whose name is stored in the stFileName variable. A For Next loop will write the PatronRec record variable to the file, 48 times. It will also change the BackColor property of each of the 48 seats to white, and change each seat's Visible property to True. (Recall that the Visible property of each seat in the lblSeat control array is initially set to False.) Before the procedure ends, it will display the current file's name, along with the name of the application (Cole's Playhouse), in the frmSeat form's title bar.

2 Enter the code and documentation shown in Figure 8-32.

```
frmSeat                                                            _ 8 X

Object:  (General)              ▼    Proc:  Initialize              ▼

Private Sub Initialize(stFileName As String)
    Dim inSeat As Integer, PatronRec As PatronStruc
    PatronRec.stName = Space(20)                      'assign spaces to field variables
    PatronRec.stPhone = Space(8)
    Close #1
    Open stFileName For Random As #1 Len = Len(PatronRec)
    For inSeat = 0 To 47
        Put #1, inSeat + 1, PatronRec               'initialize each record
        lblSeat(inSeat).BackColor = vbWhite         'change seat to white
        lblSeat(inSeat).Visible = True              'display seat
    Next inSeat
    frmSeat.Caption = stFileName & " - Cole's Playhouse"

End Sub
```

Figure 8-32: Completed Initialize procedure

tips

If you omit the Step from the For Next loop, recall that the loop uses a default step of a positive 1.

3 Close the Code window, then **save** and **run** the application.

4 Click **File**, then click **New**. When the Save As dialog box appears, save the file as **lbTest** in the Tut08 folder on your Student Disk. Because the file does not exist, the New command creates a new random access file and initializes it for 48 records. The 48 label controls appear in the form with a white background, and the name of the file appears in the form's title bar. See Figure 8-33.

open file's name

Figure 8-33: frmSeat form showing the file name in the form's title bar

> **5** Click **File**, then click **New**. When the Save As dialog box appears, click **lbTest.dat** in the filename list box, then click the **Save** button (*the OK button if you are using Windows 3.1*). Because the file already exists, the MsgBox function in the New command's Click event displays the "This file already exists. Replace existing file?" message. Click the **No** button. Visual Basic returns to the frmSeat form. The form's title bar indicates that the lbTest.dat file is still open.
>
> **6** Click **File**, then click **Exit** to end the application. Visual Basic returns to the design screen.

Next, code the File menu's Open command.

Coding the File Menu's Open Command

The Open command should allow the user to open an existing data file so he or she can continue to record reservations for the play. The pseudocode for the Open command is shown in Figure 8-34.

Pseudocode for the File menu's Open command

1. Declare the variables.

2. Begin error trapping.

3. Show the Open dialog box to get the name of an existing file from the user.

4. If the file exists then

    a. Close the currently open file, if any.

    b. Open the file whose name is stored in the cdlSeat control's Filename property.

    c. Display the file name and the application name in the frmSeat form's title bar.

    d. Repeat for each seat in the lblSeat control array

        1) Display the label control in the lblSeat control array.

        2) Read the record that corresponds to the seat in the lblSeat array.

        3) If the record contains a patron's name, then

            change the label control to red to indicate that it is reserved

        Else

            change the label control to white to indicate that it is available

        End If

    End Repeat for

  Else

    Display a message to the user indicating that the file does not exist.

  End If

5. Exit the Click event.

Figure 8-34: Pseudocode for the Open command

Most of the code for the Open command has already been entered into its Click event procedure for you.

To view the code in the Open command's Click event procedure:

1 Click **File** on the form's menu bar, then click **Open**. The Open command's Click event procedure appears. Maximize the Code window, then position the blinking insertion point as shown in Figure 8-35.

position insertion point here

```
frmSeat                                                                    _ 8 X

Object:  mnuFileOpen              ▼      Proc:  Click                       ▼

Private Sub mnuFileOpen_Click()
    Dim inSeat As Integer, PatronRec As PatronStruc, inUserAns As Integer
    Const conBtns = vbOKOnly + vbInformation + vbDefaultButton1 + vbApplicationModal
    On Error GoTo Errhandler                   'turns error trapping on
    cdlSeat.CancelError = True                 'treats Cancel button as an error
    cdlSeat.Filter = "Data (*.dat) | *.dat"    'displays only files ending in .dat
    cdlSeat.filename = ""                      'clears filename from dialog box
    cdlSeat.ShowOpen                           'displays Open dialog box
    If Dir(cdlSeat.filename) = "" Then         'if file doesn't exist
        inUserAns = MsgBox(cdlSeat.filename & " does not exist.", conBtns, "Cole's Play
    Else                                       'if file exists
        Close #1
        Open cdlSeat.filename For Random As #1 Len = Len(PatronRec)
        frmSeat.Caption = cdlSeat.filename & " - Cole's Playhouse"
        |
    End If
    Exit Sub                                   'prevents ErrHandler from being
                                               'processed when no error occurs
Errhandler:
    Exit Sub
End Sub
```

Figure 8-35: Open command's Click event procedure

After declaring three variables, as well as a constant for the MsgBox function, the procedure turns error trapping on, sets the properties of the common dialog control, and displays the Open dialog box. It then uses the Dir function to verify that the file to be opened exists. If the file does not exist, a message to that effect is displayed to the user, then the procedure ends. If, however, the file does exist, the currently open file, if any, is closed, and the file whose name is stored in the cdlSeat control's Filename property is opened. The frmSeat form's caption is then changed to reflect the name of the open file. Notice that the error handling routine, which simply exits the Click event when an error occurs, is already entered in the Code window.

According to the pseudocode, you still need to add the code that will display the lblSeat controls in the interface. You also need to add the code to read each record in the open file and, if the record contains a name, set the seat's color to red to indicate that the seat is reserved; otherwise set it to white to indicate that it is available.

First display the 48 lblSeat controls in the interface by setting each control's Visible property to True. (Recall that the Visible property of the lblSeat controls is initially set to False.) As you learned in Tutorial 5, you use both the Name property and the Index property to refer to a control in a control array. The indexes of the label controls in the lblSeat array are numbered 0 through 47.

2 With the blinking insertion point positioned as shown in Figure 8-35, type **for inSeat = 0 to 47** and press the **Enter** key.

3   Press the **Tab** key, then type **lblSeat(inSeat).visible = true** and press the **Enter** key.

Now read each seat's record from the random access file. If the record contains a name, then change the color of the corresponding seat to red, which indicates that the seat is reserved; otherwise set it to white, which indicates that it is available. Although the indexes of the controls in the lblSeat array are numbered 0 through 47, the records that store the information about each seat are numbered 1 through 48. In other words, the lblSeat(0) control's information is stored in record 1 in the random access file, the lblSeat(1) control's in record 2, and so on. Notice that the record number is always one greater than the index number.

4   Enter the code shown in Figure 8-36.

```
frmSeat                                                                   _ 8 X

Object:  mnuFileOpen            ▼        Proc:  Click                      ▼

Private Sub mnuFileOpen_Click()
    Dim inSeat As Integer, PatronRec As PatronStruc, inUserAns As Integer
    Const conBtns = vbOKOnly + vbInformation + vbDefaultButton1 + vbApplicationModal
    On Error GoTo Errhandler                    'turns error trapping on
    cdlSeat.CancelError = True                  'treats Cancel button as an error
    cdlSeat.Filter = "Data (*.dat) | *.dat"     'displays only files ending in .dat
    cdlSeat.filename = ""                       'clears filename from dialog box
    cdlSeat.ShowOpen                            'displays Open dialog box
    If Dir(cdlSeat.filename) = "" Then          'if file doesn't exist
        inUserAns = MsgBox(cdlSeat.filename & " does not exist.", conBtns, "Cole's Play
    Else                                        'if file exists
        Close #1
        Open cdlSeat.filename For Random As #1 Len = Len(PatronRec)
        frmSeat.Caption = cdlSeat.filename & " - Cole's Playhouse"
        For inSeat = 0 To 47
            lblSeat(inSeat).Visible = True
            Get #1, inSeat + 1, PatronRec
            If PatronRec.stName <> Space(20) Then
                lblSeat(inSeat).BackColor = vbRed
            Else
                lblSeat(inSeat).BackColor = vbWhite
            End If
        Next inSeat
    End If
    Exit Sub                                    'prevents ErrHandler from being
                                                'processed when no error occurs

Errhandler:
    Exit Sub
End Sub
```

enter these seven lines of code

Figure 8-36: Additional code entered in the mnuFileOpen Click event

5   Close the Code window.

6   **Save** and **run** the application.

First open a file that does exist.

7   Click **File**, then click **Open**. When the Open dialog box appears, open the **lbTest.dat** file, which is located in the Tut08 folder on your Student Disk. The form's title bar indicates that the file is open. The seats are white because you have not saved any information for this play.

Now open a data file that contains some records. You will find such a file in the Tut08 folder on your Student Disk.

8   Click **File**, then click **Open**. When the Open dialog box appears, open the **Play.dat** file, which is located in the Tut08 folder on your Student Disk. The form's title bar indicates that the file is open. The reserved seats (seats 2 and 5) are red; the others are white.

Now try opening a file that does not exist.

9 Click **File**, then click **Open**. When the Open dialog box appears, enter **t8.dat** in the File Name box, then click the **Open** button (*the OK button if you are using Windows 3.1*). A message box telling the user that the file does not exist appears on the screen. Click the **OK** button to remove the message box. Visual Basic returns to the application.

10 Click **File**, then click **Exit** to end the application. Visual Basic returns to the design screen.

You have now completed Lesson B. You can either take a break or complete the questions and exercises at the end of the lesson. You will complete the Cole's Playhouse application in Lesson C.

S U M M A R Y

To add an existing form to an application:

■ Click File, then click Add File.

To specify the startup form:

■ Click Tools on the menu bar, then click Options. When the Options dialog box appears, click the Project tab. Click the Startup Form list arrow, then click the name of the startup form in the list, and then click the OK button.

To view Visual Basic's built-in constants:

■ Click the Object Browser button 🖼 on the toolbar, or click View, then click Object Browser; you can also press the F2 key.
■ Click the Libraries/Projects list arrow, then click VB - Visual Basic objects and procedures.

To pass information to a procedure:

■ Use the Call statement. Its syntax is **Call** *name* (*argumentlist*), where *argumentlist* is the information you want passed to the procedure.

To create a user-defined sub procedure:

■ Open any Code window, then click Insert on the menu bar, then click Procedure. The Insert Procedure dialog box appears.
■ Type the procedure's name in the Name box.
■ If necessary, select the Sub option button in the Type box.
■ If the user-defined procedure will be used only by the form in which it is created, click Private in the Scope box.

To have a sub procedure receive information passed to it with the Call statement:

- List the variables in a set of parentheses following the procedure's name. The names of the receiving procedure's variables do not need to be identical to the names of the variables listed in the Call statement. The receiving procedure's variables, however, must be the same type as the passing variables, and they must be listed in the same order as the passing variables.

- Variables can be passed either by value or by reference. You control which way they are passed by including the keywords ByVal or ByRef before the variable's name in the receiving procedure arguments. When you pass a variable by value, Visual Basic creates a copy of the variable in memory, and only the copy is passed to the receiving procedure. Although the receiving procedure can change the contents of the copy, it cannot change the contents of the original variable. When you pass a variable by reference, Visual Basic passes the variable's actual address in memory. Because the actual address is passed to the receiving procedure, the contents of the variable can be permanently changed by the receiving procedure. Unless specified otherwise, all variables are passed by reference.

Q U E S T I O N S

1. When a multiform project is run, Visual Basic automatically loads and displays the _____ form.
   a. beginning
   b. first
   c. initial
   d. loaded
   e. startup

2. You use Visual Basic's _____ menu to specify the startup form.
   a. File
   b. Options
   c. Project
   d. Startup
   e. Tools

3. Which of the following will invoke the DoubleNumber procedure, passing it the contents of the inNumber variable?
   a. Call DoubleNumber inNumber
   b. Call DoubleNumber (inNumber)
   c. Call DoubleNumber(inNumber as Integer)
   d. Invoke DoubleNumber (inNumber)
   e. Sub DoubleNumber(inNumber as Integer)

4. The procedure that sends data to another procedure is called the _____ procedure.
   a. invoking
   b. receiving
   c. passing
   d. sub

5. The procedure that receives data from another procedure is called the
   _____ procedure.
   a. invoking
   b. receiving
   c. passing
   d. sub

6. Which of the following will call a procedure named PrintHeading, passing it no
   arguments?
   a. Call PrintHeading
   b. Call (PrintHeading)
   c. CallSub PrintName
   d. Invoke PrintName
   e. Sub PrintName

7. If you invoke the DisplayName procedure, passing it a String variable named stFriend,
   which of the following is a correct Private Sub statement for the DisplayName procedure?
   a. Private Sub DisplayName( )
   b. Private Sub DisplayName(Call stFriendName)
   c. Private Sub DisplayName stFriendName
   d. Private Sub DisplayName stFriendName as String
   e. Private Sub DisplayName (stFriendName as String)

8. If you invoke the UpdateAge procedure, passing it a String variable named stFriend
   and an integer variable named inAge, which of the following is a correct Private Sub
   statement for the UpdateAge procedure?
   a. Private Sub UpdateAge( )
   b. Private Sub UpdateAge(inAge as Integer, stMyFriend as String)
   c. Private Sub (UpdateAge) stMyFriend as String, inAge as Integer
   d. Private Sub UpdateAge inAge as Integer, stFriendName as String
   e. Private Sub UpdateAge (stFriendName as String, inAge as Integer)

9. You can view Visual Basic's built-in constants by displaying the _____ .
   a. Constant Browser
   b. Constant Viewer
   c. Object Browser
   d. Object Viewer

10. Which of the following is false?
    a. The names of the receiving procedure's variables must be identical to the names of
       the variables listed in the Call statement.
    b. The receiving procedure's variables must be the same type as the passing variables.
    c. The receiving procedure's variables must be listed in the same order as the passing
       variables.
    d. Variables can be passed either by value or by reference.
    e. You control which way variables are passed by including the keywords ByVal or
       ByRef before the variable's name in the receiving procedure arguments.

11. When you pass a variable _____ , Visual Basic creates a copy of the vari-
    able in memory, and only the copy is passed to the receiving procedure.
    a. by copy
    b. by original
    c. by reference
    d. by value

12. When you pass a variable _____ , Visual Basic passes the variable's actual address in memory.
    a. by copy
    b. by original
    c. by reference
    d. by value

13. When you pass a variable _____ , the receiving procedure cannot change the contents of the original variable.
    a. by copy
    b. by original
    c. by reference
    d. by value

14. When you pass a variable _____ , the contents of the variable can be permanently changed by the receiving procedure.
    a. by copy
    b. by original
    c. by reference
    d. by value

15. Unless specified otherwise, all variables are passed _____ .
    a. by copy
    b. by original
    c. by reference
    d. by value

16. Assume you want to open the file whose name is entered in the stFile variable. Which of the following could you use in an If...Then...Else statement to test if the file exists?
    a. If Dir("stFile") = True Then
    b. If Dir("stFile") = Yes Then
    c. If Dir("stFile") = "" Then
    d. If Dir(stFile) = "" Then
    e. If Dir(stFile) = True Then

17. Which of the following can you use in an If...Then...Else statement to test if the myfile.dat file exists?
    a. If Dir(myfile.dat) = True Then
    b. If Dir(myfile.dat) = Yes Then
    c. If Dir("myfile.dat") = True Then
    d. If Dir("myfile.dat") = " " Then
    e. If Dir("myfile") = " " Then

18. If the friends.dat file exists, what will the following Dir function return?

    Dir("friends.dat")

    a. FRIENDS.DAT
    b. the null string
    c. true
    d. yes

E X E R C I S E S

1. In this exercise you will observe the difference between passing arguments by reference and passing them by value.

   a. Open the lb1 (lb1.vbp) project, which is located in the Tut08 folder on your Student Disk.

   b. View the form. The interface contains a label control and two command buttons (Display and Exit).

   c. Print the application's code.

   d. Notice that the cmdDisplay control's Click event declares a local Integer variable named inNumber, to which it assigns the number 10. The procedure then calls the DoubleNumber user-defined procedure and passes it the inNumber variable. After processing the instructions in the DoubleNumber procedure, the application returns to the cmdDisplay control's Click event, where the value in the inNumber variable is displayed in the lblNumber control. Notice that the DoubleNumber procedure receives an Integer variable named inNum, which it multiplies by two. (Recall that the name of the variable in the receiving procedure does not have to match the name of the passing variable.) The DoubleNumber procedure is receiving the variable by reference, which is the default way that variables are passed to procedures. That means that although the receiving variable's name is different from the passing variable's name, they both refer to the same location in the computer's memory. Passing a variable by reference gives the receiving procedure access to the variable in memory.

   e. To see what it means to pass by reference, run (but don't save) the application. Click the Display button. The Display button's Click event calls the DoubleNumber procedure, passing it the inNumber variable, which contains the number 10. The DoubleNumber procedure multiplies the contents of the inNumber variable (10) times 2, giving 20. The value in the inNumber variable is now 20. When control returns to the Display button's Click event, the number 20 is assigned to the lblNumber control on the form. Click the Exit button to end the application.

   f. To see what it means to pass by value, open the DoubleNumber procedure, which is located in the General declarations section of the form. Change the Private Sub statement to `Private Sub DoubleNumber(ByVal inNum as Integer)`. The ByVal keyword tells Visual Basic that the inNumber variable in the passing procedure should be passed by value, and not by reference. That means that Visual Basic will pass a copy of the inNumber variable to the DoubleNumber procedure; the name of the copy will be inNum. The DoubleNumber procedure has access to the inNum variable, but not to the original inNumber variable in memory. Close the Code window.

   g. Run (but don't save) the application. Click the Display button. On the printout from step c, write down the number that displays in the lblNumber control. Also explain why the Display button printed that number. What is stored in the inNum and inNumber variables when the Display button is clicked?

   h. Exit the application. Submit the printout from step c, which includes the information from step g.

Exercises 2 and 3 are Discovery Exercises, which allow you to "discover" the solutions to problems on your own. Discovery Exercises may include topics that are not covered in the tutorial.

discovery ▶ 2. In this exercise you will create a user-defined procedure in a code module. The user-defined procedure will center a form. You will also learn about the Form object.

   Scenario: In addition to the Screen object, which you learned about in Tutorial 3, and the Printer object, which you learned about in Tutorial 6 in Lesson A's Discovery Exercise 7, Visual Basic also has a Form object. The Form object refers to the form itself. You can use the Form object to pass a form from one procedure to another.

In this exercise, you will create a user-defined procedure, called CenterForm, that will center a form. Because the CenterForm procedure will need to be used by any number of forms in a project, you will create it as a global procedure. You declare a global procedure by entering the Public statement in the General declarations section of a code mode. (Recall from Tutorial 3 that that is also the way you declare global variables.)

   a. Open a new project, if necessary. Add a Module to the project. Use the Insert menu to insert a sub procedure. Call the sub procedure CenterForm, and make its scope Public.

   b. If you want to pass a String variable to a procedure, recall that you would include an argument such as `stName as String` within the parentheses that follow the procedure's name. In this case, however, you want to pass the actual form itself, not a variable, to the CenterForm procedure. You can do so by using the argument `FormName as Form`. Change the `Public Sub CenterForm( )` statement to `Public Sub CenterForm(FormName as Form)`. The `FormName as Form` argument tells the CenterForm procedure that it will be receiving a form, and to accept the form as FormName.

   c. Enter the following two instructions in the CenterForm procedure. These instructions tell the CenterForm procedure to center the form that is passed to it.

```
FormName.Left = (Screen.Width - FormName.Width) / 2
FormName.Top = (Screen.Height - FormName.Height) / 2
```

   d. Save the module as Procs (short for "Procedures") in the Tut08 folder on your Student Disk. You do not need to save the form or the project. You should create one module that will store all of your global procedures and variables. You can then include the module in each of your projects. By doing so, the project will have access to these global procedures and variables; you won't have to retype them.

   e. Open the lb2 (lb2.vbp) project, which is located in the Tut08 folder on your Student Disk. (You do not need to save the form or the project from step d. Only the module needs to be saved as Procs.)

   f. View the frmSales form.

   g. Save the form and the project as lb2Done in the Tut08 folder on your Student Disk.

   h. Run the application. Notice that the form is not centered on the screen.

   i. Exit the application.

   j. Add the Procs.bas file to the project.

   k. Open the frmSales form's Load event. Enter the appropriate Call statement that will invoke the CenterForm procedure, passing it the frmSales form.

   l. Save and run the project. The CenterForm procedure centers the form on the screen.

   m. Exit the application.

   n. Print the application's code.

discovery ▶   **3.** In this exercise you will create two user-defined functions.

Scenario: In addition to creating a user-defined sub procedure, you can also create a user-defined function procedure. The difference between both procedures is that a function procedure returns a value, whereas a sub procedure does not. In this exercise you will create two function procedures. The first function will increase the number passed to it by 10%. The second function will calculate the square root of the number passed to it.

   a. View the Help window on the Function statement. Read the information contained in the Help window, then close the Help window.

   b. Open a new project, if necessary. Save the form and the project as lb3Done in the Tut08 folder on your Student Disk.

   c. Double-click the form to open a Code window. Use the Insert menu to insert a procedure. Create a Private Function procedure named CalcNewPrice.

d. Change the `Private Function CalcNewPrice( )` statement to `Private Function CalcNewPrice(crNum as Currency) as Currency`.

e. This function should increase the crNum variable by 10%. Enter the `CalcNewPrice = crNum * 1.1` instruction between the Private Function and End Function statements. Notice that the name of the function, CalcNewPrice, is used in the equation itself; you return a value from a function by assigning the value to the function's name.

f. Close the Code window. Place a text box and a command button on the form. Remove the contents of the text box's Text property.

g. Open the command button's Click event procedure. You can invoke the CalcNewPrice function simply by using its name in an instruction. In the command button's Click event, enter the following three instructions:

```
Dim crPrice as Currency
crPrice = Val(Text1.Text)
Text1.Text = CalcNewPrice(crPrice)
```

h. Close the Code window. Save and run the project. Enter the number 50 in the text box, then click the Command1 button. The number 55 appears in the text box.

i. Exit the application.

j. Use the Insert menu to insert another procedure. Create a Private Function procedure named SquareRoot. The SquareRoot function should receive an Integer variable named inNum. Declare the function as an Integer. This procedure will find the square root of the number passed to it. (Hint: You can use Visual Basic's Sqr function to calculate the square root.)

k. Add another command button to the form. Have this command button's Click event print, on the form, the square root of the number entered in the text box. (Be sure to invoke the SquareRoot function and use the Print method to print the square root on the form.)

l. Save and run the application. Enter the number 9 in the text box, then click the Command2 button. The number 3 should appear in the upper-left corner of the form.

m. Stop the application. Print the application's code.

In this lesson you will learn how to:

■ Refer to a control in another form

■ Clear a record from a random access file

Completing the Cole's Playhouse Application

Important Note: You will not be able to complete Lesson C if you are using the Working Model. You will need to use either the Standard Edition or Professional Edition of Visual Basic.

Coding the lblSeat Control Array

In this lesson you will complete the Cole's Playhouse application. First open the lbCole project file that you created in Lesson B.

To open the lbCole project that you created in Lesson B:

1 Start Visual Basic, if necessary. Open the **lbCole** (lbcole.vbp) project, which is in the Tut08 folder on your Student Disk.

2 If necessary, click **Patron.Frm** in the Project window. Open Visual Basic's File menu, then use the Save File As command to save the frmPatron form as **lcPatron**.

3 View the frmPatron form. See Figure 8-37.

lblNum

txtName

txtPhone

Figure 8-37: frmPatron form

Recall that this form will allow the theater manager to enter a reservation, cancel a reservation, or return to the main screen—the frmSeat form.

4 Close the frmPatron form.

5 Click **lbSeat.Frm** in the Project window. Open Visual Basic's File menu, then use the Save File As command to save the frmSeat form as **lcSeat**.

6 Open Visual Basic's File menu, then use the Save Project As command to save the project as **lcCole**.

7 View the frmSeat form. Recall that the 48 label controls, which represent the theater seats, belong to a control array named lblSeat.

The first event procedure you will code is the Click event for the lblSeat control array. The pseudocode for the lblSeat control array's Click event procedure is shown in Figure 8-38.

Pseudocode for the lblSeat control array

1. Declare an Integer variable named inSeat and a PatronStruc variable named PatronRec.

2. Add 1 to the inSeat variable.

3. Display the contents of the inSeat variable in the lblNum control, which is in the frmPatron form.

4. If the lblSeat control's BackColor property is set to red, then

    a. read the record from the random access file

    b. assign the name to the txtName control, which is in the frmPatron form

    c. assign the phone number to the txtPhone control, which is in the frmPatron form

  Else

    clear the text from the txtName and txtPhone controls, which are in the frmPatron form

  End If

5. Show the frmPatron form.

6. Set the focus in the txtName control, which is in the frmPatron form.

Figure 8-38: Pseudocode for the lblSeat control array

When the user clicks on any of the 48 label controls in the lblSeat control array, the array's Click event should display the frmPatron form on the screen, with the number of the chosen seat displayed in the lblNum control on the frmPatron form. If the seat is reserved, the Click event should also display the patron's name and phone number in the appropriate text boxes in the frmPatron form. If the seat is available, the name and phone number should be blank when the frmPatron form appears. In the next section you will learn how to refer to a control in another form.

Referencing a Control in Another Form

When writing Visual Basic code for a form or one of its controls, you can refer to another control in the same form by using the control's name. For example, if the lblNum control was in the same form as the lblSeat control array, you could refer to it as simply lblNum. In this case, however, the lblNum control is not in the same form as the control array—the lblNum control is in the frmPatron form and the control array is in the frmSeat form. To refer to a control in another form, you simply precede the control's name with the name of the form in which it is contained. You separate the form name from the control's name with a period, like this: *Form.Control*. For example, to refer to the lblNum control in the frmPatron form, you will need to use `frmPatron.lblNum`; otherwise, Visual Basic will not be able to locate the control. To refer to the property of a control contained in another form, you use the following syntax: *Form.Control.Property*.

Now code the lblSeat control array's Click event.

To code the lblSeat control array's Click event:

1 Double-click any **one of the label controls** in the lblSeat control array. Recall that the controls in a control array use the same Code window, which you can open by double-clicking any of the controls in the array. The Code window for the lblSeat control array appears.

According to the pseudocode, your first step is to declare the inSeat and PatronRec variables. InSeat (an Integer variable) will store the seat number and PatronRec (a record variable) will store the patron's record.

2 Maximize the Code window, press the **Tab** key, then type **dim inSeat as integer, PatronRec as PatronStruc** and press the **Enter** key.

Now assign the appropriate seat number to the inSeat variable. Recall that Visual Basic stores, in the Index argument, the Index property of the control that is receiving the event. In this case, for example, if the user clicks seat number 1 (the lblSeat(0) control), Visual Basic records a zero in the Index argument; if the user clicks seat number 45 (the lblSeat(44) control), Visual Basic records the number 44 in the Index argument, and so on. Notice that the Index argument is always one less than the seat number. That means that you will need to add one to the Index argument in order to display the proper seat number in the frmPatron form.

3 Type **inSeat = Index + 1** and press the **Enter** key.

Now assign the seat number to the lblNum control in the frmPatron form.

4 Type **frmPatron.lblNum.caption = inSeat** and press the **Enter** key.

According to the pseudocode, the next step is to see if the seat is reserved. In this application, recall that the reserved seats have a BackColor setting of red; the available seats have a BackColor setting of white. If the BackColor setting is red, then you will need to read the patron's name and phone number from the random access file in order to display that information in the frmPatron form. If the BackColor is not red, then the name and phone number should be blank when the frmPatron form appears. Use a selection structure to compare the BackColor property to Visual Basic's vbRed symbolic constant.

5 Enter the selection structure shown in Figure 8-39, then position the insertion point as shown in the figure.

enter this selection
structure

position insertion point
here

Figure 8-39: Selection structure entered in lblSeat Click event procedure

According to the pseudocode, you still need to display the frmPatron form on the screen and then set the focus to the txtName control. You can use the Show method, which you learned about in Tutorial 3, to display the form. Recall that the syntax of the Show method is *Form*.**Show**, where *Form* is the name of the form you want to display or show. The Show method loads the form into the computer's memory, if necessary, then displays the form on the screen.

6 With the blinking insertion point positioned as shown in Figure 8-39, type **frmPatron.show** and press the **Enter** key.

Now set the focus to the txtName control in the frmPatron form.

7 Type **frmPatron.txtName.setfocus** and press the **Enter** key.

See how the application works so far.

8 Close the Code window, then **save** and **run** the application. Click **File**, then click **New**. When the Save As dialog box appears, name the file **lcTest** and save it in the Tut08 folder on your Student Disk. Because the file does not exist, the New command calls the Initialize procedure, which creates and initializes the file. The Initialize procedure also displays the lblSeat control array in the interface, with all of the seats colored white because it is a new file.

HELP? If you are practicing this lesson again, the dialog box asking if you want to replace the file will appear. Click the Yes button.

9 Click seat number **2**. The frmPatron form appears on the screen with the number 2 in the lblNum control. The name and phone number text boxes are empty because the ticket for this seat has not yet been purchased. The focus is in the txtName control.

10 Click the frmPatron form's **Close** button ⊠ to close the frmPatron form.

Click the frmPatron form's Control menu box ⊟*, then click the Close button to close the frmPatron form.*

11 Click **File**, then click **Exit** to end the application. Visual Basic returns to the design screen.

You still need to code the frmPatron form, which allows the user to enter the ticket information, cancel the ticket information, and return to the main form—the frmSeat form. Code the Enter Ticket button first.

Coding the Enter Ticket Button

Before you can code the Enter Ticket button, you will need to display the frmPatron form.

To display the frmPatron form:

1   Close the frmSeat form. Click **lcPatron.Frm** in the Project window, then click the **View Form** button.

The pseudocode for the Enter Ticket button's Click event procedure is shown in Figure 8-40.

Pseudocode for the Enter Ticket button

1.   Declare an Integer variable named inSeat and a PatronStruc variable named PatronRec.

2.   Assign the Caption property of the lblNum control to the inSeat variable.

3.   Assign the Text property of the txtName control to the stName field variable in the PatronRec variable.

4.   Assign the Text property of the txtPhone control to the stPhone field variable in the PatronRec variable.

5.   Write the record to the open random access file.

6.   Set the BackColor property of the corresponding label control in the lblSeat array, which is located in the frmSeat form, to red.

7.   Hide the frmPatron form.

Figure 8-40: Pseudocode for the Enter Ticket button

The first step is to declare the variables. This procedure will need two variables: inSeat and PatronRec. InSeat will store the seat number, which will also be the record number in the file. PatronRec, a record variable, will store the record—the name and phone number of the patron.

To code the Enter Ticket button:

1   Double-click the **Enter Ticket** button to open its Code window. In the Click event procedure, press the **Tab** key, then type **dim inSeat as integer, PatronRec as PatronStruc** and press the **Enter** key.

The next step is to assign the appropriate values to the variables. First assign the seat number to the inSeat variable. The seat number is in the Caption property of the lblNum control.

2   Type **inSeat = lblNum.caption** and press the **Enter** key.

Now assign the name and phone number to the field variables in the PatronRec record variable. The name is in the txtName control, and the phone number is in the txtPhone control.

3   Type **PatronRec.stName = txtName.text** and press the **Enter** key, then type **PatronRec.stPhone = txtPhone.text** and press the **Enter** key.

After declaring the variables and assigning the appropriate values to them, you are ready to write the record to the random access file. Recall that you do that with the Put statement, whose syntax is **Put #** *filenumber*, [*recordnumber*], *variablename*.

4   Type **put #1, inSeat, PatronRec** and press the **Enter** key.

After a seat has been reserved, its BackColor property should be set to red. Recall that the value currently in the inSeat variable is one more than the value in the lblSeat control's Index property. So, to refer to the appropriate seat in the lblSeat array, you will need to subtract 1 from the inSeat variable. For example, if the inSeat variable contains the number 2, you will want to set the BackColor property of the control named lblSeat(1) to red.

5   Type **frmSeat.lblSeat(inSeat – 1).backcolor = vbred** and press the **Enter** key.

The last step in the pseudocode is to hide the frmPatron form, so the user can view the frmSeat form again. You can use the Hide method, which you learned about in Tutorial 3, to do so.

6   Type **frmPatron.hide** and press the **Enter** key.

7   Compare your code with the code shown in Figure 8-41 and make any needed corrections before continuing to the next step.

Figure 8-41: Code entered in the Enter Ticket button's Click event procedure

8   Close the Code window.

Now save and run the application, then test the Enter Ticket button to see if its code is working properly.

To save and run the application, then test the Enter Ticket button:

1   **Save** and **run** the application. Use the File menu's Open command to open the **lcTest.dat** file, which is located in the Tut08 folder on your Student Disk.

2   Click seat number **2**. The frmPatron form appears on the screen, with seat number 2 in the Seat number label control.

3   Type **Khalid Patel** as the name, then press the **Tab** key, and then type **444-4444** as the phone number. Click the **Enter Ticket** button. Visual Basic writes the name and phone number as the second record in the random access file. The frmSeat form now appears on the screen with seat number 2 colored red.

You can also use the Enter Ticket button to edit an existing record.

4   Click seat number **2**. The frmPatron form appears on the screen. Notice that, in addition to the seat number, the patron's name and phone number also appear in the form.

5   Change the phone number to **444-4443**, then click the **Enter Ticket** button. The new information overwrites the existing record in the file.

6   Click **File**, then click **Exit** to end the application. Visual Basic returns to the design screen.

Code the Cancel Ticket button next.

Coding the Cancel Ticket Button

The Cancel Ticket button allows the user to remove a patron's name and phone number from the random access file. The pseudocode for the Cancel Ticket button's Click event procedure is shown in Figure 8-42.

Pseudocode for the Cancel Ticket button

1. Declare an Integer variable named inSeat and a PatronStruc variable named PatronRec.

2. Assign the Caption property of the lblNum control to the inSeat variable.

3. Assign 20 spaces to the stName field variable in the PatronRec variable.

4. Assign 8 spaces to the stPhone field variable in the PatronRec variable.

5. Write the record to the open random access file.

6. Set the BackColor property of the corresponding label control in the lblSeat array, which is located in the frmSeat form, to white.

7. Hide the frmPatron form.

Figure 8-42: Pseudocode for the Cancel Ticket button

Notice that the pseudocode shown in Figure 8-42 is very similar to the pseudocode shown in Figure 8-40. That means that the code for the Cancel Ticket button will be almost identical to the code for the Enter Ticket button. Therefore, you will copy the code from the Enter Ticket button to the Cancel Ticket button, and then make the necessary changes.

To code the Cancel Ticket button, then test the application:

1   Double-click the **Enter Ticket** button. The cmdEnter control's Click event procedure displays.

2   Select all of the instructions between the Sub statement and the End Sub statement. (However, do not select either the Sub statement or the End Sub statement.) When the appropriate instructions are selected, press **Ctrl + c** to copy the instructions to the clipboard.

3   Use the Code window's Object box to open the cmdCancel control's Click event, then press **Ctrl + v** to paste the instructions in the cmdCancel control's Click event procedure.

You will need to make three changes to the code in the Code window. When a ticket is canceled, you will tell Visual Basic to write spaces over the existing name and phone number in the file. You can use the Space function to assign spaces to the stName and stPhone field variables before the PatronRec record variable is written to the file. You also need to change the BackColor property of the lblSeat control that corresponds to the canceled seat to white.

4   Enter the changes shown in Figure 8-43.

tips

To cancel a record having a numeric field, you would write a zero over the existing data in that field.

change these lines of code

change the color in this line of code

```
frmPatron

Object:  cmdCancel              Proc:  Click

Private Sub cmdCancel_Click()
    Dim inSeat As Integer, PatronRec As PatronStruc
    inSeat = lblNum.Caption
    PatronRec.stName = Space(20)
    PatronRec.stPhone = Space(8)
    Put #1, inSeat, PatronRec
    frmSeat.lblSeat(inSeat - 1).BackColor = vbWhite
    frmPatron.Hide

End Sub
```

Figure 8-43: Code entered in the Cancel Ticket button's Click event procedure

5   Close the Code window, then **save** and **run** the application. Use the File menu's Open command to open the **lcTest.dat** file. Notice that seat number 2 is colored red, which indicates that it is reserved.

6   Click seat number 2. Khalid Patel's record appears in the frmPatron form. Click the **Cancel Ticket** button. Visual Basic replaces Khalid Patel's record in the random access file with spaces. When the frmSeat form appears again, seat number 2 is colored white.

7   Click **File**, then click **Exit** to end the application.

The last control you need to code in the frmPatron form is the Return to Main button.

Coding the Return to Main Button

The Return to Main button allows the user to return to the frmSeat form without either entering or canceling a ticket. The user might need to use this button if he or she accidentally clicked the wrong seat, or he or she might simply be interested in the name and phone number of a patron. This button will simply hide the frmPatron form.

To code the Return to Main button, then test the application:

1   Double-click the **Return to Main** button. The cmdReturn control's Click event procedure appears. Press the **Tab** key, then type **frmPatron.hide** and press the **Enter** key.

2   Close the Code window, then **save** and **run** the application. Use the File menu's Open command to open the **lcTest.dat** file. The frmSeat form appears on the screen. All of the seats are colored white because no seat has yet been reserved. (Recall that you canceled seat number 2's reservation in the prior set of steps.)

3   Click seat number **33**. The frmPatron form appears. Type **Sue Billings** as the name, press the **Tab** key, then type **111-1111** as the phone number. Press the **Enter** key to select the Enter Ticket button. Visual Basic writes the record to the file, then hides the frmPatron form. When the frmSeat form reappears, seat number 33 is colored red.

Verify that you entered Sue Billings's information correctly.

4   Click seat number **33**. The frmPatron form appears with Sue Billings's information showing.

In some applications, it's convenient to be able to move a dialog box to another part of the screen. In the current application, you might want to move the frmPatron form, which is being used as a dialog box, to determine if a seat currently covered by it is reserved.

5   Place the mouse pointer on the Patron Information dialog box's title bar and drag the dialog box to another part of the screen. When the dialog box is where you want it, release the mouse button.

6   Click the **Return to Main** button. The frmSeat form appears once again.

7   Click **File**, then click **Exit**. Visual Basic returns to the design screen.

You have now completed Lesson C and the Cole's Playhouse application. You can either take a break, complete the end-of-lesson questions and exercises, or continue to the Debugging section. The Debugging section may contain information that will help you complete the end-of-lesson exercises.

S U M M A R Y

To reference the property of a control that is located in another form:

■   Use the syntax *Form.Control.Property*, where *Form* is the name of the form in which the *Control* is located.

To show a form:

■   Use the Show method. Its syntax is *Form*.**Show**.

To remove a form from the screen, but leave the form in memory:

■   Use the Hide method. Its syntax is *Form*.**Hide**.

QUESTIONS

1. Assume that you are coding an object in the frmFriends form and you want to refer to the Text property of the txtPhone text box, which is also in the frmFriends form. Which of the following could you enter into the Code window?
   a. frmFriends.text
   b. frmFriends.text.txtPhone
   c. Text.txtPhone
   d. txtPhone.text
   e. txtPhone.text.frmFriends

2. Assume that you are coding an object in the frmFriends form and you want to refer to the Text property of the txtPhone text box, which is in the frmNumbers form. Which of the following could you enter into the Code window?
   a. frmFriends.txtPhone.text
   b. frmNumbers.txtPhone.text
   c. Text.txtPhone
   d. txtPhone.text
   e. txtPhone.text.frmNumbers

3. Which of the following methods will display a form?
   a. Access
   b. Display
   c. Form
   d. Show

4. Which of the following methods will remove a form from the screen, but keep it in memory?
   a. Blank
   b. Clear
   c. Erase
   d. Hide
   e. Remove

EXERCISES

1. In this exercise you will use a control array and a random access file. (You cannot complete this exercise using the Visual Basic Working Model; you will need to use either the Standard or Professional Edition of Visual Basic.)

   Scenario: Mr. Fletcher, a fourth grade teacher, wants an application that he can use to keep track of the names and grades of his students. In this exercise you will use two forms. One form will use label controls to represent the 20 seats in the classroom. The other form will allow Mr. Fletcher to enter the student's name and grade in a random access file, remove the student from the file, and return to the main form.
   a. Open the lc1 (lc1.vbp) project, which is located in the Tut08 folder on your Student Disk.
   b. Save the frmStudent form as lc1Stud. Save the frmDesk form as lc1Desk. Save the project as lc1Done. (Save the files in the Tut08 folder on your Student Disk.)
   c. Change the frmDesk form's BorderStyle property to 1-Fixed Single.
   d. The frmDesk form should be the startup form.
   e. Add a code module to the project. Define a record structure named StudStruc. The StudStruc should contain two fields: stName and stGrade. StName is a 20-character String field and stGrade is a 1-character String field.
   f. Save the code module as lc1Done in the Tut08 folder on your Student Disk.

g. In the frmDesk form, code the File menu's New command appropriately. (You can use Tutorial 8's Figure 8-24 as a guide.)

h. Create and code the user-defined Initialize sub procedure. (You can use Tutorial 8's Figure 8-29 as a guide.)

i. In the frmDesk form, code the File menu's Open command appropriately. (You can use Tutorial 8's Figure 8-34 as a guide.) If a seat is occupied, then change its BackColor property to yellow; otherwise it should be white.

j. In the frmDesk form, code the File menu's Exit command and the form's Unload event appropriately. (Use the code for the Cole's Playhouse application as a guide.)

k. In the frmDesk form, code the lblDesk control array's Click event procedure appropriately. (You can use Tutorial 8's Figure 8-38 as a guide.) If a seat is occupied, then its BackColor property should be yellow; otherwise it should be white.

l. Code the Return to Main button in the frmStudent form so that it hides the frmStudent form.

m. Code the Enter button in the frmStudent form. (You can use Tutorial 8's Figure 8-40 as a guide.)

n. Code the Remove button in the frmStudent form. (You can use Tutorial 8's Figure 8-42 as a guide.)

o. Save and run the application. Create a new file named lc1Test.

p. Test the application by entering the following records, shown as desk number, student name, and grade. After entering each record, the seat in the lblSeat array should be yellow.

  12, Mary Jane, A
  7, Fred Jones, C
  20, Ellen Berry, B

q. Click desk number 20. Ellen Berry and a grade of B should appear in the frmStudent form.

r. Ellen Berry has moved to another school. Remove Ellen Berry from the random access file and from the classroom. Her seat in the lblSeat array should be white.

s. Click desk number 7. Fred Jones and a grade of C should appear in the frmStudent form.

t. Click the Return to Main button.

u. Use the File menu's Exit command to end the application.

v. Run the application again. Use the File menu's Open command to open the lc1Test.dat file. Add your name and grade to a seat number of your choice, then exit the application.

w. Print the application's code.

2. In this exercise you will use a control array, a random access file, and a list box. (You cannot complete this exercise using the Visual Basic Working Model; you will need to use either the Standard or Professional Edition of Visual Basic.)

Scenario: Janice and Bob own a restaurant that has a small banquet room. The banquet room, which can accommodate 40 guests, is typically rented out for small weddings. Janice and Bob would like you to create an application that they can use to keep track of each guest's name and meal preference (Steak, Fish, and Vegetarian).

a. Open the lc2 (lc2.vbp) project, which is located in the Tut08 folder on your Student Disk.

b. Save the frmBanquet form as lc2Banq. Save the frmGuest form as lc2Guest. Save the project as lc2Done. (Save the files in the Tut08 folder on your Student Disk.)

c. The frmBanquet form should be the startup form.

d. Add the Steak, Fish, and Vegetarian entries to the lstMeal list box in the frmGuest form. Set the list box's Sorted property to True. The default selection in the lstMeal list box should be Steak.

e. The frmBanquet form contains 40 image controls, which represent the 40 seats in the banquet room. The form also contains an image control, imgSmile. If a seat is occupied, then the smiling face icon should appear in the corresponding imgSeat image control.

f. Add a code module to the project. Define a record structure named GuestStruc. The GuestStruc structure should contain two fields, stName, which is a 20-character String field and inMeal, an Integer field. The stName variable will store the guest's name, which is entered in the frmGuest form. The inMeal variable will store the index of the list box selection from the frmGuest form.

g. Save the code module as lc2Done in the Tut08 folder on your Student Disk.

h. Add a File menu to the frmBanquet form. The File menu should contain New, Open, and Exit commands. You will need to add the Microsoft Common Dialog control to the application.

i. In the frmBanquet form, code the File menu's New command, Open command, and Exit command. Also code the frmBanquet form's Unload event. You will also need to create a sub procedure that will initialize the random access file and the frmBanquet form.

j. In the frmBanquet form, code the imgSeat control array appropriately. The image controls should display the frmGuest form when clicked. The guest's number and name, as well as his or her meal preference, should display in the frmGuest form.

k. In the frmGuest form, code the Enter, Delete, and Return to Main buttons' Click event procedures appropriately. Occupied seats in the imgSeat array should display the smiling face icon (imgSmile); otherwise the imgSeat control should be empty.

l. Test the application by entering the following guests anywhere you want:

Sue Shah	select Vegetarian from the List box
Ann Yonkers	select Fish from the List box
Ellen Alders	select Steak from the List box

These seats should display the smiling face icon.

m. Click the seat occupied by Ann Yonkers. Ann's number, name, and meal should appear in the frmBanquet form. Click the Delete button to remove her from the random access file; her seat in the frmBanquet form should now be unoccupied.

n. Use the File menu to exit the application. Rerun the application; the occupied seats should display the smiling face icon. Exit the application.

o. Print the application's code.

3. In this exercise you will modify the application you created in Lesson C's Exercise 1. (You cannot complete this exercise using the Visual Basic Working Model; you will need to use either the Standard or Professional Edition of Visual Basic.)

Scenario: In Exercise 1, you created an application that Mr. Fletcher could use to keep track of the names and grades of his students. You will now modify the code so that it displays the student's grade in the frmDesk form.

a. Open the lc1Done (lc1Done.vbp) project that you created in Lesson C's Exercise 1.

b. Save the lc1Stud form as lc3Stud. Save the lc1Desk form as lc3Desk. Save the lc1Done code module as lc3Done. Save the project as lc3Done. (Save the files in the Tut08 folder on your Student Disk.)

c. Modify the code so that all occupied seats will display the student's grade in addition to the seat number.

d. Save and run the application. Two grades, which correspond to the two records already in the file, should appear in the frmDesk form. (The seat numbers for these seats should also appear.) The two seats should be yellow, indicating that they are occupied.

e. Enter the following student's information in any of the unoccupied seats: Steven Ivanelli, F. Exit the application.

f. Now change the code so that the color assigned to the BackColor property of a desk depends on the grade. The desks associated with grades of A should be magenta, grades of B should be red, grades of C should be yellow, grades of D should be green, and grades of F should be blue.

g. Save and run the application. Three grades, which correspond to the three records already in the file, should appear in the frmDesk form. Each grade should be a different color.

h. Add the following two records in any unoccupied seat in the lblDesk array: Darlene Burnham, D and Jackie Bunt, B.

i. Exit the application. Print the application's code.

Exercises 4 through 6 are Discovery Exercises, which allow you to "discover" the solutions to problems on your own. Discovery Exercises may include topics that are not covered in the tutorial.

discovery ▶ 4. In this exercise you will modify the Cole's Playhouse application that you created in the tutorial. (You cannot complete this exercise using the Visual Basic Working Model; you will need to use either the Standard or Professional Edition of Visual Basic.)

Scenario: In this exercise you will modify the code in the lcCole (lcCole.vbp) project so that it allows the user to select the Enter Ticket button only when a name has been entered into the frmPatron form. You will also create a short user manual for new theater employees.

a. Theater employees mentioned that if they inadvertently click the Enter Ticket button without entering any seat information, the seat will appear to be reserved when, in fact, the entry is blank. An empty phone field is fine, but a name should be required. Use the Help menu to view the Help windows on the Change event and the Enabled property. Modify the code so that the Enter Ticket button is enabled only when the name entry is completed. (Hint: You will need to code the txtName control's Change event.)

b. Save and run the application using the current form, module, and project names. Create a new data file named lc4.dat.

c. Click an unreserved seat in the frmSeat form. The Enter Ticket button should be dimmed. Type your name into the txtName control. As soon as you type the first letter, the Enter Ticket button should darken.

d. Remove your name from the txtName control. When the entire text box is empty, the Enter Ticket button should be dimmed again.

e. Click the Return to Main button. Exit the application. Print the code for the frmPatron form only.

discovery ▶ 5. In this exercise you will create a user's manual for the Cole's Playhouse application.

Scenario: The manager of Cole's Playhouse expressed concerns about training employees to use the application you created. You have agreed to write a user manual to provide a reference for the different functions of your application.

a. Develop a user manual to be used by the employees of Cole's Playhouse. It should include step-by-step instructions for each function of the application. Use the word processor of your choice. Start by creating an outline for the different sections of the manual. Be careful not to skip any of the functions of the program—opening data files, initializing data files, reserving seats, and so on.

b. Next, create the text for each section of your outline. Proofread and edit the text as necessary. To create a truly accurate manual, you must test it. Go through each of the sections while using the program. Keep in mind that the users will not have the working knowledge of the program that you have, so don't make any assumptions.

c. Once the manual is finished, print the final copy. Be sure to have a title page and a table of contents. For more complex applications, an index is important.

discovery ▶ 6. In this exercise you will update records stored in a random access file.

Scenario: Shirts Outlet Store sells a variety of shirts manufactured by three different companies. The specific manufacturer is identified by a letter, which is added to the end of the shirt's item number. For example, the item numbers of shirts manufactured by Cody end in C, the item numbers of shirts manufactured by Adams end in A, and the item numbers of shirts manufactured by Dawn end in D.

Shirts Outlet stores the item number and price of the shirts in a random access file. Periodically a manufacturer will raise the wholesale price, which means that Shirts Outlet Store will need to raise the retail price in order to pass the increase on to the consumer. They want you to create an application that will allow them to update the prices in the random access file. The application should also allow them to print a price list on the printer. The price list should show each item's number, manufacturer (Cody, Adams, Dawn), and price. Print the price list in three columns.

a. First create a random access file that contains the following 10 records:

Item No.	Price	Item No.	Price
444C	15.75	888A	20.00
111A	16.00	777D	21.50
222A	24.30	555C	45.00
333D	21.56	123C	34.78
666D	34.57	345A	10.00

b. Next create a user interface that Shirts Outlet Store can use. Remember that you will need to get the percent increase and the manufacturer from the user. The application should update the random access by increasing the price of only the items made by that manufacturer. Also recall that the interface should allow the store to print a price list on the printer.

c. Save the form, module, and project as lc6Done in the Tut08 folder on your Student Disk.

d. Run the application. Print the price list with the original prices showing.

e. The Adams company is increasing their prices by 10%. Update the appropriate prices in the random access file.

f. Print the new price list.

g. Exit the application.

h. Print the Shirts Outlet Store's user interface. Also print the lc6Done application's code.

D E B U G G I N G

Technique

As you already know, when an error occurs in an application's code, Visual Basic displays a dialog box containing an appropriate error message. While the dialog box is on the screen, you can press the F1 key to display a Help screen that explains the error message. The Help screen will list the types of errors that generate the error message; it will also offer solutions.

Your Student Disk contains a file that you can use to practice this tutorial's debugging technique.

To debug the Debug (debug.vbp) project:

1 Start Visual Basic, if necessary, and open the **Debug** (debug.vbp) project, which is located in the Tut08 folder on your Student Disk.

2 View the form. The form contains a list box, a label control, and two command buttons.

3 **Run** (but don't save) the application. Click the **Display** button. Visual Basic displays a dialog box that contains the "Sub or Function not defined" error message.

4   Press the **F1** key to display a Help window that explains the error message. The Help window for the "Sub, Function, or Property not defined (Error 35)" error message appears.

According to the Help window, you may have mistyped the name of a procedure.

5   Close the Help window, then click the **OK** button to remove the error message. Visual Basic highlights the error—the word Upper—in the Code window. The name of the function that converts text to uppercase is UCase, not Upper. Change the highlighted Upper to **UCase**.

6   Click the **Continue** button 🔲 on the toolbar to continue the application. The "Method or data member not found" error message appears.

7   Press the **F1** key to display the "Method or data member not found" Help window.

According to the Help window, you may have misspelled an object or member name.

8   Close the Help window, then click the **OK** button to remove the error message. Visual Basic highlights the error in the Code window. The error occurred because label controls do not have a Text property.

9   Change the instruction from `lblName.Text = UCase(lstName.Text)` to **lblName.Caption = UCase(lstName.Text)**.

10 Click the **Continue** button 🔲 on the toolbar. The name selected in the list box now appears in uppercase in the label control. Click the **Exit** button to end the application. Visual Basic returns to the design screen. You do not need to save this application.

TUTORIAL

9

Variable Arrays

Creating a Personal Directory Application

case ▶ In this tutorial you will create a personal directory application. The personal directory will contain the names, phone numbers, and birthdays of your friends and relatives. The application will allow you to add information to the directory, delete information from the directory, display the phone number and birthday of a person in the directory, and display the name, phone number, and birthday of friends and relatives who were born in a specific month.

Previewing the Completed Application

As you've done in previous tutorials, you will preview the application before creating it.

To preview the completed application:

1   If necessary, start Windows, then place your Student Disk in the appropriate drive.

2   Use the Run command on the Start menu to run the **Dir95** (Dir95.exe) file, which is located in the Tut09 folder on your Student Disk. The personal directory application's user interface appears on the screen. See Figure 9-1.

WINDOWS   **3.1**

Use the Run command on the Program Manager's File menu to run the dir31.exe file, which is located in the Tut09 folder on your Student Disk. The personal directory application's user interface appears on the screen. See Figure 9-1.

combo box

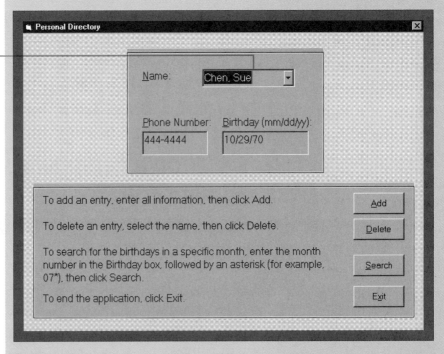

Figure 9-1: Personal directory application's user interface

When you run this application, the form's Load event reads the names of your friends and relatives, as well as their phone numbers and birthdays, from a sequential access file on your Student Disk. The Load event enters the information in a variable array in the computer's memory. You will learn about variable arrays in Lesson A.

The Load event also enters the names of your friends and relatives in a combo box control. The combo box control, which is covered in Lesson B, combines the features of a text box and a list box in that it allows the user to either type an entry or select an item from a predefined list. Open the combo box to view its list.

3   Click the **Name** list arrow to open the combo box's list. An alphabetical list of names appears.

When you click a name in the list, the application will display that person's phone number and birthday in the interface.

4   Click **Patel, Khalid** in the list. The list closes and the name "Patel, Khalid" appears in the combo box. Khalid's phone number and birthday appear in the appropriate text boxes on the form.

You can also use the application to add a person to the directory.

5   Type **James, Amos** in the combo box and press the **Tab** key, then type **333-4444** in the Phone number text box and press the **Tab** key, and then type **02/03/76** in the Birthday text box and click the **Add** button. The Add button adds the name to the combo box's list; it also adds the name, phone number, and birthday to the variable array in memory.

Verify that the name was added to the combo box's list.

6   Click the **Name** list arrow to open the list. "James, Amos" appears in the list.

The application also allows you to delete a person from the personal directory. Delete Amos James.

7   Click **James, Amos** in the list, click the **Delete** button, then click the **Yes** button.

The Delete button removes the name from the list; it also clears the name, phone number, and birthday from the variable array in memory. Verify that the application removed the name from the combo box's list.

8   Click the **Name** list arrow to open the list. Notice that the deleted name—James, Amos—does not appear in the list.

9   Click the **Name** list arrow to close the list.

You can also use the application to display the name, phone number, and birthday of friends and relatives born in a specific month. Try that now.

To display the information on friends and relatives born in a specific month:

1   Press the **Tab** key two times to move the insertion point into the Birthday text box.

To see who was born during the month of April, which is the fourth month in the year, you simply type 04 followed by an asterisk (*), like this: 04*. The 04 tells Visual Basic that the birthday must occur in month 4. The * tells Visual Basic that you don't care what characters follow the 04—in other words, you want all the birthdays during the month of April, regardless of their specific day or year.

2   Type **04*** (be sure to type a zero and not the letter O) and click the **Search** button. The name, phone number, and birthday of Khalid Patel, the first friend or relative with an April birthday, appears in the form. The dialog box tells you to press Enter or click OK to continue.

> **HELP?** If you can't see all of the information, simply drag the dialog box out of the way.

3   Click the **OK** button to continue searching for April birthdays. The name, phone number, and birthday of the next person born in April, Tom Williams, appears in the form.

4   Click the **OK** button to continue searching for April birthdays. The "Search is complete" message appears, which means that no other friends or relatives listed in your personal directory were born in April.

5   Click the **OK** button to remove the "Search is complete" message.

6   You can now experiment with the personal directory application on your own, then click the **Exit** button. If you added or deleted a friend or relative from the personal directory, the Exit button updates the sequential access file accordingly. The personal directory application then ends.

tips

· · · · · · · · · · · · · · · ·

▶ **If you want to restore the sequential access file used in this preview to its original contents, use Windows to copy the Person.bak file to the Person.dat file. Both files are in the Tut09 folder on your Student Disk.**

In Lesson A you will learn about variable arrays. The combo box control is covered in Lesson B. You will begin coding the personal directory application in Lesson B and then complete it in Lesson C.

In this lesson you will learn how to:
- Create a one-dimensional variable array
- Search a variable array
- Compute the average of an array's contents
- Find the highest entry in an array
- Update the contents of an array
- Create a two-dimensional variable array

Storing Data in a Variable Array

Variable Arrays

In addition to control arrays, which you learned how to create in Tutorial 5, Visual Basic also allows you to create variable arrays. A **variable array** is a group of variables that have the same name and data type and are related in some way. For example, each variable in the array may contain the name of a state, or each may contain an income tax rate, or each may contain an employee record (name, social security number, pay rate, and so on).

Unlike control arrays, you can't see variable arrays on the screen. It may help to picture a variable array as a group of tiny boxes inside the computer's memory. You can write information to the boxes and you can read information from the boxes; you just can't see the boxes.

Although variable arrays in Visual Basic can have as many as 60 dimensions, the most commonly used arrays in business applications are one-dimensional and two-dimensional. Figure 9-2 illustrates both a one-dimensional and a two-dimensional array. (Arrays having more than two dimensions, which are used in scientific and engineering applications, are beyond the scope of this book.)

One-dimensional array:					
Nebraska	New Jersey	New Mexico	Tennessee	Texas	Virginia

Two-dimensional array:		
Adams, Bill 111-11-1111 8.55	Asaf, Nancy 222-22-2222 10.65	Bell, Jack 333-33-3333 7.50
Celt, Carl 444-44-4444 6.35	Dorey, Jill 555-55-5555 7.65	Doty, Jim 666-66-6666 5.25

Figure 9-2: Illustrations of a one-dimensional and a two-dimensional array

As Figure 9-2 shows, a **one-dimensional array** is simply a row of variables. A **two-dimensional array**, on the other hand, resembles a table in that it has rows and columns.

It is not necessary for an array's name to include the word Array.

Similar to the way Visual Basic assigns a unique number, called an **index**, to each of the controls in a control array, Visual Basic also assigns a unique number, called a **subscript**, to each of the variables in a variable array. You refer to each variable in the array by the array's name and the variable's subscript. The subscript is specified in a set of parentheses immediately following the name. For example, StateArray(5)—read "StateArray sub five"—refers to variable number 5 in a one-dimensional array named StateArray. EmpArray(2,3)—read "EmpArray sub two comma three"—refers to the variable located in row 2, column 3, of a two-dimensional array named EmpArray. Figure 9-3 illustrates this naming convention.

One-dimensional array named StateArray:					
StateArray(1)	StateArray(2)	StateArray(3)	StateArray(4)	StateArray(5)	StateArray(6)
Nebraska	New Jersey	New Mexico	Tennessee	Texas	Virginia

Two-dimensional array named EmpArray:		
EmpArray(1,1)	EmpArray(1,2)	EmpArray(1,3)
Adams, Bill 111-11-1111 8.55	Asaf, Nancy 222-22-2222 10.65	Bell, Jack 333-33-3333 7.50
Celt, Carl 444-44-4444 6.35	Dorey, Jill 555-55-5555 7.65	Doty, Jim 666-66-6666 5.25
EmpArray(2,1)	EmpArray(2,2)	EmpArray(2,3)

Figure 9-3: Names of the variables in a one-dimensional and a two-dimensional array

Advantages of Variable Arrays

Programmers use variable arrays to store related data in the internal memory of the computer. By doing so, a programmer can increase the efficiency of an application because data stored inside the computer can be both written and read much faster than data stored in a file on a disk. The following analogy may help illustrate this point: Think of the computer's internal memory as being comparable to your brain. Now assume that someone asks you to name the first U.S. President. Because that information is already stored in your brain, you can respond almost immediately with "George Washington." Similarly, the computer has almost immediate access to the information stored in internal memory—its brain.

Now assume that someone asks you to name the eighth U.S. President. If that information is not stored in your brain, you will need to open a history book, find the page containing the listing of presidents, and then read the eighth name—a much more time-consuming process. Similarly, accessing information that is not stored in the computer's internal memory—rather, it is stored in a disk file—takes the computer much longer because it must wait for the disk drive to locate the needed information and then read that information into memory.

In addition to speedier access of information, another advantage of using a variable array is that data can be entered into an array once, usually at the beginning of the program, and can then be used by the application as many times as desired. For example, assume that you are creating a payroll program. In order to compute the net pay for an employee, his or her federal withholding tax must be calculated. By storing the federal withholding tax table in a variable array, at the beginning of the program, the application can use that stored information to calculate each employee's federal withholding tax.

Now that you know what variable arrays are and why they are used, you will learn how to create a one-dimensional array.

Creating a One-Dimensional Variable Array

As with simple variables, you must declare a variable array before you can use it. (A **simple variable** is a variable that does not belong to an array.) You declare a variable array with the Dim statement, which is the same statement you use to declare a simple variable. The syntax of the Dim statement to declare a one-dimensional array is **Dim** *arrayname*(*lower subscript* **To** *upper subscript*) **As** *datatype*. *Arrayname* is the name of the variable array; the name must follow the same rules as for simple variables. *Lower subscript* and *upper subscript* are numbers that define the lowest and the highest subscript, respectively, in the array. Although the subscripts can be numbers in the range of −32768 to 32767, inclusive, in most business applications, the lower subscript is set to either 0 (zero) or 1. (The applications in this book will use a lower subscript of 1.) *Datatype* is the type of data that the array variables will store; recall that each of the variables in the array has the same data type. The `Dim StateArray(1 to 5) as String` instruction, for example, declares a one-dimensional array named StateArray that contains five String variables. The name of the first String variable in the array is StateArray(1), the name of the second is StateArray(2), and so on. Figure 9-4 shows other examples of Dim statements that create one-dimensional variable arrays.

Dim statement	Result
Dim MonthArray(1 to 12) as String	Creates an array of 12 String variables
Dim SquareArray(1 to 5) as Integer	Creates an array of 5 Integer variables
Dim NumArray(1 to 10) as Single	Creates an array of 10 Single variables
Dim EmpArray(1 to 20) as EmpStruc	Creates an array of 20 EmpStruc variables

Figure 9-4: Examples of Dim statements

The Dim statement both creates and initializes the array variables in memory. Like simple variables, String and Variant array variables are initialized to the empty string; Integer, Long, Single, Double, and Currency array variables are initialized to 0 (zero). Array variables also can be declared as a user-defined data type, which you learned about in Tutorial 8. In those cases, the field variables that make up the data type are initialized in the same manner as simple variables.

After you declare an array, you can then store data in it.

Storing Data in a One-Dimensional Variable Array

You can enter data into a one-dimensional array in a variety of ways. The examples shown in Figure 9-5, for instance, can be used to enter data into the arrays created by the Dim statements in Figure 9-4.

Example 1:

```
MonthArray(1) = "January"
MonthArray(2) = "February"
MonthArray(3) = "March"
MonthArray(4) = "April"
MonthArray(5) = "May"
MonthArray(6) = "June"
MonthArray(7) = "July"
MonthArray(8) = "August"
MonthArray(9) = "September"
MonthArray(10) = "October"
MonthArray(11) = "November"
MonthArray(12) = "December"
```

Example 2:

```
For inNum = 1 to 5
    SquareArray(inNum) = inNum * inNum
Next inNum
```

Example 3:

```
For inNum = 1 to 10
    NumArray(inNum) = Val(InputBox("Enter a number"))
Next inNum
```

Example 4:

```
Do While Not EOF(1)
    Input #1, EmpArray(inNum).Name, EmpArray(inNum).Salary
Loop
```

Figure 9-5: Examples of entering data into an array

In the first example, the 12 assignment statements will enter the names of the 12 months into the MonthArray variable array. In the second example, a For Next loop will fill the SquareArray array with the square of the numbers from one through five. In the third example, the Inputbox function within the For Next loop will enter the user's responses into the NumArray array. In the fourth example, the Input # statement within the Do While loop will read the data from a sequential access file and store it in the EmpArray variable array.

Now look at an application that uses a one-dimensional array.

The President Application

On your Student Disk is an application that uses a one-dimensional variable array to store the names of the first 10 U.S. presidents.

To open the President application:

1 Start Visual Basic, if necessary, and open the **Pres** (pres.vbp) project, which is in the Tut09 folder on your Student Disk.

2 Save the form and the project as **laPres**.

3 Click the **View Form** button in the Project window to view the frmPres form. The frmPres form appears on the screen. See Figure 9-6.

Figure 9-6: The President application's user interface

You can use this application to study for a test on U.S. presidents. When you run the application, it will store the names of the first 10 U.S. presidents in a variable array named PresArray. The name of the first president will be stored in PresArray(1), the name of the second president will be stored in PresArray(2), and so on. You can enter a number between 1 and 10 in the Number text box and then click the Display Name button to display the corresponding president's name. You can also enter the name of a president in the Name text box and then click the Display Number button to display the president's number.

Almost all of the President application is already coded for you; only the instruction to declare the PresArray variable array is missing. You will enter that instruction next.

Coding the President Application

The Click events of both the Display Name and Display Number buttons will need to access the data stored in the PresArray array, so you will declare the variable array as a form-level array. As you learned in Tutorial 3, form-level variables are declared in the General declarations section of the form and are available to all procedures in the form.

To declare a form-level variable array:

1 Double-click the **form** to open its Code window. Use the Object box to open the General declarations section. The form's General declarations section appears with the `Option Explicit` statement already entered in the Code window.

The PresArray array will need to store 10 names, so you will declare it as a String array containing 10 variables.

2 Press ↓ on your keyboard to position the insertion point below the Option Explicit statement, then type **dim PresArray(1 to 10) as string** and press the **Enter** key.

Now view the code already entered in the form's Load event.

The Form's Load Event Procedure

The form's Load event procedure will enter the names of the presidents into the PresArray variable array as soon as the form is loaded into memory. View the code in the Load event procedure.

To view the form's Load event procedure:

1 The Code window for the form's General declarations section should be open, so you simply need to use the Object box to open the form's Load event. The form's Load event procedure appears as shown in Figure 9-7.

```
frmPres                                              _ □ ×
Object: Form                    ▼    Proc: Load              ▼
Private Sub Form_Load()
    frmPres.Left = (Screen.Width - frmPres.Width) / 2
    frmPres.Top = (Screen.Height - frmPres.Height) / 2
    PresArray(1) = "George Washington"
    PresArray(2) = "John Adams"
    PresArray(3) = "Thomas Jefferson"
    PresArray(4) = "James Madison"
    PresArray(5) = "James Monroe"
    PresArray(6) = "John Quincy Adams"
    PresArray(7) = "Andrew Jackson"
    PresArray(8) = "Martin Van Buren"
    PresArray(9) = "William Henry Harrison"
    PresArray(10) = "John Tyler"

End Sub
```

Figure 9-7: Load event procedure

When the application is run and the form is loaded into memory, the 10 assignment statements shown in Figure 9-7 will enter the names of the first 10 U.S. presidents into the PresArray variable array.

Next, view the Display Name button's Click event procedure, which will display the name of the president that corresponds to the number entered in the Number text box.

The Display Name Button

When the user enters a number in the Number text box and then clicks the Display Name button, the name of the president that corresponds to the number should appear in the Name text box. The flowchart for the Display Name button's Click event is shown in Figure 9-8.

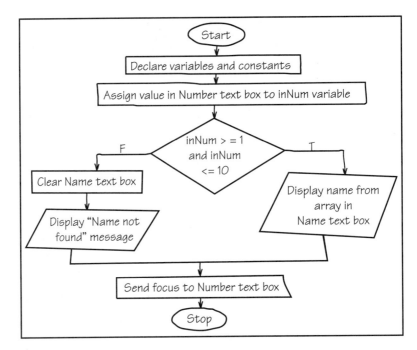

Figure 9-8: Flowchart for the Display Name button's Click event procedure

Open the Display Name button's Click event procedure and view its code.

To view the code in the Display Name button's Click event procedure:

1   Use the Code window's Object box to open the cmdName control's Click event. Maximize the Code window. See Figure 9-9.

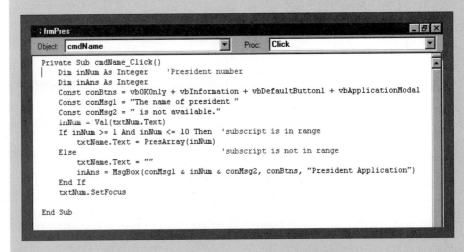

Figure 9-9: Display Name button's Click event procedure

The code first declares two local Integer variables named inNum and inAns, and three constants. The three constants and the inAns variable will be used by the MsgBox function. The code then assigns the numeric equivalent of the txtNum control's Text property to the inNum variable. The selection structure that follows the assignment statement verifies that the inNum variable contains a valid subscript, which is a subscript from 1 through 10. If inNum contains a value that is greater than or equal to one and less than or equal to 10, then the `txtName.Text` `= PresArray(inNum)` instruction assigns the contents of the PresArray variable, whose subscript is contained in the inNum variable, to the Text property of the txtName control. If, for example, the inNum variable contains the number 1, the instruction assigns the contents of the PresArray(1) variable—George Washington—to the txtName control. If, however, the subscript does not fall in the valid range, the selection structure clears the contents of the txtName control and displays a message informing the user that the president's name is not available. The `txtNum.SetFocus` instruction sends the focus to the Number text box.

2   Close the Code window.

See how the Display Name button works.

3   **Save** and **run** the application. The code contained in the form's General declarations section creates and initializes, to the empty string, a variable array named PresArray. The array contains 10 String variables; each variable is named PresArray and each has a unique subscript from 1 to 10. The form's Load event procedure then enters the names of the first 10 U.S. presidents into the array and the user interface appears on the screen. At this point the variable array in memory resembles Figure 9-10.

George Washington
John Adams
Thomas Jefferson
James Madison
James Monroe
John Quincy Adams
Andrew Jackson
Martin Van Buren
William Henry Harrison
John Tyler

Note: You can picture a one-dimensional array as either a row of variables, as shown in Figures 9-2 and 9-3, or as a column of variables, as shown in this figure.

Figure 9-10: Status of PresArray array in memory

First test the application by entering a valid number—the number 5, for example—in the Number text box.

4   Type **5** in the Number text box and click the **Display Name** button. The Click event assigns the number 5 to the inNum variable. Because you entered a valid subscript, the `txtName.Text = PresArray(inNum)` statement displays the contents of the PresArray(5) variable—James Monroe—in the txtName control.

Now see what happens if you enter a number that is not within the lower subscript and the upper subscript of the array; in other words, the number is not within the range of 1 to 10, inclusive.

5   Type **12** in the txtNum box and click the **Display Name** button. Visual Basic clears the contents of the txtName control and displays the message "The name of president 12 is not available." in the MsgBox dialog box.

6   Click the **OK** button to remove the dialog box, then click the **Exit** button to end the application. Visual Basic returns to the design screen.

tips

Always test your application with both valid and invalid data. Valid data in this application is the numbers 1 through 10, which are the valid subscripts for the array; invalid data is any number that is either less than 1 or greater than 10.

Now view the code in the Display Number button, which displays the number corresponding to the name of the president entered in the Name text box.

The Display Number Button

You can use the Display Number button to display the number of the president whose name is contained in the Name text box. Figure 9-11 shows the flowchart for the Display Number button's Click event procedure.

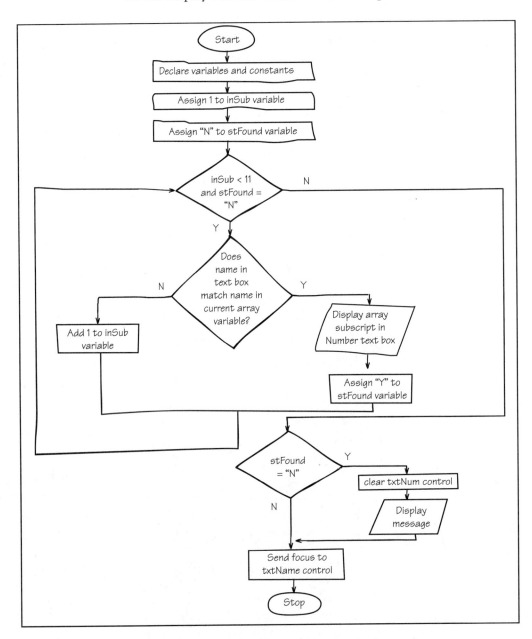

Figure 9-11: Flowchart for Display Number button's Click event procedure

Now view the code that corresponds to the flowchart. The code has already been entered in the Display Number button's Click event procedure.

To view the code in the Display Number button's Click event procedure:

1 Double-click the **Display Number** button, then maximize the Code window. The cmdNum control's Click event procedure appears as shown in Figure 9-12.

```
frmPres                                                            _ 🗗 🗙
Object:  cmdNum                    ▼      Proc:  Click                ▼

Private Sub cmdNum_Click()
    Dim inSub As Integer, inAns As Integer, stFound As String
    Const conBtns = vbOKOnly + vbInformation + vbDefaultButton1 + vbApplicationModal
    Const conMsg = "This president's number is not available."

    'initialize inSub and stFound variables
    inSub = 1
    stFound = "N"
    'search array for president's name
    Do While inSub < 11 And stFound = "N"
        If UCase(PresArray(inSub)) = UCase(txtName.Text) Then    'name is in the array
            txtNum.Text = inSub
            stFound = "Y"
        Else
            inSub = inSub + 1    'continue search
        End If
    Loop

    'determine if a match was found
    If stFound = "N" Then          'no matching name was found in the array
        txtNum.Text = ""
        inAns = MsgBox(conMsg, conBtns, "President Application")
    End If
    txtName.SetFocus

End Sub
```

Figure 9-12: Display Number button's Click event procedure

After declaring the necessary variables and constants, the code initializes the inSub variable to 1 and the stFound variable to "N". Both the inSub and stFound variables are used by the Do While loop to search each of the 10 variables in the array, one at a time, for a name that matches the one entered in the Name text box. If a matching name is found in an array variable, then the array variable's subscript, which is stored in the inSub variable, is assigned to the Number text box on the form, and the stFound variable is set to "Y" to indicate that the search was successful; otherwise the inSub variable is incremented by one so that the search can continue with the next array variable. Notice that the Do While loop continues searching the array while the inSub variable is less than 11 and the stFound variable equals the letter "N". The Do While loop will stop when either the entire array has been searched (inSub = 11) or when a match is found (stFound = "Y").

After the Do While loop completes its processing, the second selection structure in the procedure is processed. That selection structure compares the contents of the stFound variable with the letter "N". If the stFound variable contains an "N", which means that the Do While loop instructions did not find a matching name in the array, then the MsgBox function displays an appropriate message to the user. The procedure ends by sending the focus to the Name text box. Now see how the Display Number button works.

To see how the Display Number button works:

1   Close the Code window, then **run** the application.

First enter a name that is in the array.

2   Press the **Tab** key to move the insertion point into the Name text box, then type **John Adams** and click the **Display Number** button. The Display Number button's Click event procedure searches each variable in the array, looking for the name John Adams. Because that name matches the name in the second variable in the array, a 2 appears in the Number text box. John Adams, therefore, was the second U.S. president.

> **HELP?** If a 2 does not appear in the Number text box, you may have mistyped the president's name. Type John Adams in the Name text box again and click the Display Number button. Be sure to spell the name correctly and include a space between John and Adams.

Now enter a name that is not in the array.

3   Type **George Bush** in the Name text box and click the **Display Number** button. Because the name George Bush is not in the president array, the MsgBox function displays the message, "This president's number is not available."

4   Click the **OK** button to remove the message, then click the **Exit** button. Visual Basic returns to the design screen.

In the next example you will use an array to store student scores contained in a sequential access file. You will then use the information in the array to calculate the average and highest score. You will also learn how to update the contents of an array.

The Test Score Application

On your Student Disk is an application that uses a one-dimensional variable array to store the test scores earned by 20 students. The 20 test scores have already been entered into a sequential access file for you. Figure 9-13 shows the Test.dat file displayed in WordPad.

Figure 9-13: Test.dat displayed in WordPad

Open the test score application and view its code.

tips
....
▶ You can recreate the Test.dat file by using the method appropriate for your version of Windows to copy the Test.bak file to Test.dat. Both files are in the Tut09 folder on your Student Disk.

To view the code in the test score application:

1 Open the **Test** (test.vbp) file, which is located in the Tut09 folder on your Student Disk.

2 Save the form and the project as **laTest**.

3 Click the **View Form** button. The user interface appears on the screen, as shown in Figure 9-14.

Figure 9-14: Test score application's user interface

An instructor can use this application to calculate and display the average score and the highest score earned by the 20 students. He or she can also use the application to increase each student's test score by a set amount. (Some instructors give additional points to each student to compensate for poorly written test questions.) First view the code in the form's General declarations section.

4 Open any Code window, then use the Code window's Object box to open the General declarations section of the form. See Figure 9-15.

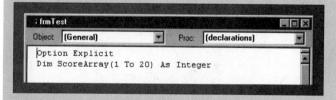

Figure 9-15: Form's General declarations section

The code begins with the `Option Explicit` statement. The `Dim ScoreArray(1 to 20) As Integer` instruction then declares a form-level array named ScoreArray, which contains 20 Integer variables. Next look at the code in the form's Load event procedure, where the array is filled with data.

5 Use the Code window's Object box to open the form's Load event, then maximize the Code window. See Figure 9-16. If your Student Disk is in the B drive, then change the drive letter in the Open statement to b:.

if your Student Disk is in the B drive, change the drive letter to b:

when you omit the Step in a For...Next statement, Visual Basic uses a default Step of 1

```
Private Sub Form_Load()
    Dim inNum As Integer
    frmTest.Left = (Screen.Width - frmTest.Width) / 2
    frmTest.Top = (Screen.Height - frmTest.Height) / 2
    Open "a:\Tut09\Test.dat" For Input As #1      'Open file
    For inNum = 1 To 20                           'Fill array with data
        Input #1, ScoreArray(inNum)
    Next inNum
    Close #1

End Sub
```

Figure 9-16: Load event procedure

When the form is loaded into memory, the Open statement will open the Test.dat sequential access file for Input. The For Next loop and the Input # statement will then read the 20 test scores from the file, one at a time, and store them in the 20 variables in the ScoreArray variable array. Notice that the For Next loop's counter variable, inNum, is used as the array subscript. When the For Next loop completes its processing, the sequential access file is closed.

The Average Score button's Click event is the next procedure you will view.

The Average Score Button

The Average Score button will calculate and display the average test score earned by the 20 students. Figure 9-17 shows the flowchart for the Average Score button's Click event procedure.

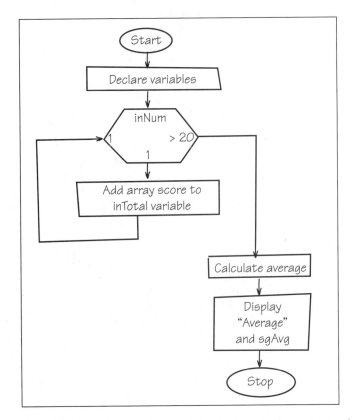

Figure 9-17: Flowchart for Average Score button's Click event procedure

Now view the code entered in the Average Score button's Click event.

To view the code entered in the Average Score button's Click event, then run the application:

1   Use the Code window's Object box to open the cmdAvg control's Click event. See Figure 9-18.

```
frmTest                                                          _ & X
Object:  cmdAvg                        ▼    Proc:  Click                ▼

Private Sub cmdAvg_Click()
    Dim inNum As Integer, inTotal As Integer, sgAvg As Single
    For inNum = 1 To 20
        inTotal = inTotal + ScoreArray(inNum)      'accumulate array scores
    Next inNum
    sgAvg = inTotal / 20                           'calculate average
    lblMsg.Caption = "Average"                     'display results
    lblAnswer.Caption = Format(sgAvg, "standard")

End Sub
```

Figure 9-18: Average Score button's Click event procedure

The code declares three local variables: inNum, inTotal, and sgAvg. The For Next loop instructions add the 20 test scores from the array, one at a time, to the inTotal variable. After the test scores are accumulated, the average score is calculated and then displayed in the appropriate label control. Observe how the Average Score button works.

2   Close the Code window, then **run** the application. The form's General declarations section creates the ScoreArray variable array. The form's Load event procedure then reads the scores from the sequential access file and enters them into the array. The user interface then appears on the screen.

3   Click the **Average Score** button. The button's Click event procedure accumulates the 20 scores. The procedure then calculates and displays the average—71.30.

4   Click the **Exit** button to end the application. Visual Basic returns to the design screen.

Now look at the Highest Score button's Click event procedure, which will display the highest test score.

The Highest Score Button

The Highest Score button will display the highest test score earned by the 20 students. Figure 9-19 shows the flowchart for the Highest Score button's Click event procedure.

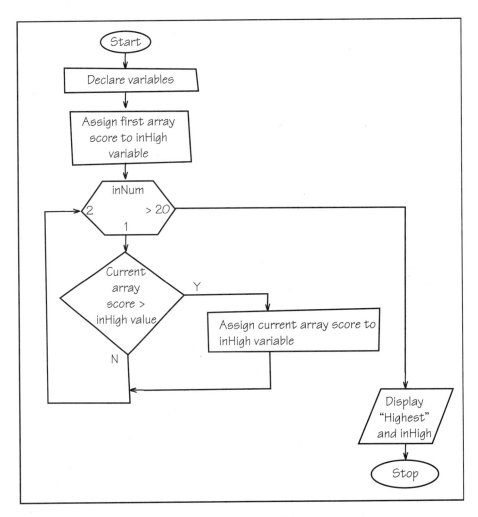

Figure 9-19: Flowchart for the Highest Score button's Click event procedure

Now view the code entered in the Highest Score button's Click event.

To view the code entered in the Highest Score button's Click event, then run the application:

1   Double-click the **Highest Score** button to open its Click event procedure, then maximize the Code window. See Figure 9-20.

Figure 9-20: Highest Score button's Click event procedure

The code first declares two local Integer variables, inNum and inHigh. It then assigns the contents of the first array variable's test score to the inHigh variable. The For Next loop compares the contents of each of the remaining variables in the array—the variables with subscripts of 2 through 20—to the contents of the inHigh variable. If the test score contained in an array variable is greater than the test score contained in the inHigh variable, then the array variable's test score is assigned to inHigh. For example, if inHigh contains the number 85 and the array variable contains the number 90, then the number 90 is assigned to inHigh. The remaining variables in the array are then compared to the number 90, the current value of inHigh. When the For Next loop completes its processing, the inHigh variable will contain the highest test score stored in the array; that score is then displayed in the appropriate label control on the form. Run the application to see how the Highest Score button works.

2 Close the Code window, then **run** the application. The user interface appears on the screen.

3 Click the **Highest Score** button. The Click event procedure searches the array for the highest test score and then displays that test score, 100, in the form.

4 Click the **Exit** button. Visual Basic returns to the design screen.

The last procedure you will view in this application is the Click event procedure for the Update Scores button.

The Update Scores Button

The Update Scores button will allow the instructor to update each student's score by a set amount. Figure 9-21 shows the flowchart for the Update Scores button's Click event procedure.

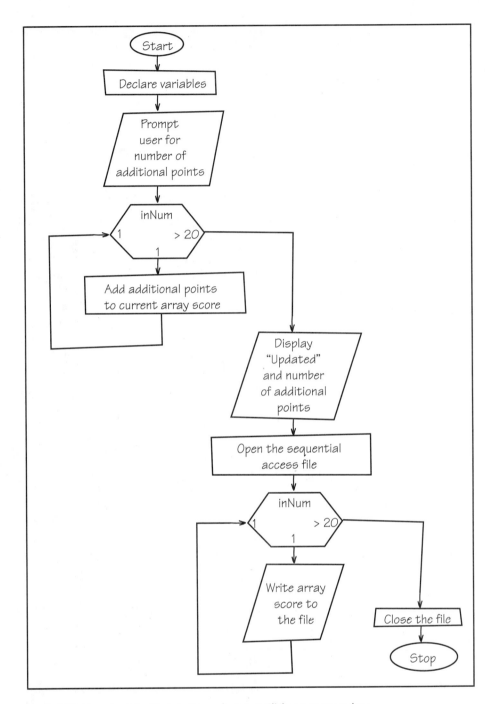

Figure 9-21: Flowchart for Update Scores button's Click event procedure

View the code entered in the Update Scores button's Click event.

To view the code entered in the Update Scores button's Click event, then run the application:

1   Double-click the **Update Scores** button to open its Click event, then maximize the Code window. The cmdUpdate control's Click event procedure appears, as shown in Figure 9-22. If your Student Disk is in the B drive, then change the drive letter in the Open statement to b:.

if your Student Disk is in the B drive, change the drive letter to b:

```
frmTest
Object: cmdUpdate          Proc: Click

Private Sub cmdUpdate_Click()
    Dim inNum As Integer, inIncrease As Integer
    inIncrease = Val(InputBox("Enter the number of additional points:"))
    For inNum = 1 To 20          'add additional points to each score in the array
        ScoreArray(inNum) = ScoreArray(inNum) + inIncrease
    Next inNum
    lblMsg.Caption = "Updated"   'display results
    lblAnswer.Caption = inIncrease

    Open "a:\Tut09\Test.dat" For Output As #1    'open file
    For inNum = 1 To 20                          'write array contents to file
        Write #1, ScoreArray(inNum)
    Next inNum
    Close #1                                     'close file

End Sub
```

Figure 9-22: Update Scores button's Click event procedure

This procedure declares two local Integer variables, inNum and inIncrease. The InputBox function, which you learned about in Tutorial 3, prompts the user to enter the number of additional points and stores the numeric equivalent of the user's response in the inIncrease variable. The For Next loop then adds the value in the inIncrease variable to each test score in the array. When the For Next loop completes its processing, the word "Updated" and the contents of the inIncrease variable are displayed on the form. The Test.dat sequential file is then opened for Output, and the updated scores are written from the array to the file on your Student Disk. The sequential file is then closed. See how the Update Scores button works.

2   Close the Code window, then **run** the application.

Add four points to each student's test score.

3   Click the **Update Scores** button. Type **4** in the dialog box, then press the **Enter** key to select the OK button. Visual Basic adds 4 to each score in the array and then writes the updated information to the sequential access file on your Student Disk. "Updated" appears in the Calculator text box; the number 4, which is the number of points added to each score, appears in the Answer text box.

One way to prove that the Update Scores button increased the test scores by 4 is to click the Highest Score button. Recall that before you updated the test scores, the highest score was 100.

4   Click the **Highest Score** button. Notice that the highest score is now 104 instead of 100.

Now add a negative four points to each test score—in other words, subtract four points from the scores.

5 Click the **Update Scores** button, type **–4** (be sure to type the minus sign) in the dialog box and press the **Enter** key. Visual Basic adds a negative 4 to each score in the array, then displays "Updated" and a –4 in the label controls on the form. Visual Basic then writes the updated information to the sequential access file on your Student Disk.

If you click the Highest Score button, the highest score should be 100 again.

6 Click the **Highest Score** button. The highest score is now 100.

7 Click the **Exit** button to end the application. Visual Basic returns to the design screen.

In the last example covered in this lesson, you will learn how to create and use a two-dimensional array.

The Classroom Application

On your Student Disk is an application that uses a two-dimensional variable array to store the names of the eight students seated in a classroom. The names of the eight students have already been entered into a sequential access file for you. Figure 9-23 shows the Class.dat file displayed in WordPad.

Figure 9-23: Class.dat file displayed in WordPad

Almost all of the classroom application is already coded for you; only the Dim statement that declares the ClassArray two-dimensional String array, which will store the names of the eight students, is missing. The syntax of the Dim statement to declare a two-dimensional array is **Dim** *arrayname*(*lower subscript* **To** *upper subscript, lower subscript* **To** *upper subscript*) **As** *datatype*. The first set of subscripts represents the number of rows in the array; the second set represents the number of columns in the array. In this case the classroom has four rows and two columns, so the proper Dim statement is `Dim ClassArray(1 to 4, 1 to 2) As String`. First you will enter the missing Dim statement; then you will view the remaining code before running the application.

To open the Class project and enter the Dim statement that declares the two-dimensional array:

1 Open the **Class** (class.vbp) project, which is located in the Tut09 folder on your Student Disk.

2   Save the form and the project as **laClass**.

3   Click the **View Form** button. The user interface appears on the screen, as shown in Figure 9-24.

lblColTwo(3)

lblColOne(3)

lblColOne(2)

lblColOne(1)

lblColOne(0)

lblColTwo(0)

lblColTwo(1)

lblColTwo(2)

Figure 9-24: Classroom application's user interface

The interface contains eight label controls and one command button. The first column of label controls belongs to a control array named lblColOne; the second column belongs to a control array named lblColTwo. Each seat in the classroom is identified by both a row number and a column number. In order to display the name of the student that sits in a particular seat, the instructor will simply need to click the appropriate label control in the interface.

First enter the Dim statement that declares the two-dimensional ClassArray variable array.

4   Double-click the **form** to open its Code window. Use the Code window's Object box to open the General declarations section. The form's General declarations section appears with the `Option Explicit` statement already entered in the Code window.

5   Press ↓ on your keyboard to position the blinking insertion point in the blank line below the `Option Explicit` statement.

6   Type **dim ClassArray(1 to 4, 1 to 2) as string** and press the **Enter** key. This instruction will create the two-dimensional variable array in the computer's memory.

The form's Load event procedure will fill the ClassArray array with the names of the eight students. Figure 9-25 shows the flowchart for the Load event procedure.

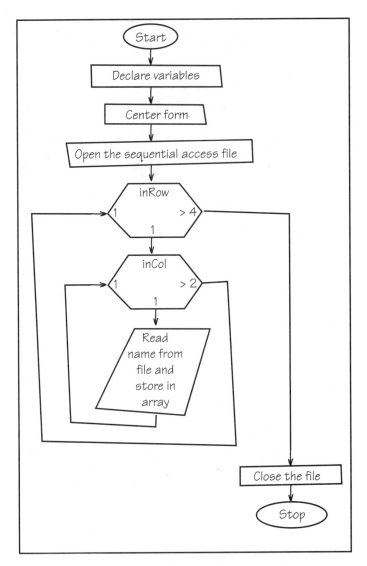

Figure 9-25: Flowchart for the form's Load event procedure

Now view the corresponding code.

To view the code entered in the form's Load event procedure:

1   The Code window should be open. Use the Object box to open the form's Load event, then maximize the Code window. The Load event procedure is shown in Figure 9-26. If your Student Disk is in the B drive, then change the drive letter in the Open statement to b:.

if your Student Disk is
in the B drive, change
the drive letter to b:

```
frmClass                                                    _ 8 X
Object: Form                        ▼    Proc: Load              ▼
Private Sub Form_Load()
    Dim inRow As Integer, inCol As Integer
    frmClass.Left = (Screen.Width - frmClass.Width) / 2
    frmClass.Top = (Screen.Height - frmClass.Height) / 2
    Open "a:\Tut09\Class.dat" For Input As #1      'Open file
    For inRow = 1 To 4                      'Fill array with data, row by row
        For inCol = 1 To 2
            Input #1, ClassArray(inRow, inCol)
        Next inCol
    Next inRow
    Close #1                                        'Close file

End Sub
```

Figure 9-26: Form's Load event procedure

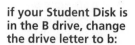

tips

● ● ● ● ● ● ● ● ● ● ● ● ● ●

▶ **You learned about nested
selection structures in
Tutorial 4. Notice that you
can also nest loops, which
means that you can place
one loop entirely inside
another loop. The two For
Next loops are referred to
as nested loops.**

After declaring the necessary variables (inRow and inCol) and centering the form, the code opens, for input, the sequential access file that contains the eight student names. The two For Next loops read the names from the file and enter each name, row by row, into the appropriate variable in the array. The first name in the sequential file (Mary) will be entered into ClassArray(1, 1) and the second name (Jesse) will be entered into ClassArray(1, 2). After entering data into the first row, the For Next loops then enter data into the second row of the array; Sharon, the third name in the sequential file, will be entered into ClassArray(2, 1) and Lisa, the fourth name in the file, will be entered into ClassArray(2, 2). The For Next loops will then fill the third row with data by entering the fifth name (Jack) into ClassArray(3, 1) and the sixth name (Khalid) into ClassArray(3, 2). Lastly, the For Next loops will fill the fourth row with data by entering the seventh name (Robert) into ClassArray (4, 1) and the eighth name (George) into ClassArray(4, 2). The sequential file is then closed. Figure 9-27 illustrates the filled array in memory, as well as the seating chart.

ClassArray(4,1)	Robert	George	ClassArray(4,2)
ClassArray(3,1)	Jack	Khalid	ClassArray(3,2)
ClassArray(2,1)	Sharon	Lisa	ClassArray(2,2)
ClassArray(1,1)	Mary	Jesse	ClassArray(1,2)

ClassArray in Memory

lblColOne(3)	Robert	George	lblColTwo(3)
lblColOne(2)	Jack	Khalid	lblColTwo(2)
lblColOne(1)	Sharon	Lisa	lblColTwo(1)
lblColOne(0)	Mary	Jesse	lblColTwo(0)

Seating chart

Figure 9-27: Status of ClassArray in memory and seating chart

Notice that the name of the student sitting in lblColOne(0) is stored in ClassArray(1, 1). The row number (1), which is the first subscript in the parentheses following ClassArray, is one more than the index of the label in the control array (0); that's because the array subscripts begin with the number 1, but the indexes of the labels in the control arrays begin with the number 0. Following this logic, notice that the name of the student sitting in lblColTwo(3) is stored in ClassArray(4, 2). Here again, the row number in the array (4) is one number greater than the index of its corresponding label control (3).

2   Close the Code window. Visual Basic returns to the design screen.

Next, view the code in the lblColOne and lblColTwo control arrays' Click events, which allow the instructor to display the name of the student sitting in a particular seat. Recall that the four label controls on the left side of the interface belong to the lblColOne control array, and the four label controls on the right side belong to the lblColTwo control array.

To view the code entered in the lblColOne and lblColTwo control arrays' Click events:

1   Double-click any one of the label controls in the first column, then maximize the Code window. The lblColOne control array's Click event procedure appears as shown in Figure 9-28.

stores the index of the label control that is receiving the event

control array name

row number

column number

Figure 9-28: The lblColOne control array's Click event procedure

tips

As you learned in Tutorial 5, the Index argument in a control array's event procedure stores the index of the control receiving the event.

When the user clicks one of the label controls in the lblColOne control array, you want the corresponding student's name, which is stored in the ClassArray array, to appear in the label control. The `lblColOne(Index).Caption = ClassArray(Index + 1, 1)` instruction tells Visual Basic to do just that. The `lblColOne(Index).Caption` part of the instruction tells Visual Basic where to display the name. The `ClassArray(Index + 1, 1)` part of the instruction tells Visual Basic that the name can be found in the ClassArray array, in the position whose row number is one number greater than the index of the label control that is receiving the event, and whose column number is 1. If, for example, the user clicks the lblColOne(2) label control, the Click event will display the name found in ClassArray(3, 1). Now view the code in the lblColTwo array's Click event.

2 Use the Object box to open the lblColTwo control array's Click event. See Figure 9-29.

stores the index of the label control that is receiving the event

control array name

row number

column number

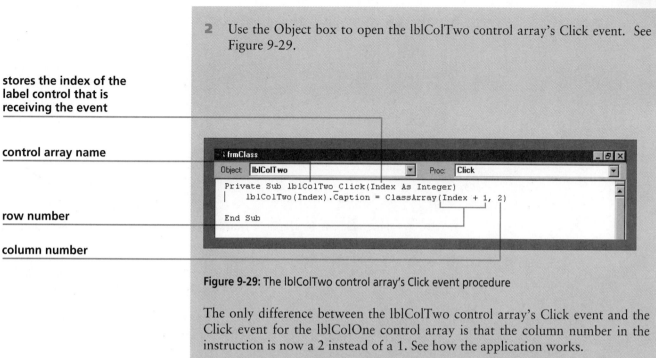

```
: frmClass                                                    _ 5 X
Object: lblColTwo              ▼    Proc: Click                    ▼
Private Sub lblColTwo_Click(Index As Integer)
    lblColTwo(Index).Caption = ClassArray(Index + 1, 2)

End Sub
```

Figure 9-29: The lblColTwo control array's Click event procedure

The only difference between the lblColTwo control array's Click event and the Click event for the lblColOne control array is that the column number in the instruction is now a 2 instead of a 1. See how the application works.

3 Close the Code window, then **save** and **run** the application.

4 Click each of the label controls, one at a time. The names of the students should appear as shown in Figure 9-30.

Figure 9-30: Label controls showing student names

5 Click the **Exit** button to exit the application. Visual Basic returns to the design screen.

You have now completed Lesson A. You can either take a break or complete the end-of-lesson questions and exercises.

S U M M A R Y

To declare a one-dimensional variable array:

- Use the Dim statement. Its syntax is: **Dim** *arrayname*(*lower subscript* **To** *upper subscript*) **As** *datatype*.
- *Arrayname* must follow the same rules as for simple variables. *Lower subscript* and *upper subscript* are numbers that define the lowest and the highest subscript, respectively, in the array. *Datatype* is the type of data the array variables will store.

To declare a two-dimensional variable array:

- Use the Dim statement. Its syntax is: **Dim** *arrayname*(*lower subscript* **To** *upper subscript*, *lower subscript* **To** *upper subscript*) **As** *datatype*.
- *Arrayname* must follow the same rules as for simple variables. *Lower subscript* and *upper subscript* are numbers that define the lowest and the highest subscript, respectively, in the array. *Datatype* is the type of data the array variables will store.

Q U E S T I O N S

1. A variable array is a group of variables that _____. (Select three)
   a. are related in some way
   b. belong to a control array
   c. have the same data type
   d. have the same index
   e. have the same name

2. Variables in an array are identified by a unique _____.
   a. data type
   b. index
   c. name
   d. order
   e. subscript

3. Stock(2) is read _____.
   a. Stock 2
   b. Stock array 2
   c. Stock parenthesis 2
   d. Stock sub 2
   e. two sub Stock

4. Which of the following is NOT an advantage of a variable array?
   a. Data stored in an array can be accessed faster than data stored in a disk file.
   b. Data stored in an array needs to be entered only once.
   c. Variable arrays use many more variable names.
   d. Variable arrays allow the programmer to store information in internal memory.
   e. When using variable arrays, you will have fewer variable names to remember.

5. Which of the following Dim statements declares a one-dimensional variable array named ItemArray that consists of five variables, each of which can store the name of an item?

    a. Dim ItemArray(5 to 1) as String

    b. Dim as String ItemArray(1 to 5)

    c. Dim String as ItemArray(1 to 5)

    d. Dim Item as StringArray(1 to 5)

    e. Dim ItemArray(1 to 5) as String

6. Which of the following is NOT true about the Dim statement?

    a. You use the Dim statement to fill an array with data.

    b. You use the Dim statement to declare a variable array.

    c. The Dim statement initializes a String variable array to null.

    d. The Dim statement initializes a Currency variable array to zero.

    e. The Dim statement creates the storage locations in memory.

Use the following array, named StudentArray, to answer questions 7 through 9. The array was created with the following Dim statement: `Dim StudentArray(1 to 5) as String`.

Tom	Mary	Suman	Patrick	Sue

7. The instruction, Printer.Print StudentArray(2), will print _____.

    a. Tom

    b. Mary

    c. Suman

    d. Patrick

    e. Sue

8. The instruction, `StudentArray(4) = "Jan"`, will _____.

    a. replace the name "Sue" with the name "Jan"

    b. replace the name "Patrick" with the name "Jan"

    c. replace the name "Jan" with the name "Patrick"

    d. concatenate the name "Jan" to the name "Patrick"

    e. have no effect on the array

9. The instruction, `StudentArray(1) = StudentArray(5)`, will _____.

    a. replace the name "Sue" with the name "Tom"

    b. replace the name "Tom" with the name "Sue"

    c. concatenate the name "Sue" to the name "Tom"

    d. concatenate the name "Tom" to the name "Sue"

    e. have no effect on the array

Use the following array, named SalesArray, to answer questions 10 through 14. The array was created with the following Dim statement: `Dim SalesArray(1 to 5) as Currency`.

10000	12000	900	500	20000

10. The instruction, `SalesArray(4) = SalesArray(4) + 10`, will _____.

    a. replace the 500 amount with 10

    b. replace the 500 amount with False

    c. replace the 500 amount with 510

    d. have no effect on the array

    e. result in an error message

11. The instruction, `SalesArray(4) = SalesArray(4-2)`, will _____ .
    a. replace the 500 amount with 12000
    b. replace the 500 amount with 498
    c. replace the 500 amount with False
    d. have no effect on the array
    e. result in an error message

12. The instruction, `Printer.Print SalesArray(1) + SalesArray(2)`, will print
    _____ .
    a. 22000
    b. 10000 + 12000
    c. SalesArray(1) + SalesArray(2)
    d. SalesArray(3)
    e. 900

13. Which of the following If clauses can be used to verify that the array subscript, called
    inX, is valid?
    a. If SalesArray(inX) >= 1 and SalesArray(inX) < 5 then
    b. If SalesArray(inX) >= 1 and SalesArray(inX) <= 5 then
    c. If SalesArray(inX) <= 1 and SalesArray(inX) >= 5 then
    d. If inX > 1 and inX < 5 then
    e. If inX >= 1 and inX <= 5 then

14. Which of the following will correctly add 100 to each variable in the SalesArray array?
    a. For inX = 1 to 5 Step 1
           inX = inX + 100
       Next inX
    b. For inX = 5 to 1 Step 1
           inX = inX + 100
       Next inX
    c. For SalesArray(inX) = 1 to 5 Step 1
           SalesArray(inX) = SalesArray(inX) + 100
       Next inX
    d. For inX = 1 to 5 Step 1
           SalesArray(inX) = SalesArray(inX) + 100
       Next inX

Use the following array, named NumArray, to answer questions 15 through 17. The array
was created with the following Dim statement: `Dim NumArray(1 to 4) as Integer.`

10	5	7	2

15. The average of the numbers in the NumArray array is _____ .
    a. 4
    b. 6
    c. 8
    d. 23.5
    e. 24

16. Which of the following will correctly calculate and print the average of the NumArray variables? Assume that inX and inTotal are declared as Integer variables. SgAvg is declared as a Single variable.

a. For inX = 1 to 4 Step 1
       NumArray(inX) = inTotal + inTotal
   Next inX
   sgAvg = inTotal / inX
   Print sgAvg

b. For inX = 1 to 4 Step 1
       inTotal = inTotal + NumArray(inX)
   Next inX
   sgAvg = inTotal / inX
   Print sgAvg

c. For inX = 1 to 4 Step 1
       NumArray(inX) = NumArray(inX) + inTotal
   Next inX
   sgAvg = inTotal / inX
   Print sgAvg

d. For inX = 1 to 4 Step 1
       inTotal = inTotal + NumArray(inX)
   Next inX
   sgAvg = inTotal / inX – 1
   Print sgAvg

e. For inX = 1 to 4 Step 1
       inTotal = inTotal + NumArray(inX)
   Next inX
   sgAvg = inTotal / (inX – 1)
   Print sgAvg

Only one of the five groups of code shown in Question 16 will print the average of the NumArray variables. What will the other groups of code print? Record your answers in questions 17 through 21.

17. The code in question 16's answer "a" will print _____ .
   a. 0
   b. 3.8
   c. 4.8
   d. 5
   e. 6

18. The code in question 16's answer "b" will print _____ .
   a. 0
   b. 3.8
   c. 4.8
   d. 5
   e. 6

19. The code in question 16's answer "c" will print _____ .
   a. 0
   b. 3.8
   c. 4.8
   d. 5
   e. 6

20. The code in question 16's answer "d" will print _____
- a. 0
- b. 3.8
- c. 4.8
- d. 5
- e. 6

21. The code in question 16's answer "e" will print _____
- a. 0
- b. 3.8
- c. 4.8
- d. 5
- e. 6

22. Which of the following Dim statements declares a two-dimensional String variable array named ItemArray that consists of three rows and four columns?
- a. Dim ItemArray(1 to 3, 1 to 4) as String
- b. Dim as String ItemArray(1 to 4, 1 to 3)
- c. Dim String as ItemArray(1 to 4, 1 to 3)
- d. Dim ItemArray as String(1 to 4, 1 to 3)
- e. Dim ItemArray(1 to 4, 1 to 3) as String

Use the following array, named NumArray, to answer questions 23 through 28. The array was created with the following Dim statement: `Dim NumArray(1 to 2, 1 to 3) as Integer`.

10	200	50
300	25	30

23. Which of the following Print statements will print the number 25 from the NumArray array?
- a. Print NumArray(1, 2)
- b. Print NumArray(2, 1)
- c. Print NumArray(2, 2)
- d. Print NumArray(1, 3)

24. Assume that a sequential access file contains the following numbers, in this order: 10, 200, 50, 300, 25, 30. Which of the following nested For Next loops will fill the NumArray as shown above?
- a. For inCol = 1 to 3 Step 1
        For inRow = 1 to 2 Step 1
            Input #1, NumArray(inRow, inCol)
        Next inRow
    Next inCol
- b. For inRow = 1 to 2 Step 1
        For inCol = 1 to 3 Step 1
            Input #1, NumArray(inRow, inCol)
        Next inCol
    Next inRow
- c. For inRow = 1 to 3 Step 1
        For inCol = 1 to 2 Step 1
            Input #1, NumArray(inRow, inCol)
        Next inCol
    Next inRow
- d. For inCol = 1 to 2 Step 1
        For inRow = 1 to 3 Step 1
            Input #1, NumArray(inRow, inCol)
        Next inRow
    Next inCol

Only one of the four groups of code shown in question 24 will fill the NumArray array as shown. What will the other groups of code do? Record your answers in questions 25 through 28.

25. Show what the NumArray array will look like in memory if you use the nested For Next loops shown in question 24's answer "a."

The code shown in question 24's answer "a" will _____ .
a. fill the array incorrectly
b. result in the "Subscript out of range." message
c. fill the array correctly

26. Show what the NumArray array will look like in memory if you use the nested For Next loops shown in question 24's answer "b."

The code shown in question 24's answer "b" will _____ .
a. fill the array incorrectly
b. result in the "Subscript out of range." message
c. fill the array correctly

27. Show what the NumArray array will look like in memory if you use the nested For Next loops shown in question 24's answer "c."

The code shown in question 24's answer "c" will _____ .
a. fill the array incorrectly
b. result in the "Subscript out of range." message
c. fill the array correctly

28. Show what the NumArray array will look like in memory if you use the nested For Next loops shown in question 24's answer "d."

The code shown in question 24's answer "d" will _____ .
a. fill the array incorrectly
b. result in the "Subscript out of range." message
c. fill the array correctly

EXERCISES

NOTE: Unless specified otherwise, write your answers on a piece of paper.

1. Write the appropriate Dim statement to declare a one-dimensional variable array named StatesArray. The array should contain 50 variables, numbered 1 through 50. Each variable will store a string.

2. Write the appropriate Dim statement to declare a one-dimensional variable array named PopulationArray. The array should contain 10 variables, numbered 1 through 10. Each variable will store an integer.

3. a. Write the appropriate Dim statement to declare a variable array named MonthsArray. The array should contain six variables, numbered 1 through 6. Each variable will store a string.
    b. Write the assignment statements that will store the first six months of the year in the array.
    c. Draw the array. Include each variable's name and its contents in the drawing.

4. a. Write the appropriate Dim statement to declare a variable array named SalesArray. The array should contain four variables, numbered 1 through 4. Each variable will store a currency type number.
    b. Write the assignment statement that will assign the following four numbers to the array: 10000, 40000, 20000, 5000.
    c. Draw the array. Include each variable's name and its contents in the drawing.

5. a. Write the appropriate Dim statement to declare a one-dimensional variable array named CityArray. The array should contain five variables, numbered 1 through 5. Each variable will store a string.
    b. Write the code that will open a sequential access file named City.dat, which contains the names of five cities. The procedure should fill the array with the data contained in the file and then close the file.

6. a. Write the appropriate Dim statement to declare a one-dimensional variable array named ScoresArray. The array should contain 10 variables, numbered 1 through 10. Each variable will store an integer.
    b. Write a procedure that will open a sequential access file named Scores.dat, which contains 10 scores. The procedure should fill the array with the data contained in the file and then close the file.

7. Write the appropriate Dim statement to declare a two-dimensional variable array named ItemArray. The array should contain three rows and four columns. (Use a lower subscript of 1.) Each variable in the array will store a string.

8. Write the appropriate Dim statement to declare a variable array named SalesArray. The array should contain 10 rows and 20 columns. (Use a lower subscript of 1.) Each variable will store an integer.

9. a. Write the appropriate Dim statement to declare a two-dimensional variable array named EmployeeArray. The array should contain three rows and two columns. (Use a lower subscript of 1.) Each variable will store a string.
    b. Write the code that will open a sequential access file named Employ.dat, which contains employee names. The procedure should fill the array with the employee data, row by row, and then close the file.
    c. Now write the code that will open a sequential access file named Employ.dat, which contains employee names. This time have the procedure fill the array with the employee data, column by column, and then close the file.

10. Assume you have used the `Dim CityArray(1 to 10) as String` instruction to declare an array named CityArray. The array contains the names of 10 cities. When the user enters a number in the txtNumber control on the form and then clicks the Display City button, he or she can display the name of the corresponding city in the lblCity control. Write the Display City button's code according to the pseudocode shown in Figure 9-31.

Pseudocode for the Display City button

1. Declare an Integer variable named inNum and constants for the MsgBox function

2. Assign the value in the txtNumber control to inNum.

3. If inNum contains a valid number then

    display the city name, which is stored in the array, in the lblCity control

    Else

    clear the lblCity control

    display a message indicating that the city is not available

    End If

Figure 9-31

11. Assume you have used the `Dim CityArray(1 to 10) as String` instruction to declare an array named CityArray. The array contains the names of 10 cities. When the user enters the name of a city in the txtCity control on the form and then clicks the Display Number button, he or she can display the number of the corresponding city in the lblNum control. Write the Display Number button's code according to the pseudocode shown in Figure 9-32.

Pseudocode for the Display Number button

1. Declare an Integer variable named inNum and a String variable named stSuccess.

2. Declare constants for the MsgBox function.

3. Assign the number 1 to the inNum variable.

4. Assign the letter "N" to the stSuccess variable.

5. Repeat while there are array variables to search and a matching city has not been found

    If the city in the txtCity text box matches the city in the current array variable then

    display array variable's subscript in the lblNum control

    assign "Y" to stSuccess variable

    Else

    add 1 to the inNum variable, which controls the subscript

    End If

    End Repeat while

6. If the city was not found in the array then

    clear the txtNum control

    display an appropriate message to the user

    End If

7. Send the focus to the txtName control

Figure 9-32

12. Assume an application uses the `Dim SalesArray(1 to 10) as Integer` instruction to declare an array named SalesArray. The array contains 10 sales amounts. When the user clicks the Display Average button on the form, he or she can calculate and display the average sales. Write the code for the Display Average button. Format the average sales to currency and display it in the lblAverage control.

13. Assume an application uses the `Dim SalesArray(1 to 10) as Integer` instruction to declare an array named SalesArray. The array contains 10 sales amounts. When the user clicks the Display Highest button on the form, he or she can display the highest sales amount. Write the code for the Display Highest button. Format the highest sales amount to currency and display it in the lblHighest control.

14. Assume an application uses the `Dim SalesArray(1 to 10) as Integer` instruction to declare an array named SalesArray. The array contains 10 sales amounts. When the user clicks the Display Lowest button on the form, he or she can display the lowest sales amount. Write the code for the Display Lowest button. Format the lowest sales amount to currency and display it in the lblLowest control.

15. Assume an application uses the `Dim SalesArray(1 to 10) as Integer` instruction to declare an array named SalesArray. The array contains 10 sales amounts. When the user clicks the Update Sales button on the form, the Click event procedure will ask him or her for a number. The procedure will then add that number to each sales amount in the array. After the sales amounts are updated, the procedure will write the updated sales to a file named Sales15.dat. Write the code for the Update Sales button.

16. Assume an application uses the `Dim SnameArray(1 to 10, 1 to 2) as String` instruction to declare a two-dimensional array named SnameArray. The array contains the names of 20 salespeople. When the user enters the row number and the column number in the txtRow and txtCol controls, respectively, and then clicks the Display Name button on the form, the Click event procedure will display the corresponding salesperson's name. Write the code for the Display Name button.

Exercises 17 through 20 are Discovery Exercises. Discovery Exercises, which may include topics that are not covered in the tutorial, allow you to "discover" the solutions to problems on your own.

discovery ▶ 17. In this exercise you will use the Redim statement.

Scenario: In Lesson A you completed the Test Score application. You saved the form and the project as laTest. Currently the application will work only when the number of records in the data file is 20. Your task in this exercise is to modify the application's code so that it works for any number of records.

a. Use the method appropriate for your version of Windows to copy the Test.bak file, which is located in the Tut09 folder on your Student Disk, to the Test.dat file.

b. Open the laTest (latest.vbp) project, which is located in the Tut09 folder on your Student Disk.

c. Save the form and the project as la17Done in the Tut09 folder on your Student Disk.

d. Change the Update button's Click event procedure so that it saves the updated records in a file named Test17.dat. By doing so, you will be leaving the original Test.dat file intact.

e. Change the form's Load event procedure so that it uses the Do While loop to read the records into the array. Be sure to count how many records are in the file. Call the counter variable inRecCount.

f. Find and then either read or print the Help window on the Redim statement.

g. Use the Redim statement to resize the array to accommodate the number of records in the file.

h. Modify the application's code so that all references to the number 20 are replaced with the inRecCount variable. Be sure that inRecCount is greater than zero before computing the average of the test scores.

i. Save and run the application. Test the Average Score, Highest Score, and Update Scores buttons, then exit the application.

j. Use WordPad (*Notepad in Windows 3.1*) to print the contents of the Test17x.dat file, which is located in the Tut09 folder on your Student Disk.

k. Modify the form's Load event procedure so that it opens the Test17x.dat file instead of the Test.dat file. (The Update button's Click event should still write the updated records to the Test17.dat file.)

l. Save and run the application. Test the Average Score and Highest Score buttons. Mark the answers down on a piece of paper.

m. Test the Update Scores button by increasing each of the scores by 10 points.

n. Exit the application, then print the code. On the printout of the code, write down the average score and the highest score.

o. Use WordPad (*Notepad in Windows 3.1*) to print the contents of the Test17.dat file, which is located in the Tut09 folder on your Student Disk.

p. Submit the printout from steps j and o and the code from step n.

discovery ▶ 18. In this exercise you will display the average, lowest, and highest sales amount contained in a two-dimensional array.

Scenario: JM Sales employs ten salespeople at each of its two locations. The manager wants an application that she can use to display the average sales amount, the lowest sales amount, and the highest sales amount. The application should also allow the manager to calculate the following year's expected sales by updating the sales figures by a percentage that she enters.

a. Open the laTest (latest.vbp) project that you created in Lesson A. The file is located in the Tut09 folder on your Student Disk.

b. Save the form and the project as la18Done in the Tut09 folder on your Student Disk.

c. Change the command button captions to <u>A</u>verage Sales, <u>H</u>ighest Sales, <u>U</u>pdate Sales.

d. Modify the code so that it uses a two-dimensional array named SalesArray. Use the `Dim SalesArray(1 to 10, 1 to 2) as Currency` instruction to create the array.

e. The 20 sales amounts are entered in the Sales.dat file, which is located in the Tut09 folder on your Student Disk. Open the Sales.dat file in WordPad (*Notepad in Windows 3.1*) and print the file. (If you need to recreate the Sales.dat file, use the method appropriate for your version of Windows to copy the Sales.bak file to Sales.dat.)

f. Modify the application's code appropriately. To keep the Sales.dat file intact, save the updated information to a file named Sales18.dat.

g. Run the application. Test the command buttons. Use .1 (10%) as the update percentage.

h. When the application is working correctly, print the application's code. Also use WordPad (*Notepad in Windows 3.1*) to print the Sales18.dat file. (Each number in the Sales18.dat file should be 10% greater than its corresponding number in the Sales.dat file.)

i. Submit the printouts from steps e and h and the code from step h.

discovery ▶ 19. Assume an application uses the `Dim SalesArray(1 to 10, 1 to 2) as Currency` instruction to declare a two-dimensional array named SalesArray. The array contains 20 sales amounts. When the user clicks the Calculate Bonus button on the form, the Click event procedure should calculate and print each salesperson's bonus. On a piece of paper, write the code for the Calculate Bonus button according to the pseudocode shown in Figure 9-33.

Pseudocode for the Calculate Bonus button

1. Declare necessary variables

2. Prompt the user to enter the bonus percentage (5% should be entered simply as 5.)

3. Convert the user's response to its decimal equivalent

4. Repeat for row number = 1 to 10

    Repeat for column number = 1 to 2

        calculate the bonus by multiplying the salesperson's sales by the bonus percentage

        print the row number, column number, and bonus on the form

    End Repeat for column number

  End Repeat for row number

Figure 9-33

discovery ▶ 20. In this exercise you will update only specific elements in an array.

Scenario: In Lesson A's Test Score example, you learned how to update each of the elements in an array. Mr. Weaver, the instructor using the application, also wants the ability to select which student's score will be updated. In other words, if the third and fifth students should receive an additional number of points, only those students' scores should be updated.

a. Use the method appropriate for your version of Windows to copy the Test.bak file, which is located in the Tut09 folder on your Student Disk, to the Test.dat file.

b. Use WordPad (*Notepad in Windows 3.1*) to print the Test.dat file.

c. Open the laTest (latest.vbp) project that you created in Lesson A. The file is located in the Tut09 folder on your Student Disk.

d. Save the form and the project as la20Done in the Tut09 folder on your Student Disk.

e. Modify the code appropriately. Save the updated scores in a file named Test20.dat.

f. Run the application. Use the Update Scores button to update only the third and fifth scores by 5 points.

g. Exit the application. Open the Update button's Click event procedure. Select the entire procedure, then use the Print command on the File menu to print only the selected code.

h. Use WordPad (*Notepad in Windows 3.1*) to print the Test20.dat file.

i. Submit the printouts from steps b and h and the code from step g.

LESSON B

objectives

In this lesson you will learn how to:

■ Set various properties of list box and combo box controls
■ Manipulate the ItemData array
■ Add a combo box control to the form
■ Store a record in an array

List Boxes, Combo Boxes, and the ItemData Array

List Box and Combo Box Controls

Most Windows applications make extensive use of list boxes (which you learned about in Tutorial 6) and combo boxes (which you will learn about in this lesson); both controls allow the user to enter data much more efficiently than can be done from the keyboard. For example, you can usually click an item in a list box or combo box faster than you can type the item into a text box. Also, because list boxes and combo boxes display a set of predefined selections for the user, typing errors and invalid data errors are minimized.

In this lesson, you will review the Text and ListIndex properties from Tutorial 6, and learn four additional properties of the list box and the combo box: List, ListCount, NewIndex, and ItemData.

The Text and ListIndex Properties

When you select an item in a list box or a combo box, Visual Basic stores the item in the control's **Text property**; it stores the index of the currently selected item in the **ListIndex property**. The index, you may remember from Tutorial 6, represents the position of the item in the control's list portion. The first item in the list has a ListIndex value of 0 (zero), the second item has a ListIndex value of 1, and so on. Assume, for example, that you enter the following five names into a list box named lstEmploy: Amy, Beth, Carol, Dan, Edward. Figure 9-34 illustrates the lstEmploy list box and its corresponding ListIndex and Text property values.

List box entry	Value in ListIndex property when item is selected	Value in Text property when item is selected
Amy	0	Amy
Beth	1	Beth
Carol	2	Carol
Dan	3	Dan
Edward	4	Edward

Figure 9-34: lstEmploy list box and corresponding ListIndex and Text property values

The value in the ListCount property is always one more than the largest index value; that's because the first index value is 0. In the lstEmploy list box shown in Figure 9-34, for example, the largest index value is 4; the ListCount value is, therefore, 5.

Using the data shown in Figure 9-34, the `Print lstEmploy.ListIndex` instruction will print 1 if Beth is selected in the list box; the instruction will print 4 if Edward is selected. The `Print lstEmploy.Text` instruction, on the other hand, will print "Beth" if Beth is selected in the list box; the instruction will print "Edward" if Edward is selected.

The ListCount Property

The number of items found in the list portion of a list box or a combo box is stored in the control's **ListCount property**. Using the lstEmploy list box shown in Figure 9-34, the instruction `Print lstEmploy.ListCount` would print 5.

The NewIndex Property

The **NewIndex property** stores the index of the item most recently added to a list box or a combo box. As you add an item to either of those controls with the AddItem method, Visual Basic inserts the item into the list portion either alphabetically (if the Sorted property is set to True) or at the end of the list (if the Sorted property is set to False). The NewIndex property tells you where in the list the new item was added. For example, assume you want to add the name Betty to the lstEmploy list box shown in Figure 9-34. If the list box's Sorted property is set to False, Visual Basic will add Betty to the end of the list and will store the number 5 in the control's NewIndex property. If, on the other hand, the control's Sorted property is set to True, Visual Basic will insert Betty after Beth in the list and will store the number 2 in the control's NewIndex property. Figure 9-35 illustrates this concept.

You learned about the AddItem method and the Sorted property in Tutorial 6. Recall that the syntax of the AddItem method is *control*.**AddItem***item*, where *item* is the string expression you want displayed in the control.

List box entries if Sorted property is set to False	Value in NewIndex property
Amy	
Beth	
Carol	
Dan	
Edward	
Betty	5

List box entries if Sorted property is set to True	Value in NewIndex property
Amy	
Beth	
Betty	2
Carol	
Dan	
Edward	

Figure 9-35: Illustration of lstEmploy list box and NewIndex property

The List and ItemData Property Arrays

When you create a list box or a combo box, Visual Basic automatically creates two property arrays for the control: the List property array and the ItemData property array. A property array is similar to a variable array in that it stores data that you can't see. Both the List and ItemData property arrays contain the same number of elements as the control's list—in other words, if the list contains five items, both property arrays will contain five items.

The **List property array**, which stores strings only, allows you to access the individual values in the list portion of the list box or combo box. The syntax of the List property array is *control*.**List**(*index*), where *control* is the name of the list box or combo box and *index* is the index of the item that you want to access. LstEmploy.List(0), for example, refers to the first item listed in Figure 9-34's list box, and lstEmploy.List(4) refers to the last item. The instruction `Print lstEmploy.List(0)` would print "Amy," and the instruction `Print lstEmploy.List(4)` would print "Edward."

Unlike the List property array, which stores strings only, the **ItemData property array** stores numbers in the Long data type range only. You can use the ItemData array to associate a specific number with each item in the list—for example, you can assign an employee number to each of the employee names in the list, as illustrated in Figure 9-36.

The difference between the Text property and the List property array is that the Text property allows you to access only the currently selected item. The List property array allows you to access each item in the list, even if the item is not selected.

List box entry	Value in List property array	Value in ItemData property array
Amy	Amy	2222
Beth	Beth	3456
Carol	Carol	2278
Dan	Dan	6698
Edward	Edward	9999

Figure 9-36: The lstEmploy list box showing values in List and ItemData property arrays

You use the ItemData property to access the items in the ItemData array. The syntax of the ItemData property is *control*.**ItemData**(*index*), where *control* is the name of the list box or combo box and *index* is the index of the item that you want to access. For example, lstEmploy.ItemData(0) refers to the first entry in the ItemData array shown in Figure 9-36. The `Print lstEmploy.ItemData(0)` instruction will print the employee number 2222. Figure 9-37 recaps the Text, ListIndex, ListCount, NewIndex, List array, and ItemData array properties.

Property	Purpose
Text	Stores the item that is currently selected in the list.
ListIndex	Stores the index of the item that is currently selected in the list.
ListCount	Stores a number that represents the number of items in the list.
NewIndex	Stores the index of the item most recently added to the list.
List array	Stores an array of strings. Each string is an item contained in the list.
ItemData array	Stores an array of numbers. Each number is associated with an item contained in the list.

Figure 9-37: Recap of list box and combo box properties

You will use all of these properties, except the Text property, in the employee application that you will run in the next section.

The Employee Application

On your Student Disk is an application that uses the ListIndex, ListCount, NewIndex, List, and ItemData properties. Open the file and view its code.

To open the employee application:

1. Start Visual Basic, if necessary. Open the **Employ** (employ.vbp) project, which is located in the Tut09 folder on your Student Disk.
2. Save the form and the project as **lbEmploy**.
3. Click the **View Form** button. The frmEmploy form appears on the screen, as shown in Figure 9-38.

list box

lblEmploy

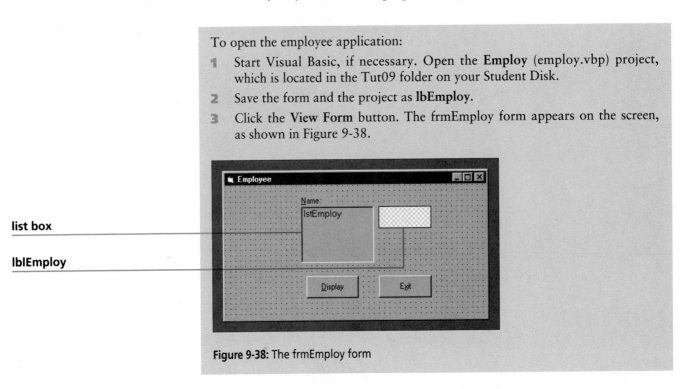

Figure 9-38: The frmEmploy form

The employee application will display an employee's number when you click the employee's name in the Name list box. Begin by viewing the code in the form's Load event, which fills the list box with data.

The Form's Load Event Procedure

When you run this application, the form's Load event procedure will enter the names of five employees into the list box; it will also enter each employee's number into the list box's ItemData array. Because the list box's Sorted property is set to False, Visual Basic will not sort the list items as they are entered into the list; rather, the items will appear in the order in which they are entered by the Load event procedure. After the list box and the ItemData array are filled with data, the Load event will select the first item in the list box before displaying the user interface on the screen.

To view the form's Load event procedure:

1 Double-click the **form** to open its Code window, then maximize the Code window. The form's Load event procedure appears, as shown in Figure 9-39.

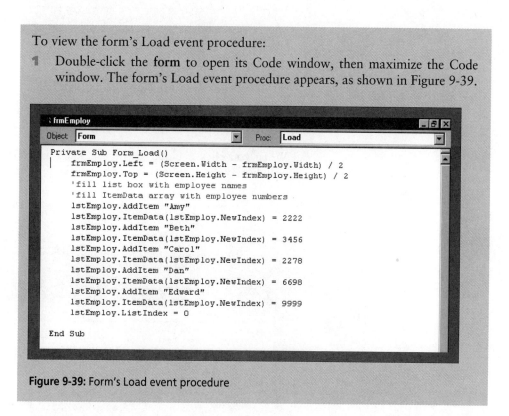

Figure 9-39: Form's Load event procedure

The `lstEmploy.AddItem "Amy"` instruction will add the name Amy to the list box. Because Amy is the first name inserted into the list, the list box's NewIndex property, which contains the index of the item most recently added to the list box, will contain a 0 (zero). Because lstEmploy.NewIndex has a value of 0, the `lstEmploy.ItemData(lstEmploy.NewIndex) = 2222` instruction will enter the number 2222 into position zero of the list box's ItemData array.

After Amy's name and number have been added to the list and the ItemData array, respectively, the `lstEmploy.AddItem "Beth"` instruction will add the name Beth as the second item in the list. The NewIndex property will contain the number 1 after Beth is added, so the `lstEmploy.ItemData (lstEmploy.NewIndex) = 3456` instruction will enter the number 3456 into position 1 of the ItemData array. The remaining code will enter each employee name into the list box and his or her employee number into the corresponding position of the ItemData array. The final instruction, `lstEmploy.ListIndex = 0`, will select the first item in the list box. As you learned in Tutorial 6, a default item should be selected in a list box when the interface first appears. Figure 9-40 illustrates the contents of the list box and its ItemData array when the Load event ends.

List box entry	Value in List property array	Value in ItemData property array
Amy	Amy	2222
Beth	Beth	3456
Carol	Carol	2278
Dan	Dan	6698
Edward	Edward	9999

Figure 9-40: Contents of list box and its List and ItemData property arrays when Load procedure ends

Next view the code in the list box's Click event procedure.

The List Box's Click Event Procedure

When you click a name in the list box's list, the control's Click event procedure will display the employee's number in the lblEmploy label control on the form.

To view the code in the list box's Click event procedure:

1 Use the Code window's Object box to open the lstEmploy control's Click event. See Figure 9-41.

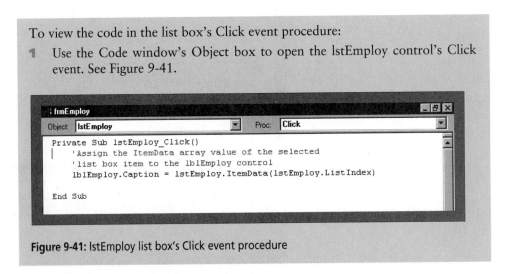

```
frmEmploy
Object: lstEmploy              Proc: Click

Private Sub lstEmploy_Click()
    'Assign the ItemData array value of the selected
    'list box item to the lblEmploy control
    lblEmploy.Caption = lstEmploy.ItemData(lstEmploy.ListIndex)

End Sub
```

Figure 9-41: lstEmploy list box's Click event procedure

The instruction in the Code window tells Visual Basic to display, in the lblEmploy control, the employee number that corresponds to the currently selected name in the lstEmploy list box. Look at each part of the instruction: lblEmploy.Caption tells Visual Basic where to display the employee number on the form. lstEmploy.ItemData tells Visual Basic that the employee number is stored in the list box's ItemData array. lstEmploy.ListIndex tells Visual Basic where in the ItemData array (in what position) to find the data. Recall that the ListIndex property contains the index of the currently selected item in the list. Therefore, if the currently selected item is Amy, lstEmploy.ListIndex will contain the number 0. The lblEmploy.Caption = lstEmploy.ItemData (lstEmploy.ListIndex) instruction will, therefore, assign the value found in position 0 of the ItemData array—2222—to the lblEmploy label control. (Recall that the first position in the ItemData array is position 0.)

The last procedure you will view is the Display button's Click event procedure.

The Display Button's Click Event Procedure

The Display button will display the contents of both the List and ItemData property arrays on the form. The Display button is included in the application for two reasons: it will allow you to verify the contents of the List and ItemData property arrays, and it will give you a chance to use the ListCount property.

To view the Display button's Click event procedure:

1 Use the Code window's Object box to open the cmdDisplay control's Click event procedure. See Figure 9-42.

```
frmEmploy
Object:  cmdDisplay                     ▼    Proc:  Click                      ▼
Private Sub cmdDisplay_Click()
    Dim inNum As Integer
    'Display the list box items and the values in the ItemData array
    For inNum = 0 To lstEmploy.ListCount - 1
        Print lstEmploy.List(inNum), lstEmploy.ItemData(inNum)
    Next inNum

End Sub
```

Figure 9-42: Display button's Click event procedure

The code first declares an Integer variable named inNum. A For Next loop is then used to display the contents of the list box's List array—lstEmploy.List(inNum)—and the contents of its ItemData array—lstEmploy.ItemData(inNum)—on the form. Notice that the For Next loop is initially set to 0—the index of the first item in each property array. The loop's ending value, which represents the index of the last item in each array, is lstEmploy.ListCount - 1. Recall that the ListCount property stores a number that represents the number of items in the list box, and the value in the ListCount property is always one more than the largest index. Run this application to see how it works.

2 Close the Code window, then **run** the application. The form's Load event procedure fills the list box with the names of the five employees; it also fills the ItemData array with the corresponding employee numbers. When the Load event selects the first name in the list box, the list box's Click event displays the corresponding number from the ItemData array.

3 Click the **Display** button to verify the contents of the List and ItemData arrays. The employee names and their corresponding numbers appear on the form, as shown in Figure 9-43.

tips
• • • • • • • • • • • • •

▶ Notice that when the lstEmploy.ListIndex = 0 instruction in the Load event selects the default item in the list box, it also triggers the list box's Click event procedure.

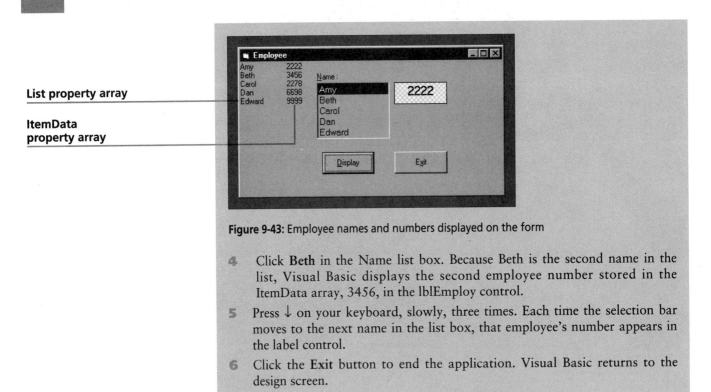

List property array

**ItemData
property array**

Figure 9-43: Employee names and numbers displayed on the form

4   Click **Beth** in the Name list box. Because Beth is the second name in the list, Visual Basic displays the second employee number stored in the ItemData array, 3456, in the lblEmploy control.

5   Press ↓ on your keyboard, slowly, three times. Each time the selection bar moves to the next name in the list box, that employee's number appears in the label control.

6   Click the **Exit** button to end the application. Visual Basic returns to the design screen.

In the next section you will modify the employee example by setting the list box's Sorted property to True and adding another employee to the list.

Modifying the Employee Example

Observe what happens to the list box and its ItemData array when you set the list box's Sorted property to True and then add another employee to the list.

To change the list box's Sorted property and then add an employee to the list:

1   Click the **lstEmploy** list box to select it. Set the list box's Sorted property to **True**.

2   Double-click the **form**. The form's Load event procedure appears.

Add Betty, who is employee number 1234, to the list of employees.

3   Maximize the Code window and enter the two lines of code shown in Figure 9-44.

enter these two lines of code

```
 frmEmploy

Object: Form                              Proc: Load

Private Sub Form_Load()
    frmEmploy.Left = (Screen.Width - frmEmploy.Width) / 2
    frmEmploy.Top = (Screen.Height - frmEmploy.Height) / 2
    'fill list box with employee names
    'fill ItemData array with employee numbers
    lstEmploy.AddItem "Amy"
    lstEmploy.ItemData(lstEmploy.NewIndex) = 2222
    lstEmploy.AddItem "Beth"
    lstEmploy.ItemData(lstEmploy.NewIndex) = 3456
    lstEmploy.AddItem "Carol"
    lstEmploy.ItemData(lstEmploy.NewIndex) = 2278
    lstEmploy.AddItem "Dan"
    lstEmploy.ItemData(lstEmploy.NewIndex) = 6698
    lstEmploy.AddItem "Edward"
    lstEmploy.ItemData(lstEmploy.NewIndex) = 9999
    lstEmploy.AddItem "Betty"
    lstEmploy.ItemData(lstEmploy.NewIndex) = 1234
    lstEmploy.ListIndex = 0

End Sub
```

Figure 9-44: Modified Load event procedure

4   Close the Code window, **save** and **run** the application.

Because the list box's Sorted property is set to True, the `lstEmploy.AddItem "Betty"` instruction inserts Betty's name after "Beth" in the list; the list box's NewIndex property now contains the number 2. The `lstEmploy.ItemData (lstEmploy.NewIndex) = 1234` instruction then stores Betty's employee number in position 2 of the ItemData array. The employee names and numbers that originally occupied positions 2, 3, and 4 in the list box and in the ItemData array, respectively, are moved down to positions 3, 4, and 5. Figure 9-45 illustrates what happens to the list box and the ItemData array when Betty's name is inserted.

List box entry	Value in List property array	Value in ItemData property array
Amy	Amy	2222
Beth	Beth	3456
Betty	Betty	1234
Carol	Carol	2278
Dan	Dan	6698
Edward	Edward	9999

Figure 9-45: New contents of list box and its List and ItemData property arrays

5   Click the **Display** button. The contents of the list box and its ItemData array appear on the form. Notice that Betty's name and number are now included in the List and ItemData arrays, respectively.

6   Click **Betty** in the list. Betty's employee number, 1234, appears in the lblEmploy control.

7   On your own, click each of the other names in the list box and verify that their employee numbers appear correctly in the label control.

8   Click the **Exit** button. Visual Basic returns to the design screen.

Now that you know how to use the ListIndex, List, ListCount, NewIndex, and ItemData properties, you can create the personal directory application that you viewed at the beginning of this tutorial.

The Personal Directory Application

In this tutorial you will create a personal directory application that will contain the names, phone numbers, and birthdays of your friends and relatives. The sketch of the user interface for this application is shown in Figure 9-46.

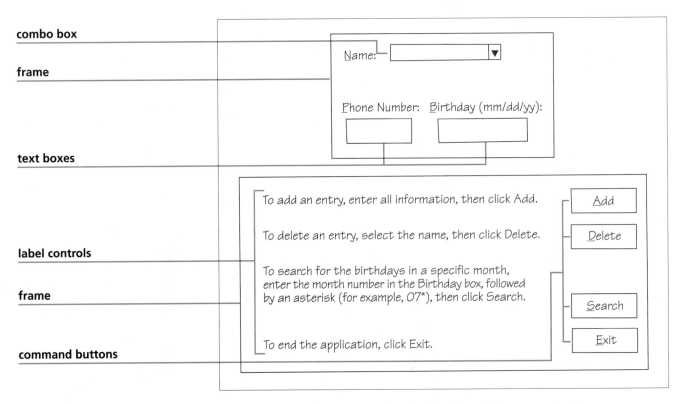

Figure 9-46: Sketch of the user interface for the personal directory application

According to the sketch, the application will contain various label controls, text boxes, command buttons, frame controls, and a combo box. To save you time, your Student Disk contains a partially completed personal directory application. When you open the application you will notice that most of the user interface has already been created. You will finish creating the user interface in this lesson. You will also begin coding the application.

To open the partially completed application:

Important Note: If you are using the Working Model, you will need to use the following procedure to open the Direct.vbp application. First open a new project, then use the File menu's Remove File command to remove the Formal form. Use the File menu's Add File command to add the Direct.frm file to the project, then use the File menu's Add File command to add the Direct.bas file to the project.

1   Open the **Direct** (direct.vbp) project, which is located in the Tut09 folder on your Student Disk.

2   Save the form, the code module, and the project as **lbDirect**. (You will need to click the Direct.Bas file name in the Project window to save the code module.)

3   Click **lbDirect.Frm** in the Project window, then click the **View Form** button. Maximize the frmDirect form. The user interface appears on the screen, as shown in Figure 9-47.

combo box control is missing

Frame1 control

txtPhone

txtBirth

Figure 9-47: Partially completed user interface for the personal directory application

One control is missing from the user interface—a combo box. You will learn how to add that control in the next section.

4   Restore the form to its standard size.

Creating a Combo Box

A **combo box** combines the features of a text box and a list box in that it allows the user to either type an entry or select an item from a predefined list. In this case the combo box will allow you to either type the name of a friend or relative in its text box portion or select the name from its list.

To create a combo box control:

1   Double-click the **ComboBox** tool 🔲 in the toolbox. A combo box control appears on the form.

You will need to cut the combo box from the form and then paste it into the frame control at the top of the form.

2   The combo box control should be selected. Click **Edit**, then click **Cut** to cut the combo box from the form. Click the **Frame1** control at the top of the form to select the frame. Sizing handles should appear around the frame. Click **Edit**, then click **Paste** to paste the combo box into the frame.

3 Set the following eight properties for the combo box:

BackColor:	**light gray**
Font:	**12** points
Left:	**1800**
Name:	**cboName** (The cbo stands for combo box.)
Sorted:	**True**
TabIndex:	**1**
Top:	**480**
Width:	**2200**

4 Remove the Text1 from the combo box control's Text property.

5 Maximize the form. The user interface appears as shown in Figure 9-48.

cboName

txtPhone

txtBirth

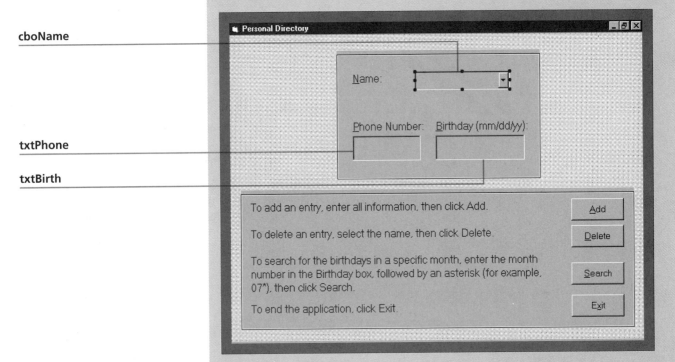

Figure 9-48: User interface with combo box added

Visual Basic offers three styles of combo boxes. You specify the style you want by setting the combo box's **Style property**. The default style, Dropdown Combo, is the one currently on the screen. A **Dropdown Combo box** allows the user to make an entry in the text box portion of the control. However, by clicking the control's list arrow, the user can also display a list of choices. Once the user makes a selection from the list, the list closes.

The second style of combo box, the **Simple Combo box,** is exactly the same as the Dropdown Combo except its list remains open at all times. Of the two styles, the Simple Combo is more convenient to use because the user doesn't have to click the list arrow to display the list. However, the Dropdown Combo takes up less space on the form, and it is the preferred choice if many items must be displayed.

The third type of combo box is the **Dropdown List box.** This style displays a list of choices when the user clicks its list arrow. Unlike the other two styles, this style of combo box does not allow the user to type an entry into the text box portion.

In deciding which of the three styles to use in this application, you rule out the Dropdown List box because you want to be able to type an entry into the text box portion. You also rule out the Simple Combo box because, considering the number of friends and relatives that you have, that style would take up too much space on the form. The Dropdown Combo style is the best to use in this situation, so you will not need to change the Style property from its default value.

Just as with the list box, you use the AddItem method to specify the items to display in a combo box; in this case you will display the names of your friends and relatives. The names, phone numbers, and birthdays of your friends and relatives have already been entered into a sequential access file for you. In a little while you will learn how to display those names in the combo box.

6   Restore the form to its standard size, then click the **Lock Controls** button on the toolbar to lock the controls in place on the form.

Combo Box Style, Default Item, and List Arrangement

- Use the Dropdown List style of combo box to display a list of choices when the user clicks its list arrow, and you don't want to allow the user to type an entry into the text box portion of the combo box.

- Use a Dropdown Combo box if you need to allow the user to make an entry in the text box portion of the control, and you have many choices to display. By clicking the control's list arrow, the user can display the list of choices; however, once the user makes a selection from the list, the list closes.

- Use the Simple Combo style of combo box if you need to allow the user to make an entry in the text box portion of the control, and you have only a few choices to display. The Simple Combo box's list remains open at all times.

- Although the Simple Combo is more convenient to use because the user doesn't have to click the list arrow to display the list, the Dropdown Combo takes up less space on the form, and it is the preferred choice if many items must be displayed.

- Select a default item in the combo box when the interface first appears.

- Combo box items are either arranged by use, with the most used entries appearing first in the list, or the items are sorted in ascending order either alphabetically, numerically, or chronologically.

You can now begin coding the application.

Coding the Personal Directory Application

The TOE chart for the personal directory application is shown in Figure 9-49.

Task	Object	Event
1. Get the name from the user 2. Display corresponding phone number and birthday in txt Phone and txtBirth controls 3. Display the name	cboName	Click
Add entry to combo box, ItemData array, and variable array	cmdAdd	Click
Delete entry from combo box, ItemData array, and variable array	cmdDelete	Click
Unload form	cmdExit	Click
Search the variable array for a birthday and display the name, phone number, and birthday in the cboName, txtPhone, and txtBirth controls, respectively	cmdSearch	Click
Read data from a sequential file into the combo box, ItemData array, and variable array	frmDirect	Load
End the application		Unload
Display phone number	txtPhone	None
Display birthday	txtBirth	None

Figure 9-49: TOE chart for the personal directory application

On your Student Disk is a sequential access file named Direct.dat that contains the names, phone numbers, and birthdays of five people. You will use this file in the personal directory application. Figure 9-50 shows the file displayed in WordPad.

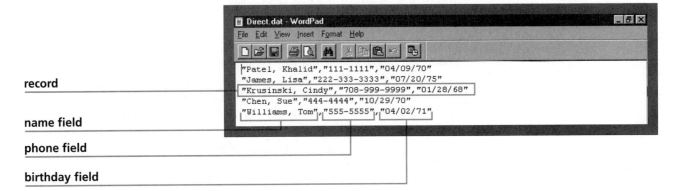

record

name field

phone field

birthday field

Figure 9-50: Direct.dat file displayed in WordPad

> **Important Note:** If this is the second or subsequent time that you are practicing this lesson, be sure to first use the method appropriate for your version of Windows to copy the Direct.bak file to Direct.dat. The Direct.bak file is in the Tut09 folder on your Student Disk.

In Tutorial 6 you learned that each line in a sequential access file represents a record and that records are composed of fields. Each record in the Direct.dat file, for example, contains three fields: name, phone number, and birthday. In this application, you will store the entire record—the three fields—in an array named DirArray. In order to store a record in an array, you need to create a record structure for the record. As you learned in Tutorial 7, you create a record structure (a user-defined data type) by entering the Type statement in a code module.

To enter the Type statement in the code module:

1   Click **lbDirect.Bas** in the Project window, then click the **View Code** button. The module's Code window appears.

The record structure will contain three String fields named stName, stPhone, and stBirth. You will name the user-defined data type DirStruc.

2   Enter the `Option Explicit` and Type statements shown in Figure 9-51.

Figure 9-51: Type statement entered in code module

Notice that the Type statement shown in Figure 9-51 does not specify the length of the String fields, as did the Type statements in Tutorial 7. Unlike the records stored in a random access file, the records stored in a variable array do not have to be the same length.

3   Close the Code window.

After creating a user-defined data type, you can then declare a variable array of that type. You will declare the array in the form's General declarations section because the array will be used by several procedures in the form.

To code the form's General declarations section, then save the application:

1   Double-click the **form** to open its Code window. Use the Code window's Object box to open the form's General declarations section. The form's General declarations section appears with the `Option Explicit` statement already entered in the Code window.

You estimate that you will need to keep track of as many as 50 people, so you will declare a one-dimensional form-level array named DirArray that can store up to 50 records. The array will have a data type of DirStruc, which means that each variable in the array will contain three fields: name, phone number, and birthday.

2   Maximize the Code window, then press ↓ on your keyboard to position the blinking insertion point in the blank line below the `Option Explicit` statement, then type **dim DirArray(1 to 50) as DirStruc** and press the **Enter** key.

The directory application will also need a variable in which it can keep track of the number of records that are both read from the file and stored in the array. You will use a form-level Integer variable named inNumRec for that purpose.

3   Type **dim inNumRec as integer**, press the **Tab** key, then type **'number of records** and press the **Enter** key.

If people are either added to the array or deleted from the array, the information in the sequential access file on your Student Disk will need to be updated to reflect the additions and deletions. You will use a form-level String variable named stUpdate to keep track of whether the file needs to be updated.

4   Type **dim stUpdate as string**, press the **Tab** key, then type **'keeps track of whether file needs updating** and press the **Enter** key.

5   Compare your code with Figure 9-52. Be sure to make any needed corrections before continuing.

```
frmDirect
Object: (General)                    Proc: (declarations)
Option Explicit
Dim DirArray(1 To 50) As DirStruc
Dim inNumRec As Integer 'number of records
Dim stUpdate As String  'keeps track of whether file needs updating
```

Figure 9-52: Code and documentation entered in the form's General declarations section

6   Close the Code window, then click the **Save Project** button on the toolbar to save the application.

The form's Load event is the next procedure you will code.

Coding the Form's Load Event Procedure

The pseudocode for the form's Load event procedure is shown in Figure 9-53.

Pseudocode for the form's Load event procedure

1. Open the sequential access file for input
2. Repeat while it is not the end of the file
        add 1 to the inNumRec variable, which keeps track of the number of records
        read a record from the file and store it in the variable array
        add the name from the array to the combo box
        store the record's array position in the combo box's ItemData array
     End Repeat while
3. Select the first item in the combo box's list
4. Close the file

Figure 9-53: Pseudocode for the form's Load event procedure

When you run the application and the form is loaded into memory, the form's Load event procedure will first open the Direct.dat sequential file that contains the names, phone numbers, and birthdays of your friends and relatives. A loop will then check if the record pointer is at the end of the file—in other words, if there are any records in the file. If the record pointer is at the end of the file, the first item in the combo box is selected, the sequential file is closed, and the Load event procedure ends. If, on the other hand, the record pointer is not at the end of the file, then the four instructions within the loop are processed as follows:

- the form-level inNumRec variable, which keeps track of the number of records, is increased by one
- the next record is read from the file and stored in the array
- the name of the friend or relative is added to the combo box
- the record's array location is stored in the combo box's ItemData array

The loop will process those four instructions for each of the records in the sequential access file. When all of the records have been read and stored in the array, the loop will stop. At that point the first item in the combo box is selected as the default item, the sequential access file is closed, and the Load event procedure ends. Now enter the corresponding code in the form's Load event procedure.

To code the form's Load event procedure:

1　Double-click the **form**. Use the Proc box to open the form's Load event procedure.

First open the Direct.dat sequential access file, which contains the names of your friends and relatives. That file is located in the Tut09 folder on your Student Disk.

2　Maximize the Code window. Press the **Tab** key, then type one of the following Open statements according to the location of your Student Disk:

　　open "a:\Tut09\Direct.dat" for input as #1

　　open "b:\Tut09\Direct.dat" for input as #1

3　Press the **Enter** key.

Now enter a Do While...Loop statement that will stop processing when all of the records in the sequential file have been read—in other words, when the record pointer reaches the end of the file. As you learned in Tutorial 6, you can use the EOF function to test for the end of the file.

4　Type **do while not eof(1)** and press the **Enter** key to begin the loop.

If it's not the end of the file, then add 1 to the form-level inNumRec variable, which keeps track of the number of records read from the file and stored in the array.

5　Press the **Tab** key, then type **inNumRec = inNumRec + 1** and press the **Enter** key.

Now use the Input # statement to read a record from the sequential file and store it in the array. The syntax of the Input # statement, you may remember from Tutorial 6, is **Input #** *filenumber, variablelist. Filenumber* is the number used in the Open statement to open the sequential access file and *variablelist* is one or more numeric or string variables, separated by a comma. In this case the *variablelist* will include the three field variables contained in the DirArray variable array. Recall that you refer to the individual field variables by preceding the field variable's name with the name of the record variable in which it is defined. You separate the record variable's name from the field variable's name with a period. Figure 9-54 illustrates the names of the record variables and the field variables in the DirArray variable array.

DirArray(1).stName	DirArray(2).stName	.....	DirArray(50).stName
DirArray(1).stPhone	DirArray(2).stPhone	.....	DirArray(50).stPhone
DirArray(1).stBirth	DirArray(2).stBirth	.....	DirArray(50).stBirth

Figure 9-54: Record variables and field variables in the DirArray array

Notice that each record variable shown in Figure 9-54 has a subscript; that's because the record variables in this application belong to an array. The subscript indicates the position of the record variable in the DirArray array. In this application you can use the inNumRec variable as the record variable's subscript; it will control into which array variable the next record will be stored. For example, if inNumRec contains the number 1, the record from the file will be stored in DirArray(1). If inNumRec contains the number 2, the record will be stored in DirArray(2), and so on. Enter the Input # statement.

6 Type **input #1, DirArray(inNumRec).stName, DirArray(inNumRec).stPhone, DirArray(inNumRec).stBirth** and press the **Enter** key.

Now enter the name, which is stored in the DirArray array, into the combo box.

7 Type **cboName.AddItem DirArray(inNumRec).stName** and press the **Enter** key.

The next step is to enter the value stored in the inNumRec variable, which represents the record's position in the DirArray array, into the combo box's ItemData array. You can use the `cboName.ItemData(cboName.NewIndex) = inNumRec` instruction to do so. (Recall that the NewIndex property specifies the index of the item most recently added to a combo box.) When a name is added to the combo box, the value in the inNumRec variable should be entered into the corresponding position of the ItemData array.

8 Type **cboName.ItemData(cboName.NewIndex) = inNumRec** and press the **Enter** key.

You can now end the loop, select the first item as the default item in the combo box, and close the sequential access file.

9 Enter the remaining code and documentation shown in Figure 9-55. Also compare your code with the code shown in the figure and make any needed corrections before continuing to the next step. (You may need to scroll the Code window to see the rest of the Input # statement.)

enter the
documentation

enter these three
lines of code

enter the
documentation

you will need to scroll
to see the remaining
code in this line

```
frmDirect
Object:  Form                                    Proc:  Load
    Private Sub Form Load()
        Open "a:\Tut09\Direct.dat" For Input As #1
        Do While Not EOF(1)
            inNumRec = inNumRec + 1                        'add 1 to number of records
            Input #1, DirArray(inNumRec).stName, DirArray(inNumRec).stPhone, DirArray(inNum
            cboName.AddItem DirArray(inNumRec).stName       'add name to combo box
            cboName.ItemData(cboName.NewIndex) = inNumRec   'store record's array position
        Loop                                                'in ItemData array
        cboName.ListIndex = 0
        Close #1

    End Sub
```

Figure 9-55: Form's Load event procedure

Now save and run the application to test the code you've entered so far.

To test the application:

1   Close the Code window, then **save** and **run** the application. The Load event procedure reads the records from the sequential file and enters each record, one at a time, into the array. The procedure also enters the names into the combo box and each name's DirArray array position into the ItemData array. Figure 9-56 illustrates the contents of the DirArray array, the list portion of the combo box, and the ItemData array when the Load event ends.

Contents of the DirArray variable array

Patel, Khalid	James, Lisa	Krusinski, Cindy	Chen, Sue	Williams, Tom
111-1111	222-333-3333	708-999-9999	444-4444	555-5555
04/09/70	07/20/75	01/28/68	10/29/70	04/02/71

Contents of the combo box	Contents of the combo box's ItemData array
Patel, Khalid	1
James, Lisa	2
Krusinski, Cindy	3
Chen, Sue	4
Williams, Tom	5

Figure 9-56: Contents of the DirArray array, the combo box, and the combo box's ItemData array

Open the combo box and verify that the names were entered correctly.

2   Click the **Name** combo box list arrow. A list showing the five names from the file appears in alphabetical order, as shown in Figure 9-57.

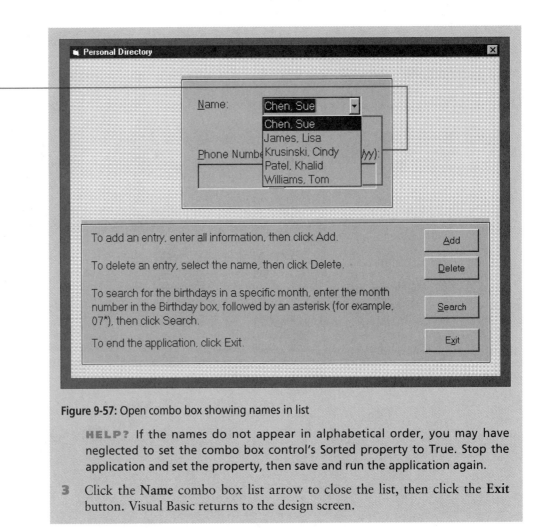

names appear in alphabetical order

Figure 9-57: Open combo box showing names in list

HELP? If the names do not appear in alphabetical order, you may have neglected to set the combo box control's Sorted property to True. Stop the application and set the property, then save and run the application again.

3 Click the **Name** combo box list arrow to close the list, then click the **Exit** button. Visual Basic returns to the design screen.

In the next section you will code the combo box so that it displays the phone number and birthday when you click a name in the list.

Coding the Combo Box

Recall that when you click a name in the Name combo box's list, Visual Basic records the name in the control's Text property. You don't need to write any code for that to happen; Visual Basic handles it automatically. You do, however, need to write the code to tell the combo box's Click event procedure what you want to happen, if anything, when a name is selected; in this case, you want to display, in the Phone Number and Birthday text boxes, the phone number and birthday that correspond to the selected name. The pseudocode for the cboName control's Click event procedure is shown in Figure 9-58.

Pseudocode for the combo box's Click event procedure

1. Declare an Integer variable named inSelection.

2. Assign the selected item's ItemData value to the inSelection variable.

3. Use the inSelection variable to display the selected item's phone number, which is stored in the array, in the txtPhone control.

4. Use the inSelection variable to display the selected item's birthday, which is stored in the array, in the txtBirth control.

Figure 9-58: Pseudocode for the combo box's Click event procedure

Now write the corresponding code in the Name combo box's Click event procedure.

To code the combo box's Click event procedure, then save and run the application:

1 Double-click the **Name combo box**. The cboName control's Change event procedure appears. Use the Code window's Proc box to open the combo box's Click event procedure, then maximize the Code window. Enter the code shown in Figure 9-59.

```
frmDirect

Object: cboName                           Proc: Click

Private Sub cboName_Click()
    Dim inSelection As Integer
    'Assign the selected item's ItemData value
    inSelection = cboName.ItemData(cboName.ListIndex)
    'Assign selected item's phone and birthday to text boxes
    txtPhone.Text = DirArray(inSelection).stPhone
    txtBirth.Text = DirArray(inSelection).stBirth

End Sub
```

Figure 9-59: Combo box's Click event procedure

The code declares a local Integer variable named inSelection. The `inSelection = cboName.ItemData(cboName.ListIndex)` instruction assigns the value contained in the selected item's ItemData property to the inSelection variable. The value in the ItemData property, remember, tells Visual Basic where the record corresponding to the name is located in the DirArray array. For example, if a name's ItemData value is 3, its record is stored in DirArray(3).

The `txtPhone.Text = DirArray(inSelection).stPhone` and `txtBirth.Text = DirArray(inSelection).stBirth` instructions display, in the appropriate text boxes on the form, the phone number and birthday that correspond to the name selected in the combo box. Save and run the application to see how the combo box's Click event procedure works.

2 Close the Code window, then **save** and **run** the application.

3 Click the **Name** combo box list arrow, then click **James, Lisa**. Lisa's name, phone number, and birthday appear on the screen, as shown in Figure 9-60.

tips

> Recall that the ListIndex property stores the index of the item currently selected in the list portion of either a combo box or a list box.

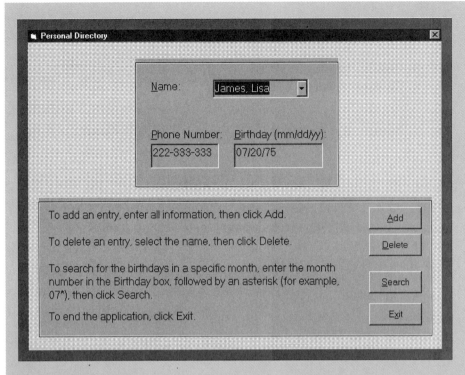

Figure 9-60: User interface showing Lisa James's information

Notice that the focus is in the combo box, as indicated by the selected name. Visual Basic automatically highlights (or selects) the text in a combo box when the control receives the focus. When you type a character into the combo box or when you click another name from its list, the new entry will replace the selected text. You can also press either the Delete key or the Backspace key to remove the selected text.

4   Click the **Exit** button. Visual Basic returns to the design screen.

You have now completed Lesson B. You will finish coding the personal directory application in Lesson C. You can now either take a break or complete the end-of-lesson questions and exercises.

S U M M A R Y

To combine the features of a text box and a list box:

■   Use the combo box control. The combo box has three styles: Dropdown Combo, Simple Combo, and Dropdown List.
■   If you want the items in the combo box to be sorted, set the combo box's Sorted property to True.

To refer to the elements in a list box or a combo box:

■   Use the Text property to determine the item that is currently selected in the list.
■   Use the ListIndex property to determine the index of the item that is currently selected in the list.

■ Use the ListCount property to determine the number of items in the list.

■ Use the NewIndex property to determine the index of the item most recently added to the list.

■ Use the List property array, which stores strings only, to access each of the items contained in the list.

■ Use the ItemData property array, which stores numbers in the Long data type only, to access the number that you have associated with each item contained in the list.

To add an item to a combo box:

■ Use the AddItem method. Its syntax is *control*.**AddItem** *item*. *Control* is the name of the control, **AddItem** is the name of the method, and *item* is the string expression you want displayed in the control. Be sure to enclose the string expression in quotation marks.

To store a record in a variable array:

■ Use the Type statement to create a record structure—a user-defined data type. Enter the Type statement in a code module.

■ Use the user-defined data type to declare the array.

Q U E S T I O N S

1. The _____ property of a list box or combo box stores the index of the item currently selected in the list.
   a. ItemData
   b. List
   c. ListCount
   d. ListIndex
   e. NewIndex

2. You use the _____ property to access the individual values in the list portion of a list box or combo box.
   a. ItemData
   b. List
   c. ListCount
   d. ListIndex
   e. NewIndex

3. The _____ property specifies the number of items in the list portion of a combo box or list box.
   a. ItemData
   b. List
   c. ListCount
   d. ListIndex
   e. NewIndex

4. The _____ property specifies the index of the item most recently added to a combo box or list box.
   a. ItemData
   b. List
   c. ListCount
   d. ListIndex
   e. NewIndex

5. You use the _____ property to access the items in the ItemData array of a list box or a combo box.
    a. ItemData
    b. List
    c. ListIndex
    d. NewIndex
    e. Text

6. The _____ property stores the item that is currently selected in the list portion of a list box or a combo box.
    a. ItemData
    b. List
    c. ListIndex
    d. NewIndex
    e. Text

Use the following information to answer questions 7 through 16:

Assume that the lstCity list box and its ItemData array, which stores the city's population, contain the following items, in the order shown:

lstCity List box	ItemData array
Glenview	10900
Boulder	35600
Watertown	5000
Amos	12000

7. lstCity.List(1) refers to _____ .
    a. Amos
    b. Boulder
    c. Glenview
    d. Watertown

8. Assume that you have clicked Glenview in the list box. Which two of the following instructions will change Glenview's population to 20000?
    a. lstCity.ItemData(0) = 20000
    b. lstCity.ItemData(0) = "20000"
    c. lstCity.ItemData(1) = 20000
    d. lstCity.ItemData(1) = "20000"
    e. lstCity.ItemData(lstCity.ListIndex) = 20000

9. If you click Watertown in the list box, the value in the lstCity.ListIndex will be _____ .
    a. 0
    b. 1
    c. 2
    d. 3
    e. 4

10. Which of the following instructions will display Boulder on the form?
    a. Print lstCity.List(0)
    b. Print lstCity.List(1)
    c. Print lstCity.ListIndex(0)
    d. Print lstCity.ListIndex(1)
    e. Print 544lstCity.Index(1)

11. The value of the lstCity control's ListCount property is _____ .

    a. 0

    b. 1

    c. 4

    d. 5

    e. 8

12. If you added the city of Carlton to the list, its NewIndex property would be

    _____ .

    a. 0

    b. 1

    c. 4

    d. 5

    e. 6

13. Which of the following instructions will display the population of Watertown on the form?

    a. Print lstCity.ItemData(2)

    b. Print lstCity.ItemData(3)

    c. Print lstCity.ListIndex(2)

    d. Print lstCity.ListIndex(3)

    e. Print lstCity.Index(2)

14. Assuming that you have clicked the city of Amos in the list box, which of the following instructions will display the population of Amos on the form?

    a. Print lstCity.ItemData(lstCity.ListIndex)

    b. Print lstCity.ItemData(lstCity.NewIndex)

    c. Print lstCity.ListIndex(lstCity.ItemData)

    d. Print lstCity.ListIndex(lstCity.ListCount)

    e. Print lstCity.Index(lstCity.List)

15. If you set the lstCity control's Sorted property to True, what will happen to the list box and the ItemData array? Show the results in the chart below.

lstCity List box	ItemData array

16. Assuming that you have set the lstCity control's Sorted property to True, if you add the city of Carlton to the list, its NewIndex property would be _____ .

    a. 0

    b. 1

    c. 2

    d. 5

    e. 6

17. The combob box control combines the features of a _____ and a
_____ .
a. command button
b. frame control
c. label control
d. list box
e. text box

18. You use this method to define the items in a combo box.
a. AddItem
b. AddList
c. ItemAdd
d. ItemDefine
e. ListAdd

19. Which of the following instructions will add the word COMPUTERS to a combo box named cboItems?
a. AddItem.cboItems COMPUTERS
b. AddItem.cboItems "COMPUTERS"
c. ItemAdd.cboItems "COMPUTERS"
d. cboItems.AddItem "COMPUTERS"
e. cboItems.ItemAdd "COMPUTERS"

20. Which of the following instructions will add the number 10 to the cboNums combo box?
a. AddItem.cboNums 10
b. AddItem.cboNums "10"
c. ItemAdd.cboNums "10"
d. cboNums.AddItem "10"
e. cboNums.ItemAdd "10"

21. This style of combo box allows the user to make an entry in the text box portion and also display a list when the down arrow button is clicked.
a. Dropdown Combo
b. Dropdown List
c. Simple Combo
d. Simple List

22. This style of combo box displays the list at all times.
a. Dropdown Combo
b. Dropdown List
c. Simple Combo
d. Simple List

23. This is the only style of combo box that does not allow the user to enter text into the box.
a. Dropdown Combo
b. Dropdown List
c. Simple Combo
d. Simple List

24. This property determines the style of the combo box.
a. BoxStyle
b. ComboStyle
c. ComboType
d. Style
e. Type

25. When set to True, the _____ property automatically sorts the items in a combo box.
   a. Alphabet
   b. Order
   c. Position
   d. Sorted
   e. Style

26. When you click an item in a combo box's list, Visual Basic automatically records the item in the control's _____ property.
   a. Caption
   b. Label
   c. Name
   d. Style
   e. Text

Use the following information to answer questions 27 through 29:
   a. You have entered the following Type statement in a code module:

   Type EmpStruc
       stId as String
       stName as String
   End Type

   b. You have entered the following Dim statement in the General declarations section of the form: Dim EmpArray(1 to 15) as EmpStruc
   c. inX, an Integer variable, is used to keep track of the array subscript.

27. You refer to the fifth Id in the array as _____ .
   a. EmpArray(5).stId
   b. EmpArray.stId(5)
   c. EmpStruc(5).stId
   d. EmpStruc.stId(5)

28. Which of the following can be used to enter the data from a sequential access file into the array? The first field in the file is the Id and the second field is the name.
   a. Input #1, EmpStruc(inX).stId, EmpStruc(inX).stName
   b. Input #1, EmpStruc.stId(inX), EmpStruc.stName(inX)
   c. Input #1, EmpArray(inX).stName, EmpArray(inX).stId
   d. Input #1, EmpArray.stId(inX), EmpArray.stName(inX)
   e. Input #1, EmpArray(inX).stId, EmpArray(inX).stName

29. Which of the following will add the Id from the array to a combo box named cboId?
   a. cboId.AddItem EmpArray(inX).stId
   b. cboId.AddItem EmpArray.stId(inX)
   c. cboId.AddItem EmpStruc(inX).stId
   d. cboId.AddItem EmpStruc.stId(inX)
   e. cboId.AddItem(inX) EmpStruc.stId

30. Which of the following is equivalent to cboName.Text?
   a. cboName.List(cboName.ListIndex)
   b. cboName.ListIndex(cboName.List)
   c. cboName.List(cboName.ListCount)
   d. cboName.ListIndex(cboName.ListCount)
   e. cboName.List(cboName.ItemData)

EXERCISES

1. In this exercise you will use a sequential access file, an array, and a combo box.
   a. Create the user interface shown in Figure 9-61.

Figure 9-61

   b. Declare a user-defined data type that consists of two string fields: stState and stCapital. Use the data type to declare a 50-element one-dimensional array.
   c. Save the form, code module, and project as lb1Done in the Tut09 folder on your Student Disk.
   d. Enter the 50 state names and their corresponding capitals into the one-dimensional array. The state names and their capitals are in the Capital.dat file, which is located in the Tut09 folder on your Student Disk. The Capital.dat file is a sequential access file. The first field in the data file is the state name and the second field is the capital.
   e. Enter the 50 state names in the combo box. The combo box should be a Dropdown List box style. Sort the names in the combo box.
   f. Code the Exit button so that it unloads the form. Code the form's Unload event so that it ends the application. Code the combo box's Click event procedure so that it displays the state's capital when you click the state's name.
   g. Save and run the application. Test the application by clicking each state name in the combo box.
   h. Exit the application. Print the form and the application's code.

2. In this exercise you will use a sequential access file, an array, and a combo box.
   a. Create the user interface shown in Figure 9-62.

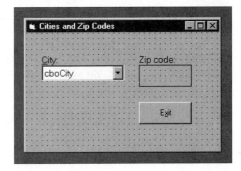

Figure 9-62

b. Declare a user-defined data type that consists of two string fields: stCity and stZipCode. Use the data type to declare a 10-element one-dimensional array.

c. Save the form, code module, and project as lb2Done in the Tut09 folder on your Student Disk.

d. Enter the 10 cities and their corresponding zip codes into the one-dimensional array. The cities and their zip codes are in the Zip.dat file, which is located in the Tut09 folder on your Student Disk. The first field in the data file is the city name and the second field is the zip code.

e. Enter the 10 cities in the combo box. The combo box should be a Dropdown List box style. Sort the cities in the combo box.

f. Code the Exit button so that it unloads the form. Code the form's Unload event so that it ends the application. Code the combo box's Click event procedure so that it displays the city's zip code when you click the city's name.

g. Save and run the application. Test the application by clicking each city name in the combo box.

h. Exit the application. Print the form and the application's code.

3. In this exercise you will use a sequential access file, an array, and a combo box.

a. Create the user interface shown in Figure 9-63. Make the Display City button the default command button.

Figure 9-63

b. Declare a user-defined data type that consists of two string fields: stCity and stZipCode. Use the data type to declare a 10-element one-dimensional array.

c. Save the form, code module, and project as lb3Done in the Tut09 folder on your Student Disk.

d. Enter the 10 cities and their corresponding zip codes into the one-dimensional array. The cities and their zip codes are in the Zip.dat file, which is located in the Tut09 folder on your Student Disk. The first field in the data file is the city name and the second field is the zip code.

e. Enter the 10 zip codes in the combo box. The combo box should be a Dropdown Combo box style. Sort the zip codes in the combo box.

f. Code the Exit button so that it unloads the form. Code the form's Unload event so that it ends the application. Code the Display City button's Click event procedure so that it displays the name of the city corresponding to the zip code entered in the combo box. If the zip code is not in the array, then display an error message.

g. Save and run the application. Test the application by clicking a zip code in the combo box and then clicking the Display City button. Then test the application by typing a zip code that you know is in the array and then clicking the Display City button. Last, test the application by typing a zip code that is not in the array and then clicking the Display City button.

h. Exit the application. Print the form and the application's code.

4. In this application you will use a sequential access file, an array, and a combo box.

    a. Create the user interface shown in Figure 9-64.

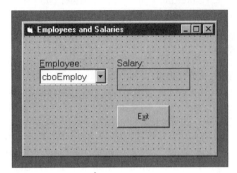

Figure 9-64

    b. Declare a user-defined data type that consists of a string field named stEmployee and a Currency field named crSalary. Use the data type to declare a 20-element one-dimensional array.

    c. Save the form, code module, and project as lb4Done in the Tut09 folder on your Student Disk.

    d. Enter the 20 employees and their corresponding salaries into the one-dimensional array. The employees and their salaries are in the Employ.dat file, which is located in the Tut09 folder on your Student Disk. The first field in the data file is the employee name and the second field is the salary.

    e. Enter the names of the 20 employees in the combo box. Enter the salaries in the combo box's ItemData array. The combo box should be a Dropdown List box style. Sort the employee names in the combo box.

    f. Code the Exit button so that it unloads the form. Code the form's Unload event so that it ends the application. Code the combo box's Click event procedure so that it displays the salary when you click the employee's name.

    g. Save and run the application. Test the application by clicking each name in the combo box.

    h. Exit the application. Print the form and the application's code.

Exercises 5 and 6 are Discovery Exercises. Discovery Exercises, which may include topics that are not covered in the tutorial, allow you to "discover" the solutions to problems on your own.

discovery ▶

5. In this exercise you will use an array to store a grading table.

    a. Open the Grade (grade.vbp) file, which is located in the Tut09 folder on your Student Disk, then click the View Form button. You can use this application to display a student's grade. You simply enter the student's total points in the txtPoints control and then click the Display Grade button. The grading scale is shown below.

Minimum Points	Maximum Points	Grade
0	299	F
300	349	D
350	399	C
400	449	B
450	500	A

b. Store the minimum points and the corresponding grade in a one-dimensional array. For example, in the first variable in the array, store the number 0 and the F grade.

c. Code the Display Grade button's Click event procedure so that it displays the grade.

d. Save the form, the code module, and the project as lb5Done in the Tut09 folder on your Student Disk.

e. Run the application. Test the application by entering the number 455 and clicking the Display Grade button; the grade should be an A. Then test the application by entering the number 210 and clicking the Display Grade button; the grade should be an F.

f. Exit the application. Print the application's code.

discovery ▶ 6. In this exercise you will modify the code contained in the lb5Done (lb5Done.vbp) application that you created in Lesson B's Exercise 5.

Important Note: If you are using the Working Model, you will need to use the following procedure to open the lb5Done.vbp application. First open a new project, then use the File menu's Remove File command to remove the Form1 form. Use the File menu's Add File command to add both the lb5Done.frm file and the lb5Done.bas file to the project.

a. Open the lb5Done (lb5Done.vbp) application that you created in Lesson B's Exercise 5. The file is located in the Tut09 folder on your Student Disk.

b. Add an InputBox statement to the form's Load event procedure. The InputBox statement should prompt the instructor for the total number of points that a student can earn in the course.

c. The form's Load event procedure contains the assignment statements that enter the data into the array. Modify the assignment statements according to the grading scale shown below. (For example, if the instructor enters the number 500 in response to the InputBox statement, the Load event should enter 450 (90% of 500) as the minimum number of points for an A. If the instructor enters the number 300, the Load event should enter 270 as the minimum number of points for an A.)

Minimum Points	Grade
Less than 60% of total points	F
60% of total points	D
70% of total points	C
80% of total points	B
90% of total of points	A

d. Save the form, the code module, and the project as lb6Done in the Tut09 folder on your Student Disk.

e. Run the application. Test the application by entering the number 300 as the total number of points possible. Then enter 185 in the txtPoints box and click the Display Grade button; the grade should be a D.

f. Exit the application. Then run the application again. This time enter 500 as the total number of points possible. Then enter 363 in the txtPoints box and click the Display Grade button; the grade should be a C.

g. Exit the application. Print the application's code.

L E S S O N   C
objectives

In this lesson you will learn how to:
- Add records to an array
- Delete records from an array
- Remove records from a combo box

Completing the Personal Directory Application

Coding the Add Button

To complete the Personal Directory application, you will need to code the Add button, the Delete button, the Search button, and the form's Unload event. You will begin with the Add button, which is responsible for adding a person to the personal directory.

To add a new person to the personal directory, you first enter his or her name in the text box portion of the combo box. When you do, Visual Basic records the name in the combo box's Text property. You then enter the phone number and birthday in the appropriate text boxes on the form and click the Add button. The pseudocode for the Add button's Click event procedure is shown in Figure 9-65.

Pseudocode for the Add button's Click event procedure

1. Declare an Integer variable named inSub and a String variable named stFound.

2. Declare variables and constants for the MsgBox function.

3. Assign 1 to the inSub variable.

4. Assign "N" to the stFound variable.

5. Repeat While there are array variables to search and a matching name has not been found

   If the name entered in the Name combo box matches the name in the current array variable then

   display "Duplicate name." message

   assign "Y" to stFound variable

   Else

   add 1 to the inSub variable

   End If

   End Repeat while

6. If a matching name was not found in the array then

    add 1 to the form-level inNumRec variable, which keeps track of the number of records

    store the name, phone number, and birthday in the array

    add the name from the array to the combo box

    store the DirArray array position in the combo box's ItemData array

    assign "Y" to the form-level stUpdate variable

  End If

7. Send the focus to the combo box

Figure 9-65: Pseudocode for the Add button's Click event procedure

Notice that, before adding a name to the personal directory, the Add button's Click event procedure will compare the name in the combo box with each name in the array. If the name in the combo box matches a name in the array, then the procedure will display a message alerting the user that the name is already in the directory. If, however, the name in the combo box does not match any of the names in the array, then the name, phone number, and birthday will be entered into the variable array. The name will also be added to the combo box's list, and the name's location in the DirArray array will be added to the combo box's ItemData array.

The code for the Add button is already entered in its Click event procedure; you will need to make only one modification to the code.

To modify the code in the Add button's Click event procedure:

Important Note: If you are using the Working Model, you will need to use the following procedure to open the lbDirect.vbp application. First open a new project, then use the File menu's Remove File command to remove the Form1 form. Use the File menu's Add File command to add both the lbDirect.frm file and the lbDirect.bas file to the project.

1 Start Visual Basic, if necessary. Open the **lbDirect** (lbDirect.vbp) project that you created in Lesson B. The file is located in the Tut09 folder on your Student Disk.

2 Save the form, the code module, and the project as **lcDirect**.

3 Click **lcDirect.Frm**, if necessary, in the Project window. Click the **View Form** button, then maximize the form. The user interface appears on the screen.

4 Double-click the **Add** button, then maximize the Code window. The cmdAdd control's Click event procedure appears.

You will need to remove the Exit Sub statement and its documentation, which are located below the `Private Sub cmdAdd_Click ()` instruction.

5 Select the `Exit Sub` statement and the documentation that follows in that line, press the **Backspace** key to delete the selected code, then press the **Backspace** key again to remove the blank line. The Code window should appear as shown in Figure 9-66.

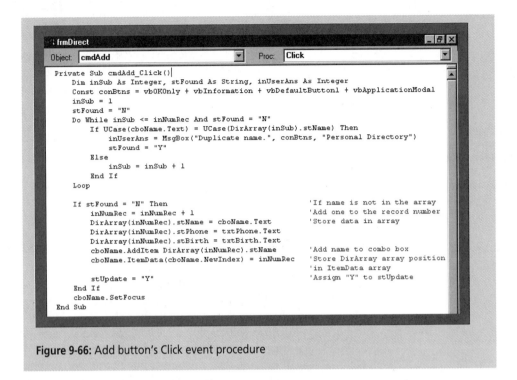

Figure 9-66: Add button's Click event procedure

After declaring the necessary variables (inSub, stFound, inUserAns) and the constant (conBtns), the code initializes the inSub variable to the number 1 and the stFound variable to the letter "N". The inSub variable will keep track of the DirArray array subscripts, and the stFound variable will keep track of whether a name matching the one entered in the combo box is found in the array. A Do While loop and a selection structure will compare the name contained in the combo box with the name stored in each array variable. If the name in the combo box matches a name in the array, then two tasks are performed. First, a "Duplicate name." message is displayed on the screen to alert the user that the name he or she entered in the combo box is already in the directory. Second, the stFound variable is set to "Y" to indicate that a name matching the one in the combo box was found in the directory.

If, on the other hand, the name in the combo box does not match the name in the current array variable, the number 1 is added to the inSub variable so that the search can continue with the next variable in the array. Notice that the loop will continue the search while there are still array elements to search and a name has not been found. The loop will stop either when it has searched each array variable or when a matching name is found, whichever occurs first.

After the Do While loop completes its processing, another selection structure compares the value in the stFound variable with the letter "N". If the stFound variable contains an "N", it means that the name in the combo box does not match any of the names in the directory. In that case, the number of records is increased by one; the name, phone number, and birthday are entered into the DirArray array; the name is added to the combo box's list; and the location of the name in the DirArray array is stored in the combo box's ItemData array. The form-level stUpdate variable is then set to "Y" to indicate that the sequential file will need to be updated so that it includes the new record. The `cboName.SetFocus` instruction, located above the `End Sub` statement, sends the focus to the combo box. That instruction is processed whether or not a matching name has been found in the array. Test the Add button to see how it works.

tips

· · · · · · · · · · · · · · · · · ·

▶ **As you learned in Tutorial 4, you can use the UCase to perform a case-insensitive comparison of two strings.**

To test the Add button:

1   Close the Code window, restore the form to its standard size, then **save** and **run** the application.

First try to add a name that is already in the directory.

2   Type **James, Lisa** and click the **Add** button. The Click event procedure searches the array for a name that matches the one in the combo box. Because Lisa James's name is already in the file, the "Duplicate name." message appears in the MsgBox function's dialog box.

> **HELP?** If the "Duplicate name." message did not appear, you may have mistyped the name. Try typing James, Lisa again. This time be sure to include the space between the comma and the letter L.

3   Click the **OK** button to remove the message. The focus moves to the Name combo box.

Now add a new person to the directory.

4   Type **Lee, Jack** in the combo box and press the **Tab** key, type **889-8888** in the Phone number text box and press the **Tab** key, and then type **12/20/48** in the Birthday text box and click the **Add** button.

The Add button's Click event procedure searches the array for a matching name. Because Jack Lee's name is not in the array, the procedure increases the number of records by 1. It then enters Jack's name, phone number, and birthday into the DirArray array. It also adds Jack's name to the combo box and his record's location in the DirArray array to the combo box's ItemData array. It also sets the value in the stUpdate variable to "Y" to indicate that the sequential access file needs to be updated to include Jack Lee's record.

5   Click the **Name** combo box list arrow. Notice that "Lee, Jack" appears, in alphabetical order, in the list.

It is important to note that, at this point, the combo box includes Jack Lee's name and the DirArray array includes his record, but Jack's information is not yet saved in the sequential access file on your Student Disk. Because the information in both the combo box and the DirArray array resides in the computer's internal memory, which is temporary, Jack Lee's information will be lost if you end the application or if the computer loses power. To make Jack's information permanent, you need to save it to the sequential access file on your Student Disk. You will write the instructions to update the sequential access file later on in this lesson.

6   Click the **Name** combo box list arrow to close the list.

7   Click the **Exit** button. Visual Basic returns to the design screen.

Next you will code the Delete button.

The Delete Button

The personal directory application should allow the user to remove a person from the directory by clicking his or her name in the combo box's list and then clicking the Delete button. The pseudocode for the Delete button's Click event procedure is shown in Figure 9-67.

Pseudocode for the Delete button's Click event procedure

1. Declare an Integer variable named inSelection

2. Declare inUserAns variable and constants for the MsgBox function

3. Ask user if he or she wants to remove the person from the directory

4. If the user wants to remove the person then

       assign, to the inSelection variable, the ItemData value of the item selected in the combo box

       clear the corresponding record from the DirArray array.

       remove the selected name from the combo box

       assign "Y" to the form-level stUpdate variable

       select the first item in the combo box

    End If

5. Send the focus to the combo box

Figure 9-67: Pseudocode for the Delete button's Click event procedure

GUI
Design Tips
Getting Verification from the User

- If a procedure is destructive, as is the Delete button's Click event, be sure to prompt the user with a warning message that verifies that he or she wants to run the procedure.

When you click a name in the combo box and then click the Delete button, the button's Click event procedure will ask the user to verify that he or she wants to remove the person from the directory. If the user wants to remove the person, the Click event clears the record whose name matches the one selected in the combo box, from the DirArray array, then removes the selected name from the combo box. The Click event procedure also assigns the letter "Y" to the stUpdate variable to indicate that the sequential file needs to be updated in order to remove the record from the file. The Click event then selects the first item in the combo box. The focus is sent to the combo box whether or not the person is removed. Before viewing the code in the Delete button's Code window, you will learn about the RemoveItem method.

The RemoveItem Method

You can use the **RemoveItem method** to remove an item from a combo box or a list box. The syntax of the RemoveItem method is *control*.**RemoveItem** *index*. *Control* is the name of the combo box or list box, **RemoveItem** is the name of the method, and *index* is an integer that represents the position of the item in the list. Recall that the first item in the list has an index of 0 (zero), the second item has an index of 1, and so on. To remove the third item from a combo box named cboName, you would use the following RemoveItem instruction: `cboName.RemoveItem 2`.

But how do you tell Visual Basic to remove the currently selected item from a combo box, as you need to do in the Delete button's Click event procedure? The answer is simple: you use the ListIndex property. The ListIndex property, recall, contains the index of the currently selected item in a list box or a combo box. The following instruction, therefore, will tell Visual Basic to remove the currently selected item from the cboName control's list: `cboName.RemoveItem cboName.ListIndex`.

The code for the Delete button has already been entered into its Click event procedure; you will need to make only one modification to it. View the code and make the modification.

To modify the code in the Delete button's Click event procedure, then save and run the application:

1   Maximize the form, double-click the **Delete** button, then maximize the Code window. The cmdDelete control's Click event procedure appears.

2   Select the `Exit Sub` statement, which is located below the `Private Sub cmdDelete_Click ()` statement, and the documentation that follows in that line, then press the **Backspace** key two times. The Code window should appear as shown in Figure 9-68.

```
frmDirect                                                          _ 8 X
Object:  cmdDelete              ▼        Proc:  Click                    ▼
Private Sub cmdDelete_Click()
    Dim inSelection As Integer, inUserAns As Integer
    Const conMsg = "Do you want to remove this person from the directory?"
    Const conBtns = vbYesNo + vbExclamation + vbDefaultButton2 + vbApplicationModal
    inUserAns = MsgBox(conMsg, conBtns, "Personal Directory")
    If inUserAns = vbYes Then
        'Assign the currently selected item's ItemData value to inSelection variable
        inSelection = cboName.ItemData(cboName.ListIndex)
        DirArray(inSelection).stName = ""       'clear record from the array
        DirArray(inSelection).stPhone = ""
        DirArray(inSelection).stBirth = ""
        cboName.RemoveItem cboName.ListIndex    'remove name from combo box
        stUpdate = "Y"                          'assign "Y" to stUpdate
        cboName.ListIndex = 0                   'select first item in combo box
    End If
    cboName.SetFocus                            'set focus

End Sub
```

Figure 9-68: Delete button's Click event procedure

tips
· · · · · · · · · · · ·
You clear a numeric field by assigning the number 0 to it.

The code declares an Integer variable named inSelection; it also declares an Integer variable named inUserAns and two constants for the MsgBox function. The MsgBox function will then prompt the user to verify that he or she wants to remove the person from the directory. If the user clicks the Yes button in the MsgBox function's dialog box, the selection structure will assign the value stored in the selected item's ItemData property to the inSelection variable. Recall that the ItemData property array contains the location of each name in the DirArray array. The `DirArray(inSelection).stName = ""`, `DirArray(inSelection).stPhone = ""`, and `DirArray(inSelection).stBirth = ""` instructions will clear the record, which corresponds to the name selected in the combo box, from the DirArray array. Notice that you clear the record by assigning the empty string to each of the field variables in the record variable. The `cboName.RemoveItem cboName.ListIndex` instruction will remove the selected name from the combo box's list. The stUpdate variable will then be set to "Y" to indicate that the sequential access file needs to be updated, and the first item in the combo box will be selected. The `cboName.SetFocus` instruction, which sends the focus to the combo box, is processed whether or not the person is removed from the directory.

3   Close the Code window, then restore the form to its standard size.

Now test the Delete button to see how it works.

4   **Save** and **run** the application. Click the **Name** list arrow, click **Chen, Sue** in the list, then click the **Delete** button. When the MsgBox function's dialog box appears, click the **No** button. Sue Chen's name remains in the combo box and her record remains in the DirArray array.

5   Click the **Name** list arrow, click **Chen, Sue** in the list, then click the **Delete** button. When the MsgBox function's dialog box appears, click the **Yes** button. Sue Chen's record is cleared from the array and her name is removed from the combo box; the first name in the combo box is then selected.

Now prove that Sue Chen's name was removed from the combo box.

6   Click the **Name** list arrow. Notice that Sue Chen's name does not appear in the list. Click the **Name** list arrow to close the list.

Now prove that Sue Chen's name was removed from the DirArray array. You can do so by simply adding Sue Chen's information to the personal directory. Recall that the Add button's Click event procedure searches the array for a name matching the one entered in the combo box. If the procedure finds a matching name in the array, then it will not allow the record to be entered in the personal directory. Only when the procedure does not find a matching name in the array does it allow the record to be entered.

7   Type **Chen, Sue** in the Name combo box and press the **Tab** key. Type **444-4444** in the Phone number text box and press the **Tab** key. Type **10/29/70** in the Birthday text box and click the **Add** button. Because Sue Chen's name is not in the array, the Add button enters her record in the personal directory; it also enters her name in the combo box and the record's location in the combo box's ItemData array.

Prove that Sue Chen's name was added to the combo box.

8   Click the **Name** list arrow. Notice that Sue Chen's name appears in the list. Click the **Name** list arrow to close the list.

Now prove that Sue Chen's name was added to the DirArray array. If her name is in the array, the "Duplicate name." message will appear in a dialog box when you try to add her information to the personal directory.

9   Click the **Add** button. The "Duplicate name." message appears.

10 Click the **OK** button to remove the message, then click the **Exit** button. Visual Basic returns to the design screen.

The next procedure you will view is the form's Unload event, which saves the personal directory information to a sequential access file.

Viewing the Form's Unload Event Procedure

When you exit the application, the form's Unload event procedure will need to check whether the stUpdate variable contains the letter "Y". If it does, then the procedure should write the array records to the sequential access file on your Student Disk. Only the records whose names appear in the combo box, however, should be written to the file. The pseudocode for the form's Unload event procedure is shown in Figure 9-69.

1. Declare two Integer variables: inSub and inNumRec

2. If the sequential file needs to be updated then

  open the file for output

  Repeat for each name in the combo box

    write the corresponding array record to the file

  End Repeat for

  close the file

  End If

3. End the application

Figure 9-69: Pseudocode for the form's Unload event procedure

The code for the form's Unload event is already entered in its Code window; you just need to make a minor modification to it.

To modify the code in the form's Unload event procedure, then save and run the application:

1 Double-click the **form**. If necessary use the Proc box to open the form's Unload event. Maximize the Code window.

2 Select the End statement, which appears below the `Private Sub Form_Unload (Cancel as Integer)` statement, and the documentation that follows on that line. Press the **Backspace** key two times. The Code window should appear as shown in Figure 9-70. If your Student Disk is in the B drive, then change the drive letter to b: in the Open statement.

if your Student Disk is in the B drive, then change the drive letter to b:

```
frmDirect                                                      _ 6 x
Object: Form                          ▼    Proc:  Unload             ▼
Private Sub Form_Unload(Cancel As Integer)

    Dim inSub As Integer, inArrayLoc As Integer
    If stUpdate = "Y" Then              'The sequential file needs updating
       Open "a:\Tut09\Direct.dat" For Output As #1
       'Write the record that corresponds to each name in the Combo box
       For inSub = 0 To cboName.ListCount - 1
          inArrayLoc = cboName.ItemData(inSub)   'Assign record number to variable
          Write #1, DirArray(inArrayLoc).stName, DirArray(inArrayLoc).stPhone, DirArr
       Next inSub
       Close #1                          'Close the sequential file
    End If
    End

End Sub
```

Figure 9-70: Form's Unload event procedure

The code declares two Integer variables, inSub and inArrayLoc. The inSub variable is used by the For Next loop to access each item in the Name combo box. The inArrayLoc variable is used to keep track of each record's location in the DirArray array. The selection structure in the Unload event compares the contents of the stUpdate variable to the letter "Y". If the stUpdate variable contains a "Y", then the sequential file is opened for Output. The For Next loop instructions look at each name in the list portion of the combo box. The `inArrayLoc = cboName.ItemData(inSub)` instruction within the loop assigns each name's array location, which is contained in the combo box's ItemData array, to the inArrayLoc variable. The Write # instruction then writes the corresponding record from the array to the sequential access file. (You may need to scroll the Code window to view all of the Write instruction. The entire instruction is: `Write #1, DirArray(inArrayLoc).stName, DirArray(inArrayLoc).stPhone, DirArray(inArrayLoc).stBirth`. Test the application to see how the Unload event works.

3   Close the Code window, then **save** and **run** the application.

First add a record.

4   Type **Lee, Jack** in the Name combo box and press the **Tab** key. Type **889-8888** in the Phone number text box and press the **Tab** key. Type **12/20/48** in the Birthday text box, then click the **Add** button. The procedure adds Jack Lee's information to the personal directory and assigns "Y" to the stUpdate variable.

Now delete a record.

5   Click the **Name** list arrow. Click **James, Lisa** in the list, then click the **Delete** button. When the MsgBox function's dialog box appears, click the **Yes** button. The Delete button's Click event procedure removes Lisa James's name from the combo box. The procedure then assigns "Y" to the stUpdate variable, selects the first item in the combo box, and then sets the focus to the combo box.

Verify both that Jack Lee's name was added to and that Lisa James's name was removed from the combo box.

6   Click the **Name** list arrow. Notice that Jack Lee's name appears in the list; Lisa James's name does not.

7   Click the **Exit** button. The Exit button's Click event procedure, which contains the `Unload frmDirect` instruction, invokes the form's Unload event. The Unload event first compares the contents of the stUpdate variable to the letter "Y". In this case the stUpdate variable does contain a "Y", so the procedure writes the records whose names appear in the combo box to the sequential access file on your Student Disk. Visual Basic then returns to the design screen.

The last procedure you will code is the Search button's Click event procedure, which allows you to search the directory for friends and relatives born in a specific month. Before coding that procedure, you will learn about the Like operator.

The Like Operator

You can use the **Like operator** to compare two string expressions. The syntax of the Like operator is *string* **Like** *pattern*, where both *string* and *pattern* are string expressions. The difference between *string* and *pattern* is that *pattern* can contain special characters, called wildcard characters, but *string* cannot. If the *string* matches the *pattern*, then the string comparison results in the Boolean value True; otherwise, it results in the Boolean value False. Keep in mind that the string comparisons made by the Like operator are case-sensitive, which means that an uppercase letter is not equivalent to a lowercase letter—in other words, "JAN" Like "JAN" is true, but "JAN" Like "jan" is false. Figure 9-71 shows other examples of the Like operator.

Expression	Result
"Alaska" Like "ALASKA"	False
"California" Like "Calif"	False
"ILLINOIS" Like "ILLINOIS"	True
UCase(stState) Like "FLORIDA"	True if the stState variable contains Florida entered in uppercase, lowercase, or any case combination; otherwise False

Figure 9-71: Examples of the Like operator

tips

As you learned in Tutorial 4, you can use the UCase function to perform a case-insensitive comparison of two strings.

As already mentioned, the *pattern* can contain wildcard characters, one of which is the asterisk (*). Similar to a wildcard in a game of poker, you can use the asterisk to represent anything you want. UCase(stState) Like "T*", for example, tells Visual Basic to compare the first character of the string contained in the stState variable, in uppercase, with the letter T; you don't care how many letters follow the T in the string, nor do you care what those letters are. The comparison will result in True if the stState variable contains either "Texas" or "Tennessee"; otherwise it will result in False. Figure 9-72 shows other examples of the Like operator using the asterisk wildcard character.

Expression	Result
"Alaska" Like "A*"	True
"C*" Like "California"	False because only the *pattern* can contain a wildcard character
"Arizona" Like "Ark*"	False
UCase(stState) Like "I*"	True only if the stState variable contains a word that begins with the letter I, entered in any case; otherwise False

Figure 9-72: Examples of the Like operator using the asterisk (*) wildcard

tips

If you want to learn more about the Like operator, use the Help menu to view the Help window on the Like operator topic.

Now use the Like operator to search for the birthdays occurring in a specific month.

The Search Button

The Search button should allow the user to search the directory for the birthdays occurring in a specific month. The pseudocode for the Search button's Click event procedure is shown in Figure 9-73.

Pseudocode for the Search button's Click event procedure

1. Declare two Integer variables (inSub and inUserAns) and one String variable (stBirthday)

2. Declare constants for the MsgBox function

3. Assign contents of Birthday text box (the pattern) to the stBirthday variable

4. Repeat for each variable in the DirArray array

     If the birthday in the array matches the pattern in the stBirthday variable then

         display the corresponding name in the cboName control

         display the corresponding phone number in the txtPhone control

         display the corresponding birthday in the txtBirth control

         display a "Press Enter or click OK to continue." message

     End If

     End Repeat for

5. Display a "Search is complete." message

6. Send the focus to the combo box

Figure 9-73: Pseudocode for the Search button's Click event procedure

To search for the birthdays occurring in a specific month, you type the month's number (01, 02, and so on) followed by an * (asterisk) in the txtBirth text box; the month's number and the asterisk will serve as the *pattern* for the Like operator. The procedure will search the array for birthdays matching the *pattern*. When a match is found, the procedure will display that person's name, phone number, and birthday in the appropriate controls on the form, along with a message that tells the user to either press Enter or click OK to continue the search. When the search is complete, a message to that effect is displayed.

The Search button's code is already entered in its Click event procedure. You need to make only one modification to it.

To view the code in the Search button:

1   Maximize the form, double-click the **Search** button, then maximize the Code window. The cmdSearch button's Click event procedure appears.

2   Select the `Exit Sub` instruction, which is below the `Private Sub cmdSearch_Click ()` statement, and the documentation on that line. Press the **Backspace** key two times. The Code window should look like Figure 9-74.

```
frmDirect                                                           _ B X
Object:  cmdSearch              ▼     Proc:  Click                        ▼

Private Sub cmdSearch_Click()|

     Dim inSub As Integer, stBirthday As String, inUserAns As Integer
     Const conMsg = "Press Enter or click OK to continue."
     Const conBtns1 = vbOKOnly + vbExclamation + vbDefaultButton1 + vbApplicationModal
     Const conBtns2 = vbOKOnly + vbInformation + vbDefaultButton1 + vbApplicationModal
     stBirthday = txtBirth.Text          'Assign stBirthday pattern to stBirthday

'Search array for birthdays matching the stBirthday pattern
     For inSub = 1 To inNumRec
         If DirArray(inSub).stBirth Like stBirthday Then  'If stBirthday matches pattern
             cboName.Text = DirArray(inSub).stName      'Assign data to controls
             txtPhone.Text = DirArray(inSub).stPhone
             txtBirth.Text = DirArray(inSub).stBirth
             inUserAns = MsgBox(conMsg, conBtns1, "Personal Directory")
         End If
     Next inSub

     inUserAns = MsgBox("Search is complete.", conBtns2, "Personal Directory")
     cboName.SetFocus

End Sub
```

Figure 9-74: Search button's Click event procedure

The code declares three local variables (inSub, stBirthday, inUserAns) and three local constants (conMsg, conBtns1, conBtns2). It then assigns the *pattern*, which is entered by the user into the txtBirth text box, to the stBirthday variable. A For Next loop then searches the entire array, looking for birthdays that match the pattern in the stBirthday variable. When a match is found, that person's name, phone number, and birthday are displayed on the form. The MsgBox statement, which displays a dialog box that contains the "Press Enter or click OK to continue." message, temporarily halts the program so that the user can read the information on the screen. After the For Next loop searches the entire array, a MsgBox statement displays the "Search is complete." message. The focus is then set to the combo box. Save and run the application to see how the Search button works.

3   Close the Code window, restore the form to its standard size, then **save** and **run** the application.

4   Press the **Tab** key two times to position the blinking insertion point in the Birthday text box.

    Search for the people born in April—the fourth month of the year.

5   Type **04*** in the txtBirth text box and click the **Search** button. The Click event procedure stores the 04* (the *pattern*) in the stBirthday variable. It then compares each of the birthdays in the array with the contents of the stBirthday variable. The information about Khalid Patel, the first friend or relative in the array whose birthday is in April, appears on the form. The MsgBox statement's dialog box tells you to press Enter or click OK to continue.

    HELP? If you can't see the name, phone number, or birthday, simply drag the dialog box to another location on the screen.

6   Click the **OK** button to continue. The name, phone number, and birthday of the next friend born in April, Tom Williams, appears. The MsgBox statement tells you to press Enter or click OK to continue.

7   Click the **OK** button to continue. The MsgBox statement displays the "Search is complete." message. Click the **OK** button to remove the "Search is complete." message. The Search button's Click event procedure ends.

8   Click the **Exit** button to end the application.

You have now completed Lesson C and the personal directory application. You can either take a break, complete the questions and exercises at the end of the lesson, or read and complete the Debugging section. The Debugging section may contain information that will help you to complete the exercises.

S U M M A R Y

To remove an item from a list box or a combo box:

■   Use the RemoveItem method. Its syntax is *control*.**RemoveItem** *index*. *Control* is the name of the list box or combo box, **RemoveItem** is the name of the method, and *index* is an integer that represents the position of the item in the list. The first item in the list has an index of 0 (zero).

To refer to the index of the currently selected item in a list box or a combo box:

■   Use the ListIndex property.

To compare two string expressions:

■   Use the Like operator. Its syntax is *string* **Like** *pattern*. The *pattern* can contain wild-card characters, such as the asterisk (*).

Q U E S T I O N S

1.   Use the _____ method to remove an item from a combo box's list.
   a.   DeleteItem
   b.   EraseItem
   c.   ItemErase
   d.   ItemRemove
   e.   RemoveItem

2.   Which of the following will remove the first item from a combo box named cboName?
   a.   cboName.DeleteItem 0
   b.   cboName.EraseItem 1
   c.   cboName.ItemErase 0
   d.   cboName.ItemRemove 1
   e.   cboName.RemoveItem 0

3. When you click an item in a combo box's list, Visual Basic records the index of that item in the _____ property.
   a. Index
   b. IndexList
   c. List
   d. ListIndex
   e. ListNumber

4. Which of the following will remove the currently selected item from a combo box named cboName?
   a. cboName.DeleteItem cboName.Index
   b. cboName.EraseItem cboName.IndexList
   c. cboName.ItemErase cboName.List
   d. cboName.ItemRemove cboName.ListNumber
   e. cboName.RemoveItem cboName.ListIndex

5. You can use this operator to compare two string expressions.
   a. Comp
   b. Compare
   c. Like
   d. Match
   e. Pair

6. Which two of the following comparisons are true?
   a. "TEXAS" Like "T*"
   b. "TEXAS" Like "t*"
   c. "Texas" Like "T"
   d. "Texas" Like "T*"
   e. "T*" Like "TEXAS"

7. If the stCity variable contains "Atlanta," which two of the following comparisons are true?
   a. stCity Like "ATL*"
   b. stCity Like "At*"
   c. stCity Like "At"
   d. "stCity" Like "A*"
   e. UCase(stCity) Like "ATLANTA"

8. If the stBirthday variable contains 07/20/50, which two of the following comparisons are true?
   a. stBirthday Like "07*"
   b. stBirthday Like "07/20"
   c. stBirthday Like "07/20*"
   d. "stBirthday" Like "07/20/50"
   e. stBirthday Like "*/20/50"

E X E R C I S E S

1. In this exercise you will add and delete records from a sequential access file, an array, and a combo box.
   a. Use the method appropriate for your version of Windows to copy the Song.bak sequential access file, which is located in the Tut09 folder on your Student Disk, to Song1.dat.
   b. Open the Song1.dat file in WordPad (*Notepad in Windows 3.1*) and print the file.
   c. Start Visual Basic, if necessary. Create the user interface shown in Figure 9-75.

txtArtist control

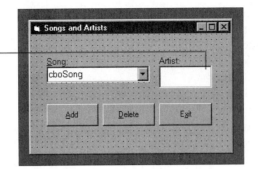

Figure 9-75

d. The combo box should be a Dropdown Combo style. Set its Sorted property to True.

e. Create a user-defined data type named SongStruc that contains two fields, stSong and stArtist.

f. Save the form, module, and project as lc1Done in the Tut09 folder on your Student Disk.

g. Declare a SongStruc array named SongArray that can contain as many as 10 records.

h. Code the form's Load event procedure so that it adds each record from the Song1.dat file to the SongArray array. The procedure should also add each song's name to the combo box and add each song's array position to the ItemData array.

i. Code the combo box so that it displays the artist when the user clicks a song in the list.

j. Code the Add button's Click event procedure so that it adds the song and the artist to the array. It should also add the song to the combo box and the song's array position to the ItemData array. Don't allow duplicate songs to be added to the array or to the combo box.

k. Code the Delete button's Click event procedure so that it clears, from the SongArray array, the record corresponding to the song selected in the combo box. The procedure should also remove the song from the combo box. Be sure to prompt the user before making the deletion.

l. Code the Exit button so that it unloads the form. Code the form's Unload event so that it saves the array records to the Song1.dat sequential file before ending the application. Don't save the records that were cleared from the array by the Delete button. Only update the data file if it needs to be updated.

m. Code the txtArtist control so that the existing text is selected when the control receives the focus.

n. Save and run the application. Test the application as follows:

1) Click a song in the combo box; the name of its artist should appear in the Artist box.

2) Enter "Persons" in the Song combo box, then enter "Barb Streis" in the Artist text box. Click the Add button. The button's Click event procedure should add the record to the array, the song's name to the combo box, and the song's array location to the ItemData array.

3) Click Blue Rain in the combo box, then click the Delete button. The button's Click event procedure should clear the record from the array and remove the name from the combo box.

4) Click the Exit button to unload the form. The form's Unload event should write the array records to the Song1.dat sequential access file on your Student Disk, then end the application.

o. Print the application's code. Also print the Song1.dat file in WordPad (*Notepad in Windows 3.1*).

p. Submit the printouts from steps b and o and the code from step o.

2. In this exercise you will use a sequential access file, an array, and a combo box.
   a. Use the method appropriate for your version of Windows to copy the Song.bak sequential access file, which is located in the Tut09 folder on your Student Disk, to Song2.dat.
   b. Open the Song2.dat file in WordPad (*Notepad in Windows 3.1*) and print the file.
   c. Launch Visual Basic, if necessary. Create the user interface shown in Figure 9-76.

lblSong control

Figure 9-76

   d. The combo box should be a Dropdown List style, which does not allow the user to enter information in the text box portion. Set the combo box's Sorted property to True.
   e. Create a user-defined data type named SongStruc that contains two fields, stSong and stArtist.
   f. Save the form, module, and project as lc2Done in the Tut09 folder on your Student Disk.
   g. Declare a SongStruc array named SongArray that can contain as many as 10 records.
   h. Code the form's Load event procedure so that it adds the following four artists to the combo box:
      Paul Jones
      Maria Casey
      Rolling Rocks
      Strawberries

   The Load event should also read the records from the Song2.dat sequential access file and store each in the SongArray array.
   i. Code the Search button's Click event procedure so that it searches the array for the artist whose name is selected in the combo box. If the artist's name is in the array, display the corresponding song or songs (one at a time) in the lblSong control.
   j. Code the Exit button so that it unloads the form. Code the Unload event so that it ends the application.
   k. Save and run the application. To test the application, click Rolling Rocks in the combo box, then click the Search button. The Search button should display this group's songs, one at a time, in the lblSong control.
   l. Print the application's code.
   m. Submit the printout from step b and the code from step l.

Exercises 3 through 7 are Discovery Exercises. Discovery Exercises, which may include topics that are not covered in the tutorial, allow you to "discover" the solutions to problems on your own.

   Important Note: If you are using the Working Model, you will need to use the following procedure to open the lcDirect.vbp application. First open a new project, then use the File menu's Remove File command to remove the Form1 form. Use the File menu's Add File command to add both the lcDirect.frm file and the lcDirect.bas file to the project.

discovery ▶ 3. In this exercise you will modify the personal directory application that you created in Lesson C.

a. Use the method appropriate for your version of Windows to copy the Direct.bak sequential access file, which is located in the Tut09 folder on your Student Disk, to Direct3.dat.

b. Open the Direct3.dat file in WordPad (*Notepad in Windows 3.1*) and print the file.

c. Start Visual Basic, if necessary. Open the lcDirect (lcDirect.vbp) project that you created in Lesson C. If you are using the Working Model, please refer to the Important Note at the beginning of the Discovery Exercises.

d. Save the form, the module, and the project as lc3Done in the Tut09 folder on your Student Disk.

e. Change the code in both the form's Load and Unload events so that the procedures open the Direct3.dat file instead of the Direct.dat file.

f. Change the Dim statement in the General declarations section from `Dim DirArray(1 to 50) As DirStruc` to `Dim DirArray(1 to 8) As DirStruc`.

The `Dim DirArray(1 to 8) As DirStruc` instruction will allow the DirArray array to store up to eight records only. Currently, if the user clicks the Add button to enter the ninth record into the array, the application will "crash" (that is, it will end unexpectedly).

g. Change the code in the Add button's Click event procedure so that it will not allow the user to have more than eight records stored in the DirArray array. Display an appropriate error message if the user tries to add more than eight records. (*Hint:* Remember that the user can use the Delete button to remove a person from the array. If an entry is removed from the array, the next record added should fill that position. In other words, if the second entry in the array was removed, the information for the next person added to the directory should be placed in the second position of the array.)

h. Save and run the application. To test the application add the following records.

Schmidt, Paul	711-1177	02/04/65
Bender, Jan	991-0002	05/06/87
Rice, Rich	334-6789	12/30/75
Zorch, Pat	123-3211	11/02/60

When you click the Add button to enter Pat Zorch's record, which will be the ninth record, an error message should be displayed. The record should not be added to the array, and the name should not be entered into the combo box.

i. Delete Jan Bender from the personal directory. Now add Pat Zorch's record to the directory. The Add button's Click event should add the record to the array; Pat Zorch's name should appear in the combo box.

j. Exit the application, then print the code. Also print the Direct3.dat file in WordPad (*Notepad in Windows 3.1*).

k. Submit the printouts from steps b and j, and the code from step j.

discovery ▶ 4. In this exercise you will modify the personal directory application that you created in Lesson C.

a. Use the method appropriate for your version of Windows to copy the Direct.bak sequential access file, which is located in the Tut09 folder on your Student Disk, to Direct4.dat.

b. Open the Direct4.dat file in WordPad (*Notepad in Windows 3.1*) and print the file.

c. Start Visual Basic, if necessary. Open the lcDirect (lcDirect.vbp) project that you created in Lesson C. If you are using the Working Model, please refer to the Important Note at the beginning of the Discovery Exercises.

d. Save the form, the module, and the project as lc4Done in the Tut09 folder on your Student Disk.

e. Change the code in both the form's Load and Unload event procedures so that the procedures open the Direct4.dat file.

f. To delete a person from the directory, you click his or her name in the combo box and then click the Delete button. Currently, the application will "crash" (that is, it will end unexpectedly) when the user clicks the Delete button if he or she types the person's name in the combo box, instead of clicking the name in the list. The application will also crash if the user clicks the Delete button when the text box portion of the combo box is empty. To see the error message, run the application, press the Backspace key to remove the entry in the text box portion of the combo box, click the Delete button, then click the Yes button. Visual Basic displays the "Invalid property array index." message. Press the F1 key to display a Help window on this error message. After reading the information in the Help window, close the Help window, then click the End button to remove the error message. Visual Basic selects the `cboName.ItemData(cboName.ListIndex)` instruction.

g. Stop the application. Based on the error message and its Help window, correct the code in the Delete button's Click event procedure so that the application does not "crash" if the user types the name in the combo box (instead of clicking it in the list) or neglects to enter a name. Rather, use the MsgBox statement to display a message telling the user that he or she must click a name in the list in order to delete a name.

h. Save and run the application. To test the application:

1) Press the Backspace key to remove the contents of the text box portion of the combo box, then click the Delete button. A message telling you to select a name to delete should appear. You should then be returned to the form.

2) Type Chen, Sue in the combo box, then click the Delete button. A message telling you to select a name to delete should appear. You should then be returned to the form.

3) Click Chen, Sue in the combo box's list, then click the Delete button. A message asking you if you want to delete Sue Chen's record should appear. Click the No button to return to the form without deleting Sue Chen's record.

4) Click Chen, Sue in the combo box's list, then click the Delete button. A message asking you if you want to delete Sue Chen's record should appear. Click the Yes button to delete Sue Chen's record.

i. Exit the application, then print the code.

j. Submit the printout from step b, and the code from step i.

discovery ▶ 5. In this exercise you will modify the personal directory application that you created in Lesson C.

a. Use the method appropriate for your version of Windows to copy the Direct.bak sequential access file, which is located in the Tut09 folder on your Student Disk, to Direct5.dat.

b. Open the Direct5.dat file in WordPad (*Notepad in Windows 3.1*) and print the file.

c. Start Visual Basic, if necessary. Open the lcDirect (lcdirect.vbp) project that you created in Lesson C. If you are using the Working Model, please refer to the Important Note at the beginning of the Discovery Exercises.

d. Save the form, the module, and the project as lc5Done in the Tut09 folder on your Student Disk.

e. Change the code in both the form's Load and Unload event procedures so that the procedures open the Direct5.dat file.

f. Change the Add button's Caption property to Add/Edit. Modify the Add/Edit button's code to allow the user to make changes to the person's phone number and birthday. In other words, if the user clicks an existing name in the combo box's list and then makes changes to either the phone number or birthday, the new information should replace the existing information in the array when the Add/Edit button is clicked. For example, assume that Sue Chen's record is stored in DirArray(4). If the user clicks Chen, Sue in the combo box's list and then changes her phone number and/or birthday, the new information should replace the existing information in DirArray(4) when the Add/Edit button is clicked.

g. Save and run the application. To test the application:

1) Enter Phillips, John in the Name combo box. Enter 222-2987 in the Phone number box. Click the Add/Edit button. The record should be added to the personal directory.

2) Click Chen, Sue in the combo box's list. Her phone number (444-4444) and birthday (10/29/70) should appear in the appropriate controls on the form. Change her phone number to 333-3333 and her birthday to 10/29/71. Click the Add/Edit button. The new phone number and birthday should replace the old phone number and birthday in the array.

3) Click Phillips, John in the combo box's list. Enter 01/05/85 in the Birthday box, then click the Add/Edit button. The birthday should be included in the array.

4) Click Chen, Sue in the combo box's list. Her phone number should appear as 333-3333, and her birthday should be 10/29/71.

5) Click Phillips, John in the combo box's list. His phone number (222-2987) and birthday (01/05/85) should appear in the appropriate controls on the form.

h. Exit the application, then print the code for the Add/Edit button's Click event procedure only. Also print the Direct5.dat file in WordPad (*Notepad in Windows 3.1*).

i. Submit the printouts from steps b and h, and the code from step h.

discovery ▶ **6.** In this exercise you will learn about the KeyUp event procedure.

a. Start Visual Basic and open a new project, if necessary. Place one combo box on the form. Set the combo box's Style to Simple Combo. Set its Sorted property to True.

b. Save the form and the project as lc6Done in the Tut09 folder on your Student Disk.

c. In the form's Load event, add the following 10 items to the combo box:

Beth	Eugene
Betty	Kim
George	Ann
Penny	Kristy
Doris	Tammy

d. Size the combo box so that all 10 items display.

e. Display, then read or print the Help window on the KeyUp event.

f. Code the combo box's KeyUp event so that it moves the selection bar to the first name that matches the first letter entered in the text box portion of the combo box. In other words, if the user enters the letter k, the selection bar in the combo box should be positioned on Kim in the list, and the name Kim should appear in the text box portion of the combo box.

g. Save and run the application. Test the application by typing the letter b. The selection bar should be positioned on Beth in the list, and the name Beth should appear in the text box portion of the combo box. Now type the letter k, the selection bar should be positioned on Kim in the combo box, and the name Kim should appear in the text box portion of the combo box. Press ↓ on your keyboard. The selection bar should now be on Kristy in the list, and the name Kristy should appear in the text box portion of the combo box.

h. Stop the application. Print the code for the KeyUp event only

discovery ▶ **7.** In this exercise you will modify the Personal Directory application that you created in Lesson C.

a. Start Visual Basic, if necessary. Open the lcDirect (lcdirect.vbp) project that you created in Lesson C. If you are using the Working Model, please refer to the Important Note at the beginning of the Discovery Exercises.

b. Save the form, the module, and the project as lc7Done in the Tut09 folder on your Student Disk.

c. Currently, the Search button's Click event will search the entire DirArray for the birthdays that occur in a specific month; the search will not stop until the entire array is searched. Modify the code in the Search button so that it allows the user to stop the search whenever he or she desires. You will need to change the type of buttons, as well as the message, used in the MsgBox function.

d. Save, run, and test the application. Then print the code for the Search button.

D E B U G G I N G

Technique

You can use Visual Basic's Debug window to help in debugging your code. The Debug window consists of the Immediate pane and the Watch pane. You will learn about the Immediate pane in this Debugging Section and the Watch pane in Tutorial 10's Debugging Section.

In the Immediate pane, which is located below the Debug window's title bar (or below the Watch pane if the Watch pane is displayed), you can enter code that you want executed immediately. You can use the Debug window for such tasks as printing the value stored in a variable or in the property of a control, changing a variable's value or a control's property, and testing the effect a new line of code will have on the application.

On your Student Disk are two projects that are not working correctly. You will use the Debug window to help you debug the projects.

Exercises

1. In this exercise you will use the Debug window to help you debug the Debug1 project.

To debug the Debug1 project:

1 Start Visual Basic, if necessary, and open the **Debug1** (debug1.vbp) project, which is in the Tut09 folder on your Student Disk. Click the **View Form** button to view the frmSales form.

2 Save the form and the project as **deb1Done** in the Tut09 folder on your Student Disk.

The three command buttons' Click events, as well as the form's Unload event, have already been coded for you. The Print the File button will print the contents of a sequential access data file named Debug.dat. The Calculate Average button will use the data in the Debug.dat file to calculate the average sales made in California and the average sales made in Oregon. The Exit button will unload the frmSales form, and the form's Unload event will end the application.

Before you can run this application, you will need to modify the Open statement entered in two of the Code windows: the Print the File button's Click event procedure and the Calculate Average button's Click event procedure.

3 Double-click the **Print the File** button to open its Code window. The Click event procedure appears.

4 Remove the <insert file name> from the Open statement and type one of the file names listed below in its place. Which file name you type will depend on the location of your Student Disk.

    a:\Tut09\debug.dat"

    b:\Tut09\debug.dat"

5 Use the Code window's Object box to open the cmdCalc control's Click event procedure, then repeat Step 4 to change the Open statement in the open Code window.

6 Close the Code window, then **save** and **run** the application.

First print the sequential access file.

7 If your computer is connected to a printer, then click the **Print the File** button. Five records should appear on the printout. The first field in each record is the state, and the second field is the sales.

Now calculate the average sales made in both states.

8 Click the **Calculate Average** button to calculate the average sales in each state. Visual Basic displays a dialog box with the "Division by zero" error message. Click the **Debug** button to remove the dialog box. Visual Basic selects the `crOreAvg = crOreAccum / inOreCount` instruction in the cmdCalc control's Click event procedure.

You will use the Debug window to verify that the inOreCount variable contains a zero.

tips

· · · · · · · · · · · · · · · · ·

▶ You can also display the Debug window by clicking View on the menu bar, then clicking Debug Window.

To use the Debug window:

1 Press **Ctrl + g** to display the Debug window. The Debug window appears, as shown in Figure 9-77.

Your screen will look different if you are using Windows 3.1.

Code window

Debug window

Figure 9-77-: Debug window

2 Type **print orecount** in the Debug window and press the **Enter** key. A 0 (zero) appears below the print instruction.

Observe why the inOreCount variable contains a zero.

3 Click the **cmdCalc_Click** event's **Code window**, then maximize the Code window. See Figure 9-78.

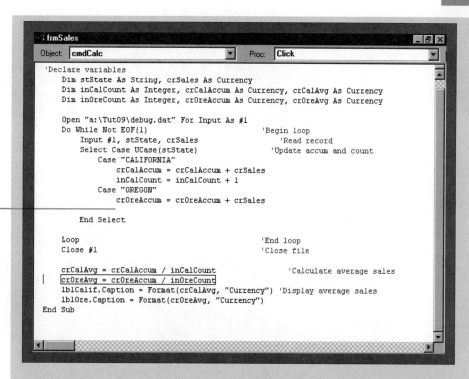

enter missing instruction here

Figure 9-78: Calculate Average button's Click event procedure

If you look closely at the code in the Case structure shown in Figure 9-78, you will notice that the assignment statement to update the inOreCount counter variable is missing. You will fix the code now.

4   Click the blank line below the `crOreAccum = crOreAccum + crSales` instruction, then type **inOreCount = inOreCount + 1**.

Now use the Debug window to change the value stored in the inOreCount variable so that processing can continue.

5   Close the Code window, then press **Ctrl + g** to display the Debug window.

To continue processing the application, you will need to change the value in inOreCount to any number other than zero. The zero in the inOreCount variable, remember, is the cause of the "Division by zero" error message. In this case the data file contains two Oregon records, so you will change the value to 2. If you didn't know how many Oregon records were in the file, you could simply change the inOreCount value to 1 and processing would continue, although the displayed average would be incorrect.

6   Type **inOreCount = 2** in the Debug window and press the **Enter** key. This statement changes the value stored in the inOreCount variable to 2.

Use the Debug window to verify the contents of the inOreCount variable.

7   Type **print inOreCount** in the Debug window and press the **Enter** key. A 2 appears in the Debug window. Close the Debug window, then close the Code window.

To continue processing the application, you simply need to press the F5 key. Processing will resume with the statement that caused the error—in this case, the crOreAvg = crOreAccum / inOreCount statement. Now, however, the inOreCount variable will contain the number 2, not a zero.

8   Press the **F5** key to resume processing of the application. The average sales made in both states ($30,000.00 and $60,000.00) appear in the label controls on the form. Click the **Exit** button to end the application.

Recall that you added the `inOreCount = inOreCount + 1` instruction to the Code window. You will need to save the application for that change to be saved.

9 **Save** the application. Now **run** the application and click the **Calculate Average** button. This time the application runs without any errors and the average sales made in both states appear on the screen.

10 Click the **Exit** button to end the application. Visual Basic returns to the design screen.

2. In this exercise you will use the Debug window to help you debug the Debug2 project.

1 Start Visual Basic, if necessary, and open the **Debug2** (debug2.vbp) project, which is in the Tut09 folder on your Student Disk. Click the **View Form** button to view the frmSales form.

2 Save the form and the project as **deb2Done** in the Tut09 folder on your Student Disk.

The application has already been coded for you. View the code in the Calculate Average button's Click event.

3 Double-click the **Calculate Average** button to open its Click event procedure. The Calculate Average button is responsible for calculating and displaying the average of the five numbers entered in the array. Close the Code window.

4 **Run** the application, then use the Debug window to help you debug the application.

5 When the application has been debugged, print the application's code.

Database Access, DDE, and OLE

Creating a Grade Application

case ▶ Now that you are in your third year in college, you realize that it won't be long before you will need to complete the necessary paperwork to apply for graduation. You realize that it would be helpful to create an application that you can use to keep track of the courses you have taken and the grades you have earned. You will create such an application in this tutorial.

Additionally, each semester you seem to run out of money quickly and have to write home for more. To make your plea to your parents more convincing, you will also create an application that includes a Microsoft Excel worksheet and a Microsoft Word document. In the Excel worksheet you will list your expenses; you will use the Word document to write the note to your parents asking them to send you more money.

Previewing the Completed Applications

You will create two applications in this tutorial: the College application and the Money application. Begin by previewing the completed College application.

To preview the completed College application:

1 If necessary, start Windows, then place your Student Disk in the appropriate drive.

2 Use the Run command on the Start menu to run one of the following files, which are located in the Tut10 folder on your Student Disk. Which file you run will depend on the location of your Student Disk.

    If your Student Disk is in drive A, then run the **Coll95A** (coll95a.exe) file.

    If your Student Disk is in drive B, then run the **Coll95B** (coll95b.exe) file.

The application's user interface appears on the screen. See Figure 10-1.

WINDOWS 3.1

Use the Run command on the Program Manager's File menu to one of the following files, which are located in the Tut10 folder on your Student Disk. Which file you run will depend on the location of your Student Disk.

If your Student Disk is in drive A, then run the coll31a.exe file.

If your Student Disk is in drive B, then run the coll31b.exe file.

The application's user interface appears on the screen. See Figure 10-1.

data control

Figure 10-1: The College application's user interface

You can use this application to keep track of the courses you have taken in college. The courses are stored in a Microsoft Access database, which was created with Data Manager. You will learn about Data Manager, an add-in program that comes with Visual Basic, in Lesson A.

The College application contains a new control, the data control, which you will learn about in Lesson B. The data control allows you to add a new record to the database, as well as edit, delete, and find an existing record in the database. First use the data control to browse through the existing records in the database. You can use the data control's First Record button ◄◄ and Last Record button ►► to display the first and last records, respectively. You can use the Previous Record button ◄ and Next Record button ► to display the previous and next records, respectively.

3   Click the data control's ►, ►►, ◄, and ◄◄ buttons to browse through the existing records.

Now add a new record to the database.

4   Click the ►► button to display the last record in the table, then click the ► button to add a new, blank record to the table.

5   Enter the following record: **Cis241, Intro to C, 5, A**, then click the ►► button to save the current record. The Cis241 record is now the last record in the table.

6   Click **File** on the form's menu bar, then click **Refresh Records**. The Refresh Records command rearranges the records in course ID order. The first record in the database appears on the screen.

Use the Find Record button to search for the Cis241 record.

7   Click the **Find Record** button. Type **cis241** in the dialog box, then click the **OK** button. Visual Basic displays the Cis241 record in the form.

Now delete the Cis241 record.

8   Click the **Delete Record** button, then click the **Yes** button to delete the Cis241 record.

9   Click **File** on the form's menu bar, then click **Exit**. Visual Basic returns to the design screen.

In addition to the College application, you will also create the Money application, which will include a Microsoft Excel worksheet and a Microsoft Word document. Preview the Money application.

> **Important Note:** In order to complete the next set of steps using the computer, you must have access to both the Microsoft Excel and the Microsoft Word applications.

To preview the Money application:

1   Use the Run command on the Start menu to run one of the following files, which are located in the Tut10 folder on your Student Disk. Which file you run will depend on the location of your Student Disk.

   If your Student Disk is in drive A, then run the **Mon95A** (mon95a.exe) file.

   If your Student Disk is in drive B, then run the **Mon95B** (mon95b.exe) file.

The application's user interface appears on the screen. See Figure 10-2.

Use the Run command on the Program Manager's File menu to run one of the following files, which are located in the Tut10 folder on your Student Disk. Which file you run will depend on the location of your Student Disk.

If your Student Disk is in drive A, then run the mon31a.exe file.

If your Student Disk is in drive B, then run the mon31b.exe file.

The application's user interface appears on the screen. See Figure 10-2.

OLE control containing
Microsoft Excel worksheet

OLE control containing
Microsoft Word document

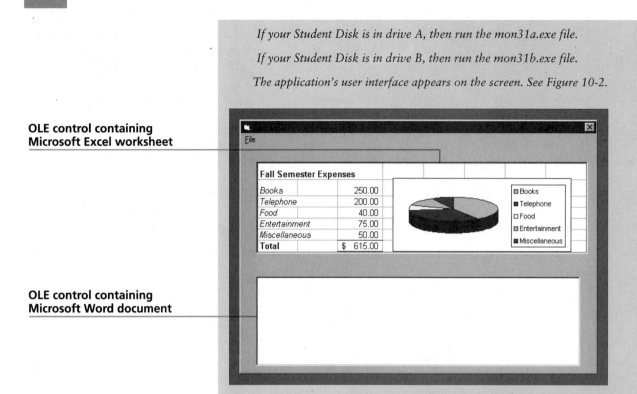

Figure 10-2: The Money application's user interface

The worksheet contains two OLE controls. One OLE control contains a Microsoft Excel worksheet; the other contains a Microsoft Word document. You use an OLE control both to embed and to link an object from one Windows application to another Windows application. You will learn about the OLE control in Lesson C.

2   Double-click the **OLE control that contains the Microsoft Excel worksheet**. The Microsoft Excel application appears as shown in Figure 10-3.

You can use the Excel application to change the data in the worksheet.

Excel application

Money application

Figure 10-3: User interface showing Excel application

3 Click the cell that contains the 50.00 Miscellaneous expense. Type **30** and press the **Enter** key.

The Excel worksheet shows that the Miscellaneous expense is now 30.00.

4 Click the **Money application** to make it the active application. Notice that the Miscellaneous expense in the form now says 30.00.

5 Click the **Excel application**. Click the cell that contains the 30.00 Miscellaneous expense. Type **50** and press the **Enter** key to change the Miscellaneous expense back to 50.00. Click **File** on Excel's menu bar, then click **Exit**. When you are asked if you want to save the changes to the worksheet, click the **No** button.

6 Double-click the **OLE** control that contains the empty Microsoft Word document. If the interface displays one or more of Word's toolbars, drag one out of the way, if necessary, until you can see the form's menu bar. Microsoft Word's menus appear on the Money application's menu bar as shown in Figure 10-4.

Word menus

Word document

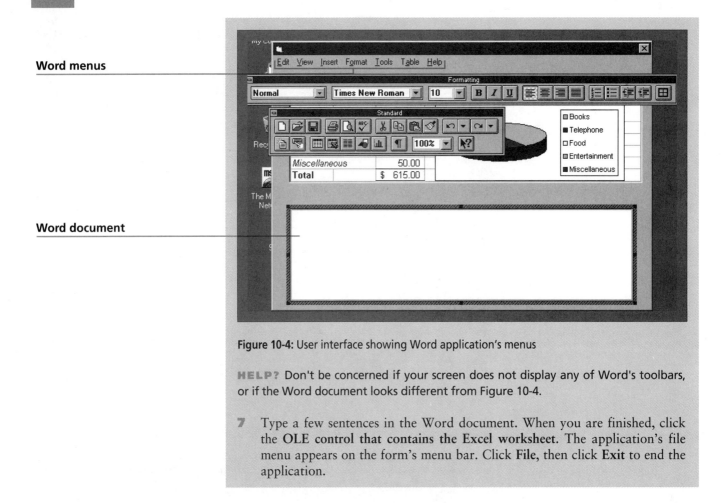

Figure 10-4: User interface showing Word application's menus

HELP? Don't be concerned if your screen does not display any of Word's toolbars, or if the Word document looks different from Figure 10-4.

7   Type a few sentences in the Word document. When you are finished, click the **OLE control that contains the Excel worksheet**. The application's file menu appears on the form's menu bar. Click **File**, then click **Exit** to end the application.

    You will learn about Data Manager in Lesson A, the data control in Lesson B, and the OLE control in Lesson C.

In this lesson you will learn how to:

- Design a database
- Create a database using Data Manager
- Create an index
- Define data validation rules and data validation text
- Add records to and delete records from a table
- Edit records in a database table
- Search a table for records that match a search criteria

tips

You don't have to be a business to make use of a database. Many people use one to keep track of their medical records, their compact disc collection, and even their golf scores.

tips

The column and row format used in a relational database is similar to the column and row format used in a spreadsheet.

Using Data Manager

Database Concepts and Terminology

In order to maintain accurate records, most businesses store information about their employees, customers, and inventory in files called databases. In general, a **database** is simply an organized collection of related information stored in a file on a disk.

Many software packages exist for creating databases; some of the most popular are Btrieve®, dBASE®, Microsoft Access™, and Paradox®. You can use Visual Basic to access the data stored in these databases. This allows a company to create a standard interface in Visual Basic that employees can use to access database information stored in a variety of formats. Instead of learning each database package's user interface, the employee only needs to know one interface. The actual format the database is in is unimportant and will be transparent to the user.

In addition to allowing you to access the data stored in databases created by other software packages, you can also use Visual Basic to create a Microsoft Access database; that's because Visual Basic contains the same Jet database engine used in Microsoft Access. The **Jet engine** allows databases created in Visual Basic to be read and manipulated by Microsoft Access, and those created in Access to be read and manipulated by Visual Basic.

The databases created by both Visual Basic and Access are relational databases. A **relational database** is one that stores information in tables, which are composed of columns and rows. Each column in a table represents a field and each row represents a record. As you learned in Tutorial 6, a **field** is a single item of information about a person, place, or thing—such as a name, address, and phone number—and a **record** is a group of related fields that contain all of the necessary data about a specific person, place, or thing. A **table** is a group of related records; each record in the group pertains to the same topic, and each contains the same type of information—in other words, the same fields.

A relational database can contain one or more tables. For example, you would typically store the information regarding the college courses you have taken in a one-table database. The table would consist of a group of related records that each contain a course ID (department and number), course title, number of credit hours, and grade. A database that stores information about a CD (compact disc) collection, on the other hand, would typically use two tables. One table would store the general information about each CD—the CD's name and the artist's name—and the other table would store the information about the songs on each CD—their title and track number.

The advantages of storing data in a relational database are many. Data stored in that format can be retrieved both quickly and easily by the computer. In addition, the data can be displayed in any order. In a CD database, for example, the information can be arranged by artist name, or it can be arranged by song title, and so on. A relational database also allows you to control how much information you want to view at a time. You can view all of the information in the CD

You will learn how to create a two-table database in Lesson A's Discovery Exercise 4.

database, or you can view only the information pertaining to a certain artist, or only the names of the songs contained on a specific CD.

In this lesson you will learn how to design and create a one-table Microsoft Access database. You will use the one-table database to keep track of the college courses you have taken.

Designing the College Database

It is important to design a database in order to assure that it meets the user's requirements. When designing a database, you should follow these basic design steps:

- Identify the information the user will need from the database
- Organize the information into one or more tables
- Establish relationships between tables (if the database contains more than one table)
- Create one or more indexes, if necessary
- Define data validation rules, if necessary

You will use these design steps to design the College database.

The first step in the design process is to identify the information the user will need from the database; this will help you decide which fields to include in the database. A database that keeps track of your college courses will typically include the following information: the course ID (department and number), course title, number of credit hours, and grade. Each piece of information will become a field in one of the database tables.

Once the information is identified, you then organize the fields into one or more tables. Fields that are logically related should be grouped in the same table. In the College database, the ID, title, credit hours, and grade are all characteristics that uniquely describe each college course you have taken, so the fields should be placed in the same table. Because the College database will contain only one table, the third design step (establish relationships between tables) is not necessary.

The fourth step in the design process is to create any necessary indexes for the tables in the database. An **index** is a special table, created and maintained by Visual Basic, that allows you to arrange the database records in a specific order, as well as to quickly search the database for information. For each record in a database table, the index stores two fields. The first field, called the **index field**, stores the values contained in the field being indexed. For example, to arrange the college records in ID order, you would create an index for the table's ID field; the index field in the index would then contain all of the course IDs in either ascending or descending order, depending on which order you selected. To arrange the records in grade order, on the other hand, you would create an index for the grade field in the table; the index field would then contain the grades you earned in each of the courses.

The second field in the index is called the **pointer field**; it stores the record number of the corresponding record found in the table. For example, if the first ID in the index field corresponds to record number 5 in the database table, then the pointer field in the index will contain the number 5. The record number in the index's pointer field points to the location of the record in the table. Figure 10-5 illustrates the concept of a table and an index using a table named Courses and an index named ID. The information in the ID index tells Visual Basic how to arrange the records in course ID order. In this case, for example, record number 6 should be first, then record number 3, and so on.

Courses Table				ID Index	
ID	Title	Credits	Grade	ID	Record
Cis106	Intro to Windows	3	A	Biol100	6
Math135	Statistics	5	B	Cis100	3
Cis100	Intro to Computers	4	B	Cis106	1
Cis110	Intro to Programming	3	B	Cis110	4
Eng101	English Composition	3	A	Eng101	5
Biol100	Biology	5	C	Math135	2

Figure 10-5: Illustration of Courses table and ID index

tips

Not every field in a table needs to be indexed. In fact, creating too many indexes can slow down database processing. Only create indexes for fields on which you want either to order records or to search.

When new records are added to a table, Visual Basic handles entering the appropriate information in the indexes. If, for example, you enter the information for a new course in the Courses table, Visual Basic will automatically enter the course's ID and corresponding record number in the appropriate position in the ID index.

A table does not have to have an index; if it does, it can have one or more. You may need to create more than one index so that the user can view the table information in different ways. In the Courses table, for example, you may want to arrange the records in ID order so that you can quickly locate all of the English courses you have taken. At another time, however, you may want to arrange the records in grade order so that you can easily find the courses in which a grade of A was earned.

In addition to allowing the *user* to locate information, an index also allows the *computer* to find information more quickly. Assume, for example, that you want the computer to locate and display only the Eng101 record. If the data you want to locate is in a field that is indexed, the computer uses the index, rather than the database table, to locate the information. In Figure 10-5's illustration, for example, the computer would search the ID index, rather than the Courses table, for the Eng101 record. Because the ID index is arranged alphabetically by ID, the computer can search the index for the desired record much faster than it can search the database table, which is not arranged in any particular order. When the computer finds the Eng101 entry in the index's index field, it uses the information in the index's pointer field to locate and then display the Eng101 record. In the Courses table, you will create an index for the ID field only.

The last step in the design process is to define any necessary data validation rules. **Data validation** refers to the process of ensuring that the data in the database meets certain criteria. A data validation rule places restrictions on the data entered in a field. An hourly wage field in an employee table, for example, would typically contain a validation rule that restricted the field data to only numbers that are greater than or equal to the minimum wage. You will include two data validation rules in the Courses table: one rule will specify that the number entered in the credit hours field must be less than or equal to 6, and the other will specify that the grade field can contain only *, A, B, C, D, or F. The asterisk (*) will indicate that the grade is not currently available because the course is not yet completed.

The final design for the College database is shown in Figure 10-6.

Courses table	
Fields:	ID, Title, Credits, Grade
Relationships:	None. The database contains only one table.
Indexes:	Create an index for the ID field
Validation Rules:	The Credits field must contain a number that is less than or equal to 6.
	The Grade field can contain an *, A, B, C, D, or F only.

Figure 10-6: Final design for the College database

Now that you have designed the College database, you can begin creating it. You will use Visual Basic's Data Manager to do so.

Using Data Manager to Create the College Database

Important Note: In order to complete the remainder of this lesson using the computer, you must be using either the Standard or Professional Edition of Visual Basic. You cannot complete the lesson using the Visual Basic Working Model.

Visual Basic comes with an application named Data Manager that you can use to create a Microsoft Access database, including the indexes and data validation rules. You can also use Data Manager to both add records to and delete records from the database, as well as to search for information in the database.

To use Data Manager to create a Microsoft Access database:

1   Start Visual Basic, if necessary.

2   Click **Add-Ins** on the menu bar, then click **Data Manager**. The Data Manager window appears.

HELP? If you are asked if you want to add the system file to the INI file, click the No button.

3   Maximize the Data Manager window.

The File menu contains the New Database command, which you use to create an Access database.

4   Click **File** on the menu bar. The File menu opens. Notice that the File menu also contains the Open Database command, which you use to open an existing database. In this case, you want to create a new database.

5   Click **New Database**. The New Database dialog box appears.

The Save as type list box (*Save file as type list box in Windows 3.1*) in the New Database dialog box contains Access (*.mdb). When you create a database in Visual Basic, the .mdb extension will be appended to the file name when the file is saved. The .mdb extension indicates that the file is a Microsoft Access database. Use the New Database dialog box to give the database a name (College) and save it on your Student Disk.

5 Type **College** in the File name text box. Save the College database in the Tut10 folder on your Student Disk. The Database window appears, as shown in Figure 10-7.

filename

database window

list box

Figure 10-7: Database window

The six buttons in the Database window allow you to open an existing table, create a new table, change the design of a table, delete a table, attach another table, or specify the relationship between tables. Because the College database does not contain any tables, only the New and Attached Tables buttons are available at this time. When the current database contains one or more tables, each table's name appears in the list box that is located in the middle of the Database window. Use the New button to create the Courses table.

The Attached Tables button allows you to attach either an external table (a non-Access table) or an Access table from another database.

To create the Courses table:

1 Click the **New** button. The Add Table dialog box appears as shown in Figure 10-8.

table name

list box displays the names of the fields in the table

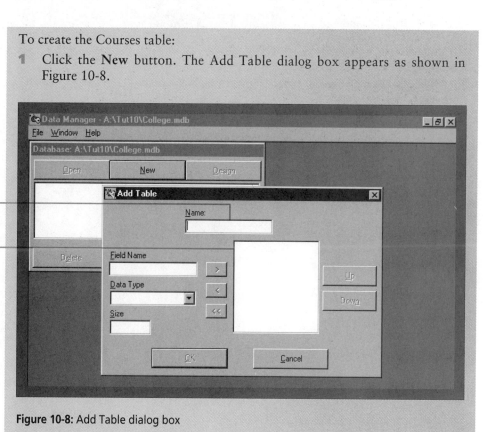

Figure 10-8: Add Table dialog box

You use the Add Table dialog box to give the table a name, and also to define the name, data type, and size of each field in the table. First give the table a name.

2   Type **Courses** in the Name text box, then press the **Tab** key to move the insertion point to the Field Name text box.

You must assign a unique name, as well as a data type and size, to each field in the table. Figure 10-9 shows the valid data types for the table fields.

Data type
Boolean
Byte
Currency
Date/Time
Double
Integer
Long Binary
Long Integer
Memo
Single
Text

Figure 10-9: Data types for table fields

For all but the Text data type, the size of the field is preset by Visual Basic and can't be changed.

Define the ID field first.

3   Type **ID** in the Field Name text box, then press the **Tab** key to move the focus to the Data Type list box.

A course ID will contain letters and numbers, so you will declare the field's data type as Text.

4   Click the **Data Type** list arrow. Scroll the list box until you see Text, then click **Text** in the list. Notice that the Size text box automatically displays 10, which is the default size for a Text field.

Recall that you can change the size of a Text field. In this case, the ID field will need to contain a maximum of eight characters only, so you will change its size from the default of 10 to 8.

5   Press the **Tab** key to move the insertion point into the Size text box. Delete the 10, then type 8 in the Size text box.

Notice that the ⊡ button in the dialog box is darkened, which means it is available. When you are finished defining a field, you must click the ⊡ button to add the field to the table.

6   Click the ⊡ button to add the ID field to the table. Visual Basic removes the field's name from the Field Name text box and adds it to the list box located to the right of the ⊡ button. As you are creating the table, the list box displays the names of all of the fields contained in the table.

In addition to the ☑ button, notice that the Add Table dialog box also contains four other buttons: ☑, ☑, Up, and Down. If you want to remove a field from the table, you select the field name in the list box, then press the ☑ button. You use the ☑ button to remove all of the fields from the table. The Up and Down buttons allow you to reposition the existing fields in the table. For example, if the ID field was the third field in the list box, and you wanted it to be the first field, you could simply click ID in the list box, then press the Up button until the ID field was listed first.

You will now complete the Courses table by defining the remaining three fields: course title, credit hours, and grade.

7 Click the **Field Name** text box to place the insertion point in that text box.

8 On your own, add the remaining three fields to the Courses table. Be sure to click the ☑ button after defining each field. Because the data type for the Credits field is Integer, you will not be able to specify a size. N/A will appear in the Size text box for that field.

Field Name	Data Type	Size
Title	Text	30
Credits	Integer	N/A
Grade	Text	1

When you have finished defining the fields, the Add Table dialog box should look like Figure 10-10.

Figure 10-10: Completed Add Table dialog box for the Courses table

HELP? If you inadvertently added an incorrect field, click the field name in the list box, then click the ☑ button. If you want to remove all of the fields so that you can define the fields again, click the ☑ button. If necessary, use the Up and Down buttons to rearrange the fields to match Figure 10-10.

When you are finished defining the fields in the table, you simply click the OK button.

9 Click the **OK** button to save the table information. The Add Table dialog box closes and Data Manager returns to the Database window. See Figure 10-11.

Figure 10-11: Database window showing Courses table

Notice that the name of the table, Courses, appears in the Database window's list box. Data Manager also opens a SQL Statement window below the Database window. SQL, pronounced like the word "sequel", stands for Structured Query Language. SQL consists of commands that allow you to access the data stored in a database, and is beyond the scope of this book. For the College application, you do not need to be concerned about the SQL Statement window.

After creating a table, you can use the Design button to display the Table Editor window, which allows you to make changes to the table, as well as to create an index for the table and define any validation rules. First create an index for the Courses table.

Creating an Index

You will create an index for the ID field in the Courses table. This will allow you to view the records in ID order, and also allow the computer to quickly search the Courses table for a specific ID. Recall that if the field you want to search is indexed, Visual Basic uses the index, rather than the database table, to find the information. Remember that the computer can search an index much faster than it can search a database table.

To create an index for the Courses table:

1   Click **Courses** in the Database window's list box. When you click the name of a table in the list, the Open, Design, and Delete buttons darken to indicate that they are now available. The Relations button, which allows you to define a relationship between two tables, is not available at this point because the College database contains only one table.

2   Click the **Design** button. The Table Editor window opens as shown in Figure 10-12.

field names

field properties

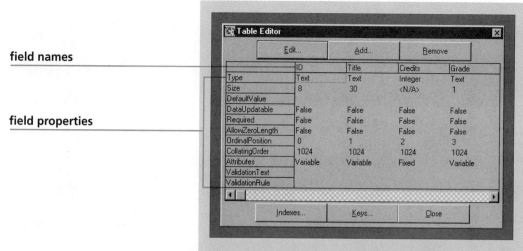

Figure 10-12: Table Editor window

The Table Editor window displays the names and properties of the table fields. (A discussion of each of these properties is beyond the scope of this book.) The three buttons at the top of the window allow you to add new fields to the table, as well as edit and remove existing fields. You can use the three buttons at the bottom of the window to define indexes and keys, and to close the Table Editor window. (The Keys button allows you to create data keys for use with multiple-table databases.)

Use the Indexes button to create an index on the ID field.

3 Click the **Indexes** button. The Indexes window opens. You use the Indexes window to add a new index to a table, and also to edit and remove an existing index. The Edit and Remove buttons are currently dimmed because the Courses table does not contain any indexes.

4 Click the **Add** button to create a new index. The Add Index dialog box opens as shown in Figure 10-13.

Figure 10-13: Add Index dialog box

First you need to give the index a name. In this case you want to create an index for the ID field, so you will name the index ID. Using the same name for the index and its corresponding field will help you remember the purpose of the index.

5 Type **ID** in the Index Name text box.

Now select the field you want to index.

6   Click **ID** in the Fields in table list box. The Add (ASC) and Add (DEC) buttons now darken to indicate that they are available.

The Add (ASC) button will arrange the records in ascending order by the ID, and the Add (DEC) button will arrange them in descending order. Arrange the records in ascending order.

7   Click the **Add (ASC)** button. Visual Basic removes the ID field from the Fields in table list box, and adds ID (ASC) to the Fields in index list box.

Selecting the Primary Index check box, which is located at the top of the Indexes window, tells Visual Basic to arrange the table records in ID order when the records are first displayed—in other words, to automatically use the ID index.

8   Click the **Primary Index** check box to select it. A check mark (*an X in Windows 3.1*) appears in the check box. Now when you display the table records, the records will appear in ID order.

A table can have only one primary index, and that primary index must contain a unique value for each record in the table. In other words, when entering a record into the Course table, you must complete the ID field, and each ID in the table must be unique. You tell Data Manager to require a unique entry in the primary index field by selecting both the Unique and Required check boxes that are located at the bottom of the Add Index dialog box.

9   Click the **Unique** check box, then click the **Required** check box. A check mark (*an X in Windows 3.1*) should appear in both check boxes.

The Add Index dialog box appears as shown in Figure 10-14.

Figure 10-14: Completed Add Index dialog box

10   Click the **OK** button both to save the index information and to close the Add Index dialog box. The Indexes window appears. Click the **Close** button to close the Indexes window. The Table Editor window appears. Click the **Close** button to close the Table Editor window. The Database and SQL Statement windows appear.

Next you will define the data validation rules for the Courses table.

Including Data Validation Rules in a Table

Recall that data validation refers to the process of ensuring that the data in the database meets certain criteria. A data validation rule places restrictions on the data that can be entered in a field. When planning the College database, recall that you identified the following data validation rules for the Courses table:

- The credit hours for a course must be less than or equal to 6.
- The grade field can contain either an *, A, B, C, D, or F only.

Data Manager stores the validation rules directly in the table itself. By doing so, any application that accesses the table records is forced to uphold the same rules; this provides consistency in the data entered into a database by different applications that have access to the same database information. Data Manager also allows you to specify the message that should appear when a validation rule is broken.

To enter the data validation rules for the Courses table:

1 Courses should be selected in the Database window's list box. Click the **Design** button. The Table Editor window opens.

First enter the validation rule for the Credits field.

2 Click the **Credits** field name in the Table Editor window, then click the **Edit** button. The Edit Field dialog box opens as shown in Figure 10-15.

name of field to edit

Figure 10-15: Edit Field dialog box

HELP? If your Edit Field dialog box does not display the information on the Credits field, then click the Cancel button to close the dialog box. Click the Credits field name in the Table Editor window and click the Edit button.

You enter the validation rule in the field's ValidationRule property. You use the ValidationText property to specify the message your application should display if the value entered by the user doesn't follow the validation rule.

3 Click the **ValidationRule** text box to place the insertion point in that box.

The validation rule should specify the valid data for that field. When entering a validation rule, you can use mathematical, relational, or logical operators, as well as numbers and strings. In this case, you will use the following validation rule to tell Visual Basic that only credit hours that are less than or equal to 6 are valid: <= 6.

4   Type **<= 6** in the ValidationRule text box.

Now enter an appropriate message in the ValidationText property.

5   Click the ValidationText text box to place the insertion point in that box. Type **The credit hours cannot be greater than 6.** in the ValidationText text box, then click the **OK** button both to save the validation information and to close the Edit Field dialog box. The Table Editor window appears.

Now enter the validation rule for the Grade field.

6   Click the **Grade** field name in the Table Editor window, then click the **Edit** button. The Edit Field dialog box opens.

7   Click the **ValidationRule** text box to place the insertion point in that box. Type **= "*" or "A" or "B" or "C" or "D" or "F"** in the ValidationRule text box.

8   Click the ValidationText text box to place the insertion point in that box. Type **The grade can be *, A, B, C, D, or F only.** in the ValidationText text box.

Before closing the Edit Field dialog box, enter a default value for the Grade field. The default value will automatically appear in the grade field when you are adding new records to the table. The default grade should be the asterisk (*), which indicates that the grade is not currently available.

9   Click the **DefaultValue** text box to place the insertion point in that box. Type ***** and then click the **OK** button both to save the field information and to close the Edit Field dialog box. The Table Editor window appears as shown in Figure 10-16.

default value

validation rules and text

Figure 10-16: Table Editor window showing validation rules, validation text, and default value

HELP? Don't be concerned if the Grade field in the Table Editor window is not selected as shown in Figure 10-16. You can select a field either by clicking its name, which selects the entire field, or by clicking one of its properties, which selects only the property.

10 Click the **Close** button to close the Table Editor window. The Database and SQL Statement windows appear.

In addition to creating a table, Data Manager also allows you to open an existing table and either view its records, add new records, delete existing records, and search the table for information.

Opening an Existing Table

After a table is created, you can use Data Manager to open the table. When a table is open, you can browse through its existing records, add new records, delete existing records, and search for specific records in the table.

To open the Courses table:

1 The Courses table should be selected in the Database window, so you simply need to click the **Open** button in order to open the table. The Table window opens as shown in Figure 10-17.

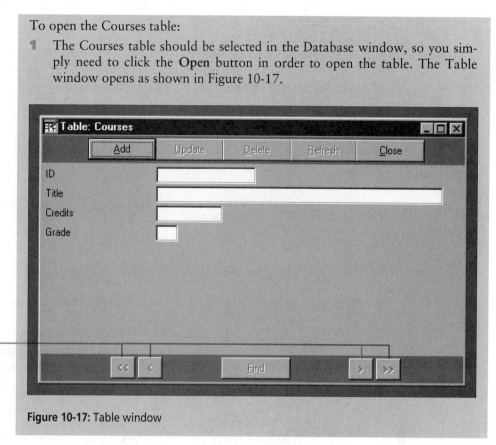

use these buttons to
navigate through the
records in a table

Figure 10-17: Table window

Five buttons appear at the top of the window. The Add button adds a new, blank record to the end of the table. You use the Update button to save the changes made to the current record. The Delete button deletes the current record from the table. The Refresh button reopens the table, and the Close button simply closes the Table window.

Five buttons also appear at the bottom of the Table window. The Find button allows you to search the table for a record that matches a search expression—for example, you can use it to search for a specific ID, or to search for all courses in which you received a grade of A. You use the First Record button ⟨⟨ and Last Record button ⟩⟩ to move to the first record and the last record, respectively, in the table. You use the Previous Record button ⟨ and Next Record button ⟩ to move from record to record. Most of the buttons in the Table window are dimmed because the table does not contain any records. Add five records to the Courses table.

To add records to the Courses table:

1 Click the **Add** button. Data Manager adds a new, blank record to the end of the Courses table. The Add button's caption changes to Cancel. If you

choose not to enter the record, you can click the Cancel button to cancel the Add operation.

2   Click the **ID** text box to place the insertion point in that box, then type **Eng101** and press the **Tab** key. Type **English Composition** in the Title text box and press the **Tab** key. Type **3** in the Credits text box and press the **Tab** key. Type **A** in the Grade text box, then click the **Update** button to save the current record in the table.

Now add another record.

3   Click the **Add** button to add another blank record to the end of the table. Click the **ID** text box to place an insertion point in that box. Enter the following record: **Cis131, Intro to Databases, 3, B**. Click the **Update** button to save the current record.

4   Use the Add button to add the following three records to the table. Be sure to click the Update button after entering each record.

    Cis100, Intro to Computers, 4, B

    Biol100, Biology, 4, C

    Cis106, Intro to Windows, 3, A

5   On your own, use the ⟪, ⟫, ⟨, and ⟩ buttons to browse through the records. As you browse, notice that the courses display in the order in which they were entered in the table, rather than in course ID order.

Although you specified the ID index as the primary index, Visual Basic uses that index to arrange the records only when the records are first displayed. Visual Basic does not automatically arrange the records in primary index order as new records are added to the table. In order to arrange the records after new records are added, you simply need to click the Refresh button. The Refresh button reopens the table and redisplays the records using the primary index.

6   Click the **Refresh** button. The Refresh button reopens the database and puts the records in order by the primary index—in this case, in ID order. You can observe this by clicking the ⟩ and ⟨ buttons to browse through the records in the table.

Recall that a unique entry is required in the primary index field. Observe what happens when you try to save a record that does not have an ID.

7   Click the ⟪ button to make the Biol100 record the current record. Select Biol100 in the ID field, then press the **Backspace** key on your keyboard to delete the ID. Click the **Update** button. Data Manager displays an error message informing you that the Field ID cannot be zero length. Click the **OK** button to remove the error message.

Now try entering a record with a duplicate ID.

8   Type **Cis131** in the ID field, then click the **Update** button. Data Manager displays an error message informing you that the changes were unsuccessful because there is a duplicate value in either an index, primary key, or relationship. Click the **OK** button to remove the error message.

Now replace the Cis131 in the current record's ID field with Biol100.

9   Select Cis131 in the ID field, then type **Biol100** in the ID field and click the **Update** button. Biol100 replaces Cis131 in the current record.

Now observe how Data Manager handles an incorrect entry in the Credits field. Recall that the data validation rule in the Credits field specifies that the field can contain only numbers that are less than or equal to six.

10 The Biol100 record should be displayed in the interface. Delete the 4 from the Credits field, then type 7 in the Credits field and click the **Update** button. The error message contained in the Credit field's ValidationText property, "The credit hours cannot be greater than 6.", appears in a message box. Click the **OK** button to remove the message box. Change the credit hours to **4**, then click the **Update** button.

Next observe how Data Manager handles an incorrect entry in the Grade field. Recall that the data validation rule in the Grade field specifies that the field can contain an *, A, B, C, D, or F only.

11 Delete the C from the Biol100 record's Grade field, then type **X** in the Grade field and click the **Update** button. The error message contained in the Grade field's ValidationText property, "The grade can be *, A, B, C, D, or F only.", appears in a message box. Click the **OK** button to remove the message box. Change the grade to **C** and click the **Update** button.

You can also edit the values in an existing record. When you click the Update button, Data Manager saves the changes you made.

12 Use the ▸ button to display the Cis100 record. Change the grade from B to **C**, then click the **Update** button to save the change.

13 To confirm that the change was saved, click the ▸ button to move to the next record, then click the ◂ button to move back to the Cis100 record. The grade is now a C.

In addition to both adding and editing records, you can also use the Table window to delete records from the table and to locate one or more records in the table. First you will delete the Cis131 record, then you will search for the Eng101 record.

tips

▸ Be careful when using the Delete button in Data Manager to delete records. The Delete button removes the record permanently. The only way to restore the record is to reenter it into the table.

To delete a record from the table, then search the table for a specific record:

1 Display the Cis131 record, then click the **Delete** button. Data Manager removes the record from the Courses table.

Now use the Find button to find and display the Eng101 record in the table.

2 Click the **Find** button. The Find Record dialog box appears.

The Find Record dialog box allows you to enter a search condition that specifies which record or records you want to find. You use the Fields list box to select the field you want to search, and you use the Operator list box to select the appropriate operator. You enter the search string—the value for which you are searching—in the Value text box. Use the Find Record dialog box to search for the Eng101 record.

3 Click **ID** in the Fields list box, then click = in the Operator list box. Click the **Value** text box to place the insertion point in that box. String comparisons made by the Find dialog box are not case sensitive; therefore, to find the Eng101 record, you can type the search string in any case. Type **eng101** in the Value text box, as shown in Figure 10-18.

Figure 10-18: Find Record dialog box containing search condition

The Operator list box will not contain scroll bars in Windows 3.1.

the Operator list box
will not contain scroll
bars in Windows 3.1

WINDOWS   **3.1**

4   Click the **OK** button in the Find Record dialog box to begin the search. The Find Record dialog box closes and the Eng101 record appears in the Table window.

Notice the ⌐«⌐ and ⌐‹⌐ buttons that appear to the immediate left of the Find button, and the ⌐›⌐ and ⌐»⌐ buttons that appear to its immediate right. You can use these buttons to display each of the records that match the search condition. In this case, because each record's ID must be unique, only one Eng101 record will be in the table. You can confirm this by clicking the Find button's ⌐›⌐ button.

5   Click the ⌐›⌐ button that is located to the right of the Find button. Data Manager displays the "Unable to find a match" message in a message box. This tells you that no other Eng101 records exist in the table. Click the **OK** button to remove the message box.

Data Manager also allows you to use the Like operator and the asterisk (*) wildcard to locate information in a table. Recall that you learned how to use the Like operator and the asterisk wildcard in Tutorial 9. Use both to search for all records whose course ID begins with Cis.

6   Click the **Find** button to display the Find Record dialog box. Click **ID** in the Fields list box. If necessary, scroll the Operator list box until you see the Like operator, then click **Like** in the list. Click the **Value** text box, then type cis* in the Value text box, as shown in Figure 10-19.

tips

Recall that the ID field is the field in the primary index, which can contain only unique values.

find all Cis records

Figure 10-19: Find Record dialog box containing Like operator and asterisk wildcard

7   Click the **OK** button in the Find Record dialog box to begin the search. The Find Record dialog box closes, and the Cis100 record—the first record in the table that matches the search condition—appears in the Table window.

8   Click the ▷ button that is located to the right of the Find button to view the next Cis record. The Cis106 record appears. Click the ▷ button again. When the "Unable to find a match" message box appears, click the **OK** button. The message box closes and the Table dialog box appears.

9   Click the **Close** button to close the Table dialog box. Click **File**, then click **Exit** to close Data Manager. Visual Basic returns to the design screen.

You have now completed Lesson A. You can either take a break or complete the questions and exercises at the end of the lesson. In Lesson B you will learn how to use Visual Basic's data control to access the records in the College database.

S U M M A R Y

To design a database, follow these basic design steps:

■   Identify the information the user will need from the database.
■   Organize the information into one or more tables.
■   Establish relationships between tables (if the database contains more than one table).
■   Create one or more indexes, if necessary.
■   Define data validation rules, if necessary.

To create a Microsoft Access database in Visual Basic:

■   Use Data Manager. You access Data Manager by clicking Add-Ins on Visual Basic's menu bar, then clicking Data Manager.
■   You must assign a unique name, as well as a data type and size, to each field in a database table.

Q U E S T I O N S

1. A(n) _____ is an organized collection of related information stored in a file on a disk.
   a. control
   b. database
   c. field
   d. object
   e. record

2. A _____ database is one that stores information in tables, which are composed of columns and rows.
   a. columnar
   b. relational
   c. sorted
   d. tabular

3. A group of related records in a database is referred to as a _____ .
   a. column
   b. field
   c. row
   d. table

4. Which of the following is true about a relational database?
   a. Data stored in a relational database can be retrieved both quickly and easily by the computer.
   b. Data stored in a relational database can be displayed in any order.
   c. A relational database stores data in a column and row format.
   d. All of the above are true.

5. A(n) _____ is a special table, created and maintained by Visual Basic, that allows you to arrange the database records in a specific order, as well as to quickly search the database for information.
   a. control
   b. field
   c. index
   d. order field
   e. sort field

6. The _____ field in an index stores the values contained in the field being indexed.
   a. index
   b. pointer
   c. primary
   d. sort
   e. table

7. The _____ field in an index stores the record number of the corresponding record found in the table.
   a. index
   b. pointer
   c. primary
   d. sort

8. Which of the following is NOT true?
   a. An index allows the user to easily locate information in a database.
   b. An index allows the computer to quickly locate information in a database.
   c. An index allows you to arrange the database records in a particular order.
   d. It takes the computer much more time to search an index than it does to search the database table itself.

9. _____ refers to the process of ensuring that the data in the database meets certain criteria.
   a. Criteria checking
   b. Data validation
   c. Rule enforcing
   d. Standard setting

10. You can use _____ , which is an application that comes with Visual Basic, to create a Microsoft Access database.
   a. Access
   b. Database Creator
   c. Data Creator
   d. Data Manager

11. A table can have _____ primary index(es).
   a. only one
   b. only two
   c. many

12. Which two of the following are true?
   a. A primary index can contain only letters.
   b. A primary index can contain only numbers.
   c. Each record in a table must have an entry in the primary index.
   d. The entries in a primary index must be unique.

13. Which of the following are true?
   a. Data Manager stores the validation rules in the table itself.
   b. Data Manager allows you to specify the message that should appear when a validation rule is broken.
   c. When entering a data validation rule, you can use mathematical, relational, or logical operators, as well as numbers and strings.
   d. All of the above are true

14. Which of the following tells Data Manager to search for all records whose ID begins with Eng?
   a. Eng*
   b. Find Eng
   c. Find Eng*
   d. Like Eng
   e. Like Eng*

EXERCISES

Important note: In order to complete this lesson's exercises, you must be using either the Standard or Professional Edition of Visual Basic. You cannot complete the exercises using the Visual Basic Working Model.

When designing the databases in these exercises, recall that the basic design steps are:
   ■ Identify the information the user will need from the database.
   ■ Organize the information into one or more tables.
   ■ Establish relationships between tables (if the database contains more than one table).
   ■ Create one or more indexes, if necessary.
   ■ Define data validation rules, if necessary.

1. In this exercise you will use Data Manager to create a one-table database. You will also define an index and a validation rule.
   a. Use Data Manager to create a one-table database that tracks the basketball scores for your favorite team. Name the database la1Done; name the table Scores. Save the

database in the Tut10 folder on your Student Disk. The Scores table should contain the name of the opposing team, the date the game was played, your team's score, and the opposing team's score.

b. Create an ascending index on the opposing team's name field. This index should be the primary index.

c. Define a data validation rule for the two fields that store the scores; the fields should allow numbers between 0 and 130 only.

d. Use Data Manager to add five records to the table, then click the Refresh button. The records should be in ascending order by the opposing team's name.

e. Submit a disk that contains the la1Done.mdb file.

2. In this exercise you will use Data Manager to create a one-table database. You will also define an index and a validation rule.

a. Use Data Manager to create a one-table database that keeps track of your monthly phone bill. Name the database la2Done; name the table Phone. Save the database in the Tut10 folder on your Student Disk. The Phone table should contain the month, the year, and the total bill. The month and year fields should be integers, and the total bill field should be currency.

b. Create an ascending index on the month field. This index should be the primary index.

c. Define a data validation rule for the month field. The field should allow only 01, 02, 03, 04, 05, 06, 07, 08, 09, 10, 11, 12.

d. Use Data Manager to add five records to the table, then click the Refresh button. The records should be in ascending order by the month.

e. Submit a disk that contains the la2Done.mdb file.

Exercises 3 and 4 are Discovery Exercises, which allow you both to "discover" the solutions to problems on your own and to experiment with material that is not covered in the tutorial.

discovery ▶ 3. In this exercise you will use Data Manager to create a one-table database. You will also define a multiple-field index and a validation rule.

a. Use Data Manager to create a one-table database that contains the names and phone numbers of your friends. Name the database la3Done; name the table Friends. Save the database in the Tut10 folder on your Student Disk. The Friends table should contain three fields: last name, first name, and phone number.

b. Because some of your friends may have the same last name, you should arrange the records by first name within last name. In other words, if four of your friends have the last name "Smith," you can tell Data Manager to arrange the Smith records in first name order. Use the Help menu's Contents command to research how to create an index that contains more than one field, then create an ascending index that includes both the last name and first name fields. This index should be the primary index.

c. Use Data Manager to add ten records to the table. Be sure that three of the records have the same last name, but different first names.

d. Click the Refresh button. The records should display in ascending last name order. The records having the same last name should display in ascending first name order.

e. Submit a disk that contains the la3done.mdb file.

discovery ▶ 4. In this exercise you will learn how to create a two-table database. You will also learn how to relate two databases.

Scenario: In this exercise you will design and create a database that you can use to keep track of your CD (compact disc) collection. Recall that the first design step is to identify the information to include in the database. A CD database will typically include the CD's name and the artist's name, as well as the song titles and their location (track number). Once the information is identified, you then organize the fields into one or more tables. Fields that are logically related should be grouped in the same table. But how do you decide how many tables to use, and which fields belong in which table? What helps here is to sketch the database using one table only. Include some sample records in the sketch, as shown in Figure 10-20.

CD Name	Artist Name	Song Title	Track Number
Country Music	Bonnie Condrell	Showdown	1
Country Music	Bonnie Condrell	Pals	2
Country Music	Bonnie Condrell	Truck Stop	3
Country Music	Bonnie Condrell	Afternoon Breeze	4
Dreaming	Janice Paige	Secrets	1
Dreaming	Janice Paige	Candlelight	2
Dreaming	Janice Paige	Dreams	3

Figure 10-20: Illustration of a CD database as one table

If you include all of the CD information in the same table, notice that you would need to enter the CD's name and the artist's name several times in the table; once for each of the songs on the CD. This repetition of data is referred to as **data redundancy**. Data redundancy has several disadvantages. In addition to wasting both time keying in the data and disk space, data redundancy makes a database difficult to maintain, which can then lead to inaccurate information. For example, assume that you made a mistake entering the name of a CD. In order to correct that error, you would need to change the name in each of the records for that CD; a time-consuming process and also one that is open to errors: What if you forget to change one of the records? A better design for the CD database would be to separate the information into two tables: one table would contain the information that describes the general characteristics of the CD (its name and the artist's name) and the other would contain the information that describes the specific characteristics of each CD (the song titles and track numbers). The modified design is shown in Figure 10-21.

CD Name	Artist Name
Country Music	Bonnie Condrell
Dreaming	Janice Paige

Song Title	Track Number
Showdown	1
Pals	2
Truck Stop	3
Afternoon Breeze	4
Secrets	1
Candlelight	2
Dreams	3

Figure 10-21: Modified design for the CD database

Although the modified design does not repeat the CD and artist names, as did the initial design, notice that the new design does not indicate on which CD the song is located. When using more than one table in a database, you need to establish a relationship between the tables. Establishing a relationship between multi-table databases is Step 3 in the design process. You relate two tables by including a common field in each one. In this case, you will assign a unique number to each CD, similar to the way the government assigns a unique number to you (your social security number). You will then add a CDNum field to both the CD table and the song table, as shown in Figure 10-22.

CD Table:

CD Number	CD Name	Artist Name
1	Country Music	Bonnie Condrell
2	Dreaming	Janice Paige

Song Table:

CD Number	Song Title	Track Number
1	Showdown	1
1	Pals	2
1	Truck Stop	3
1	Afternoon Breeze	4
2	Secrets	1
2	Candlelight	2
2	Dreams	3

Figure 10-22: Final design for the CD database

The CDNum field relates both tables. In the CD table, the CDNum field uniquely identifies each CD; in the song table, the CDNum field indicates on which CD the song is located.

a. Use the method appropriate to your version of Windows to copy the Cd(Cd.mdb) database, which is located in the Tut10 folder on your Student Disk, to la4Done.mdb. Place the la4Done.mdb file in the Tut10 folder on your Student Disk.

b. Use Data Manager to open the la4Done (la4Done.mdb) database, which is located in the Tut10 folder on your Student Disk. The CD database already contains the CD table.

c. Click the New button to add another table to the CD database. Type Song in the Name text box, then press the Tab key to move the insertion point into the Field Name text box.

d. Add the following three fields to the Song table. Be sure to click the ▶ button after defining each field.

Field Name	Data Type	Size
CdNum	Integer	N/A
Song	Text	25
Track	Integer	1

e. Close the Add Table dialog box.

f. Create an ascending primary index, named CdNum, for the CdNum field in the CD database.

g. Create an ascending index named CdNum for the CdNum field in the Song table. Do not make the CdNum index the primary index.

h. The CD table already contains the two records shown in Figure 10-22. Open the Song table and add the seven records shown in Figure 10-22.

i. Close Data Manager.

j. Submit a disk with the la4Done.mdb file on it.

In this lesson you will learn how to:

- Display database records using the Data control
- Set the EOFAction property
- Reopen a database using the Refresh method
- Delete records using the Delete and MoveNext methods
- Find a record using the FindFirst method and the NoMatch property

Using the Data Control

The College Application

Although Data Manager allows you to add, edit, delete, and search the records in a table, its user interface cannot be altered. If you want to give the user a customized interface with which he or she can access the records stored in a database, you will need to create a Visual Basic application. Your Student Disk contains a partially completed Visual Basic application that you can use to add records to the College database. You can also use the application to edit and delete records, as well as to search for a record in the database.

To open the partially completed College application:

1 Start Visual Basic, if necessary, then open the **College** (college.vbp) project, which is located in the Tut10 folder on your Student Disk.

2 Click the **View Form** button to view the frmCollege form, then save the form and the project as **lbColl**. The user interface appears on the screen as shown in Figure 10-23.

Figure 10-23: The frmCollege user interface

The College application's interface contains four text boxes, two command buttons, and two frame controls. It also includes a File menu that contains two commands: Refresh Records and Exit.

Applications that can access and manipulate the data stored in a database are referred to as **data-aware** applications. You can use Visual Basic's data control to create a data-aware application. You will use the data control to make the College application a data-aware application.

Using the Data Control

Visual Basic's data control allows you to access the data stored in any of the following database formats: Microsoft Access, Btrieve, dBase, Microsoft Excel, FoxPro, Paradox, and ODBC databases including SQL Server and Oracle®. Adding a data control to an application is the first step in making the application data-aware. The data control establishes a link between the database and the other controls in the interface.

To make the College application data-aware, then save and run the application:

1   Double-click the **Data tool** 📇 in the toolbox. The Data1 control appears on the form.

Now cut the data control from the form and paste it into the frame control located at the top of the interface.

2   Click **Edit** on the menu bar, then click **Cut**. Click the **frame** control located at the top of the interface to select it. Sizing handles should appear around the frame control. Click **Edit** on the menu bar, then click **Paste** to paste the data control into the frame.

3   Display the Properties window, then set the Data1 control's properties as follows:

Height:	375	Top:	1680
Left:	120	Width:	6255
Name:	datCollege		

4   Set the data control's Caption property to **Click the arrow buttons to view the database records.** and press the **Enter** key.

5   Click the **form** to select it, then click the **Lock Controls** button 🔒 on the toolbar to lock the controls in place. Click the **datCollege** data control in the form to select it. The interface appears as shown in Figure 10-24.

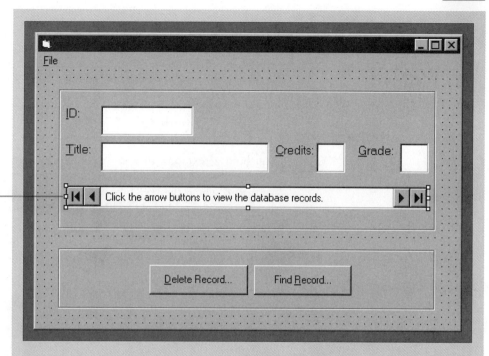

data control

Figure 10-24: Data control displayed in the interface

You use the ◄◄ and ►► buttons to display the first and last database record, respectively; you use the ◄ and ► buttons to display the previous and next database record, respectively.

After adding the data control to the interface, you then set its **DatabaseName property**, which tells Visual Basic the name of the database to connect to the data control. You will connect the datCollege data control to the College database.

6   The datCollege data control should be selected in the form. Display the Properties window. Click **DatabaseName** in the Properties list, then click the **...** button in the Settings box. The DatabaseName dialog box appears.

7   Use the dialog box to select the **College** (college.mdb) file, which is located in the Tut10 folder on your Student Disk, then click the **Open** button.

Use the dialog box to select the College (college.mdb) file, which is located in the Tut10 folder on your Student Disk, then click the OK button.

Next you need to set the data control's **RecordSource** property, which tells Visual Basic which table in the database contains the records you want to access. In this case the College database contains only one table, Courses.

8   Click **RecordSource** in the Properties window. Click the **Settings** list arrow, then click **Courses** in the list.

Notice that the method for accessing a Microsoft Access database is quite simple. You first add the data control to the form, then set its DatabaseName and RecordSource properties.

WINDOWS   3.1

tips

· · · · · · · · · · · · · · · · ·

If you need to access a database other than a Microsoft Access database, you will also need to set the data control's Connect property. You will learn about the Connect property when you access the dBASE IV database in Lesson B's Discovery Exercise 6.

Now that the data control is on the form and its DatabaseName and RecordSource properties have been set, you can connect the four text boxes in the interface to it. Connecting a control to a data control is called **binding**, and the connected controls are referred to as **data-aware controls** or **bound controls**. You can bind the following 10 controls to a data control: check box, combo box,

tips

▶ You bind any of the 10 controls to a data control in the same manner: first set the DataSource property, then set the DataField property.

dbCombo, dbGrid, dbList, image, label, list box, picture box, and text box. In the College application, you will bind the four text boxes to the datCollege data control. By binding the text boxes to the data control, the text boxes will display the data from the table specified in the data control's RecordSource property.

Binding Controls to a Data Control

You bind a text box to a data control by setting the text box's DataSource and DataField properties. In the **DataSource property** you enter the name of the data control to which the text box is to be bound. In the **DataField property** you enter the name of the table field to bind to the text box. You set the DataSource property first, then set the DataField property.

In this application, the four text boxes should be bound to the datCollege control. You can set the DataSource property for all four text boxes at the same time.

To bind the four text boxes to the datCollege control:

1   Select the ID text box, the Title text box, the Credits text box, and the Grade text box.

   HELP? To select multiple controls, recall that you click the first control, then press and hold down the Ctrl key while clicking the other controls.

2   Display the Properties window, then click **DataSource** in the Properties window. Click the **Settings** list arrow, then click **datCollege** in the list. Click the **form** to cancel the selection of the four text boxes.

Now set the DataField property, which tells Visual Basic the name of the field whose contents you want displayed in the text box. For example, in the ID text box, you want to display the contents of the ID field from the Courses table. In the Title text box, you want to display the course title. Because each text box will display a different field from the Courses table, you will need to set each control's DataField property separately.

3   Select the ID text box, then display the Properties window. Click **DataField** in the Properties window, then click the **Settings** list arrow. Click **ID** in the list.

4   Set the DataField properties for the remaining three text boxes as follows:

Text box	Field
Title	Title
Credits	Credits
Grade	Grade

Now save and run the application to see how it works so far.

5   **Save** and **run** the application.

6   Use the data control buttons to view the four records in the database. Because you defined the ID field as the primary key when you created the Courses table, the records display in course ID order.

The data control allows you to edit the database records. After making a change to a record, you need to click one of the data control's arrow buttons in order to save the change. Clicking an arrow button moves the data control to another record, which automatically saves the changes made to the current record.

7 Display the Cis100 record, then change the grade from C to **B**. Click the ▶ button to move to the next record. Visual Basic saves the change made to the Cis100 record as it moves to the next record in the table. You can prove that the change was saved by moving back to the Cis100 record.

8 Click the ◀ button to display the Cis100 record again. The grade is now a B.

9 Click **File** on the form's menu bar, then click the **Exit** button to end the application. Visual Basic returns to the design screen.

In addition to displaying and editing the records stored in a table, you can also use the data control to add records to the table. One method of doing so is to set the data control's EOFAction property.

The EOFAction Property

The **EOFAction property** contains a value that tells the data control what action to take when the user tries to move past the last record in the table. The default action is that the last record remains current—in other words, the last record remains on the screen when the ▶ button is clicked. By setting the EOFAction property to 2 - Add New, Visual Basic automatically adds a new, blank record to the end of the table when the user clicks the ▶ button while viewing the last record. The user can then enter information into the new record. Clicking the ▶ button again will save the current record and add another new record to the end of the table. Clicking any of the other three buttons in the data control will save the information in the current record without displaying a new record.

To set the datCollege control's EOFAction property, then save and run the application:

1 Click the **datCollege** control to select it. Display the Properties window, then set the EOFAction property to **2 - Add New**.

2 **Save** and **run** the application.

First display the last record in the table.

3 Click the ▶ button to display the last record in the table, then click the ▶ button to add a new, blank record to the table. Notice the * in the Grade field; when you created the College database, recall that you specified the * as the default value for this field.

4 Enter the following record: **Math135, Statistics, 5, B**, then click the ▶ button. The ▶ button saves the current record and also adds a new, blank record to the end of the table.

5 Now enter the following record: **Eng102, English II, 3, B**, then click the ▶ button. The ▶ button saves the current record and also adds a new, blank record to the end of the table.

6   Now enter the following record: **Cis110, Intro to Programming, 3, A.** This time, click the ◀ button. The ◀ button saves the current record but does not display a new record.

7   Use the ◀ and ▶ buttons to view each of the records. You will notice that the records are no longer in ID order; the new records are at the end of the table.

   HELP? If you clicked the ▶ button and a new record was added to the end of the table, simply click the ◀ button to remove the blank record from both the screen and the table.

8   Click **File** on the form's menu bar, then click **Exit**. Visual Basic returns to the design screen.

Similar to Data Manager, the data control adds the new records to the end of the table; it does not automatically place the new records in order by the primary index—in this case, by the ID. In Data Manager, recall that you needed to use the Refresh button to put the new records in their correct order. Rather than use a Refresh button, the College application will use a Refresh Records command on the File menu to rearrange the records.

Coding the File Menu's Refresh Records Command

tips

If you are using a multi-user database, it is a good practice to refresh the database periodically to make sure that the database contains the latest information, and the records are in the proper order.

After adding records to a database, you can use the data control's Refresh method to rearrange the records so they appear in order by the primary index. The Refresh method actually closes and then reopens the database. When you open a database, Visual Basic rearranges the records in order by the primary index. The syntax of the Refresh method is *datacontrol*.**Refresh**. You will use the Refresh method to code the Refresh Records command on the File menu.

To code the File menu's Refresh Records command:

1   Click **File** on the form's menu bar, then click **Refresh Records**. The mnuFileRefresh Click event procedure appears. Press **Tab**, then type **datCollege.refresh** and press the **Enter** key.

2   Close the Code window, then **save** and **run** the application. When you run the application, the data control automatically displays the records in order by the primary index—in this case, in ID order.

Add another record to the database.

3   Click the ▶ button to display the last record in the table, then click the ▶ button to add a new, blank record to the table.

4   Enter the following record: **Cis201, Intro to Visual Basic, 5, A**, then click the ▶ button to save the current record. The Cis201 record is now the last record in the table.

5   Click **File** on the form's menu bar, then click **Refresh Records**. The Refresh Records command closes the College database, then reopens the database and rearranges the records in order by ID.

6   Click the ▶ button four times to display the Cis201 record. The Cis201 record is now correctly positioned between the Cis110 record and the Eng101 record.

7 Click **File** on the form's menu bar, then click **Exit**. Visual Basic returns to the design screen.

Most applications that allow the user to add records to a database also allow the user to delete records from the database. The Delete Record button in the College application will give the user this capability.

Coding the Delete Record Button

The collection of records from one or more tables in a database is referred to as the **Recordset object**. You use the following syntax to refer to the Recordset object associated with a data control: *datacontrol*.**Recordset**. The Recordset object has its own set of methods. For example, to delete a record from a recordset, you use the Recordset object's Delete method in the following syntax: *datacontrol*.**Recordset.Delete**. This command deletes the current record from the recordset; it does not, however, remove the record from the screen. To remove the deleted record from the screen, you must move the data control to another record in the recordset. You can tell the data control to move to the next record in the recordset by using the Recordset object's MoveNext method. The syntax of the MoveNext method is *datacontrol*.**Recordset.MoveNext**.

Most of the code for the Delete Record button has already been entered in its Click event procedure for you. You will need to enter only two additional lines of code to complete the procedure.

To finish coding the Delete Record button:

1 Double-click the **Delete Record** button to open its Code window. Maximize the Code window. The cmdDelete control's Click event appears as shown in Figure 10-25.

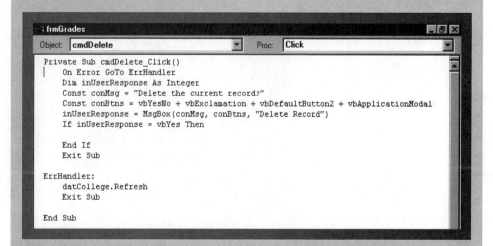

Figure 10-25: Code window for the Delete Record button

When the user clicks the Delete Record button, the MsgBox function prompts the user to confirm the deletion. You should display a message verifying that the

---

tips

▶ Although the deleted record appears on the screen until you move to another record in the recordset, you cannot save the deleted record, nor can you try to delete it again. If you do, Visual Basic will display an error message.

tips

▶ You can also use the Recordset object's Move-First, MoveLast, and Move-Previous methods to move the data control to the first record in the table, the last record in the table, and the previous record in the table, respectively.

user wants to delete the current record before you use the Delete method; the Delete method permanently deletes a record from the recordset.

The MsgBox function's dialog box contains both a Yes and a No button. If the user clicks the Yes button, the current record should be deleted. You can use the Recordset object's Delete method and its MoveNext method to remove the record from the recordset and from the screen, respectively.

2   Enter the two lines of code shown in Figure 10-26.

deletes current record from the recordset

removes deleted record from the screen

```
frmGrades
Object: cmdDelete                    Proc: Click

Private Sub cmdDelete_Click()
    On Error GoTo ErrHandler
    Dim inUserResponse As Integer
    Const conMsg = "Delete the current record?"
    Const conBtns = vbYesNo + vbExclamation + vbDefaultButton2 + vbApplicationModal
    inUserResponse = MsgBox(conMsg, conBtns, "Delete Record")
    If inUserResponse = vbYes Then
        datCollege.Recordset.Delete
        datCollege.Recordset.MoveNext
    End If
    Exit Sub

ErrHandler:
    datCollege.Refresh
    Exit Sub

End Sub
```

Figure 10-26: Completed Code window for the Delete Record button

Notice that, if an error occurs when deleting a record, the error handling routine uses the Refresh method to close and then reopen the database before exiting the procedure.

3   Close the Code window, then **save** and **run** the application. Display the Cis106 record, then click the **Delete Record** button. When the Delete Record dialog box appears, click the **Yes** button.

The `datCollege.Recordset.Delete` instruction, which you entered in the Delete Record button's Click event, deletes the record from the recordset. The `datCollege.Recordset.MoveNext` instruction then removes the deleted record from the screen by moving to the next record in the recordset.

4   Use the ◄ and ► buttons to browse through the records to confirm that the Cis106 record is no longer in the database.

   HELP? If a new record was added to the end of the table after you clicked the ► button, simply click the ◄ button to remove the blank record.

5   Click **File** on the form's menu bar, then click **Exit** to end the application.

Recall that the Data Manager application allowed you to search for specific records in a table. You will include this feature in the College application also.

Coding the Find Record Button

The Find Record button will allow the user to locate and display the information regarding a specific course by searching for the course ID. The code for the Find

Record button has already been entered into its Click event procedure for you. Before looking at the code, however, you will need to learn about the Recordset object's FindFirst method, and its NoMatch property.

The Recordset object's **FindFirst method** locates the first record in the recordset that matches a specified criteria, then makes that record the current record. The syntax of the FindFirst method is *datacontrol*.**Recordset.FindFirst** *criteria*, where *criteria* is a string expression that specifies which record or records to locate. The *criteria*, which must be enclosed in quotation marks, includes both the name of the field you want to search and the data you want to search for. For example, you would use the following instruction to tell the datCollege data control to search the recordset for the first record whose course ID is Eng101: `datCollege.Recordset.FindFirst "ID = 'eng101'"`. Notice the use of the double and single quotation marks in this instruction. Recall that the *criteria* in the FindFirst method must be enclosed in quotation marks. In this case, however, the *criteria* involves a string comparison. As you learned in previous tutorials, the string in a string comparison also must be enclosed in quotation marks. You can't use double quotation marks around both the *criteria* and the string because Visual Basic would not be able to tell where the *criteria* ends and the string begins. The solution is to enclose the *criteria* in double quotation marks and enclose the string in the comparison in single quotation marks. Figure 10-27 shows two examples of how to use the FindFirst method to search for the first course in the recordset that has an A in the Grade field.

The Recordset object also has FindLast, FindNext, and FindPrevious methods that allow you to find the last, next, or previous record in a recordset, respectively.

Example 1:

```
datCollege.Recordset.FindFirst "Grade = 'A'"
```

Example 2: Assume that the stFindString variable contains the letter A.

```
datCollege.Recordset.FindFirst "Grade = '" & stFindString & "'"
```

Figure 10-27: Examples of using the FindFirst method to search the recordset

In the first example, notice that the *criteria* is enclosed in double quotation marks and the grade—the letter A—is enclosed in single quotation marks. You can also use a variable in the *criteria*, as the second example shows, but you must be careful to position the double and single quotation marks correctly. In the second example, the `datCollege.Recordset.FindFirst "Grade = '" & stFindString & "'"` instruction uses string concatenation, which you learned about in Tutorial 3, to include the variable in the *criteria*. The instruction first concatenates the string `"Grade = '"` with the stFindString variable, then concatenates the result with the string `"'"`. Assuming the stFindString variable contains the letter grade A, this instruction is identical to the one shown in the first example.

When searching for a record in the recordset, you can use the Recordset object's **NoMatch property** to determine if a match was found. The NoMatch property will contain the Boolean value True if the desired record was not found; otherwise it will contain the Boolean value False. The code entered in the College application's Find Record button uses both the FindFirst method and the NoMatch property to allow the user to search for a specific course ID.

To view the code in the Find Record button:

1 Double-click the **Find Record** button to open its Code window, then maximize the Code window. The Click event procedure appears as shown in Figure 10-28.

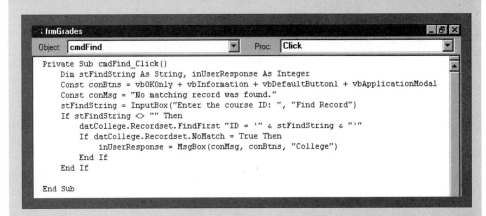

Figure 10-28: Code window for the Find Record button

The procedure begins by declaring two variables and two constants. The inUserResponse variable and the two constants are used by the MsgBox function. The code then uses the InputBox function to prompt the user to enter a course ID. The user's response is assigned to the stFindString variable.

If the stFindString variable does not contain the null string (""), which means that the user entered an ID in the InputBox function's dialog box, then the `datCollege.Recordset.FindFirst "ID = '" & stFindString & "'"` instruction tells Visual Basic to search the ID field for the ID stored in the stFindString variable. The `If datCollege.Recordset.NoMatch = True Then` instruction then uses the Recordset object's NoMatch property to determine if a matching record was found. If the NoMatch property contains the Boolean value True, then a message indicating that no matching record was found is displayed. Use the Find button to search for the Eng101 record.

2 Close the Code window, then **run** the application. Click the **Find Record** button. The InputBox function's Find Record dialog box appears and requests a course ID.

3 Type **eng101** in the Find Record dialog box, then press the **Enter** key to begin the search. The Eng101 record displays. Notice that the search performed by the FindFirst method is not case-sensitive.

Now search for a record that is not in the recordset.

4 Click the **Find Record** button. Type **cis131** in the Find Record dialog box, then press the **Enter** key. The "No matching record was found" message appears in a message box. Click the **OK** button to remove the message box.

5 Click **File**, then click **Exit** to end the application. Visual Basic returns to the design screen.

You have now completed Lesson B. You can either take a break or complete the questions and exercises at the end of the lesson. In Lesson C you will learn how to exchange information among Windows applications.

S U M M A R Y

To access the information in a database:

- Use the data control, which establishes a link between the database and the controls in the interface.
- After adding the data control to the interface, set its DatabaseName property and its RecordSource property. The DatabaseName property tells Visual Basic the name of the database to connect to the data control. The RecordSource property tells Visual Basic which table in the database to use when accessing the records.
- Bind controls to the data control by setting the DataSource and DataField properties. In the DataSource property you enter the name of the data control to which the control is to be bound. In the DataField property you enter the name of the table field to bind to the control. You set the DataSource property first, then set the DataField property.

To automatically add a new record when the user tries to move past the last record in the table:

- Set the data control's EOFAction property to 2-Add New.

To arrange an open database in order by the primary index:

- Use the data control's Refresh method. The syntax of the Refresh method is *datacontrol*.**Refresh**. The Refresh method closes the database, then reopens it using the primary index to display the records.

To delete a record from a database:

- Use the Recordset object's Delete method in the following syntax: *datacontrol*.**Recordset.Delete**. This command deletes the current record from the recordset; it does not, however, remove the record from the screen. You must move to another record in order to remove the deleted record from the screen.

To tell the data control to move to the next record in the recordset:

- Use the Recordset object's MoveNext method. The syntax of the MoveNext method is *datacontrol*.**Recordset.MoveNext**.

To locate the first record in the recordset that matches a criteria:

- Use the Recordset object's FindFirst method. The syntax of the FindFirst method is *datacontrol*.**Recordset.FindFirst** *criteria*, where *criteria* is a string expression that specifies which record or records to locate. The *criteria*, which must be enclosed in quotation marks, includes both the name of the field you want to search and the data you want to search for.

To determine if a matching record was found in the recordset:

- Use the Recordset object's NoMatch property. The syntax is *datacontrol*.**Recordset.NoMatch**. If the NoMatch property contains the Boolean value True, then no matching record was found. If, on the other hand, the NoMatch property contains the Boolean value False, then a matching record was found in the recordset.

Q U E S T I O N S

1. Applications that can access and manipulate the data stored in databases are referred to as _____ applications.
   a. corresponding
   b. cross data
   c. data-aware
   d. data-corresponding
   e. data-sharing

2. The _____ establishes a link between a database and the controls in the interface.
   a. data control
   b. database control
   c. image control
   d. text box control
   e. table control

3. The _____ property tells Visual Basic the name of the database to connect to the data control.
   a. Data
   b. DatabaseName
   c. Record
   d. RecordSource
   e. Table

4. The _____ property tells Visual Basic which table in the database to use when accessing the records.
   a. Data
   b. DatabaseName
   c. Record
   d. RecordSource
   e. Table

5. A control that is connected to a data control is called a _____ control.
   a. attached
   b. bound
   c. connected
   d. joined
   e. linked

6. To connect a text box to a data control, you must set which two of the following text box properties?
   a. BoundField
   b. ConnectField
   c. DataField
   d. DataSource
   e. RecordSource

7. The _____ property contains a value that tells the data control what action to take when the user tries to move past the last record in the table.
   a. ActionEOF
   b. ActionLast
   c. EOFAction
   d. LastAction
   e. LastEOF

8. After adding records to a database, you can use the data control's _____ method to close and then open the database, which will arrange the records in order by the primary index.
   a. Arrange
   b. Open
   c. Order
   d. Rearrange
   e. Refresh

9. The collection of records from one or more tables in a database is referred to as the _____ object.
   a. database
   b. recordset
   c. table

10. You use the _____ method to delete the current record from the recordset.
    a. Delete
    b. Erase
    c. MoveNext
    d. Remove

11. When you delete a record from the recordset, the record is not removed from the screen until you _____ .
    a. click the Delete button again
    b. click the Erase button again
    c. click the Remove button again
    d. move to another record

12. You can use the _____ method to move to another record in the recordset.
    a. Continue
    b. Move
    c. MoveNext
    d. Next
    e. NextRecord

13. You can use the _____ method to search for the first occurrence of a string in a field in the recordset.
    a. Find
    b. FindFirst
    c. First
    d. FirstFind
    e. LocateFirst

14. If the recordset's _____ property contains the Boolean value True, then a matching record was not found in the recordset.
    a. Found
    b. Match
    c. NoMatch
    d. NotFound

15. Which two of the following can you use to locate the first record that contains Cis100 in its ID field? Assume that the stSearch variable contains "Cis100" (without the quotes).
    a. `datCollege.Recordset.FindFirst "ID = 'cis100'"`
    b. `datCollege.Recordset.FindFirst "ID = '" & stSearch & "'"`
    c. `datCollege.Recordset.FindFirst "ID = 'stSearch'"`
    d. `datCollege.Recordset.FindFirst = "ID = 'cis100'"`
    e. `datCollege.Recordset.FindFirst = ID & stSearch`

E X E R C I S E S

1. In this exercise you will create an application that will allow you to add, delete, and search the la1Done.mdb database that you created in Lesson A's Exercise 1.

   Scenario: In Lesson A's Exercise 1, you created a one-table database that allows you to keep track of the basketball scores for your favorite team. The database is named la1Done (la1Done.mdb) and the table is named Scores. The table contains the name of the opposing team, the date the game was played, your team's score, and the opposing team's score. In that exercise you also created a primary index, in ascending order, for the opposing team's name field. You also defined a data validation rule for the two fields that store the scores; the fields allow numbers between 0 and 130 only. Additionally, you added five records to the table.

   a. Create an application that allows you to add records to and delete records from the la1Done.mdb database that you created in Lesson A's Exercise 1. The la1Done.mdb database is located in the Tut10 folder on your Student Disk. The application should also allow you to search the opposing team's name field for the name of a specific team. Include a File menu that allows you to refresh the database and to exit the application.

   b. Save the form and the project as lb1Done in the Tut10 folder on your Student Disk.

   c. Run the application, then test the application by adding five more entries to the database, then deleting two of the entries from the database. Search for the first record that matches a specific team's name. Also test the commands on the File menu.

   d. Stop the application and print the form and the code.

2. In this exercise you will create an application that will allow you to add, delete, and search the la2Done.mdb database that you created in Lesson A's Exercise 2.

   Scenario: In Lesson A's Exercise 2, you created a one-table database that allows you to keep track of your monthly phone bill. The database is named la2Done (la2Done.mdb) and the table is named Phone. The table contains the month, year, and total bill. In that exercise you also created a primary index, in ascending order, for the month field. You also defined a data validation rule for the month field. The month can be only 01,02, 03, 04, 05, 06, 07, 08, 09, 10, 11, or 12. Additionally, you added five records to the table.

   a. Create an application that allows you to add records to and delete records from the la2Done.mdb database that you created in Lesson A's Exercise 2. The la2Done.mdb database is located in the Tut10 folder on your Student Disk. The application should also allow you to search the month field for a specific month. Include a File menu that allows you to refresh the database and to exit the application.

   b. Save the form and the project as lb2Done in the Tut10 folder on your Student Disk.

   c. Run the application, then test the application by adding five more entries to the database, then deleting two of the entries from the database. Search for the first record that matches a specific month. Also test the commands on the File menu.

   d. Stop the application and print the form and the code.

   Exercises 3 through 6 are Discovery Exercises, which allow you both to "discover" the solutions to problems on your own and to experiment with material that is not covered in the tutorial.

discovery ▶ 3. In this exercise you will create an application that will allow you to add, delete, and search the la3Done.mdb database that you created in Lesson A's Discovery Exercise 3.

   Scenario: In Lesson A's Discovery Exercise 3, you created a one-table database that contains the names and phone numbers of your friends. The database is named la3Done (la3Done.mdb) and the table is named Friends. The table contains the last name, first name, and phone number fields. In that exercise you also created a primary index, in ascending order, that includes both the last name and first name fields. Additionally, you added ten records to the table.

a. Create an application that allows you to add records to and delete records from the la3Done.mdb database that you created in Lesson A's Exercise 3. The la3Done.mdb database is located in the Tut10 folder on your Student Disk. The application should also allow you to search the last name and first name fields for the name of a specific person. Include a way to refresh the database and also to exit the application.

b. Save the form and the project as lb3Done in the Tut10 folder on your Student Disk.

c. Run the application, then test the application by adding five more entries to the database, then deleting two of the entries from the database. Search for the first record that matches a specific person's last and first name. Also test the refresh and exit options.

d. Stop the application and print the form and the code.

discovery ▶ 4. In this exercise you will modify the College application that you created in Lesson B.

Scenario: The Find Record button in the college application currently finds only the first record that matches the search string entered by the user. You would like the application to be able to locate and display all the records that match the search string. For example, you want the application to allow the user to display all of the Cis records, one record at a time.

a. Open the lbColl (lbColl.vbp) project that you created in Lesson B.

b. Save the form and the project as lb4Done.

c. Modify the application according to the scenario.

d. Save and run the application, then test the application.

e. When the application is working correctly, print the code.

discovery ▶ 5. In this exercise you will use the CD.mdb database that you created in Lesson A's Discovery Exercise 4.

Scenario: In this exercise you will create an application that allows you to view the records in the CD.mdb Microsoft Access database that you created in Lesson A's Discovery Exercise 4. You will need to use two data controls. One of the data controls will allow the user to browse through the records in the CD table, and the other will allow the user to browse through the records in the Song table. When the user moves to a different CD number in the CD table, the first song matching the CD number should display in the interface; the user can then use the Song table's data control to view all of the songs that match the current CD number.

a. Create an appropriate interface.

b. Save the form and the project as lb5Done in the Tut10 folder on your Student Disk.

c. Use the Help menu to search for help on the Reposition event and the Fields property.

d. Code the application appropriately.

e. If necessary, use Data Manager to add records to both the CD and Song tables. Be sure that at least one of the CD's has three songs entered in the Song table.

f. Save, run, and test the application. When the application is working correctly, print the form and the code.

discovery ▶ 6. In this exercise you will use the data control to connect to a dBASE IV database.

Scenario: The procedure to connect to an external database, a database other than a Microsoft Access database, is the same as the procedure to connect to a Microsoft Access database, with one exception. When connecting to an external database, you must set the data control's Connect property. The Connect property specifies the type of database and, in some cases, the database password. You will connect to an external database created with the dBASE IV software package. The database, which is named school.dbf, is in the Tut10 folder directory on your Student Disk.

a. Open the Dbase.vbp project, which is in the Tut10 folder on your Student Disk. Save the form and the project as lb6Done. Click the View Form button.

b. Select the Data1 control. Display the Properties window, then click Connect in the Properties window. Click the Settings list arrow, then click dBASE IV; in the list. dBASEIV appears in the Properties window.

c. The DatabaseName setting for a dBASE IV database is drive:\path\. Click DatabaseName in the Properties window. Depending on the location of your Student Disk, type either a:\Tut10 or b:\Tut10 in the DatabaseName property.

d. The name of the database is school.dbf. You enter the name of the database in the RecordSource property. Click RecordSource in the Properties window. Click the Settings box list arrow, then click SCHOOL in the list.

e. Select the txtID, txtTitle, txtHours, and txtGrade text boxes. Display the Properties window, click DataSource in the Properties window, click the Settings box list arrow, then click Data1. Click the form to cancel the selection of the four text boxes.

f. Set the DataField properties for the four text boxes as follows:

Text Box	DataField
txtID	NUMBER
txtTitle	TITLE
txtCredits	HOURS
txtGrade	GRADE

g. Save and run the application. All of the buttons have already been coded. The code is identical to the College application that accessed the Access database.

h. Test the application, then click the Exit button to end the application.

i. Print the form as text.

In this lesson you will learn how to:

- Define the terms DDE, OLE, embed, link, source application, server application, destination application, and client application
- Use the clipboard to copy data from one Windows application to another
- Use DDE to copy data from one Windows application to another
- Add an OLE container control to a form
- Embed data in an application using OLE
- Link data in an application using OLE
- Update the contents of an OLE control using the Update method

Using the Clipboard, DDE, and OLE

Sharing Data Between Windows Applications

> Important Note: You must have access to Microsoft Excel to complete this section of Lesson C using the computer.

One advantage of using Windows applications is that they can share data with each other; because of this, a Windows application can include data created by other Windows applications. For example, you can create a Visual Basic application that contains records from a Microsoft Access database, data from a Microsoft Excel worksheet, and a paragraph from a Microsoft Word document. Three methods are available for sharing data between applications: the clipboard, DDE, and OLE.

Using the Clipboard to Share Data Among Windows Applications

The simplest method of exchanging data between applications is to use the clipboard. The data in one application is either cut or copied to the clipboard, then pasted into another application. Although the clipboard provides an easy way to copy data, it does have one drawback: the copied data has no link to the application that created it. In order to update the copied data, you would need to open the application that created the data, edit the data, copy the data to the clipboard, then paste it into the other application again. Observe this now by using the clipboard to copy information from a Microsoft Excel worksheet to a Visual Basic application.

To use the clipboard to copy data from Microsoft Excel to Visual Basic:

1 Start Visual Basic, if necessary. Open the **Clipbd** (clipbd.vbp) project, which is located in the Tut10 folder on your Student Disk.

2 Click the **View Form** button. The frmClipboard form appears as shown in Figure 10-29.

The form contains an Exit command button, a label control, and an image control.

3 Save the form and the project as **lcClipbd** in the Tut10 folder on your Student Disk.

imgSales

Figure 10-29: frmClipboard form

You will now copy data from an Excel worksheet to the clipboard, then paste the data in the image control in the Visual Basic form. First copy the data to the clipboard.

4   Start Microsoft Excel, then maximize Excel, if necessary.

5   Click **File** on the menu bar, then click **Open**. Open the **Sales** (sales.xls) file, which is located in the Tut10 folder on your Student Disk.

6   Select cells A1 through B6, as shown in Figure 10-30.

HELP? To select cells A1 through B6, first click cell A1 to select it. Then hold down the left mouse button and drag the mouse pointer to cell B6. When cells A1 through B6 are selected, release the mouse button.

Figure 10-30: Cells A1 through B6 selected in the Sales worksheet

7 Click **Edit** on the menu bar, then click **Copy**. Windows copies the information in the selected area to the clipboard. A moving border appears around the selected area in the worksheet. Now paste the copied information into the image control in the Visual Basic application.

8 Make Microsoft Visual Basic the active application.

HELP? You can make an application the active application by clicking its button on the taskbar.

WINDOWS 3.1

You can make an application the active application by pressing and holding down the Alt key as you tap the Tab key; when the name of the application you want to make active appears on the screen, release the Alt key. In Windows 3.1 you can also press Alt + Esc to make an application the active one.

9 Click the **imgSales** control to select it. Click **Edit** on the menu bar, then click **Paste**. (Be sure you do not click Paste Link.) Windows pastes the contents of the clipboard into the imgSales control as shown in Figure 10-31.

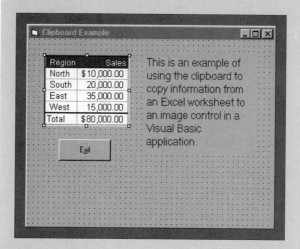

Figure 10-31: Worksheet data pasted in imgSales control

Observe what happens when you make a change to the data in the Excel worksheet.

10 Make Microsoft Excel the active application. Press the **Esc** key to remove the moving border around the selected cells, then click cell **B2**, which contains the sales for the North region. Type **20000** and press the **Enter** key. $20,000.00 appears in cell B2, and the total sales amount in cell B6 changes to $90,000.00.

11 Make Microsoft Visual Basic the active application. Notice that the image control shows that the sales for the North region are still $10,000.00.

Recall that using the clipboard to exchange information has one drawback: the only way to update the copied data is to open the application that created the data, edit the data, copy the data to the clipboard, then paste it into the other application again. Do that now.

GUI
Design Tips

Using the Clipboard to Copy Data to a Visual Basic Application

- Start the application that contains the data. Also start Visual Basic.
- Make active the application that contains the data.
- Select the data you want to copy to the Visual Basic application.
- Either copy or cut the selected data to the clipboard.
- Make the Visual Basic application the active application.
- Use the Paste command on Visual Basic's Edit menu to paste the data from the clipboard into the Visual Basic application.

Not all applications support DDE.

12 Make Microsoft Excel the active application. Select cells A1 through B6. Click **Edit** on the menu bar, then click **Copy**. Windows copies the information in the selected cells to the clipboard. A moving border appears around the selected area in the worksheet.

13 Make Microsoft Visual Basic the active application. Click the **imgSales** control to select it. Click **Edit** on the menu bar, then click **Paste**. The North region's sales are now $20,000.00, and the total sales are $90,000.00.

Now that you have observed how to use the clipboard to copy data from one Windows application to another, you can open a new project in Visual Basic and also close the Sales.xls file in Excel.

14 Visual Basic is currently the active application. Click **File** on the menu bar, then click **New Project**. When you are asked if you want to save the changes to the frmClipboard form, click the **No** button.

HELP? If a message box displays asking if you want to save the LCCLIPBD project, click the No button.

15 Make Microsoft Excel the active application. Click **File** on the menu bar, then click **Close**. When you are asked if you want to save the changes to the Sales.xls file, click the **No** button.

16 Minimize Excel, then make Visual Basic the active application, if necessary.

DDE is the second method of sharing data between Windows applications.

Using DDE to Share Data With Other Applications

Important Note: You must have access to Microsoft Excel to complete this section of Lesson C using the computer.

DDE, which stands for Dynamic Data Exchange, is another method of copying data from one Windows application to another. When using DDE, both the application that supplies the data, called the **source application**, and the application that receives the data, called the **destination application**, must be running at the same time in order for the exchange of data to occur. To update the data in the destination application, you first open the source application, then edit and save the data in the source application. The changes you make in the source application will automatically appear in the destination application. Try this by using DDE to copy data from an Excel worksheet to a Visual Basic application.

To use DDE to copy data from Microsoft Excel to Visual Basic:

1 Visual Basic should be the active application. Open the **DDE** (dde.vbp) project, which is located in the Tut10 folder on your Student Disk.

2 Click the **View Form** button to view the form. The frmDDE form appears.

3   Save the form and the project as **lcDDE** in the Tut10 folder on your Student Disk.

In Visual Basic, only the text box, picture box, and label controls support DDE; those are the only controls that you can copy data into using DDE. In the frmDDE form, you will copy information from an Excel worksheet to a picture box control. A picture box control is similar to an image control; both can be used to display a graphic.

4   Double-click the **PictureBox tool** in the toolbox. A picture box control appears in the interface. Change the picture box control's properties as follows:

AutoSize:	**True**
Left:	**360**
Top:	**360**

You will now copy the information from an Excel worksheet to the clipboard, then use DDE to paste the information into the picture box. First copy the information to the clipboard.

5   Make Microsoft Excel the active application. Open the **Bonus** (bonus.xls) file, which is located in the Tut10 folder on your Student Disk.

6   Select cells A1 through B6, as shown in Figure 10-32.

Figure 10-32: Cells A1 through B6 selected in Bonus worksheet

7   Click **Edit** on the menu bar, then click **Copy**. Windows copies the selected information to the clipboard. A moving border appears around the selected area in the worksheet.

Now use DDE to paste the information into the picture box in the Visual Basic application.

8   Make Visual Basic the active application. Click the **picture box control** to select it. Sizing handles appear around the control and the form's title bar is highlighted. Click **Edit** on the menu bar to open the Edit menu. See Figure 10-33.

Figure 10-33: Open Visual Basic Edit menu

HELP? If the Cut, Copy, and Paste commands on the Edit menu are dimmed, click Edit to close the Edit menu. Click the picture box control in the form, then click Edit to open the Edit menu again.

Notice that the Edit menu has a Paste command and a Paste Link command. As you observed when you copied the Sales worksheet information to the image control in the previous section, the Paste command merely copies the contents of the clipboard to the selected control; it does not maintain any connection between the original data and the copied data. The Paste Link command, however, not only copies the contents of the clipboard to the selected control, it also maintains a link between the original data and the copied data so that a change made to the original data affects the copied data.

9   Click **Paste Link** in the Edit menu. Windows copies the data from the clipboard into the picture box control. The Paste Link command tells Windows to maintain a link between the original data and the copied data. See Figure 10-34.

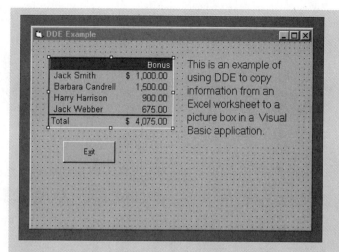

Figure 10-34: Bonus worksheet pasted in picture box control

Observe what happens when you use Excel to make a change to the Bonus worksheet. Change Jack Smith's bonus from $1,000.00 to $800.00.

10 Make Excel the active application. Press the **Esc** key to remove the moving border around the selected cells. Click cell **B2**, which contains Jack Smith's $1,000.00 bonus. Type **800** and press the **Enter** key. Jack Smith's bonus changes to $800.00, and the total bonus amount changes to $3,875.00.

11 Click **File** on Excel's menu bar, then click **Save**.

12 Make Visual Basic the active application. See Figure 10-35.

new data

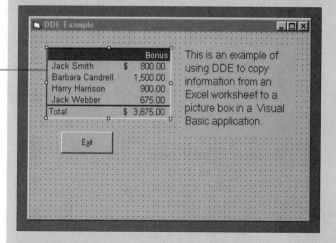

Figure 10-35: frmDDE form showing new data in the Bonus worksheet

Notice that the picture box control now shows Jack Smith's bonus is $800.00, and the total bonus amount is $3,875.00.

Now save and run the lcDDE application to confirm that Windows maintains the connection between the original data and the copied data when the lcDDE application is running.

13 **Save** and **run** the lcDDE application.

Now change Jack Smith's bonus back to $1,000.00.

14 Make Excel the active application. Click cell **B2**, which contains Jack Smith's $800.00 bonus. Type **1000** and press the **Enter** key. Jack Smith's bonus changes to $1,000.00, and the total bonus amount changes to $4,075.00.

15 Click **File** on Excel's menu bar, then click **Save**.

16 Make Visual Basic the active application. $1,000.00 displays as Jack Smith's bonus, and $4,075.00 displays as the total bonus amount. See Figure 10-36.

picture box reflects change in data

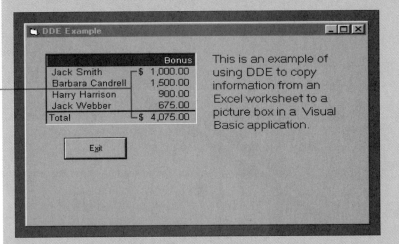

Figure 10-36: frmDDE showing changes made in the Bonus worksheet

17 Click the **Exit** button in the Visual Basic application. Visual Basic returns to the design screen. Click the **Save Project** button to save the application. Click **File** on the menu bar, then click **New Project**.

18 Make Microsoft Excel the active application. Click **File** on the menu bar, then click **Exit** to close the Excel application.

19 Make Visual Basic the active application, if necessary.

GUI
Design Tips

Using DDE to Copy Data to a Visual Basic Application

- Start the source application, then open the document that contains the data. Also start Visual Basic, and open the application to which you want to copy the data.
- Make the source application the active application.
- Select the data you want to copy to the Visual Basic application.
- Either copy or cut the selected data to the clipboard.
- Make the Visual Basic application the active application.
- Select either a picture box, text box, or label control.
- Use the Paste Link command on Visual Basic's Edit menu to paste the data from the clipboard into the selected control.

The third method of exchanging data between Windows applications is OLE.

Using OLE to Exchange Data

Important Note: You must have access to Microsoft Excel to complete the OLE sections of Lesson C using the computer.

OLE, which stands for Object Linking and Embedding and is pronounced oh-lay, is the latest mechanism for sharing data between Windows applications. The data that is copied from one application to another is referred to as an **object**. An object can be, for example, a Microsoft Excel worksheet or a Microsoft Word document. The application that created the data (object) is called the **source application** or **server application**, and the application to which the object is copied is called the **container application** or **client application**.

▶ Not all applications support OLE, and some OLE applications do not support all of the features of OLE.

Like the clipboard and DDE, OLE allows you to create an application that displays data from many different applications. Unlike the clipboard and DDE, however, OLE allows you to start a Windows application from inside another Windows application. For example, OLE enables you to start Excel from a Visual Basic application that contains an Excel worksheet. The user can then edit the data from within the application in which it was created or, in many cases, from within the Visual Basic application.

When using OLE to copy an object from a server application to a client application, you can choose to either embed the object or link the object. The difference between embedding and linking is where the object is stored. When you embed an object, the object is stored in the client application, where it exists as a separate entity; changes made to the object in the server application do not affect the object embedded in the client application, and vice versa. For example, if you embed the data from an Excel worksheet into a Visual Basic application, a copy of the worksheet data is stored in the Visual Basic application. Any changes you make to the data in the Visual Basic application affect only the copy of the data; the changes do not affect the original data. Also, any changes you make to the original data in Excel do not affect the copy of the data in the Visual Basic application.

When you link an object to a client application, on the other hand, only a pointer to the original object is stored in the client application. Changes made to the object in the server application affect the object in the client application, and vice versa.

You would embed an object, rather than link it, if you didn't want changes to the original object to affect the object in the client application, and vice versa. You would link an object, rather than embed it, if you did want changes made to the original object to be reflected in the client application, and vice versa. Assume, for example, that your duties at work require you to use a specific form letter that was created in Microsoft Word. You would like to include the Word document in a Visual Basic application; however, the document is used by a number of people in your office, and those co-workers sometimes make changes to it. If you do not want the changes that others make to the Word document to be reflected in your Visual Basic application, then you would need to embed the Word document in the application. If, on the other hand, you do want the changes to be reflected in your Visual Basic application, then you would need to link the document to the application. This concept is illustrated in Figure 10-37.

▶ An application that contains an embedded object will require more disk space when saved than an application that contains a linked object. That's because an application that contains an embedded object must store the entire object, whereas an application that contains a linked object only needs to store a pointer to the object.

Embedding:

copy of Word
document is
stored in
Visual Basic
application

Linking:

pointer to
Word
document is
stored in
Visual Basic
application

Link

Figure 10-37: Illustration of embedding and linking

You link and embed objects in Visual Basic by including the **OLE container control** in a Visual Basic application. First you will learn how to use Visual Basic's OLE control to embed an Excel worksheet in a Visual Basic application, then you will learn how to link an Excel worksheet to a Visual Basic application.

Embedding an Excel Worksheet in a Visual Basic Application

You use Visual Basic's OLE container control to embed an object in a Visual Basic application. In this case, the object will be a Microsoft Excel worksheet. Recall that when you embed an object in a client application, the object is stored in the client application.

To embed an Excel worksheet in a Visual Basic application:

1   Visual Basic should be the active application. Open the **Embed** (embed.vbp) project, which is located in the Tut10 folder on your Student Disk.

2   Click the **View Form** button to view the frmEmbed form, then save the form and the project as **lcEmbed** in the Tut10 folder on your Student Disk.

The File menu in the frmEmbed form contains Print and Exit commands only; both commands have already been coded for you.

3 Double-click the **OLE tool** 🔲 in the toolbox. An OLE container control appears momentarily, then the Insert Object dialog box appears as shown in Figure 10-38.

your Object Type list may be different

Figure 10-38: Insert Object dialog box

The Insert Object dialog box allows you to embed a new or existing file; it also allows you to link an existing file. The Object Type list box lists the type of objects that your system can either link or embed. (Your list may be different than the one shown in Figure 10-38.) The Excel worksheet that you will embed in the current application is an existing file, so you will need to select the Create from File option button.

4 Click the **Create from File** option button to select it.

The file that you will embed is named Region (region.xls) and is located in the Tut10 folder on your Student Disk.

5 Click the **Browse** button. The Browse dialog box appears. Open the Tut10 folder on your Student Disk. Click **Region** (region.xls) in the Browse dialog box, then click the **Insert** button (*the OK button in Windows 3.1*). The Browse dialog box closes and the Insert Object dialog box appears.

Because you want to embed the Excel file in the Visual Basic application, be sure that the Link check box in the Insert Object dialog box is not checked. The completed Insert Object dialog box is shown in Figure 10-39.

Figure 10-39: Completed Insert Object dialog box

6   Click the **OK** button. In a few moments the Region.xls worksheet appears inside the OLE container control. Display the Properties window, then set the OLE container control's Left property to **360** and its Top property to **360**. See Figure 10-40.

GUI
Design Tips

Using the OLE Control to Embed Data in a Visual Basic Application

- Start Visual Basic, which is the client (container) application. You do not need to start the server (source) application.

- Add an OLE container control to the Visual Basic form.

- Select either the Create New option button or the Create from File option button in the Insert Object dialog box.

- If you are embedding an existing file, select the file name in the Browse dialog box.

- Be sure the Link check box in the Insert Object dialog box is not selected.

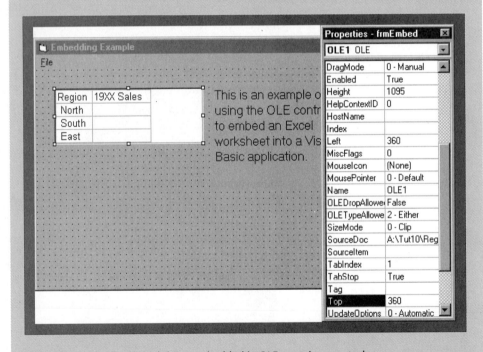

Figure 10-40: Region.xls worksheet embedded in OLE container control

The OLE container control does not display all of the Region.xls worksheet. You can use the OLE control's SizeMode property to control how much of the Excel worksheet appears inside the control.

The SizeMode Property

The **SizeMode property** contains a value that specifies how the OLE container control is sized or how its image is displayed when it contains an object. The syntax of the SizeMode property is *object*.**SizeMode** = *value*. *Value* can either be 0-Clip, 1-Stretch, 2-AutoSize, or 3-Zoom. When set to 0-Clip, which is the default setting, Visual Basic clips the image so that it fits within the OLE control's borders. When set to 1-Stretch, Visual Basic sizes the object's image to fill the OLE container control, but the image may not maintain its original proportions. When set to 2-AutoSize, Visual Basic resizes the OLE control to display the entire object. When set to 3-Zoom, Visual Basic resizes the object to fill the OLE control while maintaining the object's original proportions. Change the OLE control's SizeMode property to 2-AutoSize.

To set the OLE control's SizeMode property:

1 The OLE control is currently selected and the Properties window is currently displayed. Set the OLE control's SizeMode property to **2-AutoSize**. Visual Basic resizes the OLE control to display all of the information in the Excel worksheet.

Now change the OLE control's SizeMode property to 1-Stretch so that Visual Basic will keep the control at its current size when changes are made to the worksheet.

2 Set the OLE control's SizeMode property to **1-Stretch**.

3 Click the **form's title bar** to return to the form. See Figure 10-41.

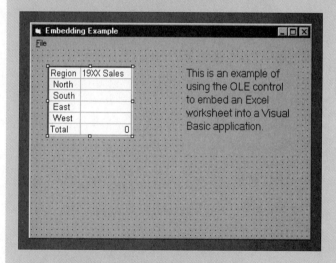

Figure 10-41: OLE control after setting the SizeMode property

The OLE control allows you to edit the Excel worksheet from within the Visual Basic application.

Editing Embedded Data

Visual Basic's OLE control allows you to use the server application's menus and/or tools to edit the embedded data in the client application. In the lcEmbed application, for example, the OLE control enables you to use Excel's menus to edit the worksheet data while you are in the Visual Basic application. Observe how this works.

To use the Visual Basic application to edit the worksheet data:

1   **Save** and **run** the lcEmbed application.

You can edit the worksheet data by simply double-clicking the OLE control in the form.

2   Double-click the **OLE control**, which contains the embedded Excel worksheet. In a few moments the interface appears as shown in Figure 10-42.

Excel menus ───────────

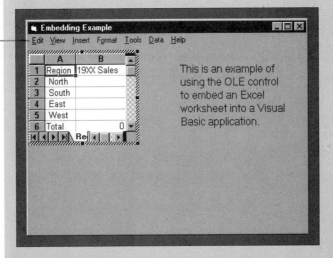

Figure 10-42: Excel menus shown in the lcEmbed Visual Basic application

The OLE control replaces the lcEmbed application's File menu with Excel's menus.

Now enter the 1998 sales for the four regions.

3   Click cell **B1** in the worksheet, then type **1998 Sales** and press the **Enter** key.

4   Type **500** in cell B2 and press the **Enter** key.

5   Type **300** in cell B3 and press the **Enter** key.

6   Type **400** in cell B4 and press the **Enter** key.

7   Type **200** in cell B5 and press the **Enter** key.

Notice that the total sales, 1400, appears in cell B6. Now use Excel's Format menu to change the appearance of the worksheet.

8   Select cells A1 through B6. Click **Format** on the form's menu bar, then click **AutoFormat**. When the AutoFormat dialog box appears, click **Accounting 3**, then click the **OK** button. The worksheet is formatted to the Accounting 3 format.

9   Press the **Esc** key to remove Excel's menus from the form's menu bar. The lcEmbed application's File menu reappears in the menu bar, as shown in Figure 10-43.

tips

In Lesson C's Discovery Exercise 4 you will learn how to display both the application's menu and Excel's menus at the same time.

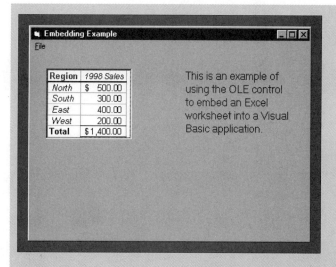

Figure 10-43: Current status of OLE control and menu bar

10 If your computer is connected to a printer, click **File** on the form's menu bar, then click **Print**.

11 Click **File** on the form's menu bar, then click **Exit**. Visual Basic returns to the design screen. The changes you made to the worksheet are not saved in the OLE control, nor are they saved in the Region.xls file.

Now learn how to link an Excel worksheet to a Visual Basic application.

Linking an Excel Worksheet to a Visual Basic Application

You also use Visual Basic's OLE container control to link an object to a Visual Basic application. In this case, you will link a Microsoft Excel worksheet.

To link an Excel worksheet to a Visual Basic application:

1 Open the **Link** (link.vbp) project, which is located in the Tut10 folder on your Student Disk.

2 Click the **View Form** button to view the frmLink form. Save the form and the project as **lcLink** in the Tut10 folder on your Student Disk. The File menu contains two commands, Print and Exit, which have already been coded for you.

3 Double-click the **OLE tool** in the toolbox. The OLE control appears momentarily, and then the Insert Object dialog box appears.

You will link an existing file named Items, which is located in the Tut10 folder on your Student Disk.

4 Click the **Create from File** option button to select it. Click the **Browse** button. The Browse dialog box appears. Open the Tut10 folder on your Student Disk. Click **Items** (items.xls) in the Browse dialog box, then click the **Insert** button (*the OK button in Windows 3.1*). The Browse dialog box closes and the Insert Object dialog box appears.

If you want to link an object, rather than embed it, you must select the Link check box.

tips

▶ **To save the changes you make to the embedded worksheet, you would need to code the Visual Basic application so that it saves the data in a separate file, then reads the file whenever the application is run.**

5 Click the **Link** check box. A check mark (*an X in Windows 3.1*) appears in the Link check box, as shown in Figure 10-44.

be sure this check box is selected

Figure 10-44: Insert Object dialog box showing link to Excel worksheet

6 Click the **OK** button. In a few moments the Excel worksheet appears inside the OLE container control.

7 Display the Properties window, then set the OLE container control's Left property to **360** and its Top property to **360**. Set its SizeMode property to **2-AutoSize**, then set its SizeMode property to **1-Stretch**.

8 Click the **form's title bar** to return to the form. Figure 10-45 shows the Excel worksheet displayed in the OLE container control.

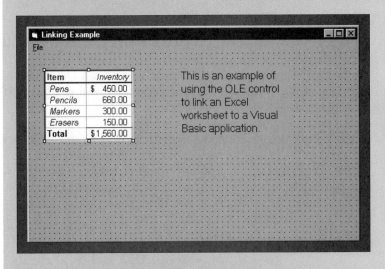

Figure 10-45: Excel worksheet displayed in OLE container control

Each time you run the current application, you want Visual Basic to use the Items.xls file on your Student Disk to update the contents of the OLE container control. In other words, if you use the Excel application to make a change to the Items.xls file, you want the current application to reflect that change. You tell Visual Basic to update the OLE container control each time the current application is run by including the OLE container control's Update method in the form's Load event.

Update Method

When an object is linked to a client application, you can use the OLE control's **Update method** to retrieve the current data from the server application before the data is displayed in the client application's OLE control. The syntax of the Update method is *object*.**Update**, where *object* is the name of the OLE container control.

To include the Update method in the form's Load event:

1 Double-click the **form** to open its Code window. The form's Load event, which contains the instructions for centering the form, appears. Position the insertion point in the line below the centering instructions. Press the **Tab** key, if necessary, then type **ole1.update** and press the **Enter** key.

2 Close the Code window, then **save** and **run** the application. In a few moments the user interface appears with the Items.xls worksheet displayed in the OLE container control, as shown in Figure 10-46.

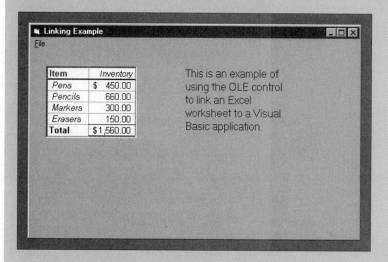

Figure 10-46: Items.xls worksheet displayed in the OLE container control

You can edit a linked object in the same manner as you edit an embedded object—by simply double-clicking the OLE control. Use the OLE control to change the Markers inventory dollar amount from $300.00 to $400.00.

3 Double-click the **OLE control**. The OLE control starts Excel and displays the Items.xls worksheet as shown in Figure 10-47.

Excel application

IcLink application

Figure 10-47: Items.xls worksheet displayed in Excel

4   Click cell **B4**, then type **400** and press the **Enter** key. The total inventory amount changes to 1,660.00.

5   Click **File** on Excel's menu bar, then click **Save** to save the changes to the Items.xls file.

6   Click **File** on Excel's menu bar, then click **Exit** to close Excel. Notice that the OLE control also shows that the inventory dollar amount for the Markers is 400.00.

7   Click **File** on the form's menu bar, then click **Exit** to end the application. Visual Basic returns to the design screen. Don't be concerned that the original inventory amount for Markers, 300.00, appears in the OLE control. When you run the lcLink application, the Update method in the form's Load event will retrieve the most current information from the Items.xls file and display it in the OLE control. Confirm that now.

8   **Save** and **run** the application. Notice that the OLE control shows the correct dollar amount for the Markers—400.00.

Now change the dollar amount for the Markers back to 300.00.

9   Double-click the **OLE control**. When the Items worksheet appears in Excel, change the 400.00 in cell B4 to **300.00**. Click **File** on Excel's menu bar, then click **Save**. Click **File** on Excel's menu bar, then click **Exit**. You are returned to the lcLink application in Visual Basic. The Markers entry is now 300.00.

10   Click **File** on the form's menu bar, then click **Exit**. Visual Basic returns to the design screen.

Now that you know how to copy data from one application to another, you can code the Money application, which you previewed at the beginning of this tutorial.

Creating the Money Application

Important Note: You must have access to Microsoft Excel to complete this section of Lesson C using the computer.

At the beginning of this tutorial you previewed two applications: the College application and the Money application. You created the College application in Lesson B; you will create the Money application in this lesson. Recall that the Money application contains an Excel worksheet that lists your college expenses for the Fall semester. The application also includes a Microsoft Word document in which you can write a note to your parents asking them to send more money.

Your Student Disk contains a partially completed Money application. You will complete the application in this lesson.

To complete the Money application:

1   Open the **Money** (Money.vbp) project, which is located in the Tutorial 10 folder on your Student Disk. Click the **View Form** button to view the frmMoney form. The form contains only a File menu with a Print and an Exit command, which have already been coded for you.

2   Save the form and the project as **lcMoney** in the Tut10 folder on your Student Disk.

Your Student Disk contains an Excel worksheet that lists your expenses for the Fall semester. The worksheet also contains a chart that displays the expenses in a 3-D pie graph. Use the OLE control to link the Excel worksheet to the Money application. The Excel file is named Expenses and is located in the Tut10 folder on your Student Disk.

3   Double-click the **OLE tool** 🖼 in the toolbox. The OLE control appears momentarily, then the Insert Object dialog box appears.

4   Click the **Create from File** option button to select it. Click the **Browse** button. The Browse dialog box appears. Open the Tut10 folder on your Student Disk. Click **Expenses** (expenses.xls) in the Browse dialog box, then click the **Insert** button (*the OK button in Windows 3.1*). The Browse dialog box closes and the Insert Object dialog box appears.

5   Click the **Link** check box to select it. A check mark (*an X in Windows 3.1*) appears in the Link check box.

6   Click the **OK** button. In a few moments the Expenses worksheet appears inside the OLE control.

7   Display the Properties window, then set the OLE container control's Left property to **360** and its Top property to **360**. Set its SizeMode property to **2-AutoSize**, then set its SizeMode property to **1-Stretch**.

8   Click the **form's title bar** to return to the form. Figure 10-48 shows the Excel worksheet displayed in the OLE container control.

GUI
Design Tips

Using the OLE Control to Link Data to a Visual Basic Application

- Start Visual Basic. You do not need to start the application that contains the data to be copied.

- Add an OLE container control to the form.

- Select the Create from File option button in the Insert Object dialog box.

- Select the file name in the Browse dialog box.

- Be sure the Link check box in the Insert Object dialog box is selected.

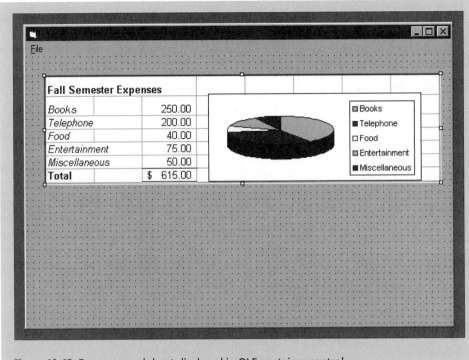

Figure 10-48: Expenses worksheet displayed in OLE container control

Each time you run the Money application, you want Visual Basic to use the Expenses.xls file on your Student Disk to update the contents of the OLE container control. Recall that you tell Visual Basic to update the OLE container control by including the control's Update method in the form's Load event.

To include the Update method in the form's Load event:

1 Double-click the **form** to open its Code window. The form's Load event procedure, which contains the instructions to center the form, appears. Position the insertion point below the centering instructions. Press the **Tab** key, if necessary, then type **ole1.update** and press the **Enter** key.

2 Close the Code window.

Now complete the Money application by embedding a new Microsoft Word document in an OLE control.

Embedding a New Microsoft Word Document in a Visual Basic Application

Important Note: You must have access to Microsoft Word to complete this section of Lesson C using the computer.

Now that the Money application contains both a listing and a graph showing your Fall semester expenses, it's time to include a note to your parents asking for more money.

To embed a new Microsoft Word document in a Visual Basic application:

1 Double-click the **OLE** tool in the toolbox. The OLE control appears momentarily, then the Insert Object dialog box appears. The Word document you will embed in the Money application is a new file.

2 The Create New option button should already be selected. Click **Microsoft Word Document** in the Object Type list box.

   HELP? Your Microsoft Word entry in the Object Type list may contain a version number.

3 Click the **OK** button. A new Word document appears inside the OLE control, as shown in Figure 10-49.

tips

▶ Existing files can only be be embedded; they cannot be linked. Only new files can be linked.

Word toolbars

new Word document

Figure 10-49: New Word document embedded in OLE control

Notice that the form now displays the menus from Microsoft Word. Your screen may also display one or more of Word's toolbars. (Don't be concerned if your screen does not display any toolbars.)

HELP? If the Word toolbars are covering the form's menu bar, drag them to another position on the screen.

4   Click the **form's title bar** to select the form.

5   The OLE control that contains the empty Word document should be selected. Click **View** on Visual Basic's menu bar, then click **Properties**. Set the OLE control's properties as follows:

Height:	2055	Top:	3000
Left:	360	Width:	7695
SizeMode:	1 - Stretch		

6   Click the **form** to select it, then click the OLE control that contains the empty Word document. See Figure 10-50.

Word document

Figure 10-50: OLE control with Word document inside

Now use the OLE control to type a brief note to your parents.

7   **Save** and **run** the application.

8   Double-click the **OLE** control that contains the Word document. The OLE control starts Microsoft Word as shown in Figure 10-51.

Word toolbars

Figure 10-51: OLE control when Money application is running

9 Type the note shown in Figure 10-52.

Figure 10-52: Note to parents

Use Word's Tools menu to verify the spelling in the document.

10 If Word's toolbars are covering the form's menu bar, drag them to a new position on the screen. Click **Tools** on the form's menu bar, then click **Spelling**. If the document contains any misspelled words, the Word spell-checker will alert you and make suggestions. Either ignore the misspelled word or accept one of Word's suggestions. When the message "The spelling check is complete" appears, click the **OK** button.

11 Press the **Esc** key on your keyboard to remove Word's menus and toolbars. If your computer is connected to a printer, click **File** on the form's menu bar then click **Print**.

12 Click **File** on the form's menu bar, then click **Exit**. Visual Basic returns to the design screen.

You have now completed Lesson C. You can either take a break, complete the questions and exercises at the end of the lesson, or read and complete the Debugging Section. The Debugging Section may contain material that will help to complete the exercises.

SUMMARY

To copy data from one Windows application to another:

■ Use one of the following: the clipboard, DDE, or OLE.

To embed or link objects to a Visual Basic application:

■ Use the OLE container control.

To control the size and display of the object in an OLE container control:

■ Set the OLE control's SizeMode property to either 0-Clip, 1-Stretch, 2-AutoSize, or 3-Zoom.

To tell Visual Basic to retrieve the current data from a server application before the data is displayed in an OLE control in the client application:

■ Use the Update method in the client application form's Load event procedure. The syntax of the Update method is *object*.**Update,** where *object* is the name of the OLE container control.

QUESTIONS

1. Which of the following can be used to copy data from one Windows application to another?
   a. clipboard
   b. DDE
   c. OLE
   d. all of the above

2. Which of the following is true?
   a. The drawback to using the clipboard to copy data is that you can't copy text.
   b. The drawback to using the clipboard to copy data is that the copied data has no link to the application that created it.
   c. In order to use the clipboard to copy data into a Visual Basic application, the Visual Basic form must include a data control.
   d. In order to use the clipboard to copy data into a Visual Basic application, the Visual Basic form must include a DDE control.
   e. In order to use the clipboard to copy data into a Visual Basic application, the Visual Basic form must include an OLE control.

3. When using DDE, the application that supplies the data is called the _____ application.
   a. active
   b. client
   c. destination
   d. source

4. When using DDE, the application that receives the data is called the _____ application.
   a. active
   b. client
   c. destination
   d. source

5. Which of the following is true?
   a. When using DDE, both the source application and the destination application must be running at the same time in order for the exchange of data to occur.
   b. When using DDE, only the source application needs to be running in order for the exchange of data to occur.
   c. When using DDE, only the destination application needs to be running in order for the exchange of data to occur.
   d. When using DDE, neither the source application nor the destination application needs to be running in order for the exchange of data to occur.

6. The Edit menu's _____ command maintains a link between the original data and the copied data.
   a. Copy
   b. Cut
   c. Paste
   d. Paste Link

7. Which of the following is false?
   a. When using OLE, you can either link or embed an existing file.
   b. When using OLE, you can either link or embed a new file.
   c. When using OLE, the application that contains the original data is called the server application.
   d. When using OLE, the application the contains the copied data is called the client application.

8. If you don't want changes to the original object to be reflected in the application that contains the copied object, and vice versa, you should _____ the object.
   a. embed
   b. link

9. If you want changes to the original object to be reflected in the application that contains the copied object, and vice versa, you should _____ the object.
   a. embed
   b. link

10. You use the _____ control both to embed and to link an object in a Visual Basic application.
    a. data
    b. frame
    c. image
    d. OLE

11. An OLE control's _____ property controls how much of an object displays in the control.
    a. AutoAdjust
    b. AutoSize
    c. Fill
    d. Size
    e. SizeMode

12. To tell Visual Basic to retrieve the current data from the server application before the data is displayed in the client application's OLE control, enter the OLE control's _____ method in the form's Load event procedure.
    a. AutoDisplay
    b. AutoSize
    c. AutoUpdate
    d. Retrieve
    e. Update

13. Assume that data in an Excel worksheet was copied to the clipboard, then pasted into a Visual Basic application. Explain how to edit the copied data.

14. Assume that you used DDE to copy the data in an Excel worksheet to a Visual Basic application. Explain how to edit the copied data.

15. Assume that you used OLE to embed an Excel worksheet object in a Visual Basic application. Explain how to edit the data in the embedded object. Does the edit have any affect on the original object?

16. Assume that you used OLE to link an Excel worksheet object to a Visual Basic application. Explain how to edit the data in the linked object. Does the edit have any affect on the original object?

E X E R C I S E S

1. In this exercise you will embed an existing Word document in a Visual Basic application. In order to complete this exercise, you will need access to Microsoft Word.
   a. Use Microsoft Word to create a two-paragraph letter of your choice. Type [Enter date here] at the top of the letter. Type [Enter name and address here] in the appropriate place in the letter. Save the letter as lc1Done.doc in the Tut10 folder on your Student Disk.
   b. Use Word to print the letter.
   c. Create a Visual Basic application that embeds the lc1Done.doc file in an OLE control. The application should allow the user to print the interface.
   d. Save the form and the project as lc1Done in the Tut10 folder on your Student Disk.
   e. Save and run the application. Test the application by entering the date, as well as the name and address of one of your friends or relatives. Print the interface, then exit the Visual Basic application.
   f. Submit the printouts from steps b and e.

2. In this exercise you will link an Excel worksheet to a Visual Basic application. In order to complete this exercise, you will need access to Microsoft Excel.

    a. Use Microsoft Excel to create a worksheet that keeps track of your yearly income and expenses for the previous two years. Enter the data into the worksheet, then save the worksheet as lc2Done.xls in the Tut10 folder on your Student Disk.

    b. Use Excel to print the lc2Done.xls worksheet.

    c. Create a Visual Basic application that links the lc2Done.xls file in an OLE control. The application should allow the user to print the interface.

    d. Save the form and the project as lc2Done in the Tut10 folder on your Student Disk.

    e. Save and run the application. Test the application by changing two of the expense amounts. Print the interface, then exit the Visual Basic application.

    f. Print the code.

    g. Use Excel to print the lc2Done.xls worksheet. On the printout, circle the two expense amounts that you changed.

    h. Submit the printouts from steps b, e, and g, and the code from step f.

3. In this exercise you will link a graphic created in Microsoft Paint (*Paintbrush in Windows 3.1*) to a Visual Basic application. In order to complete this exercise, you will need access to Microsoft Paint (*Paintbrush in Windows 3.1*).

    a. Use Microsoft Paint (*Paintbrush in Windows 3.1*) to create a graphic. Save the graphic as lc3Done in the Tut10 folder on your Student Disk.

    b. Use Paint (*Paintbrush in Windows 3.1*) to print the lc3Done graphic.

    c. Create a Visual Basic application that links the graphic file to an OLE control. The application should allow the user to print the interface.

    d. Save the form and the project as lc3Done in the Tut10 folder on your Student Disk.

    e. Save and run the application. Test the application by changing the color and size of the graphic. Print the interface, then exit the Visual Basic application.

    f. Submit the printouts from steps b and e.

Exercise 4 is a Discovery Exercise. Discovery Exercises allow you to both "discover" the solutions to problems on your own and to experiment with material that is not covered in the tutorial.

discovery ▶ 4. In this exercise you will learn about a form's NegotiateMenus property and a menu control's NegotiatePosition property.

    Scenario: Recall that when you double-clicked the Excel worksheet in the lcEmbed application, Excel's menu replaced the application's menu. In this exercise you will learn how to display both Excel's menus and the application's menu at the same time.

    a. Open the lcEmbed (lcembed.vbp), which is located in the Tut10 folder on your Student Disk.

    b. Use the Help menu to display the Help windows on a form's NegotiateMenus property and a menu control's NegotiatePosition property.

    c. Assume that you want to add Excel's menus to the end of the application's menu. What is the appropriate setting for the NegotiateMenus property and for the NegotiatePosition property?

    d. Set the NegotiateMenus property and the NegotiatePosition property in the lcEmbed application so that Excel's menus will be displayed at the end of the application's menu.

    e. Save and run the application. Double-click the Excel worksheet. Visual Basic should display Excel's menus after the application's File menu on the menu bar.

    f. Exit the application.

    g. Submit your answers to step c.

D E B U G G I N G

Technique   As you learned in Tutorial 9, you can use Visual Basic's Debug window to help in debugging your code. The Debug window, which appears only when the application is in break mode, consists of the Immediate pane and the Watch pane. You learned about the Immediate pane in Tutorial 9's Debugging section. You will learn about the Watch pane in this Debugging section. The Watch pane, which is displayed below the Debug window's title bar, appears only when the application contains watch expressions—expressions whose values you want to monitor as the application runs. This Debugging section will also show you how to set a breakpoint and how to display an instant watch.

Example 1   **Setting a Breakpoint**

On your Student Disk is a project named Debug1 that is not working correctly. You will use a breakpoint and the Debug window to help you debug the project.

To test the Debug1 project:

1   Start Visual Basic, if necessary. Open the **Debug1** (debug1.vbp) project, which is located in the Tut10 folder on your Student Disk. Click the **View Form** button to view the form.

The two command buttons have already been coded for you. The Exit button will exit the application. The Calculate Average button will calculate and display the average of two numbers that are entered by the user. Run the application and calculate the average of the numbers 5 and 7.

2   **Run,** but don't save, the application. Click the **Calculate Average** button, type 5 in the dialog box and press the **Enter** key, then type 7 in the dialog box and press the **Enter** key. The average of the numbers 5 and 7 should be 6, but it incorrectly displays on the form as 4.

3   Click the **Exit** button. Visual Basic returns to the design screen.

Now open the Calculate Average button's Code window and use a breakpoint to debug its code.

To debug the Calculate Average button's code:

1   Double-click the **Calculate Average** button to open its Code window. The cmdCalc control's Click event procedure appears, as shown in Figure 10-53.

```
frmDebug1
Object: cmdCalc          Proc: Click

Private Sub cmdCalc_Click()
    Dim inX As Integer, inNumber As Integer
    Dim inTotNum As Integer, sgAverage As Single
    Cls          'Clears text on form
    For inX = 1 To 2 Step 1
        inNumber = Val(InputBox("Enter a number"))
        Print inNumber
        inTotNum = inTotNum + inNumber
    Next inX

    sgAverage = inTotNum / inX
    Print "The average number is:", sgAverage

End Sub
```

Figure 10-53: Calculate Average button's Click event

The code declares four variables: inX, inNumber, inTotNum, and sgAverage. The inX variable, a counter variable, will be used by the For...Next loop to keep track of the number of items to request from the user—in this case, the application will request two numbers. The inNumber variable will store the user's response to the InputBox function's message. The inTotNum variable will be used to accumulate the numbers entered by the user. The sgAverage variable will store the average of the numbers.

The `sgAverage = inTotNum / inX` instruction is calculating the average incorrectly. That means that either the inTotNum variable or the inX variable contains an incorrect value. To determine which variable—inTotNum or inX—is causing the problem, you will set a breakpoint at the `sgAverage = inTotNum / inX` instruction. When Visual Basic encounters a breakpoint in the code as the application is running, Visual Basic puts the application in break mode, which temporarily halts program execution. Recall that when an application is in break mode, you can use the Debug window to debug your code. When this application is in break mode, for example, you will use the Debug window to view the values in the inTotNum and the inX variables to see which contains an incorrect value.

2 Click anywhere in the `sgAverage = inTotNum / inX` instruction. The insertion point should now be positioned somewhere in that instruction.

3 Click the **Toggle Breakpoint** button on the toolbar. Visual Basic selects the `sgAverage = inTotNum / inX` instruction to indicate that it is a breakpoint.

When you run the application, Visual Basic will put the application in break mode immediately before processing the breakpoint instruction.

4 Close the Code window, then **run**, but don't save, the application. Click the **Calculate Average** button, type **5** and press the **Enter** key, then type **7** and press the **Enter** key. Before processing the `sgAverage = inTotNum / inX` instruction, Visual Basic enters break mode. The screen appears as shown in Figure10-54.

tips

You can also toggle a breakpoint by clicking Run on the menu bar, then clicking Toggle Breakpoint. You can also press the F9 key.

breakpoint instruction

Figure 10-54: Code window showing Visual Basic in break mode

Now that you are in break mode, you can use the Debug window to view the values in both the inTotNum and the inX variables.

5 Click **View** on the menu bar, then click **Debug Window**.

First view the value in the inTotNum variable. Because you entered the numbers 5 and 7, the value in inTotNum should be 12.

tips

You can also open the Debug window by pressing Ctrl + G.

6   In the Debug window's Immediate pane, type **print inTotnum** and press the **Enter** key. The number 12, which is the sum of 5 and 7, appears in the Debug window. The inTotNum variable, therefore, contains the correct value.

Now look at the value in the inX variable. Remember that you entered two numbers, so you want the value in inX to be 2.

7   Type **print inX** and press the **Enter** key. The Debug window shows that the inX variable contains the number 3 instead of the number 2. The inX variable, therefore, is causing the average to be calculated incorrectly. Now that you know which variable is causing the problem, you need to search the code to see how inX gets its value. (It might be helpful to refer to Figure 10-54.)

The inX variable is used as the *counter* variable in the For...Next loop. Recall that the For...Next loop stops when the value in its *counter* variable is greater than the *endvalue*. In this case, the For...Next loop ends when inX reaches 3—one more than the *endvalue* of 2. So although two numbers are requested from the user, the value in inX is 3 when the For...Next loop stops. To fix the code, you simply need to change the `sgAverage = inTotNum / inX` instruction to `sgAverage = inTotNum / (inX-1)`. You can now remove the breakpoint and fix the code.

8   Click the **End** button ▣ on the toolbar to stop the application, then click the **Code window** to make it the active window. Click **Run**, then click **Clear All Breakpoints**. Visual Basic removes the breakpoint.

9   Change the `sgAverage = inTotNum / inX` instruction to **sgAverage = inTotNum / (inX–1)**. Close the Code window, then **run**, but don't save, the application.

10   Click the **Calculate Average** button, type 5 and press the **Enter** key, then type 7 and press the **Enter** key. The correct average, 6, appears on the form. Click the **Exit** button to end the application. Visual Basic returns to the design screen.

In the next example, you will learn how to display an instant watch. (You do not need to save the frmDebug1 form.)

Example 2   **Displaying an Instant Watch**

On your Student Disk is a project named Debug2 which is not working correctly. You will use a breakpoint and an instant watch to help you debug the project.

To test the Debug2 project:

1   Open the **Debug2** (debug2.vbp) project, which is located in the Tut10 folder on your Student Disk. (You do not need to save the frmDebug1 form.) Click the **View Form** button to view the form.

This application is the same one used in debugging example 1, except it contains a different bug (error). The Calculate Average button, recall, calculates and displays the average of two numbers that are entered by the user. The Exit button closes the application.

2   **Run**, but don't save, the application. Click the **Calculate Average** button, type 5 and press the **Enter** key, then type 7 and press the **Enter** key. The average should be 6, but it incorrectly displays as 7.

3   Click the **Exit** button. Visual Basic returns to the design screen.

You will now open the Calculate Average button's Code window and use a breakpoint and an instant watch to debug its code.

To debug the Calculate Average button's code:

1   Double-click the **Calculate Average** button to open its Code window. The cmdCalc control's Click event procedure appears, as shown in Figure 10-55.

```
frmDebug2
Object: cmdCalc        Proc: Click

Private Sub cmdCalc_Click()
    Dim inX As Integer, inNumber As Integer
    Dim inTotNum As Integer, sgAverage As Single
    Cls      'Clears text from form
    For inX = 1 To 2 Step 1
        inNumber = Val(InputBox("Enter a number"))
        Print inNumber
        inTotNum = inNumber + inNumber
    Next inX

    sgAverage = inTotNum / (inX - 1)
    Print "The average number is:", sgAverage

End Sub
```

Figure 10-55: Calculate Average button's Code window

The `sgAverage = inTotNum / (inX - 1)` instruction is calculating the average incorrectly. To determine the problem, you will set a breakpoint at the `sgAverage = inTotNum / (inX - 1)` instruction. This time when the application enters break mode, you will use an instant watch—instead of the Debug window, as you did in Debugging Example 1—to display the value in the inTotNum variable and in the (inX – 1) expression.

2   Click anywhere in the `sgAverage = inTotNum / (inX-1)` instruction. The insertion point should now be positioned somewhere in that instruction.

3   Click the **Toggle Breakpoint** button on the toolbar. Visual Basic selects the `sgAverage = inTotNum / (inX - 1)` instruction to indicate that it is a breakpoint.

4   Close the Code window, then **run**, but don't save, the application. Click the **Calculate Average** button, type **5** and press the **Enter** key, then type **7** and press the **Enter** key. Before processing the `sgAverage = inTotNum / (inX-1)` instruction, Visual Basic enters break mode. The Code window appears on the screen with the breakpoint instruction selected.

Now that you are in break mode, you can use an instant watch to view the values in the (inX–1) expression and in the inTotNum variable.

5   Select the (inX–1) expression, as shown in Figure 10-56.

Figure 10-56: Expression selected in Code window

select this expression

6 Click the **Instant Watch** button on the toolbar. The Instant Watch dialog box appears, as shown in Figure 10-57.

Figure 10-57: Instant Watch dialog box

The Instant Watch dialog box shows that the current value of the expression (inX–1) is 2, which is correct. (Notice that using an instant watch is much quicker than displaying the Debug window and entering a Print statement.) Next look at the value in the inTotNum variable.

7 Click the **Cancel** button to remove the Instant Watch dialog box. Select inTotNum in the Dim statement (or in any statement in which it appears), then click the **Instant Watch** button. The Instant Watch dialog box appears and shows that the current value in inTotNum is 14; you were expecting it to be 12 (the sum of the numbers 5 and 7).

Now that you know that the inTotNum variable is causing the average to be calculated incorrectly, you need to search the code for the location where the inTotNum variable gets its value.

8 Click the **Cancel** button to remove the Instant Watch dialog box, then click the **End** button to stop the application. The Code window for the cmdCalc Click event procedure appears.

tips

You can also set an instant watch by clicking Tools on the menu bar, then clicking Instant Watch; you can also press Shift + F9.

The inTotNum variable gets its value from the `inTotNum = inNumber + inNumber` instruction. That instruction, however, is incorrect. The correct instruction for updating the inTotNum variable, which is an accumulator variable, should be `inTotNum = inTotNum + inNumber`. You can now clear the breakpoint and fix the code.

To correct the code in the Calculate Average button's Code window:

1 Click **Run**, then click **Clear All Breakpoints**. Change the `inTotNum = inNumber + inNumber` instruction to **inTotNum = inTotNum + inNumber**.

2 Close the Code window, then **run**, but don't save, the application.

3 Click the **Calculate Average** button. Type **5** and press the **Enter** key, then type **7** and press the **Enter** key. This time the correct average, **6**, appears on the form.

4 Click the **Exit** button to end the application.

In the next example you will learn how to use the Debug window's Watch pane. (You do not need to save the frmDebug2 form.)

Example 3 Using the Watch Pane

On your Student Disk is a project named Debug3. You will use the Watch pane to verify the values in the variables and expressions as the application is running.

To test the Debug3 project:

1 Open the **Debug3** (debug3.vbp) project, which is located in the Tut10 folder on your Student Disk. (You do not need to save the frmDebug2 form.) Click the **View Form** button to view the form.

View the Display Total button's code.

2 Double-click the **Display Total** button. The cmdTotal control's Click event procedure appears as shown in Figure 10-58.

```
frmDebug3
Object: cmdTotal        Proc: Click

Private Sub cmdTotal_Click()
    Dim inX As Integer, inTotal As Integer
    For inX = 1 To 4 Step 1
        inTotal = inTotal + inX ^ 2
    Next inX
    Cls      'Clears text from form
    Print "The total is:", inTotal


End Sub
```

Figure 10-58: Display Total button's Click event

The code adds the squares of the numbers from 1 through 4—in other words, 1 * 1 + 2 * 2 + 3 * 3 + 4 * 4. Run the application to see if it is working correctly.

3 Close the Code window, then **run**, but don't save, the application. Click the **Display Total** button. The application displays the number 30 as the total.

4 Click the **Exit** button to end the application.

Instead of manually computing the sum of the squares to see if the number 30 is correct, you can use the Debug window's Watch pane to view the values in the variables or expressions as the application is running. In this case you will view the values in inX, inX ^ 2, and inTotal. By doing so, you will be able to see how the number 30 was reached, which will allow you to verify that it is the correct answer.

To use the Watch pane to set watch expressions:

1 Double-click the **Display Total** button to display its Click event procedure. Select inX in the Dim statement (or in any statement in which it appears), then click **Tools**, and then click **Add Watch**. The Add Watch dialog box appears as shown in Figure 10-59.

Figure 10-59: Add Watch dialog box

The Add Watch dialog box offers three watch types: Watch Expression, Break When Value Is True, and Break When Value Changes.

2 Click the **OK** button to tell Visual Basic to watch the current expression—inX.

3 Select inX ^ 2, click **Tools** on the menu bar, then click **Add Watch**, and then click the **OK** button to tell Visual Basic to watch the inX ^ 2 expression.

4 Select inTotal in the Dim statement (or in any statement in which it appears). Click **Tools** on the menu bar, then click **Add Watch**. This time, click **Break When Value Changes**, and then click the **OK** button. This tells Visual Basic to put the application in break mode each time the value in the inTotal variable changes.

5 Close the Code window.

You can verify the watch expressions by displaying the Watch dialog box. Do that before running the application.

6 Click **Tools** on the menu bar, then click **Edit Watch**. The Edit Watch dialog box appears. Click the **Cancel** button to close the Edit Watch dialog box. The Debug window appears with the watch expressions showing in the Watch pane, as shown in Figure 10-60.

Watch pane

Immediate pane

Figure 10-60: Debug window showing watch expressions in Watch pane

7 Notice the icons to the left of the expressions. The icons tell you which watch type is associated with the expression. The ᏰᏰ icon represents the "Watch Expression" type; the ⚐ icon represents the "Break When Expression Has Changed" type.

8 **Run,** but don't save, the application. Click the **Display Total** button. Visual Basic puts the application in break mode after processing the inTotal = inTotal + inX ^ 2 instruction, which is the instruction that changes the value in the inTotal variable. (You should see a rectangle around the Next inX instruction in the Code window, which is the instruction after the inTotal = inTotal + inX ^ 2 instruction.)

The Watch pane shows that the current value of inTotal, inX, and inX ^ 2 is 1. See Figure 10-61.

Watch pane

Immediate pane

Figure 10-61: Watch pane showing current values of variables and expression

9 Click the **Continue** button ▶ on the toolbar to continue processing the application. The Debug window shows that the value in the inTotal variable is now 5 (the prior value of 1 plus 4 more). The value in the inX variable is now 2, and the value of inX ^ 2 is now 4.

10 Click the **Continue** button ▸ to continue processing. The Debug window shows that the value in the inTotal variable is now 14 (the prior value of 5 plus 9 more). The value in inX is now 3, and the value of inX ^ 2 is now 9.

11 Click the **Continue** button ▸ to continue processing. The Debug window shows that the value in the inTotal variable is now 30 (the prior value of 14 plus 16 more). The value in inX is now 4, and the value of inX ^ 2 is now 16.

12 Click the **Continue** button ▸ to continue processing. The correct sum, 30, appears on the form. Click the **Exit** button to end the application. Visual Basic returns to the design screen. Now remove the watch expressions. (In this case you are removing the watch expressions for practice only. Visual Basic automatically removes watch expressions and breakpoints when you either open another application or exit Visual Basic. Visual Basic does not save watch expressions or breakpoints when you save an application.)

13 If necessary, click **View** on the menu bar, then click **Debug Window** to display the Debug window. Click **inTotal** in the Debug window's Watch pane, then press the **Delete** key. Visual Basic deletes the inTotal watch expression. Press the **Delete** key again to delete the inX watch expression, then press the **Delete** key again to delete the inX ^ 2 watch expression.

14 Close the Debug window, then close the Code window. You can now exit Visual Basic. You do not need to save the frmDebug3 form.

APPENDIX

A

Crystal Reports

Using Crystal Reports to Create a Report

Important Note: You will not be able to complete Appendix A using the Visual Basic Working Model. You will need to use either the Professional or Standard Edition of Visual Basic.

Like Data Manager, Crystal Reports is an add-in program that comes with Visual Basic. You can use Crystal Reports to create custom reports, lists, labels, and form letters using data from an existing database. Crystal Reports recognizes databases created with the following programs: Microsoft Access, dBase, Paradox, FoxPro, Clipper, Btrieve, and SQL Server (via ODBC).

In addition to displaying the database information, the reports and so on that you create can also include information that is not contained in the database. For example, you can display subtotals and grand totals for fields in the database, as well as the average, minimum, and maximum value contained in a field. You can also display an employee's raise amount in a report by multiplying his or her salary, which is stored in a database field, by a raise percentage.

Crystal Reports also allows you to limit the amount of data displayed in a report. For example, you can create a report that lists only the names of employees living in Miami, or only the names and starting dates of employees whose salary is over $25,000.

This appendix is not intended to teach you everything about Crystal Reports; it is designed merely to get you started with some of the basic features of this powerful add-in program. With just a little practice, however, you will find it extremely easy to create very impressive and useful reports.

In this appendix you will use Crystal Reports to create a report for Pro Drive Distributors.

The Pro Drive Distributors Report

Business is booming at Pro Drive Distributors, so the president of the company, Chris Timen, has decided to give each of the seven employees a seven percent raise. Ms. Timen wants a report that shows each employee's number, name, current salary, raise, and new salary.

tips

You can also start Crystal Reports while you are in Visual Basic. Simply click Add-Ins, then click Report Designer.

WINDOWS 3.1

To start Crystal Reports:

1   If necessary, start Windows, then place your Student Disk in the appropriate disk drive. Click the **Start** button on the Windows 95 taskbar, then point to **Programs** in the Start menu. The Programs menu appears. Point to **Visual Basic 4.0** in the Programs menu, then click **Crystal Reports** in the Visual Basic 4.0 menu. The Crystal Reports window appears.

If necessary, start Windows, then place your Student Disk in the appropriate disk drive. The Program Manager window should be open. Double-click the Visual Basic 4.0 (16-bit) group icon to open the Visual Basic group window, then double-click the Crystal Reports - 16-bit icon in the Visual Basic group window. The Crystal Reports window appears.

2   Maximize the Crystal Reports window. See Figure 1.

Figure 1: Maximized Crystal Reports window

The File menu contains the commands that allow you to create a new report and to open an existing report. In this case you want to create a new report.

3 Click **File** on the menu bar, then point to **New** in the File menu. A submenu appears. Click **Report** in the submenu. The New Report dialog box appears as shown in Figure 2.

Click File on the menu bar, then click New in the File menu. A submenu appears. Click Report in the submenu. The New Report dialog box appears as shown in Figure 2.

Figure 2: New Report dialog box

The New Report dialog box has both a Create new: and a from: section; you must select one of the buttons in each section. The Create new: section indicates the type of report you want to create, and the from: section tells Crystal Reports where to find the information to use when building the report. Notice that the default selections are Report and Data File. In this case you want to create a report with data that is stored in a database, so you do not need to change the selections from their default values.

4   Click the **OK** button in the New Report dialog box. The Choose Database File dialog box appears as shown in Figure 3. The report folder should be the current folder.

current folder

your dialog box will look different if you are using Windows 3.1

Figure 3: Choose Database File dialog box

HELP? If the report folder is not the current folder, first open the main Visual Basic folder on the network or local hard drive, then open the report folder, which is located in the main Visual Basic folder. In Windows 95 the main Visual Basic folder is typically named Microsoft Visual Basic. (*In Windows 3.1 the main Visual Basic folder is typically named vb.*)

The employee information for Pro Drive Distributors is stored in the Empdata.mdb database, which comes with Visual Basic.

5   Click **Empdata.mdb** in the list box, then click the **Open** button. The Report Designer window, which shows Untitled Report #1 in the title bar, appears, and so does the Insert Database Field dialog box.

Click Empdata.mdb in the list box, then click the OK button. The Report Designer window, which shows Untitled Report #1 in the title bar, appears, and so does the Insert Database Field dialog box.

WINDOWS 3.1

You design your reports, lists, labels, and form letters in the Report Designer window. The Insert Database Field dialog box contains a list of the fields in the Empdata.mdb database.

6   Maximize the Report Designer window. See Figure 4.

three sections

Report Designer window

Insert Database
Field dialog box

Figure 4: Maximized Report Designer window

HELP? If the Insert Database Field dialog box does not appear, click Insert on the menu bar, then click Database Field.

Notice that the Report Designer window contains three sections: Page header, Details, and Page footer. You use the Page header section to include information such as a report title, field headings, and the print date at the top of each page in the report. The Details section contains the body of the report—the database records, subtotals, and so on. The Page footer section usually contains the page number, if the report has more than one page, and any other information that you want to appear on the bottom of each page.

According to the Insert Database Field dialog box, the employee database contains four fields: EMPNUM, NAME, SALARY, MGRNUM. (EMPNUM stands for employee number and MGRNUM stands for manager number.) You create the report by placing one or more fields in the Details section of the Report Designer window. Place the EMPNUM field in the report first.

tips

You can use the Browse Field Data button in the Insert Database Field dialog box to view the selected field's values, as well as its data type and size.

7 EMPNUM should be selected in the Insert Database Field dialog box. Position the mouse pointer on EMPNUM in the Insert Database Field dialog box. Press and hold down the left mouse button as you drag the field into the Details section of the Report Designer window. As you drag the field into the Details section, notice that a white box appears next to the mouse pointer arrow, as shown in Figure 5.

box represents
EMPNUM field

Figure 5: White field box shown in the Details section

8 When the box is positioned as shown in Figure 5, release the mouse button to drop the EMPNUM field in the Details section. A box containing EMPNUM appears in the Page header section; this box represents the field (column) heading. Additionally, a box containing five Xs appears in the Details section directly below the heading. The five Xs indicate that the employee number field is a string field that contains a maximum of five characters.

Notice that a handle appears on both the left and right side of the employee number field box. The handles indicate that the box is selected. If you want to make any changes to the information in a box—for example, move it, delete it, change its font size, and so on—you must select it first.

Next you will include the MGRNUM (manager number) field in the report.

tips

▶ Notice that you can place the fields in any order in the report.

tips

▶ To select a group of contiguous fields, click the first field you want to select, then press and hold down the Shift key as you click the last field you want to select.

9 Click **MGRNUM** in the Insert Database Field dialog box to select the field, then drag the field into the Details section of the Report Designer window. Position the white box to the immediate right of the employee number field, then release the mouse button to drop the field in the Details section. A box containing <u>MGRNUM</u> appears in the Page header section, and a box containing five Xs appears in the Details section. The five Xs indicate that the manager number field is a 5-character string field.

HELP? If you dropped the MGRNUM field in the wrong area of the report, simply press the Delete key on your keyboard to delete the field from the report.

You can also place more than one field at a time in a report. Try that now.

10 Click **NAME** in the Insert Database Field dialog box. Press and hold down the **Ctrl** key as you click **SALARY** in the Insert Database Field dialog box. Position the mouse pointer on one of the selected fields in the dialog box, then drag the fields into the Details section. Notice that a Drag-and-drop icon, rather than a white box, appears next to the mouse pointer arrow. The Drag-and-drop icon indicates that more than one field is being dragged. See Figure 6.

drag-and-drop icon indicates that more than one field is being dragged

column (field) headings

database fields

Figure 6: Drag-and-drop icon shown in the Details section

tips

▶ You can also place one or more fields in the Details section by first selecting the field or fields in the Insert Database Field dialog box, then clicking the Insert button in the dialog box. You then use the mouse to position either the white box (if one field is selected) or the Drag-and-drop icon (if more than one field is selected) in the proper position. When positioned appropriately, you then click the left mouse button to drop the field(s) in place.

11 Position the Drag-and-drop icon to the immediate right of the manager number field in the Details section, as shown in Figure 6, then release the mouse button to drop the two fields in place. See Figure 7.

string field

numeric field

Figure 7: Name and salary fields positioned in the Details section

HELP? Don't be concerned if the fields or the headings are not positioned exactly as shown in Figure 7. In the next section you will learn how to move the boxes in the report, as well as how to delete them.

The Xs in the name field box indicate that the NAME field is a string field. The numbers in the salary field box indicate that the SALARY field is a numeric field.

12 Click in an empty area of the Report Designer window to cancel the selection of the two field boxes. The handles disappear from the boxes.

Now that the necessary fields are on the report, you can close the Insert Database Field dialog box.

13 Click the **Done** button in the Insert Database Field dialog box. The dialog box closes.

You can use the Print Preview button on the toolbar to view what the report will look like when it is printed.

14 Click the **Print Preview** button 🔍 on the toolbar. The Preview window opens, as shown in Figure 8.

tips
· · · · · · · · · · · · · ·
You do not have to include all of the database fields in a report.

tips
· · · · · · · · · · · · · ·
You can also open the Preview window by clicking File on the menu bar, then clicking Print Preview.

Close button

Figure 8: Report showing employee number, manager number, name, and salary

Notice that it is not clear whether the name and salary information belongs to the employee number or the manager number. You decide to remove the manager number information from the report.

15 Click the **Close** button, which is located at the bottom of the Preview window, to close the Preview window.

In the next section you will learn how to delete a field from a report and also how to move a field in the report.

Deleting and Moving Report Fields

Recall that you want to remove the manager number information from the report. You will need to remove the MGRNUM field and its heading, then move the name and salary fields closer to the employee number field.

To delete a field from a report, and also move a field in the report:

1 Click **MGRNUM** in the Page header section, then Ctrl + click the field box that is located directly below the **MGRNUM** heading. Both the heading and the field box are now selected, as indicated by the handles on the left and right side of each box.

2 Press the **Delete** key on your keyboard to remove the **MGRNUM** heading and its corresponding field from the report.

HELP? If you inadvertently deleted the wrong field, click Insert on the menu bar, then click Database Field. Use the Insert Database Field dialog box to insert the missing field, then close the Insert Database Field dialog box. If you inadvertently deleted the wrong heading, click Insert on the menu bar, then click Text Field. Enter the missing heading in the dialog box, then click the Accept button. Position the heading appropriately, then click the left mouse button.

Now move the name and salary columns closer to the employee number column.

3   Click <u>NAME</u> in the Page header section, then Ctrl + click the field box that is located directly below the <u>NAME</u> heading. Also Ctrl + click <u>SALARY</u> in the Page header section and Ctrl + click the field box that is located directly below the <u>SALARY</u> heading. The four boxes are now selected in the Report Designer window.

4   Position the mouse pointer on <u>NAME</u> in the Page header section. The mouse pointer should appear as an arrow (see Figure 9). Drag the selected items to the position shown in Figure 9.

new field position

Figure 9: Four boxes moved closer to employee number information

5   When the selected items are positioned as shown in Figure 9, release the mouse button.

6   Click in an empty area of the Report Designer window to cancel the selection of the four boxes.

Now save the report in the TutApA folder on your Student Disk.

7   Click **File** on the menu bar, then click **Save As**. Name the report file **ProDrive**, and save it in the TutApA folder on your Student Disk.

In the next section, you will learn how to improve the appearance of the Page Header section by including a report title and the date the report was printed.

Improving the Appearance of the Page Header Section

Recall that the information in the Page header section will print on each page. The Page header section typically includes the report's title, the field (column) headings, and the date the report was printed. You will include a title (Employee List) and the date in the Pro Driver report. You will also change the field headings from uppercase to proper case. (Proper case means that only the first letter of the word is capitalized.)

To include a report title and date at the top of the report, and also change the field headings from uppercase to proper case:

1   Click **Insert** on the menu bar. You can include a report title in a report by inserting a text field in the Page header section. Click **Text Field**. The Edit Text Field dialog box appears. Type **Employee List** in the dialog box, then click the **Accept** button.

2   Use the mouse to move the white box into the upper left corner of the Page header section. When positioning the box, don't press either of the mouse buttons; simply move the mouse.

3   When the box is positioned in the upper-left corner of the Page header section, click the left mouse button to drop the field in place, as shown in Figure 10.

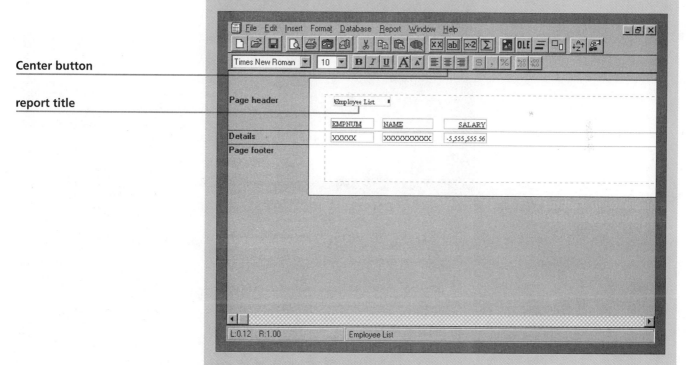

Figure 10: Report title positioned in Page header section

Report titles are typically displayed in a font size that is larger than the font size used in the body of the report. This makes the report title stand out from the rest of the report.

4 The report title box is still selected. Click **Format** on the menu bar, then click **Font**. When the Font dialog box appears, click **18** in the Size list box, then click the **OK** button.

Now center the title in the report.

5 Position the mouse pointer on the right sizing handle of the report title box until the pointer turns into a double arrow **↔**. Drag the sizing handle to the right until the right edge of the report title box is aligned with the right edge of the <u>SALARY</u> heading, then release the mouse button. Click the **Center** button 🔳 on the toolbar. See Figure 11.

Figure 11: Report title sized and centered in the Page header section

Now display the print date in the upper-right corner of the report.

6 Notice that a scroll bar appears at the bottom of the Report Designer window. Drag the scroll box in that scroll bar all the way to the right. The right side of the report displays in the Report Designer window.

7 Click **Insert** on the menu bar, then point to **Special Field**. Click **Print Date Field**. Position the white box in the upper-right corner of the Page header section, then click the left mouse button to drop the field in place. 12/31/99 appears in the Page header section, as shown in Figure 12.

Click Insert on the menu bar, then click Special Field. Click Print Date Field. Position the white box in the upper-right corner of the Page header section, then click the left mouse button to drop the field in place. 12/31/99 appears in the Page header section, as shown in Figure 12.

print date

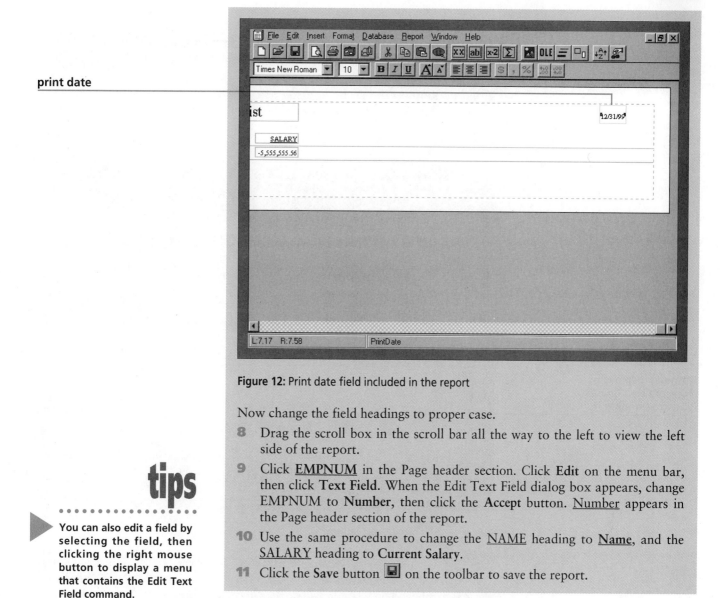

Figure 12: Print date field included in the report

Now change the field headings to proper case.

8 Drag the scroll box in the scroll bar all the way to the left to view the left side of the report.

9 Click **EMPNUM** in the Page header section. Click **Edit** on the menu bar, then click **Text Field**. When the Edit Text Field dialog box appears, change EMPNUM to **Number**, then click the **Accept** button. Number appears in the Page header section of the report.

10 Use the same procedure to change the NAME heading to **Name**, and the SALARY heading to **Current Salary**.

11 Click the **Save** button 🖫 on the toolbar to save the report.

tips

▶ You can also edit a field by selecting the field, then clicking the right mouse button to display a menu that contains the Edit Text Field command.

In the next section you will learn how to include a formula field in a report. You will use formula fields to display each employee's raise and new salary.

Including a Formula Field in a Database

Recall that Pro Drive Distributors is giving its employees a 7% raise. Ms. Timen, the company's president, wants the report to show each employee's raise amount and his or her new salary amount. To display both amounts in the report, you will need to create two formula fields: one formula field will calculate the raise and the other will calculate the new salary.

To include the two formula fields in the report:

1   Click **Insert** on the menu bar, then click **Formula Field.** The Insert Formula dialog box appears and requests the formula's name. Create the raise formula first.

2   Type **Raise** in the Formula name text box, then click the **OK** button. The Edit Formula dialog box appears as shown in Figure 13. Notice that the name of the formula field, @Raise, appears in the title bar; the @ sign indicates that the field is a formula field.

formula displays in
Formula text box as
you are building it

Figure 13: Edit Formula dialog box

The Edit Formula dialog box contains three list boxes (Fields, Functions, and Operators) and a Formula text box. You can use the list boxes to build the desired formula. The formula will appear in the text box as you are building it.

3   Scroll each of the three list boxes to view their choices.

Each employee's raise is calculated by taking his or her current salary and multiplying it by 7%.

4   Click **EMPDATA.SALARY** in the Fields list box, then click the **Select** button, which is located at the bottom of the Edit Formula dialog box. {EMP-DATA.SALARY} appears in the Formula text box.

5   Click **x * y Multiply** in the Operators list box, then click the **Select** button. An asterisk (*) appears after the {EMPDATA.SALARY} entry in the Formula text box.

6   Type **.07** in the Formula text box, as shown in Figure 14.

tips

You can also click SALARY in
the Database Field section
of the Fields list box.

database field

operator

raise percentage

enters formula in field

checks to see if formula
contains errors

Figure 14: Completed formula in the Formula text box

HELP? If one or more items in the formula is incorrect, select the incorrect item and press the Delete key on your keyboard. Then either type the correct entry or select the correct entry from the appropriate list box.

You can use the Check button to determine if the formula in the text box contains any errors.

7   Click the **Check** button in the Edit Formula dialog box. A message box appears and displays the "No errors found" message.

8   Click the **OK** button to remove the message box, then click the **Accept** button both to accept the formula and to remove the Edit Formula dialog box. A white box, which represents the formula field, appears in the Report Designer window.

9   Position the formula box about one-half of an inch to the right of the current salary box in the Details section, then click to drop the formula box in place.

Now add the New Salary field to the report.

10   Click **Insert** on the menu bar, then click **Formula Field**. The Insert Formula dialog box appears. Type **New Salary** in the Formula name text box, then click the **OK** button. The Edit Formula dialog box appears and displays @New Salary in the title bar.

Each employee's new salary is calculated by adding his or her current salary to his or her raise amount.

11   Click **EMPDATA.SALARY** in the Fields list box, then click the **Select** button. Click **x + y   Add** in the Operators list box, then click the **Select** button. Click **@Raise** in the Fields list box, then click the **Select** button. The correct formula displays as {EMPDATA.SALARY} + {@Raise}.

12 Click the **Check** button to verify that the formula is correct. When the "No errors found" message appears, click the **OK** button to remove the message box. Click the **Accept** button to accept the formula. The Edit Formula dialog box closes and a white box, which represents the current salary field, appears in the Report Designer window.

13 Position the formula box about one-half of an inch to the right of the raise field in the Details section, then click to drop the formula box in the Details section. See Figure 15.

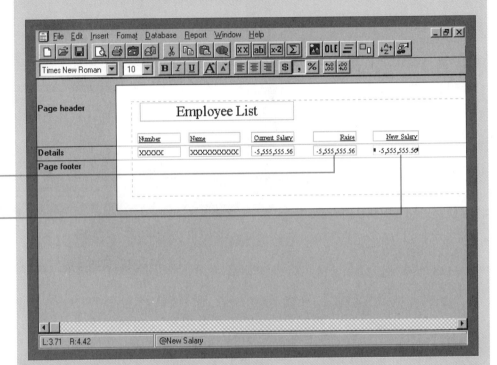

Figure 15: Raise and new salary fields included in the Report Designer window

Now that you have added two more fields to the report, the report title is no longer centered. You will fix that next.

14 Click the "Employee List" report title box. Position the mouse pointer on the right handle until it turns into a double arrow ↔. Drag the handle to the right until the right edge of the report title box is aligned with the right edge of the New Salary box, then release the mouse button.

15 Click in an empty area of the Report Designer window to cancel the selection of the report title box.

16 Click the **Print Preview** button 🔍 on the toolbar. Depending on how Crystal Reports is set up, a Saved Data dialog box may appear. If the Saved Data dialog box appears, click the **Use Saved Data** button. (The Use Saved Data button tells Crystal Reports to display the report using the same data it used when you first previewed the report. The Refresh Data button tells Crystal Reports to read the database file from the disk before displaying the report.) See Figure 16.

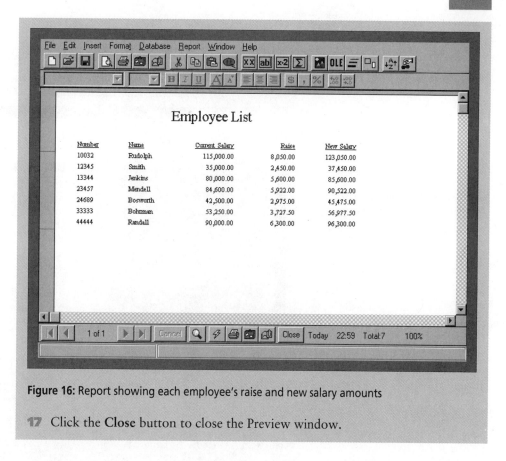

Figure 16: Report showing each employee's raise and new salary amounts

17 Click the **Close** button to close the Preview window.

Ms. Timen also wants the report to show the total amount the company is currently paying the employees, as well as the total of both the raise and new salary amounts. To display those values, you will need to include grand totals in the report.

Including Grand Totals in a Report

In order to display the total of the current salary, raise, and new salary fields, you will need to include a grand total section in the report.

If you want to delete a section, click Edit on the menu bar, then click Delete Section. Select the section you want to delete, then click the OK button.

To include grand totals in the report:

1 Click the -5,555,555.56 field box that is located directly below the <u>Current Salary</u> heading.

2 Click **Insert** on the menu bar, then click **Grand Total**. The Insert Grand Total dialog box appears. The dialog box indicates that it will insert, in the Grand total section, a field that will calculate the sum of the EMPDATA.SALARY field. Click the list arrow to view what type of grand totals can be calculated. See Figure 17.

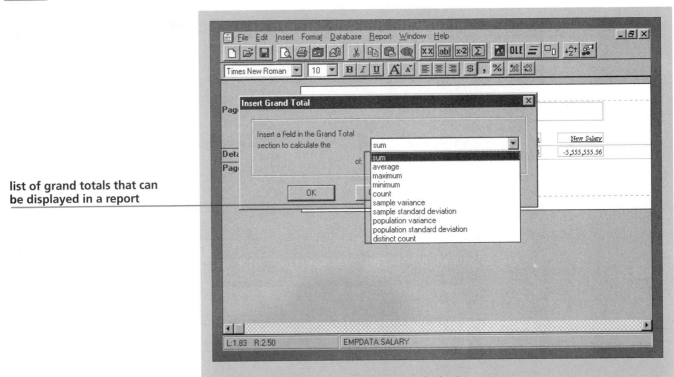

list of grand totals that can be displayed in a report

Figure 17: List of grand totals that you can display in a report

3 Click the list arrow to close the list. The list box should contain the word "sum."

4 Click the **OK** button. See Figure 18.

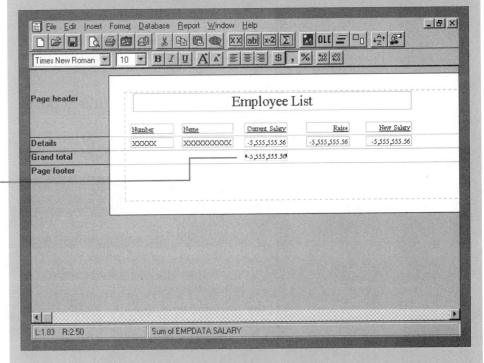

Grand total section

Figure 18: Report Designer window showing Grand total section

A Grand total section appears in the report. A box containing the number -5,555,555.56 appears in the Current Salary column in the Grand total section. Now include grand totals for the Raise and New Salary columns.

5 Click the -5,555,555.56 field box that is located directly below the <u>Raise</u> heading. Click **Insert** on the menu bar, then click **Grand Total**. The Insert Grand Total dialog box indicates that it will insert, in the Grand total section, a field that will calculate the sum of the @Raise formula field. Click the **OK** button. A box containing the number -5,555,555.56 appears in the Raise column in the Grand total section.

6 Click the -5,555,555.56 field box that is located directly below the <u>New Salary</u> heading. Click **Insert** on the menu bar, then click **Grand Total**. The Insert Grand Total dialog box indicates that it will insert, in the Grand total section, a field that will calculate the sum of the @New Salary field. Click the **OK** button. A box containing the number -5,555,555.56 appears in the New Salary column in the Grand total section.

Now place the word "Totals" in the report so the user knows what the three amounts in the Grand total section represent. You can include text in the report by simply inserting a text field.

7 Click **Insert** on the menu bar, then click **Text Field**. Type **Totals** in the Edit Text Field dialog box, then click the **Accept** button. Position the white box on the left side of the Grand total section, then click to drop the text field in place.

8 Click in an empty area of the Report Designer window to cancel the selection of the text field.

9 Click the **Print Preview** button ⬚ on the toolbar. If the Saved Data dialog box appears, click the **Use Saved Data button**. See Figure 19.

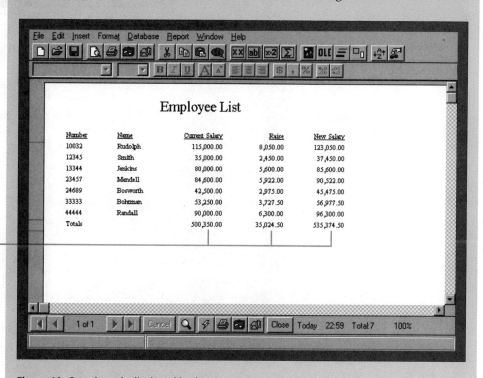

grand totals

Figure 19: Grand totals displayed in the report

10   Click the **Close** button, then click the **Save** button 🖫 in the toolbar to save the report.

After showing the report to Ms. Timen, she decides that the report would be more useful to her if the employees were grouped according to the manager number.

Grouping the Data in a Report

You can use Crystal Reports to group the data in a report. In this case, for example, you will group the employees according to the manager number.

To group the report data:

1   Click **Insert** on the menu bar, then click **Group Section**. The Insert Group Section dialog box appears.

When the report is printed, you want it sorted and grouped by the manager number.

2   Click the first list arrow, then click **MGRNUM** in the list.

Crystal Reports allows you to sort the data in either ascending or descending order. You will sort the manager numbers in ascending order, which is the default selection. The completed Insert Group Section dialog box is shown in Figure 20.

groups database records
by manager number

Figure 20: Completed Insert Group Section dialog box

3 Click the **OK** button. The Insert Group Section dialog box closes. Two new sections appear in the Report Designer window, as shown in Figure 21.

Group header section

Group footer section

Figure 21: Report Designer window showing Group header and footer sections

The #1: MGRNUM-A section located above the Details section is called the Group header section, and the #1: MGRNUM-A section located below the Details section is called the Group footer section. The information in the Group header section will appear above each group, and the information in the Group footer section will appear below each group. Include the words "Manager number:" and the manager's number in the Group header section.

4 Click **Insert** on the menu bar, then click **Text Field**. Type **Manager number:** and click the **Accept** button. Position the white box on the left side of the Group header section, then click to drop the text field in place.

5 Click **Insert** on the menu bar, then click **Database Field**. Click **MGRNUM** in the Insert Database Field dialog box. Drag the field to the immediate right of the "Manager number:" box in the Group header section, then release the mouse button to drop the database field in place.

6 Click the **Done** button to close the Insert Database Field dialog box.

tips

You can hide a section by clicking Edit on the menu bar, then clicking Show/Hide Sections.

To make the Group header information stand out from the rest of the report, you will italicize the text and also change the color of the text to red.

To change the appearance of the information in a report:

1 Click the **Manager number:** box, then Ctrl + click the MGRNUM field box in the Group header section. Both boxes are now selected.

2 Click **Format** on the menu bar, then click **Font**. When the Font dialog box appears, click **Italic** in the Font style list box, then click the **OK** button. The text in the Group header section is now italicized.

3 If you have a color monitor, click **Format** on the menu bar, then click **Border and Colors**. The first row of color squares controls the color of the text. Click the **red square** in the first row of color squares, then click the **OK** button. The color of the text in the Group header section changes to red.

4 Click in an empty area of the Report Designer window to cancel the selection of the Group header information.

5 Click the **Print Preview** button 🔍 on the toolbar. If the Saved Data dialog box appears, click the **Use Saved Data** button. See Figure 22.

database records grouped by manager number

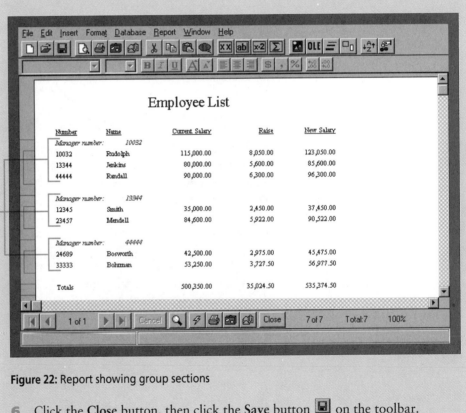

Figure 22: Report showing group sections

6 Click the **Close** button, then click the **Save** button 🖫 on the toolbar.

The final change you will make to the report is to include the company's logo in the report.

Inserting an Object into a Report

Crystal Reports supports OLE (Object Linking and Embedding), which you learned about in Tutorial 10. You will use OLE to insert the company's logo into the footer section of the current report.

To insert an object in a report:

1   Click **Insert** on the menu bar, then click **Object**. When the Insert Object dialog box appears, click the **Create from File** option button to select it.

The company's logo is stored in the Prologoc.bmp file, which is located in the report folder in the main Visual Basic folder.

2   Click the **Browse** button. If necessary, open the report folder, which is located in the main Visual Basic folder. Click **Prologoc.bmp** in the file name list box, then click the **Insert** button (*the OK button in Windows 3.1*).

So that any changes made to the logo in the Prologoc.bmp file will be reflected in the current report, you will link the Prologoc.bmp file to the report.

3   Click the **Link** check box to select it, then click the **OK** button.

4   When the white box appears in the Report Designer window, position the white box on the left side of the Page footer section, which is located at the bottom of the report, then click to drop the object in the Page footer section. See Figure 23.

company logo displayed in footer section

Figure 23: Object displayed in footer section

5   Click in an empty area of the Report Designer window to cancel the selection of the object.

6 Click the **Print Preview** button 🔳 on the toolbar. If the Saved Data dialog box appears, click the **Use Saved Data** button. The Preview window appears.

7 Click the **magnifying glass** button 🔍, which is located at the bottom of the Preview window, to compress the report so that more can be seen at one time.

Notice that the report appears unbalanced because most of the report is located on the left side of the page. To fix the problem, you can either return to the Report Designer window and move the fields, or you can move the fields in the Preview window. Most times it is easier to move the fields in the Preview window because you can see more of the page at one time. First move the New Salary column to the right side of the page.

8 Click the **New Salary** heading to select it. Ctrl + click the **first number in the new salary column** to select the new salary amounts, then Ctrl + click the **new salary's grand total number** to select it. All of the items in the new salary column should be selected.

9 Position the mouse pointer on one of the selected boxes in the new salary column, then drag the selected boxes to the right until the right edges of the boxes are aligned with the right edge of the date box, then release the mouse button.

10 Use the same process of selecting and dragging the column information to space the remaining columns in the report to your liking.

11 When you are finished moving the columns in the report, click in a blank area of the report to cancel the current selection, then click the **magnifying glass** button 🔍 to see a full-page view of the report. See Figure 24. Your report may look slightly different depending on where you chose to move each column.

full-page view of report

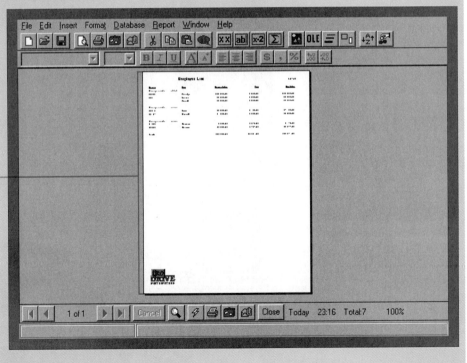

Figure 24: Full-page view of the report

12 Click the **magnifying glass** button 🔍 again to return to the normal view of the report.

13 If your computer is connected to a printer, click the **Print** button 🖨 on the toolbar, then click the OK button in the Print dialog box.

14 Click the **Close** button to close the Preview window, then click the **Save** button 💾 on the toolbar.

15 Click **File** on the menu bar, then click **Exit** to close Crystal Reports.

You have now completed the Pro Driver Distributors report. In the next section you will learn how to print the report from a Visual Basic application.

Printing a Crystal Reports Report from a Visual Basic Application

In addition to the Crystal Reports add-in program, the Professional Edition of Visual Basic also comes with the Crystal Report custom control. You can use the Crystal Report custom control to print a report while a Visual Basic application is running.

To use the Crystal Reports custom control:

1 Start Visual Basic, if necessary. Click **Tools** on the menu bar, then click **Custom Controls**. When the Custom Controls dialog box appears, click the **Crystal Report Control** check box to select it, then click the **OK** button. The CrystalReport tool appears in the toolbox as shown in Figure 25.

CrystalReport tool in toolbox

Figure 25: CrystalReport tool in the toolbox

2 Double-click the **CrystalReport tool** in the toolbox. The Crystal Report control appears on the form. Drag the control to the upper-left corner of the form, as shown in Figure 26.

Crystal Report control

Figure 26: Crystal Report control in the form

3 Display the Properties window. Change the Crystal Report control's Name property to **crpPro**.

To use the Crystal Report control to print the ProDrive report, you need to set the control's Destination property to 1 - To Printer, and its ReportFileName property to the name of the report, including the path.

4 Click **Destination** in the Properties list. Change the Destination property to **1 - To Printer.**

5 Click **ReportFileName** in the Properties list. Click the **...** in the Settings box. When the Properties dialog box appears, click the **...** button in the dialog box. The Choose Report dialog box appears.

6 Open the TutApA folder on your Student Disk, then click **ProDrive.rpt** in the file name list box. Click the **Open** button (*the OK button in Windows 3.1*), then click the **OK** button to close the Properties dialog box.

You will now put a command button on the form. When the user clicks the command button, the button's Click event procedure will use the Crystal Report control to print the report.

7 Add a command button to the form. Change its Caption to **P<u>r</u>int**, and its name to **cmdPrint**.

To tell the command button to use the Crystal Report control to print the report, you simply need to use the PrintReport command.

8 Open the command button's Click event procedure. Press the **Tab** key, then type **crpPro.printreport** and press the **Enter** key.

9 Close the Code window.

10 Save the form and the project as **AppenA** in the TutApA folder on your Student Disk.

11 **Run** the application, then click the **Print** button. The Print dialog box appears.

12 When the printing stops, stop the application. Visual Basic returns to the design screen.

E X E R C I S E S

1. a. Your Student Disk contains a database named College.mdb; the College.mdb file is located in the TutApA folder on your Student Disk. Use the database to create the report shown in Figure 27. Name the report App1Done and save it in the TutApA folder on your Student Disk. (*Hint:* Use the Report menu to sort the records by course number.)

File Edit Insert Format Database Report Window Help

College Courses

Number	Title	Credits	Grade
Biol100	Biology	4	B
Cis100	Intro to Computers	4	B
Cis110	Intro to Programming	3	A
Cis201	Intro to Visual Basic	5	A
Educ101	Intro to Education	3	F
Educ103	Primary Ed	3	D
Eng101	English Composition	3	A
Eng102	English Composition II	3	B
Hist101	Western Civilization	4	C
Math110	College Algebra	3	C
Math135	Statistics	5	B

1 of 1   Cancel   Close   11 of 11   Total:11   100%

Figure 27

b. Print the report.

Exercises 2 and 3 are Discovery Exercises, which allow you to "discover" solutions to problems on your own.

discovery ▶ 2. a. Your Student Disk contains a database named College.mdb; the College.mdb file is located in the TutApA folder on your Student Disk. Use the database to create the report shown in Figure 28. Name the report App2Done and save it in the TutApA folder on your Student Disk. Important note: The GPA is calculated by the report.

Figure 28

    b. The graphic shown in Figure 28 is named beany.bmp and is located in the bitmap\assorted folder in the main Visual Basic folder. Include the page number in the center of the Page footer section.

    c. Print the report.

discovery ▶   **3.** a. Open the AppenA (appena.vbp) project, which is located in the TutApA folder on your Student Disk. You created this project in the Appendix.

    b. Use the Crystal Reports' Help menu to research the LastErrorString property.

    c. Modify the Print button's code so that it displays the contents of the LastErrorString property in a message box if an error occurs.

    d. Save and run the application. Print the ProDrive report.

    e. Print the application's code.

    f. Submit the printouts from steps d and e.

APPENDIX

B

Visual Basic's Drag-and-Drop Feature

The Flags Application

As you already know, when you are creating a user interface during design time, you can drag controls on the form and drop them in the desired location. Visual Basic's **drag-and-drop feature** extends this ability to the user during run time by allowing the user to drag objects on the form and then drop them in either the same or a different form. The term **drag** refers to the process of holding down the left mouse button as you move the mouse; the term **drop** refers to releasing the mouse button in order to end a drag operation. You will use the drag-and-drop feature in the Flags application, which you will create in this appendix.

To create the Flags application:

1   Use the following information to create the interface shown in Figure B1. The interface contains two image control arrays: imgFlag and imgCountry. The icons in the imgFlag array are located in the main Visual Basic folder on either the network or local hard drive. Be sure to set the BorderStyle property of the controls in the imgCountry array to 1-Single. Set the Stretch property of the image controls in both arrays to True.

Control	Icon file name
imgFlag(0)	icons\flags\flgcan.ico
imgFlag(1)	icons\flags\flgfran.ico
imgFlag(2)	icons\flags\flgjapan.ico
imgFlag(3)	icons\flags\flgmex.ico

imgFlag control array

imgCountry control array

Figure B1: User-interface for the Flags application

2   Code the Exit button so it unloads the form. Code the form's Unload event so it ends the application.

3   Save the form and the project as **Flags**. You can save the file in the TutApA folder on your Student Disk.

When the user drags a flag from the imgFlag array to the corresponding country in the imgCountry array, the flag should disappear from the imgFlag array and appear in the imgCountry array. For example, if you drag Japan's flag to the imgCountry control located above the Japan label, the flag should disappear from the imgFlag(2) control and appear in the imgCountry(2) control. To use Visual Basic's drag-and-drop feature, you need to learn two properties (DragMode and DragIcon) and one event (DragDrop).

The DragMode Property

The ability to drag a control during run time is determined by the value in the control's **DragMode property**. When the DragMode property is set to 1-Automatic, you can drag the control by positioning the mouse pointer on the control and then pressing the left mouse button down as you move the mouse.

To enable dragging of the imgFlag controls:

1   Click the **imgFlag(0)** control to select it, then Ctrl + click the **imgFlag(1)**, **imgFlag(2)**, and **imgFlag(3)** controls. The four controls should be selected.

2   Display the Properties window. Change the DragMode property for the four controls to 1-**Automatic**.

3   **Save** and **run** the application. Practice dragging and dropping the flag icons anywhere on the form. Notice that the mouse pointer drags a rectangle when you drag the object. When you drop the icon, it will still be in its original location because you have not coded the application to do otherwise.

4   Click the **Exit** button. Visual Basic returns to the design screen.

The mouse pointer would look more meaningful to the user if, during the drag-and-drop operation, the pointer were the same shape as the icon you are dragging. You can control the icon that Visual Basic displays when an object is dragged by setting the control's DragIcon property.

The DragIcon Property

The **DragIcon property** determines the icon to be displayed when you are dragging a control. In this application, you will set each imgFlag control's DragIcon property to the same setting as its Picture property.

To set the DragIcon property of the imgFlag controls:

1   Click the **imgFlag(0)** control. Display the Properties window, then click **DragIcon** in the Properties list. Notice that the DragIcon property says (None). Set the DragIcon property to the **flgcan.ico** file, which is located in the icons\flags folder in the main Visual Basic folder. The DragIcon property now says (Icon).

2   Change the DragIcon property for the remaining imgFlag controls as follows:

Control	Icon File Name
imgFlag(1)	icons\flags\flgfran.ico
imgFlag(2)	icons\flags\flgjapan.ico
imgFlag(3)	icons\flags\flgmex.ico

3   **Save** and **run** the application. Practice dragging and dropping the flags on the form. Notice that the mouse pointer turns into the appropriate icon during the drag operation.

4   Click the **Exit** button. Visual Basic returns to the design screen.

Now that the icons can be dragged, the next step is to tell the imgCountry array how to respond when the user drops an icon into one of the controls in the array. You will do so by coding the imgCountry array's DragDrop event.

The DragDrop Event

When you drag a control over an object and release the mouse button, the object's **DragDrop event** occurs. The control being dragged is referred to as the **source**, and the object on which it is dropped is referred to as the **target**.

To code the imgCountry array's DragDrop event:

1 Double-click one of the controls in the imgCountry array. Use the Proc box to open the control array's DragDrop event.

2 Maximize the Code window.

The DragDrop event displays four arguments within the set of parentheses: Index As Integer, Source As Control, X As Single, and Y As Single. The Index argument, you may remember from Tutorial 5, keeps track of which control is receiving the event. The Source argument refers to the control being dragged. You can use this argument to refer to the properties and methods of that control—for example, Source.Visible would refer to the Visible property of the control that is being dragged. The X and Y arguments in the DragDrop event procedure refer to the horizontal and vertical position of the mouse pointer within the target object.

In this case, if the index of the imgFlag control being dragged matches the index of the imgCountry control on which it is being dropped, then you want to remove the flag from the imgFlag control and place it in the imgCountry control.

3 Press the **Tab** key, then type **if Index = Source.Index then** and press the **Enter** key.

4 Press the **Tab** key, then type **imgCountry(index).picture = source.picture** and press the Enter key. This will assign the icon in the imgFlag control to the image control in the imgCountry array.

5 Type **source.picture = loadpicture( )** and press the **Enter** key. This instruction will remove the flag from the imgFlag control.

6 Press the **Backspace** key, then type **end if** and press the **Enter** key.

7 Close the Code window, then **save** and **run** the application. Practice dragging and dropping the flags into the imgCountry controls. Be sure to try to drop a flag in an incorrect country. When you drop a flag into its matching country, the flag disappears from the imgFlag control and appears in the imgCountry control.

8 Click the **Exit** button. Visual Basic returns to the design screen.

Next you will code the New button.

Coding the New Button

When the user clicks the New button, its Click event should remove the flags from the imgCountry control array and place them back into the imgFlag control array.

To code the New button:

1 Double-click the **New** button to open its Click event procedure.
2 Press the **Tab** key, then type **dim inX as integer** and press the **Enter** key.
3 Type **for inX = 0 To 3** and press the **Enter** key.
4 Press the **Tab** key, then type **if imgFlag(inX).picture = 0 then** and press the **Enter** key.
5 Type **imgFlag(inX).picture = imgCountry(inX).picture** and press the **Enter** key.
6 Type **imgCountry(inX).picture = LoadPicture( )** and press the **Enter** key. This instruction will remove the flag from the imgCountry control.
7 Press the **Backspace** key, then type **end if** and press the **Enter** key.
8 Press the **Backspace** key, then type **next inX** and press the **Enter** key.
9 Close the Code window. **Save** and **run** the application. Practice dragging and dropping the flag icons, then click the **New** button. The New button's Click event removes the flags from the imgCountry controls and places them in the imgFlag controls.
10 Click the **Exit** button. Visual Basic returns to the design screen.

Currently, the flag icons are located immediately above their corresponding countries. To make the application more challenging, you will arrange the imgCountry controls, along with their corresponding label controls, so that they are not immediately below their respective flags.

11 Drag the imgCountry controls and their corresponding label controls so that the controls are not immediately below their respective flags.
12 **Save** and **run** the application. Practice dragging and dropping the flag icons.
13 Click the **Exit** button. Visual Basic returns to the design screen.

You have now completed the Flags application and Appendix B.

E X E R C I S E S

1. Use the drag-and-drop feature to create a tic-tac-toe game. Print the form and the code.

Index

C

G

LICENSE AGREEMENT FOR MICROSOFT® VISUAL BASIC® WORKING MODEL

<u>READ THIS FIRST</u>. Your use of the Microsoft software (the "SOFTWARE") is governed by the legal agreement below.

BY OPENING THE SEALED DISKETTE PACKAGE YOU ARE AGREEING TO BE BOUND BY THE TERMS AND CONDITIONS SET BELOW. IF YOU DO NOT AGREE WITH SUCH TERMS AND CONDITIONS, YOU SHOULD RETURN THE UNOPENED DISKETTE PACKAGE TOGETHER WITH THE BOOK TO THE PLACE YOU OBTAINED THEM FOR A REFUND.

1. <u>GRANT OF LICENSE</u>. Microsoft grants to you the right to use one copy of the enclosed SOFTWARE on a single terminal connected to a single computer (i.e. with a single CPU). You must not network the SOFTWARE or otherwise use it on more than one computer or computer terminal at the same time.
2. <u>COPYRIGHT</u>. The SOFTWARE is owned by Microsoft or its suppliers and is protected by United States copyright laws and international treaty provisions. Therefore, you must treat the SOFTWARE like any other copyrighted material (e.g. a BOOK or musical recording) <u>except</u> that you may either (a) make one copy of the SOFTWARE solely for backup or archival purposes, or (b) transfer the SOFTWARE to a single hard disk provided you keep the original solely for backup or archival purposes. You may not copy the written materials.
3. <u>OTHER RESTRICTIONS</u>. You may not rent or lease the SOFTWARE, but you may transfer the SOFTWARE and written materials on a permanent basis provided you retain no copies and the recipient agrees to the terms of this Agreement. You may not reverse engineer, decompile, or disasseceble the SOFTWARE.

Microsoft warrants to the original LICENSEE that (a) the disk(s) on which the SOFTWARE is recorded is free from defects in materials and workmanship under normal use and service for a period of ninety (90) days from the date of delivery as evidenced by a copy of the receipt. Further, Microsoft hereby limits the duration of any implied warranty(ies) on the disk to the respective periods stated above. Some states do not allow limitations on duration of an implied warranty, so the above limitation may not apply to you.

Microsoft's entire liability and your exclusive remedy as to the disk(s) shall be at Microsoft's option, either (a) return of the purchase price or (b) replacement of the disk that does not meet Microsoft's Limited Warranty and which is returned to Course Technology, the place you obtained them, with a copy of the receipt. If failure of the disk has resulted from accident, abuse, or misapplication, Microsoft shall have no responsibility to replace the disk or refund the purchase price. Any replacement disk will be warranted for the remainder of the original warranty period or thirty (30) days, whichever is longer.

<u>NO OTHER WARRANTIES</u>. MICROSOFT DISCLAIMS ALL OTHER WARRANTIES, EITHER EXPRESS OR IMPLIED, INCLUDING BUT NOT LIMITED TO IMPLIED WARRANTIES OF MERCHANTABILITY AND FITNESS FOR A PARTICULAR PURPOSE, WITH RESPECT TO THE SOFTWARE AND ANY ACCOMPANYING HARDWARE. THIS LIMITED WARRANTY GIVES YOU SPECIFIC LEGAL RIGHTS. YOU MAY HAVE OTHERS, WHICH VARY FROM STATE TO STATE.

<u>NO LIABILITY FOR CONSEQUENTIAL DAMAGES</u>. IN NO EVENT SHALL MICROSOFT OR ITS SUPPLIERS BE LIABLE FOR ANY DAMAGES WHATSOEVER (INCLUDING WITHOUT LIMITATION DAMAGES FOR LOSS OF BUSINESS PROFITS, BUSINESS INTERRUPTION, LOSS OF BUSINESS INFORMATION, OR OTHER PECUNIARY LOSS) ARISING OUT OF THE USE OR INABILITY TO USE THIS MICROSOFT PRODUCT EVEN IF MICROSOFT HAS BEEN ADVISED OF THE POSSIBILITY OF SUCH DAMAGES. BECAUSE SOME STATES DO NOT ALLOW THE EXCLUSION OR LIMITATION OF LIABILITY FOR CONSEQUENTIAL OR INCIDENTAL DAMAGES, THE ABOVE LIMITATION MAY NOT APPLY TO YOU.

U.S. GOVERNMENT RESTRICTED RIGHTS

The software and any associated Microsoft documentation is provided with RESTRICTED RIGHTS. Use, duplication or disclosure by the Government is subject to restrictions as set forth in subparagraph (c) (1) (ii) of The Rights in Technical Data and Computer Software clause at DFARS 252.227-7013 or subparagraphs (c)(1) and (2) of the Commercial Computer Software—Restricted Rights 48 CFR 52.227-19, as applicable. Contractor/manufacturer is Microsoft Corporation/One Microsoft Way/Redmond, WA 98052-6399.

This Agreement is governed by the laws of the State of Washington.